PHL
54060000163427

KT-414-181

A MEDIEVAL HERBAL

A FACSIMILE

A MEDIEVAL HERBAL

A FACSIMILE OF BRITISH LIBRARY EGERTON MS 747

Introduction by
MINTA COLLINS

List of Plants by
SANDRA RAPHAEL

THE BRITISH LIBRARY
2003

First published 2002 by The Folio Society
This edition published 2003 by
The British Library
96 Euston Road
London NW1 2DB

British Library Cataloguing in Publication Data
A CIP record for this book is available from The British Library

ISBN 0 7123 4789 5

Photography by Laurence Pordes
Facsimile production supervised by Joe Whitlock Blundell
Designed and typeset by Bob Elliott
Printed and bound in Great Britain by Bath Colourbooks

INTRODUCTION

MINTA COLLINS

THE MAGNIFICENT herbal reproduced for the first time in this facsimile is one of the many rare and precious manuscripts in the collections of The British Library.[1] It is an illustrated treatise on herbs, the *Tractatus de herbis*, which is part of a collection of pharmacological texts written in southern Italy around AD 1300, known as British Library Egerton MS 747.[2] From the moment the reader opens the manuscript it is evident that it is an exceptional and costly production. Its impressive size and the large number of paintings arranged throughout the text were most unusual features in all but the most expensive books of the period and are an indication of the value attached to the contents.[3] The *Tractatus de herbis* is a unique link in the transmission of knowledge of medicinal simples between the ancient world and modern times, and Egerton MS 747 is particularly important because it is the first surviving, and probably the original, manuscript of this treatise. It contains a vast corpus of information about plants and their medicinal uses, inherited from Greek, Roman and Arabic sources. This information is combined with paintings of plants which, in their observation of nature, anticipate modern botanical illustration. Such observation had not been seen since Late Antiquity and it is these plant paintings which make the manuscript exceptional. The *Tractatus de herbis* is a type of herbal which was to become one of the most influential texts on medicinal plants between the fourteenth and sixteenth centuries.[4]

A herbal is a book containing the names and descriptions of plants with their properties and virtues, in particular their medicinal uses.[5] Antique and medieval herbals were originally conceived as books of simples, a simple being a medicament composed of only one constituent, especially of one herb or plant. Herbals were one of the most ancient types of illustrated book and fragments of a papyrus roll with illustrations of medicinal herbs have been discovered which date from the second century AD.[6] From the fourth century onwards the herbal, like most other books, took the form of a codex, the type of book with which we are still familiar today, but which was then made of parchment (prepared animal skin) and contained one or more texts written by hand – *manu scriptum,* hence the word 'manuscript'. This was the format used throughout the Middle Ages until the invention of printing in the fifteenth century. The *Tractatus de herbis* is therefore an illustrated manuscript treatise and will be referred to as 'the manuscript' to distinguish it from 'the codex', the complete book of texts of which it is part.

The illustrations of plants in ancient Greek and Latin herbals were originally drawn from life to produce identifiable likenesses, but over the centuries these herbals were copied repeatedly by scribes and artists who were anxious to reproduce the text and images in the books in front of them.[7] Haste, lack of skill and misunderstandings frequently resulted in plant images that were simplified, distorted and often unrecognisable, but the artists never again tried to paint the plants from life until the end of the thirteenth century.

[1] Sandra Raphael has generously given her advice and support throughout the preparation of this commentary and I thank her and all concerned at The British Library for their contribution.

[2] The first scholar to draw attention to Egerton MS 747 was Pächt 1950, p. 28, since then the manuscript has featured in B. Degenhart and A. Schmitt, *Corpus der Italienischen Zeichnungen 1300–1450*, 1, Berlin 1968, pp. 52–54, 2, 1980, p. 243; Baumann 1974, pp. 99–125; Blunt and Raphael 1994, pp. 56–61; Toresella 1990; Collins 2000, pp. 239–265. The facsimile was first published in a limited edition by the Folio Society: *Tractatus de Herbis, British Library Egerton MS 747,* with a commentary by Minta Collins and a list of plants by Sandra Raphael, London 2002. The present edition is a revised version. A transcription of the text for a CD-Rom interactive version by Yolanda Ventura and Paola Capone is promised in the near future, followed by a translation into Italian. This should make the text more accessible for research into the medical and botanical aspects of the manuscript.

[3] Previous herbals were illustrated throughout but with fewer illustrations, none of them observed from life, and with less intricate layouts.

[4] Baumann 1974, pp. 99–125, 131–179; Opsomer 1984, *passim*; S. Toresella, 'Alla ricerca di antichi erbari', *Erboristeria domani*, 9 (196), September 1996, pp. 84–90; Collins 2000, pp. 239–298; Platearius 1986.

[5] For general histories of herbals see Singer 1927; Nissen 1958; Arber 1986 (printed herbals); Blunt and Raphael 1994; Collins 2000.

[6] London, Wellcome Institute for the History of Medicine, MS. 5753. Called the Johnson Papyrus, this fragment was found by J. de M. Johnson in 1904 at Antinoe. J. de M. Johnson, 'A botanical papyrus with illustrations', *Archiv für die Geschichte der Naturwissenschaften und der Technik*, 4, 1913, pp. 403–408. It is described by Singer 1927, pp. 31–33, see also V. Nutton, 'Scriptorium, Wellcome Library', *Kos*, 1, no. 6, 1984, pp. 7, 9; and M. H. Marganne, *Inventaire analytique des papyrus grecs de médecine*, Geneva 1987, pp. 51–52.

[7] An example of Greek illustrations is reproduced in Mazal 1998, and a late medieval Latin herbal in Zotter 1996.

The present *Tractatus de herbis* is, therefore, of exceptional interest in the history of herbals and of plant painting in general, because, for the first time since Antiquity, the artist actually looked at the plants and drew them from life wherever possible (except for the imported and exotic plants and products, which were available only in dried form). The paintings seem rather stiff and two-dimensional to us, as though they were drawn from a pressed specimen or a plant laid out on a flat surface, but at the time they were created they were amazingly innovative. Even in panel and wall paintings of this period there are no comparable pictures of recognisable plants in western art. It is difficult to imagine that at the end of the thirteenth century artists in the West were only just beginning to try to observe and paint animals, birds, plants and landscapes and to attempt to make them look 'naturalistic'.[8]

The manuscript itself is something of an enigma. It is not dated and its place of origin is not recorded, the signature it bears is not necessarily that of the person who made it, there is no trace of who the early owners were and no contemporary documents mention it. However, close examination of its physical characteristics and its contents helps to disclose when, where and for what sort of person the manuscript was made.

INTERPRETING THE MANUSCRIPT

The large size of the codex shows that it was an expensive production. When it was first made it probably measured a maximum 400 × 250 mm, but the cropping of some of the illustrations shows that the edges of the parchment folios were severely trimmed at some time, perhaps when it was rebound, and it now measures 360 × 242 mm. The *Tractatus de herbis* itself has 106 folios, and three further folios of illustrations only, but the complete codex consists of 148 folios (the other texts, which are not illustrated, are not reproduced in the present facsimile). They are bound in twelve gatherings of twelve folios each, with partly framed catchwords at the end of every gathering (e.g. folio 12v '*unde dr*') to help the binder match the first words of the following gathering and keep the right order. This is typical of university books made in Naples at the end of the thirteenth and in the fourteenth century.[9] In contrast, books made for the Angevin royal family in the same city during this period had gatherings of ten folios, i.e. five bifolia, with roman numerals marking the beginning and end of the gatherings.[10] The parchment of codices produced for the court is usually fine and very well prepared, which is not the case of the *Tractatus de herbis*; this indicates that the codex was not a royal commission.[11]

Nevertheless, the skins needed to produce so many large bifolia would have been very costly, even though the parchment is not very fine and its pigmentation is pronounced, suggesting perhaps that the skin is of calf rather than sheep or goat. The quality of the skins is unequal and their preparation uneven, with occasional bruise holes (e.g. folios 34, 43, 50, 73, 86), which may indicate that good-quality skins were difficult to obtain locally, or that they were chosen for reasons of economy.[12] This indicates that the manuscript was not made in Bologna, the major centre of book production in Italy. Comparison with datable manuscripts from Naples and Salerno reveals similar characteristics and we know that, thanks to the royal court, Naples had a lively book trade at this time and there were stationers who provided ready-prepared gatherings of parchment.[13] The leaves are disposed so that flesh-side faces flesh and hair faces hair (the latter more yellow and showing the follicles, but holding ink better, e.g. folio 34).

[8] See for example the contemporary frescoes of the *Life of St Francis* in the Upper Church at Assisi, with experiments in modelling the human figure, depicting animals, birds, trees and landscape.

[9] J. Destrez, *La pecia dans les manuscrits universitaires du XIIIe et du XIVe siècle*, Paris 1935, pp. 44 *et seq.*

[10] P. Supino Martini, 'Linee metodologiche per lo studio dei manoscritti in *litterae textuales* prodotti in Italia nei secoli XIII–XIV', *Scrittura e Civiltà XVII*, 1993, pp. 43–101, p. 54.

[11] e.g. Paris, Bibliothèque Nationale, MS lat. 6912, and Vatican, Biblioteca Apostolica, MS lat. 2398, two copies of al-Razi, *Havi seu continens.* See *Dix siècles d'enluminure italienne VI–XVI siècles*, ed. F. Avril (ex. cat. Bibliothèque Nationale) Paris 1984, pp. 68–69 with bibliography.

[12] Commissions for copies of medical texts for Charles of Anjou, *c.*1278–85, frequently stipulate the use of ox-skin, *parchemin theurosin* (*theurotin, thauratino*) as opposed to *haedina*, goatskin; see N. Barone, *Archivio storico per le provincie napolitane*, 10, p. 420 (1278), p. 425 (1280), p. 428 (1281). The cost of kidskin is documented as being half as much as the work of the scribes according to C. Coulter, 'The library of the Angevin kings at Naples', *Transactions and Proceedings of the American Philological Association*, 75, 1944, pp. 141–155.

[13] I am grateful to Professor Vivian Nutton who made corrections and suggestions to this commentary in its early stages, and drew my attention to London, Wellcome Institute Library, Wellcome MS 286, which he considers was written and illuminated in court circles in Naples around 1348, and which is similar in format, layout, and quality of parchment but has gatherings of 8–10 folios. For the context in which such manuscripts were produced see R. Weiss, *Medieval and Humanist Greek Collected Essays*, Padua 1977 (first published in 1950).

The layout of the text is also typical of university books: two columns are ruled for a maximum of fifty-five lines each and each alphabetical section (except for H) has a list or index of chapter headings at the beginning. The chapter initials are alternately in red and blue ink, with decorative penwork in the contrasting colour for many of them. We can tell that these were rubricated (a term derived from the Latin for red earth, *rubrica*) after the text was written and after most of the paintings were completed, because occasionally an initial was omitted, leaving visible the tiny guide letter in the gap (folios 28v, 40v, 41 margins). Sometimes an initial is repeated (*E endivia,* folio 34). This suggests that the rubricator was not the same person as the scribe who wrote the main text but was probably a professional employed to provide the finishing touches.

All the texts in the codex are in a round Italian Gothic book-hand (*littera gothica textualis rotunda media*) which 'points to an Italian scribe and to a date in the last quarter of the thirteenth century or first quarter of the fourteenth'.[14] The extensive use of abbreviations throughout the text indicates that the codex was made for a learned reader who was acquainted with the specialist medical vocabulary. The physical characteristics of the codex are therefore typical of university books from Naples but do not necessarily prove conclusively that it was produced there, since it is likely that similar books were made for medical men in Salerno. Although this is an academic book it is not an inexpensive production, as we have seen from its size and the professional rubrication. Furthermore a professional illuminator was employed, once the codex was completed, to decorate the frontispiece pages of the two main treatises with splendid illuminated initials and borders. The half-length 'author portrait' in the frontispiece initial 'C' on folio 1 represents a *magister*, wearing the dress typical of a university doctor in Italy at this time, the miniver-lined and trimmed blue cape over a red tunic, and double-pointed cap over a white coif.[15] He writes the first two words of the *incipit*, the opening sentence of the text, '*Circa instans*', with a stylus on an open bifolium in front of him and represents the author of that treatise, Platearius (see page 9) or perhaps, by extension, the compiler of the *Tractatus de herbis* himself.

The initial C and its blue background, with small triple dots in white and red, are sadly abraded, but gold leaf is still visible behind the figure. Long, thin, curving, stylised acanthus foliage extends from the initial to form a frame round the two columns of text, ending in the right margin in thin, curling, penwork arabesques scattered with tiny circles. The foliage is grey-blue, madder-pink and light brick red and the linking stems are decorated with knots, balls and buds in gold leaf. In the two lower corners small roundels with 'wings' of acanthus leaves surround a tonsured head to the left and a dragon's head to the right, both set against gold-leaf backgrounds. There is a distinctive interlace pattern at the centre of the lower border surrounded by gold balls.

The style of this frontispiece decoration is typical of Italian illumination at the end of the thirteenth century, especially of a number of manuscripts made in Bologna, Palermo, Salerno and Naples; it closely resembles that of the artist Jacobellus of Salerno, who was active in the last years of the thirteenth and in the early fourteenth century in both Salerno and Bologna. The decoration of the manuscript may well be by a follower of his working in the Naples/Salerno area.[16]

Academic texts of this period were not usually illustrated throughout, and it is evident that the scribe and illustrator were finding solutions to problems as the work progressed. For example, at the beginning of the manuscript the illustrations were painted in the ruled column above the relevant text so that the chapter title served for the illustration as well. This led to irregular layouts on the page, but, more significantly, the paint of the illustrations tended to gather in the incised lines of the ruling, e.g. folio 23. By folio 76 this method was corrected and only the top half of the column was ruled, and the illustrations were placed mainly in the lower half of the page, each with their own titles to avoid confusion when the text followed on the verso.

Furthermore, at some time during the making of the manuscript, additional passages were written in a smaller script, either fitted tightly into the available column space or spreading into the margins. These are excerpts from Isaac Judaeus's treatise on diet, *Liber dietarum universalium et particularium,* and treat of

[14] Dr Michelle Brown of The British Library kindly helped to date and localise the script.

[15] See W. N. Hargreaves-Mawdsley, *A history of academical dress in Europe until the end of the eighteenth century*, Oxford 1963.

[16] Several manuscripts of this period with similar decoration which were probably made in the region are still in libraries in Naples, Salerno and Messina. A. Daneu-Lattanzi, *Lineamenti di storia della miniatura in Sicilia*, Florence 1966, p. 66. A. Daneu-Lattanzi, *I manoscritti ed incunaboli miniati della Sicilia*, Palermo 1984, p. 148. Collins 2000, p. 245.

food plants and their dietary and medicinal value.[17] Those excerpts appended to an existing chapter benefited from its illustration (*cepa,* onion, folio 29) but when a new simple was introduced no new illustration was provided (*caules,* cabbage, and *cicer,* chick pea, folios 27v, 28), which suggests that the inclusions were an afterthought. Both these procedures indicate that this manuscript of the *Tractatus de herbis* was not copied directly from one pre-existing illustrated model but was an original compilation. The rather informal, almost unplanned nature of the layout indicates that the artist (or artists) of the illustrations in the text was probably not the professional who did the initials, and that he worked very closely with the scribe.[18] The paintings are arranged in the text area, without frames, and many extend into the margins, with a maximum of four per page. Some of them appear to have been painted before the writing of the text because the script is written over the illustration (*bardana,* folio 17v), and others, where the paint runs over the script, were done after the text was written (*bursa pastoris,* folio 16v).

The 406 pen-and-wash paintings of plants are remarkably varied but neither they, nor the illustrations of simples of mineral and animal origin, seem to have been executed by a large number of different hands and, as will be seen when they are described below, it is possible that the majority of them were painted by the compiler himself.

On folios 106–109 there are a number of plants which are not part of the *Tractatus de herbis.* They have almost no accompanying text, the titles are written in an ink of higher carbon content than the main text, and the initials were never completed, which indicates that the rubricator was no longer available to complete the decoration. This, and the fact that the paintings are among the more accomplished in the manuscript, may mean that they were added later and perhaps by another hand, although the pigments and drawing techniques do not seem to differ from the other plant illustrations. Titles to plants in similarly dark ink elsewhere in the manuscript may also be later additions.

The folios were originally foliated (numbered) three times, each folio having its recto (r) and verso (v). According to the first foliation (not visible in the facsimile), the present folio 3 was numbered 6 and the present folio 145 was 149. This indicates a loss of two folios preceding the *incipit* to *Tractatus de herbis.* Judging from related manuscripts there may have been a separate prefatory bifolium, as a preface to the treatise, with a series of paintings of famous medical authors of the past, perhaps the authors mentioned below.[19]

Who wrote *Tractatus de herbis,* where and when?

The *explicit,* or closing lines of the treatise, on folio 106 reads:

> Explicit tractatus h[e]rbar[um] Diascorides &
> Platone adqu[e] Galienus & Macronem tra[n]s
> latate manu & i[n]tellectu bartholomei mini
> d[e] senis i[n] arte speciarie se[m]p[er] i[n]fusus d[e]o gra[tia]s am[en]
>
> Q[u]i scripsit scribat se[m]p[er] cu[m] d[omi]no vivat.
> Vivat i[n] celis bartho[lo]m[eu]s i[n] no[m]i[n]e felix[20]

'Here ends the treatise of herbs, Diascorides, Plato (Platonicus), Galen and Macer, interpreted by the hand and mind of Bartholomeus Mini of Siena, well versed in the knowledge of drugs and spices. Thanks be to God, Amen.
May he who wrote (this) write and live always with the Lord, may Bartholomeus live blessed (?) in heaven.'

The 'signature' Bartholomeus Mini de Senis is repeated in abbreviated form, 'barthoms', in the scribe's finishing couplet, and many scholars choose to accept that Bartholomeus was the compiler of the *Tractatus de herbis.* However in 1950, the distinguished scholar Otto Pächt first drew attention to the importance of this manuscript in an article entitled 'Early Italian nature studies and the early calendar landscape' in which he pointed out that the signature was written over an erasure.[21] On close examination it is evident that both

[17] Isaac Judaeus (Ishak b. Sulayman al-Israili) was active in Egypt *c.*850–941 and his treatise was translated by Constantine the African at the end of the eleventh century.

[18] Although it is possible that the artist/artists was/were female it is more probable that he/they were male, and the masculine gender is used throughout to avoid clumsy repetition of 'he/she/they'.

[19] See Collins 2000, pp. 265, 272.

[20] Dr Scot McKendrick and Dr Peter Kidd kindly helped me with this transcription and translation. I also acknowledge gratefully advice from Professor O. Fatio and Dr B. Nicollier.

[21] Pächt 1950, p. 28, n.3.

signatures are in blacker ink than the surrounding text and are written over two erasures.[22] This in itself is suspicious, but perhaps more strange is the repetition of the same name both for the compiler of the text and for the scribe who copied it out in the handsome gothic script. Normally an author or compiler who wrote out his own text might sign his name once at the end. On the other hand a scribe who copied out a text by another author would usually write the author's name in the explicit and sign his own name separately, if at all, perhaps using one of the popular *scripsit* formulae, as here.

Even with modern technical means it is not possible to detect the names which were erased, so it is unlikely that the identity of the original compiler will ever be discovered. As for Bartholomeus Mini of Siena, it is difficult to understand why he should have been so anxious to substitute his name for the others. The most probable reason is that he added or completed some of the titles or text at a later date (perhaps the additional titles written in very black ink referred to above) and considered that he was justified in altering the authorship.

For the present, the identity of Bartholomeus Mini of Siena remains a mystery. The Italian scholar Sergio Toresella has pointed out that the name and arms of a Bartholomeus Mini feature among those of the rectors of Siena Cathedral on the ceiling of a second-floor room in the Museo dell'Opera del Duomo.[23] The earliest date for this decoration is 1347, which, if this were the same man, would give us an approximate date for his intervention in the herbal.[24]

Even if we do not know, and sadly may never know, the name of the real compiler of the *Tractatus de herbis,* our study of the manuscript enables us to glean some idea of what type of person it was made for. We have seen that the physical characteristics are typical of university books produced in Naples in the late thirteenth and early fourteenth century, that it is possible that the compiler illustrated the manuscript himself, and that the much-abbreviated text indicates that the codex must have been written for a learned medical man. Moreover, besides the *Tractatus de herbis,* the additional texts in the codex, not reproduced here, were apparently written in the same hand and at the same time. They are all associated with drugs and their preparation and include the *Antidotarium Nicolai* (folios 112–124), a series of medical recipes of Salernitan origin demonstrating the use of compound medicines, which complements the information on simple medicines in the *Tractatus de herbis.*[25] A list of synonyms on folio 128v gives the names of simples used by earlier authors, including references to the Arab scholars Avicenna, Serapion and 'Almansore'.[26] This selection of texts enabled the reader not only to identify and name the medicinal simples and be aware of how they were used in compound medicines but also to find their equivalents in newly favoured Arabic treatises. Such a selection confirms that the book was conceived by and for a physician or apothecary who was not only erudite and acquainted with learned medical texts and with the plants themselves, but was also wealthy enough to afford the expense involved in producing a herbal of this size with so many illustrations, which would have put it beyond the reach of the average druggist.

Illustrated herbals were not the most common means to learn about simples in the Middle Ages. Knowledge of herbs and herbal medicine would normally be passed on orally from the *rustici* (country people) to herb-gatherers, from apothecaries to their apprentices, or in the monasteries from one *infirmarius* to another. The scholar Rufinus, in his *Liber de virtutibus herbarum* (see below, page 11) referred to the *herbolarii* and the *ypothecarii* of Bologna and Naples.[27] The distinction he made between the herb-gatherers and the apothecaries draws attention to the different responsibilities involved in the obtaining, preparing and prescribing of simple remedies. The *herbolarii* or rhizotomists gathered the herbs and roots both in the wild and from their own gardens of simples and usually sold them to the *ypothecarii.*

[22] Toresella 1990, pp. 302–303, did not think that the signature had been changed.

[23] Toresella 1990, p. 304. Preliminary research in published biographical lists, kindly conducted for me by Dottoressa M. A. Ceppari of the Archivio di Stato di Siena, has not yet yielded further details.

[24] Another 'Bartalomeo d'Antonio di Mino' resident in the Kamollia terzo is mentioned several times between 1453–74 in the guild lists of apothecaries of Siena; see G. Cecchini, G. Prunai, *Breve degli speziali 1356–1542*, Siena 1942, Biblioteca Comunale, Siena, but this connection is improbable because of the late date.

[25] The *Antidotarium Nicolai* can be dated to the twelfth century because Mattheus Platearius wrote a commentary on it at that time. The attribution to Nicolaus is not certain but dates at least from the thirteenth century; see Kristeller 1956, pp. 511, 513. Folios 124–148v of Egerton MS 747 contain a series of small texts on dosages, substitute medicines, weights, measures, synonyms and additional recipes; see The 'Contents of the Codex' on page 23.

[26] *Incipiunt sinonima Galieni & Avicenne atque Serapiones & Almansore & Grecorum omnia simul.* 'Almansore' refers to a compendium of medicine by al-Razi (Rhazes, d. 925) the *Liber (ad) almansor(em).* Translations of Avicenna, Serapion and 'Almansore' were completed by Gerard of Cremona in Toledo in the twelfth century but were only really used by medical scholars from the mid-thirteenth century. See Jacquart 1990, pp. 150, 175.

[27] Thorndike, 1945, pp. 19, 79.

From those simples the apothecary prepared the medicaments and ointments. In theory the *speciarii,* or spicers, bought and sold spices, sugar, wine and, as we will see below, imported exotic substances (including pigments and artists' materials), whereas the apothecaries, who specialised in drugs, bought the prepared herbs and sold the preparations to the doctor's prescription.[28] However, the terms *apothecarius* and *speciarius, confectionarius* and sometimes *piperarius* (literally pepper-seller) seem to be interchangeable in the documents. Strict legislation surrounded their activities but, as the *Tractatus de herbis* points out, it was not enough to prevent fraudulent practice.

Frederick II Hohenstaufen had decreed in 1231 that only a limited number of pharmacists should be allowed to practise in his south Italian kingdom and that the making of medicines should be by two pharmacists controlled by masters of medicine. Doctors were not permitted to sell medicines, and all doctors had to swear to denounce ill practice among the pharmacists.[29] The compiler of the *Tractatus de herbis* claimed in his explicit that he was 'well-versed in the knowledge of *speciarie*', which might imply that he was an apothecary, a master in medicine, or a master of pharmacy like Magister Johannis de Casamicciola, revered professor of medical science and *magister specialis* in Naples under Charles I of Anjou.[30]

It has been suggested here, and in the absence of definite written evidence it can only be a suggestion, that the *Tractatus de herbis* was made in the Naples/Salerno region at the end of the thirteenth or the beginning of the fourteenth century. However, it is perhaps possible to date it more precisely. The main treatises contained in the codex are all Salernitan works. Isaac's treatise on diet (from which excerpts were added as an afterthought) was adopted as compulsory reading for the students of medicine in Naples from 1278 and in Salerno from 1280.[31] The texts chosen may point therefore to a Naples/Salerno connection, although they were widely copied elsewhere. An extensive lexicon of medicinal simples, the *Clavis sanationis,* compiled by Simone Januensis (Simon of Genoa) was completed *c.*1296 and Matthaeus Silvaticus dedicated his *Opus pandectarum medicinae* in 1317.[32] The compiler of the *Tractatus de herbis* would almost certainly have been aware of the last two lexicons if they had been in circulation at the time he was writing, so it is probable that his compilation was completed before. The physical characteristics and the contents suggest, therefore, that *Tractatus de herbis* was produced in the region of Naples or Salerno sometime after 1280, perhaps before 1296 and definitely before 1317.[33]

Precedents

All herbals are essentially compilations of material from a number of sources, whether written or oral, and the *Tractatus de herbis* is no exception. In fact the whole treatise might be envisaged as having been conceived in layers and these should be explained before we look at the contents of the manuscript. First came the ancient Greek and Latin medical authors. Their writings, together with some later Arab texts, were the sources used in the twelfth century by the *author* Platearius, who wrote the treatise on herbs, *Circa instans.* In the late thirteenth century the unnamed *compiler* of our manuscript adopted the *Circa instans,* word for word, as the main part of the text of his *Tractatus de herbis,* to which he added chapters from various other sources (and probably, like a modern editor, arranged for the layout, decoration and illustrations, which he may have done himself). At this stage the scribe copied out the text in the formal script.

The *explicit* on folio 106 quoted above names four ancient authors as sources: Diascorides & Platone adqu[e] Galienus & Macrone[us]...

Diascorides is the medieval Latin name for Pedanius Dioscorides, a Greek military physician of the first century AD, who gathered together a corpus of material from earlier written sources, oral traditions and his own experience to produce a comprehensive treatise in Greek on medicinal simples and their properties.[34]

[28] S. de Renzi, *Storia documentata della Scuola medica di Salerno,* Naples 1857, pp. 530–537, mentions Pietro di Salerno '*herbularius del Re*' and Goffredo de Nuco *apothecarius & speciarius* in Naples in 1324.

[29] Kristeller 1956, pp. 530–531.

[30] Casamicciola was a Palatine count; he practised and taught in Naples from 1250 and had a *viridarium,* a garden or orchard. He died in 1282. S. de Renzi, op. cit. p. 538.

[31] Kristeller 1956, pp. 509, 535.

[32] See notes 71, 72.

[33] Toresella 1990, pp. 302–304, considered that the Bartolomeus Mini de Senis signature was original; he therefore located the origin of the manuscript to Siena and dated it to approximately 1340.

[34] For Dioscorides generally see Riddle 1971 and 1985 with extensive bibliographies.

His treatise on *materia medica* was originally arranged in five books and dealt with oils, perfumes and simples from trees, shrubs and animals, with cereals, roots, herbs, wines and medicines from mineral sources.

Dioscorides' great merit was the exhaustive treatment of his subject and his systematic naming, classification and description of each substance, particularly of over six hundred plants. Every chapter gave the Greek name of the plant, a list of synonyms, a description of the plant, its origin or habitat, the preparation of the medicines from it and its medicinal properties. Dioscorides' treatise is the most influential treatise on herbs ever written; it was used by pharmacists for at least fifteen centuries and was plundered by other authors of works on simples in all languages. Many of the plant names used by Dioscorides were adopted by Linnaeus when he established his binomial nomenclature for plants in the eighteenth century, and thus are still in use today, though not always for the same plants.

Dioscorides' original treatise, in Greek, was probably not illustrated, but in the fourth century a shortened version was made which was devoted only to plant simples and was embellished with magnificent paintings of herbs drawn from nature. The earliest surviving codex of this version was made for the Byzantine princess Juliana Anicia, *c.*612.[35] After more than 900 years and many vicissitudes this exceptional volume was discovered in Constantinople in 1562 by Ogier Ghiselin de Busbecq (1522–92), ambassador from the Emperor Ferdinand to the Sublime Porte. He eventually took it to Vienna where, seven years later, it entered the Imperial Library.[36] Known as *Codex Vindobonensis*, it is now Cod.med. gr.1 in the National Library in Vienna. Several splendid copies of it were made over the centuries in Byzantine Imperial circles.[37]

An Arabic translation of Dioscorides' original treatise was made in Baghdad in the ninth century and this formed the basis of most early Arabic pharmacological texts.[38] The influence of Arab botanists in the west is often cited, but early Arabic herbals with illustrations are translations of Dioscorides and their plant paintings are on the whole stiff and stylised descendants of the Greek models.[39] Even if one of these rare Arabic herbals had been available to the compiler of Egerton MS 747 it is unlikely that it could have been a model for the more naturalistic paintings in the *Tractatus de herbis.* On the other hand, Arab interest in botany flourished during the twelfth and thirteenth centuries and we know that Arab botanists drew plants from nature, even if their drawings do not appear to have affected the illustrators of the traditional herbals.[40]

In western Europe, a Latin translation of the whole treatise, *De materia medica,* was made in the sixth century and there is a single illustrated copy, the tenth-century Munich, Bayerische Staatsbibliothek Clm 337.[41] This Old Latin translation was completely superseded by an alphabetical arrangement compiled in the late eleventh or early twelfth century, known as *Liber Dyascorides* (or *Diascorides*) *de simplici medicina.*[42] This is the Diascorides referred to in the *explicit* of *Tractatus de herbis.*

A small illustrated treatise of seventy-one chapters taken from Dioscorides, the *Liber medicinae ex herbis femininis* is included in a compendium of illustrated Latin texts on medicinal simples compiled before the

[35] Vienna, Österreichische Nationalbibliothek, MS med. gr. 1; see Mazal 1998 for a reduced-size facsimile of this manuscript (the first volume) and *Dioskurides:Codex Vindobonensis med. gr. 1 der Österreichischen Nationalbibliothek*, commentary H. Gerstinger, Graz 1970, with bibliography.

[36] Gerstinger 1970 op. cit. p. 4 and n. 18.

[37] Among the fully illustrated copies are Naples, Biblioteca Nazionale MS gr. 1, and New York, Pierpont Morgan Library M.652. In the fourteenth century a number of more practical academic manuscripts were made of the Greek *De materia medica* in five books, with small illustrations copied from the illustrated version; see Collins 2000, chapter 2.

[38] M. M. Sadek, *The Arabic Materia medica of Dioscorides*, Quebec 1983.

[39] S. Toresella, 'Il Dioscoride di Istanbul e le prime figurazioni naturalistiche botaniche,' *Atti e memorie, Accademia Italiana di Storia della Farmacia*, September 1995. Collins 2000 pp. 115–147.

[40] The botanist Rashid al-Din b. Essoury went plant-hunting in the mountains of Lebanon, accompanied by a painter in the middle of the thirteenth century; see L. Leclerc, *Histoire de la médecine Arabe,* 2 vols, Paris 1876, 2, p. 228. Arab compilers of botanical treatises, al-Ghafiki, al-Idrisi and Ibn al-Baytar travelled and went plant-hunting and significantly increased the botanical and medical data in their compilations; see Collins 2000 p. 138, note 133.

[41] Collins 2000, pp. 149–154. This codex is mentioned by almost every author of works on herbals and Dioscorides but see: *Catalogus Codicum Latinorum Bibliothecae Regiae Monacensis* 1, Munich 1892, p. 86. K. Hoffmann and T. M. Auracher, 'Der Longobardische Dioskorides des Marcellus Virgilius,' *Romanische Forschungen*, 1, 1882, pp. 49–105, who began editing the text, a task continued by H. Stadler between 1897 and 1903. Beccaria 1956, pp. 222–223. G. Cavallo, 'La trasmissione dei testi nell'area beneventano-cassinese' in *La cultura antica nell'occidente latino dal VII all'XI secolo*, Settimane di studio del centro italiano di studi sull'alto medioevo, 22, Spoleto 1975, pp. 357–414, pp. 376–382; Riddle 1971, p. 123 and ibid. 1980, pp. 20–23 and bibliography; Touwaide 1993, pp. 299 et seq. and bibliography; G. Orofino, in *Virgilio e il Chiostro*, ed. M. dell'Olmo, Rome 1996, no. 41, p. 174.

[42] J. M. Riddle, 'Dioscorides', in F. O. Kranz, P. O. Kristeller, *Catalogus translationum et commentariorum*, 4, Medieval and Renaissance Latin translations and commentaries, Washington DC 1980, pp. 1–145.

sixth century.[43] It is always found together with another herbal which is known as the *Herbarius* of Apuleius Platonicus.[44] The *Platone* mentioned in the *explicit* of *Tractatis de herbis* therefore refers to Apuleius Platonicus, the assumed name of the author of the *Herbarius* (although it is possible that the compiler confused him with Plato). The *Herbarius* consists of 131 chapters dealing with medicinal plants. Each chapter has a representation of the plant with its name and a list of synonyms for that plant in a number of different ancient languages.[45] The text is mostly devoted to the complaints that the plant can be used to cure, enumerated *a capite ad calcem*, 'from head to heel'. In the *Herbarius* valid prescriptions go side by side with myth and superstition. Betony, for example, was prescribed as a shield 'against monstrous nocturnal visitors and against frightful visions and dreams', and a sprig of pennyroyal placed behind the ear was supposed to ward off 'summer torpor' or sunstroke. Some manuscripts of the *Herbarius* retain pagan prayers, inherited from Late Antiquity, to be invoked when gathering certain plants. Occasionally the myths and superstitions are graphically illustrated; for example, the mandrake is shown with a root in human form attached to a dog straining at the leash, a reference to the legend surrounding its gathering. Among many superstitions connected with the mandrake was the belief that its roots were in human form, and that it shrieked when pulled and caused death on contact. To avoid this it was recommended to attach the root to a dog, the dog was offered food, and when he strained at the leash he unearthed the mandrake, but died in the process! This superstition is not reproduced in this *Tractatus de herbis*.[46]

Amazing though it may seem, with the exception of the single illustrated Latin Dioscorides, Munich Clm 337, the *Herbarius* compilation was the only illustrated herbal available in the Latin West from the sixth to the thirteenth century. Over sixty manuscript copies survive, most of which were copied before the late thirteenth century, and many can be associated with major ecclesiastical houses, renowned for their libraries and learning.[47] This is not a great number when one considers that these herbals were produced over seven centuries and throughout the Latin West; even taking losses into account, it does not allow for a copy in every monastic infirmary. The *Herbarius* was therefore essential source material for the compiler of the *Tractatus de herbis* for some of his text and he may also have used it as a model for the basic schemata of some of the illustrations.[48] He must have had access to a manuscript of this popular treatise, but it will be seen below that he was selective in his use of it.

Galienus, the third of the authors cited in the *explicit*, refers to Galen (AD 129–*c*.216/217), the Greek author whose vast corpus of writings dominated medical teaching in the West up to the seventeenth century. He was one of the greatest scientists of Antiquity and wrote on almost every aspect of medicine, relating his experience as a practising doctor as well as synthesising the entire heritage of ancient Greek medicine. As a result he became the most widely read and emulated author in the medical field throughout the Middle Ages.

Galen's legacy to the *Tractatus de herbis* comes less from his treatises on medicinal simples than from his influential doctrine of humours. This theory underlay all pathology and treatment in the Middle Ages, including the use of medicinal simples. It is based on Hippocratic writings, but derived originally from the Aristotelian system of the four elements which compose the universe: earth, water, air and fire. According to this theory each element is the result of the action of elementary qualities, one active and one passive; earth is cold and dry, water is cold and humid, air is hot and humid, fire is hot and dry. All living beings contain these elements and in the human body they are represented by the four humours. Black bile (predominant in the spleen) is cold and dry like the earth, phlegm (predominant in the brain) is cold and humid like water, blood is hot and wet like air, and yellow bile (predominant in the liver) is hot and dry like

[43] See J. M. Riddle, 'Medieval medical botany', *Journal of the History of Biology*, 14, no. 1, 1981, pp. 43–81 and bibliography. Also known as *Pseudo-Dioscorides de herbis feminis*, this treatise is found in the compendium with the *Herbarius* and the *Liber medicinae ex animalibus* by Sextus Placitus; see Hunger 1935.

[44] The facsimile of the old English version of the *Herbarius* is *The Old English illustrated pharmacopoeia, British Library, Cotton Vitellius C. iii*, ed. M. A. D'Aronco and M. L. Cameron, Early English manuscripts in facsimile, 27, Copenhagen 1998. A thirteenth-century Italian manuscript of the Latin *Herbarius* is published in facsimile in Zotte 1996. See also Blunt and Raphael 1994, pp. 32–46 and Collins 2000, pp. 165–238.

[45] Synonyms from a treatise on plants by Pamphilos (1st century AD) with a series of names used by the Latins, Etruscans, Egyptians, Africans, Gauls, Spanish, Syrians and by the Magi, the Prophets and others (*alii*) are included in manuscripts of Dioscorides. The synonyms in the *Herbarius* may come from the same source but the 'languages' are often indicated only by *alii* (others), as they are often in Egerton MS 747.

[46] See for example *The Old English illustrated pharmacopoeia*, 1998, British Library, Cotton Vitellius C iii, folio 57v.

[47] Manuscripts of the *Herbarius* were made at the monasteries of Montecassino, Fleury, St Gall, Canterbury, Bury St Edmunds and Stavelot among others.

[48] See for example *grias* (folio 45r) and *mori* and *rubus* (folios 64v and 85v).

fire. A person is healthy when the humours are perfectly balanced. In a normally constituted human being the predominance of one of the humours determines his 'complexion' or temperament (melancholic, phlegmatic, sanguine or choleric). Illness or disease is the result of an imbalance of the humours; for example an excess of phlegm, which is cold and wet, might take the form of a cold. In theory, food, drink and medicinal simples are all composed of the four elements, and all affect the humours. Thus a balanced and temperate diet assures good health. Disease, however, should be treated with a remedy whose qualities counterbalance the humoral disorder. In the case of a head cold, the cold and wet phlegm should be counteracted by a simple which is categorised as hot and dry, such as mint, hyssop or the imported spice, pepper. To complicate matters further the quality of each substance has four degrees of intensity (occasionally themselves subdivided) to allow for modification. Hyssop, for example, is hot and dry in the third degree and pepper is hot 'in the beginning of the fourth degree and dry in the middle of it' (folio 72v).[49] Every simple in the *Tractatus de herbis* is introduced with a description of its qualities and the degrees of intensity according to Galen's theories. The scribe of our manuscript has reduced these to the most basic abbreviations, intelligible only to the initiated, for example for hyssop (folio 48), we read *Isopus . ca. è. &. sic. ì . iii. g.* (*Isopus calidus est et siccus in tertiu gradu*), 'Hyssop is hot and dry in the third degree.'

The last name in the *explicit*, *Macrone[us]*, refers to Macer Floridus, thought to be the pseudonym of Odo Magdunensis (from Meung on the Loire), a French cleric and doctor, who sometime in the early eleventh century composed a poem of 2269 hexameters, *De viribus herbarum*, 'About the virtues of herbs'.[50] This related the properties of seventy-seven plants, many of which retained their Greek and Latin names, and many references to classical mythology. This was the first treatise of medicinal simples composed during the Middle Ages rather than during Antiquity and for this reason it was widely copied and extensively cited in later medieval texts.

The compiler of the *Tractatus de herbis* therefore referred in his *explicit* to the four greatest authorities on simples prior to the twelfth century. He failed to mention the most important source of his text, the treatise on which the whole of the *Tractatus de herbis* is based, the famous book of medicinal simples known as *Circa instans*. The *Circa instans* takes its name from the first two words of its introduction, but it is also known as the *Liber de simplici medicina, Liber simplicium medicinarum, Secreta salernitana, Opera Salernitana* and *Compendium Salernitanum.* It was written during the first half of the twelfth century by Matthaeus Platearius, a member of a distinguished medical family in Salerno. Platearius probably based his alphabetical arrangement of simples on a treatise written by Constantine the African (d. *c.*1087), *De gradibus simplicium,* which included much from Dioscorides and Galen but also, for the first time in the West, material drawn from Arabic sources. Platearius added information from other Salernitan writers and from his own experience.[51]

The original *Circa instans* described *c.*273 medicinal simples: 229 plants, fourteen of animal origin and thirty minerals and other substances.[52] A longer version with 432 chapters (many on animal products) featured in a famous southern Italian manuscript also dating from the twelfth century, the *Codex salernitanus.*[53] The *Circa instans* was translated into French as early as the thirteenth century and in the fifteenth century was the official pharmacological text for herbalists in France.[54] No illustrated manuscript of the original *Circa instans* exists, but the much enlarged and revised version, the *Tractatus de herbis* of Egerton MS 747, is the earliest attempt to provide images for this text.[55]

The arrangement of the text of the *Tractatus de herbis*

Having understood the authorities and texts that were used by the author of the *Tractatus de herbis*, it is comparatively straightforward to work out how the text was compiled. Platearius's introduction to the *Circa instans* was copied in its entirety (folio 1). It begins with the words: *Circa instans negotium in simplicibus medicinis,* 'In this present work, our aim and intention is to deal with simple medicines,' and continues: 'it should be known that a medicine is called simple if it is used in its natural state, like the clove

[49] For Galen's theory on humours see for example Siraisi 1990, pp. 4, 104 et seq.

[50] *A Middle English translation of Macer Floridus de viribus herbarum*, ed. G. Frisk, Uppsala 1945.

[51] P. Dorveaux, *Le livre des simples médecines*, Publications de la Société française d'histoire de la médecine, Paris 1913; Platéarius 1986, pp. 285–286.

[52] Camus 1886 generally; Opsomer 1984, p. 10.

[53] This codex was in Wroclaw from 1865 until its destruction in the war; see S. de Renzi, *Collectio Salernitana*, Naples, 1852–1859.

[54] Dorveaux, op. cit.

[55] Opsomer 1984, p. 11.

or the nutmeg, or if, although undergoing some artificial preparation, it is not mixed with another medicine.'[56] It explains that there are simple medicines with virtues which counterbalance most ailments, but that sometimes the complexity of an illness calls for a compound medicine, one composed of several substances, and examples are given. Finally the arrangement of the individual chapters is explained:

> For each simple we shall indicate its complexion, that is, whether it is hot, dry, moist or cold. Then we shall say whether it is a tree, shrub, plant, root, flower, seed, leaf, stone, juice or other substance. We shall also explain which varieties of it exist, where they are to be found, and which are the best. Concerning the remedies which are put together, we shall say how they are made, how they are counterfeited and how to detect this imitation. We shall explain how long they can be kept, and how to administer them. We will arrange them alphabetically.

The compiler of the *Tractatus de herbis* used the prologue of the *Circa instans* for his own introduction and then copied the chapters on simples of the earlier treatise, according to the letter of the alphabet, arranging them, on the whole, in the same order and including the same information. Sometimes he inserted a chapter from another source, like the *Herbarius*, into Platearius's arrangement, but other additional chapters were appended at the end.[57] For the letter A for example he took the first twenty-nine entries from the *Circa Instans*, then added a further seventeen from other sources (plus three more from the *Circa Instans* but out of order). The other sources are Dioscorides (2), *Herbarius* (4), Macer (2), Constantine (1), Isaac (2) and six entries of uncertain origin some of which may come from early Salernitan authors such as Copho.[58] The additions from Isaac differ from the other added chapters because, as we saw above, they are not incorporated in the text but were added as an afterthought in a smaller script.

Salerno, Naples and the revival of natural science studies

The alternative titles for the *Circa instans*: *Secreta salernitana*, *Opera Salernitana* and *Compendium Salernitanum*, and the fact that Matthaeus Platearius belonged to a family of Salernitan doctors, leave us in no doubt about the place of origin of this important treatise. The city of Salerno is strategically situated on the gulf of the same name, south of Naples and east of Amalfi. Renowned for its medicine from the early Middle Ages onwards, it flourished particularly during the late eleventh and early twelfth centuries, when it was the thriving capital of the Norman kingdom in Southern Italy. Salerno was a cultural crossroads. It was well situated for access to the Greek monasteries in Puglia and Calabria, to the Benedictine monastery of Cava nearby and to that of Montecassino to the north, with its incomparable library. Cultural and linguistic exchanges with Arab and Jewish communities in Sicily and North Africa were possible, and Jewish doctors were tolerated in this city when they were persecuted elsewhere.[59] Recent research suggests that from the tenth to the twelfth centuries the famous *Scuola medica salernitana,* the School of Medicine of Salerno, was not an established academic institution but a loose association or gathering of doctors who practised, taught and wrote in the city, placing emphasis mainly on the practical aspects of the subject.[60]

In about 1077 the famous scholar and translator, Constantine the African, arrived from Carthage and spent the last ten years of his life at the Abbey of Montecassino. He translated a number of works from Greek, Arabic and Hebrew medical authorities, and wrote on many aspects of medicine, including medicinal simples.[61] His writings were first made available to Latin scholars through the compilations and commentaries made by Salernitan scholars, including Platearius, during the twelfth century, when the city was at the height of its fame.[62]

By the end of the thirteenth century the association of learned medical men in Salerno had assumed the official status of an academic *studium,* a university status approved and regulated by the Angevin rulers (following decrees first issued for Naples by Frederick II in 1231).[63] According to these, no-one could take the title of *magister,* or practise the profession of doctor in the realm, without first being examined by the

[56] The two facsimiles of *Le Livre des simples médecines*, Opsomer 1984 and Platéarius 1986, with their commentaries, have been invaluable for reference and providing the basis of the loose translations of the text.

[57] For example the entries for *bectonica* (folio 14r) and *grias* (folio 45r) come from the *Herbarius.*

[58] Opsomer 1984, pp. 253–263.

[59] R. Davico, 'Cultura araba ed ebraica nella scuola medica salernitana del medioevo', in Gallo 1994, pp. 53–87, esp. p. 73.

[60] Gallo 1994, *passim.*

[61] G. Vitolo, 'Origine e sviluppi instituzionali della scuola medica salernitana', in Gallo 1994, pp. 17–53, esp. p. 37.

[62] Vitolo, op. cit. p. 42. See also *The Trotula: a medieval compendium of women's medicine*, edited and translated by M. Green, Philadelphia, 2001, pp. 3–9.

[63] Kristeller 1956, pp. 530–531.

masters of Salerno and obtaining the approval of the royal representatives. A candidate had to have studied medicine for fifty-six months and had to undertake to teach at Salerno for sixteen months. From 1269 students residing in Salerno were exempt from tax and in 1280 the privilege was extended to professors, evidently to encourage doctors to settle there. The academic teaching at Salerno at this time was based on a corpus of translations from, and compendia of, Greek and Arab authors with commentaries by the famous twelfth-century Salernitan masters. This was known as the *Articella.*[64] Among other Salernitan texts in use were the *Circa instans* and the *Antidotarium* of Nicolaus with a commentary by Matthaeus Platearius, both of which are included in Egerton MS 747. Similar conditions applied at the *studium* in Naples.[65]

During the thirteenth century there was an increasing awareness of nature and natural history in general. One of the most famous original works of natural history was *De arte venandi cum avibus,* 'The art of hunting with birds', compiled *c.*1241 by the Emperor Frederick II.[66] Frederick's intention was to 'show things that are as they are', *'manifestare . . . ea que sunt, sicut sunt'.* This he achieved by drawing on his own practical experience of hunting with falcons, and by providing his manuscript with a series of illustrations of birds observed from life (for the first time since Antiquity).[67] The enlightened attitude of Frederick towards scientific matters and the artist's observation from life contributed to a revival of the depiction of nature at the end of the thirteenth and throughout the fourteenth century.

Between 1280 and 1320 many important treatises on medicine and natural science were produced or translated in Italy, especially in the south.[68] Authors then, as now, sought patronage, and much of the work in this field was produced for, or dedicated to, the Angevin rulers of the Kingdom of Naples.[69] For example, Charles of Anjou commissioned the first translation into Latin of al-Razi's encyclopaedic work, the *Continens,* which was completed in Naples between 1278 and 1282.[70] The translations of treatises from Greek and Arabic accentuated the problems involved in naming and identifying plants, and several important lexicons of medicinal simples were produced at this time. Simone Januensis completed his *Clavis sanationis* at the Papal court in Rome before 1296.[71] In 1317 Matthaeus Silvaticus dedicated his vast encyclopaedia, *Opus pandectarum medicinae,* or *Pandects,* to Robert of Anjou, King of Naples. Matthaeus Silvaticus was a doctor from a distinguished Salernitan family, who certainly wrote from his own experience since he mentions he had a garden in Salerno where he grew simples, some of them 'exotic'.[72]

Another herbal treatise, the *Liber de virtutibus herbarum,* was compiled between 1287 and 1300 by Rufinus, at some time penitentiary to the Archbishop of Genoa. He explained in his introduction that he studied the seven liberal arts at Naples and Bologna and became a master of astrology at Bologna university before devoting himself to the science of herbs, implying that it was one of the highest forms of study.[73] Rufinus's treatise was based on the same sources as the contemporary *Tractatus de herbis* but incorporated many of his own observations on the plants. There are few personal observations in the text of the *Tractatus de herbis* but it is similar in conception to Rufinus's treatise and was almost certainly produced for an equally educated scholar. Its originality lies in the observation evident in the plant illustrations. Both treatises are products of the general cultural climate of the time.

[64] The texts included in the *Articella* varied but the following were constant: the *Isagoge* of Johannitius (Hunayn b. Ishak) translated by Constantine, the *Aforismi* and *Pronostici* of Hippocrates, *De urinis* of Theophilus, *De pulsibus* of Philaretus and the *Ars parva* of Galen, probably translated by Constantine.

[65] Vitolo, op. cit. pp. 47–48.

[66] An accessible facsimile in reduced size of the *De arte venandi cum avibus,* Vatican Biblioteca Apostolica MS Pal. Lat. 107 is *Das Falkenbuch Kaiser Friedrichs II,* with a commentary by C. A. Willemsen, Dortmund 1980. The recent publication of the text in French, Frédéric II de Hohenstaufen, *L'art de chasser avec les oiseaux,* Nogent-le-Roi 2000, has an excellent introduction by A. Paulus and B. van den Abeele and a bibliography.

[67] Paulus and van den Abeele, op. cit. pp. 38–42.

[68] M. Oldoni, 'Letteratura medica a Salerno nel Basso medioevo', in Gallo 1994, pp. 121–162. For example, in Rome a new translation from Arabic into Hebrew of Avicenna's *Canon* was completed by Nathan ben Eliezer ha Me'ati.

[69] Petrus Crescentius's treatise on agriculture, gardens and plants, *Liber ruralium commodorum,* was dedicated to Robert of Anjou in Naples in 1305. The Spanish scholar Arnaldus de Villanova taught in Salerno before going to Montpellier. He wrote his verse compendium of Salernitan medical knowledge, the *Regimen sanitatis salernitanum* or *Flos medicinae Salerni,* some time before 1312.

[70] See *Dix siècles d'enluminure italienne VI–XVI siècles,* ed. F. Avril (ex. cat. Bibliothèque Nationale) Paris 1984, pp. 68–69 with bibliography.

[71] Simon of Genoa's *Clavis sanationis* is a comprehensive glossary of Greek, Arabic and Latin medical terms, particularly of simples. Simon claimed to have researched this material for thirty years in libraries all over Europe as well as in the field. He probably composed his treatise while he was at the Papal court during the pontificate of Boniface VIII and completed it there before 1296; see A. Paravicini Bagliani, *Medicina e scienze della natura alla corte dei papi nel duecento,* Spoleto 1991, pp. 191–197 and 247–251 and notes. See also Simon Januensis, *Clavis sanationis,* Venetiis 1507.

[72] There is no reference in Egerton MS 747 to the *Liber pandectarum medicinae* of Matthaeus Silvaticus, probably written between 1309 and 1316. See *Mater herbarum: fonti e tradizione del giardino dei semplici della Scuola Medica Salernitana,* ed. M. V. Ferriolo, Milan 1995, p. 21.

[73] Thorndike 1945, p. 1.

THE BOTANICAL AND MEDICAL CONTENT

The *Tractatus de herbis* is arranged in alphabetical sections. There are approximately 500 entries, over 420 of which treat simples of plant origin (including gums and resins) and the remaining chapters deal with animal and mineral substances. The entries follow the traditional pattern of the earlier herbals.

The illustration usually precedes the chapter of text (some chapters are not illustrated), and each chapter gives some or all of the following information: the Latin name of the simple, abbreviated details of its Galenic complexion, the synonyms, the nature of the simple (whether it is tree, shrub, herb, bark, seed, gum, animal part, stone, etc.) and any different species. The place of origin is sometimes mentioned and an indication of its habitat: 'dry places and in the mountains', 'stony places and by the sea', 'near hedges and in ditches', 'in damp hollows and in fields'. Often, but not always, the simple or its parts are described: the shape or colour of the leaves or flowers and the height or thickness of the stem; for example *sigillum sancte marie,* Solomon's seal (text folio 99v) has 'leaves like those of *persicaria* (redshank or water pepper) and flowers small and white, and it produces red seeds one by the other like little apples'.

Instructions follow as to when and how to gather and prepare the simple, its virtues and healing properties, and the form in which it should be used for each ailment. There may be up to forty-seven such items for a single herb (e.g. *bectonica,* betony, folio 14r). For the chapters on imported simples there are lengthy instructions as to how to detect falsifications and substitutes. Because of the amount of information given it is not possible to enumerate in detail here the different uses and methods of preparation, much less to compare them with those used today, but a selective overview gives an idea of the variety and complexity of the material.

Names and identification

One of the major problems in the study of medieval herbals is the interpretation of the names and the identification of the plants. The *Tractatus de herbis* was written four and a half centuries before Linnaeus introduced the binomial nomenclature that could be used to classify plants internationally. Medieval herbals and lexicons of plant names drew on numerous sources, and the Greek and Arabic names they quoted were often transcribed directly into Latin, whether or not a native equivalent existed. Many of the names in the *Tractatus de herbis* are Latinised versions of the Greek names used by Dioscorides: e.g. *aristolongia, camedreos, camepitheos.* Fewer Arabic names are used, but *karabe* or *kekabre* is described as the 'gum of a tree or a sort of varnish'; the illustration (folio 51r) of a small, unspecified tree does not help to identify the fossil resin amber.

The *Tractatus de herbis,* following the tradition of Dioscorides and the *Herbarius,* gives the synonyms of the plant names in a number of different languages and dialects.[74] Frequently these are not recognisable, but some help to identify the plants and have survived in the modern names. For example, among the twenty synonyms for *penthaphilon* (folio 78v) the Roman name, listed as *quinquefolium,* is echoed in the modern English name, creeping cinquefoil. *Ippirum* (folio 49v) has seven synonyms; one of them, *cauda equina,* is translated in the English name, horsetail.

Sometimes the same plant features under two names (*herpillos* and *serpillum,* folios 47, 96, for *Thymus serpyllum*), or similar names are used for different plants: the three '*arthemisia*' on folios 7v–8 can be identified as mugwort (*arthemisia maior*) and tansy (*arthemisia media*) and, less certain, feverfew (*arthemisia leptaphilos*). In the latter case the illustrations aid identification, but this is not always the case.[75]

The identification of the 420 plants named in the text must have been a problem for the person who was painting the illustrations. He must have had intimate knowledge of the plants involved in order to find the correct models to portray. The majority were familiar plants found growing locally, or in the herb garden or orchard, and were easily available. Plants native to other regions, such as lavender or aubergine, might have been more difficult to obtain. Perhaps the artist travelled with a sketch-book or plants were brought to him. For imported exotica and other substances we will see that he invented other solutions.

[74] See n. 45 above; the synonyms in the *Tractatus de herbis* are occasionally taken from Pamphilos, but other names have been added from Arabic and oral sources.

[75] Other examples of the same plant featuring twice are *mori* and *rubus* (blackberry, folios 64v and 85v) and *camelleunta nigra* and *virga pastoris* (teasel, folios 28v and 103v).

The plant paintings

Turning the pages of the manuscript we can only marvel at the extraordinary achievement of those who planned, wrote and illustrated it. It is intriguing to consider how many people were involved, how the tasks were distributed and how long it took to paint over 400 illustrations of different simples. It was suggested above that the author/compiler and the scribe were two different people. The scribe and artist were also different, although they worked in close collaboration (it is unlikely that the scribe did the illustrations or he would have spelt the titles of the illustrations the same way as he wrote them in the text). It is more difficult to judge whether one, two or several artists were involved. Although the treatment of the plant illustrations is very varied, the way they were observed and depicted is consistent throughout the manuscript.

The stems are shown springing from the root, singly, several, or branching, according to the plant's habit, but with little attention paid to details such as whether they are ribbed or have bristles. Their colour varies, green for most of the herbaceous plants and occasionally brown for a tree or shrub, but this is not always true to the plant. The leaves are shown seen from above or frontally, to show their characteristic shapes, and occasionally some smaller leaves or those on the stem are shown from the side, e.g. *consolida*, comfrey (folio 30v). On the whole, less importance was accorded to the flowers, because they are not always shown, e.g. *gentiana*, yellow gentian (folio 42v), or sometimes the shape or colour of the flower is incorrect, e.g. *linaria*, toadflax (folio 56v), which should have flowers similar to those of a snapdragon, not trumpet-shaped. The flowers are frequently replaced by the fruit or seed heads, perhaps corresponding to the uses of the plant described in the text, e.g. *ciminum*, cumin (folio 24) 'the seed of a plant which grows in such quantity that it is never counterfeited'.

Usually the most distinctive details of a plant are indicated, such as the overall shape of the leaf, the number of leaflets, type of lobe or indentation, whether they are toothed or not, and sometimes the shape of the flower or seed head, e.g. *nigella*, love-in-a-mist (folio 68v). The dimensions of the individual paintings can be misleading because they are not always in proportion with the size of the plants; for example, the two large-leaved plants of the cucumber family trail delicately in the margin of folio 26v, much smaller than the relatively short celandine on the facing folio. The paintings of trees are often the smallest, partly in order to fit the whole plant into the space available on the page, e.g. *cerasorum*, cherry (folio 31r).

The roots were rather roughly painted after the rest of the plants, in varying shades of ochre, brown or black, perhaps done in series with a brush full of the same pigment. Only occasionally do they have a distinctive colour or shape, like the long, white radish and large, divided rhubarb root (both folio 84r) or the tuberous root of *consolida media*, *Symphytum tuberosum* (folio 30v) which helps to identify the plant as tuberous comfrey.

The techniques used and the shades of green vary from one plant to another, but are consistent throughout the manuscript. Occasionally preliminary drawing or outlines in hard point can be seen, for example under the rather roughly painted *brictanica* (folio 16v) and the neater *oleander* (folio 71v). Other plants are outlined with a fine brush in ink, especially many of those with toothed leaves like *sambucus* (folio 94r), and where petals are outlined to delineate white flowers as for *lilium, saponaria* and *vilubidis* (folios 52r, 89r and 104v), yet others have contours painted with a fine brush in brown, black or green paint, like *muscata* (folio 65v). However the majority of plants, particularly those with finely cut leaves like *cicuta* (folio 24r), do not seem to have been outlined and are painted freely onto the parchment.

Different greens are used to create a varied visual effect, not always corresponding to the plants' natural colour; for example, on folio 57r the light and dark green leaves are inverted in two very similar plants of the Boraginaceae, hound's tongue and viper's bugloss, the latter shown with its speckled stalk. On folios 80v and 81r, the lighter greens of *pinpinella*, great burnet, and *pilosela*, mouse-ear hawkweed, contrast appropriately with the darker green of the periwinkle and the two greens are combined in the spotted leaf of the orchid. Other pages and openings show equal concern for pleasing presentation with plants overlapping each other and the text to avoid the repetitious boxed-in effect of each illustration in the column width (e.g. folio 16v and especially folio 103v where the bryony trails through the neighbouring teasel).

Some veining shows darker green than the rest of the leaf, for example *nux vomica* (folio 68r), and elsewhere it is lighter, made perhaps by dragging the end of the brush through the wet paint, for example *acantum* and *eruca* (folios 9r, 36v). Colours of flowers and berries, where they appear, are more or less correct, like the saffron crocus (folio 24v) with its lax red styles and yellow stamens, but petals blue rather than true purple, a colour more difficult to obtain or mix.

With this subtle and recurring variety of techniques and colours it is difficult to identify different hands or to say that one artist painted one particular way, for example all the more delicate trees, or that another used pen or brush outlines or did or did not do preliminary drawing. However, it is evident that some illustrations are less accomplished and more clumsily painted, for example most of the bulbous plants such as *cepa* (folio 29r), the left-hand *allium* and *anfodillus* (folio 5r) and the stiff representations of *camelleunta nigra* and *camomilla* (folio 28v). The person who painted these is unlikely to have been the same as the artist of the accomplished *capragine* (folio 31v), *flamula* (folio 38r) and *sanbacus* or *sambacus* (folio 98r). This can be seen clearly by comparing the painting of *camalleunta nigra* (folio 28v) with another representation of the same plant, *virga pastoris* (folio 103v).

There were, therefore, at least two people of different ability painting the illustrations. It seems unlikely that they were professional illuminators, unlike the artist of the frontispiece illustrations which do not seem to have been painted by the same hand. The overall intent to represent the plants so that they could be clearly recognised, and the consistency of the observation and of the variety of techniques used to achieve the likenesses, point to one person having supervised and organised the illustration of the herbal. This person must have been familiar with all the healing plants mentioned in the text of the *Circa instans* and with the other plants he added, which were not always medicinal simples, for example box, *buxus* (folio 17v) of which he simply says, 'box is a tree whose wood is used for many building purposes, its leaves are like those of myrtle and it has round red seeds.' (In this instance the description is not correct because box has dry brown seed capsules with black seeds, but the artist has not shown either.) It is therefore possible that the compiler of the *Tractatus de herbis* painted most of the illustrations himself, with the help of a less accomplished assistant or apprentice.[76]

Comparison of the plant paintings with modern botanical drawings or photographs shows similar simplification of visual information.[77] The botanical verisimilitude of the paintings should not be exaggerated, but it is interesting to see how the illustrator represented enough of the characteristics of each specimen to aid identification even where the name of the plant may be confusing. In doubtful cases the synonyms in the text are helpful, as are the descriptions of the plant, its habitat and its medicinal uses. The three *arthemisia* (folio 7v–8r) have already been mentioned above, and among many other examples only a few can be cited here. Of the three *consolida* (folio 30v), *consolida maior* represents *Symphytum officinalis,* common comfrey, and *consolida media* either the white version or perhaps *Symphytum tuberosum*, tuberous comfrey, because of its tuberous roots. *Consolida minor* shows clearly *Prunella vulgaris,* self-heal, with its distinctive flower spike with stalkless leaves beneath. Self-heal was probably included among the *consolida* because, like comfrey, it was used for healing wounds (the Greek, Latin and English names for comfrey all come from words meaning to bind or unite).

'*Git*', 'Gith' (folio 43v) was the medieval name for the seeds of *Nigella damascena*, love-in-a-mist.[78] It was often confused with the seeds of *Agrostemma githago*, corncockle, as it is in our manuscript where the plant is shown with its unmistakeable linear, lanceolate leaves, pronounced calyx and long leaf-like sepals. The text recommends it as diuretic, vermifuge and against swollen haemorrhoids. The distinctive blue flowers, feathery leaves and blister-like fruit of love-in-a-mist are shown under the name *nigella* (folio 68v).

Alleluia (folio 12r) is still one of the popular names for *Oxalis acetosella*, wood sorrel, because it flowers around Easter, and the synonym given in the text, 'pane de cuccho', cuckoo's bread, is also one of its names in France today. The image in the manuscript corresponds to the description in Grieve's *Modern Herbal*, 'a plant of dainty character with slender irregular rootstock, thin, delicate leaves each composed of three heart-shaped leaflets, the long slender leaf stalks often reddish towards the base'.[79] However, instead of the typical white flowers with five petals, the illustrator has depicted the small yellow flowers of *Oxalis corniculata*, which is native to the Mediterranean.[80] In the illustration beneath it, the leaves of *acetosa* are clearly shown with the two backward-pointing basal lobes typical of *Rumex acetosa* and the branched spikes

[76] See note 18 above.

[77] For example R. Phillips, *Wild flowers of Britain*, London 1977; *The encyclopedia of herbs and herbalism*, ed. M. Stuart, London 1979; O. Polunin, A. Huxley, *Flowers of the Mediterranean*, 3rd edition, London 1987. M. Blamey, C. Grey-Wilson, *Mediterranean wild flowers*, St Helier 1993; R. Mabey, *The complete new herbal*, London 1988.

[78] Platéarius 1986, p. 338, *nielle des blés* and *nigelle.*

[79] Grieve 1974, p. 751.

[80] Platéarius 1986, p. 340.

of tiny flowers and seeds. The text refers to the sour taste of both these plants. Neither of them featured in the *Circa instans* and they must have been introduced into the *Tractatus de herbis* by the compiler, who was familiar with their names, appearance and their uses. *Alleluia* was used in a composite ointment 'to comfort the limbs and banish pains of the nerves', whereas *acetosa* was recommended for skin disorders and in a syrup for three-day fever 'and many other things'.

From the name alone *eliotropion* (folio 37v) might be identified with *Heliotropium europaeum*. The illustration shows the angular, branching flower stems with bright blue flowers in the angles and fruit crowned with a ring of ragged-edged scales, the pinnately-lobed basal leaves and small lanceolate upper leaves, typical of *Cichorium intybus*, chicory, or wild succory. The modern botanical name is confirmed by two of the thirteen synonyms given in the text, *cicorea* and *intiba*. Other synonyms, *sponsa solis*, bride of the sun, and *solsequium* refer to the flower's habit of opening with the sun in the morning and closing about midday or in dull weather, mentioned in the text as 'divining the course of the sun'. Chicory is recommended here as a cure for poisonous bites and liver problems. On folio 91r a less clumsy rendering of the same plant illustrates the title *sponsa solis*, with almost identical text.

If we can rely to this extent on the illustrations to identify the plants, when there is ambiguity should we believe the illustrator or the information in the text? The text for *primula veris* (folio 79r) might describe the cowslip because one of the synonyms is 'herb of Saint Peter', an association common in the Middle Ages because of that flower's likeness to a bunch of keys.[81] The second synonym [*herba*] *p*[*ar*]*alisis* was another popular name for the cowslip because it was considered beneficial in all paralytic ailments. However the text for *primula veris* in the *Tractatus de herbis* does not refer to its use as a remedy for palsy, but to its properties for healing fractures of the head and limbs, wounds, and bleeding veins, and as a diuretic, uses which correspond to those of the daisy, also called bruisewort. The illustration resembles the daisy, *Bellis perennis*, and may perhaps be identified as such.

The twelve plants on folios 106v–109 are among the more accomplished paintings and it has been argued above that they may have been added by another hand after completion of the *Tractatus de herbis*, but comparison of the painting of *orobum* (folio 106v) with *spargula* and *sambacus* (folios 97v, 98r) is not conclusive. The criteria of observation and the techniques used are similar and they are all healing herbs. As they did not feature in the *Circa instans*, it seems likely that they were added as an afterthought with their titles, but the text was never completed. The use of the Arabic name *suchar* for *Cnicus benedictus* may substantiate the southern provenance of the manuscript.

There are a number of gaps in the text left for illustrations which were never completed. Perhaps these were casual omissions, or perhaps the artist was not able to find the relevant plant or had difficulty in identifying the specific herb mentioned in the text. Most of them were plants which must have been familiar: aniseed (folio 6r), bistort (folio 15r), poppy (folio 31r), *piretrum*, probably pellitory root (folio 72r), stavesacre (folio 95r), sanicle (folio 99r), and *vitis alba*, probably white bryony (folio 105r). The artist might not have known *sesame* (folio 100) although the text stipulates that 'it grows in Sicily'. On the whole, where the artist was not familiar with a plant or a simple of mineral or animal origin, he either invented an image or did not illustrate it at all, as will be seen below.

Simples from minerals and animals

One of the original features of *Tractatus de herbis* is the number of small, sketchy landscapes or scenes with figures. These illustrate the gathering of simples from mineral or animal sources, and five of them are variations of the same composition: *alumen*, alum (folio 3r), *antimonium*, sulphide of antimony (folio 4r), *auripigmentum*, orpiment (folio 9r), *bolus*, Armenian bole (folio 12v) and *sulfur*, sulphur (folio 88v). They show a man with a mattock or pick in the practical dress typically worn by countrymen and hunters of the period, a short tunic tucked up diagonally in front and a brimmed, peaked hat.[82] The landscape is indicated by a roughly-drawn hill scattered with stylised green plants. Glass, *vitrum* (folio 103r) is illustrated by a similar figure tending a glass furnace, one of the earliest representations of this subject. In the illustration for *auripigmentum* a second, dark-skinned figure bears a basket towards a tower on the right and a blob of yellow paint indicates the mineral orpiment.

[81] Grieve 1974, p. 230.

[82] See for example the figure drinking in the contemporary fresco of *The Miracle of the Spring* in the Upper Church at Assisi.

It would have been repetitive to illustrate all mineral simples in this way and no spaces were made in our manuscript for illustrations of stones, *lapis* (folio 55r), salts, *sal* (folio 92v) or pumice, *spuma mare* (folio 99r). In later French versions of the treatise *Le livre des simples médecines* the artists contrived a decorative way to illustrate these substances arranged on shelves.[83] Many of the imported gums, resins and some of the animal products (e.g. *tela aranea*, spider's web) were not illustrated in our manuscript. *Aurum*, gold (folio 2r) represents a *magister* seated with a long-handled fan and globe (the original silver is now oxidised). A grey wash of bitumen engulfs the outline of a townscape to illustrate *aspaltum* (folio 9r) 'which some say comes from the foam of a lake hardened with chalk, a lake where Sodom and Gomorrah perished, but wherever it comes from it has the virtue of knitting bones, consuming and drawing out. '

Castoreum (folio 22r) shows a huntsman and his dogs pursuing the beaver. The artist cannot have known this northern animal, which he represented as a deer-like creature with pronounced testicles from which the imported *castoreum* of the text was traditionally thought to derive. In fact *castoreum* is a product of the animal's glands and was used as an antispasmodic. The text recommends that it be inserted in the nostrils or be drunk in a decoction of rue as a cure for epilepsy, and taken in wine flavoured with rue and sage against paralysis. A similar illustration shows another antispasmodic drug, *muscus* (folio 63r), a dried product obtained from the glands of the Indian or Tibetan musk-deer. After a lengthy account of how musk was obtained, the three different available sorts are described: very black, reddish-black and 'the best . . . completely red . . . and a little bitter, and when tasted it should fill the head with its smell, it mustn't be too hard but shouldn't melt in the mouth'. After explaining how to counterfeit it and how to keep it, the text lists recipes for its use as a stimulant.

Simple pen sketches represent a variety of substances drawn from animal sources as varied and exotic as coral (*corallus*, folio 25v), pearls (*margarita*, folio 60v) shown incorrectly in a helicoid shell rather than the bivalve oyster, honey (*mel*, folio 62v), molluscs (*blacte bisancie*, folio 18v), powders of bone of deer's heart and cuttlebone (*os de cor de cervi* and *os sepie*, folio 71r) and calcined elephant ivory (*spodium*, folio 91r), preserved skink lizards from Arabia and North Africa (*stinci*, folio 91v), and powder from embalmed mummies (*mumia*, folio 60v). The whale on folio 7r illustrates the chapter *ambra*; at the time ambergris was thought to be either the hardened sperm or the afterbirth of the whale, an identification not so far removed from the genuine, delicately perfumed secretion from the intestines of the sperm whale. It was prescribed in pill form for a weak heart, as an inhalation against epilepsy and as a fumigation for 'suffocating' of the womb. Many of these representations are among the earliest of their kind.

Lively marginal illustrations of serpents, scorpions, spiders and dogs draw attention to the antidotes recommended for their bites in the text, for example *allium*, garlic (folio 5r), *aristolongia*, birthwort (folio 7r) and *plantago*, plantain (folio 78r). This preoccupation with poisonous bites was one of the legacies of ancient herbals, and similar marginal drawings are found in the early medieval *Herbarius* manuscripts.

Gathering and methods of preparation

The chapter on the rose, *Rosa gallica* (folio 83r) shows how precise the instructions for gathering the herbs can be:

> The rose is cold in the first degree and dry in the second. In medicine both dry and fresh roses can be used. Some people pick them when mature but they do not keep well. They should be picked when the leaves (petals) are open and red; white, colourless or blackened roses should not be used in medicine. Pick them as indicated and dry them in the sun and they will keep three years. Many things can be done with fresh roses but when the recipes say roses, they mean dried roses, because they can be ground and powdered more easily. Fresh roses can be used to make honey of roses, rose sugar, rosewater, oil and syrup of roses.

Detailed instructions are given as to how to make each of these different preparations and their uses.

The variety of methods for preparing the herbs is astonishing. The roots, leaves and seeds are the most frequently used parts of the plants; the bark or flowers feature less often, and the text indicates if the dried or fresh substance is best for each medicament. Infusions of the herb in water or wine are prescribed for internal use, as well as decoctions and syrups (mixed with sugar, honey, wine, rosewater or vinegar). Powders may either be mixed with animal fats, honey, mastic or gum arabic, or made into pills or

[83] Platéarius 1986, p. 240.

suppositories. Externally the same powders can be applied as poultices or ointments, mixed with a variety of binding substances. Compresses, fumigations, inhalations, lotions and baths made from fresh or dried leaves are recommended, even for internal problems, far more frequently than in modern medicine. Alternatively the crushed herbs may be put into a sachet and laid on the painful area, like *maiorana*, sweet marjoram (folio 64r) placed on the stomach to relieve wind pain. The fresh herb or seeds may be made into tarts or pancakes to be eaten over a period of time, e.g. *matrisilva,* honeysuckle (folio 65r) or *paritaria,* pellitory (folio 75v).

Ailments

Medieval men and women, like the Greeks and Romans before them, suffered from the same common health problems as our own. Headache, migraine, toothache, colds, coughs, asthma and respiratory disorders are mentioned as often as heart problems, liver and kidney complaints, pain of the stomach and bowel, indigestion and flatulence. Pain from stones in the kidney or bladder, malfunction of the urinary tract, gout and piles are among the most frequently cited ailments.

The vast choice of possible remedies for such afflictions in the *Tractatus de herbis* must have been confusing for anyone who did not already have practical experience of preparing drugs. A limited selection of much-condensed recipes for a few familiar plants demonstrates how difficult it must have been to use this huge encyclopaedia.

Chamomile flowers, fresh or dried, are recommended as follows (folio 28v): in decoctions of wine or water for urinary problems, stones, obstruction of the liver and spleen, pain and swelling of the stomach and to prevent premature birth; steeped in water as a bath to help menstruation; as an oil friction to relieve daily fevers, headaches caused by cold, and wounds; in honey to remove scabs and scaly skin from the face; a drachma of their powder with wine taken for forty days to 'relieve and cure' ills of the spleen; chewed to make a compress to reduce swollen eyelids; in a vinegar rinse to eliminate scalp disease; with other simples as a vapour bath for diarrhoea, and finally in wine as a protection against poisonous bites. This is not one of the longer entries!

The root of iris (folio 48v) as a diuretic, if taken in wine 'unblocks' the urinary tract, liver and spleen and relieves pains of the chest, respiratory organs and stomach; its powder removes dead skin from wounds and, mixed with rosewater, is an eyewash against hardening of the conjunctiva. Aniseed, caraway and cumin are all recommended as diuretics and to stimulate the appetite, help digestion and alleviate wind, uses that are still recognised today.

Women's health problems are dealt with extensively and there are numerous recipes to help regulate menstrual flow, induce birth, prevent miscarriage, clean the womb and abort a dead foetus (birthwort, chamomile, plantain, madder, mallow, peony, and mugwort). These may be a legacy of the practices of the medical women of Salerno whose fame is associated with gynaecological tracts.[84] The aphrodisiac power of herbs is not ignored; the text proposes powdered seeds of rocket, mixed with honey and applied as a poultice to the back 'to incite lust', and for this reason apparently rocket was banned from monastery gardens. Roots of parsnip and wild orchid (*satirion*, folio 90v) candied with honey and dates, or tying the root of *malva ortensis* with a linen thread to the lower abdomen are also recommended as effective ways to 'stimulate *luxuria*' (folio 59r).

Disorders of the nervous system are mentioned frequently: insomnia could be treated with poultices of lettuce, mandrake or poppy, and the last two (both narcotics recognised today) are prescribed for anaesthetic purposes. An abundance of phlegm is the cause of melancholy which may be dispelled by a number of plants: aloe (folio 1r), fumitory (folio 38v, the fresh juice taken with water and sugar), celery-leaved buttercup (folio 3v, taken in a decoction with wine) and hellebore (folio 36r, much diluted with honey). Hellebore is among the twenty-two cures suggested for another nervous disorder, epilepsy, with the warning that this herb (which is extremely toxic) should always be used 'with discretion and prudence' because of its violent action. Another herb advocated for epilepsy is the peony (folio 72v), which indicates that the sedative and anti-convulsant effects were already recognised in ancient medicine.

Fortunately, enormous advances have been made and some of the problems that recur in the treatise are seldom encountered today. Leprosy, for example, is no longer the common affliction in Europe that it used

[84] Platéarius 1986, p. 304.

to be in the Middle Ages. Modern hygiene has reduced the need for a number of remedies to expel worms from the stomach and ears (garlic, plantain, costus, or white horehound for the former; aloe and hellebore for the latter). Today we suffer less often from *apostema*, usually abbreviated in the text to *ap'ea*, a word which covers many types of swelling, tumours, abscesses, boils or ulcers and for which there are endless compresses, poultices and ointments. The use of purgatives has long been abandoned, but it was common practice in the Middle Ages, and numerous purges feature in the *Tractatus de herbis*, accompanied by warnings about the dangers of using such violent methods (hellebore, spurge and wild cucumber).

Exotica

About seventy of the plant drugs mentioned are of foreign origin. They are mainly dried roots and seeds but there are also gums and resins, which come from 'beyond the sea', from India, Persia, Arabia, Syria, Greece, Alexandria and Babylon. They include: aloe and its wood, amomum, gum ammoniac, asafetida, balm, banana, camphor, cardamom, cinnamon, cloves, coconut, cubebs, dates, dragon's blood resin, frankincense, galingale, ginger, grains of paradise, gum arabic, henna, laudanum, mace, marking-nut, mastic, myrobalan plum, myrrh, nutmeg, nux vomica, pepper, pistachio, purging cassia, rhubarb, sandalwood, sebesten plum, senna, spikenard, storax, sumac, tamarind, turpeth root and zedoary.

These drugs from the Orient were not recent introductions. Between the ninth and eleventh century such 'exotica' were frequently found in monastic receptaries and antidotaries.[85] Drugs and spices formed a major part of exports from the East, and were imported and exported through the *apotheca* (drug storehouses) of the Byzantine world. The problems involved in their use are clearly defined in the relevant chapters of the *Tractatus de herbis*. Platearius (writing, it must be remembered, in the twelfth century) clearly stated in the chapter on aloe that he would 'reveal the way to counterfeit remedies', not because he encouraged such practice but 'so that people may know how to detect them (the counterfeits) without being deceived by those that sell them' (folio 1v).

The illustration for *balsamus* (folio 12r) shows a man in peaked hat and skullcap preparing to 'cut the branches with a knife and collect the sap which flows' in his glass phials. In this instance the shrub bears no resemblance to the exotic *Commiphora opobalsamum* (balm of Gilead) that it is supposed to represent. Following the description in the text the artist has drawn an orchard with seven well-like fountains or springs:

> Circa babillonia[m]| rep[er]it[ur] in quoda[m] campo i[n] quo su[n]t septe[m]| fontes. Si aut[em] alias trasfertur nec flores| nec fluctus faceret.
>
> It is found near Babylon, in a field where spring seven sources and if it is transplanted elsewhere it produces neither flowers nor flowing (sap).

The Babylon in question was the Roman-Byzantine fortified town which resisted the Arabs when they founded Al-Fustat and which survives today in the Coptic quarter of Old Cairo. However by drawing a wall around the field the artist showed that he knew the legend about the plant, which was grown outside 'Babylon' and was fiercely protected by the Arabs so that they could preserve the monopoly of this rare and expensive substance.[86]

The text distinguishes between *opobalsamum*, the juice or balm, *xillobalsamum*, the cut and dried branches, and *carpobalsamum*, the fruit. After defining the length of time each product can be kept and its virtues (warming and strengthening, because it is hot and dry to the second degree), the author warned that 'as it is costly it is counterfeited in several ways'. He described at length eleven different ways to falsify balm and how to test for them. Finally he listed ten uses for the drug including humours in the womb, stone in the bladder, earache, toothache, and embalming corpses to preserve them from corruption.

The artist of the *Tractatus de herbis* would not have known the exotic plants from which the dried drugs and spices came, but he dealt very deftly with the problem of illustrating them. The four nut trees on folios 67v–68r, which at first appear to be convincing representations, are fantasy images based on the text

[85] Riddle 1974, p. 167 et seq.

[86] See W. B. Kubiak, *Al-Fustat: its foundation and early urban development*, Cairo 1987; D. J. A. Ross, 'Nectanebanus in his palace: a problem of Alexander iconography', *Journal of the Warburg and Courtauld Institutes*, 15, 1952, pp. 67–87, discussed the early travellers' accounts of Babylon and its iconography. See also Platéarius 1986, p. 318: *baume*.

descriptions. Nutmeg, coconut and *nux sciarca* have leaves which resemble the common hazel but are distinguished by the fruits they bear: the nutmeg is shown with its envelope of mace, the coconut is large and oval, and the grains of paradise, *Aframomum melegueta,* imported from 'beyond the sea', are depicted as visible red seeds in the nut casing. The leaves of *nux vomica,* on the right, resemble those of the sweet chestnut. Most of the trees of overseas origin are fancifully represented and decorative but drawn with less confident, lighter strokes, e.g. *cubebe* (folio 22v), *sebesten* (folio 98v). For the latter the artist has shown the dried pod or the part of the plant with which he was familiar, borne on a fantasy plant. While these methods were obviously expedient, it indicates that the artist did not expect the paintings of trees to be useful to the reader for identifying the simple in question. This is evident in the elegant representation of the jasmine (folio 98r) which illustrates the chapter *sanbaco* or *sambacus* 'which is called *gessominus*'. The artist has provided the first known image in the West of *Jasminum officinale,* but the text refers to the plant *Jasminum sambac,* a plant of Indian origin from which the Arabs obtained Zambak oil.[87]

On folio 66 there is the chapter for *musa* which appears to have been added as an afterthought; there is no accompanying illustration of bananas, which the artist cannot have known first-hand although the text refers to them as 'fruit which look like gherkins and which others call apples of Paradise'. This is one of the earliest references in the West to the banana, which was not introduced into Europe until the seventeenth century at the earliest.[88]

Mediterranean plants

The great majority of plants included in the herbal were native to Europe, over twenty per cent to the Mediterranean basin, and many of them grew in the area around Salerno. Only occasionally did Platearius or the thirteenth-century compiler of *Tractatus de herbis* feel the need to name specific locations for these. We learn, for example, that although aloes and capers were mostly imported they also grew in Puglia, and that *golgemma* (folio 45v), probably lavender, 'grows in the mountains and especially in Provence, near Montpellier.'

The trees are mainly nut and fruit trees that were grown in southern Italy at the time, often as major commercial crops.[89] Nuts include almonds (bitter and sweet), sweet chestnut, hazelnut and walnut. The chapters dealing with fruits emphasise their dietary value as much as the medicinal properties. They include apricot, apple, cherry, fig, lemon, medlar, olive, peach, pear, plum, pomegranate, and quince. It is recommended that certain fruits should only be eaten on an empty stomach, such as pears, peaches 'which are good to eat', and apricots, *grisomilus* which 'are harmful whichever way one takes them', although their oil is good for haemorrhoids (folio 45r, margin). The lengthy entry on the quince, *mala citonia* (folio 61v), with an illustration which is not very recognisable, recommends its astringent properties as a remedy for vomiting, and includes a recipe for a compound medicine called *Diacydonium,* a quince paste, 'good for digestion and for convalescents'.

To give an idea of the contents of such entries the chapter on plums, *pruna* (folio 74v) is short enough to quote in full: 'Plums are cold and wet. There are two sorts, black and red. The firm black ones are best, and best of all are those called Damascus plums (damsons). They should be picked ripe and for keeping should be split and dried in the sun for fifteen days, then sprinkled with vinegar and kept in a wooden box. They cool and soften the bowels and are good for acute fevers. Anyone with constipation (because of dryness or drying choleric humour) should eat fresh plums, if they have them, or cook dried ones (prunes) in water, eat them and drink the water.'

Like the entries on fruits, soft fruits and grains, most of the chapters on vegetables have passages added from Isaac's treatise on diet, where the emphasis is on their general health-giving properties. Common crops that are documented as growing in the kitchen gardens of Salerno from an early date are all represented: garlic, leek, onion, scallion, lentils and white beans.[90] It is recommended that they should all be cooked in two waters to moderate the gases they provoke. Less common were cucumber, wild and cultivated lettuce, asparagus, spinach and the Indian vegetable fruit, aubergine.

Both spinach (*spinacha,* folio 97r) and aubergine (*mellongiano,* folio 66r) had been introduced to Europe comparatively recently by the Arabs, and this is the first known European mention of the aubergine,

87 Platéarius 1986, p. 333, *jasmin.* 88 Platéarius 1986, p. 318.
89 H. Besc, 'Les jardins de Palerme (1290–1460)', *Mélanges de l'école française de Rome,* tome 84, 1972. 90 Skinner, 1997, p. 7.

complete with instructions as to how to salt and drain it before cooking. The artist has illustrated the text 'these are fruits as large and fat as pears' but he has not drawn the plant from nature, unlike the artist of Paris Bibliothèque Nationale MS lat. 6823, a manuscript probably copied from Egerton MS 747 about thirty years later, where the purple aubergine is correctly portrayed.[91]

The bulk of the plant simples represented are the common herbs that are labelled as wild flowers, culinary herbs, aromatics and cultivated flowers. Occasionally a distinction is made between wild and garden flowers, for example two sorts of lily (folio 52r), the cultivated lily, *domesticum* (i.e. *Lilium candidum*) and the wild, *silvestrum,* of which there are two sorts, the one with a dark red flower (*Lilium martagon*) and the other yellow (*Lilium croceum*). *Rosa* (folio 83r) is the cultivated rose, *Rosa gallica*; whereas cyclamen, scabious, peony, violet, bugloss and periwinkle are the wild species.

The common herbs that are associated today with cooking and flavouring, such as aniseed, basil, cumin, dill, fennel, marjoram, parsley, rosemary, sage and thyme are included in the *Tractatus de herbis* for their medicinal value. However, there are a few references to their culinary uses: chervil (*cerffolium,* folio 27v) 'is a herb which is good for cooking'; 'excellent sauces can be made with cultivated parsley' (*petrosellinum,* folio 74), and ground coriander (*coliandrum,* folio 27v) which has 'a sweet and aromatic smell', 'gives meat a good flavour'. These herbs are prescribed, among many other uses, to be taken with food to prevent indigestion.

Myths and superstitions

The *Tractatus de herbis* is comparatively free of myths and superstitions, and those that feature were inherited from the *Herbarius* or from Macer. *Arthemisia* 'or by another name *mater herbarum,* mother of herbs' (folio 7v) refers to the herb which bears the name of the Greek goddess of hunting and chastity who the Romans identified with Diana, the goddess of nature, forests and the moon. Much of the text for the three *arthemisia* is taken from the *Herbarius* of Apuleius Platonicus. This includes the long list of twenty-two synonyms for *arthemisia leptaphilos* and the myth of the discovery of these herbs by Diana: 'and this herb Diana herself gave to Chiron the Centaur and he proved its virtues to many. On account of Diana he called the herb Arthemisia.' (Chiron was believed to have taught mankind the medicinal use of herbs.)

A few lines above the Arthemisia passage is the advice that 'this herb placed at the entrance of a house (prevents) either man or woman from harming it.' The chapter on *leontopodion* (folio 56r) recommends that a married man who 'cannot approach his wife' should pick a stem of the herb . . . when the moon is on the wane, steep it in water . . . wash his whole body, and after a fumigation of birthwort he should go into his house without a backward glance. Peony 'has special and secret virtues against epilepsy,' because Galen recounted that a child had been cured after peony root was hung round his neck and *Paeonia mascula* (folio 72v) is shown with its single flowers, distinctive seed pods, less divided leaves and tuberous root. Whoever carries fresh rue on his person 'can safely go and kill the basilisk', says the text on folio 85r, with the fabled reptile close by in the margin; whereas *herba vitis,* squinancy root (folio 46r) protects house and inhabitants from demons.

Another legacy from the *Herbarius* is the occasional prayer or incantation like that at the end of the chapter on *agrimonia* (folio 9v). As a cure for fistulas three roots of the plant should be gathered 'while in a state of reverence and the Ave Maria should be cited three times and three times the Pater noster. The roots should be hung over smoke with the name of the patient until dry and the fistula will heal.' Similar prayers are found in the chapters *camomilla* (folio 28v) and *polligonia* (knotgrass, folio 78v).

The lengthy text for betony (folios 13v–14r) was also taken mostly from the *Herbarius.*[92] After the list of

[91] This manuscript has not yet been published in facsimile. See E. Pellegrin, *La bibliothèque des Visconti et des Sforza ducs de Milan au XVe siècle,* Paris 1955, pp. 278–279 and supplement (T. de Marinis) 1969, p. 7. B. Degenhart and A. Schmitt, *Corpus der Italienischen Zeichnungen 1300–1450,* 1, Berlin 1968, pp. 53–55; 2, 1980, pp. 337–350. Baumann 1974, pp. 102–3; C. Opsomer, 'Un botaniste du XIVe siècle: Manfredus de Monte Imperiale', in *XVth Congress of the History of Science, Abstracts of Scientific Section Papers,* Edinburgh 1978, p. 38; *Dix siècles d'enluminure italienne, VIe–XVIe siècle,* ed. F. Avril (ex. cat. Bibliothèque Nationale) Paris 1984; *La médecine médiévale à travers les manuscrits de la Bibliothèque Nationale,* ed. M. J. Imbault Huart, L. Dubief (ex. cat. Bibliothèque Nationale) Paris 1983, p. 40. *La scuola medica* 1988, p. 115; Platéarius 1986, p. 268; Toresella 1990, p. 302–303; Collins 2000, pp. 268–273.

[92] Originally the chapter on betony was a short independent treatise, purportedly addressed to Marcus Agrippus by Antonius Musa the personal physician of Augustus, but it was in fact written during the fourth or fifth century AD and included later in the *Herbarius.* It was published by E. Howald and H. E. Sigerist (eds), *Apuleius Barbarus, Antonii Musae De herba vettonica liber, Pseudo-Apulei Herbarius, Anonymi De taxone liber, Sexti Placiti Liber medicinae ex animalibus etc,* Corpus Medicorum Latinorum, 4, Leipzig 1927.

synonyms the text at the bottom of folio 13v describes where the herb grows and states 'it safeguards both the soul and body of man and keeps safe those who go by night in holy places and is called holy by everyone. It should be gathered in the month of August, *but before picking the following prayer should be said with a devout* heart '*Herb betony, first found by* Aesculapius, I beg you with this prayer, you who are called queen of herbs, and by him who ordained that you should be created to work in so many medicines, forty-seven in number, *I beg you to help me in the things that* I wish for.' The passages italicised here were erased in the manuscript at some point, perhaps by a devout reader disturbed by the heretical nature of a prayer to a herb.

We have a rare personal glimpse of the scientific twelfth-century author of the *Circa instans* in the entry for the mandrake (folio 61r) where the root is not depicted as a female form, as in many of the earlier herbals and particularly in the *Herbarius* manuscripts. Platearius pointed out that there are two types, 'male' and 'female', but dismissed the legend that the root has a female form because 'nature would never give human shape to a herb', and praised its astringent, cooling and narcotic properties.

Domestic uses

A preoccupation with the cosmetic uses of herbs is seen in the chapters on the two arums, *iarus* (folio 48v) and *serpentaria* (folio 93v) and in those for lily, melon and cuttlebone. The recipe is more or less the same for all of them; the simple is ground to a powder, mixed with rosewater and dried in the sun several times to provide a paste which lightens the complexion, clears the skin and improves its colour. A decoction of madder root can be used to dye hair red (*rubea*, folio 84v), and orpiment mixed with lime is a depilatory (folio 9r).

No mention is made about the use of orpiment as a golden-yellow pigment. Strangely enough, there is no mention of the use of herbs or other substances for artists' pigments, and yet an apothecary would have also provided the raw materials from which painters and illuminators ground and made their colours. In the early fourteenth century Florentine painters were members of the same guild as doctors and apothecaries, the *Arte dei medici e speciali*. The compiler of the *Tractatus de herbis* might have made some reference to the artists' use of a number of other substances, including *lapis lazuli*, the precious ultramarine (folio 51v) and *bolus*, Armenian bole, used for gesso grounds (folio 12v). He did, however, mention the use of pumice, evocatively called *spuma maris* 'foam of the sea', to smooth parchment (folio 99r).

Occasionally we catch a glimpse of more frivolous uses for the herbs. The short entry on *provinca* (folio 81r) says that it is 'quite a common herb of which women make crowns' and extols it as a cure for 'bleeding of the nose and other parts of the head'. According to modern herbals periwinkle reduces blood pressure and dilates both coronary and peripheral blood vessels.[93] Women also grew *calendula*, marigolds (folio 30r) in their gardens, in order to make crowns of them 'because of their beautiful yellow and russet colours'; this is one of the few occasions when the author mentions the beauty of a plant. The name *calendula* refers to the frequency of its blooming i.e. on the calends, the first days of every month.

DESCENDANTS, FATE AND FORTUNE

Despite its format and appearance, the *Tractatus de herbis* bears no *pecia* marks to indicate that it was copied in sections by professional scribes for distribution to students or other scholars, as was the case with many university texts.[94] The first and last folios of the codex are in poor condition, a sign that the codex had no binding for some time, but the rest of the manuscript is comparatively clean, with few annotations in the margin, either contemporary or later, and no stains which might point to use by an apothecary as a practical manual or recipe book. Its appearance and condition suggest that it was used for private reference.

Few manuscripts directly related to this *Tractatus de herbis* survive, which indicate that it probably remained in private hands, or, perhaps because of the 406 plant paintings, it was too expensive to reproduce often. However, we know that in 1458 the codex was in France, at Bourg-en-Bresse, where a faithful copy of the text was made by a scribe called 'le petit pelous' (Modena, Biblioteca Estense, MS lat. 993). This is the only other copy of the *Tractatus de herbis* with the *explicit* with Bartholomeus's signature. The sumptuous

93 *The encyclopedia of herbs and herbalism*, ed. M. Stuart, London 1979, p. 281.

94 J. Destrez, *La pecia dans les manuscrits universitaires du XIIIe et XIV siècle*, Paris 1935.

illustrations are copies of those in our manuscript but were brought up to date in the French style of the mid-fifteenth century by the Master of 'le Prince de Piemont', an artist who worked for the future Amadeus IX of Savoy.[95]

There is no further indication of the whereabouts of our codex until the eighteenth century when it belonged to the Reverend John Josias Conybeare (1779–1824), Vicar of Batheaston in Somerset, a scholar and geologist. It was acquired for the British Museum on 10 July 1839, with money from the Egerton fund, from a sale of books at Southgates, a London book dealer. [96]

The earliest surviving manuscript which derives from the present *Tractatus de herbis* is not an identical copy. It was compiled by Manfredus de Monte Imperiale, probably in Naples, *c.*1330–40 (Paris, Bibliothèque Nationale, MS lat. 6823). [97] Manfredus edited and expanded the text and elaborated the basic illustrations to make them more 'naturalistic'. By the end of the fourteenth century Manfredus's codex was in the library of the Visconti at Pavia and was the model for a limited number of exquisitely illustrated copies, one of which belonged to Wenceslas IV, King of Bohemia.[98] At least three copies of Manfredus's manuscript consisted of illustrations only, and as the *Tractatus de herbis* does not appear to have been translated into Italian, other illustrated herbals eventually supplanted it in Italy.[99]

The French translation of the treatise, made at the end of the fourteenth or early in the fifteenth century, had a far greater impact on the history of herbals.[100] The *Livre des simples médecines*, with the illustrations of the Egerton MS 747 tradition, was copied in France throughout the fifteenth century in expensive codices made for wealthy patrons. It was the model for the first printed herbals in French (the *Arboleyre*, *c.*1486–88, later called *Le grant herbier*) and in English (*The grete herball*, 1526) and was thus, apart from copies of the *Herbarius*, almost the only illustrated text on medicinal simples available in those two countries until the middle of the sixteenth century.[101]

When we leaf through the manuscript it is apparent that the *Tractatus de herbis* cannot have been easy to use in a practical way. The codex is too large and cumbersome (and too precious) to take into the country to identify herbs in the wild. The vast number of simples described in the treatise, compounded by the number and complexity of the remedies and recipes and the need for compatibility of the humours, makes it difficult to use as an everyday apothecary's 'recipe book'. It is almost inconceivable that an apothecary would have stocked all the simples listed in all their different forms, nor would a practising doctor have found it easy to choose a cure for a specific ailment, especially considering the uncertainty surrounding the names of the plants. J. M. Riddle, the outstanding American scholar in this field, was convinced that at this time 'the working pharmacopoeia must have been much smaller than the learned knowledge of pharmacy'.[102] The compendium of the *Tractatus de herbis* is a testimony of the learned knowledge of pharmacy at the end of the thirteenth century.

Charles Singer, writing in 1927, might have dismissed herbal remedies as being 'quite devoid of any rational basis', but recent pharmacological research suggests that this extraordinary encyclopedia of simples has not yet revealed all its secrets.[103] However, the value of the reference material in the text should not be allowed to overshadow the artistic accomplishment of the illustrations. The innovation and variety of the plant paintings and the decorative way in which they are arranged on the page show that this was a book created by someone who had a passionate interest in his subject, an interest which we are fortunate to be able to share after seven centuries.

[95] F. Avril, N. Reynaud, *Les manuscrits à peintures en France, 1440–1520,* (ex. cat. Bibliothèque Nationale, October 1993–January 1994) Paris 1993, p. 209.

[96] The British Library *Catalogue of Additions 1836–1840,* 1839. p. 15, and information kindly given by Michelle Brown.

[97] See note 91.

[98] Rome, Biblioteca Casanatense, MS 459. Baumann 1974, pp. 105–106, with bibliography and figs, pp. 119, 125; Collins 2000, pp. 275–278.

[99] Copies of the illustrations of Paris, Bibliothèque Nationale, MS lat. 6823, are New York, Pierpont Morgan Library, M. 873; Paris, Bibliothèque de l'Ecole des Beaux-Arts MS Masson 116, both fourteenth-century, and a direct fifteenth-century copy of the latter, British Library, Sloane MS 4016; Collins 2000, pp. 273–275.

[100] An unfinished French manuscript with abbreviated text also derived from Egerton MS 747, Florence, Biblioteca Nazionale, MS Pal. 586 was produced partly in Provence and partly in Paris. E. Berti-Toesca, 'Un erbolario del '300', *La Biblofilia*, 39, 1937, pp. 341–353 described Pal. 586 as an illuminated *Tacuinum sanitatis.* Pächt 1950, p. 34 corrected this misapprehension. Baumann 1974, p. 107 (with bibliography and figs. pp. 131–154) reconstructed the order of the manuscript on pp. 172–178. Collins 2000, pp. 264–268.

[101] See note 4; Blunt and Raphael 1994, pp. 114, 163; for the printed herbals see Arber 1986, pp. 26, 28 *et passim.*

[102] Riddle 1974, p. 175.

[103] C. Singer, 'The herbal in antiquity and its transmission to later ages', *Journal of Hellenic Studies,* XLVII, 1927, pp. 1–52.

BRITISH LIBRARY EGERTON MS 747

A TECHNICAL DESCRIPTION OF THE CODEX

Tractatus de herbis, (reproduced here in facsimile) and other pharmaceutical texts written in Latin on 148 parchment folios, arranged in 12 quires of 12 folios and one quire of four folios (folios 108–112), measuring 360 × 242 mm. with evidence of trimming.

The written area measures 260 × 168 mm overall, divided into two columns of text *c.*78 mm. wide with a maximum of 55 lines per column. The ruling, in hard-point, consists of four or five vertical rulings with double lines ruled top and bottom of the text area. The inner margin measures *c.*30 mm. and the lower margins now *c.*75 mm. Pricking for the ruling is no longer visible. Most of the gatherings have catchwords in simple penwork frames at the bottom of the verso of the last folio. The manuscript is in its original order, but lacks folios at the beginning and end. The fact that the Egerton bookplate appears on the first and last folios suggests that the manuscript was incomplete when it was acquired by the British Museum in 1839.

The parchment is not very fine and its pigmentation is pronounced, indicating that it is of goat or calf skin. The leaves are arranged with hair-side to hair and flesh to flesh.

The main text is written in two columns in brown ink in *littera gothica textualis rotunda media,* a round Italian Gothic bookhand, of medium grade, with features that point to an Italian scribe writing in the last quarter of the thirteenth century or the first quarter of the fourteenth. The chapter initials are alternately blue and red, frequently with simple penwork in the contrasting colour. In-text capitals and paragraph marks are touched in red and blue throughout, including the lists of chapter headings that precede each alphabetical section and many titles to the illustrations. Abbreviations are used extensively. Passages of text from Isaac Judaeus's treatise are in a minute *littera gothica glossularis,* most probably written by the scribe of the main text e.g. folios 27v, 28r, 28v, 29r.

Additional titles or synonyms to some of the illustrations were written by another hand in an ink of higher carbon content, similar to that of the titles to the illustrations on folios 106–109 and of the alterations to the *explicit* on folio 106. Later annotations, usually synonyms, are found on folios 64v, 81v.

Two *incipit* pages (folios 1 and 112) have illuminated borders and initials, and the *Tractatus* section has 406 illustrations of plants and 25 of other simples interspersed in the text and some marginal representations of snakes, dogs and serpents..

The modern red leather binding is stamped in gold on the front with the Egerton crest and on the spine with the titles 'Bartholomeus Minus, *Tractatus de Herbis,* Nicholaus *de Medicamentis.* Brit. Mus. Egerton Ms 747.'

The manuscript has three foliations. According to the first foliation, not visible in this facsimile, written in light brown ink in Arabic numerals in the upper outer corner of the recto of each folio, the present folio 3 was numbered 6 and the present folio 145 was 149. This indicates a loss of three folios preceding the present *incipit* to the *Tractatus.* The second foliation, in Roman numerals in pale-brown ink, and starting from the present folio 1, was written after the lunar calendar (folio 110) was written and after the loss of the three prefatory folios (cx and cxix of this foliation were omitted). The most recent foliation is in Arabic numerals written in pencil in the upper, outer corner of the recto of each folio, 1–147 (the folio between 111 and 112 is not numbered.)

THE CONTENTS OF THE CODEX

Egerton MS 747 contains a collection of texts written in Latin of which the longest is the illustrated *Tractatus de herbis* on folios 1–106. Folios 106–109 have a number of illustrations of plants with titles but no text, which follow on from the *Tractatus* but are not part of it and which may have been added some time after the *Tractatus* was completed. The remainder of the codex, not reproduced here, contains the following texts with no illustrations: folios 108–112 in a separate gathering which, following the plant paintings on the recto of folio 109, now has a series of texts written in cursive script which may be dated to the mid-fourteenth century: folio 109v, *Prognostica Galieni*; folio 110, a lunar calendar for the Metonic cycle; folio 111, a canon for the lunar calendar. *Antidotarium Nicolai* occupies folios 112–24, followed on folios 124–48v by complementary information on dosages and possible substitute medicines: Nicolaus *De dosibus medicinarum*, folio 124v; a *quid pro quo*: *Quando una res potest poni pro alia que non reperitur*, folio 125v; several short texts on weights and measures of medicaments, folios 127v–8; a list of synonyms for the plants used by earlier authors, *Incipiunt sinonima Galieni & Avicenne atque Serapiones & Almansore & Grecorum omnia simul*, folio 128v; and on folio 146v, *Confectiones et medicine que non sunt in Antidotario Nicolai*, which is incomplete.[104] All these texts appear to have been written by the same scribe and were obviously planned as complementary material.

[104] L. Thorndike and P. Kibre, *A catalogue of incipits of mediaeval scientific writings in Latin*, London 1963, columns 1231, 1059, 439, 740, 27.

SELECTED BIBLIOGRAPHY

ANDERSON 1977. F. J. Anderson, *An illustrated history of the herbals*, New York 1977.

ARBER 1986. A. Arber, *Herbals, their origin and evolution 1470–1670*, 3rd edn. Cambridge 1986, (with extensive bibliography). [First published in 1912, second edition 1938.]

BAUMANN 1974. F. A. Baumann, *Das Erbario Carrarese*, Berne 1974.

BLUNT AND RAPHAEL 1994. W. Blunt and S. Raphael, *The illustrated Herbal*, 2nd edn. London 1994. [First published in 1979.]

CAMUS 1886. G. Camus, 'L'opera salernitana "Circa instans" ed il testo primitivo del "Grant Herbier en François"', *Memorie della regia accademia di scienze, lettere ed arti in Modena,* serie 2, 4, 1886, sezione di lettere, pp. 49–199.

COLLINS 2000. M. Collins, *Medieval herbals, the illustrative traditions*, London and Toronto 2000.

GALLO 1994. *Salerno e la sua Scuola medica, ed.* I. Gallo, Salerno 1994

GRIEVE 1982. M. Grieve, *A modern Herbal*, Harmondsworth, 6th edn. 1982, edited and introduced by C. F. Leyel. [First published in 1931.]

DE HAMEL 1994. C. de Hamel, *A history of illuminated manuscripts*, Oxford 1986, 2nd edn, London 1994.

HUNGER 1935. F. W. T. Hunger, *The Herbal of Pseudo-Apuleius (Codex Casinensis 97)*, Leiden 1935.

JACQUART 1990. D.Jacquart and F. Micheau, *La Médecine arabe et l'occident médiéval,* Paris 1990.

JONES 1985. P. M. Jones, *Secreta salernitana* in *Kos* I, 1, 1984, pp. 33–50.

KRISTELLER 1956. P. O. Kristeller, 'The school of Salerno. Its development and its contribution to the history of learning', *Studies in Renaissance thought and letters*, Rome 1956, pp. 495–551.

LA SCUOLA MEDICA 1988. *La scuola medica Salernitana; storia, immagini, manoscritti, dall' XI al XIII secolo,* ed. M. Pasca, Naples 1988.

MAZAL 1998. O. Mazal, *Der Wiener Dioskurides. Codex medicus Graecus 1 der Österreichischen Nationalbibliothek,* 1. Commentary and facsimile, Graz 1998.

NISSEN 1958. C. Nissen, *Herbals of five centuries*, Zurich 1958.

OPSOMER 1984. C. Opsomer, *Le Livre des simples médecines, Codex Bruxellensis IV. 1024. A 15th-century French Herbal*, English trans. by E. Roberts and W. T. Stearn; commentaries by C. Opsomer and W. T. Stearn, Antwerp 1984.

PÄCHT 1950. O. Pächt, 'Early Italian nature studies and the early calendar landscape', *Journal of the Warburg and Courtauld Institutes*, 13, 1950, pp. 13–47.

PLATÉARIUS 1986. *Platéarius, Le livre des simples médecines, d'après le manuscrit français 12322 de la Bibliothèque nationale de Paris,* translation and adaptation by G. Malandin, commentaries by F. Avril, P. Lieutaghi, G. Malandin, Paris 1986.

RIDDLE 1971. J. M. Riddle, 'Dioscorides', in *Dictionary of scientific biography*, 4, New York 1971, pp. 119–23.

—— 1974. J. M. Riddle, 'Theory and practice in Medieval medicine', *Viator. Medieval and Renaissance studies,* 5, 1974, pp. 157–184.

—— 1985. J. M. Riddle, *Dioscorides on pharmacy and medicine*, Austin, Texas 1985.

SINGER 1927. C. Singer, 'The Herbal in Antiquity and its transmission to later ages', *Journal of Hellenic Studies*, XLVII, 1927, pp. 1–52.

SIRAISI 1990. N. G. Siraisi, *Medieval and early renaissance medicine*; Chicago 1990.

SKINNER 1997. P. Skinner, *Health and medicine in early medieval southern Italy*, Leiden, New York, Cologne 1997

THORNDIKE 1945. L. Thorndike, *The Herbal of Rufinus*, Chicago 1945

TORESELLA 1990. S. Toresella, 'Sono senesi i primi erbari figurati', *Congresso nazionale dell'accademia italiana di storia della farmacia*; Università degli studi di Siena, Facoltà di farmacia, 750° anno accademico, Siena, 9–11 novembre 1990, pp. 297–305.

ZOTTER 1996. *Medicina antiqua, Codex Vindobonensis 93 der Österreichischen Nationalbibliothek*, commentary by Hans Zotter, Graz 1996.

PLANTS AND OTHER MEDICINAL SIMPLES LISTED IN EGERTON MS 747

SANDRA RAPHAEL

* indicates a description with no illustration   † indicates a medicinal simple other than a plant product

fol. 1r Aloen _Aloe vera_ aloe
fol. 2r Aloen lignum _Aquillaria agallochia_ aloe wood
fol. 2r †Aurum gold
fol. 2v *†Argentum vivum mercury, quicksilver
fol. 2v *Asa fetida _Ferula assa-foetida_ asafetida
fol. 3r Agnus castus _Vitex agnus-castus_ chaste tree
fol. 3r †Alumen alum
fol. 3r Appium commune _Apium graveolens_ celery
fol. 3v Appium raninum _Ranunculus_ species buttercup
fol. 3v Appium risus _Ranunculus sceleratus_ celery-leaved buttercup
fol. 4r Appium emoroidarum _Ranunculus ficaria_ lesser celandine, pilewort
fol. 4r †Amidum starch
fol. 4r *†Antimonium (sulphide of) antimony
fol. 4r Acatia _Prunus spinosa_ blackthorn
fol. 4v Arbor abiete _Abies_ species fir tree
fol. 4v Agaricus _Laricifomes officinale_ white or larch agaric (around the roots of) Arbor abiete
fol. 4v Anetum _Anethum graveolens_ dill
fol. 5r Anfodillum _Asphodelus_ species asphodel
fol. 5r Allium domesticum _Allium sativum_ garlic
fol. 5r Allium silvestre _Allium vineale_ wild garlic
fol. 5v Acorus _Iris pseudacorus_ yellow flag
fol. 5v *Armoniacum _Dorema armoniacum_ or _D. aucheri_ gum ammoniac
fol. 6r *Anisum _Pimpinella anisum_ aniseed
fol. 6r Absinthium _Artemisia absinthium_ or _A. pontica_ wormwood
fol. 6v Anacardi _Semecarpus anacardium_ marking nut, oriental cashew nut
fol. 6v *Amigdales dulces _Prunus dulcis_ var. _dulcis_ (formerly _P. amygdalus_) sweet almond
fol. 6v *Amigdales amare _Prunus dulcis_ var. _amara_ (formerly _P. amygdalus_) bitter almond
fol. 7r Aristolongia _Aristolochia rotunda_ round-rooted birthwort
fol. 7r Aristolongia longa _Aristolochia longa_ long-rooted birthwort
fol. 7r †Ambra ambergris (hardened secretions from the intestines of sperm whales)
fol. 7v Artemisia maior _Artemisia vulgaris_ mugwort
fol. 8r Arthemisia media _Tanacetum vulgare_ tansy
fol. 8r Arthemisia leptaphilos _Tanacetum parthenium_ feverfew
fol. 8v †Acetum vinegar
fol. 8v Alcanna _Lawsonia alba_ or _Alkanna tinctorium_ henna or dyer's alkanet
fol. 9r †Auripigmentum extracting orpiment (trisulphide of arsenic)
fol. 9r †Aspaltum asphalt, bitumen (mineral pitch from Palestine and Babylon)
fol. 9r *Anabulla a cross-reference to titimallium (see folio 101)
fol. 9r Acantum possibly _Acanthus_ species
fol. 9v Adianthos _Adiantum capillus-veneris_ maidenhair fern
fol. 9v Agrimonia _Agrimonia eupatoria_ agrimony
fol. 10r Appollinaris _Tussilago farfara_ coltsfoot
fol. 10r Alteam _Althaea officinalis_ marshmallow
fol. 10v Astula regia possibly _Asphodeline lutea_ yellow asphodel, king's spear
fol. 10v Anbroxiana _Ambrosia maritima_ ambrosia
fol. 10v Asara _Asarum europaeum_ asarabacca
fol. 11r Atriplex _Atriplex hortensis_ garden orach
fol. 11r Anthera conspicuous stamens of a rose, possibly _Rosa gallica_
fol. 11r Anthora _Aconitum anthora_ anthora monkshood
fol. 11v Avena _Avena sativa_ oats
fol. 11v Ameos _Carum carvi_ caraway
fol. 11v Amomum _Amomum_ species
fol. 12r Alleluia _Oxalis acetosella_ wood sorrel
fol. 12r Acetosa _Rumex acetosa_ sorrel
fol. 12r *Avellanarum _Corylus avellana_ or _C. maxima_ hazel or filbert
fol. 12r Albatra _Arbutus unedo_ strawberry tree
fol. 12r *Antiformacum _Vincetoxicum officinale_ swallow wort
fol. 12r Balsamus _Commiphora opobalsamum_ balsam, balm of Gilead
fol. 12v †Bolus bole armeniac or Armenian bole
fol. 13r Balaustia _Punica granatum_ (dried flowers of) pomegranate
fol. 13r Borrago _Borago officinalis_ borage
fol. 13v Baucia _Pastinaca sativa_ parsnip
fol. 13v *†Borax borax, acid borate of sodium
fol. 14r Bectonica _Stachys officinalis_ (formerly _Betonica officinalis_) betony
fol. 14v *†Bernix _Tetraclinis articulata_ vernix, a gum from this tree
fol. 14v Branca ursina _Acanthus mollis_ acanthus
fol. 15r Berberi _Berberis vulgaris_ or _Crataegus_ species barberry or hawthorn

fol. 15r *†Belliculi marini shells of marine molluscs
fol. 15r *Bistorta *Polygonum bistorta* bistort
fol. 15r Bombax *Gossypium herbaceum* cotton
fol. 15v Buglossa *Anchusa officinalis* or *A. arvensis* alkanet or bugloss
fol. 15v *†Butirum butter
fol. 16r Berbena *Vervena officinalis* vervain
fol. 16v Brictanica *Rumex* species, perhaps *R. acetosa* or *R. hydrolapathum* sorrel or water dock
fol. 16v Bursa pastoris *Capsella bursa-pastoris* shepherd's purse
fol. 16v Brionia *Bryonia dioica* white bryony
fol. 17r Bedeguard *Silybum marianum* milk thistle
fol. 17r *Bdellium *Commiphora roxburghii* bdellium gum
fol. 17v Bardana *Arctium lappa* great burdock
fol. 17v Buxus *Buxus sempervirens* box
fol. 18r Bracillum *Caesalpinia sappan* brazilwood
fol. 18r Bruscus *Ruscus aculeatus* butcher's broom
fol. 18r Bleta *Beta vulgaris* beet
fol. 18r †Blacte bisancie mollusc shell from Byzantium
fol. 18v Beem album possibly *Amaranthus* species
fol. 18v Beem rubeum possibly *Amaranthus* species
fol. 18v Ciclamen *Cyclamen hederifolium* cyclamen, sowbread
fol. 19r *Canphora *Cinnamomum camphora* camphor
fol. 19v Coloquintida *Citrullus colocynthis* colocynth
fol. 19v Cassia fistula *Cassia fistula* Indian laburnum, purging cassia
fol. 20r Cuscute *Cuscuta epilinum* flax dodder
fol. 20r Cardamomum *Elettaria cardamomum* cardamom
fol. 20v *†Cerusa ceruse, white lead
fol. 20v Capparis *Capparis spinosa* capers
fol. 21r Calamentum *Calamintha sylvatica* or *C. officinalis* wood calamint or common calamint
fol. 21r Centaurea minor, maior *Centaurea* species, possibly *C. erythraea* common centaury
fol. 21v Cassia ligne *Cinnamomum aromaticum* formerly *C.cassia* cassia bark
fol. 22r Castoreum ointment from glands of beaver (castor)
fol. 22v Cubebe *Piper cubeba* cubebs
fol. 22v Capillus veneris *Adiantum capillus-veneris* maidenhair fern
fol. 22v Cipressus *Cupressus sempervirens* common cypress
fol. 23r Cinnamomum *Cinnamomum zeylanicum* cinnamon
fol. 23r Camedreos *Veronica chamaedrys* germander speedwell
fol. 23v Camepitheos *Ajuga chamaepitys* ground-pine
fol. 24r Carui *Carum carvi* caraway
fol. 24r Ciminum *Cuminum cyminum* cumin
fol. 24r Cicuta *Conium maculatum* or *C. virosa* hemlock or cowbane
fol. 24v Croci orientalis *Crocus sativus* saffron crocus
fol. 24v Crocus ortensis, cartamen *Carthamus tinctorius* safflower (still used as false saffron)
fol. 25r Ciperus *Cyperus rotundus* or *C. longus* rush or galingale
fol. 25r Calamus *Acorus calamus* sweet flag
fol. 25v †Corallus coral
fol. 25v Cataputia *Euphorbia lathyris* caper spurge
fol. 26r Cretanus *Crithmum maritimum* rock samphire
fol. 26r Costus *Saussurea lappa* costus
fol. 26v *Cantabrum *Triticum aestivum* wheatbran
fol. 26v *Colofonia pine resin, colophony
fol. 26v Cucurbita *Lagenaria siceraria* gourd
fol. 27r Citruli *Citrullus lanatus* watermelon
fol. 27r Celidonia *Chelidonium majus* greater celandine
fol. 27r *Cucumeris *Cucumis sativus* cucumber
fol. 27v Coliandrum *Coriandrum sativum* coriander
fol. 27v *†Calx lime, quicklime
fol. 27v Cerfollium *Anthriscus cerefolium* chervil
fol. 27v *Caules *Brassica* species or *Crambe maritima* cabbage or sea-kale
fol. 28r Canapa *Cannabis sativa* hemp
fol. 28r Camelleunta alba possibly *Carlina* species or *Atractylis gummifera* thistle
fol. 28r *Cicer *Cicer arietinum* chick pea
fol. 28v Camelleunta nigra *Dipsacus* species teasel
fol. 28v Camomilla *Chamaemelum nobile* sweet chamomile
fol. 28v *Castanee *Castanea sativa* sweet chestnut
fol. 29r *Cotula fetida *Anthemis cotula* mayweed, dog fennel, stinking chamomile
fol. 29r Cottilidon *Umbilicus rupestris* navelwort
fol. 29r Cepa domestica *Allium cepa* onion
fol. 29v Cornucervino *Coronopus squamatus* or *Plantago coronopus* swine cress or buck's horn plantain
fol. 29v *Culcasia *Colocasia esculenta* dasheen
fol. 29v Canna *Phragmites australis* reed
fol. 29v *Canna mellis *Saccharum officinalis* sugar-cane
fol. 30r Calendula *Calendula officinalis* pot marigold
fol. 30r Ceterach *Ceterach officinarum* rustyback (fern)
fol. 30r Candellaria possibly *Lithospermum* species
fol. 30v Consolida maior *Symphytum officinalis* comfrey
fol. 30v Consolida media *Symphytum tuberosum* tuberous comfrey
fol. 30v Consolida minor *Prunella vulgaris* self-heal
fol. 31r Cotonaria *Otanthus maritimus* cottonweed
fol. 31r *Cennerugio *Glaucium corniculatum* red horned poppy
fol. 31r Cerasorum *Prunus cerasus* cherry
fol. 31v Capragine *Galega officinalis* goat's rue
fol. 31v Caprifollium *Lonicera caprifolium* honeysuckle
fol. 32r Diagridium *Convolvulus scammonia* scammony (juice)

fol. 32v Dragagantum (from *Astragalus gummifera* and other species) gum tragacanth
fol. 33r Daucus *Daucus carota* carrot
fol. 33r *†Dragantum vitriolum possibly vitriol
fol. 33r Diptamus *Dictamnus albus* fraxinella, dittany
fol. 33v Deronici possibly *Doronicum* species or *Potentilla erecta* tormentil
fol. 33v Dactilis *Phoenix dactylifera* date
fol. 34r Endivia *Cichorium endiva* or *Sonchus oleraceus* endive or sowthistle
fol. 34r Epithimum *Cuscuta epithymum* dodder
fol. 34v Enula *Inula helenium* elecampane
fol. 34v Euforbium *Euphorbia resinifera* the resin, officinal spurge
fol. 35r Eupatorium *Salvia* species or *Agrimonia eupatorium* agrimony
fol. 35r Enblici *Phyllanthus emblica* emblic, myrobalan
fol. 35v Epatica *Marchantia polymorpha* or *Hepatica nobilis* or *Anemone hepatica* liverwort
fol. 35v *†Es ustu *aesustum* powder of bronze?
fol. 35v Electerium *Ecballium elaterium* squirting cucumber
fol. 36r Elleborus album *Veratrum album* white or false hellebore
fol. 36r Elleborus niger *Helleborus niger* black hellebore
fol. 36v Esula *Euphorbia esula* leafy spurge
fol. 36v Eruca *Eruca sativa* wild rocket
fol. 37r *†Emathites lapis haematite
fol. 37r Ebulus *Sambucus ebulus* dwarf elder
fol. 37r Edera nigra *Hedera helix* ivy
fol. 37v Exifion *Iris foetidissima* stinking iris
fol. 37v Eliotropion *Cichorium intybus* chicory, wild succory
fol. 38r Eufragia *Euphrasia* species eyebright
fol. 38r Flamula *Clematis flammula*
fol. 38v *†Ferrum iron
fol. 38v Fumus terre *Fumaria officinalis* fumitory
fol. 38v Fu idest Valeriana *Valeriana phu* or *V. officinalis* valerian
fol. 39r Fillipendula *Filipendula vulgaris* dropwort
fol. 39r Fraxinus *Fraxinus excelsior* ash
fol. 39v Feniculus *Foeniculum vulgare* fennel
fol. 39v Fenugrecum *Trigonella foenum-graecum* fenugreek
fol. 40r Filices possibly *Polypodium vulgare* or *Dryopteris filix-mas* polypody or male fern
fol. 40r Fragia sive fragula *Fragaria vesca* wild strawberry
fol. 40v Fistularia *Helianthemum origanifolium* or *H. nummularium* rock rose
fol. 40v Fusago *Euonymus europaeus* spindle
fol. 40v Facius vidon possibly *Daphne laureola* spurge laurel
fol. 40v *Fagioli *Lablab niger* (or *Dolichos lablab*) hyacinth bean or *Vigna unguiculata* cowpea
fol. 41r Faba inversa *Solanum* species or *Atropa belladonna* nightshade
fol. 41r Faba grassa *Sedum telephium* orpine
fol. 41r Faba comunes *Vicia faba* broad bean
fol. 41v *Fungi agarics or mushrooms
fol. 41v Ferula *Ferula communis* (ssp. *nodiflora?*) or their resin
fol. 41v Ficubus *Ficus carica* fig
fol. 41v *Filicis masculus *Dryopteris filix-mas* male fern
fol. 41v *†Fuligo soot
fol. 42r Gariofili *Syzygium aromaticum* (formerly *Eugenia caryophyllata*) cloves
fol. 42v Gentiana *Gentiana lutea* yellow gentian
fol. 42v Galanga *Kaempferia galanga* greater galangal
fol. 43r Galbanum *Ferula gumosa* (formerly *F. galbaniflua*) resin
fol. 43r *Gummi arabici gum arabic from *Acacia* species
fol. 43v Gariofilata *Geum urbanum* wood avens
fol. 43v Git *Agrostemma githago* corncockle
fol. 44r Granum solis *Lithospermum officinale* common gromwell
fol. 44r Gallitricum *Salvia pratensis* or *S. sclarea* meadow clary or clary
fol. 44r Galla galls on oak twigs
fol. 44v *Glandes acorns of *Quercus* species oaks
fol. 44v *†Galia muscata a mixture of mastic, gum arabic, camphor, rosewater, and other ingredients
fol. 44v Genestinsula *Osyris alba* osyris
fol. 44v Genestra *Genista* species or *Cytisus scoparius* broom
fol. 45r Gramen *Agropyron repens* couch grass
fol. 45r *Grias *Rubia tinctorum* madder?
fol. 45r *Gumma elemin resin, perhaps from a species of *Canarium*
fol. 45r *Granum fractum unidentified 'crushed seeds'
fol. 45r *Grisomilus *Prunus armeniaca* apricot
fol. 45v Gratia deo *Gratiola officinalis* gratiola
fol. 45v Golgemma *Lavandula* species lavender
fol. 45v Gelesia *Amaranthus tricolor* Joseph's coat
fol. 46r Hermodactilis *Hermodactylus tuberosus* snakeshead iris
fol. 46r Herba vitis *Asperula cynanchica* squinancy root
fol. 46v Herba rabiosa *Heliotropium europaeum* heliotrope, turnsole
fol. 46v Hecinum a purple-flowered thistle, possibly *Sonchus* species
fol. 47r Herpillos *Thymus serpillum* thyme
fol. 47r *Herba tue (ture) unidentified
fol. 47v Herba sancte marie *Tanacetum balsamita* costmary
fol. 47v Herba paralisis traditionally *Primula vulgaris* primrose but here a plant like rue
fol. 47v Iusquiamus *Hyoscyamus niger* henbane
fol. 48r Isopus minor *Acinos arvensis* basil thyme
fol. 48r Isopus maior *Hyssopus officinalis* hyssop
fol. 48v Iarus *Arum maculatum* lords and ladies

fol. 48v Iris *Iris florentina, I. germanica, I. pseudacorus, I. foetidissima*
fol. 49r Ipoquistidos *Cytinus hypocistis* cytinus
fol. 49r Iuniperus *Juniperus communis* juniper
fol. 49v Ipericon perforata, herba sancti johannis *Hypericum perforatum* St John's wort
fol. 49v Ippirum *Equisetum* species horsetail
fol. 50r Inantes *Vitis vinifera* grapevine
fol. 50r Indacus *Isatis tinctoria* woad
fol. 50v Iva *Ajuga chamaepitys* ground-pine
fol. 50v Incensaria possibly *Primula vulgaris* primrose
fol. 50v Ieribulbus *Allium* species, possibly *A. sativum* garlic
fol. 51r Inmolum album *A. moly* or *A. nigra* moly
fol. 51r Karabe amber, fossilized resin, possibly from *Tetraclinis articulata*
fol. 51r Laudanum gum from *Cistus creticus* or *C. ladanifer*
fol. 51v Liquiritia *Glycyrrhiza glabra* liquorice
fol. 51v †Lapis lazuli semi-precious, deep blue stone
fol. 52r Lilium album *Lilium candidum* white (Madonna) lily (and others perhaps *L. martagon,* martagon or Turk's cap, and *L. bulbiferum* var. *croceum,* yellow lily)
fol. 52r of Litium possibly *Lycium* boxthorn or Duke Argyll's tea-tree
fol. 52v Lingua avis *Fraxinus* species winged seeds of ash
fol. 52v Linochis *Mercurialis annua* mercury
fol. 53r Lapatium *Rumex* species dock
fol. 53r *†Litargirium litharge, protoxide of lead
fol. 53v Lactuca *Lactuca sativa* lettuce
fol. 53v *Lactuca silvestris *Lactuca serriola* or *L. virosa* prickly lettuce or opium lettuce
fol. 53v Lupinus *Lupinus albus* or *L. luteus* lupin
fol. 54r Laurus *Laurus nobilis* bay laurel
fol. 54r Lentiscus *Pistacia lentiscus* lentisk, mastic
fol. 54v Lenticula *Lens culinaris* lentil
fol. 54v Laureola *Daphne laureola* or *Daphne mezereum* spurge laurel or mezereon
fol. 55r Levisticus *Levisticum officinale* lovage
fol. 55r *†Lapis magnetis magnet
fol. 55r *†Lapis agapis possibly fossilised spines of sea urchins
fol. 55r *†Lapis lincis lynx stone, possibly yellow amber
fol. 55r *†Lapis armenicus a blue copper carbonate
fol. 55r *†Lapis spongie stones found in sponges
fol. 55r *†Lapis demonis a black stone
fol. 55v Lollium *Lolium temulentum* darnel
fol. 55v Luppulus *Humulus lupulus* hop
fol. 56r Leontopodium possibly *Tragopogon pratensis* goat's beard
fol. 56r Lactuca silvatica *Lactuca serriola* prickly lettuce
fol. 56v Linosa *Linum usitatissimum* flax
fol. 56v Linaria *Linaria vulgaris* toadflax
fol. 56v Lenticule aquatice *Lemna minor* duckweed
fol. 57r Lingua canis *Cynoglossum officinale* hound's tongue
fol. 57r Lingua ircina *Echium vulgare* viper's bugloss
fol. 57r of *†Lacca lac, the dark red resinous secretion *Coccus lacca,* an insect
fol. 57v Lanceolata *Plantago lanceolata* ribwort plantain
fol. 57v Lactuca leporina *Sonchus oleraceus* common sow thistle, hare's lettuce
fol. 57v *†Lepidos calcis unidentified
fol. 57v Lappaccioli *Arctium lappa* burdock
fol. 58r Mirtus *Vaccinium myrtillus* bilberry
fol.58r *†Manna perhaps a substance from *Fraxinus ornus* flowering or manna ash
fol. 58v Mellilotus *Melilotus officinalis* or *Trigonella foenum-graecum* melilot, yellow medick, or fenugreek
fol. 58v Malva *Althaea officinalis* marsh mallow
fol. 58v *Malvaviscus *Malva sylvestris* common mallow
fol. 59r Malva ortensis possibly a species of *Lavatera*
fol. 59r *†Mastix gum resin from *Pistacia lentiscus* mastic
fol. 59v Menta *Mentha viridis* spearmint
fol. 60r Menta romana *Mentha piperata* peppermint
fol. 60r Mentastrum *Mentha aquatica* or *Mentha rotundifolia* water or apple mint
fol. 60v †Margarita pearls (in a shell of the wrong shape)
fol. 60v †Mumia rare powder from embalmed mummies
fol. 61r Mandragora *Mandragora officinarum* mandrake
fol. 61r Meu *Meum athamanticum* baldmoney, meu, spignel
fol. 61v Mala citonia *Cydonia oblonga* quince
fol. 62r Malorum granatorum *Punica granatum* pomegranate
fol. 62r Mala matiana *Malus sylvestris* crabapple
fol. 62v Marubium *Marrubium vulgare* white horehound
fol. 62v †Mel honey, with bees on a honeycomb
fol. 63r †Muscus musk from the glands of hunted deer
fol. 63v *Myroballani possibly *Prunus cerasifera* or the plum-like fruit of *Terminalia* species myrobalan plum or Indian myrobalan
fol. 64r Maca *Myristica fragrans* mace
fol. 64r *Mirra *Commiphora myrrha* myrrh
fol. 64r Maiorana *Origanum majorana* sweet marjoram
fol. 64r *Milium *Panicum miliaceum* millet
fol. 64v Melissa *Melissa officinalis* lemon balm
fol. 64v Mori *Morus nigra* or *Rubus fruticosus* mulberry or blackberry
fol. 65r Matrisilva *Lonicera caprifolium* honeysuckle
fol. 65r Macedonia *Smyrnium olusatrum* alexanders
fol. 65v Morsus diaboli *Succisa pratensis* devil's bit scabious
fol. 65v Muscata maior *Geranium* species perhaps *G. robertianum* herb robert
fol. 65v Muscata minor possibly *Erodium moschatum* storksbill

fol. 66r Millefolium *Achillea millefolium* yarrow
fol. 66r *Musa *Musa × paradisiaca* banana
fol. 66r Mellongiano *Solanum melongena* aubergine
fol. 66v Melonis *Cucumis melo* melon
fol. 66v Nasturcium *Rorippa nasturtium-aquaticum* watercress
fol. 67r Nasturcium agreste *Lepidium campestre* pepperwort
fol 67r Nitrus nitrate of potassium
fol. 67r Nenufar *Nymphaea alba* waterlily
fol. 67v Nux muscata *Myristica fragrans* nutmeg
fol. 67v Nux indica *Cocos nucifera* coconut
fol. 68r Nux sciarca *Aframomum melegueta* Melegueta pepper, grains of paradise
fol. 68r Nux vomica *Strychnos nux-vomica* nux vomica
fol. 68v Nigella *Nigella sativa* love-in-a-mist (with edible seeds)
fol. 68v Narciscus perhaps *Pancratium maritimum* sea daffodil
fol. 69r Nespile *Mespilus germanica* medlar
fol. 69r Ocimum *Ocimum basilicum* sweet basil
fol. 69v Oppoponax *Opopanax chironium* gum
fol. 70r *Opium from *Papaver somniferum*
fol. 70r Origanum *Origanum vulgare* wild marjoram
fol. 70v Oxifenicia *Tamarindus indica* tamarind
fol. 70v Ordum *Hordeum vulgare* barley
fol. 71r †Os de cor de cervi hardened cartilage from the hearts of deer
fol. 71r †Os sepie cuttlebone (from squid, *Sepia officinalis*)
fol. 71r Olibanum *Boswellia* species, possibly *B. carteri* frankincense
fol. 71r *Oliva *Olea europaea* olive
fol. 71r *Oleu olive oil
fol. 71v Oleander *Nerium oleander* oleander
fol. 71v Ostriago possibly *Parietaria officinalis* pellitory
fol. 72r *Piretrum *Tanacetum parthenium* or *Anacyclus pyrethrum* feverfew or Roman pellitory
fol. 72r Piper *Piper nigrum* pepper
fol. 72v Peonia *Paeonia officinalis* or *P. mascula* peony
fol. 73r Papaver nigrum *Papaver* species
fol. 73r Papaver album *Papaver somniferum* opium poppy
fol. 73v Papaver rubeum *Papaver rhoeas* corn poppy
fol. 73v Peucedanum *Peucedanum officinale* hog's fennel
fol. 74r Petrosellinum *Petroselinum crispum* parsley
fol. 74r Policaria *Pulicaria dysenterica* fleabane
fol. 74v Pinea *Pinus pinea* stone pine
fol. 74v Pruna *Prunus domestica* plum
fol. 75r †Pennidum a confection like barley sugar
fol. 75r Psillium *Plantago afra* psyllium plantain, fleawort
fol. 75r Polipodium *Polypodium vulgare* polypody
fol. 75v *†Petroleum petroleum
fol. 75v Paritaria *Parietaria officinalis* pellitory-of-the-wall
fol. 76r Portulaca *Portulaca oleracea* purslane
fol. 76r Pulegium *Mentha pulegium* pennyroyal
fol. 76v Pira *Pyrus communis* pear
fol. 76v Pomum citrinum *Citrus medica* citron
fol. 77r Passulis *Vitis vinifera* grapevine (raisins)
fol. 77r Pistacee *Pistacea vera* pistachio
fol. 77v *†Plumbum lead
fol. 77v Polium *Teucrium polium* mountain germander
fol. 77v *†Pix pine pitch
fol. 77v Plantago maior *Plantago major* greater plantain
fol. 78r Plantago minor possibly *Plantago lanceolata* ribwort plantain
fol. 78r †Panicum *Panicum miliaceum* broomcorn
fol. 78v Penthaphilon *Potentilla reptans* creeping cinquefoil
fol. 78v Polligonia *Polygonum aviculare* knotgrass
fol. 79r Politricum *Asplenium trichomanes* maidenhair spleenwort
fol. 79r Primula veris *Bellis perennis* daisy, bruisewort
fol. 79v Palatio leporis *Asparagus officinalis* asparagus
fol. 79v Pulmonaria *Pulmonaria officinalis* lungwort
fol. 80r Persicaria *Polygonum persicaria* redshank
fol. 80r Paratella *Abrus precatorius* jequerity, Indian liquorice
fol. 80v Pinpinella *Sanguisorba officinalis* great burnet
fol. 80v Pilosella *Hieracium pilosella* mouse-ear hawkweed
fol. 81r Provinca *Vinca major* periwinkle
fol. 81r Palma christi *Dactylorhiza* species spotted orchid
fol. 81v Persica *Prunus persica* peach
fol. 81v *Pes vituli, Barba Aaron, see Iarus fol. 48v
fol. 82r Pes leporinus possibly *Leontodon tuberosus* tuberous hawkbit
fol. 82r Palleo *Hordeum murinum* wall barley
fol. 82v Pes columbinus *Geranium molle* or *G. columbinum* dove's-foot cranesbill
fol. 82v Porrus *Allium porrum* leek
fol. 83r Rosa *Rosa gallica*
fol. 83v Raphanus *Armoracia rusticana* horseradish
fol. 84r Radix *Raphanus sativus* radish
fol. 84r Reubarbarum *Rheum* species rhubarb
fol. 84v Reuponticum *Leuzea rhapontica*
fol. 84v Rubea *Rubia tinctorum* madder
fol. 85r Ruta *Ruta graveolens* rue
fol. 85r *Ruta agrestis *Ruta montana* wild rue
fol. 85v Rosmarinus *Rosmarinus officinalis* rosemary
fol. 85v Rubus *Rubus fruticosus* blackberry
fol. 86r Rodalda *Lepidium latifolium* dittander
fol. 86r Rabiosa possibly *Heliotropium europaeum* heliotrope, turnsole
fol. 86v Risus *Oryza sativa* rice
fol. 86v *Robillum *Lathyrus cicera* or *L. sativus* chickling vetch
fol. 86v Rapistrum *Raphanus raphanistrum* wild radish
fol. 87r Rapa *Brassica rapa* turnip

fol. 87v Spica nardi *Nardostachys grandiflora* or *Valeriana celtica* Indian or Celtic spikenard
fol. 88r Strignum, morella *Solanum nigrum* black nightshade
fol. 88r Solatrum rusticum *Physalis alkekengi* Chinese lantern
fol. 88r *Serapinum *Ferula* species serapin or sagapenum gum
fol. 88v Semperviva *Sempervivum tectorum* houseleek
fol. 88v †Sulfur sulphur
fol. 89r *Siselios *Laserpitium* species, possibly *L. siler*
fol. 89r Saponaria *Saponaria officinalis* soapwort
fol. 89r Sanguis draconis *Dracaena draco* or *D. cinnabari* dragon's blood resin
fol. 89v Squinantum *Cymbopogon schoenanthus* camel grass
fol. 89v Sinapis *Sinapis alba* white mustard
fol. 90r Sarcocolla resin from *Astragalus fasciculifolius*
fol. 90r Sticados citrinus *Helichrysum stoechas* helichrysum
fol. 90v Sticados arabicus *Lavandula stoechas* French lavender
fol. 90v Satirion *Orchis* species orchid
fol. 91r Sponsa solis *Cichorium intybus* chicory
fol. 91r Scrofularia *Scrophularia nodosa* figwort
fol. 91r Spodium white calcined elephant ivory
fol. 91v Strucium *Crambe maritima* sea-kale
fol. 91v Stinci *Scincus officinalis* small dried lizards from Arabia, Egypt, or the Sudan
fol. 91v *Scordeon *Allium vineale* wild onion, crow garlic
fol. 92r *†Sapo soap
fol. 92r Sparagus *Asparagus officinalis* asparagus
fol. 92r Savina *Juniperus sabina* savin
fol. 92v Saxifraga *Pimpinella saxifraga* burnet saxifrage
fol. 92v Sal, sal armoniacum, sal gemma sea salt, sal-ammoniac, rock salt
fol. 92v Sisinbrium *Mentha aquatica* water mint
fol. 93r Salvia *Salvia officinalis* sage
fol. 93r Scabiosa *Scabiosa columbaria* or *S. arvensis* scabious
fol. 93v Senationes *Rorippa nasturtium-aquaticum* or *Lepidum sativum* watercress ot garden cress
fol. 93v *Sanationum unidentified
fol. 93r Serpentaria *Dracunculus vulgaris* dragon arum
fol. 94r Salix *Salix* species willow
fol. 94r Sambucus *Sambucus nigra* elder
fol. 94v Squilla *Urginea maritima* squill, sea onion
fol. 94v *†Storax resin from *Styrax officinalis* or *Liquidambar orientalis*
fol. 95r Sumac *Rhus coriaria* Sicilian sumach
fol. 95r *Staphisagria *Delphinium staphisagria* stavesacre
fol. 95v Sandali *Santalum album* white sandalwood
fol. 95v Sene *Cassia acutifolia* Alexandrian senna
fol. 96r Serpillum *Thymus serpyllum* wild thyme
fol. 96r Saturegia *Satureja hortensis* or *S. montana* summer or winter savory
fol. 96v Sanguinaria *Digitaria sanguinalis* crab-grass
fol. 96v Scolopendria *Asplenium scolopendrium* hart's-tongue (fern)
fol. 97r Soldanella *Calystegia soldanella* sea bindweed
fol. 97r Spinacha *Spinacea oleracea* spinach
fol.97v [S]icla *Beta vulgaris* spinach beet
fol. 97v Scalognum *Allium cepa* scallion, spring onion
fol. 97v Spargula *Galium aparine* cleavers, goose-grass
fol. 98r Silfu possibly *Thalictrum flavum* common meadow rue
fol. 98r Sanbacus or Sambacus *Jasminum officinale* jasmine
fol. 98v Spina benedicta *Paliurus spina-christi* Christ's thorn
fol. 98v Secchacul *Centaurea calcitrapa* star-thistle
fol. 98v Sebesten *Cordia myxa* Sebesten plum, Assyrian plum
fol. 99r *Sistra *Meum athamanticum* baldmoney, meu, spignel
fol. 99r *Salvinca possibly *Valeriana officinalis* or *Sanicula officinalis* valerian or wood sanicle
fol. 99r *†Spuma maris 'sea-foam', pumice
fol. 99r *†Spongia sponge
fol. 99r Sigillum sce marie *Polygonatum odoratum* Solomon's seal
fol. 99v Sorbastrella *Sanguisorba minor* burnet
fol. 99v Sorbe *Sorbus domestica*
fol. 100r Sinoni perhaps *Aethusa cynapium* fool's parsley
fol. 100r *Sissamus *Sesamum indicum* sesame
fol. 100v Tartatum tartar, salts of tartaric acid
fol. 100v Tamariscus *Tamarix* species tamarisk
fol. 100v *†Terra sigillata small cakes of red bole from Lemnos and elsewhere, with seals to guarantee them
fol. 100v Tetrahit unidentified, possibly *Galeopsis tetrahit* hempnettle
fol. 101r Anabulla *Euphorbia* species spurge
fol. 101r Tithimalus *Euphorbia cyparissias* cypress spurge
fol. 101r Turbit *Operculina turpethum* turpeth root
fol. 101v Tapsia *Thapsia garganica* Spanish turpeth root
fol. 101v Tela aranee spiders' webs
fol. 101v Tassus verbassus *Verbascum thapsus* Aaron's rod, mullein
fol. 102r Terbentina turpentine from various conifers
fol. 102r Tribuli marini *Tribulus terrestris* caltrops, devil's thorn
fol. 102r Trinitas *Trifolium* species clover
fol. 102v Torbentilla *Potentilla erecta* tormentil
fol. 102v Trifolium acutus *Trifolium angustifolium* clover
fol. 103r *†Terre stelle a mineral-like nitrate
fol. 103r Viola *Viola odorata* sweet violet
fol. 103r †Vitrum glass (and the furnace used to make it)
fol. 103r *Uvi *Vitis vinifera* grapes

fol. 103v Virga pastoris *Dipsacus fullonum* teasel
fol. 103v Viticella *Tamus communis* black bryony
fol. 104r Viperina *Lamium purpureum* purple dead-nettle
fol. 104r Urtica *Urtica dioica* stinging nettle
fol. 104v Vermicularis *Sedum acre* stonecrop, wall pepper
fol. 104v Vilubidis/Volubilis *Calystegia sepium* bindweed
fol. 105r Vincetoxicum *Vincetoxicum hirundinaria* swallow wort
fol. 105r Valdebona possibly *Petroselinum crispum* parsley
fol. 105r *Vitis alba possibly *Brionia alba* black-berried white bryony
fol. 105r *Uva acerba & matura *Vitis vinifera* sour and ripe grapes
fol. 105v Zinziber *Zingiber officinale* ginger
fol. 105v Zedoar *Curcuma zedoaria* zedoary, turmeric
fol. 106r Zucchar *Saccharum officinale* sugar-cane
fol. 106r *Zizania *Lolium temulentum* darnel
fol. 106r *†Zibulla a sort of fritter made of flour and oil
fol. 106v Orobum *Lathyrus* species, perhaps *L. odoratus* sweet pea
fol. 106v Crispula *Achillea millefolium* yarrow
fol. 107r Ypie *Anagallis* species three pimpernels
fol. 107v Ghimandrea perhaps *Teucrium chamaedrys* wall germander
fol. 107v Andronica possibly *Urtica* species
fol. 108r Peristereon *Verbena officinalis* vervain
fol. 108r Suchae/suchaar possibly *Cnicus benedictus* blessed thistle
fol. 108v Herba san cristoforo *Campanula rapunculus* rampion bellflower (though herb Christopher is also an English name for *Actaea spicata* baneberry)
fol. 108v Monachella/Calacantha probably *Delphinium consolida* field larkspur
fol. 109r [unlabelled] possibly *Ruscus aculeatus* butcher's broom

THE FACSIMILE

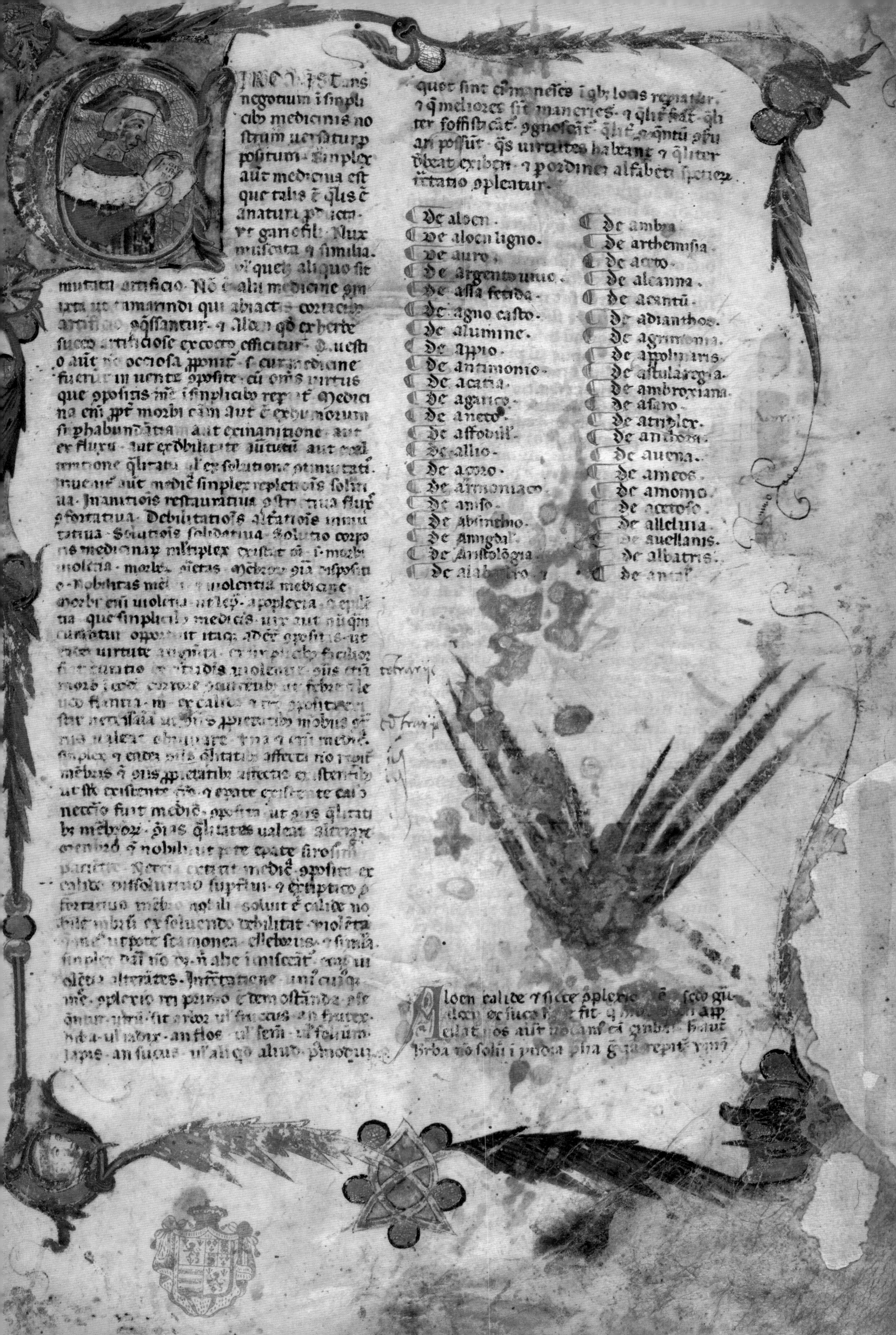

Circa instans negotium in simplicibus medicinis nostrum versatur propositum. Simplex autem medicina est que talis est qualis a natura producitur, ut gariofili, nux muscata et similia, vel que ex aliquo sit mutata artificio. Non est alii medicine composita ut tamarindi qui abiectis corticibus artificio conservantur, et aloen quod ex herbe succo artificiose excocto efficitur. Questio autem non ociosa proponitur scilicet cur medicine fuerunt invente composite, cum omnis virtus que compositis inest in simplicibus reperiatur. Medicina enim propter morbi causam aut est exhibenda, morbum autem sive per habundantiam aut exinanitionem, aut ex fluxu, aut ex debilitate virtutum, aut commutatione qualitatum vel ex solutione continuitatis. Invenitur autem medicina simplex repletionis solutiva, inanitionis restaurativa, constrictiva fluxus, confortativa debilitationis, alterationis immutativa, solutionis solidativa. Solutio corporis medicinarum multiplex existit: [illegible] scilicet morbi violentia, morbus, [illegible] etas, membrorum [illegible] dispositio, nobilitas membri, [illegible] violentia medicine. Morbi enim violentia, ut lepra, apoplexia et epilentia, que simplicibus medicinis vix aut numquam curantur. Oportuit itaque adinvenire compositas ut [illegible] virtute augmentata [illegible] facilior fieret curatio [illegible] violentie. Quandoque enim morbi [illegible] contrariis [illegible] ut febre [illegible] fluxus [illegible] ex calido [illegible] compositam fieri necessariam [illegible] morbus [illegible] valeat obviare [illegible] medicina simplex [illegible] qualitatis affecta [illegible] membris [illegible] existentibus ut [illegible] existente [illegible] existente [illegible] necessario fuit medicine composita ut [illegible] qualitatibus membrorum [illegible] qualitates valeat alterare membro [illegible] nobili ut [illegible] epate [illegible] patientie. [illegible] medicine composita ex calida dissolutiva [illegible] et [illegible] confortativa membro nobili. Solutive calide nobile membrum ex solvendo debilitant. Violenta medicine ut scamonea, elleborus et similia simplex dari non [illegible] alie immisceantur [illegible] violentie alterantes. Investigatione unicuique medicine complexio in primo et tertio ostendam esse [illegible] utrum sit arbor vel fructus an frutex, herba vel radix an flos vel semen vel folium, lapis an sucus vel aliquid aliud producens, quot sint eius maneries, in quibus locis reperiatur, et que meliores sint maneries, et qualiter falsificatur, qualiter falsificate cognoscantur, qualiter conservatum [illegible] possunt, quas virtutes habeant et qualiter debeat exiberi, et per ordinem alfabeti specierum tractatio compleatur.

De aloen.
De aloen ligno.
De auro.
De argento vivo.
De assa fetida.
De agno casto.
De alumine.
De appio.
De antimonio.
De acatia.
De agarico.
De aneto.
De affodill'.
De allio.
De aceto.
De armoniaco.
De aniso.
De absinthio.
De amigdal'.
De aristologia.
De alabastro.
De ambra.
De arthemisia.
De aceto.
De alcanna.
De acantũ.
De adianthos.
De agrimonia.
De appolinaris.
De astula regia.
De ambroxiana.
De asaro.
De atriplex.
De [illegible].
De avena.
De ameos.
De amomo.
De acetoso.
De alleluia.
De avellanis.
De albatris.
De anti[illegible].

Aloen calide et sicce complexionis est [illegible] sicco gradu. Aloen ex succo herbe fit [illegible] appellatur [illegible] aut vocant [illegible] habent herba non solum in [illegible] repitur [illegible]

i anpulia. Aloe tria gña sũt. Cicotrinũ. epa
ticũ. et caballinũ. fit aũt aloe h' m̃ herba teri
tur. succus extrahit'. et ad ignẽ poĩt'. quousq;
bulliat. p'quã uõ bullierit. ab igne remo
uet'. soli expoĩt' et exsiccat'. et ut qdã di
cũt qđ supius colligit' purũ ẽ. et cicot
nũ d'r. qđ i medio min' purũ ẽ et epaticũ
appellat'. qđ in fũdo feculẽtũ et caballinũ
noĩat'. quoꝝ oppinio falsa ẽ. Nos aũt
dicim' qđ diuerse sũt herbe nõ i gñe s; i
bonitate. ex qb; iste tres maneries aloe
fiũt. Sic diuerse sũt uue ñ i gñe s; i bo
nitate ex qb; uina sũt diffra. Optimũ
aũt aloen et cicotrinũ discñit' ex citrino colo
re seu ruffo. et p'cipue cũ plũs ei' frangit'
apparet q̃si plũs croci ẽẽt. et ex clara sba
maxĩe cũ p minuta frusta frãgit'. ut pu
ram et sbtilẽ. et q̃si ꝯfectiuã hãt subam que
leuit' frãgit'. et ex eo q' ñ ẽ fetidũ. ñ ualđ
amarũ. qñ; guosũ. qñ; frãgibile. Epati
cũ aũt colori epatis assimilat'. ht' ẽ co
lore epaticũ. i. sb nigrũ. et hĩc in foramĩa
ht' ut hora uenarũ. obtusã ht' sbam. et ñ
clarã et alia signa p'dictis silia. q; ea ht'
oĩa remissiora et maxĩe colorẽ. Caballinũ
aũt nigrũ obscurũ ht' suba; et feculẽtã. a
marissimũ. et orribilẽ p'cedit odorẽ. q' ual
de fedidẽ ẽ. Sophisticatur aũt qñ; caballinũ
ut cicotrinũ seu epaticũ uidat'. qđ aũt de
sophisticatiõe h'. et aliaꝝ sp'ciꝝ rogatu so
cioꝝ scripsim'. ad uitãdas sophisticatiões
et fraudulẽtias ꝯficiẽtiũ et uẽdẽtiũ. ñ ut a
ab aliquo ꝯmictat' sophio. s; ut fraudulẽ
tia uitet' deceptio. Virtus ẽ hẽe dilig. asp
naturq; gña. nec potest uitari uitiũ nisi c
cogñtũ. Sophisticat' aũt h' m̃. bulliat acetũ.
addito c'co oriẽtal'. et modico plũe nuc'. m.
ul' alteri sp'ei odorifere. caballinũ aloen p
frusta parua dimissũ. fillis ligent'. et aceto
bulliẽti i mictat'. et s… eleuet' et exsiccat'
modice dimictat'. et … ces. ul' aplĩ fiat
ita qđ e color i mutit'. qđ uid' ẽẽ epati
cũ seu cicotrinũ. et difficile discẽit' qđ uõ m
ñ sit. Discernit' aũt q' ꝯfrãgit' stati feti
dissimũ sẽtit'. qđ nõ ẽ i epatico seu cicot
no. Et nota qđ oẽ qđ d' natura ẽ aromatic'
q̃nto magis est arromaticũ tãto melius.
et oẽ qđ d' na. d; ẽẽ fetidũ. q̃nto fetid' tã
to meli' p'ter aloen. oẽ et qđ d; h'ẽ aliq;
saporẽ q̃nto i suo sapore i tẽsiu' ẽ. tãto me
lius excepto aloen. qđ cũ sit d' natura
amar… q̃nto min' amarũ. tãto laudabili'.
¶ Aloen uirtutẽ ht' pũgẽdi flã et mũdifi
candi meliã. ht' et uirtutẽ ꝯfortãdi mẽbra
nuosa. Vñ ual' ꝯt sup'fluitatẽ frõꝝ huoꝝ

i stõ ꝯtentorũ. Ip'm aũt stomac' ꝯfortat. caput
a dolore releuat. qui fit ex in aniti masin. i. ex fũosi
tate stõi. uisu; clarificat. oppilationẽ splẽis et e
cpĩs. mẽstrua p'uocat. sup'fluitates cir
ca puđeda si sit ex frã cã abstgit. et scabie; cu
rat. corpũ discoloratũ. coloratũ reddit si fuĩt
discoloratio ex p'cedẽte egritudine. ualet ad ex
tingẽdũ sãguinẽ d' uulnere et ad ꝯsolidãdũ
fco in ep'lm cũ uitello oui et olo et sep' suppo
nat'. ualet et ꝯt oppilitiã ex casu capilloꝝ.
Si huores flãtici ul' melãcolici hũndauẽit i
stõ et p't digestionẽ det'. ℥. ij. aloes cũ ℥. i.
mastic'. stõm mũdificat. et eudẽ i firmũ. et
d'bilitat' ꝯfortat. addite gñũ aloe cũ melle
exhitũ ualet. stõm mũdificat et digestione;
p'curat et nota qđ aloẽ et mastix d'bet teri et i
uino al' d'cotto d'bet dari. ¶ Ad idẽ exhatur
lingua abhore et p'ea inigat' p' ysofigum
duo gña aloes. q'a uis ẽ aloes sit amar
ori. dulce tñ ẽ stõm. pigodostoma di
amar' stõ. ¶ ꝯt dol' capĩs ual'. yerapig'
galieni. ad uisũ clarificãdũ i qua optim'
ẽ aloen. simplicit' ul' cũ mirob. addito enud'
ato et cotto. d'tur. ℥. ij. aloes et ℥. i. mastic'.
ul' draggti. addito syr'. et aq' tepida exp
tissimũ eni ẽ. Ad uisũ clarificãdũ et oppil'
tiõe; splẽis et epĩs fiãt aloes cũ calido su
co. appii. p'et. bruschi. et sp'agi. poĩat'. ℥. ij.
aloes. ul' ℥. iii. et ℥. s. mastic'. et d't. bis
ul' ter i septĩana. tal' ẽ d'cottio mẽstrua
educit. Suppositoriũ fcm ex tersa mag
plũis aloes sup aspgat'. ꝯt discolora tio
ne; corp'is q' ẽ ex frãte stõi. ul' p'cedẽte
egritudine. et maxĩe si fuẽit ex oppilatiõe
epĩs. d't. ℥. i. aloes. et i. mastic'. cũ ℥. s.
succi absinthii. mane et bis i die ¶ Et etiã
p'seuerat corp' ab ydrope. et i p'ncipio cu
rat sic p'bauim'. ¶ plũis et cũ melle dat'
lũbricos i t'ficit. cũ succo p'sicaie auri
b; stillat' uermes necat. ꝯt alopitia;
et casu' capilloꝝ i fortiõ aceto bulliat
radix oliue uetuste. p'ea colet'. et i cola
tuã poĩat' due p'tes farine lupinoꝝ a
maroꝝ et t'tia aloes. siml' ꝯficiat'. et ad
dat' plũis staphisage et m̃ i ugat' cap.
p' discrimĩalia. ¶ ꝯt artheticos d't suc'
bardane ¶ ꝯt scabie; et putredinẽ pude
doꝝ aloe cũ aceto ꝯfectũ et i uctu; ua
let. ¶ Nota q' aloen. t'tũ cũ aq' rosa. et
i uino al'. distep'atũ ad p'runitũ oculoꝝ
ualet. ꝯt timores auriũ fũdat' ipa her
ba. et iter poĩat' ciminũ et p'ea assetur p'a s
sb igne et exthaat' hec calida sup poĩat' et
mirabilit' p'dest.

Aloen lignū · ca · ē · ⁊ siccū ī · ii · gū · repit̄
aūt ī magno fluīne sup̄ioris babillōie
cui ꝯiungit fluui͛ paradisi · vn̄ q̄dā dicūt
q̄ ī pl'sione fluuīi ab arboribꝫ t̄rrestis pa
radisi ꝯducit̄ · Nullius tn̄ hui͛ arboris fert
uidisse origīe͡ȝ · alii ā̄ dicūt q̄ ī cacūinibꝫ
mōtiū ꝺ̄ stoꝝ locoꝝ circa p̄ad̄m locū existē
tiū oriat̄ h̄ lignū q̄ ī pl'su ueti aut tēpōi
uetustate cadit ī fluuiū apꝺ̄ dictis mō
tibꝫ remotissimū inponūt · retia ⁊ sic lign̄
īt̄rcipit̄ ·

Sut̄ aut̄ tria gn̄a lignorū aloes · ut ꝯst̄
diat̄ ē unū q̄ repit̄ ī isule q̄ dr̄ cume ⁊
ē laudabili͛ ceteris ē ⁊ alius q̄ repit̄ ī in
sula q̄ dr̄ cumear · ⁊ ē min͛ laudabile · ē
t̄rtiū q̄ repit̄ ītr̄ia īsula q̄ dr̄ xamie ⁊
illud ē peius ceteris · p̄mū itaq; ꝯgnoscit̄
q̄d optimū est · ex eo q̄ ē ualde ponderosū
⁊ nodorosū ⁊ aromaticū ⁊ s̄b amari sapo
ris · coloris s̄b nigri seu s̄b rufi · ꝯttioi de
tiū nō oīo resistēs dū ī mastigat̄ statim
odor aromatic͛ · uid̄t̄ atingē cerebrū · ⁊
quodāmō replē · Secd̄m gen͛ ē min͛ pōdero
sū · nec adeo amarū · seu odoriferū ⁊ ibi
medioc͛ · Tertiū gen͛ ē s̄b albidū leue u
alde nec amarū · Inmo quasi nullius saporis
ñ aroātic͛ n̄ sit artificio coaptatū · ⁊ dr̄ fer
ruleū · Sophisticat̄ aut̄ sic · In mōtan̄ ama
lphie repit̄ q̄dā lignū · ligno aloes · ualde
simil' pōderosū ⁊ nodosū ⁊ modicū arom̄
⁊ aq̄bꝫ dā lignū alos dr̄ h̄ aut̄ plūbo seu
stāgno ꝯficiat̄ ut mutet̄ color addita a
uriū sup̄fluitate ut amarū fiat ⁊ aliq̄n
tulū rufū · posmodū ī uino decotiōis pl'
ueris opti ligni al' addito modico mō
ut fiat ualde aroātic͛ · sic ī fit ut uix aut
nū̄q̄ discernit̄ ab optio discēnit̄ aut̄ q̄r pu
triū · durissimū ē ⁊ ꝯttioni dētiū oīo re
sistit · ⁊ q̄ ī terius ē dū cū masticat̄ non
sentit̄ amar̄ · L lignū aut̄ aloes ·

stomacū ꝯfortat digestionē ꝓcurat · Cꝯt debi
litatē cordis · ⁊ cēbri · ⁊ ꝯt cardiacā passione͡ȝ ·
⁊ sincopī · ꝯt retētionē mēstruoꝝ · ⁊ ꝯt oēs pās
⁊ debilitates cordis ex f̄rīate ꝓueniēte ualet ·
C Vinū d̄cotis ligni al' digestione͡ȝ ꝯfort̄ ·
⁊ stom̄ īf̄rātū cal'facit · ⁊ si abhoīnabile͡ȝ fue
rit pōat̄ parū lig̃ al' · integrū ꝑ nocte͡ȝ mañ
uinū exibeat̄ · C Adide͡ȝ d̄cotio ligni aloes ·
gariōfal' ⁊ mastic · digestionē ꝓcurat sto
macū ꝯfortat ⁊ cerebrū ualꝺ̄ delicatis fiat
hoc m̄ pōant̄ · ii · ʒ · ligni al' · ⁊ gariofil' ⁊ dimi
ictāt̄ ꝑ nocte͡ȝ ī uino · ī mañ suāt̄ uinū cum
aq̄ · ro · tale lignū pōt diu suāi · uinū ē mlt̄
tum īmutatur a ligno · C ꝯt sincopī ⁊ de
bilitate͡ȝ cerebri d̄t̄ sir̄ fcō ex aq̄ · ī q̄ pluī
lig̃ al' · ossis de corde cerui · gariōf ⁊ ros̄ dec̄oc
te fuerit addito zuchro · C Suffumigiū lig̃
aloes · repuocat ⁊ suffucatiōi matrī medet̄ ·
Sit tañ mulier pānis coopta ūdiq; ne fu
mus nares attingat · Si mulier t̄fera mag̃
sūpta cū uino d̄cotiōis lig̃ al' · ꝯ menstrua ꝓ
uocat ul' d̄t̄ priu͛ t̄fera · oꝫ · ⁊ pēā d̄cotio lign̄
aloes · Eiu͛ fumi͛ ꝑ nares recept͛ cerebrū in
f̄rātū · cal'facit · ⁊ d̄bilitatū ꝯfortat · ut bre
uiter ꝯcludā ei͛ laudes ualde ꝯfortat oīa
mēbra toti͛ corporis d̄bilitati ·

Avrum tēperatiu͛ ē quolibet metallo
ē aut̄ aur̄ · ca · f̄ caliditas mediocris
est ī eo excessus ī gr̄du nō locat̄ · aurū de
uena terre fit ꝑ excoctiōe͡ȝ · i · ītractiōe q̄ sup̄
fluū ē ab auro separ̄ · ī chatimia seu spu
ma auri dr̄ q̄ aut̄ quales sit ei͛ uarietas
tes ⁊ qualiter ꝯgnoscāt̄ ꝓ t̄rmictimus
q̄r nichil ad nos · uirtute͡ȝ h̄t · C Virtute͡ȝ
h̄t ꝯfortādi ⁊ d̄purādi un̄ ualꝫ ꝯt elephā
tia͡ȝ cardiacā pāss ⁊ sincopī · splenē · ⁊ ī
f̄rāti oēs stomici · limatura auri ꝯ epilēciā
data ī potu ul' cibo ualet depurando sup̄
fluitate͡ȝ hūorū ⁊ ext̄gēdo · pōt ī dari ꝯ
hāc pāss · ꝯ yera logodiō · ul' theodoricō an̄ ·

ul' ī potu bis ī septimana ⁊ utiliter ualet ad pser
uationē. ¶ Ex exhibita limatura auri cū su
co boragis. aut cū pl'uere ossis de corde cerui. ⁊
cū tali sir̄ zuchro sincopizātib; auxiliatur.
ul' fiat sirupus de suco boragis ⁊ zuchro ap
posito pl'uere ossis de corde cerui ⁊ cū tali sir̄
dt̄ limatura auri ⁊ siñ hēt dt̄ cū aliq̄ alio
vinū sir. in quo exstīcte fuerit lamine auree cād;
tes freneticos iuuat. q̄ si hēri nō possūt ex ca
libe idē fiat. ¶ Cōt ī frātionē stōi dt̄ limatura a
auri ī potu ul' cibo cū aūt ustūre dēbēt fieri eb;
facte ex aureo īstrumēto meliores erūt quā
ex alio metallo pl'uis cathimie more colli
rii ul' simpliciter ocul' ī posit' maculas oculorū
corrodit. ¶ Querit' uñ ⁊ q' aurū confortat ꝯ nec
ī corporet' nec mēbra nutriat. ad q' dicimus
q̄d cor̄ q̄ confortāt aliī confortāt mēbra repārā
tm̄ sp̄s. ut aromatica. alia restaurādo mēbra
ut cibi ⁊ potus. alia restrīgēdo mēbrū rela
xatū sic ē ēpl'm factū de mastice. ¶ alia alterādo
q̄litate distēpātiā ⁊ mēbrorū debilitatē. sic
dia storacos. stō. ex frāte distēpato ⁊ debilita
to apposito. alia confortāt depurādo superfluitatē
q̄ oprimēdo debilitat. sic sūt medicine laxē
⁊ mlta alia depurāda sūt. q̄m aurū confortat
dū asp̄itate sua extergit superflua.

Argentū uiuū. ca. ē. ⁊ hu. ī. iiij. gū. ī nq̄b;
dā libris repit' q' ē frīz. ī. iiij. gū. effectu.
aut pbat' ēē. ca. q' dissoluit. incidit. penetrat.
s; q' ē actualiter ualde frigidū. frīm ab auc
torib; iudicat'. dicūt aut' q'dā argētū uiuū
de uena terre p excotiōē fieri. q' falsū ē q'a
ex actione ignis facile extenuat' ī fumū. Ge
nerat' aut' ī terra ⁊ tale q̄le appet extra. q'
aq̄ fluēs pducit'. diutissie conseruat'. ī uase
aut' solido conseruat' ī loco frō. ¶ Virtutē hēt
dissoluēdi ⁊ penetrādi. farina lupinorū
amarorū decoquit' ī aceto forti usq; ad spi
situdinē ⁊ addita. ʒ. [illegible] argēti uiui. fi
at ī mixtio. ⁊ cap' pati[illegible]e exhūdātia pe
diclor' pūgat' p discriminalia. ¶ Extīgitur
aut' cū saliua ul' confricat' cū saliua ⁊ cinē aut
cū capill' ⁊ saliua. cū pl'uē ossis sipie. sed
saliua meliꝰ. nisi ē sic extīguat' ipius ad
aliud nō pot fieri īmixtio. ¶ Nota ī re actu
aliter calidā nō ēē ponēdū argētū uiuū.
fumꝰ enī argē[illegible] uiui astātib; obest q' remo
lliendo neruos palisī opat'. ¶ Ore ō rece
ptū ul' aurib; īmissū occidit. dissipando
mēbra. si aut' fuerit ore receptū. dt̄ lac ca
prinū ī mlta q̄ntitate ⁊ patiēs sit ī motu.
⁊ dt̄ uinū decotis ysopi ⁊ absinthii. hec aut'
sūt ad salutē remedia. ¶ Cōt scabiē olō

q' extenuat' ī fumū

nucis par. cal'fm ad misce acetū ō ī litargir
⁊ cerusā pl'uerizata ī eadē q̄ntitate bullias ad
spissitudinē mell'. refrigerat' hus ī pōe argētū
uiuū conmisce ⁊ usui reserua. ul' argētū uiuū
cū axūgia gallinacea ⁊ cerusa conficiat'. ex hac
facies īuncta clarificat' ⁊ dealbat'. Vl' sic acc.
bellicalos marinos. olm. ro. ⁊ cerusā. ⁊ adi
pe gallinaceā resolutā ad ignē hās ⁊ colatā
pōdis appoñ. ⁊ ad ultīo argētū uiuū mortifi
catū cū cinē ⁊ sputo conmisce ⁊ usui reserua.

Asa fetida. ca. ē. ⁊ sic. ī. oī gū.
Gūmi arboris ē. ī ultramarīs ptib; nascē
tis. ex estiuo tpr̄ colligit' ⁊ q' maxē fetet dr̄
asa fetida diu absque corruptionē conseruatū
in sicco mediocriter loco conseruari dēbet. Et
nota q' q̄ñ ē fetidior ⁊ purior. tāto me
lior ē. ¶ virtutē hēt dissoluēdi attrahē
di. consumēdi. vñ pill' ex asa formate simp
liciter. ul' cū ouo sorbil' ī sero exhibite as
matis ex humida causa laborātib; maxīe psūt
ul' cū sir̄ uiol'. ¶ Cōt quartanā ⁊ cotidianā
p̄gationē p̄cedēte. v. ʒ. ase decoq̄nt' ī uino
in malo terre concauato ⁊ colā addito melle
ul' zuchro. añ horā acc. dt̄ patiēti. ¶ Supposito
riū ex asa ⁊ galbano. ul' ex asa ⁊ armoniaco ⁊ se
rapino ul' ex sola asa. ī unctū priꝰ olō ul' mel'
ul' butiro. ne ledet īteriora miro mō mēstru
a. educit ⁊ secūdinā. ⁊ confortat. ¶ Vngt' ex
asa fetida fcm̄ ⁊ armoniaco. cera ⁊ olō splēn
mollificat. ⁊ lac ī mamill' coagolatū dissol
uit. ¶ Asa foramī dentis īmissa dolorē pla
cat. ¶ Gargarissimū fcm̄ ex aceto et aq̄ de
cotiōis ase ⁊ rosar. vuā tumefactā ex humore
hūdātia desiccat. ¶ Cōt palisim ⁊ podagrā
arthticā. ⁊ epilētiā. ⁊ ꝯ. ōēs uitiū humoris fri
gidi ⁊ frē nate. acc. asā fetidā ⁊ ptr'lū simil'
resoluat' ad ignē ⁊ ī tali liq̄re pl'uēs resol
uat' castorei. euforbii. sulphuris uiui ⁊ ad
dita cera fiat ungt' ceroctū ⁊ loco patiēti
supponāt'. ul' īūgat' patiēs. si fiat epilētia ui
tio capis tūc īungat' circa spatulas ⁊ collū
⁊ ī capō. ¶ Si uitio stōi tūc ps illa īūgatur
si uitio īferior ptiū īūgat' īferiorē ptes.
Circa alia egtudines simili' īūgat' loca
patiētia.

Agnus castus. ca. ē. ⁊ s. ī. iii. gradu
Agnus castus. frutex ē simil' arbor.
cuiꝰ folia ⁊ magis flores usui conpetunt
medicine ⁊ nō radices. flos aut' agni cas
ti. agnꝰ castꝰ appellat'. Cū ī ueīt' receptio ag
casti ponē debēmꝰ flores eiꝰ. agnus castus
oī tēpōr uiridis pōt repiri. ⁊ ī aq̄sis locꝭ

agnus castus

magis. In siccis u͛o min͛. flores ī autūno. colligūt͛. p annū nō ampli͛ ī mlta efficitia ꝯ uāt͛. Viridis aūt agn͛ cast͛ maioris ē effi cacie. q̄ exsiccat͛. Dr̄ aūt agn͛ castus q2 libi dinē reprimēdo castū reddit ut agnū. Lectus ergo ex eo factus libidinē reprimit. fomētet ī genitalia ex aq̄ dcoctiōis ipiu͛. su cus q̄ potes. in suco ipi͛ dcoquāt͛ castoreū. ꝗ dt͛ ī potu. Ct gomorreā folea q̄ ul͛ florē ꝯlinquāt͛ ī aceto addito fenu g͛co ꝗ cata pletur genitalia. Nota q̄ qdā extigūt libi dinē ī spissando spma. ut sem̄ lactuc. psi liū. citrol͛. melōis. cucu. ꝗ cucur. portulac̄ scariol͛. acetū. agsta. sūmat caphā. ꝗ simil͛. alia maniedo spās. ꝗ ꝯsumēdo spma. ut ruta. cimīnū. calamētū. anetū. Sūt enī ca. ista ꝗ apitissiā ꝗ uētositatē soluūt. In succo agni casti. ꝗ sem̄ feni. ꝗ ʒ. ii. esul͛. de coq̄nt͛ man̄ dt͛ leuco flatico colatiuā. Vin̄ q̄ dcoctiōis ei͛ agni casti ꝯfert eis. agn͛ cast͛ dimictit͛ ī amurca oli ut putrē fiat ꝗ addi to uino forti fiat dcoctio col͛nt͛ ꝗ addita cerā ꝗ olō fiat ungt͛. q͛ splenis duritiē remol lit. C fomētū fem̄ ex aq̄ dcotīs. agni casti matricē exsiccat supfluitates ꝗ q̄ ipi͛ āgu stat orificiū. C Ad mēstrua puocāda. fiat fomētū ex aq̄ dcotīs ipi͛ ꝗ cētū galli. C ɔt litargiā. acc̄ agnū castū. ꝗ appiū. ꝗ saluiam ꝗ fiat dcoctio ī aq̄ salsa ꝗ friget͛ fortiter pōsterior ps capīs.

Alumē

Alumen. ca. ē. ꝗ s. ī. iii. gu͛. Alumē ē trē maneries. scd̄m quosdā. scd̄m alios uena tīe ē q̄ ppt͛ nimiā excoctiōē calois ī albū colorem ꝯducit͛ ꝗ efficit͛. Alumē ī regiōē ualdē calidis. ꝯcreat͛ ꝗ ꝯpapue ī locis sulphureis ꝗ igni tis. qd albū est illud ē meli͛. ꝗ acutū ꝗ salsug gini ī mixtū. Qz aūt feculētū ē ꝗ terreū ē n̄ ē bonū. Diu absq; corruptiōē ꝯsuat͛. Virtutē ht͛ ꝯsumēdi ꝗ uehemēter ꝯsiccādi. Ct cācrū pluis alumis ꝗ carnis maiē ꝯfetus cū uermi bz īuētis ītera pigui ꝗ impositus ualet. Clicīm ū q̄ extal ꝯfectiōē ī uētū orificio fistul͛ ī unc tū mell͛ sup aspso pluis aluminē ī mictat͛ sz pri lauet͛ cancrū cū aceto. C ɔt īflactiōē gigiuar. loco hoc cū aceto prius. ꝗ p̄modū ex aceto ꝗ al lumine fiat ꝯfricatio pcedēte tn̄ appositiōē ue tosar ꝯscarificatiōē circa collū ꝗ spatulas. ul͛ sic scarificēs pri͛ pteriōē pte capīs tcīa die p̄ scari ficatiōē apponas sangsugas. ipi͛ gingiuas ꝗ mō lauet͛ os ex aceto dcoctiōīs alumīs. gallar ꝗ pos͛ lauet͛ os bis ul͛ t͛. ī die ex illo aceto. ꝗ ita laues usq; ad quartū diē mltū ualet. C ɔt scabiem sulphur uiuū. litargiriū ꝗ alum̄ bulliātur ī aceto ꝗ olō nucis. ꝗ uad ad balneū. ꝗ ablue pte dolētē ꝗ aq̄ calda ꝗ pea ī ūgas balneū aq̄ aq̄ alui nos. ꝯfert idropicē. ꝗ scabiosis et arthtic. Si tn̄ nō īuenit͛ naturale. fiat artifici osū hoc mō. sal. ꝗ alumē buliāt ī aq̄ feruēti bz lapidibz fūdo sūp aspgāt͛. aq̄ calda ꝗ patiēs ī medio tuse sedēs sudet ꝗ pea ex aq̄ lauētū. Quidā dicūt q̄ alumē sassuz ꝗ nitrū sūt idē.

Appium acē

…ā rustic̄ hūtē tibia exsl̄ac̄ salsocū
…ita ꝑigine ꝑ ij āno nō pot̄ sanāz
…r q̄dā mulier … fust̄es appij a
… tere q; sucū in expmie ⁊ cū san
… ttia tucta eplm sr̄ pone ⁊ reno
… b̄ i die · folia uō apij elim ute
…c rustic̄ ille semꝑ ipō ꝑbauit q
…berat ē i viij · diebȝ · dixit e act
…e ⁊ ꝯsolidat · ꝑigines expellit

Appiū cōe · ca · ē i pri apio
tertii gdi · s · i medio · eidē hrba ē satis
comune cui^9 sem̄ ē maioris efficacie scd̄o radix
tīio hrba cū ergo iuenit^r i medicina appii si
plicit^r receptioib; sem̄ ē apponēdū ipm̄ aūt se
men appiū appellat^r · alio noīe sellinō dr̄ · ali
alexcarasis · ul' alcarapsi · i · sem̄ eidē · ¶ Sucus ap
pii · i quo decta sit saxi fraga strāguriosis di
suriosis scuriosis sbuenit · s; colatū sit ma
ne ul' sero dt^r q̄ sic fit · saxifraga grā sol' ⁊ silli
ꝑēcula lapis lincis · coq̄nt^r i suco appii ⁊ i co
latura addito zuchro fia sir^9 ⁊ dt^r man̄ cū ca
lida ¶ Sucus appii decotis tamarisci · spleni
⁊ epis oppilatiōez soluit ⁊ duritiē · s; ꝑpre sp
lenis · aliud sumat^r decotiōis radicū appii · fen · petrsli ·
¶ ꝯt ycteritiā · fiat syrup^9 · ex suco appii ⁊ sca
riol' · ⁊ dt^r cū cal'a · ¶ ꝯt ydropisim ⁊ yctericiā
radices appii ⁊ fen · bulliat in suco fumi tre
⁊ i decotiōe adito zuchro · fiat sir^9 · miro mō ꝯsu
mit fl'a · ¶ fiat ēt iste sir^9 · leucofl'aticus ⁊ y
posartiā laborātib; · q; R̸ suci appii · l' · i · suci
scariol' · l' · s · mastic̄ · ʒ · i · fca decotiōe colt^r · ⁊ ꝑ^9
modū addito zuchro fiat sir^9 · ⁊ circa finē de
cotiōis addat^r pl'uis esul' · ʒ · ii · ⁊ pl'uis reu
barbari · ʒ · s · mane exibeat^r cū calida · ¶ ꝯt
frenesim sucus appii · ag̃sti ul' acetū ⁊ olū uiolac̄
ul' rosaceū admisceāt^r ⁊ bulliāt i uase uitreo ad
ignē · ⁊ tali olo calido capud pacieti i ūgat^r · rasu
tm̄ pri^9 · ¶ ꝯt efimerā ꝑecedat ꝑgatio d im̄ coq̄nt^r
agaricū ꝯ suco appii i pomo colloqntid ul' malo
tre ꝯcauato ⁊ talis decotio dt^r pacieti · ¶ Nota
q; appiū nocet ꝑgnātib; qa uirtutē suā resol
uit retinacula fetus · Epileticc obest qa dissol
uit ⁊ mouet materiā ad actionē ⁊ remouet
ad iferiora · Nocet pueris illa ē etas ꝑpt hui
ditatis mltitudinez ⁊ uirtutis dbilitatē ⁊ me
atū ꝯstrictionez · parata ē ad epilētiā · Sūt
⁊ alie maneries appii · s · appiū raninū · appi
um risus · ⁊ appiū emoroidū ¶ Appiū raninū
coctū i uino ⁊ olo ⁊ cataplasmatu renib; ⁊
pectini · renū ad dolore releuat ⁊ stanguriam
mitigat · uñ appiū raninū dr̄ qa renib; obstu
latur · ul' raninū qa i locis quos rane habitāt
ꝑcipue repit^r · ut pote i aquosis locis · ꝑdictū
q̄ ēplastū dolorē i testinorꝫ mitigat · ¶ ꝯt te
tasmō colatā illi^9 cotti ī aq̄ cātabri ꝑ clistere
i iciat^r · ¶ ꝯt uitiū spleis ex suco ei^9 ⁊ cera et
olō · fiat ceroctū · ⁊ cataplēt^r · ¶ Appiū risus i
uino ⁊ olo · ꝯputrescat · decoq̄nt^r ⁊ ꝑmodū exp̄u
māt^r ꝑ pānū, addita cera fiat ungtȝ splene
ticos ualō ꝯfert · uñ appiū risū · dr̄ q2 melāco
nicū hūorē hn̄dāte ꝯsumit · exctui adbūdātia
a fit tstitia excipi^9 itaq; i anitione effect^9 ꝯri
seqt^r s; risus^9 in letitia ¶ Vnde dr̄ splen nō
re facit · q2 cāz tstitie hūorez ꝯpurat · ¶ Appiū
risū decoct^9 i aq̄ ul' uino · ualet ꝯt strāguriam
⁊ dissuriā ⁊ scuriā · ⁊ ꝑcipue ꝯt lapidē dt^r eiu^9
decotio ꝑse · dt^r ⁊ litotripō i eadē decotiōe ¶ Ad
mēstrua ꝑuocāda · fiat fumigiū · ul' sucus eiu^9
tepid^9 i iciat^r · ¶ Appiū emoroidar coctū in
uino natib; cataplātū emoroidas iflatas de
siccat · Cauēdū tm̄ ē ne eis fluetib; hoc fiat ·
si sine fluxū cū tumore dolorē ⁊ extēsionez
dissoluit · ¶ pl'uis hui^9 appii excusti melli
mixtus ⁊ suppoīt^r emoroidas exsiccat ⁊ ob hoc
patietib; · appiū emoroidarū dr̄ ·

Appiū raninū nascit^r iusta aq̄s ⁊ i aq̄ · alij
uocāt appiū siluestre · d sua uirtute dixi
mus cū appio cōe

Appiū risus · nascit^r locis sablosis ⁊ i ca
pis renosis · alii uocāt botraciō · alii · co
ras · alii nilion · alii · stati cōe · alij · atirtoris ·

alii. cloropir. alii. russellinō. alii. asticon.
alii. cataltice. alii. effistiō. alii. licopnum.
alii. bellinō agriō. alii. bnecō. alii. h̄rbasce
lerata. alii. appio rustico. alii. appiū risu.
d' effectu ⁊ virtute eiđ satis diximꝰ ubi appi
um cōe. ⁊ iteꝝ ualet ꝯt plagā chironiā. ap
ium risus bn̄ tere ī mortario cū stercore pō
cino ⁊ fac ēplastrū ⁊ suppē strumis. siue
ferrūculū. siū apꝫā. stati īfra pauca hora ru
pit. pōt eā legi oī tpr̄.

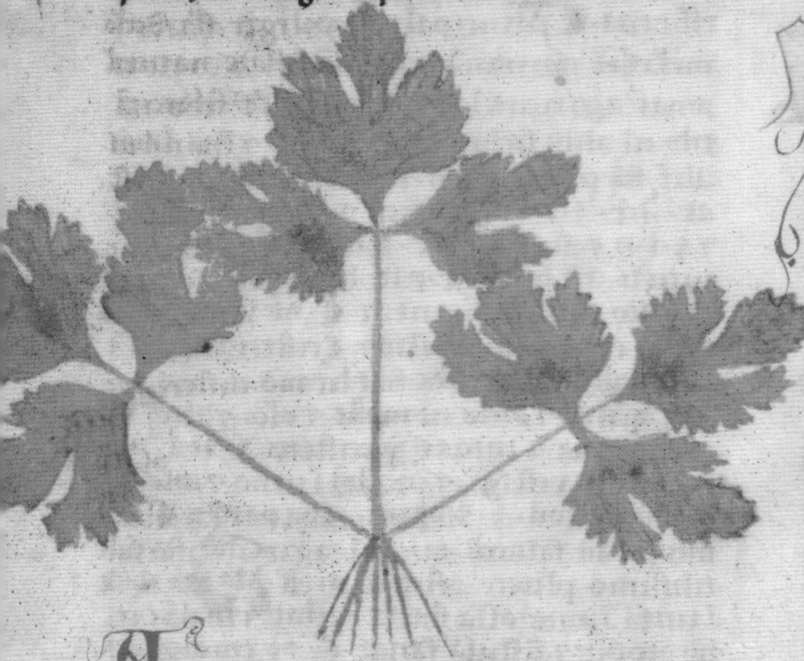

Appiū emoroidaꝝ. q alio noīe botracion
staticere appellat. alii dicūt vian. alii di
cūt cutrada. nascit locis sablosis ⁊ ī campis
⁊ hꝫ radicē simil' uerticulo ⁊ pue. d' ꝓprietate
⁊ uirtute sua diximꝰ ubi appiū cōe. ꝫt valꝫ
ꝯt lunaticos. h̄rba botraciō staticē. si obli
gata ul' supposita ī capite lunatico ⁊ lino
rubro luna crescēte ⁊ sit ī signo tauro. siū
scorpionē ī prima pte. stati sanitatē reddit
ꝯt cicatrices nigras. botraciō staticē totā
h̄rba cū suis radicibꝫ bn̄ tere addito modi
co forti aceto ⁊ supposita cicatricē nigram
mirabilit' stati mundificat ⁊ mala cāne
expellit ⁊ sanat.

Amidū. tēpato. calidū ⁊ hu. q̄ fit hoc mō
frumētū ī aq̄ frā ponit ⁊ ibi ꝑ die ⁊ nocte
morat ⁊ d' die ī die renouat aq̄ quusq; fru
mētū uideat putrefactū ⁊ post modū re
mota aq̄ optie ꝯterit ⁊ sic addita eadem
aq̄ ꝯficitur ⁊ exprimit ꝑ pannū ⁊ soli ex
ponit quousq; ad aq̄ ꝯsūptioēꝫ. frequēter
remouet aq̄ frā usꝫ ad dealbationeꝫ eī qđ
residet ꝑ mīcte ꝯsiccā ⁊ īdurari. ⁊ amilū
dr̄. q̄ sine mola fit. Ex ordeo mūdato sil'r
potest fieri. Valet aūt amidū ꝯt apꝫā spu
aliū ⁊ tussim. coctū ī aq̄ ordi ꝯditū cū lac
te amigdalino addito penidiis.

Antimonium. c. ē. ⁊ s. ī. iiii. g.
Vena tēre ē ⁊ metallo assimilat. stagno
precipue discernit aūt a metallo qa an
timoniū facile urit ⁊ terit ⁊ metallū non.
metallū fundit. anthimoniū urit. Anthi
moniū quāto clarius tāto meli'. puluis
anthimonii cū sapone spataretō ul' gal
lico ꝯficiat ⁊ liciniū ībibitū ī tintū orifici
o fistule ī ponat. puluis ē eī. cancro come
denti suppōit aut carni supflue optimū ē
remediū. ꝯt polipū magdaliō ex apos
tolicō formatus ⁊ aspsus pluēꝫ anthiōi
naribꝫ ī mictat. ꝯt maclaꝫ oculoꝝ fiat
colliriū ex pluē anthimoī ⁊ pluē nucle
orū mirob' cū pūdē addita aq̄ ro. ul' pon
ꝯtutia cū pluere anthimoī. si habes. ꝯt
fluxū sanguīs e naribꝫ bōbax ī tinctum
ī suco sanguinarie ⁊ pluē anthi. naribꝫ
in mictatur. puluis anti. cū suco tap
si barbassi ꝯficiat ⁊ bōbix ī tīcta suppositū
ad emoroidas exsiccādas. Aliud inie
sucū peucedani ꝑ clistere. si sit iterūꝰ pl'
uis iniciat cū calamo ī posito ī uexica in
flata. pl'uis ellebori nigri ualet tātūdeꝫ
ī hoc expimeto ad emoroidas q̄tū pluens
anthimoī.

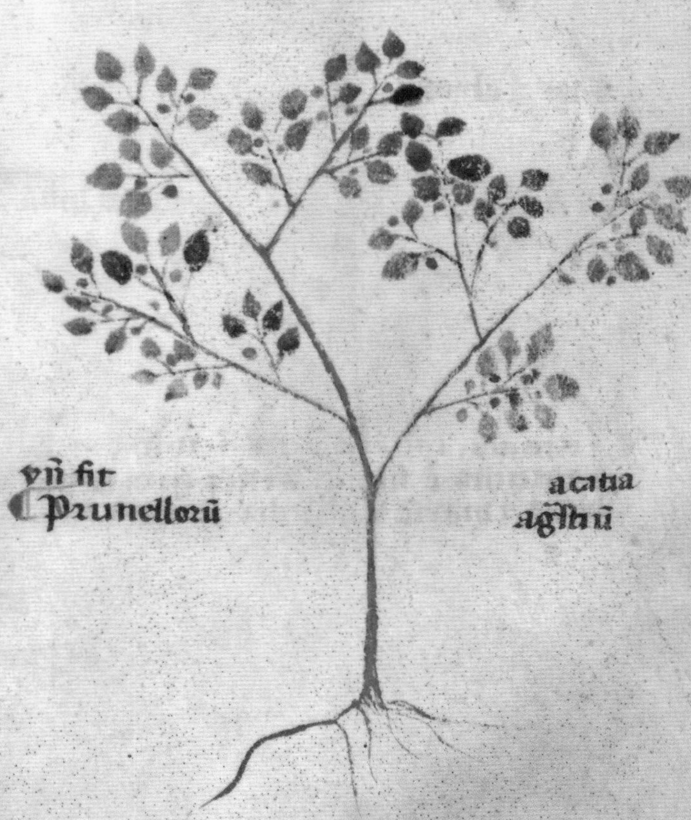

Acatia · frigida ē ⁊ sicca ī · ii · gū:
est aūt acatia sucus prunellaꝝ ī ma
turarū agrestiū · fit aūt sic · añ tp̄e matu
ritatis colligūt̄ prunell' ⁊ sucus eoꝝ extra
itur ⁊ ad solem exsiccat̄ · huiꝰmodi sucus
dsiccatꝰ acatia dr̄ · p annū pōt ſuari · ħt aūt
uirtutē ↄstringendi ⁊ ↄfortādi · Cōt uomit
colericū ex d'bilitate uirtutis retētiue · acc̄.
acatiā · mumiā · ⁊ dragātū · gūi arab · distēpē
tur cū oui albumine ⁊ fiat īn crispelle in sā
tagine ⁊ dēt̄ · ul fiat ēplastū sup furculam
pectoris ul' fiat īn crispell' cū aq̄ pluuiali
ul' aq̄ rōs distēpēt̄ ⁊ dēt̄ i potu ↄt fluxū uē
tris · idez pōt fieri ↄt fluxū mēstruoꝝ · Acc̄.
acatiā · lapidē ematitē ⁊ ipoqstidos · ⁊ cū
aq̄ rōs · ul' pluuiali ↄficiāt̄ ⁊ dēt̄. Cōt flux
sanguīs enarib; ⁊ mestruorū · d acatia et
⁊ succo sāguinaīe fiat suppositoriū ad mat̄
cez · pōt ⁊ fieri ēplm · ↄt uomitū ⁊ fluxū uētris ·
ex acatia · sanguīs dracōis · mastic · dragāt ·
olo rōs ⁊ oui albuīne. Cōt apostema · ca · ualt
acatia distēpatū cū suco plātagīs ul' corigi
ole ul' alicuiꝰ hꝰbe frē sup cataplasma ī pri
cipio ·

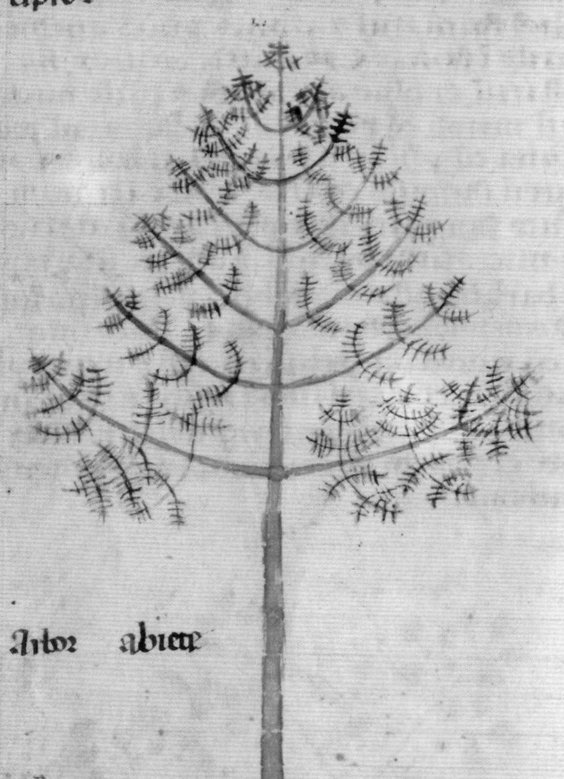

Agaricus · calidus ē ⁊ s · ī · ii · g̃.
Agaricus ē fūgus crescēs circa radicē
abietis ⁊ maxīe ī lūbardia · Sūt aūt due
spēs · s; · masculinū ⁊ femīnū · s; femininum
meliꝰ ⁊ ħt rotūdā formā · dsiccatꝰ ⁊ fit albi
simū · masculinū ħt fīgām oblōgā ⁊ nō adeo
albū · femininū ē albū ⁊ frāgibile ⁊ leue.
⁊ ħt qsdā tuberositates ītus ⁊ qdā frustula
qi diuisa · masculū nō ħt ⁊ nō ē adeo frāgibi
le s; ē ↄtinuū nec ē ita albū · s; leuitas eiꝰ
tm̄ pōt eē bonitate cū manib; tractatꝰ facilis
sime · pluēizat̄ ⁊ manꝰ est in pluēizata · s; ē
ex bonitate nō pōt ↄſuari p · iiii ānos ī multa
efficatia · C principaliter purgat flā · s; cdo
melā · Cōt cotitianā ⁊ qrtanā d flāte natural'
ponat̄ agaricus ī decoctiōe aliq̄ q dēt̄ febricitā
tib; cū aliis ſpēb; ut cū sq̄nāto ⁊ similibus ·
alit̄ fcā pūgatiōe · q̄ · si frebris adhuc ī fest
at · acc̄ · ʒ · i · ⁊ s · agarici · ⁊ ʒ · i · ⁊ s · suci fen̄.
⁊ ʒ · i · ⁊ s · suci fūi tīre · ↄmisceāt̄ ⁊ d h' dētur
patiēti · añ horā acc̄ · p sex horas · d h' solo ex
pimēto mlti dlibrantur · Cōt yliaci pass'
ualet eodez mō · ul' aliter. Cristerigēt̄ · patiēs
pri' mollificatīs ⁊ pōa fiat h' mō clistere · acc̄.
ʒ · i · agarici ⁊ ↄfice cū melle ⁊ olo · ⁊ aliq̄ aq̄
mitigatiua ⁊ iniciat̄ p cristere · Cōt dissinte
riā · acc̄ · saxifragā · ⁊ coq̄ bn̄ ī uino ⁊ cola · ⁊
ī colatuā · pon̄ · ʒ · s · agarici · ⁊ da patiēti · Cōt
fistulā · acc̄ salcoctū · tartarū · agaricū · ⁊ fcō sub
tilissimo pluere · ↄfice cū mell' · ⁊ tentā ibidē
ī tinctā īpone · ossa fracta extħit; ⁊ malā car
nē ↄrodit ⁊ fistulā sanat · Cōt emoroidas
acc̄ sbtilissimū pluēz agarici · ⁊ ↄfice ↄ suco
plātagīs · ⁊ olo ⁊ calfac ad ignē ⁊ bōbice iīti
ta suppoāt̄ · Cōt morsfeā acc̄ pluēz p'dictū
s; · sal cocti · tartari · agarici · ⁊ scarificatiōe facta
suppōe pluēz ⁊ frica · C decoctio agarici · casto
reum · sq̄nāti · ⁊ sene · dol' capis fcm ex hab
ūdātia flatis mitigat · ⁊ stom̄ ↄfortat · ul'
fiat pill' d p'dictis ⁊ tēpent̄ ↄ suco feniculi
ul' absinthi ⁊ idez opetur.

Anetū

Anetum . c . ē . 7 s . i . scđo gu .
Anetū herba est cui⁹ sem principalit usui
medicine cpetit . scđo radix . tcio herba . vn̄
cū īuenit in receptiōib; anetū ītelli
gendū . In uere aut̄ debȝ colligi semē ab ipa
herba desiccatū fuari aut̄ pōt p trennū ī multa
efficacia . melius tn̄ ē si singlis annis renou
tur . Radix eius exsiccata . aut nulli ē efficatie
aut modice . herba uō diuretica ē . Contra
eius uals stranguiosis 7 dissuriosis . valet 7 cō
litotripō Valet ad idem dissicatis . hec exde
cotione eius 7 zuchro . detur mane cū electuar an
ti . plures fiat circa pectine cataplasmata ex a
neto cocto ī uino 7 oleo . Contra dol matricis
bulliat fasciculi duo aneti ī uino 7 catap
lasmet . ul' tuniones eius bulliat ī uino 7 fiat
suppositoriū sic extergit frigidas supfluitates .
secūdinā 7 mestruā educit . Contra uitiū pec
toris ex frīgte parat qnq; ficus sicce . i . li . iiij
suci aneti ptoti noctes mane 7 sero adiūga
to modicū uini 7 bulliat bn̄ 7 dēt colatura .
Contra emoroidas . acc plures urtice 7 plures
aneti 7 cōfice cū melle 7 emoroida ī ūge . ul'
sic anetū 7 ecantū . i . semē urtice sicca pul'
uerzā 7 fac emplastrm ul' suppositoriū 7 ipone
si fluat emoroide . appone plures tn̄ similiter
eni cstringit . si fuerit uene inflate cōfice plures
cū melle 7 albumine oui appone Valet hec
cōt ficū si fit iter anū . decotio aneti 7 mastic
cōt uomitū 7 singultū ex frīgte . ualt narib;
appositū ul' cōmasticatū ul' cū carne coctū
ul' potatū . cōfortat stomacū 7 cerebrū .

Affodillū . centū capita . albucciū . dr̄ .
herba ē . que dicitur porrus ceruin⁹ . Greci
uocant asphodillos . Dyaceos dicit polioctis . al
ii . uocāt bulbuncus . alii Raboio . alii asir
cus . alii . affiut . alii . fistilā . alii . apullacia .
hec herba . calida . ē . 7 sicca . ī scđo gu . cui⁹ fo
lia sūt similia foliis porrorū . Radix cpetit
usui medicine magis quā folia . uiridis
melior ē quā siccata . Radices eius inuenitū tū
qi qda capita ī modū testicloꝝ . diuretica ht
uirtutē . Valet ad pdicta . eodē mō excepto qd
ualet ad morphea 7 alopitiā . sic acc apes com
bustas 7 cap plures cōmisce cū suco affodilli 7 oleo
ungēm cōueniēs ē pdca . Contra stranguriā 7 dissuri
am . 3 . iii . suci affodillorū resolue . 3 . i . saxifra
ghe . 7 3 . i . mili sol' puluerizate 7 bulliat usque
ad cōsūptione duarū partiū . da patienti cū zuchro .
Contra yposisim . mediam corticis sambuci 7 fi
lipendule . ana 3 . iii . bulliat 7 in ā . iii . suci af
fodillorū 7 dēt . cōt leuco flantia . purpue . Contra
maculā 7 cōt uitiū oculorū . acc . 3 . iii . sarcocolla . 7 3 .
i . mirre . bulliat ī lib . i . mell' 7 li . s . boni uini
rubi . 7 suci affodillorū . li . s . usq; ad cōsupti
onē medie ptis ul' ponāt ad solē p plures dies
ut ad medietatē reducatur ī uase eneo . deinde po
ni . mirro mō prodest . Valet cōt alopitiā impeti
gines ut dictū ē 7 alopitiā

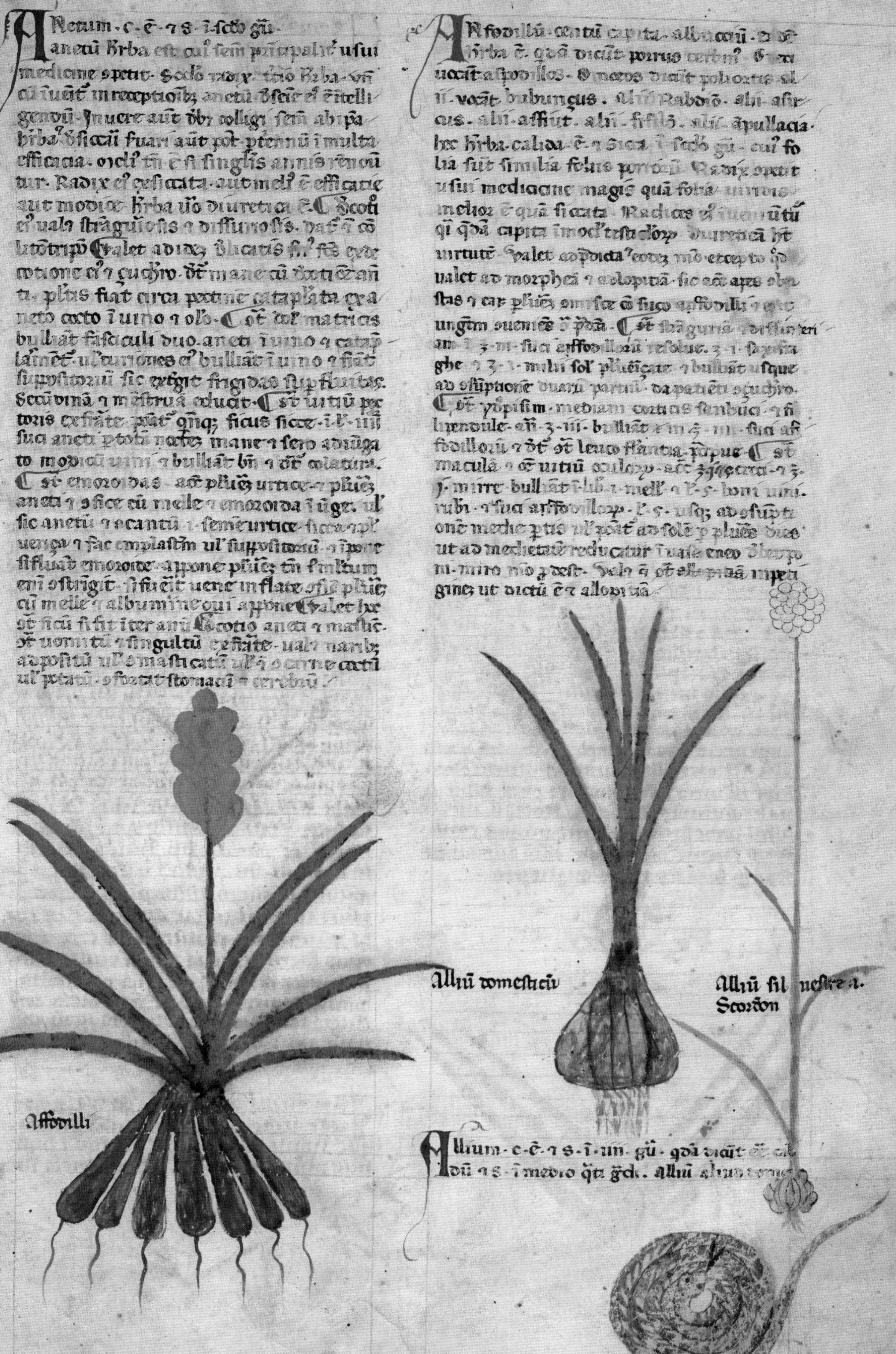

Allium . c . ē . 7 s . i . iii . gu . qda dicūt ī scđo
dū 7 s . ī medio qrti grdi . allū album . . .

sticū· aliud siluestre· qd̄ Scordon appellat᷑ 7 ē
c· 7 s· minus tn̄ q̄ domesticū· s; nō hēmus
d̄terminatū ab auctorib;· ī quo g̃du sit eius exc̄
sus· mediocriter tn̄ sic opat᷑· vn̄ ī receptioib;
d̄bet poni siluestrū 7 nō domesticū· domestic̄
ē cū ī petu opat᷑· Illud aūt nō· aliū siluestris.
florib; utimur· d̄bet itaq; colligi· ī fine ueīs
et ī ūbra suspēdi 7 d̄siccari· p biennū possūt
ꝑuari· ī mlt̄a efficacia· meli᷒ ē tn̄ si singlis an
nis renouetur· ¶ Virtutē hēt· dissoluendi cō
sumēdi 7 expellēdi uenenū· ¶ Cōt morsū uen̄
natorū aīaliū· acc̄· allia· 7 tere 7 cataplentū.
¶ Sucus ē īterius corp̄ receptus discutit uen̄
nū un̄ dicit᷑ tiriaca rusticorp̄· ¶ Cōt lūbricos.
acc̄· allia· pip· par petrosli 7 sucū mēte et
acetū 7 fac salsamētū et ītingat patiens
cibū 7 cōmedat· ¶ Ad apiendas uias epa
tis 7 urinales meatus· fiat salsamētū
similiter 7 distēpent᷑ cū uino 7 suco di
ureticar̄ h̄rbar̄· 7 d̄nt᷑· ¶ Cō straguriam
7 dissuriam· 7 dolores iliorū· acc̄· allia.
et coq; ī olo 7 fac in ēplastū 7 pone super
pectinē 7 circa uirgā 7 loco dolētiū sati᷒
ualet· ¶ Ad mēstrua ꝓuocanda· d̄pilētū
dens uni᷒ allii 7 bn̄ mūdtur 7 poāt᷑ ī orifi
cio matricis· mēstruā ꝓuocat ut dicit cō
stantin᷒· ul᷑ sic coquātū allia ī aq̄· 7 ī tali
aq̄ sedat mulier· usq; ad ūbelicū· ul᷑ bul
liat allia 7 fiat suppositoriū· ¶ locus ū fiat
morsea scarificetur· 7 pēa cū allio trito scari
ficetur 7 cataplet᷑· etiā acc̄ allia 7 pip 7 tere
7 fac ēplm̄ materiā ꝯsūmit· cōt crpetē estio
menū· idē mō opet᷑· ¶ Vsui obest q2 d̄siccat
7 toti corpori nocet si ultra modū sūatur.
q2 generat leprā· appoplesiā· maniā· 7 mlt̄a
alia· ¶ Flores allii· siluestris diuretici sūt· 7
ī syr᷒ ul᷑ uino ul᷑ aliquo alio potu sūpti· u
ualēt dissiriā 7 straguriā· Notidū aūt qd̄
alliū domesticū· raro aut nūquā ī anti
dotis īuenit᷑ medicinale· alliū aūt siluestr̄
sepi᷒ ꝓp suas tēpatiōes qualitates·

Acorus· c· ē· 7 s· in· ii· gu· h̄rba ē qd̄
greci simili noīe appellat᷑· alii· uocāt
afrodisius· alii· pip apiū· alii· ueneriā·
alii· radix nutica· alii· Singētiana· est
aūt radix gladioli· q nō tn̄ ī aquosis lo
cis uerū ē ī siccis repit᷑ 7 marinis ꝑtib;
crescit᷑· Acorus aūt ī pricipio estatis d̄b;
colligi· 7 ī· iiii· ptes findi· remotis· extrīs
cis supfluitatib; cū cultello 7 ad solē ex
siccari· ne siccū· hūitate sua remaneat
citius putrescat· pōt aūt ꝑ triēniū ī ml᷑
ta efficacia ꝑuari· hēt aūt uirtutē· diure
ticā· apitiuā· 7 dissolutiuam· ¶ Ad du
riciem spleīs 7 epīs· acc̄· l᷑· i· radix acori.
aliqntulū ꝯtriti 7 maceretur ꝑ tres dies
7 noctes ī aceto· pēa coqnt᷑· ad medietatē
aceti pēa colētur· colatē addat᷑ mel 7 itē
coquat᷑ ad ꝯsūptionē aceti· Istud aūt oxi
oximell᷑ d̄t cotidie mane 7 sero· paciētē
cū d̄coctione acori· ¶ Accipe· l᷑· i· suci aco
ri· pl᷑uis ei᷒· l᷑· s· aceti· l᷑· s· olii· l᷑· s· armo
niaci· ʒ· i· serapini· ʒ· ii· dimictāt᷑ ꝑ noc
tem ī aceto mane coq; usq; ad medietatē
d̄inde pone pl᷑uē ipi᷒ acori· 7 ex tali ungto
splen 7 epar īungatur manib; malaxan
do· et simis facē ceroctū d̄coctioī appones
cerā 7 ex tali ceroto suppoātur ad modū em
plastri· ¶ Vinū ī d̄coctionis eius ualet ad
idē· s; tn̄ nō d̄bet dari febricitāti· ¶ Cōt ycte
riciā coqnt᷑· radix acori· ī aq̄ 7 colētur et
colatē addat᷑ cicer rubrū 7 d̄tur patiēti
sūmū remediū est· si fuerit sin̄ febre· Si
nō cū frebre lēta· fiat eis balneū d̄ radice
acori· si pōt hēre ul᷑ si nō ē copia poātur
pl᷑uis eius· in balneo 7 ī sacculo pri᷒ poītu.
¶ Vl᷑ sic d̄coqnt᷑ acorus ī magna qn̄tita
te ī aqua· 7 ponat᷑ ī balneo pēa patiēs
sedeāt sup aqua ūdiq; pannis bn̄ coopt᷒
ut sudet ī tali d̄sudatiōe optīe pūgat col
lera· ¶ Cōt pānū oculi· sucū acori· 7 su
co feniculi· an̄· poātur ī uase 7 soli expo
natur ut hūitas ꝯsumetur· 7 pēa ponat᷑
pl᷑uis aloes· 7 bulliat ad ignē· pas 7 co
la ꝑ pannū pēa poātur ī uase ereo 7 cum
opus fuerit cū pēna poāt᷑ ī oculis· ¶ aerē
infrigidat hoc mō spgat᷑ folia ꝑ pauimētū
domus 7 mire actualiter fraternitate aerē
īfrigidat· ¶ etiā d̄r si adligabis acorū ad
uasa apiū· apes nūq̄ fugiūt s; multipli
cāt et aliae ibi ueniēt·

Armoniacum· c· ē· 7 s· i siccū· gu· s· i· tertio ē
aūt armoniacū gūmi cuiusdā arboris·
que simili noīe appellat᷑ cū rami ī super
ficie minutati ī cidūt᷑ estiuis dieb; ide

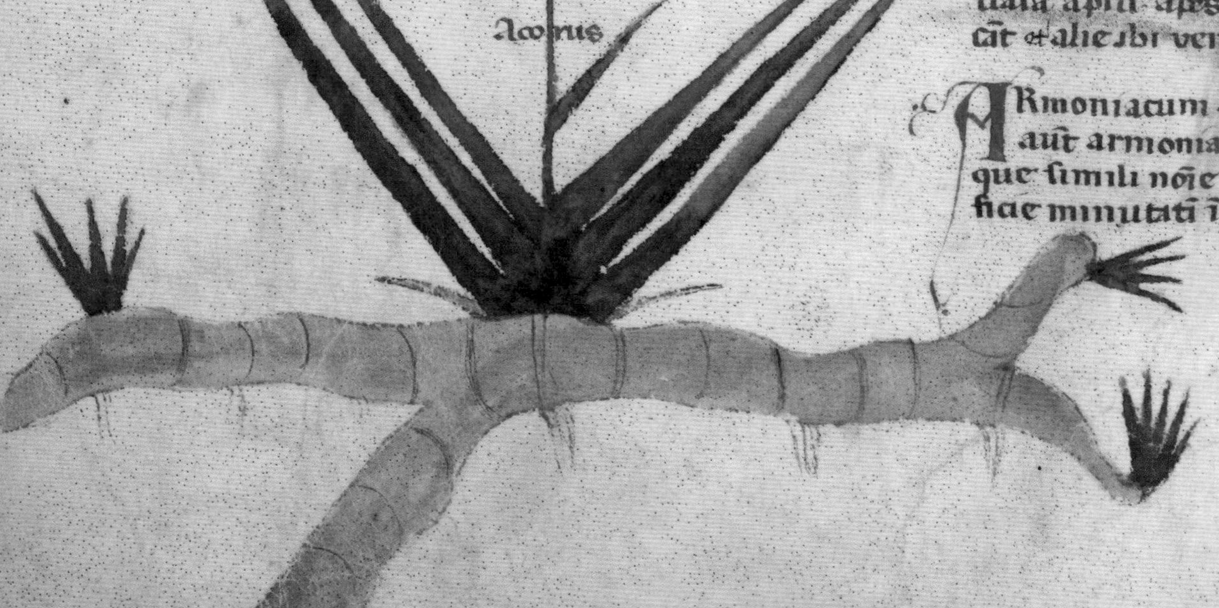

liquor qui distillat ibidem siccatur ⁊ ī durā
tur ⁊ uocat͛ armoniacū. Illud u͛o elligēdū
est q͛ puri͛ est ⁊ albius ⁊ cū terra nō admi
scetur. bonū ē assimilat͛ albumē oui coc
to. h͞t aūt uirtutē laxādi ⁊ dissoluēdi.
¶ Ꝯt tussim antiquā umectā ⁊ asma ex
uiscoso flatu. tres gutte armoniaci accipi
atur ī ouo sorbili ul͛ distēpēt͛ cū mell͛ et
d͛t. pectore t̄n prius mollificato cū dialtea ⁊
butyro ⁊ semine lini ul͛ brāce ursine. ¶ Ꝯt
scrofulas ī pricipio. acc͞e armoniacū ⁊ sal
gēmā. nitrū ⁊ sucū marrubii ⁊ cerā ⁊ resol
ue ⁊ ī unge. ¶ Ꝯt uitiū spleīs. acc͞e armo
niacum ⁊ galbanū eq͛ pōdere ⁊ resoluas ī aceto
cū cera additis pl͛ueribꝫ costi ⁊ absinthii
⁊ facias cerotū siū ungtū ⁊ sup splenem
unge. ¶ Ad menstrua puocāda ex solo armo
niaco fac suppositoriū ul͛ sufumiga. d͛ arō
niaco ⁊ asa fetida. ¶ Ꝯt lūbricos d͛tur d͛e
armoniacus ꝯ suco absinthii ul͛ persicarie
addito melle pl͛ueris gl͞o uic͞e hic ē d͛ād.
acc͞e armoniacū sucū absinthii ⁊ psicarie.
⁊ resolue ī aceto ⁊ fac ēplm̄ sup ūbellicū.

p̄ tres annos. Virtutē h͞t dissoluēdi ⁊ cōsum
di. ¶ Ꝯt uētositatē ī digestionē ⁊ acidā eruc
tationē. d͛t uinū d͛coctiōis eī anisi. costi. ma
sticis. ul͛ pl͛ueris istaꝝ addito pl͛ueꝝ cinamomi
⁊ mastic. ual͛ ꝯ ī digestionē ⁊ dolorē ītestīo
rū ex frīgīte ul͛ aliq͛ cllīm d͛t cū tali decoctiōe.
¶ Val͛ ī ꝯ dolorē ⁊ uētositatē ad positū cū pa
ritaria. ¶ Ꝯ dolorē auriū et maxīe si ex hūi
tate. fiat d͛coctio eī ī suco porri ⁊ olō ī corti
ce cepull͛ auribꝫ stilletur tepid͛. ¶ Ꝯt uitiū
matricis. d͛t ūfera magna cū d͛cotiōe eī. de
cotio anisi cū aliis h͛bis diureticis. solū
oppilationē epis ⁊ splenis. ¶ Ꝯt liuorē et
percussionē ⁊ p͞cipue si fit ī facie ⁊ circa
collū ꝯterātur cū cimino ⁊ supponat͛ cum
cera calfci. ¶ Ad augmētationē lactis et sp͛
matis. ual͛ pl͛ueris anisi sūptus ī cibo
ul͛ potu h͛ aūt facit apiendo meatus taꝝ
lactis quā spmatis calore suo.

Anisum. ca. est ⁊ sic. ī t͛tio gū. alio no
mine d͛r ciminū dulce. sem̄ ē cuidā
h͛be q͛ simili noīe appellatur. seruat͛

Absinthium. c. ē ⁊. s. ī. ii. gū. q͞dā dicūt
ēē c. ī. primo gū. s. ī. scd͛o. ¶ Absinthii
duo sūt gn͞a. unū q͛ d͛r pōticū. ul͛ q͛r

i ponto isula repit. ul qa pôticu hʒ saporez.
ꝫ amarissimu ꝫ colorez ī uiridez. aliud repi
tur sub albidu ꝫ minus amarū ꝫ tale mi
noris est efficacie. ꝑ sine ueris ꝺʒ collige
ꝫ ī ubra exsiccari. ꝑ annū ſuatur. absinth
ium dr hre duas ptes ſbas. ſ. laxatiuāz
ex caliditate ꝫ amaritudine. ꝫ ostrictiuaʒ
ex grossitudine sube ꝫ pôticitate. C Grossa
dr hre ſbām. ꝑt pôticitatē ꝫ amaritudinē.
amaru ē ꝫ pōtica grossa dr hre ſbas. q si
interi recipiat. ſ. existēte opacta cū gros
sicie sua opactiore reddit. caliditate sua ab
os hu. dissoluit. ꝫ sic ōtria ōpatur. qr nō ē
dandū ī materia existēte digesta. ut dige
stam dissoluat sua caliditate ꝫ dissolutaʒ
sua pôticitate opriēte expellat. C ꝯ. lubri
ī inferiorib; intestinis existētib; dē succus absi
thii cū puluere bectonice ul cētauree. ul ꝑsica
rie. ul nucleor ꝑsicor. ul folior. C ꝯt oppila
tionez splenis dē succus ei cū pluē costi. Idē
ualet ꝯ oppilationez epis extra cū. C ꝯ oppila
tionez epis. ꝫ ictericiā dē succus ei ꝫ scario
le. ul ex his fiat syr ꝫ dē cū calida. C Ad. ꝓ.
ꝓuocādā pessarizet succus ei. ul fiat supposi
toriū. ex absinthio ꝫ arthmisia coctis ī olō co
muni. ul mustellino q mēlr ē. C ꝯ. dolorem
capis exhantimasi stōi. ſ. ex fumositate stōi dē
succus ei cū calida ꝫ çacchara. C ꝯ ebrietatē dē
succus ei cū melle ꝫ calida. C ꝯ suffocationē
ex fūgis dē cū aceto ꝫ calida. C ꝯ. duriciez spl
nis. absinthiū coctū ī olō catapl. ul fiat ugt.
ex succo ei ꝫ aceto. armoniaco. cera ꝫ olō. ꝫ ī u
gatur. ad solez ul ad ignē. manib; malaxādo.
C ꝯ liuorez ꝫ dolorez mēbror ex pcussione. ex
pcussione suco absinthii ꝫ pluē cimini fiat
eplm. C ꝯt uermes auriū ī stilletur succus
succus ei potatus. uisū clarificat. ꝫ ocul' ip
situs ruborem ꝫ pānū remouet. C ꝯt libros ꝫ pan
nos cōctos a muribz custodit. teste diasco
rides ꝫ macro. C Dbet aūt colligi circa mediū
madiū ꝑpt suco tm̄. si aūt uolueris suari. dbz
colligi qn̄ ꝓducit florez ꝫ ī ubra desiccari. potest
aūt suari ꝑ duos ānos ī multa efficacia.

Anacardi. ca. sūt ꝫ s. ī. iii. gu. qdā dicūt
ī. iiii. g. sūt aūt fructus cuidā arboris ī
india nascētis. qdā dicūt q sūt pediculi el'
fantū q falsū est. pōderosi ꝫ humorosi. me
liores sūt. diu possūt suari. s. ꝑ. xxx. annos
ī loco nec nimis humido. nec nimis sicco.
anacardi. ꝓsūt sūpti. leprā ul mortē īducū
nt. C ꝯ obliuionez decoqt castoreū ī forti a

aceto ꝑea adde humositatē anacardor ab
iectis exteriorib; ꝫ ī ugāt ꝑterior ps capis
precedēte scarificatione. C ꝯ ꝑrigine ꝫ ī peti
ginez ofice auripigmtū osuco anacardor
ꝫ abluto loco patiēti cū aq calā supponas.

ad ugtū. caue tn̄ ne diu dimictat qr nimiā
faceret īcisionez. sʒ illo emoto itez ablue a
qua calā ꝫ itez ī unge ꝫ facias multotiēs in
ungēdo ꝫ lauādo. C ꝯ. morpheā. saluiā. ab
sinthiū. ī tenora colongntīd pluērisati. ofice
osuco anacardor ꝫ suppone. ul sic ita ofiat
cū aceto ꝫ fiat decoctio ex illis sic decoctis fiat
eplastrū. C Electuariū anacardinū. ualet ōtra
obliuionez ꝫ curat leprā.

Amigdalis amare. c. sūt ꝫ sicce ī scdō g.
amare opetūt ī medicis. dulces esui. ꝯ
asma ꝫ tussī ex frigiditate terat amigdal' amare
ꝫ addito çuccaro ad reprimēdū malū saporez
fiat pilles. C ꝯt surditatē terat ōtrite ponatur
iter duo folia sub cinere feruētissimo. ꝫ ind
exprimatur ꝫ illo olm. q in fluit ī stilletur
auribus cū aliqs humorū īpedit auditum
ul qn̄ sanies egreditur. C ꝯt lumbricos ofi
ciatur cibz ex tali olō ꝫ farina lupinorū
amaror ꝫ dē. ul fiat hoc eplm circa umbili
cum. mestrua ꝓuocat. si ex tali olō fiat pes
sariū. ul suppositoriū. ī liniat extra. ꝯ.
ꝫ ex tali olō fiat suppositorium.

Aristologia. diuerse sūt sps. ſ. longe et
rotūda. utraq. c. ē ꝫ sicca ī. scdō g. dicit

Amigdale dlces. ca. sūt ꝫ hu. ī medio p. g. ... [illegible] ... amaritudine ... [illegible]
... [illegible] ... acerbo ... [illegible] ...
... [illegible] ... Amigdale ... [illegible] ...
... [illegible] ... amare ... [illegible] ...
Amigdale amare ... [illegible] ... splenis ... [illegible] ...
... [illegible] ... colon ... [illegible] ...
... [illegible] ... lapides ... [illegible] ...
... [illegible] ... febrib; ... [illegible]

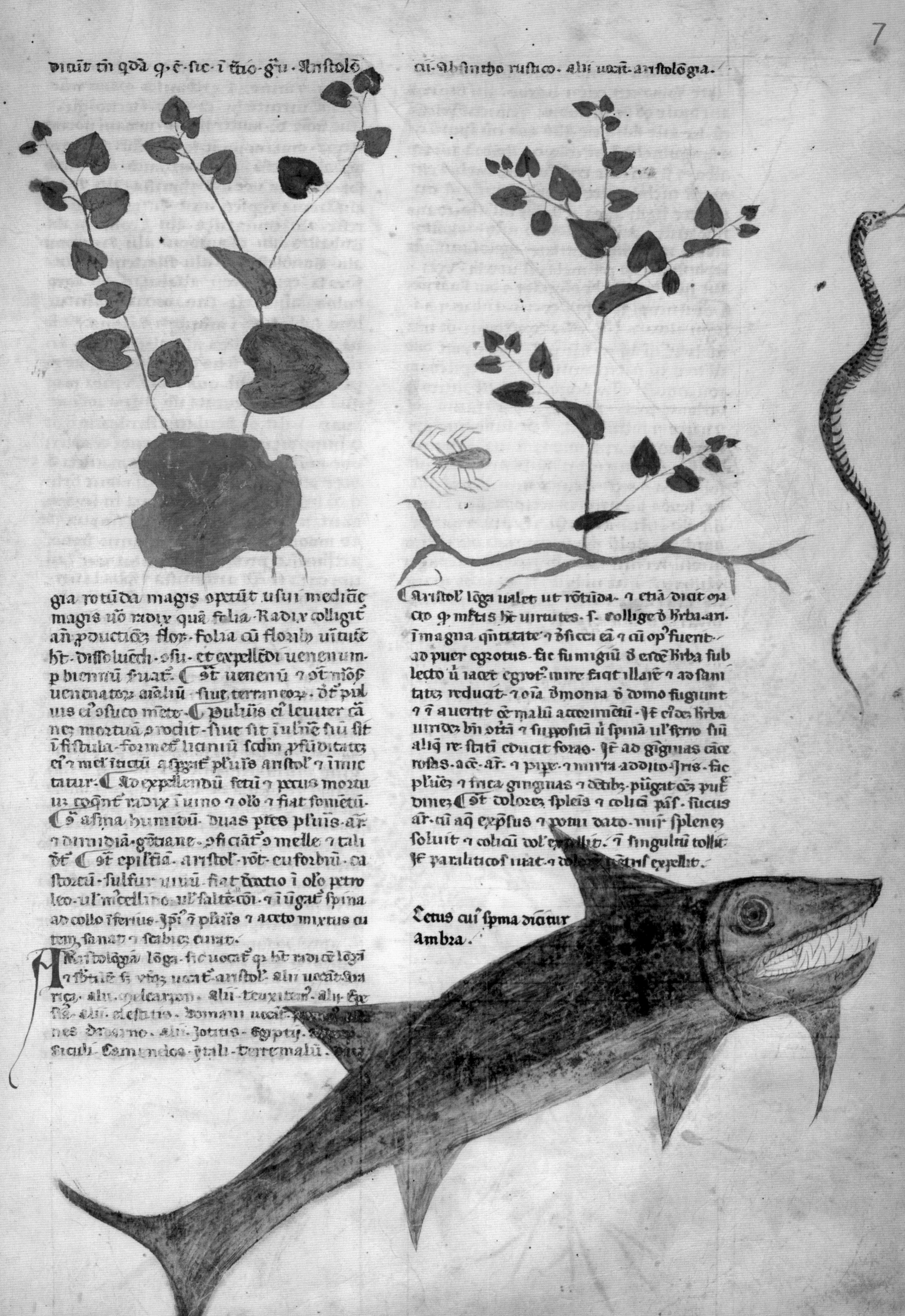

dicit tn̄ qdā q̄ ē sic ī ttio g̃u. Aristolō cū absinthio rustico. alii uocāt aristologia.

gia rotūda magis opetūt usui mediciñe magis uō radix quā folia. Radix colligit̃ añ pductioē flor. folia cū florib; uirtute ht̃. dissoluēdi. osu. et expellēdi uenenum. p biennū suat̃. Ꞇ ɔt uenenū ⁊ ɔt mors uenenatoꝝ aīaliū. siue terraneoꝝ. d̃t pulu̾is ei᷒ ɔsuco mēte. Ꞇ puluis ei᷒ leuiter cāneꝫ mortuā ɔrodit. siue sit ī uulnē siu sit ī fistula. formet̃ liciniū scđm pfūditateꝫ ei᷒ ⁊ mel īiectū aspgat̃ pluis aristol̓ ⁊ īmictatur. Ꞇ Ad expellendū fetū ⁊ pectus mortuū coq̄nt̃ radix ī uino ⁊ olō ⁊ fiat fomētū. Ꞇ ɔ̃ asina humidū. duas ptes pluis. ar̄. ⁊ dimidiā. gēciane. ɔficiāt̃ ɔ melle ⁊ tali d̃t. Ꞇ ɔt epilēā. aristol̓. rot. euforbiū. castoreū. sulfur uiuū. fiat decoctio ī olō petroleo. ul̓ mecllino. ul̓ saltē cōi. ⁊ ī ūgat̃ spina ad collo īferius. Ipi᷒ ī pluis ⁊ aceto mixtus cuteꝫ sanat ⁊ scabieꝫ curat.

Aristologia lōga. sic uocat̃ q̄ ht̃ radicē lōgā ⁊ sbtilē. ꝑ uīgꝫ uocat̃. aristol̓. alii uocāt. [illegible]rica. alii. epelcarpon. alii. teuxiton. alii. Ep[illegible]. alii. elestitis. Romani uocāt [illegible] nes drosino. alii. Iotitis. Egyptii. [illegible] Siculi. Camenclos. ytali. terremalū. [illegible]

Ꞇ Aristol̓ lōga ualet ut rōtūda. ⁊ etiā dicit oracio q̄ mltas ht̃ uirtutes. s. colligē d̃ herba. ar. ī magna q̄ntitate ⁊ d̄siccē eā ⁊ cū op᷒ fuerit. ad puer egrotus. fic fumigiū d̃ eadē herba sub lecto ū iacet egrot᷒. mire facit illarē ⁊ ad sanitateꝫ reducit. ⁊ oīa d̃monia d̃ domo fugiunt ⁊ ī aūertit oē malū accidentū. It eadeꝫ herba uirideꝫ bn̄ ɔtrita ⁊ supposita ū spinā ul̓ ferro siu aliq̄ re. stati educit foras. It ad gingiuas cācerosas. ac̄e. ar̄. ⁊ pipe. ⁊ mirra addito. sīs. fac pluēꝫ ⁊ frica gingiuas ⁊ dētib;. pūgat oēꝫ putredineꝫ. Ꞇ ɔt doloreꝫ spleīs ⁊ colicā pas̄. sucus ar̄. cū aq̄ expssus ⁊ potui dato. mir̄ spleneꝫ soluit ⁊ colicā dol̓ expellit. ⁊ singultū tollit. It paraliticos iuuat. ⁊ dolore [illegible] expellit.

Cetus cui᷒ spma dicitur ambra.

Ambra · ca · ē · ⁊ sic · ī · scdō · gū · Ambra dr̄
eē · spma ceti · cete · i · balene · alii dicūt eē
alii dicūt qd sit ɔ̄secūdina q̄ emictit post pa
tū · hec aūt falsū est · Illd aūt cū ipurū ē
⁊ sanguinolētū ħt colorē · Ambrā aūt est
alba · ⁊ si iueniatur crisei coloris melior est ·
nigrū nichil ualet · Sophisticatr̄ aūt cū
pl'uere ligni · aloes · ⁊ storac cal' ⁊ laudano
resoluūt ī aq̄ · ros · addito mco · ⁊ apposita
ambra in modica qntitate · Cognoscatur aūt
sophisticata q2 pot malaxari ut cera · Vera ·
aūt nō · Virtute ħt ɔ̄fortādi ⁊ diu suari pot ·
Cōt sincopī fiat pill' ex · ʒ · i · ambre · ⁊ · ʒ · i ·
ligni aloes ⁊ · ʒ · ii · ossis d' cord' cerui · q2 trita
resoluat' cū aq̄ · ro · ⁊ fiat pill' · d'q accipiat duo
ul' tres cū uadit dormitū · Cōt epilētiam
poni · ambrā · ossis d' cord' cui · ī uase uitreo sup
carbones poat' ⁊ patiēs recipiat fumū p os
⁊ nares · ⁊ mltū ualet · Cōt suffocationem
matricis qn aprimit spūalia · ponatur
simlr ī uase uitreo cū aliis aromatic ul'
sola ābra · ⁊ recipiatur p fumus p os uul
ue · fetida uō p nares recipiat' sic ē licinī
ū ī olō itīctū accensū ⁊ extītū ⁊ narib3
appositū · Solū mō licinio tali olō itīctō
accēsū ⁊ extītū ⁊ narib3 appōitū · cō · pūgat
⁊ librauit qdā nobilē · Nota q' ɔ̄t matri
cis cās d'b3 poni ifeꝰ fetida uō supi · aro
matica ɔ̄ suffocatiōē ⁊ ɔ̄uerso ·

Artemisia · tria sūt gnā · s3 · maior · me
dia · ⁊ minor · d' arthimisia · maior nūc
dicamꝰ · uirtutē ħt · ca · ⁊ sic · ī tertio · gū ·
alio noīe dr̄ · mater herbar̄ · romani uocant
Regia · omiani · uocāt · karistellū · alii · toxo
ter · alii · Epesia · alii · parthnicō · alii · appoli
sos · Simachi uocāt · Arthmisia · alii · Sogusa ·
alii · lioptas · pfeti uocāt · Entropū · alii · te
tesie · alii · Onicatisça · alii · Teonisis · alii ·
Bubastes · alii · Ostantōpu · alii · Emeronu ·
alii · Gonoscefestus · alii · filacterion · alii ·
sexasa · egipti uocāt alsabasar · alii · toxo
bulus · alii uocāt · Canapaccia · Nascitur
locis sablosis ⁊ ī mōtib3 ⁊ ī ī ortis · ħt fo
lia subalbida ⁊ lōga · asimilat' canapa · Ar
thimisia maior · folia ei' ⁊ flores · sō pue ɔ̄
petit usui medic' · quā radix · viuida mag
quā exiccata · exiccata uō p ānū possunt
suari · Valet ɔ̄t sterilatio sterilitatio q̄ fit
ex humiditate · Satis pot ɔ̄pendi ex ɔ̄plexi
one · mulieris · si fit piguis · an macilēta ɔ̄
d'bet pl'ueriçari · arthimisia cū radice herbe
q̄ dr̄ bistorta · ⁊ cū nuce micati sit ī eadem
qntitate · ɔ̄ficiat' pluis cū mell' sinplici ⁊ d'et
ad modū elli · mañ ⁊ sero · cū uino d'coctiōis
arthimisie · pcest tn̄ magis si balneet' ī aq̄
ubi cocta fuēit arthimisia ⁊ folia lauri
ul' si fomētet ex tali aq̄ · Valet ēt arthimisia
cocta ī olō cōi · ul' olō nucū · Ad menstrua ·
puocādū · fiat pessariū · ex suco ei' · ul' ei' d'coctio
pessariçet' · Cōt tetasmō ex frāte · patiēs fumū
colofonie posite sup carbones p anū recipiat
d'in cal'fiat arthimisiā sup tegulā ⁊ cal' fūin
poat' sup lapidē molarē ⁊ d'supsedeat ifir
mus pb' ē · Cōt glādula q nascūt' iux̄ anū
q̄ uocat' attı · fiat ipi ɔ̄fricatio pea p̄atur ·
d' sup pluis arthimisie ⁊ marubū · Cōt emi
graneā ⁊ cephaleā ɔ̄t aliq̄ aq̄ opiata calida
cū uino d'coctiōis arthimisie · Itē d' herba ar
thimisia quicūq; secū portauēit ī uiatico nō
se fatigatus · ut dicit macro · It ualet ɔ̄t malō
medicamētos ⁊ aduertit oculos d' malo · ⁊
oīa d'monia fugiūt aduersus eā ubicūq; ipa
herba fuēit · Cōt dol' pectū · herba arthimisia bn̄
ɔ̄trita cū axūgia ⁊ supposita mirab' dol' tollit
Ad dol' itestinor̄ · herba arthimisia fac puluē
⁊ cū mlsa potui dab' mir̄ dol' tollit · ⁊ ad mlt'
tas alias īfirmitates sbuenit hec dicit m
mac' · Ad menstruis ⁊ matricis · arthimisia
d'coq; ī aq̄ ⁊ potui dab' · It fumigatio ex ea
ifeꝰ receptū · menstrua puocat · Itē uinū d'co
tionis ei' sepe bibitū · mulierib; nō d'micit ·

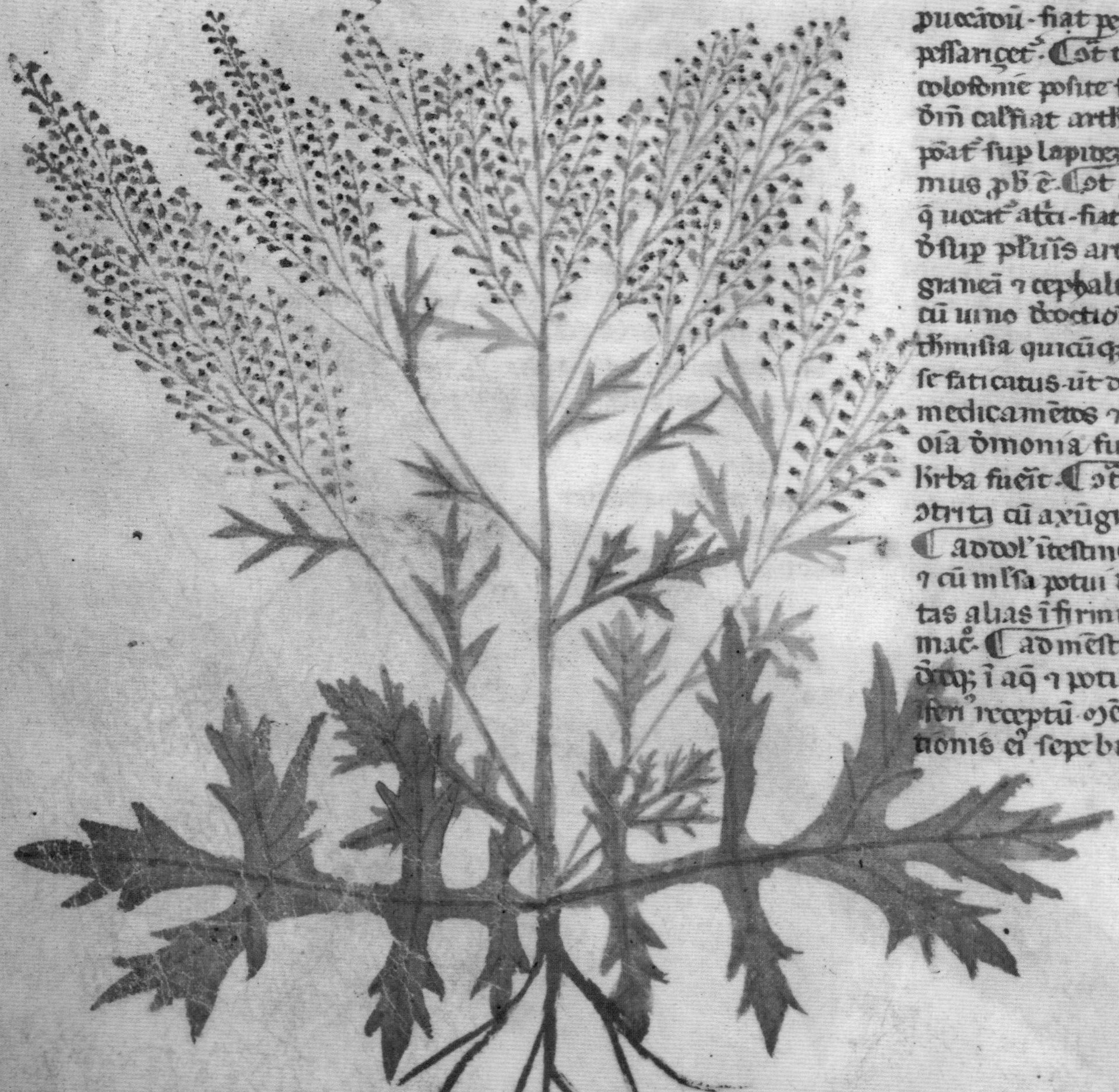

abortum an̄ tẽpus. ul' ipa herba contrita ⁊ super umbelicũ ligata in nocte cito facit. Item eodem modo supposita omnem duriciã siue inflactiones matris dissolluit. ⁊ ad multa alia facit. Item uocat' arthemisia monodos.

letus fiat puer siue infans. acc fasciculũ arthemisie tagantes ⁊ fac fumigiũ sub lecto puerorum infantibus auertit eos ab omni aduenimento ⁊ leterit.

Arthemisia media quã greci uocant tagantes. Romani uocant. Grisantemis. egipti uocant. Alim romani. tanium. alii uocant tanaciata. alii tanacipa. c. c. ⁊ s. i. m. gũ. alii uocant taneta. Contra dol' uexice ⁊ contra stranguriã ⁊ disuriã. acc de arthemisia tagantes ℥. i. ⁊ uino gactos .i. da patienti non febricitantibus. si uero febricitat dab eũ aq' cocti uino. ⁊ uidebis effectũ bonũ. Contra dol' coxiarum herba cũ axũgia bene tere addito modicũ de aceto ⁊ facto emplim sup pon̄ ad tertio die liberatus erit. Contra dol' neruorũ. ipa herba contrita ⁊ coacta in oleo com̄ ⁊ superposita mirifice sanat. Contra dol' pedũ siahausq; nisi tu tormentat' fuerit. radix ipius arthemisie cũ mell' comedat post cenã. mirifice liberauit. Nota quod impossibile est ad credendũ magnas uirtutes que sunt in ipa herba. Contra omnes febres. sucus arthemisie tagantes ⁊ tere oleo ro. simul cal'facto ⁊ pungeris. mir expellit febrẽ. Ut

Arthemisia leptaphilos ⁊ di minor. sed matricaria. flos ei similat' camomilla et ht odorem sanbuci quinq; ei tursens. Contra dol' stomachi ex frigiditate acc. herba arthemisia uiride bene tere ⁊ cũ oleo amigdalino simul cal'facto ⁊ ad modũ emplastri sup stomachum pon̄. ad quinto die erit liberatus. Item herba sup ostiũ de domo iposita. aliquis uir ul' femina non poterit nocere in illa domo. Contra dol' ⁊ tremorem neruorum. herba arthemisia leptaphilis sucus cũ oleo ro. simul cal'facto ⁊ loca dolentia punctis. omnem dol' ⁊ tremorem atque omnem uitiũ reumaticũ mirabiliter expellit. Et nota quod iste tres arthemisie inuenit diana ⁊ in uirtutes earum ⁊ medicamenta de herbe ipa diana dedit ad chiro centauro que uirtutes iste probauit ad oculis. ⁊ pro diana uocauit nomen herbe arthemisie. Legis hec mense madio ul' Julio.

Acetum · frigidu est 7 s · i secdo gu · penetratiua hz uirtutem ex substaa
et diuisiua · et ostrictiua ex qualitatib3 · Acetu
pot fieri hoc mo · ponatur uinu bonu i uase
ita q uas sit semiplenu tn discoopertu 7 ita
pot fieri acetu · ul' sic cicius facere uolueris ca
le facias calibem · ul' lapides · 7 pone i uino o
ore uasis manente discoperto · ul' uas cu uio
ponit p duos dies ad solez · ul' p tres · pbare
debes hoc mo acetu pone sup terra ul' sup ferru
frigidu · si bullierit bonu est · sin aut no e bon.
Ct uomitu 7 fluxu uetris · bulliat i ace
to tatu3 rose · galle · i tinguat ibi lana ul' sp
gia 7 ponat sup stom si sit uomit9 si aut fluxu
ponat sup renes 7 sup ubellicu · Valz 7 sir
acetosus · ad simplicez 7 duplicez tertiana 7
ad cotidiana3 de flate salso · 7 ad cez acutas.
sidet i mane · cu aq cal'a · Syr acetos dissoluo
dit materia · 7 fit hoc mo quidam ubi resol
ui i aceto ut coquitur donec adhereat cachi
e · 7 si uis facere duru mag coquitur · Syr aceto
sus · ualet ? calida materia · ualet etia ?
fria3 materia q2 ex aceto 7 melle fit oximel
qnq3 simplx qnq3 opositu · Simplex fit ex du
abus ptib3 aceti 7 tertia mell' siml' cognati
ad spissitudinez mell' Copositu aut fit
hoc modo · acc · radices feniculi · appii · petrs
ote aliqtulu 7 p diez 7 noctez pmictat in
aceto · scdo die coq3 siml' 7 pea cola · 7 i illo a
ceto 7 colato pone mel ad tertia ptez 7 coq3 ut s
fit i oximell' sqllitig hoc mo · acc sqlla 7 dim
icte p diez 7 noctez i aceto 7 coq3 7 cola · Oport3
tn exteriora 7 iteriora · sqlle abici 7 mediana
uo amisceri · deinde ad misceas mel ut s · 7 si n
habes sqlla · acc radicez rafani 7 similit fac ea
sicut supi Syr acetos dat ? calida3 materia
Ita oximel simplx ul' copositu · dari debet ?
fria3 q digerit ea Acetu ofortat apetitu hoc
mo · acc saluia 7 petrslinu · pipe 7 meta et o
tere 7 distepa cu aceto · tale salsametu otu
pictamesiu · Jt si carnes edatur solu mo cu
aceto appetit augmetat · Nota si acetu inue
nit · stom · plenu tuc laxat uetrez · si aut iuent
uacuu tuc strigit · Valet ? debilitates exe
gritudine · acc acetu 7 pone itus panez assu
et ex tali pane sic madificato ugeos 7 nares
7 labia patietis · 7 uenas pl'satiles · 7 i bra
chio · 7 ibi q s uenas lega tales panez assu3
· s · i aceto madefactu in stu ofortat patientez.
Valet 7 acetu ? litargia 7 frenesim si
fiat fricatio circa uolas manuu 7 pedu
o sal' 7 aceto · Ad casses passioes ualet si
raso capite · prius lauetur cap ex decotione ace
ti et castorei.

Alchanna · fria · e · i primo gu · sicca i principio
scdi · Alchana e herba q i cta simals ptibus i
uenit · Quia uo no ubiq3 iuenit q ea hnt pl'
pluericat · pl'uericata deportat p diuersas corpo
ris regiones · pl'uis sbnigri coloris e · Virtu
tez hz ofortadi 7 extergedi 7 solidandi.

Alcanna.

Alcanna · valet ? ... cationez cutis
hoc mo · q ult ... ficare 7 atenuare cute
suaz i brachio siue i alio corpore · eat ad b
alnea 7 ablutis ptib3 cu aq · ca · distepetu
alcana cu albumine oui 7 aceto 7 i ugat.
7 paulo post ptes i ucte · 7 bis aq · ca · ablu
antur · 7 i scda die abluat aq · ca · sic 7 tertia
et quarta · Nota tn q i prima die partes
iucte apparebut deformes · scdo die min · et tertio
Quarto aut lucidissime apparebut · hoc eti
modo curatur herpes ?ulosus · Ad ?solida
tionez uulneris ualet si supponat solu mo · ut
est i aure 7 naso 7 i alijs cartillaginosis lo
cis 7 albi · Nota q si no hns alcana ad ?so
lidatioez · ualet tantudez pl'uis cinamoi · Si
uis ungere ungues ul' capillos ul' alias pte
rubeo colore distepa alcana cu aceto ul' aqua.
Si uo uolueris nigro colore tingere · ipam distepa
cu oleo 7 ptes iniuncta permicte siccari · uix po
stea recedit tintura illa nisi ? suco pomaru
adrange ul' cantabro et aceto.

Auripigmentū · c · ē · 7 · s · ī quarto gu · due
na terre fit · dissoluit actrahit 7 mūdifi
cat · due st spēs auripigmēti · ē ē rubeus et
citrinū · citrinū ɔpetit medic̄ · ɔt asma
ex humiditate · ponat̄ · auripigmētū sup̄ prunā
et inclinato capite erectis pedib; 7 patiens
recipiat fumū p̄ ebotū · valet ēt ad idē · ʒ ·
iii · ex auripimēto 7 alee cū ouo sorbili · bis
ul' semel ī septimanā · Nota q̄ ad tussim ī pue
ris q̄ ē canina dr̄ · auripigmēti · ʒ · i · datū
ī ouo sorbili uel uino ul' cū lacte semel
ī ebdomadā mltū ualet ¶ Ex calce uiua et
auripigmēti fiat psilotrū · acc̄ · ʒ · iiii · a
calcis uiue 7 resolue ī aq̄ 7 bliat 7 adde
· ʒ · ii · auripigmēti 7 coq̄; · Signū aūt de
coctiōis est qn̄ pēna ī missa stati excocta le
uiter manib; d̄pilatur · Si uō uis remouere
pilos oportet ēē ī loco calido inunge pātē
illā illo psilotro · p̄ea ablue aq̄ tepida · qr̄
aliter excoriaret si fria ul' nimis calida ·
ablueretur · alii addut̄ ciminū 7 aloen ·
ut nō excoriet · ¶ ɔt ipetigines 7 sp̄pigines
acc̄ duas ptes saponis spataretī 7 t'tiā au
ri pigmēti 7 distēpa 7 fac ungt̄; 7 ūge p̄u
uō aq̄ · ca · abluas p̄t̄ illā 7 post ī unctiōē
similiter qa sidiu remaneret · vngt̄; tā bo
nā quā malā carnē corrodet · t' · ul' quat
ita ablue 7 unge pilos radicitus euelle
7 p̄ea ī unge ex ol'o īqami · et pone ī foliis
7 micte s̄b cinerib; calis 7 coq; et postea in
manib; exp̄me · et illō ualō bonū est ¶ ul'
aliter coq; sem̄ y'qami cū ol'o coi 7 p̄ea
cola 7 usui reserua · ¶ Ad ungues repandā
acc̄ serapinū 7 misce simil' cū eo pluē; aūri
pigmēti · 7 mō fac ēplastū; 7 pōe sup ūguē; ·

Aspaltū · i · butimen iudaicū · ca · ē 7 sic ·
ī t'tio gu · t'ra qdā ē q̄ uenit d̄ ultramaris
ptib; · d̄ iudea 7 nigri coloris est · 7 pōderosa
alii dicūt q̄ sit d̄ spuā cuidā lacus · cum
creta 7 ī durata · ī quo · s · laci sodome · et

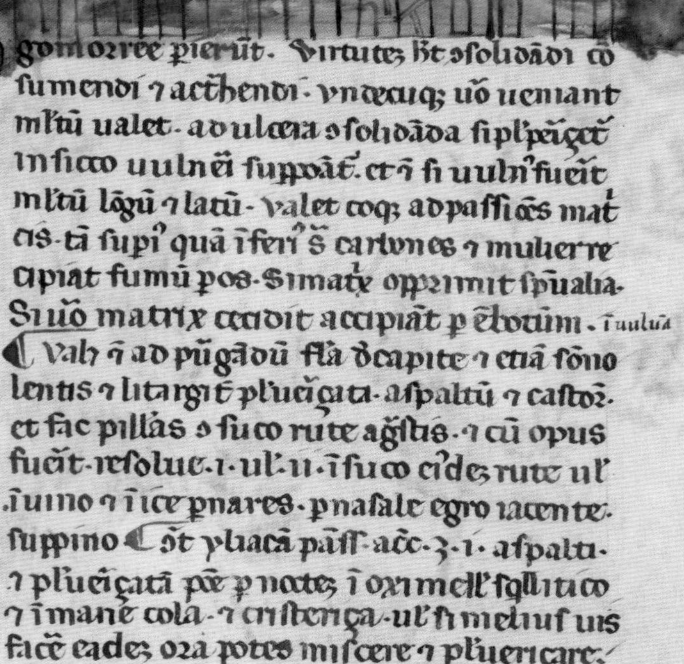

gomorree perierūt · Virtutē; h̄t ɔsolidādi cō
sumendi 7 acthendi · vndecuq; uō ueniant
mltū ualet · ad ulcera ɔsolidāda sipl' p̄ergēt
in sicco uulnēi suppoāt · et ēt si uuln' fueit
mltū lōgū 7 latū · valet coq; ad passiōēs mat
cis · tā supi' quā īferi' s̄ carbones 7 mulier re
cipiat fumū pos · Si matx̄ opprimit spūalia ·
Si uō matrix cecidit accipiāt p̄ ebotum · ī uulua
¶ Vali; ēt ad pūgādū flā d̄ capite 7 etiā sōno
lentis 7 litargit pluēigata · aspaltū 7 castor ·
et fac pillās ɔ suco rute agistis · 7 cū opus
fueīt · resolue · i · ul' · ii · ī suco eid; rute ul'
ī uino 7 ī ice pnares · p nasale egro iacente ·
suppino ¶ ɔt yliacā pass · acc̄ · ʒ · i · aspalti ·
7 pluēiçatā pōe p̄ noctē; ī oximell' sqllitico
7 ī mane cola · 7 cristeriça · ul' si melius uis
facē eade; orā potes miscere 7 pluēriçare ·

Anabulla d̄ ea modo nō loqm' qr̄ eā īuenies
ubi titimalliū ·

Acantū h'ba est q̄ alii uocāt · melāfilon
alii uocāt · pederon · Nascit' locis d̄lic
tibil' 7 īaquosis 7 h̄t folia pār mag' lactuē
sive sic erucā 7 uirid' mltū q̄si sbnigre · 7
braxica ei' ē lenior 7 lōga duob; gubitis 7
grossa ad modū digito ·

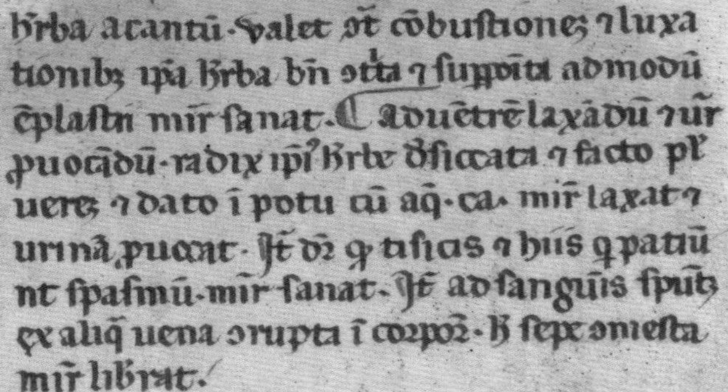

herba acantū. valet ꝯt cōbustiones ⁊ luxa
tionib; ipa herba bn̄ ꝯtrita ⁊ supposita ad modū
ēplastri mir sanat. ¶ Ad uētrē laxādū ⁊ uī
puocādū. radix ipi' herbe dsiccata ⁊ facto pl'
uere; ⁊ dato ī potu cū aq. ca. mir laxat ⁊
urinā pucat. It dr̄ ꝙ tisicis ⁊ hiis ꝙ patiū
nt spasmū. mir sanat. It ad sanguīs sput;
ex aliq uena ꝯrupta ī corpor. h sepe ꝯmesta
mir librat.

sistit. ꝯt dol' stōi hr̄ adiātos bn̄ ꝯtrita et
supposita ī modū ēplastri. stati mitigat dolore;
It ꝯtrita ⁊ supposita morsū canis mir sanat.
Nota ꝙ uiridis ualet meli' ꝙ exsiccata.

Salvia vita.

Adianthos. herba ē ꝙ simili noīe appellat.
alii uō uocāt eā. Gallitricos. alii. pollit
cos. s; alia herba ē illa ꝙ dr̄ pollitricū. h aūt
herba adiātos hūs folia simil' coliandro
⁊ ht̄ fusticulū sb̄ nigro ⁊ radix pua. Nasci
tur locis obscuris ⁊ max ī sepib;. foliis
utim̄ ī medicīs ⁊ nō radicē qr nichil ē util'
Virtutē ht̄. ca. ⁊. h. ī. i. gu. ¶ Ɔt suspiriosos
⁊ ytericos ⁊ ꝯt stranguriā ⁊ diss. ⁊ lapidez
ī uexica frāgēdā. aq decotiōis andiātos fit
syr' ꝯ zuchero ⁊ dt̄ ī mane ī aurora cū eadē
decotiōe calā. plenū ciatū ⁊ da patieti feb
citātib;. si uō nō febricitāt fac sir' cū mell'
⁊ da cū deā decotiōe ibi addita radix. fenicli
pets. appii. spagi. ⁊ bruschi. ⁊ similia. ul' da
cū uino ⁊ mirabris. It ualet oppilationi
epis ꝯt splēis ꝯ fri. ca. It pse coctū ī aq ul'
uino ⁊ utē. ꝯ ꝯestuā pucat. fluxū uetri

Eupatorius.

Agrimonia. ē herba ꝙ silit' appellat. dom
ani uō uocāt eā. ynone. alii uocāt. vin
unia. Romani. argemonoz. alii. liburrna.
alii. herbalis maior. alii. Cordialis. alii. R
Rucilia. alii. Ruminalis. alii. domitris
gallica. alii. sarcacolla. alii. arcella. alii.
agrimatū. alii. abrella. Nascit' ī mōtibus
⁊ ī planis u' c'ca sepib;. prima cura eī ad
dol' ⁊ uitia oculoꝝ. herba agrimoīa uirides bn̄
tere ⁊ suppōe ocul'. oēs liuore ⁊ īflactiōes mi
rabiliter expellit. Nota si nō iueniūt uirides
acc dsicca ⁊ macerab in aq calā. pdicē. ¶ Ad
dol' uētris. agrimoīa cū suis radicib; potui
data mir pficit. ¶ Ad fetidez canceromat
agrimoīa uides bn̄ ꝯtrita ⁊ supposita ministrat
sanare. ¶ Ɔt illuxatiōe. agrimoīa cū axū
gia bn̄ ꝯtere ⁊ fac ēplm ⁊ suppone. oēs
īflactiones ⁊ dol' expellit. ¶ Ɔt morsū spe

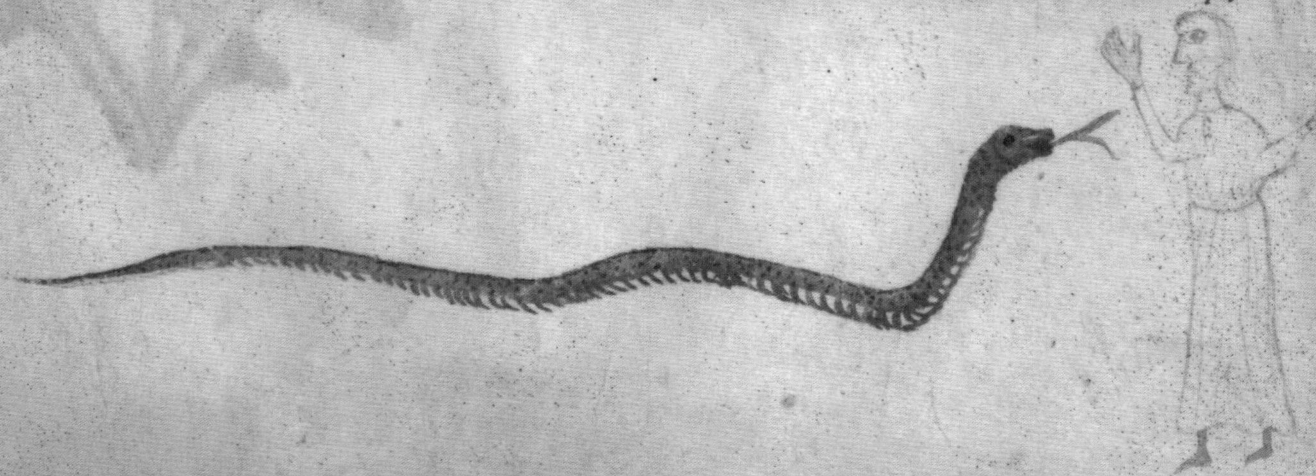

tibus ⁊ oīuz reptiliū uenenātiū. pluūs agri monie. ʒ. ii. ⁊ uino qactos. ii. potui dato oēs uenenū. mir̄ discutit ⁊ expellit. ¶ Ad uulneratus lanceā ul' aliqd ferro. hrba agrimonia cū aceto bn̄ tere ⁊ suppōe plag̃ cito sanabit. ¶ Ꝯt dol' splenis. agrimonia sepe comesta. mir̄ splenē curat ⁊ ī qsūt sede. ¶ Contra apēa. agrimoīaz cū asūgiā fco emplm. et suppone cito apit ⁊ sanat. ¶ Ad fistulā collige trib; radicib; agrimoīe ⁊ collige eā cū reuerētia adeo ⁊ oratiōe. s; tres aue m̄ ⁊ tres pat̄ nr̄. pēī suspēde adfuo ī noīe patiētis. dr̄ q. cū radice ipī' fit ōsiccata ⁊ fistulā erit sanata.

hrba appollinaīa. uirtutē ht̄ pncipaliter ad fetidas chironias ⁊ terraneor morsus. hba h' uiride fasciculū. i. ⁊ axūgiā sin̄ sal' simil' coteris ⁊ addito uinū ueter optimo qactos. ⁊ coq; ad ōsūptiōez uini ⁊ fac ēplastrū ⁊ suppon̄. ⁊ cito librat' erit.

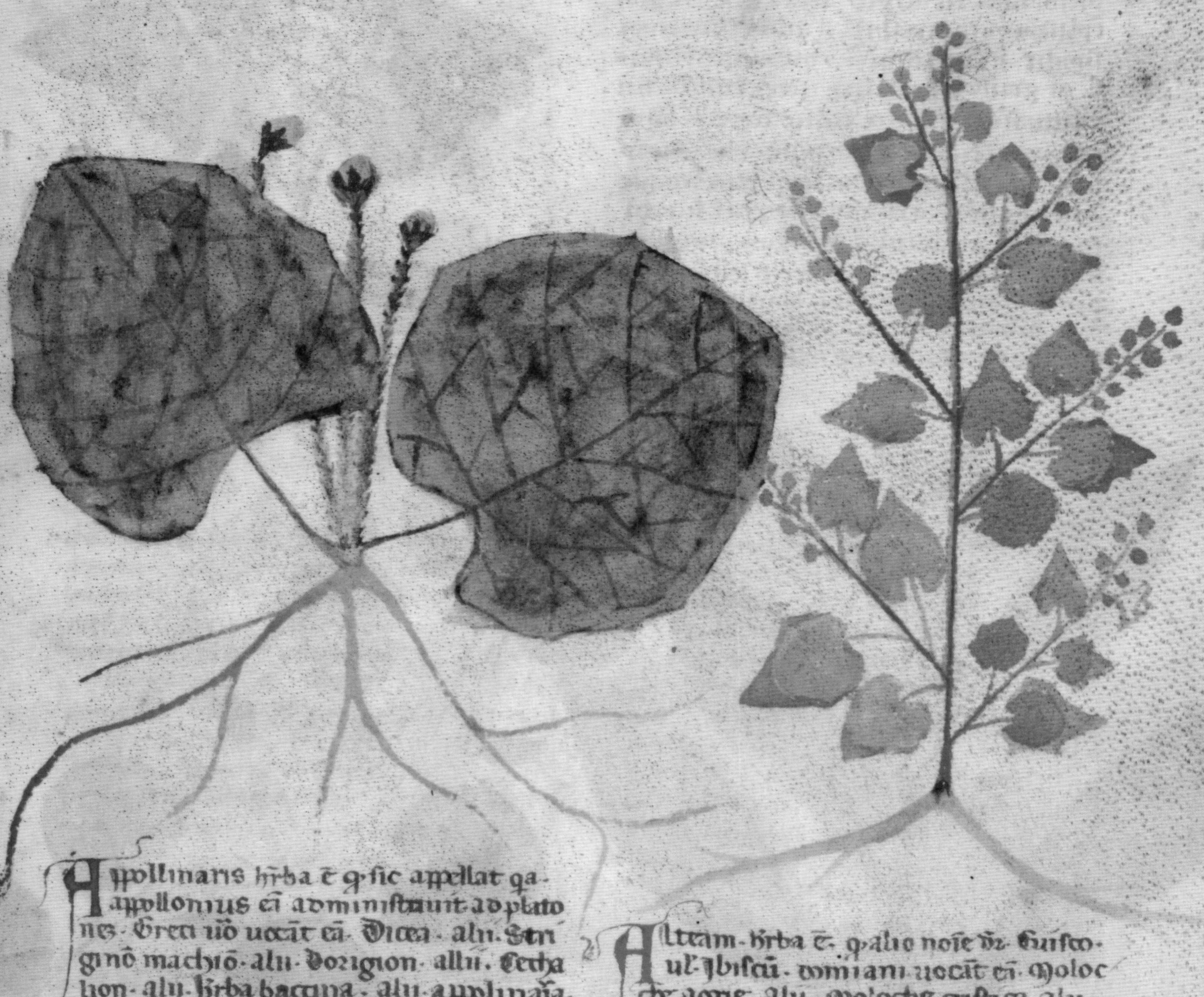

Appollinaris hrba ē q. sic appellat qa appollonius eā administrauit ad platones. Greci uō uocāt eā. Dicea. alii. Strignō machiō. alii. Dorigion. allii. Cethalion. alii. hrba baccina. alii. appolinaīa. Nascitur

Alteam. hrba ē. q. alio noīe dr̄. Euiscoul'. Ibiscū. romiani uocāt eā. Moloche agrie. alii. Moloche cristica. alii. Molochin. alii. Siccofillon. alii. higemōs alii· Ribiscu· alii· albacus· alii· maluacu scus· alii· Bruiscus· alii· Baucilus· Nasci tur locis humidis 7 i capis· radix ei ime dicis opetit 7 sem u iuenit bismalua d suo seie itelligit. Virtute ht· calida 7 hu· i so gu. Cont podagra· radix altea i aq bn dcoque 7 cu axugia uete bn otere 7 suppone eplas tu· adtio die erit liberatus 7 pbatu est ad mltis sapietib; hoc expimetu. Cad onnes apostei siu iflactiones i quacuq; ptes co poris fuerit siu inguines· radix altee dcoc ta ut sups diximus 7 bn pistata cu axugia uete addito farina fenugci 7 seie lini· et suppone eplastu· pfectissime remollit et maturat 7 q rupit si sepe renoueb drecet. Cc dol neruoz 7 iucturis. aq dcoctiois dra dicib; suis 7 fenugco· ablue loca 7 suppon eplastru· mir sanabit. Cad dol intestinoz similit ablue 7 suppon 7 mirabeis d bn ficio. Cct graue 7 sicca adq; uetez tussim· fiat ellactuariu; ex radice euisco dcocto 7 bn m dato 7 cu cisorie bn minutu itciso 7 accip lib· i· 7 mell albi· lib· ii· simil bene dcoque diu amiscedo 7 cu uolueis pbar si coctu fueit pon aliqntul s marmor 7 pmicte in frigidai 7 si digitis no adheret coctu e· dpoa tur ab igne· 7 addat ibi· gingiber pluericat ℥· ii· pineaz mudatoz· lib· s· 7 cu bn admi sto record 7 usui mane 7 sero· usq; libret·

Astula regia· hrba e q simili noie appellatur 7 valet adu itia 7 putredine oris· Radix astule regie uinu dcoctiois ei ore retento statim sentiet bnficiu·

Abroxiana· hrba est simil eupatorium. s; no est adeo logiora 7 magis similat mctistri. Ct oppilatioez epis 7 spleis· 7 ydropisi i pri cipio egritudis 7 q eot uermes siu lubricos aq ul uinu dcoctis eidez hrbe sepe potat mir librabit si fuerit extri. ca·

Nom hrbe astul regie.

Nom hrbe asarum·

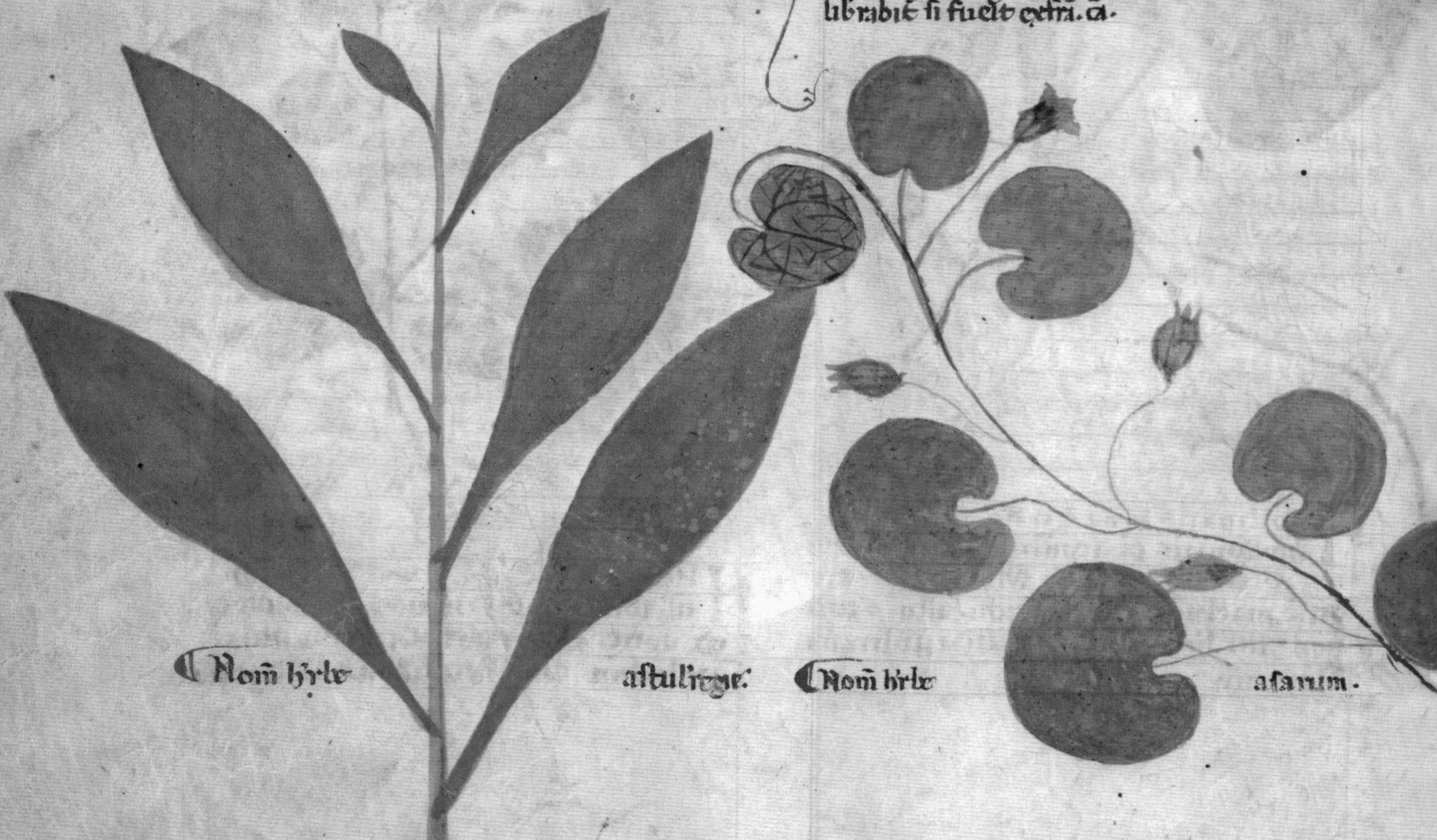

Asara vel asar. i. q̄ bachara. latini vocant eam. vul
gago. c. ē 7 s. i. iii. gu. vinum vel aqua decoctis
eius urinam 7 menstrua provocat. dolorem 7 opilationem
epatis extensam et 7 splenem mirabiliter proficit. Ydropisim 7
sciaticis si sepe bibita valde iuvat. Item similiter
potata dolorem sive morbo matricis expellit. Ictericos
bonos colores reddit. Item purgat ventrem
7 maxime flam p os q̄ provocat vomitum 7 ē q̄si
violete sic eleborum albo s̄ non adeo tamen fortis q̄
debet considerare etas 7 virtus accipientis. si pin
guis aut macilentus. si regione frigida vel calida q̄
melius potest dari pinguis quam macilenti 7 mag in
regione frigida quia calida. 7 nota come debet dari ¶ Acc
folia. xx. asar viridis folia. xxx. prepara sic
ponatur illa in vino ut cooperiat 7 ibi maneat
per noctem ut maceretur. mane vero tere ipsa in
mortario 7 resolve in eodem vino 7 da in potu
vel ponatur in cogna vel decocta sit carnes porcina
pinguis 7 da comedere patienti postea da sibi de op
timo vino al quantum vult bibere. hoc numerum
debet dari fortiores nature. aliis vero secundum nature
7 etatis. Nota q̄ cum reperitur in medicinis. asari. debet
poni de radice eius 7 non folia.

Atriplex. frigidum ē in. i. gu. hu. in secundo. alio
nomine dicitur. Atriplex. alii. Arcapassis. alii.
Crisolacana. Atriplex utimur in cogna sive in
cibis virtutem habet ad ventrem solvendum 7 laxan
dum 7 s̄ narrat duritiam solvit 7 remollit. oppi
lationem curat. Item emplastrata cruda vel cocta
expellit ungulam tortuam 7 corruptam. ¶ Contra ygnem
sacrum. trita 7 supposita mirabiliter sanat. ¶ Contra podagram.
Atriplex bene cocto cum melle 7 aceto 7 supposito mirabiliter
curat 7 sanat. Contra yctericia morbo ut dicit
galienus. vinum decoctionis seminis eius sepe bibito
multum valet. Item aqua decoctionis seminis atriplicis 7 ra
dix rafani addito modico aceto. in multa quantita
te bibita. stomacum purgat per os. flam 7 s̄ colleram.

Nasc aut c q̄t. Atriplex paynnes c
ē liquor ē agstis eius eiec. nemini
in. ppter viscositates q̄z causa pl
alim apper. illud refrigerat maxime
sic crisipilla. semen eius multi ficatu
ē 7 colaturi. pin utile ē hicteritis
hominibus q̄z nascitur de epatis oppilatione
dosis. n. 3. cum melle 7 aqua ca potu
tis colleram nostris provocat.

Anthera dicitur flos rose i. semen q̄ reperitur in medio
rose. precipue valet contra fluxum ventris et
vomitum. valet in contra humiditatem uve. supponitur
vel capienti 7 plus cinamomi. mirabiliter humiditatem
uve consumit exhibiore fluente ad caput. Item
contra ragadias. pulvis anthere superspergatur vel
cum aqua dragaganti illiniatur. cum dentes extrahuntur 7 fluit
sanguis fac gargarismum ex aceto decoctionis
anthere vel cum tota rosa.

Anthora herba ē q̄ filii nomine appellatur. ipsi

radix ē parua asimilat qsi testiculi galli ⁊ ht
nigrum colorez exteriꝰ intus uō alba sa
porez ht sb amar ⁊ ualō ꝑticā i modum
calami aromatici. Nascit i mags motibus
⁊ i ꝯstis. Virtutez ht. ca. ⁊ siccā. ualet ꝓpe
ē. ꝯt dolorez matricis ⁊ dolori uetris ⁊ stoi.
ex fiā. ca. uinū decoctis eiꝰ potui dato uel de
radice eiꝰ fac pluez ⁊ tepa cū uino calido.
ul fac elctm d puluē ipiꝰ ⁊ mell ⁊ dab ieiu
no stō cū uino calido. mir oēz dolorez expe
llit. Jt lobricos necat. ⁊ ē ꝯt uenenū ⁊ oi
um reptiliū aīaliū.

Avena hrba est cuiꝰ sem̄ sibi nōie appellat
auena. f. ē. ⁊ hu. i. i. gu. uirtutez ht sic
farina ordi. ul ut far. auena bn̄ mūdata
articlm abiectis corticib; ꝑcā i mortario be
ne pistata ⁊ addito aq tepida p linteo raro
bn̄ colet ⁊ expmat cū maib; ⁊ tali colatura
coqnt ad spissitudinez ⁊ fiat ptes ⁊ i fine
dcoctiōis addat lacte amigdalino suffici
enti ⁊ çucharo albo i bona qntitate. hoc
mltū ualet febricitātib; ttianariis. sinoc.
⁊ causon. fit ꝯpetēs cib; laborātib; appcāte.
spūaliū ⁊ nutritor. apeā maturat. maturata
relaxat. ⁊ optimū nutmetū est.

Ameos. pipcula. karui agstis. curminel
la. idez est. due sut ē spēs. s. maiꝰ ⁊ minuꝰ
et utz ht una cadez uirtut. s. ē maiꝰ qr m
agna hn̄s folia ⁊ ꝓpt magnā efficaciā. mi
nor aut ht parua folia ⁊ modic crescit
⁊ ē ualō aromaticū q; maiꝰ ⁊ ht sapore
qsi ut pipe. Nota q illud q i motib; crescat
mag aromaticū ē. Virtutez ht. c. ⁊ s. in
iii. gu. Menstruā ⁊ urinā d grosso flāte.
ꝯstipata ꝓuocat. cū mell potatꝰ lūbricos
cucurbitinos ⁊ ascarides mir occidit.
Grossa dissoluit uētositatez. lapides i ue
xica frāgit. Stomacū cal fac. Mis ꝑ tractus
renez ⁊ uuluā mūdificat. tritꝰ ⁊ cū mell
ꝯpatus. potū q; datꝰ flāticā febrez ⁊ mo
sum reptiliū curat. asue factos tn̄ aut
cataplātus cuti citrinū colorez acomo
dat.

Amomū. c. ē. ⁊ s. i. iii. gu. sem̄ ē cuidam
hrbe. mulieri i eiꝰ apposimate sedenti
dol uulue placat. pessariū idez opat. mstrā
ꝓuoc. appōa eiꝰ potatū ē epil. nefretic. ⁊ podagc.

Albatra arbor ē cui⁹ fructus simil' ē cerase.

Alleluia · herba ē q̄ alio noīe dr̄ pane de
cuccho · herba nascit' oīb; locis ⁊ circa
uiā ⁊ ad pedē parietib; ⁊ similat' trifolium
s; h̄t saporē acetosū · flores h̄t croceū hec
herba ponit' ī marciatō q̄r ꝯfortat mēbra
⁊ dissoluit · ⁊ dol' neruoꝝ expellit.

Asti formacū · i · q̄ uincetoxicū · Nascit' ī
mōtib; ⁊ crescēs ī lōgitudine uni⁹ cubti
hec ponit' ī metridat' ⁊ ī alijs antidotis ꝯt dol'
matricis ⁊ ī ualet ꝯt uenenū ⁊ oīu̅ reptili
um uenenatoꝝ · d' ipso dicerem⁹ ante ū dr̄ uin
cetosicum.

Acetosa siuē acedula · herba est similat' spi
nach ⁊ meli⁹ asimilat' lapaciū rotūdū ⁊ h̄t
saporē acetosū · sem̄ ei⁹ ē simil' lapaciū acuti
uirtute; h̄t frā; ⁊ s · Valet ꝑncipue scabiosis
⁊ auriginosis sucū ei⁹ · ī syr̄ · ul' oximell' factū
d' suco suū tere ⁊ c · ul' ꝑse ꝯmesta · mir̄ scabi
em ⁊ pruriginē; tollit · si fit ex colera ru · et
sanguine putrefactō · It sem̄ ei⁹ decoctus ī siru
pis ꝯt lōgā egritudinē; ꝯtia febre · mirab'
ꝓficit · ⁊ ad m̄lta alia facit.

Auellanarū siue auellane nucib; s̄t frigi
diores ⁊ grossiores · Sīt ē corpora subtiliori
⁊ spissiōra · unctuositate carētia hac d' cā plurimib;
s̄it corpori nutriue · tardiores tām ad digerēd'
⁊ ad descēdend' corpē · īflatiō; uentre gn̄at · ma
xīe si cū iteriori suꝑficie comedāt' q̄ ablato me
lius digerūt' · Valēs s̄it antiquā h̄ntib; tussi;
precipue si pistate comedāt' cū melle · Et ei q̄ cū
modico piper assi ul' falsas reuma patietes ex
celenter adiuuat · Et tame nō asse ieiunis sūpte
fiūt ꝯt uenenū · ꝑterea si cū exteriori cortice asse pistēt' ā
ueteri adipe suis · ul' ursi · fiūt allopicias h̄ntib; iu
natiue · locis q̄ denudatis capillo reuocāt · q̄dā dix ad
hoies nimis pingues uolēs ex macillēt · ipse sartagin
florib; auellanaꝝ ⁊ ꝯfuso uino cōmuni fortie ⁊ obliat
die ac nocte ⁊ diu eū sicerit ī ferē uinū q̄ colato bibat
ieiun · ʒ · iij · p · v · dieb; ⁊ comedat apndum · hoc fiat
mēse febrario.

De balsamo.
De bolo armenico.
De balaustia.
De borrago.
De baucia.
De borace.
De bectonica.
De bernice.
De branca ursina.
De berberis.
De belliculi.
De bistorta.
De bonbace.
De buglosa.

De butyro.
De berbena.
De brictanica.
De bursa pastoris.
De brionia.
De bedeguard.
De boeslio.
De bardana.
De buxo.
De braxillo.
De brusca.
De bleta.
De blacte bisantis.

Balsamus arbor est ut quidam dicunt
vel frutex quod verius est. adtestante
diascoride. et etiam illud quod dicunt
quod nunquam crescit nisi in quantitate duorum
cubitorum. ad plus. Circa babilloniam
reperitur in quodam campo in quo sunt septem
fontes. Si autem alias transfertur. nec flores
nec fructus faceret. in tempore autem estivo
inciduntur rami aliquantulum cum cultello non
penitus postea guttatim emanans colligitur
in vase vitreo scissure suspenso. In uno anno colliguntur xl. libre illius succi qui dicitur opobalsamum. frutex dicitur balsamus.
postea rami incisi aliquantulum desiccantur
et colliguntur et dicitur xillobalsamum fructum
qui in fructice reperitur dicitur carpobalsamum
qui non potest servari nisi ad plus per iiii. annos
postea enim incipit putrefieri. Est ergo illud
bonum quod recens est. vel quod non est perforatum. significat vetustitatem esse consumptum. Xillo
balsamum per duos annos servatur. postea
putrefit. est ergo eligendum quod cum frangitur
aliquid gumositas sive glutinositas habet
interius. quod sit etiam solidum interius. sed nec
multum liquidum nec multum solidum et non pulverizetur. quia sic significat vetustatem esse consumptum. Ista scilicet xillobalsamum et carpobalsamum virtutem habent calefaciendi et confortandi. Oppo
balsamum potentissimam habet virtutem. quod calidum est et siccum
in secundo gradu. sed quia carissimum est multis modis sophisticatur. Quidam vendunt terbentinam pro oppo
balsamum. quidam admiscent partem balsami terbentine ita habent odorem balsami et similitudinem.
Alii accipiunt succum melogelli vel foliorum citri
et admiscent terbentine addito croco orientali.
alii admiscent oleum nardinum terbentinum. Quidam auctores dicunt quod sic discernitur. quia
si ponatur in stilli puncta et accendatur ardet.
Similiter et terbentina. Diascorides dicit quod si
gutta oppobalsami ponatur in lacte caprino lac coa-
gulatur et gutta descendit ad fundum. sed sunt
multa alia coagulativa. alii dicunt quod pannus
subtilissimus madefactus oppobalsamo et ablutus si
in nulla parte remanet infectus purum fuit.
oppobalsamum est citrinum et multum clarum. dignoscitur
sic a sophisticato. si cum stillo ponatur suaviter in
superiori parte aque ibi remanet si in medio et
ibi remanet. est et alia probatio pone aquam
in aliquo vase et in illa aqua ponatur oppobalsamum
postea moveatur cum aliquo ligno. similiter sophisticatum vel terbentina turbatur. Si vero fit purum oppobalsamum non turbatur. Alia probatio ablue

manus per partem. postea pone aquam mundissimam
in vase argenteo. mundissimo vel alio vase postea pone oppobalsamum et panno subtilissimo et mundissimo puncturato tamen prius balsamo. postea ablue in vase illo. quod purum est ad unam partem aggregabit
vel illud vivum argentum. Si aliquid gummi ibi fuerit
remanebit in alia parte. vel si aliqua sophisti-
catio ibi affuerit pannus inficietur. Si vero pu-
rum fuerit oppobalsamum non inficietur. sed etiam erit eiusdem ponderis
cum prius fuerit. Alia probatio ponderetur parum oppobalsami
in aliquo vase. et postea deponatur et postea ponderetur
terbentina in eodem vase vel simili. si fuerit oppobalsamum
purum ponderabit in triplo plus quam terbentina. si
vero non ponderat plus vel parum plus quam terbentina
constat esse sophisticatum. Dicunt enim quidam quod si ponatur
in volis manuum penetrat volas quod falsum est.
sed si parum oppobalsami ponatur in palato cerebrum ita
calefacit quod videtur succendi. Virtutem habet dissolvendi et attrahendi. Oppobalsamum ʒ i. datus cum
vino matricis superfluitates mundificat. fetum
mortuum et secundinam educit. menstrua provo-
cat in oppobalsamo bombice intincta et supposita. Contra dis-
uriam vel stranguriam. vel lapidem vesice. si etiam oppilatio fuerit ex frigido humore detur cum vino vel virga
pari erecta et ex aqua calida iniciatur cum oleo musce-
leo vel nardino. Contra dolorem yliacum vel dolorem stomachi ex frigida causa detur modicum oppobalsami cum vino tepido. Contra omnes passiones capitis inveteratas detur cum aqua
opiata passioni illi congruenti. Contra cicatrices
removendas misceatur cera cum balsamo et ponatur super cicatrices per x. dies quia cum cera potest du-
rare et sic per xl. dies fiat si necesse fuerit.
Contra quartanam et cotidianam. postea prius purgatione detur cum vino. Contra tinitum aurium parum stilletur. Contra tinitum aurium de humore calido
aliquid in aure iniciatur. Corpora mortuorum in-
corrupta conservat quia quantum dissolvit tantum consumit.

Bolus f. et s. in secundo gradu. bolus quedam vena terre est que precipue in armenia reperitur.

Unde dicitur

unde dr̄ bolus armenicus · Nō sophisticatur
ꝑpt̄ mlt̄a ei᷒ copiā · p · c · ānos pōt ꝯuari · Vir
tutē hͣt ɔstrīgēdi · ē · tn̄ elligendū q̄ rubic
us ē · & · oēs ptes nō habēs colores distintos
aliq̄ntulū fragibiles · boli aūt sit talis usū ·
C ɔt emoptoicā passioē · s · sanguīs fluxū uel
uōitu; sāguīs p os · si fiat uitio spūaliū me
broꝝ · ɔfic̄ pillās ex pl̄ue boli · ⁊ gūi · arab · et
p̄enidioꝝ cū aq̄ ordei ī fusiōis draggti · q̄ sic fit ·
In aq̄ ordi pōn̄ dragāt · p nocte ⁊ fiat q̄dā ɔge
latio ex aqua ɔgelatus ɔficiātū pill᷑ quas ten̄
at patiēs s᷑b lingua ut sic dissolute cū sali
ua trāseant ad spūalia · Si ex uitio nutritiuo
rū · ei᷒ plius cū pl̄uere gūi ār · exusti ɔfecto
cō suco plātagīs potui det᷑ · C ɔ dissinteriā ul᷑
fluxū uētris sanguineū ɔmisce pl̄ue; boli ·
cū albumine oui ul᷑ cū toto ouo · ⁊ fac c̄ptel
las et da mane · ii · ul᷑ tres ul᷑ sic ɔfice puluē;
boli cū suco plātagīs · et p os d̄t᷑ ul᷑ iniciat᷑
p clistere fc̄a tn̄ prius purgatiōe · si sit ex su
periori intestino p hos · Si ex īferiori p anū;
iniciat᷑ · ul᷑ fiat hoc emplastm̄ ɔfice cū pl̄ue; boli
albumine oui et modico aceto · C ɔ fluxum
matricis ɔmisce bolū ɔ suco plātagīs ⁊ suppo
sitoriū d̄ bonbice fc̄m et ītinctū suppoāt᷑ · C ɔt
fluxū sanguīs e narib; hoc mō ɔfice bolum
ɔ suco sanguinaīe ⁊ fac tuellū · et pone nāi
bus · ul᷑ puluis solus cū bōbice narib; imic
tatur · ul᷑ fac pl̄uē; liq̄dā s᷑bam d̄ bolo ⁊ suco
sanguinaīe ⁊ patiēs sugat narib; · fiat eti
am emplm̄ sic ɔfice pl̄ue; boli cū albumi
ne oui ⁊ succo sanguinarie et fac ēplastm̄
et sup tīpora ei pone ·

B alaustia · fria ē · ⁊ sic · ī · s° · gū · dicitur aūt
balaustiā flos caducus mali ḡnati · Cū
aūt ē arbor fructus dē pducē flores in qua
dā tuberositate ɔglutināt᷑ · ⁊ q̄nq; ab ar
bore cadūt ⁊ q̄nq; sūmūtur · ꝯuari possūt
p duos annos ī mlt̄a efficatia · Psidia dr̄
cortex mali ḡnati · et d̄bent accipi cortices
cū pomū est maturū · seminib; eiectis · ad
oīa ualet at q; bolus · et p̄terea ad uomitū
collr̄icū ⁊ fluxū ~~sanguīs~~ uentris ex d̄bilitat᷑
uirtutis ɔtentiue · C ɔ uōitu; collr̄icū cū;
balaustia ⁊ cortex mali ḡnati ɔterant᷑ et coq̄
ntur ī aceto spōgiā ītinctā sup furculā pecto
ris ponātur · C ɔt fluxū uentris ex d̄fectu
uirtutis ɔtētiue decoquat᷑ ī aq̄ pluuiali et
fiat fomētu; · C puluis balaustie uulne
ra ɔsolidat · Nota q᷑ · in loco boli pōt pōi pl̄ui
balaustie et generale sit tibi ī oīb; q᷑ cum
aliqua sp̄es pōit᷑ in receptione aliqua · ali
am loco ei᷒ nō ponas · si potes eam habere ·

Balaustia ·

B orago · ca · ē · ⁊ hu · in primo ·
gū · herba q̄dā est satis cōs
aspa hn̄s folia q̄ dū uirida s̄t
precipue ɔpetūt usui mebrane ·

exsiccata nõ sanio seia. Virtutez hŗt generãdi bonũ sãguinem. Vñ oualescẽtibꝫ ex egritudine sincopiçantibus cardiacis melãcõicis. omesta cũ carnibꝫ ul' saginime. Cõt sincopi ꝛ õt tussim talis sit usus ex succo borragiẽ ꝛ çuchĩro fiat sir'. Cõ cardiacã pãssione. et epilẽtiẽ. fiat sir' ex succo eĩ ĩ çuccõ addito pluẽ ð osse ð cord' cerui. Cõ melãconicã passionez. fiat ĩ sucũ eĩ decctio señ ĩ colatura fiat sir'. sic ẽ hrba sem. decoquat' ĩ aq̃ iq̃ colatã fiat sir'. Nota q̃ seia ĩ magna efficatia suatur p. ii. ãnos. radix nõ oppetit m usui. hrba in cruda omesta bonũ sanguinez gñat. Cõ yctericiã omedatũ freqñt' cũ carnibꝫ cocta. et succo eĩ ex scatiole patiẽs impotu utat'.

Baucia. cã. ẽ. ĩ medio si. gdi. et hu. in pricipio eiðz. huĩ modi hrbe duplex ẽ maneriẽ domestica. s. ꝛ agstis. h hrba. alio nomine appellat' pastinaca. alii. agriostasilõ. dictĩ plus õpetit cibo q̃ medicine. Virtutez hŗt generandi bonũ sanguinez spissũ ꝛ mltũz. Vñ augmentatur libidinez. Cõ ualescẽtibꝫ et melancõic. ualet cruda ul' cocta omesta. uiridis et nõ siccata. sit q̃ õ gingiber õditum ad coitũ excitandũ. ꝛ digestionez õfortãd. acc' radices ꝛ coq̃ bñ coctas minutatĩ ĩcide et exprime aq̃ in form̃ magdaliones qbꝫ addat' mel despumatũ sufficiẽti ꝛ coq̃tur ad mell' õsuptionez. et õtinuo moueat' ne adhereat cacabo. In medio uõ decctionis si habes pone amigdalas et ĩ fine pineas mũdatas si habes. pĩea apponas spẽs arromaticas.

Borax. cã. ẽ. ꝛ sic. i. iiii. gu. ẽ aũt gũmi cuidã arboris. ĩ ultramaris ptibꝫ nascẽtis. In estate fluit uiscositas q̃dã. pura ex actione caloris. cõtẽpsatur ꝛ induratẽ et effluit etiaz q̃dã impurũ. q̃ aliq̃ntulũ molle ẽ et feculentũ. et q̃i tereũ. borax est elligẽda q̃ alba est lucida ꝛ dura. Si aũt hẽs sup̃ fluitates abiciat'. Virtutez hŗt astergẽdi et acthendi. Cã d faciez clarificãdã et pãnũ faciei remouendũ. maxiẽ si sit p̃ partũ. et etiaz si fiat ex calore aeris. pl'uis eĩ õficiat' cũ aq̃. ro. illiniat'. Cã d facies mũdificãdã et õpurand' cõficiunt' mulieres cũ mell' albo et mũdo. õficiũt etiã cũ unguẽto citrĩo. õficiũt ĩ unguẽtuz ex gallinacea asũgia resoluta ꝛ pulue borac. et facies illiniũt. No q̃ ĩ tribus. ʒ. aq̃. ro. possũt poĩ. ʒ. iii. ĩ lib mell'. ʒ. i. borac. Cã d mestr' puoc. et ad fetũ mortũ educend'. et sima. fiat suppositoriũ ex borace et succo centrũgalli.

Bectonica. cã. ẽ. ꝛ sic. ĩ tiio. gu. cuius folia p̃cipue õpetũt usui medicẽ. uirida et siccata mlt'e sũt efficacie. Vñ cũ inuenitur ĩ receptione. folia ponẽda sũt. h sũt alia noĩa bectonicẽ. Greci uocãt eam. Censtros. alii. Indicez. alii. Cosinice. alii. Sicotrofos. alii. Tiarica. alii. peropomon. alii. Cirone. alii. Teriopomon. alii. pantoma. alii. yeracha. alii. Seracatulã. hrba h nascitur ĩ planis. uidꝫ ĩ siluis ꝛ etiã ĩ mõtibꝫ ꝛ locis mũdis et unbrosis ul' circa arboribꝫ ꝛ custodit animẽ ꝛ cõpora humanũ ꝛ eũtes ĩ nocte. ꝛ locis scĩs. et scã ðz ab oĩbꝫ psonis. Nota q̃ q̃n legis eã. colliges mẽse augusto [illegible]

cord. Herba bectonica q primu inventa
fuisti ab escolapio tibi quero ppt penti
o ista tu qes vocata dña oia herbar et
p ille qte precepit q creata fuisses et ad
mltis remediis opata vid; p numeru
xlvii tu dignare me adiuvare in hiis
oia q tibi voluero ¶ prima cura ei ad
fracturã siũ vuln̄ i capite. herba bectoĩc
viridẽ bñ 9trita i mortario 1 suppõita.
mir sanabit 1 meli erit si a ttio die re
noveb̄ 9tinẽte; usq; q san erit 1 etia;
dr̄ q extrahit ossa fracta. ¶ ad dol' fc̄; s. ex
frã. cã. s. capis inco existẽte fiat garga
rismus. ex colatã dcoctiõis bectonĩc cum
staphisagria. i. aceto si fiat exanathiãsi
stõi et fuositate. dt vinũ dcoctis bectoĩc.
¶ 9t. dol' stõi. dt dcoctio supi cũ suco ab
sinthii cũ calida. Si adsit vehemẽs 9sti
patio. ut i yliacã. pass. pcedẽte existen

fiat h et ẽ remediũ. ¶ ad matricẽ; mũ
dificandã. et 9ceptũ adiuvãd. fiat fo
mentũ ex aq̃ dcoctiõis bectonĩc. ¶ fiat ẽ
suppositoriũ. ht ẽ esst 9fortũ ex eis pluere.
cũ mell'. ¶ 9t vitia 1 dol' oculor. herba bec
tonica cũ aq̃ a ttio dcocta 1 ocul' lava. folias
eidẽ 9tẽ 1 fac eplm sup frõtẽ; siũ i ocul' mi
rabilẽ bonũ effectũ senties. ¶ 9 vitia 1 dol'
auriũ. succus bectoĩc 1 olo rõx simil' calfcis
1 cũ licinio aurib' iiec pea cũ lana bñ obtu
ra. mir pficit. ¶ 9 obscuritatẽ; oculor. ʒ. i.
pluis bectoĩc cũ aq̃ cala ieiuno potui dab'
mir caligine oculor expellit. 1 pter oculor
ĩfenorẽ ubi galigo nascit mltũ subtiliat.
¶ 9t fluxũ sanguĩs e narib; pluẽ; bectoĩc
1 tãtud; sal' simil 9misce 1 acce p qntũ accipi
pot cũ duob; digitis pollic 1 narib; imic
te. stati sistet sanguine;. ¶ 9t vitia 1 dol'
dẽtium. herba bectoĩc dcoq; i vino ul' aceto
1 diu i ore teneat mir dol' expellit. ¶ 9t
vomitũ 1 suspiriosos 1 toracis dol. plũ
bectoĩce ʒ. i. 1 s. 1 qactos. v. aq̃ tepid dab'
ieiuno 1 mirabilẽ effectũ bonũ. ¶ ad
ptisicos 1 his q purulẽtũ excreãt. pul
vis bect. ʒ. iii. 1 mell'. ʒ. i. dab' ieiuno.
¶ ad stõi dol' pluis bectoĩc. ʒ. iii. i vice tib;
dieb; cũ aq̃ frã ciatos. iiii. 1 sanitatẽ redu
cit. ¶ ad iecoreris dol'. pluis. b. ʒ. iii. aq̃. c.
qactos. iiii. p dnũ potui dab' mir sanabi
tur. 9t dol' splẽis. vinũ dcoctiõis. bectõ.
bibit. mir pficit. ¶ ad dol' renũ. pl'uis. b.
ʒ. ii. 1 mlsa. qactos. ii. potui dab' 1 sanab'
¶ 9t colica pas. pluis. b. ʒ. iii. 1 vino
vetero opto. qactos. trib; pipis. g. 1 9.
i vino facto pluẽ distẽpa i pdõ vino et
da paciẽti ieiuno stõ. ¶ ad lũbor dolor.
pl'uis. b. ʒ. iii. 1 pipe. g. xvii. vini ami
nei. qactos. iii. calo dab' paciẽti ieiuno.
¶ ad dol' vẽtris. plũ. b. ʒ. i. aq̃. cal'. qactos
duos. potui dato. et ẽ valz ad dol' itestinor.
¶ ad laxãdũ vẽtrẽ; plũ. b. ʒ. iiii. ydro
mell'. qactos. novẽ; potui dato. stati laxt
vẽtrẽ; ¶ ad dol' d collo. vinũ dcoctis. bẽ
potui vtẽ mir pficit. ¶ ad gue; tussim
ellim 9fectũ. ex pluẽ. b. 1 mell'. da mane
et sero p. viii. dieb. et videris bñficium.
¶ ad cotidianã febrẽ. pl'uis. b. ʒ. ii.
suci arnoglos. ʒ. i. aq̃. ca. qacti. iiii. potũ
dab' paciẽti i hora access. mir sanabitur.
¶ ad Tertianã. f. pluis. b. et pulegio
tantũdẽ. ana ʒ. i. aq̃. ca. qactos. x. dab'
paciẽti i hora acc. 1 sanabit. ¶ ad qrtã;

febrez. pl'uis bectonic. ʒ. iii. mell' attici ℥. i.
aq. calid. ciatos. ccc. dab' patienti ante horaz
accessionis. sine molestia sanus erit. Contra uerice
dol'. becto. ʒ. iiii. radicum appii numero iiii. fiat decoctio in aq ad consumptionez medietatis. decoq; radices p̄sea adde pl'uez becto. et bibat patiens et librabit' ppetue. Contra lapidez in uexica frangendaz
pl'uis becto. ʒ. iii. aceti sqll' et mell' an ℥. i.
aq ciatos nouez sepe accipiat in potu. im-
mediate lapidez frangit et expellit foras. Ad mulieres que in partu laborant et febricitant. pl'uis b. ʒ. ii.
aq. ca. ciatos. iiii. dab' potui. si uero non febricitant
da cum mulsa et mirabaris. Ad paraliticos. bec-
uiridis. bene contrita et supposita mire sanat. et in neruos incisos consolidat et coniungit. Ad timorosos
pl'uis b. ʒ. ii. aq. ca. et uino adustero. an. ciac-
tos duos. simul potui dab' i hora acc. Ad mulieres locosas an loca sunt mortua ppter frigus. pl'ui
bect. ʒ. iii. aq. ca. ciati. iii. dab' potui ptribus diebus. ieiuno stomacho. et sanabit. Ad eos qui sanguinez per os eiciunt et purulentum excreant. pl'uis.
b. ʒ. iii. uini ueteris ciati. iii. dab' potui ptribus
diebus et librabit' cito. Ut numquam ebrius eris
herba. b. comesta antequam bibat. in illa die ebrius
non fiet. Ad euersos cuculculos. b. pl'uis.
ʒ. iii. et uino uetero calido ciati. ii. dab' potui.
Ad ytericos siue morboregio qui sunt auri-
riginosis. pl'uis. b. cum uino adustero sepius
accepta. pbatum remedium est. Ad carbunculos. pl'.
b. ʒ. i. aq. ciati. ii. dab' potui. Item herba cum axungia madefacta et supposita mire sanat. Ad eos
qui patiuntur psulcationes. pl'uis. b. ℥. i. et ciato
tribus uini optimi. potuiq; dato ptribus diebus mire
sanabit. Ad laxis uentris. pl'uis. b. ʒ. i. oximell'. ℥. i. dab' potui cum aq. ca. Ad cibos fas-
tidios. ex egritudine. pl'ui. b. ʒ. ii. et mulsa ciati. iii. da potui. mire fastidium tollit. Ut leuiter concoquat. etiam confectum ex pl'ue. b. et melle. uidez. ʒ. iii. b. et ℥. i. mell' da cum aq. ca. ciac-
ii. mire pficit. Contra uomitum. pl'uis. b. ʒ. iiii.
mell' cocti. ℥. i. fac pastillos admodum macha-
roni et da ieiuno ut comedat uno quolibet die
ptribus diebus. sunt dissolue cum aq. ca. et bibat. Ad
inflationez uirge et dol'. herba. b. in uino decoq;
p̄sea contere et fac emplim suppon. Contra uenenum.
pl'ui. b. ʒ. iii. et uino. ciati. iiii. potuiq; dato
statim uenenum eicit. contra omnia ualet quodcumque iec-
turum uenenatum. Ad morsum canis rabidi. b.
uiridez bene contrita et supposita mire curat et sanat.
Ad fistulam. b. uiridis bene contere cum modico sale
et fac tenta et pone intus et in suppon. emplim. mire pgat
et sanat. Ad dol' lumborum et lateris. pl'uis. b.
ʒ. ii. mulsa ciatos. i. da ei si non febricitat. si uero
febr. da cum aq. ca. Contra podagram. aq decoctionis becto
sepe bibita et etiam eadez herba desup implastata pedibus. mire dol' mitigat. ut dixerunt illi qui pbaue-
runt eaz.

Bernix. frē. et sic. conplexionis est in scdo gradu. Et est
gumi cuidam arboris in ultramarinis ptibus nascentis. ppter estuum quedam gumositatis effluit que actione
caloris exsiccatur et indurat'. et bernix dr. cuius in-
sunt spēs. quedam est sbcitrina coloris est quedam sbrufi. quedam sballbidi. quecumq; sit dum modo sit lucida
et clara eligenda. habet aut' uirtutem conglutinandi
ex gumositate sua. clarificandi et conseruandi quod satis
patet pictores est sup alios colores consueuerunt diu
suari pot cuius usus sit tal'. Contra fluxum sanguinis
e naribus. pl'uis eius confectus cum albumine oui tiporib et fronti suppoatur et dr. simpasma. quod fit ex eo
glutinantibus. pl'uis eius in naribus iniciat'. Contra uomitum
colericum. fiat emplim ex pl'ue eius. olibani et oui
albumine et furcule pectoris suppoatur. Contra dissinteriaz. fiat addito aceto et suppoat' pectini. Contra
uomitum colericum et dissinteriam. pl'uis eius cum ouo sorbili datus confert. ualet etiam pl'uis eius contra interiorez
et exteriorez solutionez. pl'uez eius apponunt mulieres faciei. et Nota quod bernix. kecabre. uernic.
dr.

Branca ursina · ca · ē · 7 hu · i primo · gu · virtu
tē hꝫ mollificādi · maturandi · 7 leniendi · Cō
sirā apcata utilis ē cui usus hec mō folia decoqnt
7 terat cū asungia porcina 7 suppoat · Cō apcata
spūaliū decoquat i aq̄ prius 7 cocta suppoatur.
Cō uitiū splenis 7 ariditate nervorū fiat un
guētū ex brā ca ur cocta 7 macerata diu in olo
colati addat cera · et fiat unguētū ut predcā
Nota folia recētia sep sūt ponenda i unguētis.

Berberi · fri · sūt 7 sicca · in 2° · gū · sūt aūt fruc
tus cuidā arboris rotūdi aliqtulū lōgi 7 ali
qtulū subnigri elligēdi sūt cōtinui · febriles nō
pforati · valēt cō febriles discrasiā ut i sir
fiat eorū decoctio i aq̄ addito zuchero · colature
fiat syr · Cō calfactiōē epis · pl'ius eorū cōfi
ciat cū succo solatri 7 epati suppoatur · Cō
dol' capis ex calliditate tota nocte dimictat
i aq̄ macerari mane dēt potui · No · q · p · vij ·
annos possūt suari ·

Belliculi marini · fri · sūt 7 sic · s; eorū excessus
nō determinat abauctoribꝫ · Sūt aūt ūbelli
ci circa litora maris repuītur · In ūguentis
ad faciē clarificādā ponūtur · et i ūnguēto
citrino quorū us sit tal' · Ad faciē clarificā
dā · pl'ius eorū subtilissime resoluāt cū asūge
gallinacea pri resoluti 7 fiat unguētū · et ·
no · q · di possūt suari ·

Bistorta fria · ē 7 sic · licet ei excessus eorū nō de
minat abauctoribꝫ ex ponticitate aūt cōnicit
eē fria · 7 sic · i ttio · gu · hꝫ aūt uirtutē · cōstrin
gendi · cōsolidandi · 7 cōfortandi · cōceptuꝫ · Cō
uomitū ex debilitate ul' feruore colle · pl'ui
eorū cōficiat cū albumine oui et suptegu
lam decoquat · et dēt patienti · Cō dissinteriā
dēt cū succo plātagis · Cō ad mēstrua cōstri
genda fiat fomētū ex aq̄ pluuiali decocti
onis pl'uis ei · Cō ad cōceptū adiuuandū fiat
cēlls ex pl'ue bistorte inquītitate · l' · s · 7 sperie
aromaticarū i eadē q̄ntitate · fiat ī p̄dictū
fomentū · qa p̄dcā adiuuāt cōceptū · s; q̄ cō
fortat uirtutē retētiuā matricis · Cō pl'uis
bistorte uulnera cōsolidat · et cōglutinat · No ·
q · bistorta hba ē cui radix bistorta appellat
qa est tortuosa · 7 simil' galange · s; nō habet
acumen ·

Bonbax

Bonbax siue cotone; unū ? idē; ē. ē herba q̄ in
ultramarinis ptib; etiā sicilia ī multa q̄ntita
te cresscit. vn̄ flos ei' fit bōbax. repitur ītus
q̄dā semē q̄ in medicinis ponit' ? ppē ī syru
pis ? ī electuariis resūptiuis. vn̄ cū repi
tur ī restaurātiuo sēis bōbacis. ōbet poni
sine corticib; b̄n mūdate. valet. asmaticis.
ptisicis ? ōsūptis.

Buglossa herba ē q̄ grē. bugloss' dr̄. latini
uō. lingua bouina uocāt. pseti uocāt. cono
sellurū. ostani uocāt. anich ul' aniti. egip
tii. antiesigillitos. romani. lingua bubu
la. lucani. corrago. daci. budama. libu.
sassinfach. alii. aleptosilō. q̄dā uocant
borrago agrestis. nascit' locis cultis ? sablo
sis. ? ōbet eā legi mēse iunio ul' iulio. h̄t
aut uirtutē. ca. ? hu. ī primo. g. sic borra
go. herba lingua bouina q̄ facit tres ramu
los ad se ie. colligē radice; suā ? ī aq̄ b̄n ǫq̄;
? ō tali aq̄ dab' potui febricitātib; s. tertiana
riis. mir' pficit. C ōt q̄rtā; febre; īueni es
herbā linguā bou. q̄ h̄t. iiii. ramulos. radix
ei' ǫq̄; simili mō ? bibat sepe. C ad apēa ta
herba ip̄' b̄n ōteris addito mell' ? medulla
panis. ? fac ēplm̄ ? suppon̄. mir' rūpit ? pu
gat. C ad suspiriosos succus cū mell' potuq;
dato suspiriosos curat ut dicēs macro. ō
collerā rubam. uinū ǫctiois. bugl'. sepe bi
bitū. collerā. ru. ? adustā. mir' pūgat. C ōt
cardiacā pass' q̄ fit ex collera. nig'. similiter
accepta mir' librat. C ad pl'mone; ex humo
ribus. lingua bouina cocta ul' cruda.
sepe ōmesta nociuos. hu. a pulmo
ne expellit. C ad guttam sciaticā. suc
cus eide; potui utere mir' pficit. C ad
memoriā ōfuādā. h' herba sepe ōme
sta. memoriā mir' auget ut dic multos
sapiētes. It libidinē puoc. no. si ōme
dēt cū lactuc̄ bōnū tēpamētū fit ? bon
sanguine; gnāt. q̄a frīdite; lact. tēperat
caliditate suā. C ut illares fiut oēs q̄
fiut ad ōuiuiū. aq̄ ǫctiois lingue bo.
aspge iter ōuiuium oēs fiut leti. Nota
q̄ hec herba lingua bouina sūt tres spē
s. pma q̄ pducit flore colore cel'stis quasi
borago ? radix ei' ē s' rubea. alia pducit
flore; albū ? radix nig' it' uō alba ? facit
ramulos magnos similat' cauda gatti.
alia pducit flore ī citrino colore ? h̄t mo
dice folia ? ē uald' aspa q̄ a multis dr̄
asprago. illa aūt q̄ h̄t flore celestinum
melior ē q̄ ipa ōbet pōi ī medicīs.

Buturum. ca. ē ī. i. g. h. ī sc̄o. pigu edo
ē q̄ fit ō lacte ouiū. uaccar; ? bubuli
linū uniuscuiq; bonū est ? max. uaccinū
? ouinū ? q̄nto recētī tāto meli'. C a tussi;
siccā ? asma. ? ptisicis ? ōsūptis exsiccāt
butirū recēte; ōmestū ī cogna ? ī cibis ?
ō ipō ōditis ul' cū pane cal'o ī' positus
? ōmestus mir' restaurat ? tussi; expellit
C ōt dol' neruor; ? pcussiōe;. butirū ueter
sepe ī uctū ad balneū ul' ad igne;. mir' dol'
mitigat ? neruos ōfortat. C ōt ad postea
calin. butyrū ueterē ul' recētē; cū herbe
brāce ursine ? uiolarie pri' ǫcte pēa ad
dito butiro ? fcō ēplm̄ suppone. mirab'
maturat apēa ? mitigat dolore;. Hinc igr̄
Butyrū. vulnerib; pectoris q̄ pl'mōis q̄ diafragmatis ē ouem
ens. ōmūdificat ē q̄ colat atq; uulnera ad maturitate; pdu
cit. gingiuas ā īfantiū dolētib; p' dētes ei nascētes dat mi
tigatione; q̄ si cū melle potui ōtur. fiet q̄ uenenū. s; tam
assue fcm̄ nocet stō q̄ uillos stō q̄ aspiratē lenificat.

BErbena· uerminaca· idez ē· herba ē q̄ alio no
dr̄ Colūbarā· siciliani uocāt eā· Pensterēō·
Greci uocāt· hierobotanez· alii Diosatiz·
domiani· Trigonion· africani· Sanguinaīā
alii· Petoromon· alii· Collesis· romani·
Sidericis· alii· ciparissus· pfeti· Persefo
nion· tuscij· Demetria· alii· pancroma· Egi
pti· Penpetar· pictagoris· Eriseeptron· Ita
liani· Verminacia· alii· Licima· alii· Slus
trago· Captupanus uocāt· Colūbina· alii·
Militaria· alii· Uertipediū· Nascitur oīb3
locis planis ⁊ humosis· Virtutez hēt· friā; ⁊ siccā;
s; excessus eī nō ōterminat ab autorib3· C ō
fetidez ⁊ pariotidas· radix uerminacie ad collo
suspēsa mirr̄ sanat· C Ad strumas et pariot
das· herba uerminacia cū asūgia sinē sal' bn̄
ōtrita ⁊ supposita mirr̄ sanat· C Ad eos q̄ indu

rate sūt uene ⁊ cibos nō accipiūt· herba uer
minacia succus cū mell' uino ⁊ aq̄· simil' bulia
bullitionez unā potū q; dab' ieiuno ciatū· i·
i uice· ad sanitatez reducit· C ō dol' ō corata
p'luis· uerminacia q̄ collecta sit solsticio· dab'
fortiores· coclaria· v· cū uino calb' ciatos· trib3
dab' potui· ōbilis uo da secdm uirtutez tps ⁊
etas· C Ad lapidez i uexica frāgēdā· p'luis ō
radicib3 uerminacie cū mel'sa potui dab'· statī
senties bn̄ficiū ⁊ etiā pucat urinā· C Ad dol'
capis· fac coronā ⁊ porta sup capite mirr̄ dol'
tollit C ō spentib' ⁊ oīa reptilia· uerminacia
cū radice sua q̄cūq; secū portauerit ul' corona
ō ipā cinta erit securus ad spētib3· C Ad p
cussionez araneor' q̄ gr̄ci spalagion uocāt
uinū decoctiōis herbe uerminacie potui dab'
⁊ eidez folis ōtūdes ⁊ suppone plage cito ad sa
nitatez reducit· C Ad morsuz canis rabiosi ⁊
corrosobi· uermin̄· folis bn̄ ōteris ⁊ suppon̄
opimū est· si aūt cognoscere uolueris si libe
retur ul' nō· acc̄· xv· gr̄na· frumenti ⁊ pōe i uul
nus ⁊ dimicte usq; uidēt grossū ut ōberet na
nascere ⁊ pice ad pullos ut manducēt cū
alio frumēto· si pulli ōmedūt illū q̄ mansit
in uulnus certū ē q̄ liberabit' si aūt nō ōme
dūt morit'· C Ad fetidas recētes· Ver· cū
butiro bn̄ ōcta ⁊ fetide i pōsita uelocissime
sanabit'· C Ad spētiū morsus· fosticulos siu
ramulos· manipul'· i· in uino decoq3 ⁊ inla
ua ⁊ folis bn̄ ōteres ⁊ suppone· ōez iflactiōez
soluit ⁊ apit· ⁊ pōea cū mell' bn̄ ōcta ⁊ supposita
sepe ōsolidat ⁊ sanat· C Ad yctericos siū
morbo regio q̄ dr̄ aurigīnosis· uerminacia
sicca· ʒ· i· nardo obulos trib3· ⁊ pap' mirr̄
dab' potui pacientis cū ca· aq̄· ciatos trib3·
fiat ōlecta mēse augusto· certū ē remedi
u3· C Ad fetidis ⁊ putredinez oris· sucū ei'
i ore retento· fetidis purgat ⁊ sanat· Itez
succus ei' dez tepido fcō gargarismo· putredi
nez oris mirr̄ expellit· Itez succus ei' bibitū
ōez uenenū discutit· C ōt· Tertianā et q̄rtā
febrez· herba· uer· trib3 radicib3· ⁊ trib3 folis in
aq̄ resolue ⁊ da patiēti an̄ horā· acc̄· liberabit'·
C Vt leti fiāt illi q̄ siūt ad ōuiuiū· acc̄· iiij·
folis ⁊ iiij· radicib3· uerminacie· i uino decō
que ⁊ illō uinū aspge iter ōuiuiū· ōes ga
uisi siūt· C Siuis scire· uitā· ul' mortem
alicui' i firmi· herba· uermin̄· porta tecū in
dextā manū· usq3 ad lectū egri ⁊ q̄re egrū
cōmodo stat· si respōdēs bn̄· certū eris q̄d li
berabit si aūt· respōdēs male· scias q̄ morit'·
C Ad habēdū gr̄az ul' amorez alicui' uir·

unge te manus · succo berbene · ⁊ tange cuiq;
gratiaz cupis habere ·

Brictanica · h'ba ē · omocos uocāt eā · Dama
simius · pfeti · Elluros · romani uocāt · Bri
tanica · itali dicāt · Beata piantauiana ·
prima cura ei · ¶ Ad uitia ⁊ putredinē oris
h'rba brictanica uiridez omesti ī modū lactu
ce · mir' sanat · ¶ Cō dol' dentiū et ōmouētiū
h'ba brictaīca h't magnā uirtutē; q2 ī estate
d'bȝ colligere ⁊ dsiccari ⁊ ī pluēr; redigē ⁊ reo
dere ⁊ ōsuare inuase argenteo ⁊ cū op' fu
erit dab' potui cū uino calō ⁊ etiā ī ore tene
at · mir' dol' dētiū discutit ⁊ ualō ōfirmat
pbatū est · ¶ Cō paraliticos · succus cū uino q
acti tribȝ · potui dato optīe iuuat tere h'rbā
cū radicē suā · ¶ Ad uentrē laxandū · succū
bric · potui dato scdm uirtutē accipiētis si
ne piculo uētrē purgat ⁊ laxat · ¶ Ad spl'
nis dol' · h' h'rba cū radicibȝ suis cū uino po
tui dab' qacti duobȝ · mir' pficit · ¶ Ad ingui
nē; q' greci uocāt sinācē · radix h'b brictaīe
collige eā añ q' audies aliqt tronū ī illo an
no · d'q' radix ōmedat toto anno uidz · semel
ī die · ⁊ nūq' sentient dol' īguinē;

Bursa pastoris · h'rba ē q' sili noīe appellatur
alio noīe dī · Sanguinariaz · q2 fluxu san
guinis enarib; sistit · h'ūs folia simil' eruce
pūe · semē ei similat' bursa · ⁊ radix modica
h't uirtutē; termātica; ⁊ obcultā · Nascit' oīb;
locis circa uiā · legis eā mēse · Iunio · luna de
crescente · ¶ Ad alī ōt fluxū sanguis enarib;
h' h'rba · bursā pastorē uiridē; ul' siccatā da
paciēti duplicitā ī manu dextera · stati sistet
sanguinē; · ¶ Ad crepatos · pluie ei cū uino
potui data cū uino optīe hec fiat sepe ⁊ mire
ōsolidat · ⁊ sanat.

xviij 17

Brionia · cucurbita agrestis · vitis alba · idem est · alia nomina dicitur · anpelloleuci · alii · austannura · alii · alpesar · Nascitur locis sablosis et humorosis et in sepibus · et habet magna radix · sunt autem due species · scilicet alba et nigra · semen producit rubeum et illa dicitur nigra · alia facit scilicet album · nigra autem melior est et efficacius ut inquit ypocras. ¶ Precipue valet contra spasmum quem alii dicunt guttam cadiam · radix eius ad collum pacienti suspensa statim liberabitur · ¶ Contra dissintericos et his qui eiciunt sanguinem per os · succus eius potatus ciatum unum iuice hoc fiat ter vel quater · mirabiliter liberat. ¶ Ne ebrietatem timeas · succi brionie et tantum dem aceto potui quod dato per totam ebdomadam non erit ebrius ex superfluo vino. ¶ Contra yliacam et colicam passionem · aqua decoctionis foliorum eius cum melle potui dato · statim expellit dolorem ¶ Contra scrofulas et gangulas et etiam contra cancrum et plagas chironie · radix brionie · et aristologie rotunde partes equales tere addito melle vel assungia fiat emplastrum et superpone · ¶ Contra dissinteriam et dolorem ani et in osso fractum in manibus vel in aliquo alio loco corpore · accipe · cimas · xl · brionie · et quinque · iii · gallas que sint et bulliatur in tribus ciatos vini · usque ad reddat · colentur et detur patienti · mirabiliter sanabitur · ypocras dicens fuit quidam homo qui tota digita manuum habebat cerosam per infirmitatem et precurauit hoc medicamentum et liberauit · ¶ Contra porros vel verucas · accensa cum fistucibus · b · et comburere ut fiat cinis et cum succo eiusdem herbe confice admodum unguenti et sepe unge porros scilicet statim expellit eos · Item similiter facit · stercus aquile suppositum ut dicit ypocras. Item aginguas cancerosas · succus · b · cum melle in ore receptum liberat. ¶ Ad matricem mundificandam et menstruam educendam · fumigium aque decoctionis foliorum brionie recepto vulue mundificat. ¶ Ad mamillas dolorem et ubi sit lac coagulatum et corruptum · eadem decoctione calida lavetur mirabiliter purgat. Item laxat ventrem · ¶ Contra quartanam · semen · b · iuuenile · iiii · similiter · da pacienti in hora accessionis ut comedat · vel bibat cum vino · ¶ Ad urinam prouocandam · aqua decoctionis cimarum eius potui data · mirabiliter proficit. ¶ Ad mulieres que habent non possunt lactem · cimarum · b · comedat in cogna decocte et abbundauerit lac in multa quantitate.

Bedeguard · spina alba · id est · frigida est in primo · gradu · et in medio eius virtus siccitatem · et hu · dicunt quidam bedeguard esse quandam superfluitas que nascitur supra fustum rose quod falsum est. est autem bedeguar herba que nascitur locis solidis et in planis et habet folia pingua et fixa similiter erucee et extendit per terram et in medio producit spinam albam que multum

barbiez

152

pungit et hoc est quod non pura est. crescit autem in quantitate unius cubiti et non amplius et multa producit de his spinis et habet florem purpureum. Confortat stomachum. Febrem diuturnam mitigat. et contra spasmum quod est ex defectione stomachi sit. contra asticatam supposita morsurum reptilium · dolorem mitigat. ¶ Contra fluxum sanguinis et ventris valet quod cataplasmata membra confortat · unde expellit humores ad ea fluentes · humidam in apposita dissoluit de cuius approximate ossis fuerit locum dolentium placabit · huius arboris cortex et rami sunt frigidi et sicci · in · ii · gradu · eius floribus cum aceto cataplasmatis scabies pustulas et plage uniuntur ¶ Cortice eius extus cum vino vel aqua potui dato · humores flati plecantur · cum aceto temperato cutis · mollificant sanatis ex ea in uncta mundificat · superflacturam positus cito sanat.

Bdellium · calidum est in · ii · gradu · humidum · in · i · gummi arboris est que in ultimis partibus reperitur scilicet · dicitur quidam quod sit id quod reperitur in fraquidam rotundum similiter galange · quod in arbore ulmi fit · gluttinosam habet summam virtutem habet constringendi et actrahendi dissinterie de acuta farmacia facte repugnat ¶ Ad poenta inuncta extus sanat · lapidem frangit · Tussim mitigat ¶ Morsum reptilium curat temperatum cum aceto et sapa · crepaturam ex eo in uncta · et etiam acetum cum cerusa et sapa similiter commixtis et apposita testiculorum in vetis mirabiliter sanat.

oĩa simil' fac unguẽtũ ⁊ suppõe ⁊ sanabitur
cito. Ad dol' uisceru. succus folioꝶ barda
ne. ciatũ .i. ⁊ mell'. ʒ. ii. simil' potui dabis
mir' sanabitur.

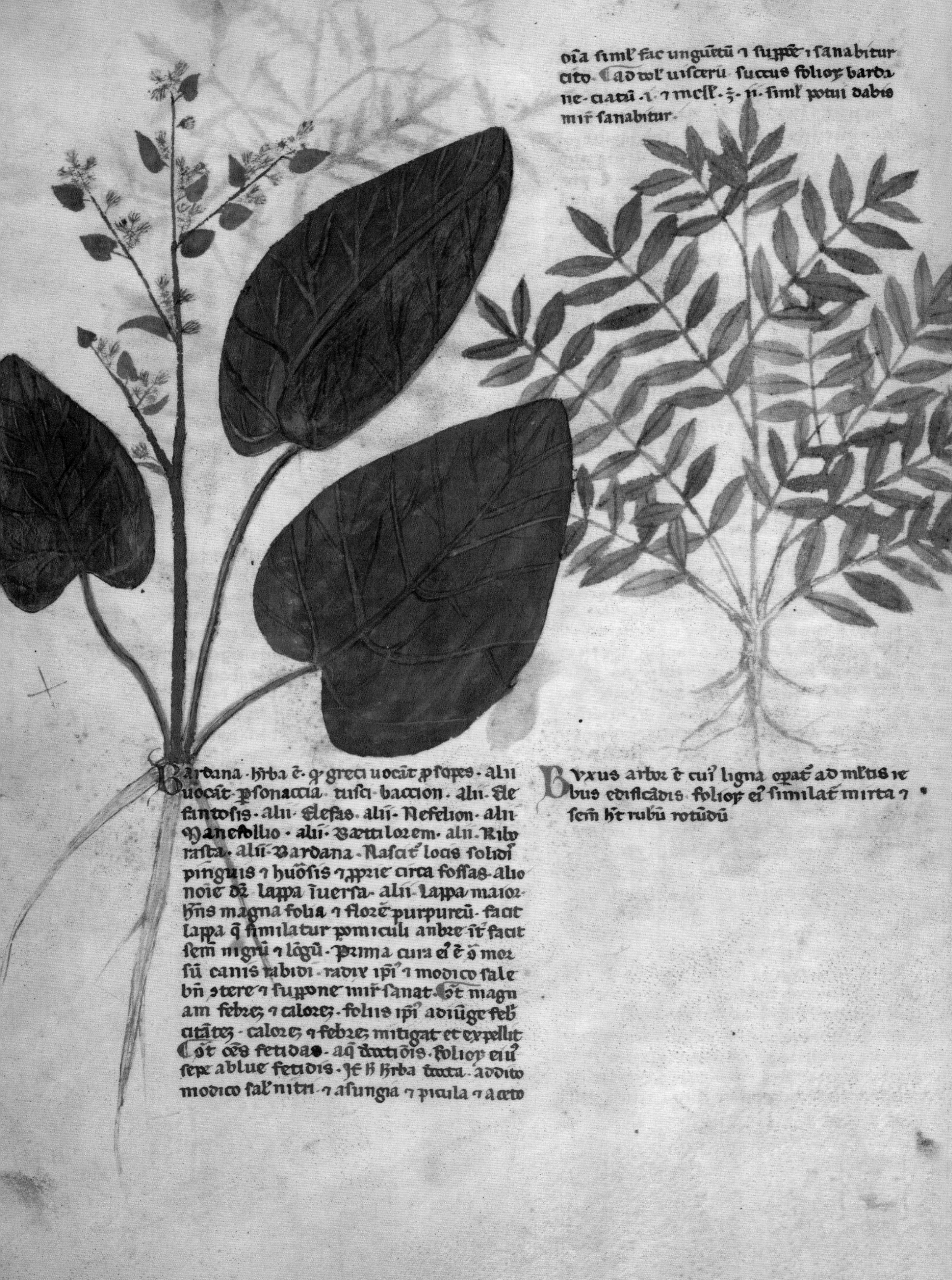

Bardana. hrba ẽ. q' greci uocãt ꝓsopes. alii
uocãt ꝓsonaccia. tusci baccion. alii. Ele
fantosis. alii. Elefas. alii. Nefelion. alii
Manefollio. alii. Bacti lorem. alii. Ribo
rasta. alii. Bardana. Nascit' locis solidis
pinguis ⁊ hũosis ⁊ ꝓprie circa fossas. alio
noie dr̃ lappa ĩuersa. alii. lappa maior.
hñs magna folia ⁊ florẽ purpureũ. facit
lappa q̃ similatur pomiculi anbre it' facit
sem̃ nigrũ ⁊ lõgũ. Prima cura ei' ẽ ꝯ mor
sũ canis rabidi. radix ipi' ⁊ modico sale
bñ ꝯtere ⁊ suppone mir' sanat. Ꝯt magn
am febreꝫ ⁊ caloreꝫ. foliis ipi' adiũge feb
citãteꝫ. caloreꝫ ⁊ febreꝫ mitigat et expellit
Ꝯt oẽs fetidas. aq̃ dcctiõis. folioꝶ ei'
sepe ablue fetidis. It' h' hrba trita. addito
modico sal' nitri. ⁊ asungia ⁊ picula ⁊ aceto

Buxus arbor ẽ cui' ligna opat' ad m'ltis re
bus edificadis. folioꝶ ei' similat' mirta ⁊
sem̃ h't rubũ rotũdũ

Brusci siue bruscus. ca. ẽ ⁊ sic. i. iii. g.
i multa ꝗ copia repit. Radix ⁊ sẽia ponit
i medicis. virtutẽ hẽt diureticã. ⁊ dissolutiuã.
Cõt ydropisiz i pricipio. aq̃ decoctiõis radicũ brusci ⁊ spagi. fen. pets. appii. addito
mell sufficienti potui dato sepe ⁊ etiã cõt
duritiẽ spleĩs mirabilit opat. Jt valꝫ
ꝯ stranguriaz ⁊ dissuriã ⁊ yliacã pass. semẽ
ipĩ ⁊ sem. an ⁊ fen. fac pl'uẽ ⁊ apponat tãtũ
dẽ zuchiro ⁊ accipia coclariũ. i. ieiuno stõ
cũ optio uino si aũt febricitat da cũ aq̃
ca. decoctiõis eadẽ sẽia. Cõt tumorẽ et
dol' genicul'. radicũ. bru. bn decoq̃ ⁊ fac
emplm itẽ pone ꝯ saluiã ⁊ axũgia ⁊ fa
sciã suppone. oẽs tumorẽ ⁊ dol' placat.

Bracillũ siue bergnũ arbor ẽ tortuosũ
⁊ valde rubũ ꝗ lignũ similat sandali. ru.
repit i ultmarinis ptib; ꝗ; lignũ tĩctorẽ
opat ad tingẽdũ.

Brusci siu bruscai

Bleta hrba ẽ q̃ greci uocãt. Zicla. alii
uocãt. Crisocantis. h hrba satis cõpetit
esui. ca. ẽ. i. i. g. hu. i. scdo. hẽt aũt uirtu
nutriendi ⁊ bonũ sanguinẽ gnandi decocta
etiã cũ carnẽ pinguaz ⁊ comestã. mirab
laxat uẽtrẽ. Jt cõstipatiõẽ uẽtris exsicci
tate ⁊ cal'. ꝯ succo ei' ⁊ sal' ⁊ olo cẽteri gẽt.

Blacte biçantie.
Beā. sūt ⁊ sicce in
scd'o. g. ē aūt blac
te biçātie. oculus
q̄dā pisciū simil'
limaccia. q repitū
i mari. ⁊ h't sustāti
az ossiū. virtutez
h't ɔfortādi ⁊ mū
dificādi

De Cidamine.
De Canphora.
De Cologntida.
De Cassia fistula.
De Cuscute.
De Cardamomo.
De Cerusa.
De Capparo.
De Calamento.
De Centaurea.
De Cassia lignea.
De Castoreo.
De Cubebe.
De Cipresso.
De Cinnamomo.
De Camedreos.
De Camepitheos.
De Carui.
De Cimino.
De Cicuta.
De Croco.
De Cipero.
De Capillo uenē.
De Calamo aromatico.
De Corallo.
De Cattaputia.
De Cretano
De Costo.
De Cantabro.
De Colofonia.
De Cucurbita.
De Celidonia.
De Coliandro.
De Calce uiua.
De Celtica.
De Cerfollio.

De Canapa.
De Camelleunta.
De Camomilla.
De Cotula fetida.
De Cottilidon.
De Cepa.
De Canna.
De Calendula.
De Cornu ceruino.
De Candellaria.
De Caprifollio.
De Consolida.
De Ceterach.
De Cotonaria.
De Cennerugio.
De Cerasarū
De Capragine.
De Cicerū
De Cera.
De Crispula.
De Castanee.
De Calacantū.
De Cartamo.
De Cimolea.
De Copporoso.
De Calcum.
De Curcuma.
De Canphorata.
De Carabe.
De Cucumeris.

Ciclamen. ca. e. 7 sic. i. t'cio. g. q' i cassam.
panis porcin. Malu terre. appellat. omeceos uo
cat. Ceseron. alii. ation. alii. cassophilos. alii.
Chedonion. alii. Stinpaitos. alii. Ostanes.
alii. asphet. tusci. Maalpa. egipti. Patalia
romani. Terremalu. ytalii. Orbiculares. alii.
rapu terre. alii. Rapu porcinu. alii. Clargia.
Nascitur locis cultiuis 7 mo'tuosis. quasdaz
habes tuberositates. q' q'n sut maiores ta'to ef
ficatiores. Radix itaq; 7 recens 7 exsiccata ma
gnaz h't efficaciaz. s; recens maiorez. d3 aut cir
ca finez autuni colligi. et i. iiii. ptes findi. et p
filuz suspendi. i unbroso loco ul' ad solez. parum
pot aut p triennuz i magna efficatia suari.
H't aut uirtutez dissolutiuam. osuptiuaz 7 ac
tractiuaz. Cui usus sit talis ad Emoroidas
i flatas. 7 no fluentes et exterius adparentes
sup asp'gat. p'l'uis ei ul' ilimiatur ex succo ei. p'a
sp's'gatur. p'l'uis elli. nigri. et rosaru. Si iteru
latitet. iniciatur. in modica q'ntitate peniste.
ul' fiat suppositoriu 7 p'a iniciat. p'l'uis predcus
cu cristeri. h' mo p'oat i cristeri. p'a i suflet cu por
cina uesica. ul' sili i flata aere. Quedam aut mu
lier salernitana. pbauit q' sic ualet. ad dees
ficus 7 emoroid'. ad mistruaz puoc et matrez
mudificadam. trifera. o3. resolue i ol'o m' uel
coi 7 bliat ad ignez i ciclamine. 7 d' lonbic
i hec ol'o iticto. fiat suppositoriuz. C' tenasm
on ex flate uitreo. succus radic. cu ol'o coi. 7
i ipo pomo bliat. 7 bobix iticta suppoat. C' otr
quartanaz. acc ipm et pista cu seie atplicis
et fac blire cu uino usq; du recsat. ad medi
etatez 7 da pacienti. an hora accessioe sustinat
se ad potu qtu potuerit 7 p'a da ei bibe paru
uini et fac cu dormire. C' spl'nis uitium
malu tre i ml'ta q'titate mudata 7 otrita p. xv.
dies in uino 7 ol'o maceret. cui colate. adda
tur cera. 7 par acti. 7 d'coq't ad spissitudiez
precedetib; aliis mollificatiuis. h' efficax e.
Si p'a i ungat. ul' ex succo ei. ul' ex p'l'ue sic'e
succu' ofice cu ol'o 7 cera i modu ungueti. sepi
pbatu est. Mulieres etiaz salrnitane. i ultimo
die iouis luna d' crescete. accipiut ciclam et
ponut sup splenez et cu securi i ciduntur i tre
ptes sup limen hostii dicetes ter. q' d' icidis
7 paties. Rx. splenez meuz. 7 p'a suspedut in
fumo. ad desiccadu dicetes sic d'siccat ptes
illius ciclamis ita d'siccet splenez. tal. 7 p'a
i ungut ungto pretio. C' ot apcata ex fri. ca.
q' no possut rupi. ppt spissitudiez cutis pomu
ipm oteratur. 7 in ol'o bliat. 7 calid' suppoat.
aut p exteriora aut p interiora purgabitur

C' fistulaz tentaz d' radice fra. in ponat. os am
plificat. os i si aliq' intus fuerit attrahit ul' penit.
ul' ut cu tenaculis meli' auferri p'sit. C' p'l'uis ei
carnez supfluaz corrodit. C' polippu p'l'uis eiu
asp'gat sup aliq' stuellu q' naribz i ponat. ad
spleneticos. ciclam' a collo suspesu; ut tangat
splenez mirabilit' sanat.

Camphora. fra. e 7 sic. i t'cio. gu. dicut q'da. caphoraz
ee gu' i arboris q' falsu est. e succus cuida herbe
testante diascorid' 7 aliis ml'tis q' caphata d'
herba ml'tu est silis nre caphate. s; mag' e aro
matica. h' aut herba i fine ueris colligit' 7 terit'.
7 succus exp'mit'. q' feculetu; e residet 7 abicit'
q' puruz e. 7 liqdus retinet'. soli expoitur. et ex
siccatur. exsiccatu u'o i sub'a caphe reducitur.
maxie aut et ei ofectioe sophicat' ex amixtioe
p'l'uis. ul' alteri' succi 7 ita efficit'. dupla ul' tri
pla q'titas caphe. Est aut elligenda. alba et
lucida. turbuleta no est adeo bona. Que ac
cedit ad croceu colorez no e adeo bona. So
phisticat' aut ex amixtioe. kekabre. i. uer
nicis. e aut uernix i sb'a silis caphe. et ex in
mistioe silis caphe et i odore discernit'. n
q' uernix h't solida sb'az et difficile frangit'.
Canpha u'o cito et si manib; tractet' ad fa
cili p'l'uericat'. No. nisi caph'a. artificiose
suetur. facile d'pdit'. e aut aroatica et oe
aroaticu; fuosuz. et cito esoluitur i fuosita
te. citoq; pditur. Pot aut suari i uase ma
moreo. et meli' in alabastro. suat' aut i seie
lini. ul' psiliuz. ul' milio. ul' alio sili. suat'
i ml'ta efficacia p. xl. annos. C' gomorre
az. i. i uoluntaria. spmatis emissioez p'l'uis ca
phe. distepet' cu mucillagie ul' psilii. ul' ag'
sta. l' succo solatri. et i tictis plagell' poatur
sup pectinez. et renes et puteda. C' diabete
idez fiat. 7 p't sppoatur lamia plubea. C' ca
lefactioez epis p'l'uis ei cu suco solatri oficia
tur. i quo plagelle i ticte sepi' epi suppoat'. C'
fluxu saguis enarib; fiat magdaliones ex p'l'
uere ei' 7 p'l'ue seis urtice usti ofectus cu suc
co sanguinarie narib; q; i poatur. Si aut fiat
sanguis fluxus ex ipi' ebullitioe. ul' ex epe cu
aq' fra. oficiat' p'l'uis caphe et plagelle i fus
fronti 7 tiporib; et gule. et epi sppoat'. C' ma
cula oculi tal' sit us' oficiat' p'l'uis ei cu aq. ro.
addito succo feniculi. et poatur i uase ereo.
C' pannu faciei 7 ad faciez d'purdaz ofi
ciatur cu aq. ro. addito mell' albo 7 mudissi
mo. C' libidinez odoret' caph'a. spus eni
actioe nimia fratis otepsat spma i spissat.
in spissatu retinet retineto libidinez aufert.

corpus īfrāndo · ꝑ illud catapl'a ꝑ nares
castrat odorē nares · No · satis ɔpetēter
pōitur ī sir' · ꝯ acutas egritudiēs · No · ꝙ̄ ·
ꝙ ī frenesi ɔpetēt ꝓuocat sternutatiōe
si pl'uis eī cū ol'o · ro · distēpet' · ⁊ ꝑēnā iuc
taȝ nāibꝫ iungātur · ⁊ ī alijs febribꝫ acu
tis qꝛ ñ augmentat calorē nec matēiā
sic si fieēt sternutatio ex ell'o · pipe ul' pire
tro · Jdē ualet ad ruborē ⁊ ardorē oculoꝝ ·

Cologntida · Celena · andale · idē ē · ca · ē
ī ttio gu · sic · ī · ꝯo · cologrita pomū ē cui
daȝ fructis nascētis ī ultmaīs ptibꝫ circa
regiōēȝ gerusalēȝ · ꝙ dr̄ etiā Jelela ⁊ Cucur
bita alexādrina appellat' · No · ꝙ tā pomū
ꝙ̄ fructex cologntda appellat' · ꝙ aūt sola re
pitur mortifera ē sic sqlla ꝙ sola īuenit'
dia scorid teste ⁊ etiā ɔstantin' · hʒ autem
medullā sem̄ ⁊ corticē · medullā pōtissiā
ē usui · m̄ · sem̄ ꝑario · cortex aūt hʒ efficaci
aȝ modicā · vn̄ si īueiatur ī receptiōe deb
ent pōi ꝑmia cū medulla · ē aūt cologn
tida elligenda · qꝛ hʒ medullā cōtinuaȝ
et albā m'ltū · seia medulle bn̄ insita · Jlla
uero ē abiciendū ꝙ cū ɔcutit' m'ltū sonat · Si
aūt īueniant' interiora cū sēibꝫ ul' fr̄i sēibus ·
ꝙ facile pl'uericant' · cū tractāt' manibꝫ abicien
da sūt · Possūt aūt ꝯuaī ꝑ sex annos et meli'
in pomo ipō · hʒ autēȝ uirtutēȝ dissoluēdi et ɔ
sumēdi · et ex amaritudine etiā uirtutēȝ di
ureticaȝ purgat qd flāȝ principalit' · ꝯo · me
lācoliaȝ · un̄ eius tal' sit usus · C ꝯ cotidianā
ʒ · ꝯ · interioꝝ cologntid · cū · ʒ · ii · ul' · iii · suc
ci ebuli · coqn̄tur ī pomo cologntid ⁊ col'ntū
et colatē addat' · zuccūȝ ⁊ dtur patiēti · ī sero
an̄ accessiōēȝ ꝑcedentibꝫ tn̄ digestiuis ⁊ purga
tionibꝫ · hec aūt fiat · si post purgationēȝ rem
anꝑrit accessio · C ꝯ quartāȝ aq̄ decoctiōis se
ne pōatur · ī pomo cologntid · addita · ʒ · ꝯ ·
interioꝝ cologntid fiat decoctio colatē addāt'
zuccūȝ ⁊ dt' patiēti an̄ horā acc' · ꝑcedētibꝫ dig
stiuis · ꝯ · ut dcūȝ ē hec fiat · Si post pūgatiōnēȝ
febris remāꝑrit · B nō ualet tn̄ ad qr̄tāȝ · ꝯȝ etiā
ad scabiēȝ uetustissimā · C ꝯ dolorē dntiū fi
at gargarissim' · ex aceto decoctiōis īterioꝝ co
logntid · C ꝯ lūbricos pl'uis eī cū mell' ɔfec
tus patiēti offerat' · pluris fiat epl'm ex pl'
uere eī et succo absinthi · circa umbellicū · C ꝯ
uermes auriū iniciat' pl'uis eī cū succo per
sicarie · C ꝯ spl'nis ⁊ epis duritiēȝ · dt' succus
decoctiōis feri · īterioꝝ cologntid ul' etiā pul
uis cū ipō succo · C ad matricēȝ mūdificand ·
et · mestr' · ꝓuocandaȝ · fiat fomētūȝ ex aq̄ de
coctiōis cologntid · eī etiaȝ pl'uis cū aq̄ ⁊ ol'o
decoq̄t' ī ipō pomo ⁊ ītincta bōbice fiat supposi
toriūȝ · C ad emoroidas · coqnt' ol'm nuciȝ
ī pomo cologtid · etiaȝ ī tingat' bonbix ⁊ sup
pōat' freq̄nter ·

Cassia fistula

Cassia fistula. ca. ē. 7 hu. i fra ḡ. G. q̄ppius ē ei⁹ excessus ab optiā tēpantia.
tūc fructus cuidā arboris q̄ī seīa longa
pducētis. tpr̄e p̄ea succedente elōgat᷑ et
ingrossat᷑. exteriora ī choacti ōe caloris ɔ
dēp̄sāt᷑ medulla īteriu⁹ existente. ī una co
pula inueniuntur. xx. ul'. xxx. sichītia.
Elligēda ē q̄ grossa est q⁹ significat hūita
te; m̄ltā. et magnā q̄ sigficat maturitatē.
et q̄ cū ɔcutitur non sonat interiu⁹. Q; so
nat puā h̄t hūitate; 7 seīa h̄t sepatā ad
medulla. pōt aūt ſuāī pbiēnū. Notidū;
q̄ cū inueīt᷑ cassia fistula ī receptiōe ab
auctorib;. ɔposita ul' ɔfecta ī qn̄titate. iii.
ʒ. ul'. in alia qn̄titate. ōbēt pōc̄īari ut a
lia. medulla etiā sīn̄ seminib; pōd̄rari ōb;
si pōt. S; q̄a nō patiūt᷑ apotecarii. appōātu
seīa. ut si ōbeat ɔfici aliq̄. medicina. cū sir
in quo ōbet resolui. cassia. f. nō bliat cū;
eo. s; ī feruēti ul' m̄l'tū calido resoluat᷑. cū;
manib; q̄usq; tota resoluta fueīt. p̄ea p
ciatur. seīa cū catia. et sic pficiat᷑. m̄. cū ea.
ī decoctioib; nō. cū inueīt᷑. ʒ. ii. cassie. f. ōbēt
pōd̄rari. cū cortice. p̄ea resoluāt᷑ sola medull̄
in feruēti aq̄. abiectis seib; p̄ea īpoāt᷑ pl'uī
reubrbari ul' mirob. ul' pl'uis aliis cū q̄ ōb;
fieī purgatio. No. q̄ cassia fistula. ī nulla
medicīe. pōit᷑ in aq̄ ut bulliat p̄ter quā ī oxi
7 trifera saī. ī qb; etiā ī m̄l'ta q̄ntitate pōit᷑.
h̄t aūt uirtute; leniendi et mūdificandi.
feruore; sanguīs mirabilit᷑ mitigat san
guine;. cola ōpurat. uñ ualet ī acutis fe
brib;. Cassia. f. cū aqua data ul' p se ante
purgatione. uentre; mollit et aptū pū
gationi reddit.

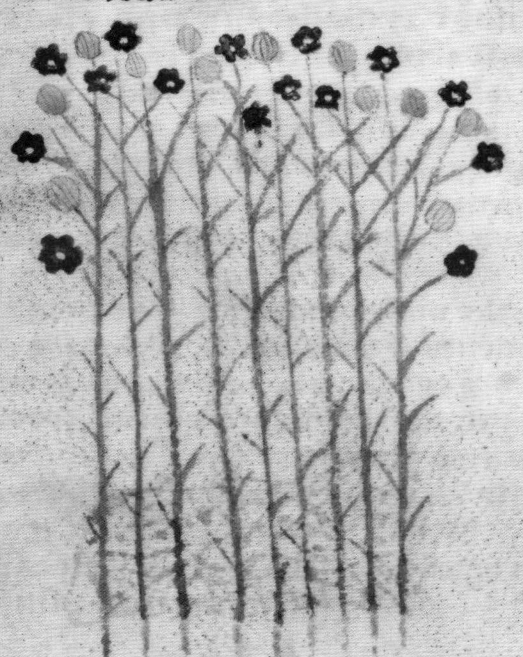

Cuscute. ca. ē ī primo. g. sicī ſo. Est aūt
cuscute podagra lini q̄ heres circa linum
cū florib; ōbet ɔligi p duos annos pōt ſu
ari. h̄t aūt uirtute; principaliter. purgādi
melā;. ſo. ſl'a. uñ ɔpetēter pōitū ī decoctiōi
bus purgātib; melā; et ſl'a;. aq̄ decoctiōis
ei⁹. C ualet ɔ̄ stranguriā. 7 dissuriā. S; ī pōt
haberi h'rba ī magna q̄ntitate. ipsā; h'rbā
in uino bñ decoctā; 7 ol'o. renib; pectini q;
7 aliis ptib; dolentib; cataplāatis.

Cardamomū. ca. ē 7 sic. ī ſo. g. ē aūt. fruc
tus cuiᷤdā arboris. ul' potius semē arbor au
te; tp̄r ueris pducēs fructus quasdā fac̄ tu
borositates. sic̄ ē sem̄ rute. ul' sem̄ fusagis
ul' similes uuis ī qb; seīa ɔducūt᷑. Cui⁹ due
sūt maneries. s. maius 7 min⁹. cardamom̄
mai⁹ meli⁹ est. q̄z magis aromaticū et dōe
sticū est. Est aūt elligendū illud q̄ maius
ē 7 h̄t aliq̄ntulū acuminis et dl'cedine; ī
īmixtā. et q̄ ē sbrufi coloris. q̄ aūt sballi
dū ē. 7 palosū abiciēdū est. Cū aūt ponitū
in medicīs ōbēt abici lapilluli 7 etiā ōbē
ɔfricari cū pannis pp̄t pl'uē; abiciētes fu
stes. p. x. annos pōt ſuari. Virtute; h̄t ɔ
fortandi. ex aromaticitate dissoluendi et
ɔsumendi. ex q̄litatib;. C ɔ̄ sincopi; et cardi
acam pas. ex fīā. ca. fiat decoctio ei⁹ ī uino
odorifero. addita aq̄. ro. et ōt patiēti. C st

debilitatem stomachi et digestionem confortandam pulvis kardamomi cum semine anisi detur iab.

Ad appetitum provocandum et etiam contra vomitum ex frigida causa pulvis eius cum suco mente confectatum et ibi iniecti ibidem confortat. pulvis etiam cardamomum cum menta viridi vel sicca in aceto et aqua salmitina coquatur et spongia intincta oris stomachi superponatur.

Contra debilitatem cerebri pulvis eius naribus applicetur. si fiat reuma ponatur pulvis cum oleo in scellino in testa ovi super cineres calidos usque dum bulliat postea ungatur caput.

Cerusa. frigida est et sicca in secundo gradu. cerusa flos plumbi sive gerse appellatur de cerusa fit autem sic. accipe laminas plumbeas quadratas in quantitate unius libre vel plus et pone in vasa terrea sepium mediocriter angusta in latitudine pedis .i. et sint vasis tamen impletis aceto fortissimo. pone baculos super orificia vasorum ab una extremitate ad aliam et suspende laminas plumbeas perforatas per spatium .iiii. digitorum ab aceto cum filis et postea cooperi orificia et vas similiter cooperies et pone in obscuro loco. et claude ostium et ita dimitte per .iiii. menses. in fine quarti mensis aperi hostium. ut fortis vis aceti exalet et invenieris quasdam tuberositates et mucillagines circa plumbum quod invenitur in minori quantitate quam prius fuerit. Illas cultello abradas. et pone in vas magnum et apposita aqua pedibus malaxa postea aquam illam abice et pone substantiam que remanet in vase aliquantulum concavatum et apposita aqua soli expone autem aquam illam consumpta aliam appone. et ita facias quousque sit albissima. et tunc deponatur de vase illo in vase concavo. Unde etiam rotundam cerusa invenitur. Notandum quod hii qui cerusam faciunt. sepius incurrunt apoplexiam epilensiam. paralisim et arthriticam. propter frigiditatem mortificatam. Habet autem virtutem mundificandi et extergendi superfluitates unde quedam mulieres sic ea utuntur. primo faciem abluunt postea pulverem cerusse subtilissimum mediocriter superducuntur. alie autem melius faciunt. quia cerusa aliquantulum fetida est. conficiunt cerusam cum aqua rosarum. et exponunt soli maxime in estate. quo consumpta aliam apponunt. et hoc faciunt donec sit albissima et aliquantulum aromatica postea informatam pillas. et faciei imponunt. alie autem apponunt pulverem boracis vel camphore vel utriusque. et bellicculi mani melius operantur. Nota quod longo tempore qui utuntur additione cerusse dentium dolorem incurrunt. et putrefactionem eiusque fetorem.

Capparis sive capparus. calida est et sicca in secundo gradu. est autem capparus ut quidam dicunt herba

alii quod frutex in transmarinis partibus. etiam in apulia et in aliis partibus reperitur. alia nomina vocitatur fillis. Alichacalon. alipmor. Cortex radicis flores et folia competunt usui medicine. precipue tamen cortices dicunt autem cortex colligi in principio veris in umbra suspendi. et desiccari vel etiam ad solem per .v. annos in maxima efficacia servatur. Est autem eligendum cortex eius quod cum frangitur non pluciçatur et quod aliquantulum subrufus est. et subalbidum amarus. Flores autem eius cum adhuc sunt coibrosi et non dilatatum debet colligi. quia cum dilatati sunt flores non valent. accipiunt cum sole et aceto conditur. servantur per annum vel per duos annos. Virtutem habet incitandi appetitum humorem more stomachi consistente. et extergendi stomachum confortat. infrigidatum calefaciunt. cibus enim ei est ut medicina. Contra splenis vitium et epatis duritiem valet vinum decoctionis capparis fiat etiam hoc unguentum quod potissimum est. non minus etiam valens. quod agrippa. pulvis eius in magna quantitate conficiatur cum suco marathri per modum addito vino et oleo fiat decoctio usque ad spissitudinem addito aliquantulum cera fiat unguentum. Valet etiam ad idem ellectuarium quod dia capparum appellatur et non minus hoc ellectuarium quod [illegible] .ii. pulvis radicis capparis .3 .i. corticis radicis tamarisci pulvis con

ↄficiat cū melle et decoctioē radicis tamarisci.
¶ Succus foliorū capparū aurib; imissus ue'
mes necat et pl'uis corticē ī oleo coquat' colatu
ra aurib; īstillet' nō solū uermes necat sz ī
surditati ſbuenit et auribus fistulosis. ¶ Cō
lūbricos pl'uis ei' ↄfectus cū melle patiēti d'.
¶ Cō scrofulas nouellas d' aq' decoctiōis corticē
capparis. brusci et spagi. ¶ Fit ut ungat' ī hoc
ungto. acc rufū spentez. et scid' cap' ↄ caudaz
psspatiū. IIII. digitorū pēa pōc ī olla inferiū mi
nutatī pforata. et illa olla ī alia ītegra ponat'.
ita q' fūdus ille pforate sit ī orificio alterius
olle p'mo modū ita pōāt'tur ī caldario aq' pleno et
bulliat diu et excalore aq' resoluatur spēs cui'
pinguedo ad inferiorā ollā ↄfluēs. huiūtate
aque ↄsuat'. Ex illa pinguedine et pulue' elle
bori nigri. et pl'uē radicē capparis. fiat ungtm
quo etiā ungant' scrofule nouelle. Sētāt' etiā
patiētes aq' predicta. ¶ Cō yliacā pās' et artē
acc. lib'. I. corticē pl'ueris capparis. et decoquat'
ī succo corticis. radicis ebuli addatū zuccū'
et fiat sir'. d' aūt bis ī septiāna. sero ul' manē
cū calida. Nota. q' cū iuenitur ei' receptioni.
medicis. cortex radicē eius. debz poni.

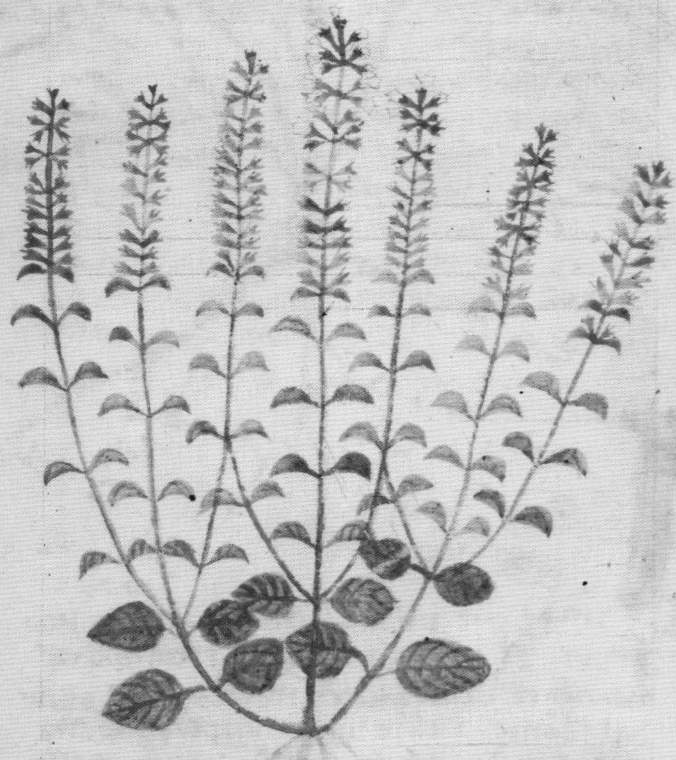

Calamentū. ca. ē. et sic. ī tio. g. ē aūt her
ba q' alio noīē nepita. d'. alii. calamites. ul'
nepitella uocat'. Calamentū mōtanū meliū
est. q2 magis sicce. cū flores pducit d; colli

gi. pannū pōt suari. in unbroso loco suspēs
et ibi d'b; dsiccari. Ht aūt uirtutez dissoluē
di ↄ ↄsumendi. ¶ Cō frīgz tussi; et firm asma licet
antiq dicitur uinū decoctionis ↄ uue passe. et
liqritie. ul' uinū decoctiōis pl'ueris ei'. et ficuū
siccarū. Valet eītiā q' dia calamentū d'. eti
hoc. q' ē. pluēz calamēti ī magna qūtitate pl'
uerez gentiane. ↄ liqritie. ī ītia ul' qta pte cum
melle potissimū e. Cō predicta etiā d' pl'uis ei'
in ouo sorbili. Crispelle ī fiāt d' pl'uere. et fari
na ordei. ¶ Cō dolorez stōi. et frāter ītestinorūm
utat' patiēs pl'uē ei' ī cibis et uino decoctionis
ei'. ¶ Cō frīgz reuma ungat' occipitiū ex mell' decoc
tionis pl'ueris ei'. p' fiat sacellatio ex pl'uē ei'
calefacto ī olla rudi. ul' ex ipā h'rba m'ltū ↄfēt.
¶ Cō relaxatiōēz uue fiat gargarism' ex aceto de
coctiōis pl'uēis ei'. ↄ pl'uē rosaz. et calamenti
ſbleuatur uuā satis ↄpetenter. ¶ Cō tetasmo ex
flate uitreo ul' alio frīo huōre. Inūgāt' renes ex
melle solo. ul' ex melle decoctiōis pl'ueris ei' pēa.
aspgat' solo pl'uere. colofonie et calamenti.
fortiter cū aliquo pāno ligent'. Cū etiā ass
ellat pl'uis cū bonbice ano sppōātur. pōe dē
te suffumigatio colofonie sic liberat' est. Ma
thus d' plata. ↄ mat' magistri plateari. ¶ Ad
excitcādu; supfluitatez matricē ↄ huītate: fiat
fomētu; ex aq' decoctiōis ei'. hoc ut mulieres sa
lernitane. satis ualet. Calamentū sup morsū
reptiliū cataplā ab interiorib' ad exteri
ora uenenū trahit. ¶ Succus ei' aurib; īstilla
tus. uermes occidit. et coitū mō ul' ueē
libidinez extiguat. Lepre pēst. uiridis in ui
no cocta. sup maculas ponat' eas mūdificat.

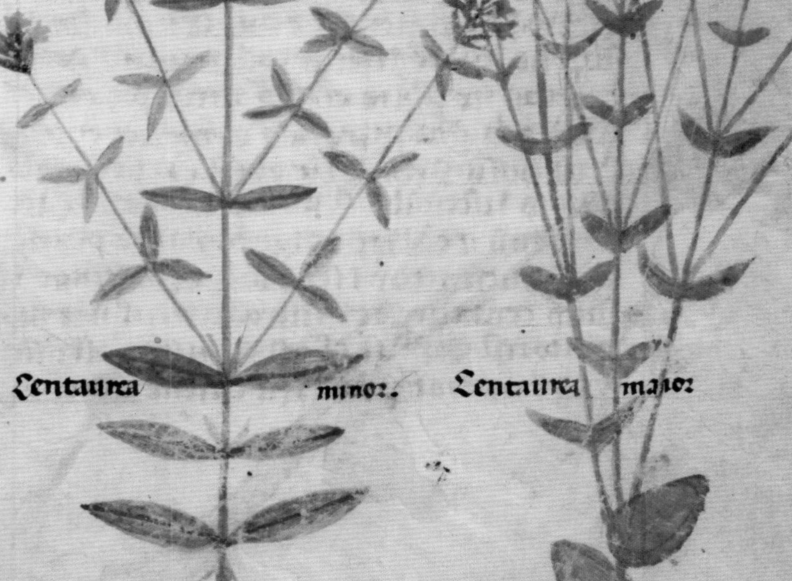

Centaurea. ca. ē ⁊ sic. i. iii. g. ē aūt h'
ba amarissima uno alio noīe dr̄ fel terr'
ul' febrifuga. est aūt cētaurea maior que
maioris est efficacie. et minor q minori.
dicit aūt ɔstatinꝰ q̄d radix maioris. ca. ē
⁊ sic. in scd̄o. g. et h̄t amaritudinē cum
q̄daz dulcedinez. h̄t etiā ɔticitatez. unď
h̄t uirtutez ɔglutinandi ex amaritudīe
nō diureticā. Centaurea maiorez. h̄t effi
caciaz. s; foliā ⁊ flores. Vn̄ ɔincipit flores
ɔducē. d; colligi. et in ūbroso loco suspē
di ⁊ ɔsiccari ꝑ annū ī mxta efficatia ꝑua
tur actractiuā ⁊ ɔsūptiuā. Cū aūt ī me
dicinis repit' cētaureā. maior ɔbet poni.
C Vinū ɔcoctiōis cētauree addito çucha
ro. valet ɔ̄ opilatiōez ul' splenis ul' epatis
et renū ⁊ uexice. stranguriaz et dissuriā. h' ɔ̄
iuino et olō ipa ɔcocta renib; et pectini ū
ca pudēda et peritoneon cataplasmata.
et etiā supsplenez ɔfert. Vngt; ī factū ex
pl'uē ei' ul' succo addita cera ⁊ olō ualet ɔ̄
splenez. C Ad epis et sinplicis duritiez fiā
sir' hoc mō. in succo cetauree. coq; radicē appi
feñ. ⁊ petr' qb; ɔcoctis cola ⁊ colatuē addat
çuccāz. et fiat sir'. Valet ɔ̄. adlōgā ycteri
am. sin h̄t succū. In decoctiōe appi. feñ. petr'
pone pl'uez. addito çucho fiat sir'. C ɔ̄ iliacā;
pass. puluis ei' cū aqua salmacina. et olō ꝑ
cristē iniciatur ꝑcedente cristeri mollitiuo
ďt etiā ꝑ os. v. ʒ. pl'ueris ei' cū benedicta.
ɔ aqua. ca. eodez mō ɔ̄ palisim C ɔ̄ uermes
auriuz iniciat' succus ei' cū succo porrorum
auribus. C ɔ̄ lūbricos ďt succus ei' ul' pul
uis cū mell'. C Ad uisū clarificādū succū
radic cētauree maioris cū aq. ro. ɔmisceā
tur ⁊ illineatur ocul'. Ad ulcera ɔsolidād
terat' radix ⁊ suppōatur ɔsolidat. cui rei ar
gumētu; ē q si ɔ̄patur cū carne icisa ɔsoli
dat ut dic ɔstantinus. C Ad maculā fiā
colliriū d pl'uē ei'. ⁊ aq. ro. h' mltū ualet si
magna sit macl'a. si aūt sit ꝑua nō ɔbet
appoi. q̄a ɔsumeret sbā oculi. C ɔ̄ emoroidas
suppone bōbice itictuz ī olō muscelli cui ad
mixtus sit pl'uis ei'. C ɔ̄ uitiū pectoris. ac
succū ⁊ ta gūa purissimi armoiaci et ɔficee
tur ua iussū. si tn̄ fuerit ex fiā. ca. ꝑcedentib;
calidis iūctiōib;. C Ad mestr' ꝑuocād. acc
serapinū ⁊ cal'fiat adignez ⁊ adde pl'uere
ut ɔglutinetur. i serapino ⁊ pecia stinge i
suco centauree et suppōatur. ul' fiat sup
positoriū ex pl'uē ei' cū amurca oli ɔfec
to. It iniciat' pessariū cū felle taurino
resoluto in suco cētauree mestrua educat
secūdina ⁊ mortuū fetū. ad idez valet aq
ɔcoctiōis ei'. ɔstātinꝰ dicit q h' aq et sagapi
nū intus ɔcoctū uulnera ɔsolidat. Cen
tauree exagiū unū ɔuino ꝑpinetur ɔ̄ do
lori uentris et putrefactionis ɔ̄ grossis
hūorib; et grosse uentositati subuenit.
C Succus ei' cū melle mistus oculorum clarifi
cat obscuritatez.

Cassia lignea. ul' xillocassia. ca. ē. ⁊ sic. ī tio
gradu. est aūt cortex cuidā arboris q cas
sia lignea ďr. ul' fructex. nascēs iuxta ɔfiñe
babillonie. Cassie lignee duplex ē mane
ries. s. cassia fistula et cassia lignea. Cassia
fistula nūq repitur sin ɔterminatione. i
receptiōib;. cassia ligā. ul' xillocassia q̄d. i.
ē. cui due sūt spēs una q est simile cinamō
q oīno sbrusa est ⁊ rotūda. ⁊ nota q ɔsoli
daz h̄t subam et ɔfrāgitū nō duplicat s; sin

plicatura resistit actu h̃t saporem dulcedi
ni amixtus cũ aromaticitate ⁊ h̃c meli
or· nõ tamẽ ea utimur in medicinis· Alia sp
ecies est q̃ sb̃ rufa est· parũ h̃ns colores
distinctos· Elligenda est ergo q̃ nõ frangi
tur facile s̃ plicatur ⁊ cõfrangit̃ colores
sub albidos intus ⁊ distinctos h̃t· ⁊ plures
sub rufos saporem h̃t acutũ dulcedini in
mixtũ cũ aromaticitate· Põt aut̃ s̃uari p
x· annos· sophisticatur aut̃ q̃nq̃ ex ad
mistione radicis capparis s̃ sic discerni
tur q̃ cortex capparis sb̃ amari saporis ẽ·
H̃t aũt uirtutem diureticã ex sbtili substã
cõsũptiuã ex q̃litatib; cõfortatiuã ex arõat
Cõt̃ frĩm reuma· ul' alias cãs frĩas capitis ul' e
pilẽ· dnt̃· iii· pill' ex pl'ue cassie lignee ⁊
laudano optĩe cõfecte mir̃ cõfortãt cerebrũ
fiat ĩfumigatio hoc mõ· C pl'uis cassie
lige s̃ cãbones p̃iat· s̃ uitrũ ⁊ aq̃· ro· sp
asp̃gat et recipiat patiẽs fumũ· C cõ stra
guriã ⁊ diss· ⁊ pãs renũ· ⁊ uesic dẽt uinũ d
cectionis ei patienti· ul' saltem cõi decoc̃
ex quo ĩiũgatur uirga· et piteneon et pectẽ
dolentes· C cõt oppilatiões splenis ⁊ epati
renũ ⁊ uexice· Valet si ĩ aquis et syrup
cõponat̃· C cõ frĩtatem stõi· ⁊ etiã cõ pre
dicta cãs· Valet uinũ decoctiõis ei· ⁊ masc̃
et fen̄ sẽis· Ieiun̄ datũ pigmẽtum· et factũ
ex melle et uino ĩ quo decocta sit cassia· li
stõm ĩfrĩatũ calfac̃· et digestionem adiu
uat· C cõ fetorem oris fiat pill' ex pl'ue cassi
e lige· ⁊ storac̃ cal'· q̃ stõr cal'· bñ manib;
malaxatĩ· põt hec· aut̃ pill' ad cõm dolorem
itianeorum fc̃m ex frĩa ca· ualẽt· C cõ fetorem
ascellarũ· ⁊ corruptiõem gingiuarum· abrasis
prius pilis abluãtur p̃ri loca cũ uino ⁊ aq̃·
ro· decoctiõis pl'ucis cassie lig· C cõ corrup
tionem gĩgiuarum fiat gargarism̃ ex predcĩs·
C cõ fectorem oris· cassia liga· ĩ ore masticã
ta· omnẽ fetorem tollit· aut p̃salitem palli
at· C ad· cõ· p̃uoc ⁊ matric cõfortãdã fiã
suppositoriũ ex bõbice ĩtincto ĩ olo m̃· ul' cõi·
decoctis pl'uis cassie lig· Cortex ẽ ei bullit̃
cũ olo m̃· ĩtegr' suppõitas mẽstrua p̃uocat·
C cõ uitiũ splenis· ⁊ epis ĩ olo decocta ⁊ cat
plasmata uitiũ eorũdem tollit· h̃ ĩ modo
s̃ppõita· tetasmo medet̃ ex frĩat p̃ueniẽte·
C cõ carcliacã ⁊ sincopi· Valet syrũ factũ
ex pl'ue ei et rosarũ et osse d corde ceruĩ·

Castoreum· ca· ẽ· ĩ· iii· g̃· sic· ĩ· scđo· est
aut̃ castoreũ testicl' cuiusdã aĩal'· q̃ castor
appellatur· s· beuens· Quidã dicũt q̃ ipm̃ aĩal
presentiẽs uenatores· insequi eũ testiculos
absidit dentibus ⁊ p̃icuit· credẽs uenatores
tm̃ testiculos curare· q̃ falsũ est· nõ eni tãte ẽ
discretionis· Ipi etiã eũ mag̃ ĩsecũt p̃pt pellẽ
quã p̃pt testiculos· Testiculi absisi in ũbro
sõ loco suspẽsi d̃siccant̃· et Nota q̃ iuuenis
castoris· testicul' nõ tante efficacie ẽ· sicut
senis· Ille aut̃ testicul' d̃siccat̃ alb' ẽ ⁊ mol
lis· Si aũt testicul' castoris nõ ĩ iuuẽtute
existẽtis· ul' parũ iuuentutem excedentis·
Illud optimũ ẽ· Si aũt sit castoris ĩ decrepita
etate existẽtis nõ ẽ tãte efficacie· Adulte
ratur aut̃ ad q̃b; dã sic· accipiũt pellem ĩ qua
fuit castoreũ· et aliis testiculis recẽs acci
pit̃ et inplẽt sanguinem et neruis addito
pl'ue castorei· ut hãt odorem castorei· alii
ponũt sanguinẽ ⁊ terrã· alii meli' sophisti
cant inponũt sanguinem· pip· ⁊ sarapinũ
et neruos· pip apponũt ut sit acuti saporis·
C Elligendũ aũt q̃ mediocriter h̃t acutũ saporem
q̃ si h̃t acutũ saporem· et sit q̃i terreũ sophistica
tum est· ⁊ si nõ h̃t neruos intricatos· Bonũ aũt
castoreũ h̃t saporem mediocriter acutũ· et ẽ glu
tinosũ ⁊ mltũ h̃t saporem orribilem· ⁊ neruos h̃t
ĩtrincatos· ⁊ pellicul' adherentes ⁊ cõuenientes
ad alterã extremitatem· p· vi· annos ĩ mlta effica
cia põt s̃uari· Melius tñ ẽ q̃to recentiũ· In me
dicĩs d̃bet põi abiecta pellicula exteriori· Virtutem
h̃t· dissoluendi cõsumendi ⁊ attenuandi· ⁊ max

loca neruosa ↄfortādi. C Cōt epilēcias et alia
frās capīs pass. detᵉ castoreū ī qntitate ʒ.ᵃ s.
et iniciatur p nares. detᵉ etiā ī qntitate iii.
ul' ii. ʒ. castorei ↄ suco rute ī potu ul' uino decoc
tiōis eiᵘˢ. C Cō palisim lingue pl'uis eiᵘ s̄b lingua
poṅatur donec p se resoluatur 7 ↄsumatᵘʳ. C Cō
palisim totiᵘˢ corporis. dᵉᵗ uinu decoctiōis eius
et rute et saluie. C Cō palisim uirge. fiat fom
tuᵉ circa pectinē ex uino decoctiōis eius frequēt
7 sic cataplēt. C Cōt gomorreā fiat decoctio eius
ↄ succo agni casti addito modico aceto 7 cata
plasmetur pecca s̄ renes 7 uirgā. 7 pectē. C Cō
litargiā puocanō sternutatio ex castoreo. cere
brū ↄmouet et ↄfortat. ul' fiat decotio eiᵘ et mē
ta. 7 suco rute 7 modico aceto et abraso occipiti
fricetur bene manibᵘ 7 sup cataplēt. Puluis
etiā ↄ suco rute naribᵘ iniciatur. ul' fumᵘ p nare
recipiat.

Cubebarū

Cvbebe. ca. ē 7 sic. tn̄ tenpate ē aūt fructus cuiᵘ
arboris ī trasmarīs ptibᵘ nascētis ī india. p. x.
annos potᵉ suari ī mlta efficacia. Elligenda est
q̄ mediocriter h̄t acutū saporē cū mlta aroatic
vñ ↄt sincopī ualet hec mō. Pl'uis eiᵘ ī qntitate.
iiii. ʒ. dᵉᵗ cū succo borragīs. ul' sucū radicū pasᵗ
nace. ul' folioꝝ eiᵘ mltū ↄfert. C Cō frīz reuā capīᵗ
7 ad cerebrū ↄfortādū odoretur. et frequēter nari
bus apponatᵘʳ. C Cō frātē stōi 7 discolorationē
ex frāte. dᵉᵗ pl'uis eiᵘ ī cibis. C Cō discolorationē
fiat pigmentū ex uino et melle 7 aliis spēbᵘ
posita cubēbe ī maiori qn̄titate.

Capillus ueneris. alio noīe. alicon. dr̄. ca. ē 7 sic
tēpate tn̄ ex s̄btili s̄ba. Virtutē h̄t diureticā.
recēs mlte est efficatie. paruū potᵉ suari. hrba
util' ē 7 nō radix. Nascitᵘʳ iuxta aquas cursiuas
C Valet ↄ cal'factionē epīs dᵉᵗ aq̄ decoctionis
eiᵘ et gucco. fiat syrᵘ. Si sit ī uitiū splēnis adda
tur aliquot calidū diureticū. plagelle etiā ī
tincte ī succo ipīus suppoatur. ul' etiā ipa hrb
trita. C Et succus eiᵘ cū uino bibitus uenenᵒ
et humoribᵘ ad stoīn fluentibᵘ resistit. C Cata
plasmatus ualet ad lopitie et scrofule decocᵗⁱ
etiā cū aq̄. 7 exeo capite loto pustulas et putᵉ
factionē mundificat. Valet etiā oībᵘ tussi
entibᵘ s̄ ēpiās ptisicās 7 pipleumonicas 7 oī
pl'mcōīs uitia. fiat exeo uinō ī mlta qntitate ī
aq̄ decoctū fuerit 7 tali decoctione potata ualere
pᵇ ē.

C Cipressus ca. ē 7 i. ḡ
sic. i. ii. arborē cuiᵘ poma.

lignū ꝛ folia ꝯpetit usui medic. Sz poma stiptica sūt ꝛ ꝯsolidatiua. lignū ꝛ folia diuretica. Cō fluxū uētris ex debilitate uirtutis ꝯtētiuē comedat patiēs poma recētia ul' pl'uis pomi sica. in cib' dēt. bibat ī aqua decōctiōis ipi'. fiat ī decoctio ī aqua pluuiali. ex qua ī uinū eius linphetur. Cō diss. pomā ī aqua pluuiali decōta renib' ꝛ stō ꝛ pectini cataplētur. Cō stranguriā et diss. dēt pl'uis ei' ligni ꝛ foliorū ei'. Jn dolio cū uino et maxīe musto ponat'. tale uinū ꝯsuat corp' ab yliacā pass. uinū etiā decoctiōis pl'uis ligni ul' foliorū ei' ī ipā accessione datū miro mō ꝓdest.

Cinnamomū. ca. ē ī iij g. sic ī sc'do. duo sūt gnā cinamomi. s. grossū ꝛ spissū et parū cauatū. q' cortex ē cuiusdā arboris ꝛ subtile. q' cauatū est et nō spissuz q' cortex ē cuiusdā arboris fructice. utrūq; in india aurop a repitur. q' grossuz est ī uomitiis medicīs ponendū est. q' subtilis ē ī aliis medicīs. Elligendū est illud q' subtile ē ꝛ acutū hēt saporem dulcedini emixtū cū m'ta aromaticitate. et dē atinos ꝛ est subrufū. q' aūt subalbidū ē. ul' nigrū abiciendū ē hī est ꝓpua electio. cū aūt elligit' ꝓgustū decēnitur bonū ꝛ abluatur lingua saliua ul' aqua q' bonū ita inficit gustū. q' malū ī gustū bonū uidatur. p. x. annos pōt suari. Ex aromatici uirtutez hēt ꝯfortandi cerebrū. Ex glutiositate ꝯsolidandi. Cō debilitatē stōi et digestiōne debilitatā. exsiāte dēt pl'uis subtil' cinamomi cū pl'uere carui ī cibis. Jon petēter ī salsamētis ponit' ad apetitū ꝓuocandū et sup fluitatibus ꝓdictū hoc mō. cū petrosill' saluia modico aceto et pl'ueribz predictis fiat salsamētū. Cō adoris aromaticitatē ꝯmasticet'. Et notādū q' ī decōctione ex usu quorūdā aromaticorū lz hos ad tps redatur aromaticū ī posterū tū corrūpitur. uel ex usu m'tū calidorū. ut gariofilorū et similiuz q' calliditate dissoluūt. unū fit putrefactio. Cinamomū uō nō ē adeo calidū ut dissoluat. est aūt glutinatiuuz. Cō ad nouas scissuras labiorū ul' aliorū ulcerū. ꝓatur puluis ei' in scissura. et pēa fiat sutura ul' ligetur bene. Cō corruptiōēz gingiuarū fiat lotura gingiuarū ex aqua salsa. et fricēt bene ut sanguis exeat et ut putride hūiditates inde fluant. ex uīo decoctiōis pl'ueris ei' abluat os pēa. pl'uis fōs de duobz ptib' sinphiti ī ꝯsolida. m. ꝛ tertia cinamomi apponatur miro mō ualet. Cō sincopī ꝛ cardiacaz dēt pl'uis ei' cū pl'uere foliorū gariofilorū. Grossuz cinnamomū in uomitiis medicīs. pōt nūquā pse nō ēz infert tātā abominatiōēz sz uiolentiā aliarū sinpliciū. ut capsie ꝛ ꝯsiliuz. repmit stomaccum ꝯfortat. unū duplex ē ꝯmod.

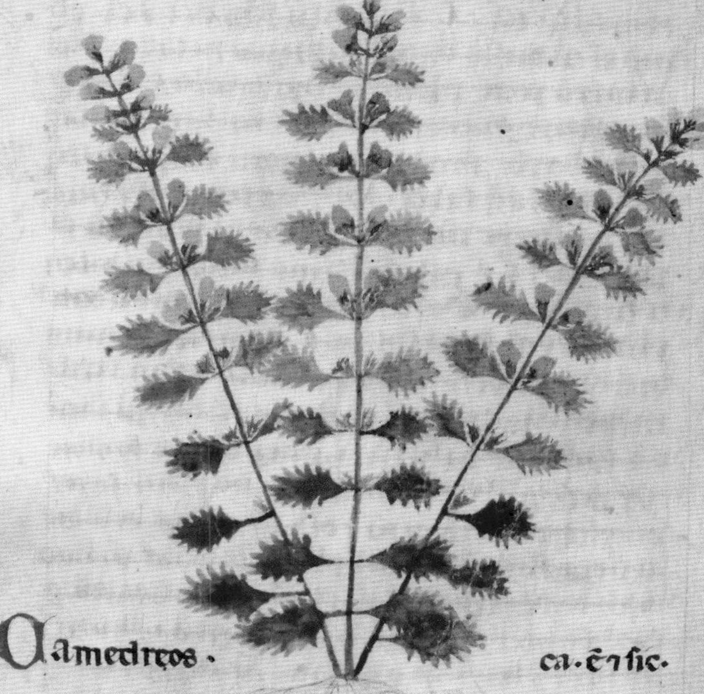

Camedreos. ca. ē ī sic.

in .iii. gu. Camedreos qrcula minor appellat
virtutē hēt diureticā et mundificatiua et
q2 simil' earū uirtus de eisdē termināt tractat
alia noīa dr̄ camerobs. alii. amarola. alii.
camedreū. h herba. Jn fine ueris cū florib3
pducūtur colligi dicetur. herbe cū foliis et flo
ribus abiectis radicib3 ī umbra dsiccetū p
annū ī m'ta efficatia suatur. C's stagun
am et dissur. yliacā pass. oppilatioēs splenis
et epīs. ipa herba ul' altera tm̄ ī aqua salm
cina decta pudēdis pectini. renib3 catapla
ment. dt etiā uinū decctiōis ei cū pl'uē bac
car lauri. C's yliacā pass. pl'uis ei cū aqua
salmacina melle ⁊ olo iniciat p cristere. c'
oppilatiōē splenis et epīs et renū. et urinali
um uiarū herbe ī uino etiā decte suplocum
cataplet. dt etiā ellē q cōficitur ex melle
et duab3 ptib3 pl'ueris utrisq3 ul' alteri et
una pte lapidis lincis ⁊ saxifrice. et n̄ op
portebit qrere litotripo. ul' elltm ducis. her
habito q2 mirabile ē. ad strān. dissur ⁊ cōtra
lapidē. C's duritiē splenis ⁊ epīs fiat decctio
pl'ueris ul' utriq3. ul' alterius solo. et epi et
splei. suppoatur. Siuiridis herbe habueris.
poat in uino p .viii. dies. ut ibi cputrescat
pea bulliat ad cōsuptionē uini. fere pea ex
primat p pannū sollidū. et forte ut tota huosi
tas exeat. et de illa huositate. et olo ⁊ cera fiat
unguentū exptus ad splē et epar. C's uomi
tū fcm̄ ex cā calida. ul' ex aliqua. cā. frā. coq
tur herbe ipē. ul' pl'uis diutissīe ī aq salina
cina ul' aq naturalr̄ salsa et addito olo ⁊ mo
dico aceto. fiat catapla sup pectus maximū
remediū est. C' ūt uomitū fcm̄ ex frā cā. pl'
uis ei cū melle datus lūbricos necat. c'tra
catarrū poat pl'ue cali ī sacello et capiti
suppoatur optimū est. C's furfurisicas cap
tis ul barbe. farina lupinorū amarorū decq
quātur ī aq salsa. addito aceto ⁊ icolatiā
pōito pl'uere utriq3 ul' alteri ea ptmodū ca
tapletur. C's paralisi ī uino decte loco dolen
ti suppoatur. C' ulcera et uulnera csolidati
pl'uis eorū supaspsus. C' ad matricē mun
dificandā et mestrua pucād. et matricē
infirāndā ex supfluitatib3 flatus cal'facie
dā coqntur herbe ipē ī aqua diu et fomete
tur mō mulier. et herbe ipē catapletū super
putellā pl'uis earū ī olo dcoquat et lōbix
in ticta suppoatur. ul' pl'uis cōficiat cū suco
mali terre ⁊ suppoatū. et Nota q sic itellig
es d Camepiteos sic d camedreos ī oi uirt
ut supi diximus q2 una ⁊ idē hēt efficatiā.

Camepitheos. c. ē. ⁊ s. ī. iii. gu. alio noīe
quercula maior. appellatur. alii. alothito.

Nascit ī magnis mōtib3 ⁊ locis asperis ⁊ lapi
dosis. Ventositatē ⁊ iflacioēs dissoluit. la
xatiuū est. huorū grossorū et atenuatiuū
et interiorū menbrorū cfortatiuū. oppilatio
nes epīs ⁊ splenis aperit ⁊ matricis. urinā
⁊ mestrua pucat. yctericiā curat. d quo
si duo exagia cū siccarū ficuū apposimate
dt. Nefresim extirpat. Vnū exagiū p uino
suptū supiora intestina cui apposima bibi
tū cū melle dolorē femorū ⁊ coxarū mitig
at. ul'nera putrida csolidat loca putrida ca
taplasmata dsiccat. duritiē mamillarū
dissoluit ⁊ tēpat.

Carui. ca. ē ⁊ sic. ī iio. gu. carui herba et
sem sic appellatur. itrasmarīs ptib3 ⁊ etiam
ī sicilia ī m'ta quantitate repitur. per qnq3
annos potest seruari. Virtutem habet di
ureticam. unde uinū decoctionis eius str
guriam et dissuriā cfert ⁊ pl'uis eius in
cibis sumptus digestionem confortat.
Ventositatem excludit in salsamentis po
situs appetitum pucat. Nota q semine

gu. alio noīe appellat. Damone abiel. Cimiñ
aūt est semē h̄be ī magna q̄ntitate nascētis
nō sophisticatur ꝓpt ip̄ius copiā. p. x. annos.
pōt s̄uari. Virtutē h̄t diureticā et fūmositatē
subtiliādi. Vñ sūptū ī cibis et potib;. et salsam
tis digestionē ꝯfortat. Vinū d̄coctionis eius
et sem̄. dolores stō̄i et tortionē ītestinorū ex uē
tositate mitigat. Cō̄ frīā tussim d̄t uinū de
coctiōis ficuū siccarū ⁊ cimini. Ellactuariū
etiā ꝯfectū ex cimino. sem̄ seie. brusco ⁊ melle.
utile est ꝯtra frigidā tussim. nec oportet diayris
ul' diaciminū h̄abito. Cō̄ dolores et tumores
faucīū. ciminū et ficus sicco. bene trite ī uino
d̄coquatur et in̄ empl'm f̄cm sup locū dolentē
inponatur. Cō̄ frīm reuma p'luis ei⁹ ⁊ baccarū
lauri. simil' trita ⁊ in testa cal'fcā. ī sacell' ponat
et capiti suppōatur. Cō̄ strāgurī ⁊ dissur. et aliōs
dolores ex frīāte ciminū ī uino d̄coctū supcata
plasmetur. Cō̄ sanguinē oculorū nō ī princi
pio dū fluxus ē. s; post p'luis ciminū cū uite
llo oui ꝯfectū sup testā calidā coquatur q̄ di
uisus ī duas medietates suppōatur sepius.
Alii etiā alio mō opant. ꝯ masticatū ciminū
inter d̄etes ī suflatur ī oculū aierē tm̄. Cō̄ liu
uorē ex contuxiōe ul' alio mō f̄cm dū recēs ē pul
uis ei⁹ sbtil' cū cera adignē; bn̄ ꝯfectus certū est
remediū. Ex freq̄nti usu cimini. fit discolora
tio.

tm̄ carui utimur.

Ciminum .ca. ē ⁊ sic. ī .ij.

Cicuta .ca. ē. ⁊ sic. ī. iij. g.

Macer dicens cicuta ee frigidā 7 sic . naturalit'.
Virtutē h̄t dissoluendi . attrahendi . ↄsum̄
di . ea nō utimur i interiorib; qa uenenosa
est . et i subā . cq̄litatib; suis dissoluit ē tn̄
q. sp̄us inaniuntur . ex quorū manitione
membra mortificātur . antiq aūt i medicinis
ponebatur . qa tnc corpora erāt fortiora . Vi
tutē h̄t potentissimā fr̄adiē secūdariaz . s. cali
dā et sic . s. folia . Maiorē frāz 7 sic . s. semen
Vn̄ sem̄ ei' q̄nq; ponim' i medicinis ↄ uitium
splenis tal' sit usus . tota h'rba i aceto . lī . 1.
7 lī . s . armoniaci sit p . ix . dies . decimo die
bulliāt ad ignē quousq; bn̄ resolutū fue
rit . armoniacū p'ea colet' p pannū forte . illa
liquorositas iterū . ad ignē bulliat bn̄ et a
addi cera . et olo fiat unguentū . h̄ ē ungt̄
cicute ↄ splinē potissimū . et ↄ dura apl'ata .
C ↄ ap'ata decoquatur i uino p'ea pistetur
cū assungia . 7 ponat' sup ap'a q' fluū expelli
dolorē . C ↄ asma decoquatur i aq̄ et cataplet'
an̄ et retro a cingulo supius usq; . ad gulam
ad arthticā 7 epilentiā ī ual3 . teste ↄstātino
C ↄt arthticā et podagrā . coq' radices i pasta
p'ea fisse p mediū . poāt' sup arthticā . certissi;
remediū ē . C ↄt yliacā pas' . str' . 7 dis' . frā deco
tione ei' i uino forti 7 olo . loca dolentia catap
lasmēt' . C ad matricē mūdificādā ex frigis
humoib; 7 gluctinosis . et mīstrā pu'ocādā . fi
at fomentū ex uino 7 aq̄ salsa decoctis ei' . C ↄ
grofulas siccas . frō usū diureticarū h'rbar'
fiāt cataplāta ex duab; ptib; cicute 7 una sca
biose . Nota si aliqui acceprint ↄcicuta i cibo ł
potu . mortal' est . stati; bibat satis de aceto 7 libe
rabitur . C ad episforas oculorum i estate ip'a h'rba
ↄt'ta 7 supposita mir' ualet . It ↄ ignē sacrū simili'
pficit 7 sanat . 7 i erpetē . C anasim teste si puella
uirgo accipit sucus cicute 7 d' ip'o illinient m
mamille nō pmictit i grossare nec cresce' . s; siut
parue 7 fixe . It h' h'rba uiridē supposita mamill'
lactē ↄsicat . It luxuriā stinguit suppectinē
cataplā . C ↄ podagrā sucū ei' 7 litargirio sup
unctū mir' est salutiferū medicamētū . 7 etiā p
se ualet ad oēs tumores q̄ fit ex nimio calore .

CRoci due sūt sūt sp'es . ortensis ab orto dcūs
in quo nasci' 7 oriental' q' i oriente crescit
sic appellatur . Iste crocus i medicinis nō uomici
pōitur . cū flores pducit i medio florē . tres
ul' quatuor flores pduc' i medio florē . Elligē
di sūt rufi ul' subrufi odo . q h̄nt aūt aliqt citri
nitatis abiciatur . It si inter manus fricatus
ↄ facili manus tingat . Signū est q'm sophisti

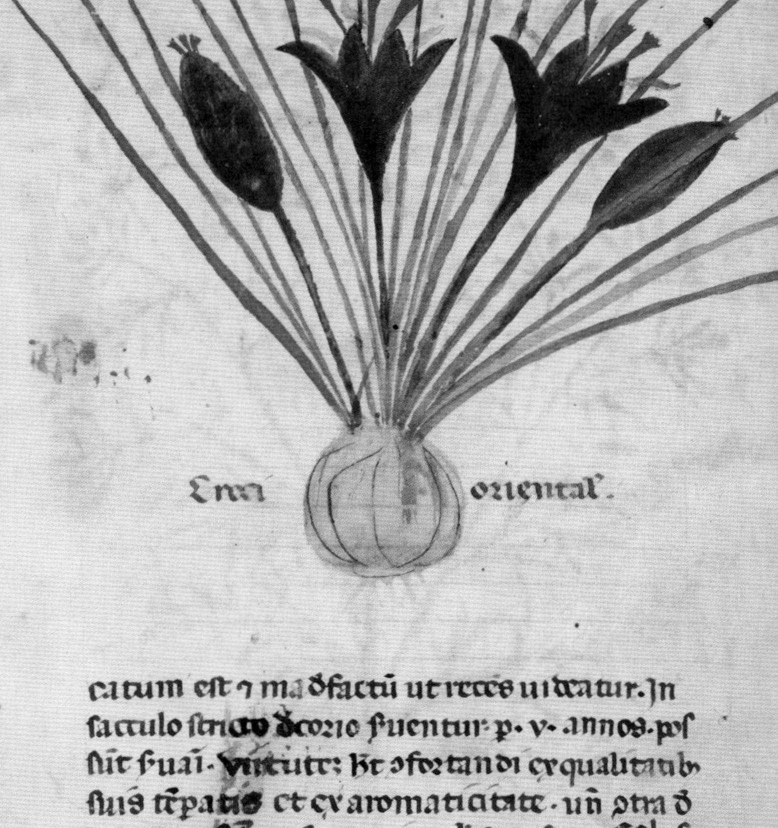

catum est 7 ma ↄfactū ut recēs uideatur . In
sacculo stricto de corio sruentur p . v . annos . pos
sūt sruari . Virtutē h̄t ↄfortandi ex qualitatib;
suis tēpatis et ex aromaticitate . un̄ ↄtra d
bilitatē stōi 7 sincopī; tal' sit usus . Calef
facta testa suppōatur crocus oriental' . et ↄsic
catus puluerizet' . et cū brodio si caro coqtur
i aqua ul' uino ul' aceto distempet in fine
decoctionis qa plus tnc tingit . ʒ . 1 . quā . ii
aliter . Et nota si fiat eius mltū usus abom
inationē facit . Collencius aūt nō debet dari
uomitū ei' puocat . C ↄ rubore oculorum et
sanguinē 7 maculā fiat plus de croco orien
tali nō siccato ut diximus ↄficiat' cū uitello
oui et bonbix i tictus oculis suppoāt' .

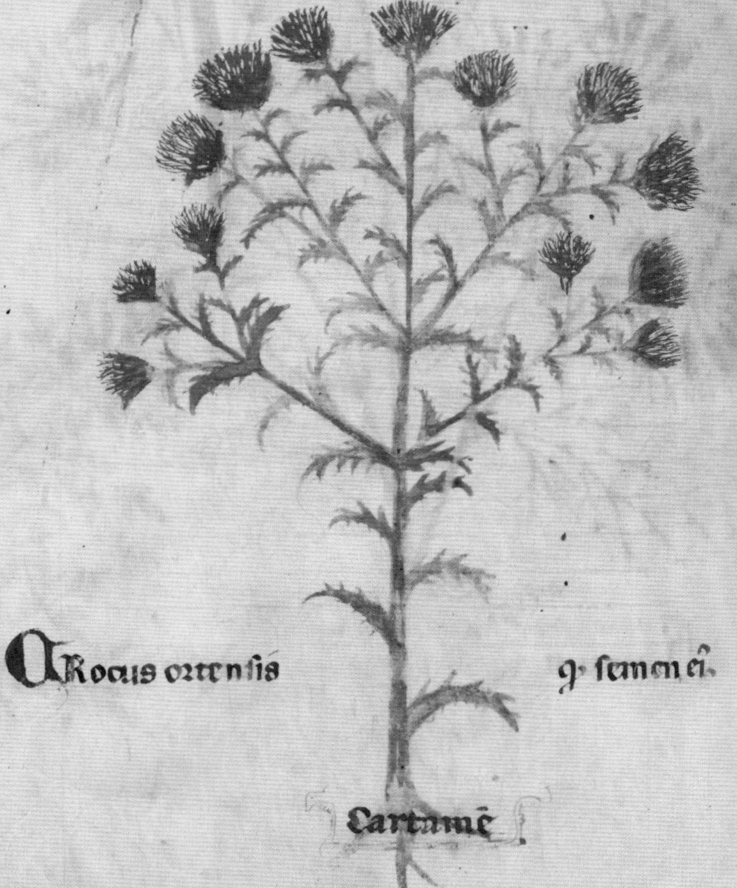

Cartamen uocatur. flos aūt eī dr̄ cassflor. tito
res ipm utut adtingendū. Crocus ortensis nō
pse datus s; imedicīs uomicis apetenter po
nitur. ¶ cō yliacam. pās. str. 7 dis. fca dectio
ne eī mediocriter icolco 7 locis dolentibus ca
taplasmetur.

Ciperus. ca. ē. 7 sic. ī. ii. gū. ē aūt ciperus.
substācia qdā modica otinua 7 rubrosa ē
aūt radix iūci triangularis q̄ iultramaīs
ptib; nascitur. melior ē 7 maior et pbien
nū suatur. quō īnr̄is regiōib; repit' minō
est. 7 nō tante efficacie. p annū suat'. Ellig
dū est tn̄ ramosus et cū frāgitur iteri. q̄ si
citinū pcedit colore; 7 nō facile pl'uericat'.
ht' aūt ex sūe sbtilitate; uirtute; diureticā;
Inqlibet tp̄e. pōt repiri. 7 colligi. s; precipue
ifine ueris tribus dieb; sole expōe et ihui
ditate putrefiat. pea iumbroso loco ponat'.
¶ cō strāguir. 7 dis. cipri simlta q̄titate aliq
tulū quassati i olō bn̄ coq̄t'. pea pectini 7 pe
ritenicon catapl'ati p certo puoē ur. humor'
dissoluūt. ¶ Ad idē. cipi bn̄ tti. cū olō miscel'
bulliāt aliq̄tulū et liquor colatus psiringā
iiectus etiā lapide; frāgit. ¶ cō dol' stōi et i

testinoz. ex frīgte ul' uētositate. Valet predic
tū catapl'a. q' fit cō str. 7 dis. fiat ī h q' precipu
ū est. dr̄ uinū dectiōis eī 7 mastic. ul' ex aq
dectiōis eī uinū limphet'. hec ī digestiōnem
ofortat. Ad ide; succus eī i uino dat' dolor'
stōi ex uentositate ul' frīgte 7 etiā itestinozū
tollit dolore;. ¶ cō litagiā. cipi. bn̄ otti in olō
ferue usq; ad osuptiōe; bulliāt pea illud to
tu; sup carbones pōat'. et fumū recipiat pa
tiens p os 7 nares. optimū ē ē puluis eī uul
nerib; iposit' putredine; tollit. abluta p
putredine;. nō ē ponedū. q' corrodit. s; pon
da sūt oglutinatiua. Cipus q albū ht co
lore; ul' terreū ul' pallidū abiciens ē.

Calamus aromaticus. calidū. ē. 7 sic. ī.
scdō. g. ē aūt radix cuidā fructicis 7 ca
lame asilat'. 7 ualō aromaticus 7 ocauus.
qa cū colligitur extit' q̄dā lignū intenus
existēs. duplicē manerie est. q̄dā dicunt
q' repit' ipsia. q citinus est. 7 eo nō utim' a
lius i india. q sb albidus ē. 7 eo utimur ē
ergo elligendū calamus sb albidi coloris.
q; cū frāgit' nō facile pl'uericatur. p tres
annos suat'. ht aūt uirtutes ofortādi. ¶ cō
stōi 7 i testinoz. dol'. ex frīgte ul' uentositate

certū est remediū. pl'uis ei' īqtitate. ʒ. iii.
ꝯficiat' cū suco absinthi addito uino calō.
∂tur pacienti mane ieiuno. ¶ Ad digestio
nē ꝯfortandā ∂t' pl'uis ei' cū pl'uē cinaōi
hoc etiā ualet ꝯtra cardiacā. ¶ ꝯ cardia
cā ∂coq̄tur calam' aroāticus integer ī aq̄
ro. ꝛ exca inpletur uinū pacietis. ¶ ꝯtra
tenasmō ex frā. cā. pl'uis ei' cū bonbice ano
addit extrinū' existēte supponat'.

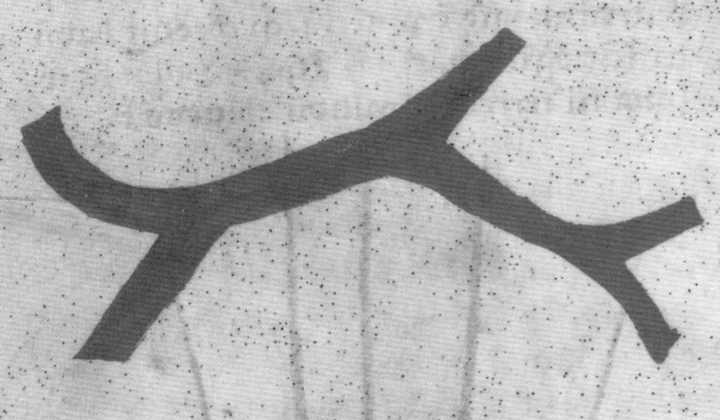

Corallus. f. ē. ꝛ. sic. ī scdo. gu. ē aūt q∂ā sb
stācia tirea q̄ ī locis maritimis repitur et
maxīe ī cauernosis mōtibꝫ ī mari existen
tibus. Quedā ē glucti nositas huōsa lap
pidibus adherēs exsiccitate ꝓpria. et mari'
callidi tate. ꝛ siccitate ꝯtēpsata ī sbstāꝫ lap
pideā tn̄smutatū. q maiorē ht. ptē igni'
fit rubus. q maiorē aquositatis fit alb'.
albus. frs ꝛ siccū' nimis. Rubus. f. ꝛ s. mi
nus quā alb'. Cāꝫ albꝫ q̄ rubus ꝯpetit usui
medicine. Sꝫ nūq̄ dꝫ pōi ī medicis nisi cū
∂terminatiōe. Cū īuenit sinpliciter cora
llus. rubeus ∂bet pōi. licet utrāqꝫ q∂ā po
nāt. Utqꝫ uō nō dꝫ pōi nisi ∂termi netur
sic. Re. coralli. al. ꝛ rubi. est ergo rubus
elligēd' q grossus ē et plan'. ꝛ clarus ꝛ q̄to
plus accedit ad ruborē tanto melior etq
nullā ht foramina. ul' pauca. ¶ Albꝫ ellig̃
dus est q grossus ē ꝛ planus. ꝛ q̄to magis
intēdit ī allbedinē tanto meli or q etiā n̄
est foratus ꝑuis foramibꝫ ita dꝫ elligi.
cū ponendū ē ī medicis ad faciē. Cū pon
dus ē ī medicis ore recipiendis nō ē curā
dū. ꝛ si nō sit adeo albꝫ. pot aūt suari utqꝫ
ꝑ ifinitos ānos. Virtutē ht ꝯfortā∂i ꝛ ꝯsti
gē∂i et depurā∂i. Ocultā etiāꝫ uirtutē ht
ꝯtra epilis. dicit etiā q∂ā q rubus ꝑs ua
domus a fulmine. ¶ ꝯ fluxū sanguini'
et naribꝫ īpoāt pl'uis ei' cū succo sangui
narie. et pille īde facte naribꝫ īponat'. ¶ ꝯt
emoctoicā. pas. i. uōitū sanguineū si fiat ui
tio spūaliū ex duabꝫ ptibꝫ coralli sbtilissīe
pl'uerīgati fiat ꝯfectio cū aq̄ ordi īfusiōis
dragāti. et fiāt pille quas teneat patiēs
singlās diu ī ore. ꝛ ꝑea resolutas trāsglu
ciat gnale enīꝫ est. q q ꝯtra uitiū spūa
liūꝫ dent'. dꝫ pri' ī ore tenēi. ut cūꝫ saliua
trāsducāt' ad spūalia. Si fiat uitio nut'
tiuorꝫ ∂t ꝯ suco plātagīs. eodē modo ua
let ꝯ dissinteria factā uitio supiorū. ¶ ꝯ
dissinteriāꝫ fcām uitio supiorūꝫ ∂t pl'
uis ei' cū ouo sorbili si fiat uitio īferiorꝫ
iniciatur ꝑ cristē cūꝫ succo plātagis. ¶ ꝯ
fluxuꝫ matris. pluis ei'. cū athanasia
ul' cū solo succo plātagis ꝯficiat' ꝛ fiat
suppositoriū. ul' ī pl'uis sol' cū bōbice tūc
ꝯstringit. ¶ ꝯ ꝯrosionē oris ꝛ gingiuār
cū aq̄ salmacina ul' aluminosa. abluā
tur gingiue. et fricē pl'ue ∂ duabꝫ ptibꝫ
coralli. ꝛ tcia rosaꝝ ꝑoāt' spgigiuas.
¶ ꝯ fluxū sāguīs ex gingiuis pl'uis co
ralli. ꝛ anthere sꝑsꝑgat'. ul' cū melle ꝯfici
atur. et illiniant' gigiē. pl'uis ī coralli.
ulceribꝫ īpōitus. ea ꝯglutinat.

Catapucia. ca. ē ī. iii. g. hu. ī ꝑmo. ē aūt

fructus ul' sem̃ cuidã h'be simili noie app
ellate. cũ i recepticle repit' fruct'. nõ h'ba
ↄ̃let p̃ti et remocto exteriori cortic̃. pot aut' p
annũ s'uari i mlta efficatia. Eligenda ẽ cata
putia uiridis ñ i teriorib; pforata nec liuid
s; alba. Virtutẽ h't pricipaliter purgandi
flã. secũdario colã ⁊ melancoliã. h't aut' uirtu
tẽ pũgãdi p supiora. ex uentuositate ⁊ leui
tate. Vñ qnq; dat' sanis ad ↄ̃suationem
sanitatis. qnq; egris ad remouendũ egri
tudinẽ. C ↄ̃ cotidianã ↄ̃flãte salso. ⁊ sca
bież. ↄteratˉ catapu'tie i mlta qntitate. ⁊
p̃ea foliis cauliũ i uolute sb cinẽ poãtur
diu ut bñ coqnt' p̃ea extracte exprimãtur.
olũ q' effluit reserue'. ⁊ cũ necesse fuerit det'
patiẽti i cibis. ul' aliquo alio mõ ita posũt
ↄ̃cipi mlti. C ad idẽ fiat claretũ hoc mõ
Cataputie bñ ↄtrite cũ melle ↄ̃qnt cũ tali
melle ⁊ uino fiat clarectũ. Nota q' ad xx
lib. uini sufficit. l. i. cataputiarũ. pot fieri
modiolũ clareti. i uire ĩ pisaũ ul' carni
um ul' aliorũ ciborũ p̃sũt poñ cataputie
ↄtrite. cõmeste ĩ mltũ ualẽt san' ⁊ egris
⁊ i predictis modis. C ↄ̃ quotidianã de
flãte salso fera atriplic̃. rape. radic̃. abla
tentur. i aq̃ feruẽti. addita tria pte ℥. ca
taputie. ⁊ dent' cũ syrup' acetos'. C ↄ̃ quo
tidianã ↄ̃ flãte uitreo precedentib; diuis'
bulliat ℥. iii. l. ii. castorei i uino fortissim'
addat' tria p̃s ℥. cataputiarũ excorticat'
p't colatura cũ oximelle d'. C ↄ̃ yliacam
pas. bulliant i aq̃ radices. fen. et cassie lig.
illa aq̃ addat' tria p̃s ℥. catapucie ⁊ inie
atur p cristẽ. p̃cedẽte tñ cristẽi mollifica
tiuo. C ↄ̃ artheticã. ⁊ paliś. dosis simpliciˉ
bñdicte cũ uino hoc modo dato ⁊ etia ℥.
cataputiar. d'. C ad p̃suationẽ sanitati
fructus. cataputie. uirides siccantur. bñ
mũdati ⁊ ↄtriti ouo mixti. i iuscello ponã
tur siñ molestia purgat. Vl' cataputie bñ
trite pri' mũdate cũ esula poãt i uino ⁊ ad
dito cinamomo ⁊ aliis sp̃eb; aromaticis
detur. C ad uomitũ puocãdũ si materia fue
rit frã et i ore stõi ⁊ i egris. ⁊ i sanis cata
putie bñ trite cũ olo siccionino ↄficiantur
⁊ orificio stõi i ponat'. Nota oleũ p̃dictũ
ex cataputiis fcm̃ p annũ s'uari pot.

et ↄ̃ yliacã pas. h' h'ba i mlta q̃titate bulliat
i aq̃ salsa ⁊ uino ⁊ olo et i aq̃ sedeat patiens
usq; ad ũbelicũ. Si aut' i tãta qntitate habẽ
neq̃as cataplent'. sup loca dolentia. h'ba
etiaz ↄmesta. ul' uinũ decoctiõis ei poteter
puocaˉ ur'. C ↄ̃ yliacã pas. h'ba decoquitur i aq̃
salsa. ex q̃ addito melle et olo fiat cristere.
precedẽte alio cristẽ mollificatiuo.

CRetanus. ca. ẽ ⁊ sic. i. iii. g'. h'ba ẽ q' in
maris locis repit'. alio nomine d'r bacch
Virtutẽ h't ualdẽ diureticã ex sbtilitate
sbe. C ↄ̃ dissur' uitiũ lapidis. ⁊ strãgur'

C Costus. ca. ẽ ⁊ sic. i. iii. g.

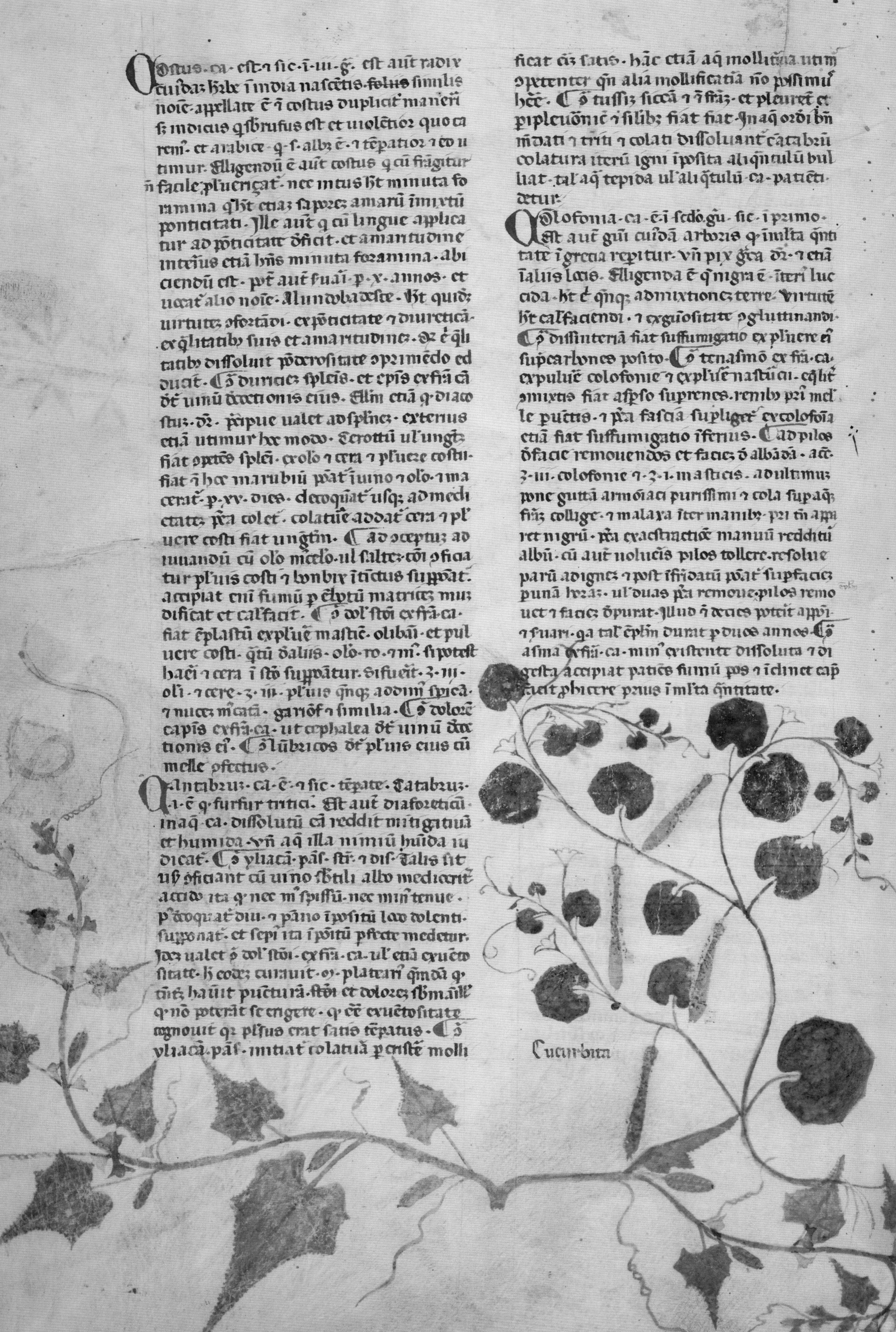

Costus. ca. est et sic. in iii. g. Est aut radix cuiusdam herbe in india nascentis foliis similis noie appellate et costus dupliciter manerierum s. indicus qui subrufus est et violentior quo caremus et arabicus q. s. albus est et temperatior et eo utimur. Eligendum est aut costus qui cum frangitur non facile pulverizatur nec intus hit minuta foramina q hit etiam saporem amarum immixtum ponticitati. Ille aut qui cum lingue applicatur ad ponticitatem deficit et amaritudine interius etiam habens minuta foramina abiciendum est. post aut servari p. x. annos. et vocatur alio noie alumdolabdeste. Hit quidem virtutem confortandi ex ponticitate et diureticam ex qualitatibus suis et amaritudine. et est qualitatibus dissolvit ponderositatem comprimendo educit. Contra duricies splenis et epatis ex fra ca detur vinum decoctionis eius. Illum etiam q diacostum dicitur. precipue valet ad splenem. exterius etiam utimur hoc modo. Cerotum vel ungtm fiat competens spleni. ex oleo et cera et pulvere costi fiat et hoc marubium ponatur in vino et oleo et maceratur p. xv. dies. decoquatur usque ad medietatem postea coletur. colature addatur cera et pulvere costi fiat ungtm. Contra conceptum adiuvandum cum oleo mellino vel saltem communi conficiatur pulvis costi et bombix intinctus supponatur. accipiat etiam fumum per clystum matricem mundificat et calefacit. Contra dolorem stomaci ex fra ca. fiat emplastrum ex pulvere mastice. olibani et pulvere costi. quantum sufficit. oleo ro. et m. si potest haberi et cera in stomaco supponatur. Si fuerit. 3. iii. oli. et cere. 3. iii. pulvis quinque addimus spica et nucem muscatam. gariof. et similia. Contra dolorem capitis ex fra ca. ut cephalea detur vinum decoctionis eius. Contra lumbricos detur pulvis eius cum melle confectus.

Cantabrum. ca. est et sic. temperate. Cantabrum id est quod furfur tritici. Est aut diaforeticum in aqua ca. dissolutum eam reddit mitigativam et humidam. unde aqua illa nimium humida iudicatur. Contra yliacam passionem stomachi et dis. talis sit usus conficiant cum vino subtili albo mediocriter acido ita quod nec multum spissum nec minus tenue. postea decoquatur diu et panno impositum loco dolenti supponatur et sepe ita impositum perfecte medetur. Idem valet contra dolorem stomaci ex fra. ca. vel etiam ex ventositate. Hic codex curavit eum platearius quendam qui continue habuit puncturam stomaci et dolorem sub mamilla quod non poterat se erigere. quod esse ex ventositate cognovit quia plus erat satis temperatus. Contra yliacam passionem initiatur colatura percussione molli ficiat ea satis. hac etiam aqua mollitiva utimur competenter quando alia mollificativa non possimus habere. Contra tussim siccam et frigidam et pleuresim et peripleumoniam et similibus fiat fiat in aqua ordei bene mundati et triti et colati dissolvatur cantabrum colatura iterum igni imposita aliquantulum bulliat. tal aqua tepida vel aliquantulum ca. patienti detur.

Colofonia ca. est in secundo gradu sic in primo. Est aut gummi cuiusdam arboris que in multa quantitate in grecia reperitur. unde pix greca dicitur et etiam in aliis locis. Eligenda est que nigra est interius lucida. hic est quamque admixtionem terre. Virtutem hit calefaciendi et ex viscositate conglutinandi. Contra dissinteriam fiat suffumigatio ex pulvere eius super carbones posito. Contra tenasmon ex fra ca. ex pulvere colofonie et ex pulvere mastici. cum his commixtis fiat aspersio supra renes. renibus prius melle punctis et postea fascia superligetur ex colofonia etiam fiat suffumigatio inferius. Contra ad pilos de facie removendos et faciem dealbandam. accipe 3. iii. colofonie et 3. i. masticis. ad ultimum pone guttam armoniaci purissimi et cola super aqua frigida collige et malaxa inter manibus. prius tamen apparet nigrum. postea ex attractione manuum redditur album. cum aut volueris pilos tollere resolve parum ad ignem et post infrigidatum ponatur super faciem punam horam vel duas postea remove pilos removet et faciem depurat. Illud in decies poterit apponi et servari ca. tale emplastrum durat per duos annos. Contra asma ex fra ca. minus existente dissoluta et digesta accipiat patiens fumum post et inclinet caput faciat [illegible] prius in multa quantitate.

Cucurbita et Citruli · fri̅ · su̅t · ⁊ hu̅idi · i̅q̅litati
bus suis tepati · Jn calidis regioi̅b; precipue
repiuntur · Se̅ia artificiose terre i̅iecta · te̅
pore ueris p̅reat̅ h̅rba̅ · q̅ fructus p̅ducit in
medicis · o̅pete̅s · Cucurbita ⁊ citruli · ante
maturitate̅ colliguntur · et p̅ citruli crudi
et an̅ maturitate̅ ⁊ p̅ possu̅t o̅medi · Cucur
bita u̅o no̅ cruda · s̅ elixa · ul' assata · Se̅ia ̅
diuretica su̅t · p̅p̅t s̅btile̅ s̅ba̅ · ⁊ p̅cipue med'
o̅petu̅t · C̅ o̅ opilatione̅ e̅pis renu̅ ⁊ uesice ·
⁊ o̅tra asp̅a̅ca pectoris · C se̅ia b̅n mu̅data a co̅
ticib; exterioꝛib; b̅n co̅tera̅tur et i̅ aq̅ ordi a
aliq̅tulu̅ coq̅ntur · ul' ablactentu̅ · et aqua
colata patienti d̅tur · Si aut̅ no̅ p̅t accipere
aqua̅ fiat sirupu̅ ex aq̅ illa et d̅t · No q̅ ma
ioꝛe̅ h̅t efficatia̅ si no̅ bullierit · s̅ ablactent
ꝑ · No q̅ a corticib; mu̅data d̅bet po̅i i̅ medi
cinis · C Jn acutis aut̅ febrib; d̅tur aq̅ ul' ̅
sir̅ · ex aq̅ fc̅u̅s · cucurbita cocta cu̅ carnibus
maxi̅e o̅fert collericis in estate · C a cutis siue
febricita̅tib; elixe cucurbite si̅n aliquo o̅di
mento ul' i̅ assate cu̅ ag̅sta date ⁊ cib; su̅t
⁊ mediciña · C Coq̅ cucurbitas i̅ pasta b̅n · q;
cocte i̅ aq̅ tote dissolu̅u̅tur ex aqua · aqua ⁊
zuchro fiat sir̅ · optim̅ acutissime febricita̅
tibus · et e̅pic̅ ⁊ ethic̅ · et p̅t da̅i a p̅ricipio m
materia̅ dig̅it · ⁊ purgat p̅ urina̅ aliqua̅tul'
etia̅ laxat · C o̅ e̅pis calefactio̅e̅ rasura cucur
bite terantur · ⁊ succo expresso ⁊ addito aceto
ul' ag̅sta pannus i̅tictus suppoatur · No p̅t
maturitate̅ cucurbita d̅bet colligi · et suspe̅
di cu̅ se̅ib; ⁊ ita siccentur · se̅a p̅p̅t o̅glutino
sitatem ablua̅tur · cu̅ aq̅ ⁊ soli exsiccentur · s;
loco sicco o̅seruent · ne p̅p̅t hu̅itate̅ m̅lta̅ o̅ru̅
pantur · p̅ triennu̅ s̅uatur · No ubi se̅ia ista h̅ri
no̅ possu̅t · seminib; maloru̅ o̅l'cu̅ uti possimu̅
q; secu̅dario ide̅ o̅patur ·

Celidonia · ca · e̅ · ⁊ sic̅ · i · iii · g̅u̅ · cui̅ duplex est
maneries · s · indica q̅ maioꝛi̅ e̅ efficacie · et
citrina̅ h̅t radicem · ⁊ co̅is q̅ i̅ n̅ris p̅tibus re
pitur · q̅ e̅ minoris efficacie · altera t̅n p̅ al
tera p̅t po̅i · Teste o̅s̅ · Cu̅ i̅ receptioi̅b; repi
tur · radix no̅ h̅rba d; po̅ni · et radix · p · iii ·
annos · p̅t s̅uari i̅ m̅lta efficacia · ex q̅lita
tib; suis ⁊ s̅ba · alia no̅ia celidonie · Glauc
os · rixa : o̅ttonica · mopop · aru̅dinina · ul'
h̅rba aru̅dinea · h̅ort i̅ t̅p̅e cu̅ ueniu̅t · arudi
nes pullos · ⁊ similit̅ o̅siccat̅ q̅nq; separa̅t q̅ꝛ
ip̅a uocat̅ arudinea · ul' celidonia q̅ Greci
uoca̅t celidonia · i · aru̅dina aues · ̅ d; q̅ a
rundine reddu̅t lume̅ ocul' ad filioꝝ eoꝝ cu̅
ipa h̅rba q̅ꝛ uocat̅ celidonia · C Virtute̅ h̅t
dissoluendi o̅sumendi ⁊ atrahendi · C o̅t
doloꝛe̅ d̅ntiu̅ exs̅ra̅ · ca · radix aliq̅tulu̅ trita
inter dentes dolentes ⁊ d̅te̅ s̅b positu̅ teneat̅ ·
C ad cap̅ purga̅d̅ ⁊ uua̅ repleta̅ s̅ro · hu · rad'
ces b̅n trite i̅ uino d̅coq̅tu̅ patie̅s p̅ os fumu̅
recipiat · p̅a uinu̅ gargariçatu̅ q̅ uulnera̅
o̅siccat · et caput p̅u̅gat · C o̅ colica̅ pa̅ss̅ ·
h̅rba t̅ta ⁊ i̅ uino d̅cocta suppo̅at̅ · ul' spongia
i̅fusa i̅ uino d̅coctio̅is p̅l'ueis radic̅ · eius se̅p̅
s̅ppo̅atur · C ad o̅estr̅ · p̅uoc̅ ⁊ matric̅ mu̅di
mu̅dificа̅da̅ fiat fomentu̅ ex aq̅ d̅coctio̅is ip̅i ·
C ad cancru̅ oris ul' exterioru̅ · p̅l'uis radic̅
eius cu̅ p̅l'ue̅ rosaru̅ o̅ficiantur cu̅ aceto et
d̅coquatu̅ usq; ad mediet atate̅ spissitudinem
ad modu̅ sinapismi ⁊ iunga̅t p̅tes cancro̅
se ul' ca̅crose ul' ca̅cerose m̅l'tu̅ o̅fert · C o̅
fistula̅ p̅l'uis ei̅ capitello p̅oat̅ · ⁊ o̅ficiatu̅ cu̅
stuello o̅ꝛi fistule i̅ mictat̅ · C ad caligine̅ siu̅
obtalmia̅ ocul' ul' scabie̅ i̅eis · succus radic̅
celido̅ie cu̅ uino optio̅ ⁊ mell' attico ⁊ pipere
al · fac colliriu̅ ⁊ ocul' ute̅ h̅ o̅magnu̅ expime̅tu̅
e̅ ⁊ adm̅l'tis p̅b̅ · aliu̅ i̅ponu̅t ocul' lac radic̅

Celidonia.

Cucumeris · f · s̅ ⁊ hu · i · ii · g̅ · cucum̅is gen̅ su̅t ac̅li · s̅ su̅t e̅ssi o̅dun ad digen̅d ⁊ tard a s̅to o̅sc̅edu̅t · s̅to s̅ nociu · neruositate̅ tame̅
et p̅tutu̅t · q̅ cibu̅ aliq̅n i̅uenientes cu̅ su̅ s̅rate illu̅ s̅uat e̅llu̅ s̅ o̅mnicu̅t a s̅to dissolui · s; ta̅n mi̅ s̅to nocet q̅ melones q̅ꝛ cu
cumeres digestiue · i obedie̅tes i̅tuiti sicut i̅ s̅to la̅b̅o̅re̅ · Melones u̅ s̅ba̅ s̅to̅ emolliu̅t · ⁊ gn̅u̅t i̅ uenenoso̅ huo̅res · q̅b; s̅to
mac̅ p̅cutit · Vera̅m melones si b̅n digesti fugint · meliores q̅ cucume̅s g̅n̅at chimo̅ q̅ cucumeis chim̅ e̅ e̅ssus · s̅lati u̅ trico
uenus · Vn̅ ypo̅c · cucume̅s s̅ e̅ssi ⁊ difficiles ad digen̅d q̅ magis q̅ melones · Vrina̅ p̅uocat̅ ⁊ uetre̅ humectat̅ ·
Citroli su̅t s̅rioꝛes e̅ssioꝛes cucumeib; s̅situto e̅ eoꝝ e̅ i̅ fine · ii · g̅ · p̅in̅ g̅n̅at e̅ssu̅ s̅la · ⁊ u̅uositati s̅to̅i cucumeib; mag̅ nocent ·
Rurs̅ p̅p̅ sua̅ duritie̅ ⁊ s̅rate̅ s̅ e̅ssioꝝ huo̅ꝝ q; s̅roꝝ g̅n̅antiu̅ · Q̅ certificat̅ q̅ꝛ crudi i̅ s̅to mora̅ facientes · coꝛruptio̅e̅
uenenatoꝝ s̅bueu̅t huo̅ꝝ · Citroli g̅ mag̅ o̅ib; s̅to nocet · medulla ta̅n eoꝝ p̅fectioꝛe̅ cibu̅ g̅n̅at ·

celidonie ⁊ mltū ꝯfert. Ad idem succus folioꝝ
⁊ florib; celidonie ⁊ mell' attico simil' ī uase
ereo inuoluto cine. decoq; ad pfectionem artēdā
pēa recond ⁊ ute. singulare ē remediū ad
caliginem oculorū ⁊ mir curat. Ut sagitt
ul' spina exeat sine dolor. manu euelle. radi
cē arundineā cū melle tere ⁊ suppone. pb ē.

Oaulle. albesthr. alnesthron. calcis uiua. i.
calida. ē. ī. sic. ī. tcio. gū. mixta ꝯstuo
⁊ olo pustulas ⁊ putrida appbata sentes
iuuat uulnera ⁊ oem scisionem bn̄ ꝯsoli
dat.

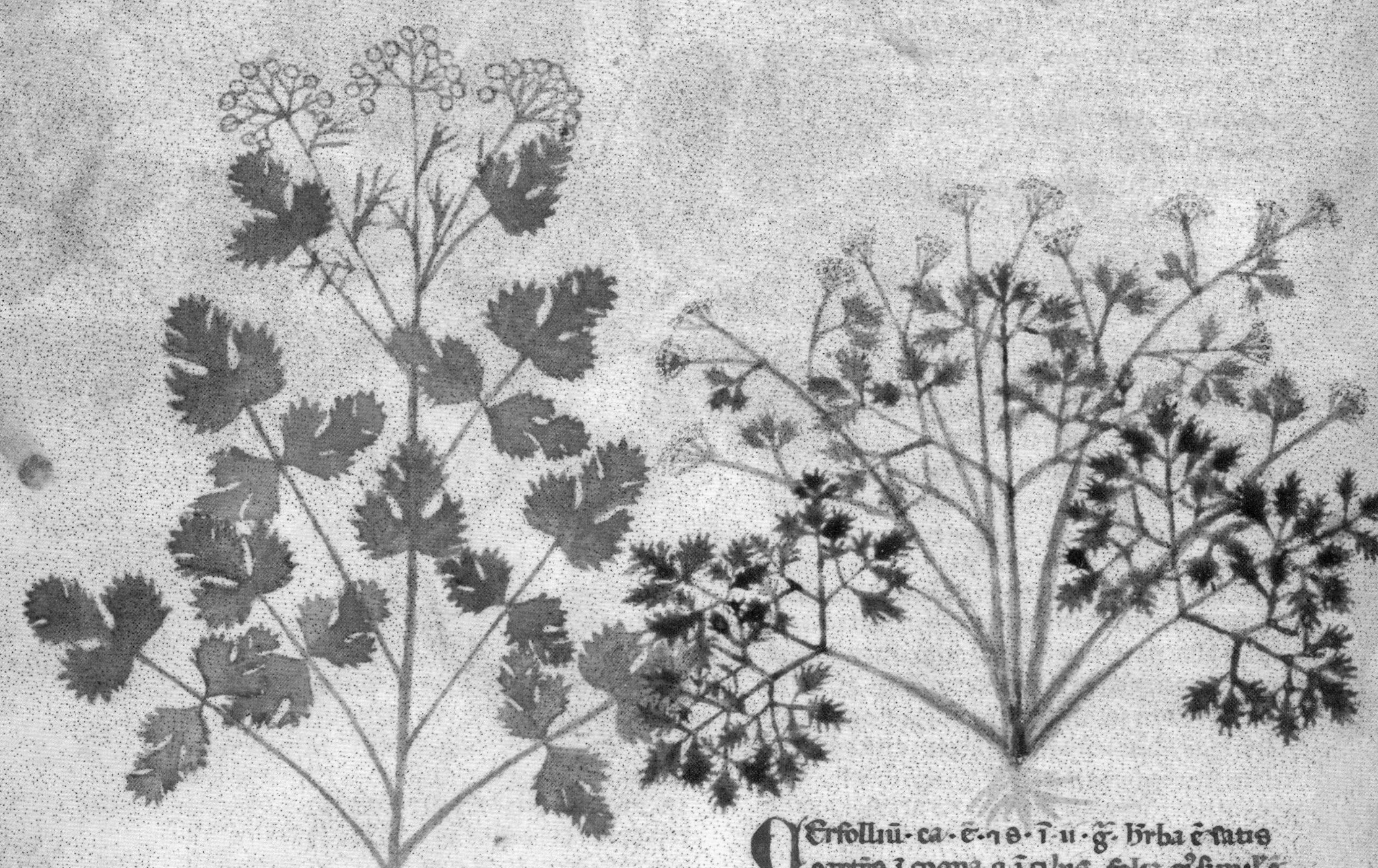

Coliandrū. alcosbara. alcosulibar. alcorbosē
idem ē. ca. e. ⁊. sic. ī. ii. gū. hrba ē satis cois
cui receptionib; poni dr. q̄n īuenit ei receptio ī
aliq. medic sem. p. ii. ānos. post suam ī multa
efficatia. Uirtutē h̄t ꝯfortādi ex qlitatib;
suis sem aliqtulā aroāticitatē. Ad digestionem
ꝯfortād ⁊ dol' stoī ceuetos dē sem ei ī cibis ⁊ in
ductionis ei. pluis seis sup carnes aspsu
eas saporitas reddit. Ad dol' auriū. succu
hrbe ipi ⁊ lacte mulieris masclm nutentis
tātū dem simil' tepid aurib; stilab. mir dol' toll'.

Cerfolliū. ca. ē. ⁊. s. ī. ii. g. hrba ē satis
ꝯpetēs ī coqna ⁊ ī cibis. folia ei simil' ē
petrosilino. precipue ualet. Ꝯt dol' stōaci
acc cimas trib; cerfolii uiridis ⁊ aliqtulū
pulegio ꝯtere ī mortario ligneo ⁊ adde co
cleariū melle. oīa fac bullire ⁊ fiat eplin.
stōm suppone. Ad cancrū. hrba ipi bn̄ ꝯt
ta ⁊ supposita cancrū mir curat. Ad dolorem
lateris ⁊ ī ꝯt colicā pass. strāgur ⁊ dissur
succus ei cū uino potui dato mir ꝯfert. Ꝯt
foliorū ei bn̄ ꝯteris ⁊ calidū suppone mire
dol' expellit. Eodem modo bibita. lonbricos
occidit ⁊ ī tinee. ⁊ mestruā educ. urina p
uocat. Ꝯt olim tcotionis ipi ī uetto febricita
te ī hora acess. ad frigorem librat ⁊ expellit
ad parotidas ⁊ īflactionem. Cerfolliū cū
cera uirgine ⁊ axūgia ueter. suppone solet

aulos. [illegible] turbidū ⁊ melācolicū gnat sanguinem [illegible] Oz duplex ē [illegible]
[illegible] cambiā [illegible] duob;
modis [illegible]
[illegible]
[illegible]
[illegible]
[illegible]

curare et reprimere pariotidas ul' aliq̄ isflatione ubiq; fuerit. C. ↄ̄ uomitū. cerfolliū cū aceto ↄmedat patiēs. statī retinē facit et stom̄ ↄfortat. ⁊ etiā uentrē laxat. C. ad puoc̄ urinā succus ei' potui dato ⁊ ī h'ba ↄtrita ⁊ suppectinē cataplā mir' puoc̄ urinā. it' sepi' ↄmesta ualet oppilatiōi epis ⁊ spli. Nota siū pōt hr̄ erbā acc̄ sem̄ ipi' ⁊ ↄmedat ul' bibat plus ei.

et punge loca. mir' dolorē expellit.

Canapa aut̄ domestica. fructus ei' ↄmestū lac mulierib; hūdare fac̄ ualet etiā ↄ̄ fiāte; pectoris ⁊ tussi;. ⁊ lōbricos occidit ī corpore.

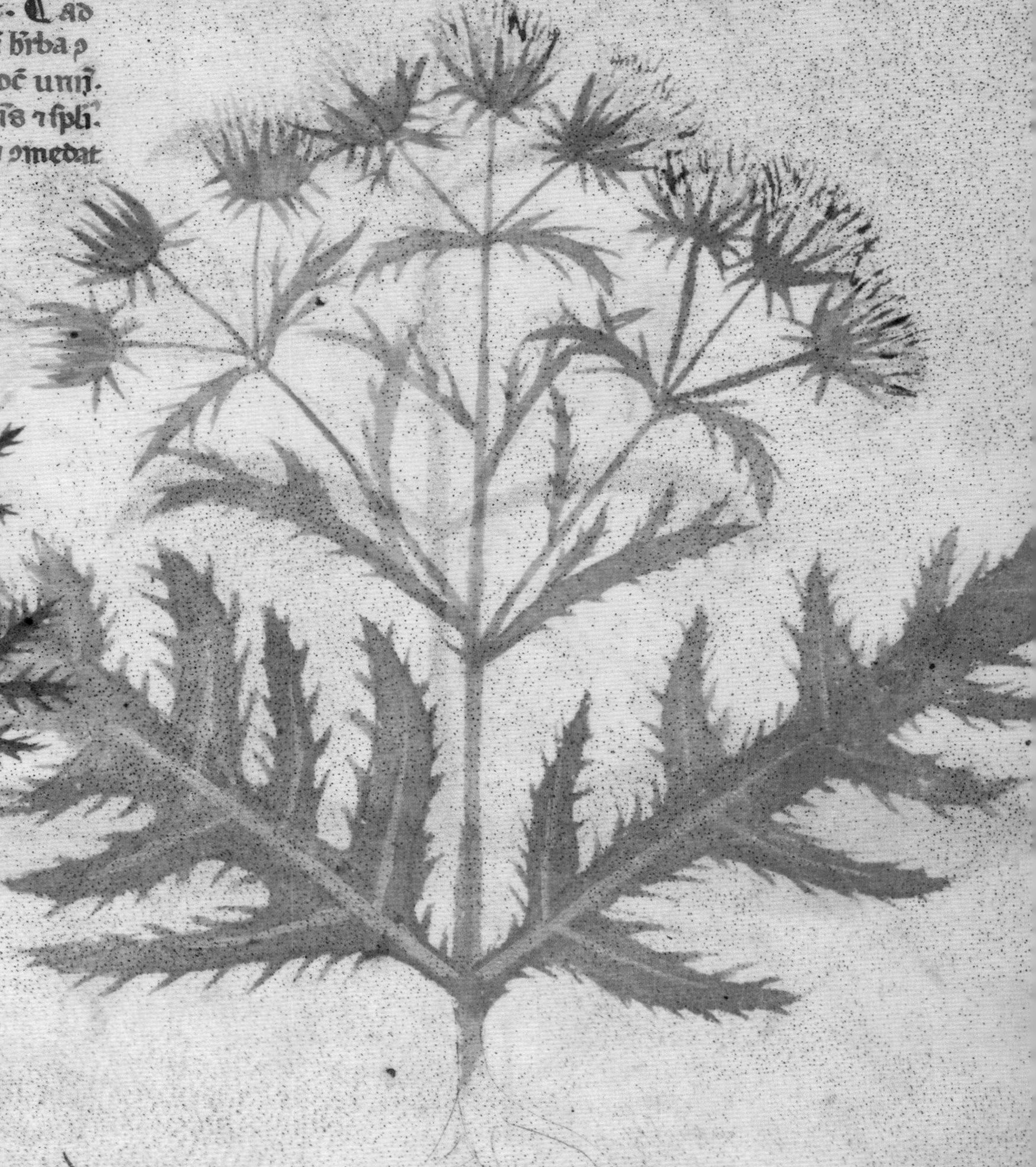

Canapa. h'rba ē. cui' duplex ē maneries. s. domestica q̄ satis ē cōis. ⁊ siluatica cui' uirtus nūc dicēe uolumu'. Canapa siluatica. ē ⁊ hu. ī. ii. gu. alio noīe dr̄. agriō canabin. prima cura ei. addol' ⁊ īflactiōēs mamillarū. h'rba ipi' cū axūgiā fcō ēplim et ↄ̄pōita sin̄ mora oē; dolorē mitigat ⁊ īflactiōē; soluit ⁊ etiā; apēata maturat ⁊ ↄ̄ſgit. ad frigore. fruct' ei' ⁊ sem̄ urtic̄ cū aceto fac̄ enplm̄ ⁊ ſppoñ ⁊ uides effectū bonū. C. ad reumā ul' gutta extrā. ca. ⁊ ī q̄cūq; loco cōporis fuerit. succus ↄ̄radicib; ei' ⁊ statūde; pinguediē ultuuis fcō ungt' addito modico aceto

Camelleunta. alba. h'rba ē q̄ alio nomīe dr̄ camelleon. licum uocat. yxiam. ⁊ h't folia aspa ⁊ ī medio h't ī modū echino marino rotūdo ⁊ spinoso ⁊ uestito floribus purpureis ⁊ sem̄ h't albū ⁊ radicē albā ⁊ odo rosa;. Succus radix ipi' ul' pluis exca fcō cū uino ⁊ aq̄ decoq; ī origano ⁊ potui dato pduc̄ foras lōbricos latos. C. ↄ̄ idropici in ī pē egtudīs eode; mō potata addito. ʒ. ī. cimino īflactiōēs ypopisim dsiccat. et etiā h't uirtutē ut tyriacā ↄ̄ oē; uenenum ↄ̄ difficultatē urine mir' apit.

Iecor plis ē nutrimēti uētrē; huectat. urinā mouet. ↄ̄stā pligat. uētrē ī tantū tam cēt ⁊ īflactiōēs. decco ↄ̄pma auget ...
ↄfortat. ē ciccr duo ī. ↄpletū ē siccū. atq; ↄpletū. ...

[illegible]

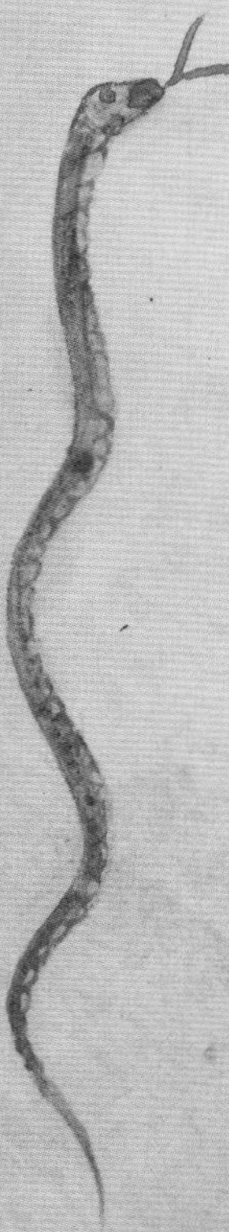

Camelleunta nigra herba est q. alii uocant Camelleam. alii Corcodrillon. alii Dipsacū. pfeti uocant Onocardion. egiptii Sencor. siculi Afrodicteloter. alii Smelita. alii Labrū ueneris. alii Cecerustico. alii Statinus. alii Mostarion. alii Alentidiū. alii Scire. alii Calos cardiacos. alii Cerbasten. alii Psalpo. alii Alipodius. Nascit iuxta sepibz et i fossatis. pōt legi eā oī tpe. Valet precipue 9 dol' capis n̄ febricitātē. sucū ei cū uino potui dabis si n̄o febricitat da cū aq. mir dol' tollit. Contra uenenū. plius ei cū uino potū q: dato q actos mi. oē uenenū eicē facit. Contra yd'opisiz. puluis eius 7 plue: camedreos 7 camepithios eqli pōdere i q̄titat. ʒ. iii. cū uino potui dabis si uir: si aut' mulier da ʒ. ii. si n̄o puer da ʒ. i. statī: oē: uenenū d' corpore 7 flāticos hu. 7 aqtosos expellit foras. Et urinā mir puocat.

Camomilla herba ē. q alio noīe dr̄. parthenicon. alii. Diacolosat. a. Trociscos ciatos. a. Aperitos. a. Nipeos. a. yeroantemi. a. Alionpotres. Itali bn̄olorosa. alii. Supba. a. Apirretos. a. Antes. romani. Bene olēte. a. Supperi. a. Solisaciū. egipti. Tiorin. galli. Oblacdia. campani. Obulacia. a. Amulla. tusci. Abiana. daci. Amulusta. a. Anasmis. a. Babonica. Nascit' locis cultis 7 i planis 1 etiā int' frumentū 7 i lino. Prima cura ē a dol' 7 uitia oculorū. herba camōilla iuenies eā an̄ sol' ortū 7 dic sup eā precatio ista ego accipio te p albuginē 7 dol' oculorū q tu michi sbueniés. 7 ollige eā 7 porta tecū ad collo suspēsa. Si aut' uis scire uirtutē uiu' h'e collige eā q̄n sol fit i signo ariete. Floribz suis coq: i olo oliue 7 unge patienti ad mod' a gomestico 7 coopi cū diligenter 7 da sibi potui d' aq. ca. i mixta q̄titate. si sudauerit.

Castanee. ca sūt i medio p̄ g. sic i. 1. significatio eorū caloris 7 dulcedo eorū q sapores 7 poticatis inuat' ... ad gladiū ... sūt ad digend' faciles 7 nutribiles. ... si emedat' iflactios dat 7 capis dolores faciūt. ... digestiois durita. 7 fumū ... si aliis nocumentū auferent si aq tepida ... q eorū ... tepat ... difficultate dissoluit cū zuchare eas omedūt ... cū melle. ... Collina ... [illegible]

bonū signū ē librabit. Si uō nō sudauerit
malū. morietr teste macr. Cō str 7 dissuriā
7 lapidē frāgendā. uinū ul' aq decoctiōis cam
mille sepi bibita mir̄ ofert. Cō oppilatiōez
epatis 7 splenis simil' potui data mir̄ pficit.
Cō dol' stōi 7 iflactiōez. 7 ī dol' uētris ex frā ca
ul' ex uentositate. uinū decoctiōis ei' potui da
to. dol' expellit stati. Ad menstrua puocād aq
decoctiōis ei'. mulier se abluet uluā. 7 pūgab
mestr. Ut mulier nō pareat an̄ tps. uinū
decoctiōis ei' sepe bibitus nō pmictit abortū. Cō
quotid febrē. olū exea fcū unge febricitātem
mir̄ calfacit 7 febrez discutit. Ad squamez
ī facie camomilla uidez cū melle decoq 7 faciē illi
nias. Cō morsū pestiferū spentez. ʒ. i. camoill'
7 uino calido qactos. ii. potui dato. nō potent
sibi nocē uenenū. Cō uitiū spleis. teste plin
ius. si patiēs splenetico accipit p. xl. diebu.
ʒ. i. camoill' pluerizate cū uino purissimo opto
qlibz mane ieiuno. mir̄ sanat splēz. Ad egi
lopie. i. cānositatē palpebrarū ocul'. camoilla
omasticata 7 supposita mir̄ sanat. Ad fetidi
core mo supposita. purgat 7 sanat. Cō dolorē
7 grauedinē capis ex febre. olū camoill' frōte
ūge. stati mitigat dol'. Cō tineaz capis qd
greci uocāt exantimatos. camoillā uiridē
cū aceto ate 7 ex tali aceto ablue cap sepi' sī
aliq medicamētū cito sanabit. Ad dolorē ca
momillā ī olo decoctā. uiridē cōtrā 7 supposita
plage. pducit huores ū fuerūt collecti ex expel
foras. No. cū repit caoilla ī medicis. florū ei
itelligit. nō si adest dūdez acc dsiccaz. Cō
fluxū uētris ex frāte ul' debilitate uirtutis et
erit sīn febre. acc. camoill'. rosarū foliorū
fuctibz. al. 7 polligoniā. an̄. ʒ. i. fiat decoctio
ī aq pluuiali. ul' salte aq cisturnā. 7 patiēs re
cipiat fum' iferi'. pea ablue pedes 7 crura. mir̄
confortat egrū. fluxū ostigit. 7 dol' 7 iflactiōez
pedū placat.

Cotula fetida. herba est q multū similat camo
milla. s; feculēta ē ualde. camomilla uō
olens odorē bonū 7 suauis. Cotula aūt. ca
est 7 sic. mag quā camoilla. sūt enī due m
maneries. s; maior 7 minor 7 una ht effica
ciā. ualet precipue Cō strangurā 7 dissur
7 lapidē ī uesica frāgendā. uinū ul' aquā
decoctionis flor ei' potui dato mir̄ pfert. Ad
mestruā puocand 7 matricē mūdificandā
7 ex supfluitate hūiditatis dsiccādā. aquā
decoctiōis ei' sepius ablue uuluā. 7 etiā olo.
exea fcm cū bōbice itintus 7 ipositus mir̄
medetur.

Cotiliidon. herba ē q alio noie dr̄ saler. alii
cinbalaria uocāt. alii umbellici ueneris.
alii cepsa fordites. alii gessiinphalos. habet
folia rotundā 7 pingua 7 crescut sup tectibz 7
antiqs edificiis. virtutē ht friā. 7 hu. ī iiio
g. Cō strumas. herba cinbalaris 7 sepo ouiū
sīn sale. tantūdē fac emplm 7 calidū suppone
et uidebis effectū bonū. Ad pedignonez q uocāt
sponaia. oleū oliue cū ipa decoq addito mo
dico cere al. fiat ungt q utē. Colligi tpr e
stiuo 7 tpr ueris.

Cepa domestica

ysaac iqt. Cepe cal'e sūt ī iiij. g. ī ttio hūide. pp sui acumē 7 hūitate malos ī sto
gnāt hu. siti iflactiōez uētositatez. capis dol'. atqz ī saniā fac pp fumū as
cēdentez ad cebrū pruētez. uī assuescētes illud ī maniā cadūt 7 sopnia tibi
lia 7 melācolica cernūt. psti si cōstudie exeūtes ea mādūcauerit. Si aūt ppi
fi co opportet mādūcē calorez ī ducit. extenuat 7 icidit huōres crssos. 7 uisco
sos. ora. uenaz apit. v. 7 mēstrā puocā. oxtremiā mitigat. appetitū augmētat.
supficiē rarificat. Iocūdo sudorez 7 egionez puocāt. Vētrez irritat. cū suo calore
7 siccitate spma cū sua hūitate augmētat. malū tm̄ fac nutimētū. Cocta u con
mesta. nichil nutimēti corpori ēbuit. s; si elixet ī aq q piciettis ī alia recipit. dat
nutimētū bonū 7 plurimū maxie si cū pigssima coedit carne 7 cū bono odimēto
7 odorifero ōdiatur. alia aūt par nutiūt. sūt nociua colicis 7 calorez ūles hntibz
q si facīt cōsta frigē 7 hūiois medētibz ī sepit. elixet ea h 8 mō ōdiat eā cū aceto 7
obsomogaro. sūt q h m qz morsibz rabiosi remediū pstat. q si post coēstionez cor
uinū forte bibitū fuit. ualebūt ot morsū spētiū. psūt q eis q ueneno sūt ifecti
7 frās passiōēs hntibz ceu tyriaca mag.

Cepa domestica . ca . ē . i . s . i tcio gu . teste raxis auicenna uō dixit . cepa ca . ē . i . tcio . gu . hu . i . ii . hȝ aūt uirtutē uiscosā stipticā ⁊ uenenosā . undē cepā longā magis q̄ rotundā . ruba aūt ē stiptica plus q̄ alba . cruda ē uiscosa magis q̄ decocta . Cepa sepi comesta i flactionē ⁊ grauedinē capitis pducere solet . qa diascorides ⁊ alii medici nullo mō consentire uidētur . hȝ comesta magnā sitī īducit ⁊ mal' odorē oris tollit . uentrē ī remollit . Succ' ex foliorū ei' anū īunctū emoroid' dissiccat . Jt' succū ei' cū oleo admixto anū pūcto . uētrē laxat . Asclepius dicēs . cepa stōm confortat . bon' colorē reddit . appetitū icitat . Contra morsum canis . cepā cū melle trita ⁊ aceto . ul' cocta cū uino ⁊ melle ⁊ supposita ad modū eplastri mir' curat . Diascorides iubet . cepā cū sale ⁊ ruta simul' contritis mō fcō cataplā sup inguē . p t'bȝ diebȝ trasaptis mir' soluit . Jt' succus cū late mulieris amixto ⁊ auribȝ stillatum magnū adqȝ grauē dol' auriū tollit . Succ' ei' cū aq̄ bibit' subito morbo mir' iuuat . Jte succū cepe ī naribȝ īiectū humores nociuos a capite pūgat . Jt' supposite ul' potate tardātia menstruos pduc' ⁊ purgat . Jt' contrite ⁊ supposit' iflactioni pedū ⁊ duritiā sanat . ul' sepe supiūcto ex succo cepe ⁊ pinguedīs galle fcō ūgtō . Jt' si mane cū cepa dentibȝ psricab' ul' succu' eius ī ore teneat . dol' dentiū nūq̄ sentiet . Jt' cū pane comesta ulcerā oris sanat . Jt' ūgtū fcm ex succo ei' ⁊ pīguīs galle ualet ulceratioi auriū . Jt' succus ei' bibitu' ualet litargicos . Jt' comesta sopnū pduc' . Galien' dixit et adfirmat . Cepa nocet collericos . flematicos uō iuuat .

q. alio noie dr' . Scorna motone . alii uocāt ferrariā . Nascit' sup lapides p uia ⁊ extēdit' similat' nastūciū ⁊ īmeduc' sem simil' plataginis . uirtutē hȝ actrahēdi . expellēdi ⁊ cōsumēdi . Cō stragur' ⁊ diss' ⁊ lapidē ī uexica ⁊ ī cō opilatioē renū . epīs ⁊ splēis . succus ei' sepe bibito mir' medet' .

Culcasia ē radix plimū ī pte egipti nascēs . aliq̄tulū pōticitate acūme hn̄s . Vn mostrat' esse cā ⁊ sic . q̄si eluēt' acumen pcut' āmictit ⁊ uiscositas q̄ pu' lateter habeb[illegible] ēa apte . Jdeo ēēt duriq nutimēti . ē gn̄atiua . [illegible] sui pōticitate stōm cofortat . ⁊ uētrē cōstipat . tam si modrate comedat' bonū gn̄at nutimētū . ualet cō dissinterias cū uetositate ex pōticitate [illegible] .

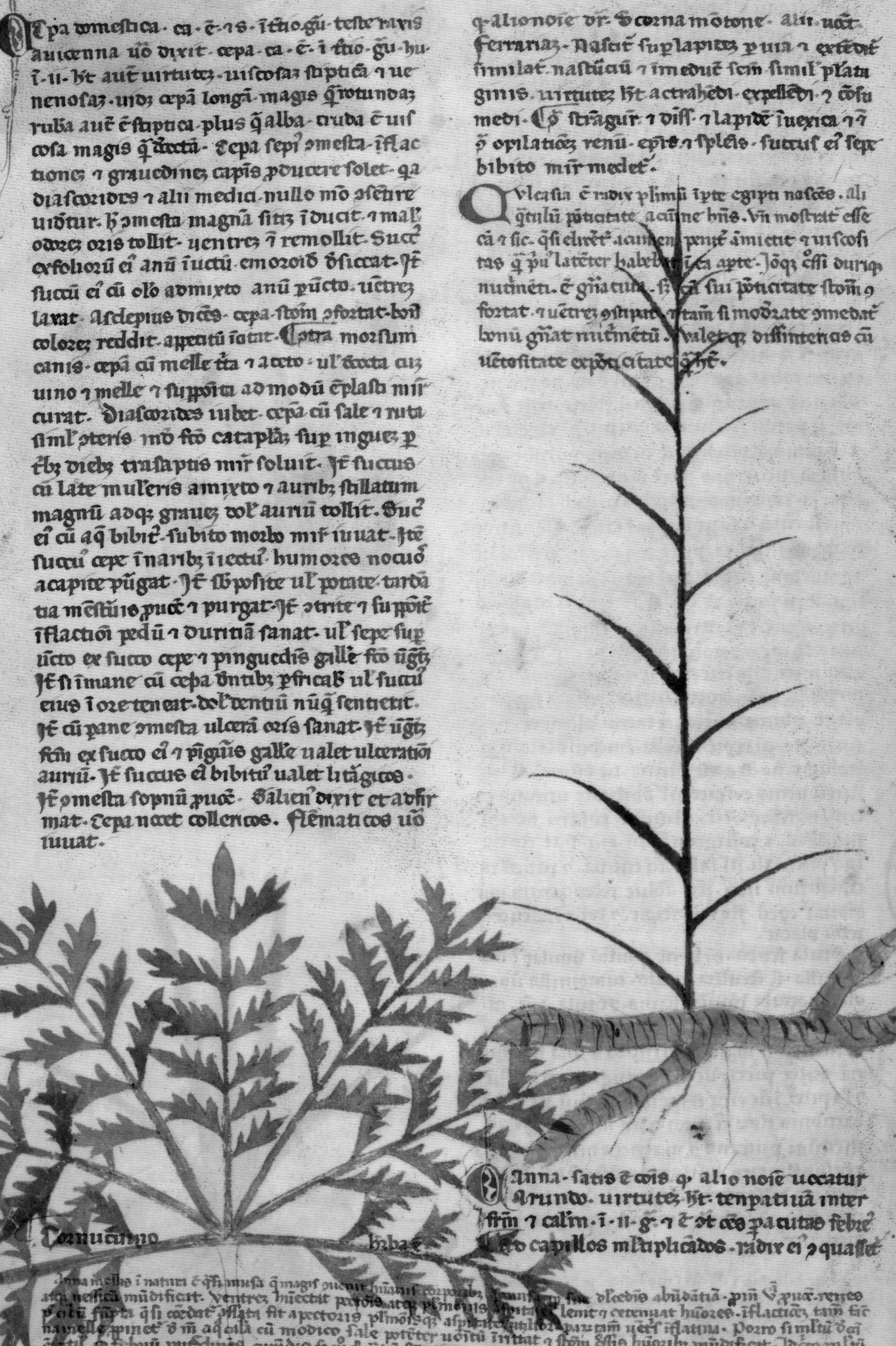

Canna . satis ē cois q. alio noie uocatur arundo . uirtutē hȝ . tenpatiuā inter frīm ⁊ calīn . ī . ii . g' ⁊ ē cō cos pacitus febre [illegible] capillos mltiplicados . radix ei' conquasset

Canna mellis i natura ē q̄si musa q̄ magis cōuenit humanis corporibȝ [illegible] dulcedis abūdātiā . pīn' [illegible] pduc' . renes atq̄ uesicā mūdificat . Ventrē mollit[illegible] pectoris atq̄ plmonis [illegible] lenit ⁊ ceteruat huōres . iflactioē tam fac p cibū sūpta q̄si cedat' cōflata fit a pectoris plmōis q̄ aspitatē [illegible] pax tam uētis iflatiua . Porro simultū dēci nanelle puncē d m aq̄ calā cū modico sale potēter uomitū īrritat ⁊ stōm cōsīs huōribȝ mūdificat . Jdeo mltū cōtil ad febriū pucdines curādis si m sup dō fiat .

et decoquat̃ i lexiua ⁊ i(n)d ablue caput. capillos m(u)ltiplicat ⁊ crescere facit. Ad sagittã u(e)l lãceã u(e)l spinã extrahendã. radix arũdinis .i. canna. ⁊ cũ melle tere ⁊ suppone. sine dolore exit.

Calendula. h(er)ba ẽ q(ue) alio noĩe d(icitu)r florũ oĩm mese alii. flores rancij. Nascit(ur) locis humorosis ⁊ etiã mulieres ponũt i ortis p(ro)pt(er) faciendũ corinã q(ue) h(abe)nt pl(ur)ros colores citrinos (et) rufos. ⁊ d(icitu)r calendula q(ui)a oĩz mensez gen(er)at florez. Ad menstruaz p(ro)uocad(um) succus calendul(e) bibit(ur) u(e)l h(er)ba cũ ouo (com)mesta u(e)l cũ farina facto crispelle. mi(ra)b(ilite)r menstr(ua) educit ⁊ etiã (con)fortat stõm. Ad dol(orem) dentiũ suc(cus) kalendul(e) ĩiectus narib(us) (con)t(ra)rio dolorez d(e)ntiuz tollit. q(ui)dã homo exp(er)imẽtator dixit. succus calendul(e) ⁊ aptano. ungat semet ip(su)m i nocte cũ uadit dormitũ. mane uo se i(n)ueniet traslatato i alio loco.

Ceterach

Ceterach. h(er)ba ẽ q(ue) nascit(ur) i parietib(us) ⁊ muris ⁊ etiã sup(er) lapidib(us) ⁊ antiq(ui)s locis. Ceterach (con)fiã ẽ ⁊ hu(mida) i .i. g(radu). uñ ponit(ur) i sir(upo) (com)posit(o) ad istãd. ualet ĩ p(ro) opilatiõez epatis ⁊ spleñs ⁊ p(ro) lõgã febrez. ualet ĩ acutis ⁊ pacutis febrib(us) ⁊ tertianariis ⁊ sinoc(hi)s. Ap(ro)l(i)uis etiaz extea f(a)c(t)os uulnera recẽtia mi(ra)b(ilite)r (con)solidat.

Candelaria.

Candellaria h(er)ba ẽ. cresc(en)s i magni mõtib(us) ⁊ maxĩe locis obscuris ⁊ humorosis. folia eius similat(ur) sigillũ salomonis ⁊ h(abe)t radix simil(em) candelã d(e) cera q(ue) uocat(ur) candellaria. h(ec) h(er)ba est termãtica. ualet paciẽte(s) p(ate)nt(ur) arthticã ⁊ sciaticã pass(ionem). ⁊ guttã fiã; i q(ua)cũq(ue) p(ar)tes corporis fuerit acc(ipe) totã h(er)bã totã cũ radicib(us) suis ⁊ tere cũ pinguedine s(er)pentib(us) ursine. marmotanee. ⁊ gatt(i) h(ec) oĩa simil bulliant(ur) ⁊ colẽt(ur) ⁊ fiat ung(uentum). d(e) quo ũgat(ur) sepi(us) ⁊ mi(ra)b(i)lis.

Consolida maior. h(er)ba ẽ q(ue) alii uocãt. Nagalicon. alio noĩe. Sinphitũ maius. Nascitur i ortis ⁊ locis humorosis ⁊ h(abe)t folia magna ampla ⁊ lõga. florez h(abe)t purpureũ. radix (e)st nigra intus uo alba ⁊ odorosa. radix colligit(ur) et cũ cultello (con)findit(ur). soli expõit(ur) ⁊ (con)siccatur ⁊ suspendit(ur) i saculo. p(er) iiii. annos s(er)uatũ i m(u)lta efficacia. Et uirtutez h(abe)t (con)glutinãdi ⁊ (con)solidandi.

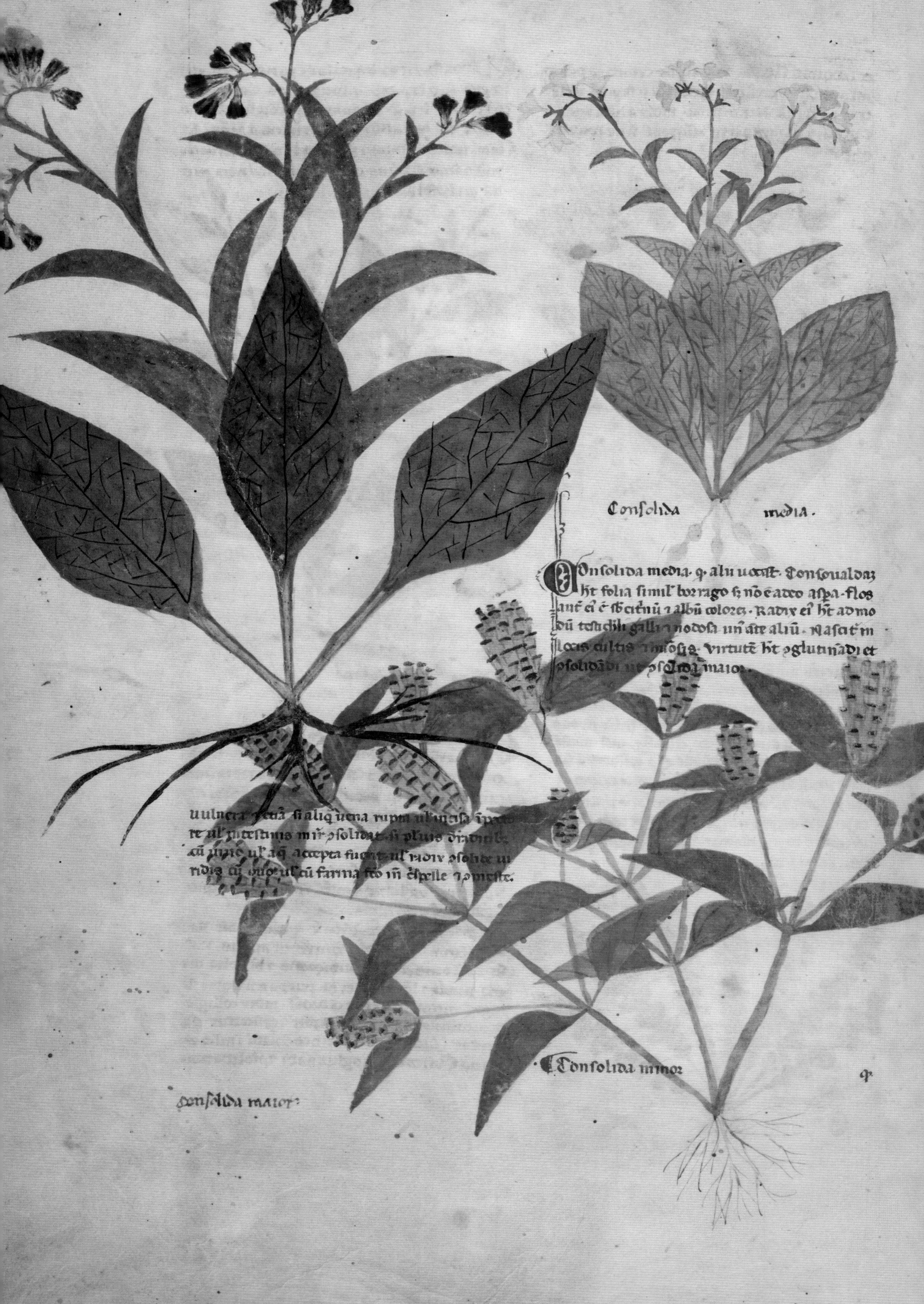

Consolida media. q. alii uocant. Consoualdaz
ht folia simil' borrago s; nō e adeo aspa. flos
aut ei ē sbcitnū 7 albū colorē. Radix ei ht ad mo
dū testiculi galli 7 nodosa unū ante aliū. Nascit in
locis cultis 7 umosis. virtutē ht ꝯglutinādi et
ꝯsolidādi ut ꝯsolida maior.

uulnera recentia si aliq uena rupta ul' incisa spe
te ul' intestinis mir' ꝯsolidat. si plus ꝯianibus
cū uino ul' aq accepta fuerit. ul' radix ꝯsolide ui
ridis cū ouo. ul' cū farina frō iñ ēspelle 7 ꝯmiscē.

alii uocant Citasana. alii uocant vinc toxicu(m). folia ei similat menta ortulana flos aut(em) ei h(abe)t colorez purpureu(m) simil' sticados arabice. Nascit(ur) iuxta fossas loco aq(uo)so (et) hu(m)oso. h(ec) (com)mesta i(n) c(om)pell' ul' cu(m) ouo. ualet (contra) uenenu(m) (et) o(mn)ez i(n)cisionez (con)solida(n)dam herba ipi(us) ui(ri)dez (con)tere (et) suppone uuln(er)i mi(ra)b(ilite)r mu(n)dificat acthit (et) (con)solidat. C(ontra) morsu(m) reptiliu(m) (con)trita (et) sup(er)posita mi(ra)b(ilite)r (con)fert.

Coronaria.

Coronaria herba est. simil' polligonie. folia ei(us) tu(m) s(cilicet) est alba (et) pilosa pili ut fuerit bonbix q(ua)re d(icitu)r Cotonaria. su(n)t due sp(eci)es s(cilicet) maior (et) minor. maior aut(em) nascit(ur) locis ma(ri)n(i)s sup(er) mo(n)tib(us) (et) lapidosis locis (et) e(st) uald(e) pelosa (et) alba. cui(us) uirtus e(st) ad uulnera (con)solida(n)d(a) s(ed) recentez uuln(er)a. plus ex cotonarie m(u)n(di)fica(n)s (et) sup(er) asp(er)sus sepe mi(ra)b(ilite)r (con)solidat. Cotonaria minor nascit(ur) locis solidis (et) i(n) planis (et) h(abe)t flore paruu(m) s(e)c(un)d(u)m citrinu(m) albu(m) q(uo)d paru(m) discernit(ur). h(ec) herba crescit ad plus i(n) q(ua)ntitate uni(us) palmi. maior aut(em) crescit i(n) q(ua)ntitate uni(us) bracchii. Cotonaria minor. virtutez h(abe)t mu(n)dificandi (con)fortandi (et) (con)solida(n)di. C(ontra) macula(m) siue obtalmia(m) ocul' succus cotonarie m(u)n(di) p(re)sse ul' cu(m) mell' attico. f(a)c(t)o collriu(m) ocul(is)q(ue) sepe d(i)stillab(itu)r mi(ra)b(ilite)r expellit maculam (et) sanat p(ro)b(atu)m e(st). fuit q(ui)da(m) expimentator q(ui) sic p(ro)bauit ea(m). accepit q(ui)da(m) gallu(m) ul' catulu(m) (et) punxit ei ocul' cu(m) aculo ul' stillo ut tot ocul' uid(e)batur crepati q(ui) nu(m)q(uam) uid(er)ent. (et) supposuit h(anc) herba (con)trita loco mu(n)do (et) b(e)n(e) cu(m) faxia obligauit (et) sic dimisit usq(ue) ad altera(m) diez. p(ost)ea. eleuauit faxia(m) (et) i(n)uenit ocul' p(er)fectissimi ut p(ri)(us) era(n)t. d(e) q(uo) mult(um) miratus fuit. p(ost)ea p(ro)bauit ad mult(i)s. Valet etia(m) ad ulcera (con)solida(n)daz puluis ei(us) sep(er) superpositus mi(ra)b(ilite)r (con)solidat. C(ontra) uitiu(m) ep(at)is et splen(i)s uinu(m) decoctio(n)is d(e)tur potui.

Gennerugio. herba e(st) simil' celidonia. q(uam) q(ui)da(m) uocant celidoniu(m) mascul' q(ui)a folia h(abe)t colorez simil' celidonie. florez gerit purpureu(m) i(n) medio s(ed) albidu(m). radix s(e)c(un)d(u)m nigra i(n)t(us) u(er)o alba cresce(n)s i(n) q(ua)ntitate duor(um) cubitor(um). Nascitur i(n) fossatis (et) locis obscuris (et) aq(uo)sis. i(n)uenies ea(m) p(ro)pt(er) florez. mense ap(ri)l' (et) madii. valet ...p(er)... (contra) oppilatio(n)ez ep(at)is (et) splen(i)s. ren(um). (et) uexic(e). (et) (contra) stra(n)guir(iam) (et) dissur(iam) (et) lapid(em) fra(n)gend(um). uinu(m) decoctio(n)is radicib(us) ei(us) potui dato. mi(ra)b(ilite)r med(e)t(ur). Valet etia(m) ad matric(em) col' (et) (contra) morbo regio. bonu(m) colorez (con)fert.

Cerasoru(m) due su(n)t

Cerasorũ siue ceragie· frutex arbor est satis
cõis cui duplex est maneries uidelicet ĩ
sapore ⁊ etiã ĩ uirtute· sũt eñ ceragie ualde
acre s. amari saporis ⁊ accetosi q. ad q̃bdã uocã
tur amarene· alii uocãt· Agriotte· q. tal' ge
rase ꝯpetũt esui ⁊ maxĩe collericis ⁊ iuenis
qa· fr̃e sũt ⁊ sicce ĩ· ii· gũ· appetitũ ĩcitãt et
stom̃ ꝯfortãt ⁊ expellit dol' ĩ eo q fit ex calõ· hu·
Sũt aũt alie ceragie dulci saporis ⁊ mlt̃e sũt
eñ maneries ĩ sapore ⁊ ĩ ĩ bonitate sic diuers
pire ⁊ similia. ceresie quãto dulciores ⁊ nig
sũt tãto meliores· sũt eñ· fr̃e· ⁊· hu· ĩ· i· g̃· Vir
tutez h̃t ꝯfortãdi ⁊ bonũ sanguinez g̃nandi
⁊ humiditatez restaurandi· ualet etiaz ꝯ dol'
epatis ⁊ morboregio· uentrez lavãt urinã p
uocãt sitiz reprimũt· bonũ colorez ꝯferunt
Nucleis eoꝝ acorticib; mũdatorũ ualet ꝯtra
stranguriã ⁊ dissũr ⁊ lapidez frãgendã pluis
eoꝝ cũ uino potui dato mir ẽ remediũ· Gũma
hui' arboris ualet ꝯ ĩpetiginẽ ⁊ s. pigine ⁊ uola
tice· cũ aceto sepe supfricata mir̃ sanat. pbe.

Caprago herba ẽ q. alio noĩe dr· Galligana
nascit' locis cultiuis ⁊ huosis· uirtutez h̃t
stiẽz ⁊ sic· Cõ fluxũ uetris aq̃ pluuial' decoctiõis
ei ablue pedes ⁊ tibia mir̃ ꝯstrĩgit ⁊ dolõr toll

Cõt ꝯ prurigine tibiarũ ex flãte salso· ĩ aq̃ pluuial'
decoquãt herba capraginez ⁊ plãtaginez ⁊ senatio
nẽ· pẽa cũ spõgia illiniãt.

Caprifoliũ siũ caprificus· herba ẽ q. alii uo
cãt oriolã· hũs folia simil' matrisilue s; ma
ior ẽ· qdã uocãt matrisiluã s; nictiut· qa matris
siluã ꝑducit fructus rubũ· caprifoliũ uõ nigrz
⁊ maĩ ⁊ foli magis uiridis· illã uõ albã· Nas
scit' ĩ uallib; ⁊ ĩ fossatis locis obscuris· cresc͡s
ĩ q̃titate duoꝝ cubitoꝝ ⁊ h̃t stipita sic arbor
florez citrinũ· sem̃ ĩmaturũ uiridez s. rubeuz
maturũ uõ fit nigrz ut sem̃ ꝑioĩe· succus
ipĩ' sem̃· ocul' ĩstillat' obtalmiã et macula mi
rab ꝯsũmit· Cõ oĩa uulnera sanãda folis
oriole ĩtegre suppoñ ⁊ liga ⁊ remoue directe
mane ⁊ sero ⁊ sanabit siñ aliquo unguẽto
qa ꝓbatũ ẽ admlt̃is q. acthit mũdificat ⁊ sanat.

De diagridio.
De dragagãto .i. uitolũ.
De dauco.
De draggãto.
De diptamo.
De deronici.
De dactillis.

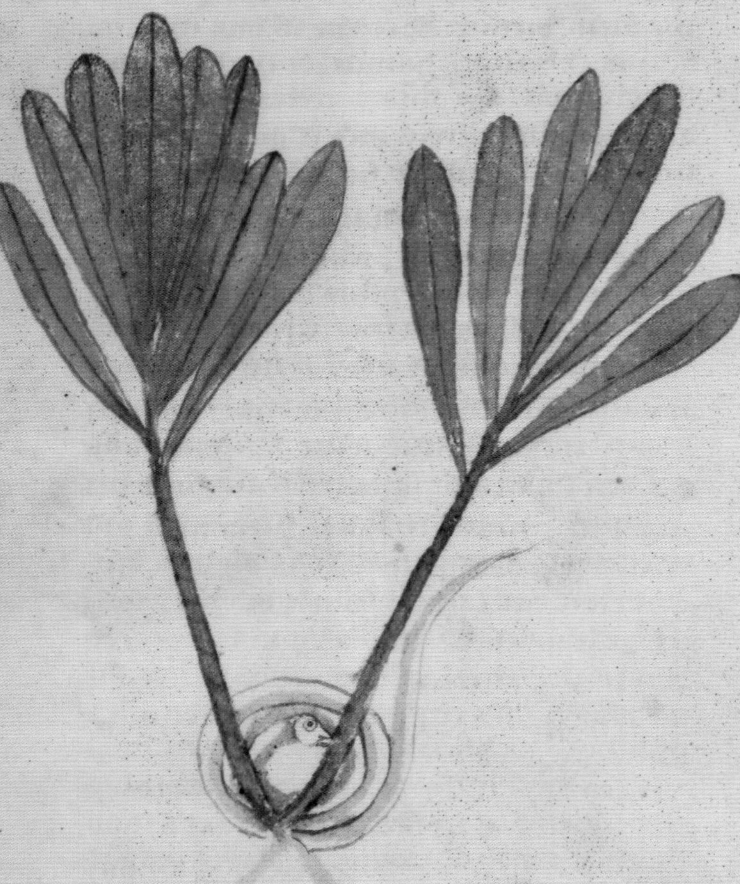

Diagridiũ . ca . ẽ . & sic . i . iiii . gñ . ẽ aut̃ succus
cuidã h̃rbe nascentis ĩ trãsmarinis ptib;
q̃ est spẽs titimalli & ĩ canicularib; diebus
rũpunt̃ . sũt enĩ . vii . spẽs . titimalli . susp
titates illius h̃rbe lac effluens ↄlligit̃ in
ũasis puis q̃ soli expoĩt̃ et ↄ̃siccatur & ĩ sbã;
diagridii trãsmutat̃ . cũ sit q̃nq; sophisticat̃
ex amistione alterius titimalli & tũc forti
us opatur . q̃ bonũ est & suauius laudabil̃ .
Sophisticat̃ ĩ q̃nq; ex amistiõe pl̃uis sbtil̃
colophonie q̃ pix g̃ca d̃r . q̃nq; ĩ frusta colof
fonie inter diagridiũ ũedunt̃ . p diagridio ẽ
aut̃ illd̃ elligendũ; q̃ albũ est ul̃ nigrũ; ul̃
sbnigrũ ĩ colore & ĩ sbã; p totũ clarũ & frãgi
bile; . licet colophonia faciliter frãgat̃ nõ tñ
adeo cito q̃ ĩ sb amarũ h̃t saporẽ; aliq̃ntul;
et nõ abhoĩnamile mĩl̃tũ; . d̃r eĩ; abhoĩnabil̃
ẽ mĩl̃tũ; ĩ saporẽ . sophisticatũ est ex alterius lac
tis admistiõe . d̃r etiã insipidũ uel nullũ ex ad
mistiõe colophonie . q̃ q̃ndã ptẽ; clarã; . q̃ndã
ũo obscurã; abiciendũ est . Est etiã elligendũ
q̃ cũ sputo h̃ũectat̃ ↄtinuo in albũ uertitur .
colorẽ; ad naturã lactis reddit . Grossum ĩẽ
elligendũ; . et ĩ medicis ponendũ . pl̃uis eĩ; ex
amixtiõe pl̃uis colophonie facile pot̃ sophisti
cari . et nõ tñ diu s̃uatur quã diu grossũ; .
Grossũ; eĩ; p . x . annos pot̃ s̃uari . ul̃ . xx . ĩ
medicinis pons̃tur . ad aciendũ q̃ ĩ pua
q̃ntitat̃ pot̃ acuere et q̃ nõ mĩl̃tũ uiole
ter duc̃ & nõ mĩl̃tã facit abhoĩnationem
nũquã p se dat̃ . Silicet nõ mĩl̃tũ sit uiole
tũ; . violentiã aut̃ ei repmimus . Nota
in dosi sufficiũt̃ . ii . ʒ . ad plus . ʒ . iii . ĩ . ʒ̃ . i . ʒ .
i . ℈ . s . S; tam̃ ei uiolentiã; reprimim̃ cũ;
aut̃ medicinã acuere uolueris . sic est faci
endũ; . acc̃ . scamonee . ʒ . ii . ul̃ . iii . pl̃ueri
ça sic noli cribare ñ terẽ sic alias spẽs q̃ a
ex sbtilitate sua & etiã; uiscositate uillis sto
maci adheret . et p̃ea dũ adhuc calidũ; est
ellt̃; ĩ pñat̃ pl̃uis scam̃ addito pl̃uere ma
sticis . in minori q̃titate parũ ul̃ ĩ media
q̃ntit̃e scam̃ . et sẽp p interuallũ . pon pl̃ueẽ
diag̃dii & ↄtinuo moueat̃ ne ĩ uiscetur . quia
si totũ pon eẽt̃ ĩ simul̃ p uiscaretũ . scam̃ ĩ calido
poĩt̃ . q̃ ex calore repẽ̃itur ei uiolentiã . S; h
tale ellt̃; nõ pot̃ dari añ . xv . dies . ul̃ . xx . uel
sic acc̃ . ʒ . i . ul̃ . ii . ul̃ . iii . ul̃ . iiii . scam̃ . hoc autẽ;
dico q̃a plus opatur . i . ʒ . ĩ calida regione & in
calido tp̃e quã duo ul̃ tres . ĩ fñã regiõe & ĩ frõ
tp̃e . pl̃uerizet . sbtil̃me . & pñat̃ in aqua ordi per
totã noctẽ; . cũ illa aq̃ acuatur medicina . uel
cũ colatura ipĩ aq̃ si tebil̃ sit . paties . Sic aut̃
possũt dari d̃licatis hoĩb; sine molestia . et ti
more & etiã; acute febricitãtib; . S; nota q̃ sca
moñ ĩ maiori q̃ntitate ẽ sic ponenda quã
alio mõ . aqua autẽ; sit tepida ul̃ fñã . Nec h
etiã ellt̃; dandũ est añ . vii . dies . ul̃ . x . S; q̃a
sepe cogimur dare medicinã . & oportet nos
acuere ĩ ipã die sic est faciendũ; . pl̃uerizã . ii .
ʒ . ul̃ . iii . diagridii s; nõ mĩl̃tũ sbtiliter . et pl̃
uerizã ↄ̃ mastic̃ et acue medicinã; . aliter ĩ
fit q̃ possit dari medicinã ĩ ipã die . acc̃ scamõã;
integrã & pone ĩ pasta ul̃ ĩ pomo g̃nato & cop
bñ . ut sic reprimat̃ eius uiolentiã; . et p̃ea
pl̃uerizetur et modicũ; mastic̃ addat̃ et in
acuatur medic̃ . Et no . q̃ . diagridio p̃nci
paliter mastix admiscetur . s̃ano . bdellium .
ttio . gũi . ar . Scamonea p̃ncipalr̃ pũgat .

coliaz. secũdario flã. 7 melia. No. q medicina
scam. nũquã d3 dari cũ frã aq. Ex frãte eiz aq3
pot scam ĩ infrigidari. ullis stoi. pot ĩ fieri potu
laxatiuũ. panis laxatiuũ. 7 fructus laxatiuus.
Et aũt fit claretũ. ul' nectar inter alias spe
cies poat. scam pluerizet etiaz addito mastix
poat ĩ pasta et coquetur et sic fit panis laxa
tiuus. Scamonea etiaz ĩtegra ĩ arborez fixã
nõ uersus terraz mĩttaz. s3 in medio. ponat
in qntitate. unĩ. l. ul. s. 7 pannus circuz p
natur. 7 cortex d sup et litargea. 7 bn ligẽt
plãta illa. humorositas. aut arboris et nut
mentũ sursuz todẽs efficaciaz scam secũ fert
ad ramos. Vñ fit fructus laxatiuũ. Et no. q ei
agrimoniũ cũ pricipalr purget colaz. sario flã.
et meliaz. cũ diuersis mediciis põituz diuisos
huores pricipalr purgat. Si eiz poat cũ oxi la
xatiuo ul' elĩo frõ ul' tfera sarac. principalr col
raz purgat. Si cũ blãca. ul' bndcã flã. cũ teodo
riton. anacardino. ul' dia sene. melia. Et no. q
diucius suatur qñ poit elio ofecto cũ melle.
q. p. ii. annos. ul' iii. ad plus. q põitur elio ofec
to ɔ sir. Et no. q si fricetur scam. cũ olo uiol
bn addito mastic. et actuat medic in ipõ die
ul' so pot dari.

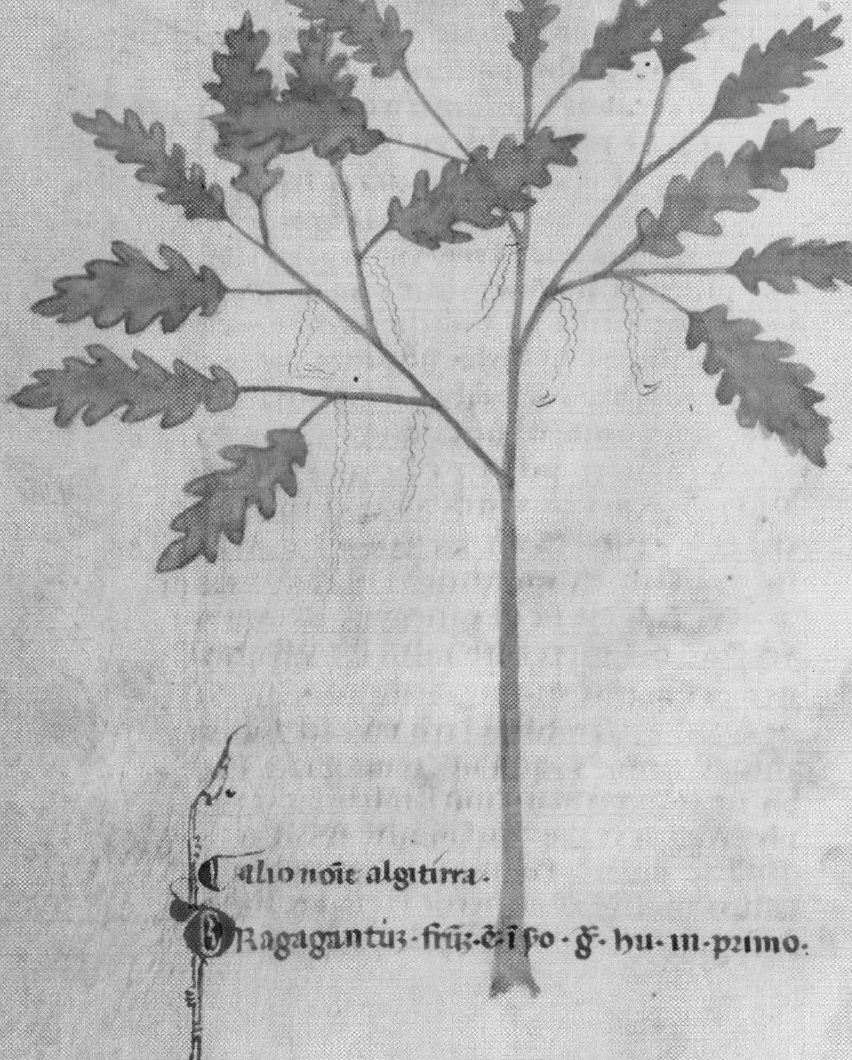

alio noie algitirra.

Dragagantũ. frĩz. ẽ ĩ sõ. g. hu. in primo.

est aut' gũi cuiusdã arboris. ĩ ultimaris ptibz nascẽ
tis. huitas eiz effluẽs exactiõe caloris ɔdẽpsatur
et ĩ gũi sba trasmutat. Eius tplex ẽ maneries.
s3. dragggtz albũ. q. meliũ ẽ si clar. fit et pur.
est ĩ sbrufuz 7 citinuz. q. nõ ẽ adeo bonũ. 7 ẽ
elligendũ. q. nõ est obscuruz. s3 clar. nec terre
stris admixtionez. Et no. q. abũ ĩ ssis mediciis.
sbrufuz ul' citinuz. incalidis d3 poi. p. l. annos
pot suari. Virtutez ht ex frãte ĩfrãndi et mundi
ficandi ex huĩtate. humectãdi exglutinosita
te. ɔglutinãdi. Cõ frĩtatez pectoris talis sit us.
aq. dragagãti decctiõis ordi et gũi. ar. dẽ patiẽ
ti. Cõ calidaz tussiz et siccã dẽ. aqua ordei.
decctiõis succi liqritie. i aq. dissolutuz fuerit
dragggtz p noctez unã. p pannũ exprimat cũ ui
scositate. ipiũ ɔficiat plius dragggti et fiant
pille. quas sb lingua teneat patiẽs. q ita di
solute trãsglutiat. Valet ĩ ɔ siti excaliditat
spũaliũ. Estz etiaz ɔfectuz ex duabz ptibz dra
gagãti. et etiaz liqritie. ualet ɔ predicta tussiz.
Cõ sitiz dẽ aq. ordi ĩ qua dissolutũ fuerit dra
gagantũ. p noctez etiaz fiat sir. ex aqua ordi
decoctiõis ipĩ dragagãti. ul' ĩ aq. dissolutũ fuit
q. pucient dat ĩ acutis febribz. dragggtz ĩ sb lig
sit teneat ualet. Cõ scissuras oris 7 labiorũ et
palati ulceratiões. ul' excoriatiões. ĩ aq. ro. dis
soluat dragggtz et p pannũ exprimatur cuz
glutinositate ɔficiatur plius amidi. intinga
tur penna et inliniat lingua. ul' labia sepi
cito curatur. Cõ ad faciez dealband et pannũ
supfluũ remouend ponũt mulieres dragggtz
in aq. ro. p noctez mane addita borace uel
cãphã ĩ parua qñtitate faciez freqñt illini
unt. Cõ callida apẽata ĩ pricipio exprimat
succus uermicularis 7 ĩ eo dragggtz dissolua
tur p noctez ĩ pannis intictus sup calida ap
posita in pricipio ponat. Eodez mõ ɔ arth
riticos dolores ex colica materia. Cõ ɔbusti
ones eodez mõ ĩ scda die ul' tcia. s3 ĩ prima
die ɔbustiones dbet poi actualit calida ĩ
actualiter frĩa. ut fumositates exalẽt. vñ qñz
primo ĩ ugim sapone. Cõ dissinteriaz ĩ aqua pl
uiali dissoluat et ĩ cateez decoqtur plius q dt
patienti. Eadez aq. aliqntulũ tepida p cristẽ
iniciat si sit excuitio ĩferiorũ ĩtestinorũ. si ex
uitio supiorũ dẽ succo plãtagis. ĩ quo p noc
tez iacuerit. et dissolutũ fuerit dragggtz. Et no
tandũ q. cũ poit ĩ mediciis. pse dbt teri. quia
ɔtrictiõi resistit. Si eiz cũ aliis spẽbz cũ teret
plus ĩ fumũ resoluetur alie species quam
dragagantum. ɔteratur. Vnde ĩ dia dragaz
to pse teruntur.

Daucus · ca · ⁊ sic · in · iii · g̃ · cuius duplex est maneries · s · daucus · creticus qui maioris ē efficacie · et dicitur creticus quia precipue i creta isula · repitur et daucus asininus quia cibus asinorũ ē precipue daucus asininus peretico ponitur · quia illius pura ē quantitas · Ht aut maiorez efficaciaz secundum herbã ⁊ florez · nullã aut modicã secundum radicez · Debet herba cũ floribus colligi cũ flores producit abiectis radicibus et i unbroso loco desiccari pãnũ seruat̃ in multa efficacia · Singul' annis renouet̃ ·

Virtutez ht dissoluendi · consumendi · ⁊ atenuandi ex qualitatibus suis · diuretica ex subtilitate substantie · Contra frigidaz asma ⁊ contra fiãz ⁊ hu · tussiz · detur uinũ decoctionis eius ⁊ ficuũ siccarũ · Contra frigidaz reuma sattellet capitis expluere facto ex ipsa herba · bene pri calefacto · Contra dolorez stomachi ex frigiditate ul' uentositate ⁊ contra stranguriã ⁊ dissuriã · colicã ⁊ iliacaz passionez · detur uinũ decoctionis eius · herba etiã ipsa i multa quantitate i uino ⁊ oleo cocta sup locũ dolentez ponatur · Contra stranguriã et dissuriã ⁊ uitiũ lapidis detur uinũ decoctionis seminis eius ⁊ saxifrage · Contra opilationez splenis ⁊ epatis ex frigida ca · ⁊ ydropisiz · fiat sirupus ex succo feniculi · decoctionis eius · Contra duritiez splenis ⁊ epatis ponatur herba i multa quantitate i uino ⁊ oleo ⁊ maceret̃ ibi · p · x · dies · decoquatur i · x̊ · die quousque redigatur i olim · exprimatur · herba bene ⁊ colet̃ colatura ponatur ad ignẽ et i ponatur cera · et fiat cerotũ contra duritiez ⁊ sc̃

...alia aperata · satis competẽs est ·

Dragantuz · i · uitriolũ · ca · ē ⁊ sic · i · iii · g̃ · sunt autez maneries · iiii · s · indicus qui i india reperitur · ⁊ est albũ ⁊ arabicũ quod in arabia reperit̃ · ⁊ est citrinũ ⁊ ciprinũ quod in ciprio isula reperit̃ · et ē uiridis coloris ⁊ tercia frãcigena · s · acetramentuz · quod i gallia reperit̃ · Illud ē elligendũ quod uiridi coloris est ⁊ claruz · Est aut̃ quoddã humosuz ⁊ terreũ quod debet frangi et gutta que interius reperit̃ debet poni in mediciniis · Et nota · quod quedã uena terre ē per · x · annos seruat̃ · Virtutez ht dissoluendi ⁊ consumendi · ⁊ corrodendi · Contra fistulã talis sit usus puluis ipsius cũ duabus partibus farine fabe fracte · cum capitello ul' sapone gallico conficiat̃ · ex quo licinium i tantuz · fistul' imponat̃ · os fistule elargat̃ · quod etiã fracta ossa si sint competenter possũt extrahi · Contra polippũ stuellũ ex apostolicon ul' ex bõbice · aqua salsa madefactũ pluere eius aspsũ naribus imponatur · Ad carnez supfluã corrodendã · solus puluis supponat̃ · Contra fluxũ sanguinis ⁊ naribus puluis ipsius combusti cũ pluere carte combuste et pluere mastic · conficiat̃ cũ succo sanguinarie · cũ quo lapis emathites fuerit cotez fricat̃ fuerit stuellũ in fine naribus i ponatur · Sic uratur dragantum in testa sicca sine liquore ponat̃ sup carbones et sic urat̃ donec uertant̃ i nigrũ colorez · Contra profluuiuz mulierũ fiat suppositoriũ ex eisdez confectis cum succo plãtaginis cũ quo fricatus fuerit lapis ematithes · Ex eisdez fiat suppositoriũ contra emoroidas fluentes eas constringit ⁊ i flatis desiccat · et conficiat̃ cũ succo tassi barbassi · Et no · quod dum comburit̃ calor eius suffocat̃ · extinguit̃ et i frãtur · unde cũ siccitate constringit · dragãtuz i amixtionem aliorũ denigrat ·

Diptamus

Diptamus. ca. 7 sicce. 9plexiois ē i scdo. g.
herba ē cui radix sili noie appellat. alio
noie dr. arthis. i locis calidis. 7 i fris et lapi
dosis precipue repit. cui folia similat fraxini.
radix collecta et exsiccata. p. ii. annos sua
tur. i multa efficacia. Eligitur q interius ht.
solida. sbaz 7 no pforata. q etia ofragit non
pluericat. Virtute ht osumendi 7 actrahendi
uenenu. Co morsu uenenatoru aialium
7 ppt uenenu. ipa herba otrita suppat. 7 suc
in uino dt. Co puluis ipius oficiat cu succo
mente 7 sr poatur 7 i potu dt. No q mitri
datu pot fieri. hns uirtutes tyriace. et pp pro
batioez addito pluere. diptami. costi. genti
ane. aristolgie logie. 7 addito pluere ui
trioli. ut denigretur sz ad plus no ualet.
nisi p duos annos. Co stranguria 7 disu
dt uinu decoctiois pluis ei. Co sim asma.
ficus sicce 7 uue passe bulliat i uino forti co
lentur. 7 colatura addat ʒ. 5. pluis diptai
mltu ualet si sit difficultas i spirandi ex
frigite. Co ad mortuu fetu 7 secudinaz educe
da. fiat iniectio pluis ei cu succo herbe ipi
ul arthmisie. ul fiat suppositoriu ex plue
eius ofecto cu succo herbe ipi ul arthmisie
Co epilētia pluis ei cu plue castorei. cu
succo rute p os dt. Et colatura p nares in
iciatur. paleticu excitat ofectioe cu sota inu
gatur 7 fricetur.

Deronia. ca. 7 sicc. i iii. g. herba ē q simi
li noie appellat. sit tn radix sbalbida parue
qi nodose admodu polipodii. Co uol dissolui
et grossa uentositate maxie i uulua osistite
placat. 7 morsus reptiliu curat. ideoqz qda
miscet eas magis antidotis ot uenenu osisti
tib. similit ualet galiga.

Dactilis. ca. sut 7 hu. i 1o 7 2 g. grossi sang gnati
tiui 7 difficiles digestioi. sicubz tn siccis di
gestibiliores. magqz urina puoc. si illud assue
scentes epis ac splinis opilatione duritia effi
ciez patiut gingiuis. atqz detibz sut nociui do
lorez i ore stoi faciut. Quaru tn actiōes f regioni
uarietatez. Q dā ē i fria qda i cala nascit regioe
alij u i medioc. cala hntes regioez sut dulcissimi
7 uiscosi. p uu pan nutiut cito ē digerut 7 uētres
huefaciut pl i cetis opilatioez epis ac splis 7 no
cumētu capi oriqz stoi faciut. Rursu q i fria sunt na
scut. i sua echitate poticitate 7 siccitate pmanet.
qz cetis sut sicciores 7 min oibz sut nutiti. ac
duri ad digerendu. tardiqz o sto ascēdendi. Cetie
tn aplius ofortāt. In medioc nascentes regi
onem. licz i pfecta ostent maturitate. tanta
illud ab est siccitas. ubi i maturitate seruari
queant. qm i eis queda liquoris supfluitas ē
... replēt dccopia crudoz huoz. q sut
... diuturne 7 prolice febris. ad dissol
... inobedientes.

Endiuia. fri. e. et sic. i. primo. g. q alio noie scariola dr. teia et folia. 9petūt medicīe. folia i usu abrorum. Secdm radicem nullam ħt uirtutem. folia uirida sūt maxīe efficacie sicca nullius aliqtulā ħt amaritudinem et ponticitatem un sūt diuretica. vn̄ uirtutem ex s'bāte ħnt alterandi et 9fortandi un̄ ualēt 9t opilatiōem epatis et splenis ex colica cā. C 9 yctericia simplicem et duplicem t'tianā. et 9 opilatiōem epis calfactionem et calā apeata. 9 oīa predicta ualent elixe ul' crude 9mesta. Succus etiā cum aq calida datus ualet. Succus etiā cū cū t'fera sarac. cala dt. C 9 oppilatiōes predictas et sinplicem et duplicem tertianā. mā. existente digesta et 9 calfactiōem epis et mar. C 9 yctericiā croceā ualet. Syr' etiam fiat ò lica tis ex succo ei. S; qa ò succis fit turbolentus fiat sic et ita ò oībz alus succis fiat clarus bulliat succus scariol aliqtulū. pa residat q feculētū ē residet. q clarū sr natat. Cola p pannū suauiter et n̄ exp'mas ne p'ithetur succus et ex illa colatura q uidr aq ee addito zucco fiat sir. Si clariorem uis face pon albumē oui. 9 febrem et yctericiam ualet hic sir. et calorem epis quē siuolucis face laxatā i fine decoctiōis. sir plus s'btil'sim opti reubri p'oat. et cola si placet p'p'e amaritudinem aliqtulam s; nō est tāte efficacie qnte ē sinō coletur. C 9 febres fcās i colra i. iiii. ul' vi. die. digesta. m̄. dt. adirem etiam ualet si succū ei cū reubro dt cū calida. C 9 febres ex apeātibz et ad saniem etiam p'gātā ualet sir' iem. et succus ei et t'fera sarac cū calida. C 9 calorem epis et cala apeata. ualet etiā h'ba 9trita et sr posita. adirem ualet sir epithimat'. No. q. cū nō huīs folia h'be. seīn cogmus i aqua prius bn̄ tritum. q'nq; p'mus seīn cū succis aliqbz curando passionem.

Epithimū. ca. ē. et sic. i. iii. g. est aute

herba precipue i locis calidis · crescens herba
aute̅ co̅atedit q̃n q3 circa thimu̅ · s · quadam
herba et flos ei̅ inde di̅ epithimu̅ q̃i sup̃ cre
sce̅s · flos aute̅ 7 no̅ herba · in medicis ponit̃
p̃ quo po̅it̃ q̃n q3 · cuscute · cu̅ p̃ducit flores
flores colligunt̃ · ht aute̅ uirtute3 purga̅d
principaliter melãcoĩa3 · s3 cu̅ aĩo flã non p̃se
ponit̃ · s3 p̃ueniente̅ po̅it̃ i medicis · pu̅gan
tib3 mela̅3 · C̃ ꝯ quarta̅3 fiat ꝺecoctio i aqua
ʒ · i · s · epithi · 7 m̃lta ꝺecoctio̅ 7 i tali po̅at̃ · ʒ · ii ·
lapis laçuli ul̃ armenici · et digesta iiii · ꝺe̅.
patie̅ti · m̃lti librantur · no · q̃ eade3 ꝺecoctio
et purgatio ualet emoroiꝺ ex melãco̅ sa̅gui
ne · C̃ ꝯ melãco̅ica̅ pas · ꝺe̅ uinu̅ ꝺecoctionis
ei̅ · C̃ ꝯ sincopi fia̅3 ex uentositate̅ mela̅3 fiat
sir̃ · ex aqua ꝺecoctio̅is sene 7 epithi · C̃ solus i
ei̅ ut dicit ꝯst̃ · sple̅ cataplãta splene3 exte
nuat̃ eade3 i uino et olo̅ ꝺecta 7 cataplãta ·
stra̅gur̃ soluit ·

Enula · ca · e̅ · i fine · iii · g̃ · hu · i p̃rincipio
cui̅ duplex est maneries · s · ortulana · et
capana · q̃ maioris est efficacie · s · radices co̅
ligu̅t̃ · colligit̃ radix i p̃ricipio estatis · soli ex
siccatur ne hu̅itate ꝯru̅pat̃ · Radix in medici
nis ꝺe̅bet po̅i no̅ herba · p̃ bie̅niu̅ pot̃ s̃uari · ht
aut̃ uirtute3 leniendi · 7 mu̅dificandi ui̅ uale
ꝯ neruos ex fri̅ate i doignatos · C̃ ꝯ dol̃ sto̅i ex
fri̅a · ca · ul̃ uentositate ꝺe̅ uinu̅ ꝺecoctio̅is radic̃
ul̃ pl̃uis radic̃ · C̃ ꝯ dol̃ sp̃ualiu̅ ex fri̅a ca̅ ul̃
ue̅tositate ꝺe̅ uinu̅ ꝺecoctio̅is ei̅ iuxta illud
Enula ca̅pana reddit p̃cordia sana · C̃ ꝯ fri̅a3
tussi3 · ualet ide3 uinu̅ pl̃uis eius cu̅ puluer̃
cinamo̅i i ꝺe̅licatis soluit uentre̅ et dolore̅
sp̃ualiu̅ herba tota i uino et olo̅ ꝺecta ꝯ folli̅
si ha̅be̅t pot̃ et cataplãta yliaca3 · 7 colicam ꝯ
stra̅gur̃ solu̅ · C̃ ꝯ fri̅3 asma ꝺecoq̃t ordu̅ optie̅
ut fiat spissa aqua sic̃ otisana et cu̅ aqua
illa ꝺecoq̃tur optie̅ pl̃uis radic̃ 7 ꝺe̅ patie̅ti.

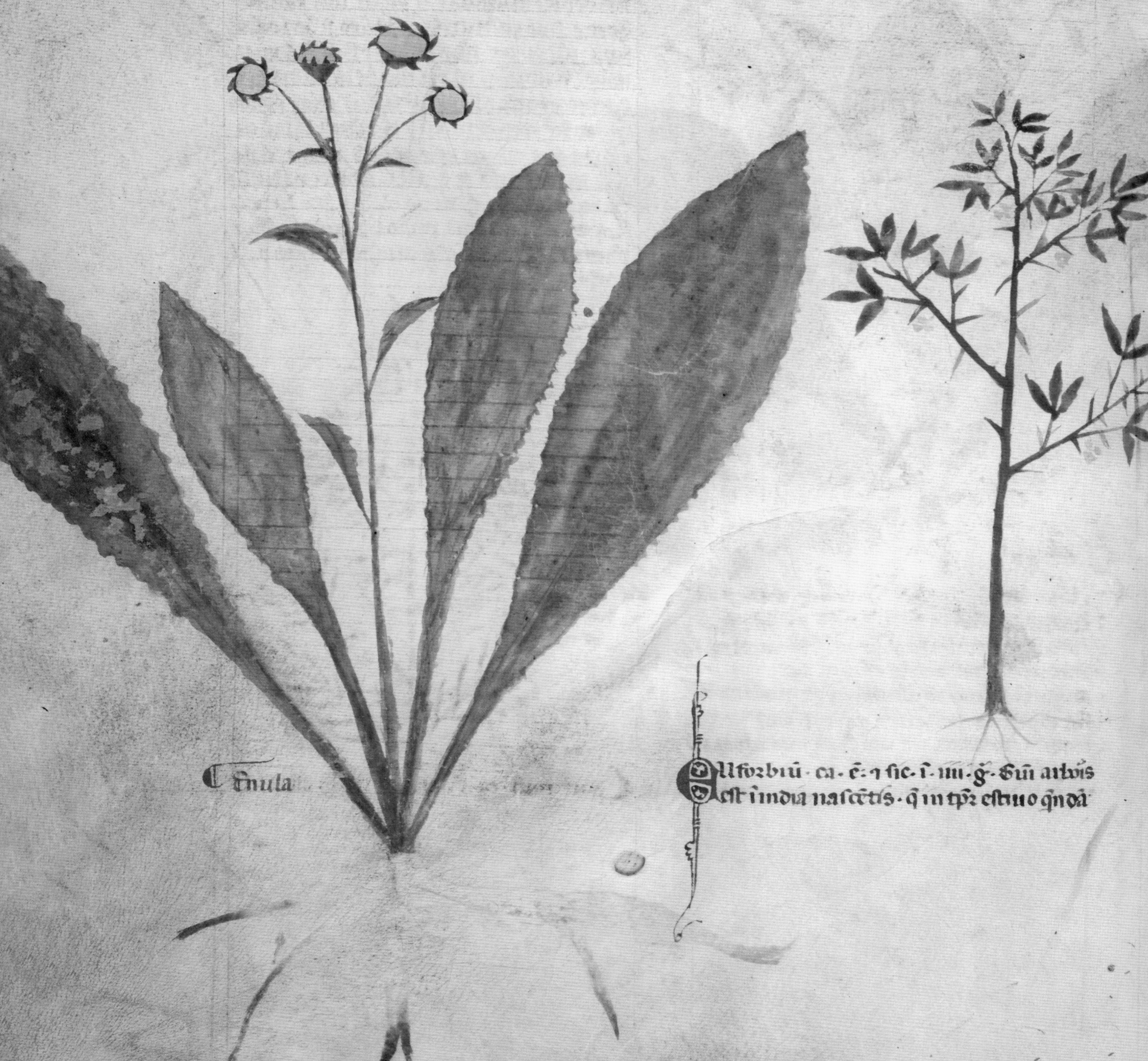

Euforbiu̅ · ca · e̅ · 7 sic · i · iiii · g̃ · succu̅ arboris
est i india nasce̅tis · q̃ in tp̃r̃ estiuo q̃nda̅

emittat quositate; q circa arbores agitur tinata; i sba euforbii trasit. q da ps ista cadit et tre ht amixtioe; q minutum est n est bonu qa tre ht admixtione. Eligedu est q grossu; claru et puru in colore 7 in substacia sbrufu; e ul citinu q sb albidu est. p. xl. annos pot suai. minutu qnq; so phisticat. examixtioe draggti rubi. Virtu te; ht dissoluendi actrahendi laxadi osu mendi et principalr fla. sario melia; et artemotis ptib; sartti 7 poda. capis 7 alus. o q libet arthtica sciatica 7 podag. et tirag; exfrate. 7 ylliaca pas. actiat bu dca. ex. iii. 3. ul. ii. euforbii. 7. iii. bdellii. ul mastic et dt bu dcu cu aq dcoctiois seis fen. ul radic eius. 7 o yliaca pas. iniciat p cristere cu; aliquo liquore maxie ualet si predce pas exflatico huore fiat. Co cephalea 7 epil. et apoplxia exflatico huore pdicto mo actiat yeralogodio ul blacha 7 dt patieti. ad psua tioe; ul p accessioe. Co litargia; puocatur strnutatio cu pluere eius narib; imisso. ul ex plue eius i panno i panno sbtili et raro posito 7 pcusso ad nares cu digito. Qnq; au no possut excitati. un oficiat ei pluis cu olo ro. et iungat pena 7 nares mugat. ectius bu i profundo. Eode; mo pot pucui strnuta tio. epil. et apopletic. i accessioe ipa. Co litargia et epil fiat iungtu. ex pluere eufo bii 7 castorei. cera. 7 olo. m. ul salte; coi. epil. a psteriori pte iungat. tota spina. litargic ab radat obcipitiu 7 iungat bn fricado fortiter Et ad memoria recupanda fiat eltm ex du obus ptib; ligni al. 7 cassie ligne. et tcia pt euforbii et anacardoru et melle dt qnq; in pua qntitate. Ca ide; aliud sit us radat occipitiu; et abluat bu cu uino calo pea sca rificetur 7 statim fit ofricatio ex dcoctioe eu forbii. 7 iteriori sbe anacardoru i sucto pi gani. Co asma ex frate dt euforbiu cu mo dica mastice in ouo sorbili. Cot uitiu spl nis actiat diasene ex euforbio addita ma stice et dt precedetib; tn mlti digestiuis. Co uete; yctericia; fca; ex opilatioe epatis. ii. 3. euforbii. in ouo sorbili dati ualent. pluis euforbii carnem supflua; rodit.

Eupatoriu. ca. e. i. i. g. sic. i. ii. ide; est q salvia agrestis. uiridis maioris e ef ficacie q siccata. ualet aut ot uniuersale tal sit usus. Castoreu bulliatur i succo salue agstis. 7 succo caulis agrestis et dnt pluerisata ponatur sb lingua fiat etia; gar garismus ex aqua dcoctiois istaru spey pce dente tn minutioe d duab; uenis q sunt sb lingua. Valet 7 saluia agstis his q in febrib; pdidrut uoces 7 ydropicis et yc tericis si fiat ex opilatioe splenis 7 epis talis sit usus. 3. i. saluie agstis bibat i. 3. s. suci appii. 7 dt tal dcoctio. Cot lubricos nu dei psicos tnti osucto saluie agrestis ualent.

Eupa torium.

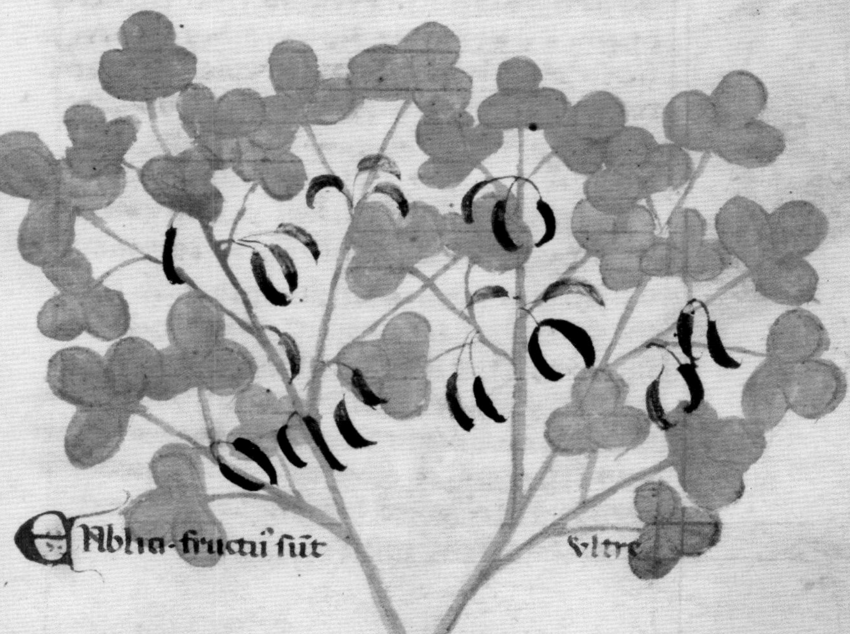

mannis ptib; crescentis. Purgat fleuma et
melacoia. un valet ot egritudines ex tali
bus huorib; puenientes. ut i quartana ad
ponitur ʒ. s. i decoctione valet ot emoroidas
sipulius distenpet cu succo tassi barbassi su
posito. Cot casuz capillor. pluis eblici cuz
pl'uere allees distenpent i oleo i iungat ca
put. Sz cadut capilli ex asp'itat porroru
ex caliditatis ml'tu valet qa curat poros.

Epatica. fra. e. i. sic i primo. g. Est aut quoda
herba crescens i aquosis locis i precipue la
pidosis. minuta hns folia. tre et lapidib
adherentia. Quato aut maiora ht folia
tato melior et dr epatica q epati precipue
e iuuatiua. Virtutez ht i frigidadi i est diu
retica. ex sbtilitate sue. unde valet. C opila
tionez splnis i epis ex ca'la. ca. et epis calo
rez i icteritia. aqua decoctiois ei. Si r fcus ex
aq decoctiois ei addito reubaro. i fine decoctionis
optim e o veteriaz. Ro. q. i oib; aquis ergb;
fit sir ot calefactioez dz poi epis epatica mi
tuz eiz iuuat. C ot callida apeata trita poatu
i principio opat eiz prepcussi oez.

Es. ustu. ca. e. i sic. i. iiii. g. alio noie. Cal
cucecaumenon. appellat. Artificio quodaz
coaptat. et oburit ut psit pl'uerizari. In olla
fcra d creta ponat es rubuz illud. s. q a fabris
fabricatu est et i fornace. Vbi fit otinuus igni
poatur. p. xx. dies pea pl'uericetur. In ex coctio
ne eiz nimia augmetat ptes terestres et dimi
nuuntur aquos. Virtutez ht dissoluedi. osu
mendi. i melacoici hu. pugadi et extenua
di. un ouenient poit i eplis extenuatiuis

ut apostolico i eplastis o splnez. carnez supflu
az orrodit. C o fistulaz osiciat pluis ei cu melle
ul cu sapone spatarenti. ul gallico tecta i tenta
poat os fistul' elargat. et etia curat. C o polip
puz fiat stuellu d apostolico ul cerocto sp'sp
gatur pluis ei et narib; i mittat. C o disto
lorationez ex hudatia melic huoris i splni
ul ex crudis huorib; i isto ex diuturnitate tpri
tal' sit usus. pluis eris usti. decies ul' plures
ad modu lapis laculi lauetur i det o succo
feni ul' oximelle i aq. cal'a. melacoicu huore
purgat sz violeter i angustiose p supiora.

Cucumer agreste

Electeriuz. ca. e. i. sic. i. iiii. g. aliud est
lacterides sut eiz cataputie. aliud electe
rides qr cucumer agstis. alio noie dr sicci
duz. aliud elethriuz. Electeriuz e fructus
cucumeris agstis i canicularib; dieb; fruc
tus cucumeris agstis olligutur et oteru
tur succus expressus soli expoit et d siccat.
C Quidaz ad ignez decoqut succu cuz melle

fere ad ↄsũptiõẽ; succi · et ĩ modũ elli dãt laxat
p̃ inferiora ⁊ supiora · p · ii · ãnos ĩ mlt̃a effica
tia ſuatur · pp̃a ↄ̃ficit uirtus ei · h̃t aũt uirtu
tez pũgãdi p̃ncipalr̃ · fla · ſb̃ · melia · ¶ Cõ ar
thriticaz pod · et iliacã · pass · plinnger electe
rii ʒ · ⁊ mirra · ãn · ʒ · ii · ⁊ fiunt bñ cũ olo · ro.
dnt pp̃a cũ succo feñ calido · ĩ ill̃ tñ pass · ſcedat
aliq̃ cristẽ mollitiuũ · et pp̃a illð ex aq̃ mal
uarũ olo ⁊ melle · ⁊ · ʒ · v · ul̃ · vi · electẽi addito
mastic cũ aq̃ · ca · herba ip̃a si h̃ri pot̃ · aliq̃tu
lũz ↄterãt · ⁊ decocta ĩ uino ⁊ olo loco dolenti
sr̃ põita · striãgur̃ · yliacã · arthriticã · pod · sbue
nit · ¶ Ad mestr̃ · puocãdaz pluis electẽi co
ficiat cũ olo ni̊ · ul̃ cõi · et bonbix ĩticta sup
põat · ¶ Ad ap̃a ca maturãda et rũpenda ·
electẽi · ʒ · vi · ul̃ · v · cũ faĩna ordi ↄficiat cũ
uitello oui et suppoat · Jtez ualet ↄ̃ calã ap̃
temata · s; uid ne sit mltũ calida nec ↄ̃lect
põi ĩ p̃ncipio · ¶ Ad ap̃a rũpenda optimuz
fit ruptoriũ · ex electerio ⁊ terbentina · ¶ Ad
uermes auriuz ↄficiat electeriuz ĩ q̃titate
g̃norũ · v · cũ modico aceto · et tepid ĩfudat ·
¶ Ad oẽz dol̃ stõi ex sr̃a · ca · inũgatur ex ↄfec
tione ellectẽi et aceti · ¶ Ad lentigines faci
ei · ⁊ oẽz supfluitatez ei remouendã · acc · ce
rusaz · et canphaz · ⁊ electeriuz in q̃titate il
lorz duorz ↄficiat cũ aceto ĩ modũ ungti ·
ĩ mortario plũbeo · et cũ pistello plũbeo et
põat ĩ uase uitreo · p · xv · dies et p̃ iteruz
ĩ eodez mortario · et predicto pistello moue
atũ addito aceto si durũ fit · et ĩungatur
facies oẽs abstergit ⁊ panũ et lẽtigines ·

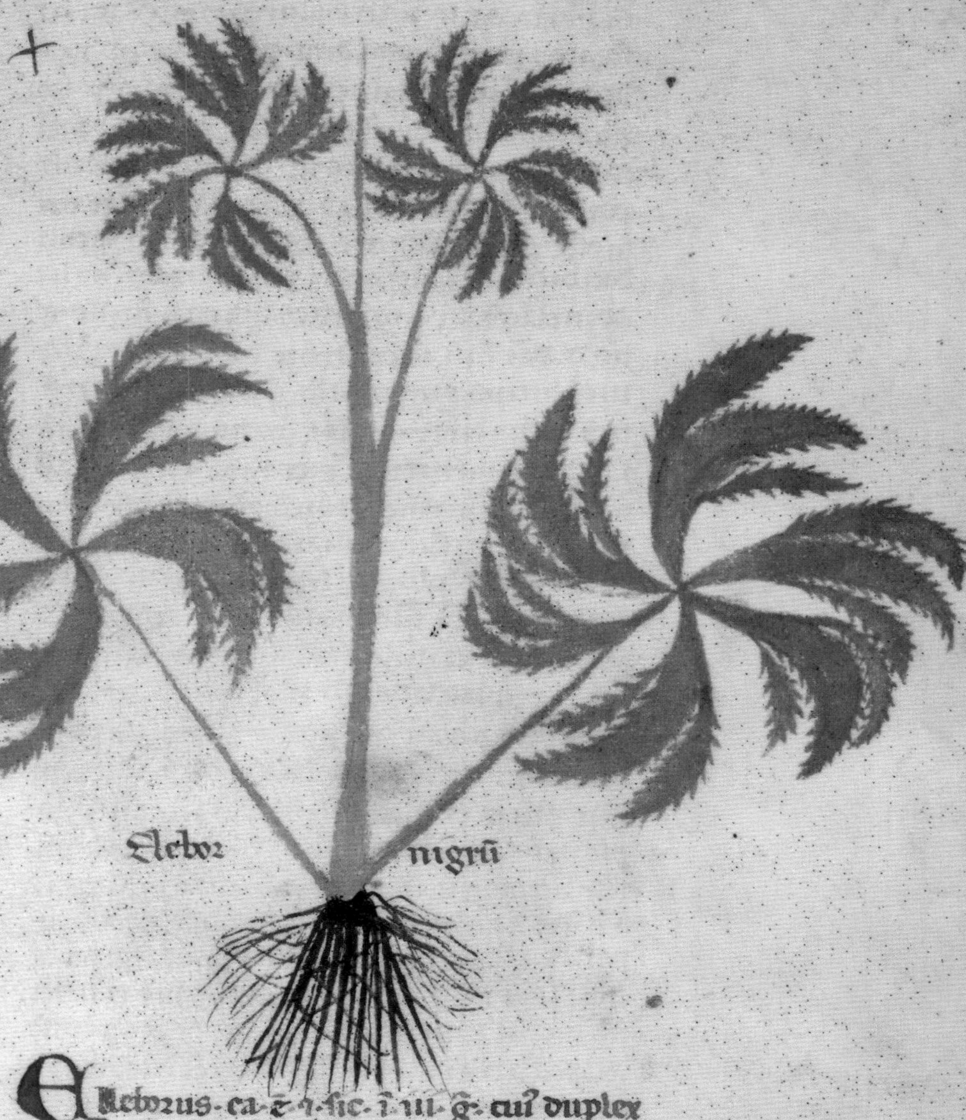

Elleborus · ca · ẽ ⁊ · sic · ĩ · iii · g̃ · cui9 duplex
est maneries · s̃ · albus ita dĩus q2 radices
h̃t albas · ul̃ q2 albos purgat · hu · s̃ · flaticos
et niger q2 nigras h̃t radices ul̃ q2 nigros
purgat · hu · s̃ · melãcolicos · cui9 ĩ medicinis
repit̃ ei receptio radix dz põi · antiq̃ ĩ pũga
tioib; utebãtur · ello sic nos nũc scamonea
corporea · ẽr̃ tũc robũstiora · violentiorez
medicinã · siue molesti pati poterãt · Nunc
uõ ↄ̃bilia ei uiolentiaz nõ sbstineret · vñ
cũ sũma cautella danda est medic̃ · q̃ Rz ell̃
borũ cũ ĩueitur · Rz elli sinpliciter · albus dz
ĩtelligi ⁊ albz dz põi · q̃ utrinq; · Rz elli al̃ ⁊ ni̊
utrinq; dz põi q2 utzq; purgat · hu · Nõ q̃ ↄ̃
bili ⁊ h̃nti pect̃ strictu; ⁊ macilentũ nõ dz
dãi q2 uõitũz puocat ⁊ p̃ inferiora ⁊ p̃ supiora
purgat · forti uõ ⁊ nõ facile mouenti pot̃
dari · ¶ Cõ quotidianaz ↄ̃ flãte naturali et
flãte uitreo · arth · pod · et ciragraz · valet
oximel fcũ ↄ̃ radicib; elli albi · fiat autez
oximelle · sic · pp̃ora radices feniculi ul̃ ra

phani cum esula et immicte radices ellebori al
bi. terra effossa circa radices imponantur caue
tamen ne rumpatur. Radix plures radices ita per
forate et parte sub terra dimictantur. per. xx. uel. xxx.
dies. ut accipiant uirtutes ab elleboro. postea
abiectis radicibus ellebori. alie radices conteran
tur. et in aceto per tres dies uel quatuor. ponantur
postea fiat decoctio ex tali aceto et melle fiat oxi
melle competens predictis casibus. ¶ Oximel factum
de radicibus elli magis eodem modo preparatis. ualet
ad melancoliam purgandam et quartanam. Sed. No. q.
non debet dari nisi materia existente digesta. No. et. q.
uiolentius purgat albus quam niger. ¶ Contra arthe
ticam pod. et ciragram. fiat decoctio ipsius herbe in aqua
salsa. et fomentetur. partes herbe in ipsa cataplas
mat. ¶ Ad uermes aurium conficiatur modicum
pulueris elli cum succo persicarie et auribus imponatur
statim exeunt. puluis eius superpositus carnem superflu
am corrodit. ¶ Contra furfures capitis et pediculos
bulliat farina lupinorum amarorum in aceto postea
coletur. colature admisceatur puluis elli ut quasi si
napismum ungatur caput per discriminalia. post mo
dum lauetur cum aqua calida. ¶ Contra scabiem
fiat puluis ex ellebo. al. bene trito. ℥. i. et litargio
per se trito. ℥. ii. oleum nucis uel com. in patella pona
tur. litargirum conficiatur bene cum aceto et ponatur in
oleo illo ad ultimum pulueris istum apposito. inungatur
patiens in balneo multum ualet. ¶ Contra litargiam et
epilensiam prouocetur sternutatio ex puluere eius naribus
immisso uel in panno posito et ad nares percusso.
¶ Diascorides dicit quod si puluis eius cum farina et
aqua conficiatur et fiat tortellus. mures occidit si
eum comederint.

Esula. ca. est et sicca. in. iii. gradu. frutex est
cuius radices cortices cortic. tamen. in. competunt.
In uere colliguntur. per biennium in multa efficacia ser
uatur. Melius tamen est ut singulis annis reno
uetur. Esula uirtutem habet purgandi principaliter
flaticos humores unde ualet contra egritudines ex fla
te. no. quod licet ea quacumque suo purgat. post sca
moneam utilior est esula. et securius potest dari.
non eius est multum abhominabilis. ¶ Contra quotidianam
de flate naturali. artheticam. pod. ciragram. paralisim.
et yliacam. pas. et leuco flatico. detur puluis istius.
petrum celli. quod R. esule. ℥. iii. modicum cinamomi
seminis feniculi. et ani. et mastic. Sanis flaticis ad pre
seruationem ualet. et contra predictas. pas. ualet cum uino
calido. uel aqua calida uel ouo sorbili datur uel cum bro
dio uel cum uiscello. ¶ Benedicta esulata ualet
contra predictas. pas. et maxime contra yliacam. passionem
iniciatur in perisstere cum aqua salsa et oleo. et mell.
optimum est. ¶ Contra leuco flantiam precipue tal.
sit usus bulliat succus feniculi aliquantulum postea
residat aquam claram supernatantem. acc. et addie
to puluere eius et succo. detur uel fiat sir. multum competens.
Sillicatis medicis orientibus ponatur puluis eius
decoquendum cum carnibus. uel cortices esul. et car
nes comedant. et brodium accipiant contra predicta. pas
siones. ualet. fiat etiam claretum ex puluere eius uino
et melle et aliis speciebus. non eius est ualde abhominabi
lis. teodoritum anacardinum. et yeralogodion.
competenter acuuntur ex esula contra predicta.

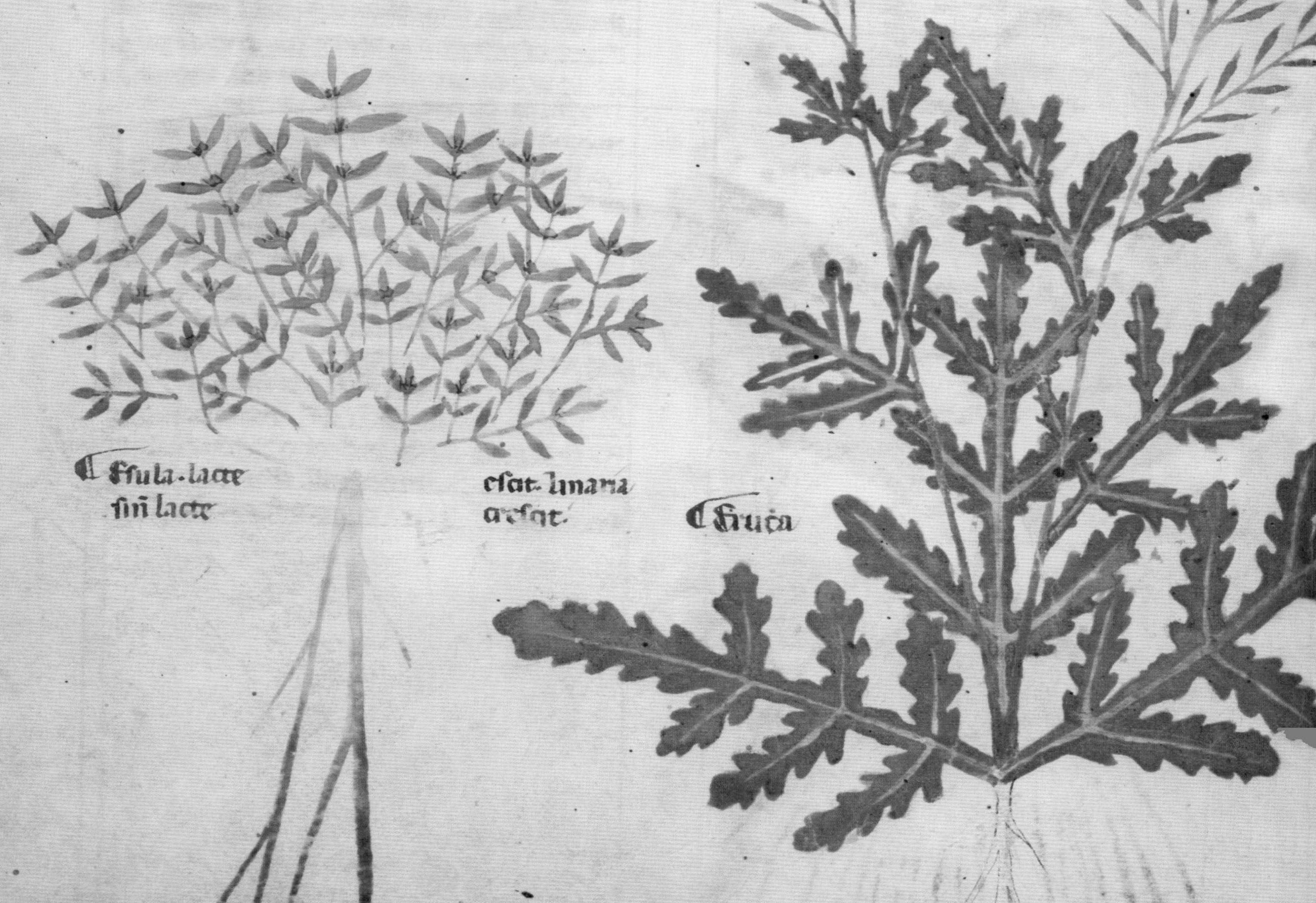

Eruca · ca · e · et · sic · in · iii · g · est aut domestica et silvestris · domestica maioris est efficacie silvestris minoris · usui medicine competunt principue semina · [?] folia · virtutem habet consumendi et coitum incitandi · Contra ad coitum incitandum · stranguiriam · et dissuriam · et palisim dicta cocta cum carnibus · pt predicta · herba ipsa decocta in vino et renibus cataplata libidinem incitat · et urinam provocat · pulvis seminis cum vino et melle conficiatur cataplasatum renibus · incitat libidinem ·

Emathites · frigida · e · et · sic · est aut lapis qui in occidentali et orientali parte reperitur · diutissime servatur · Virtutem habet constringendi fluxum sanguinis · inde dicitur emathites ab ema quod est sanguis et tithes quod est sistens · Contra fluxum sanguinis e naribus fricetur emathites cum succo sanguinarie · super cotem vel marmor · et in tali confectione intinctus bonbix naribus imponatur · Contra emoptoicam pas · scilicet vitio spiritualium fricetur cum aqua · ro · infusionis dragaganti super marmor et cum tali confectione conficiat pulvis gumi ar · et fiat pillule quas teneat sub lingua et transglutiat dissolutas si fiat vitio spiritualium nutritivorum fricetur cum succo plantaginis addito pulvere sinphiti detur pacienti · Contra dissinteriam si sit usus · et si potest iniciatur per clistere · fiat in hoc emplastrum ex albumine ovi · oleo · ro · et aceto et pulvere eius · super renes et pectines fiat sinpasma · Contra fluxum · [?] fricetur cum succo plantaginis · et addito pulvere bistorte supponatur ·

Ebulus

Ebulus · ca · e · et · sic · alio nomine dicitur camea[?] alii vocant · Abuiani · alii · [?]odactulon[?] cuius radices cortices et turiones precipue competunt usui medicine · cortices radices in vere colliguntur · soli exsiccantur per annum servantur · habet aut virtutem dissolvendi consumendi · consumendi purgandi principaliter flegma · Contra quotidianam de flegmate naturali · arthriticam · podagram et ciragram · detur succus eius radicibus · cum pulvere esule · addito cucumere · vel saltem succus turionum eius cum predictis vel pulvis radicis eius cum succo feniculi detur et precipue valet sic contra leucoflantiam · Contra timorem extremitatum · fiat fomentum ex aqua salsa decoctionis radicis et turionum totiusque herbe · Contra balneum factum ex aqua salsa decoctionis ipsius herbe valet contra artheticam et leucoflantiam ·

Edera nigra · arbor est · greci vocant · cissomelle · galli vocant · Bullussero · daci ·

uocāt· Arpropia· ytali· Edera nigra· alii· Edera
arborea· alii uocāt· Edera trestis· alii· Clamat·
Prima cura ei ad lapidē ī uexica frāgendū· Acc̄
bacchas edere nūo· vii· ul̄· xi· ⁊ bn̄ tere ⁊ cū aq
calā potui dab̄ mir̄ lapidē frāgit· Cōt dolorē
capis succus edre ⁊ modico aceto· ⁊ olō· roso·
simul̄ ꝯmisce ⁊ fronti illinias· dol̄ tollit. Cōt
dol̄ splenis ⁊ ꝯ morsꝫ spalāgionū· succus eius·
ul̄ uinū decoctiōis radic̄ edere potui dato mir̄
pdest· Vinū etiā decoctiōis folioꝝ edere uulne
ribꝫ ⁊ plage sepe ablute ⁊ ī folia ꝯtrite ⁊ sup̄poīe
mir̄ curat ⁊ sanat. Cōs polippos· succus edere
naribꝫ īiectus mir̄ sanat. Cōt dol̄ auriuꝫ et
ꝯt surditatē succus edere cū modico uino
p linteo expssus ⁊ tepid̄ auribꝫ stillat̄ mir̄ e
pficit Coīa edere poīt īuguētis ⁊ ꝯp̄ī· ī dialtea
uirtutē hṫ cal̄faciēdi ꝯ siccādi ⁊ ꝯsumendi·

tale· alii· Spatula fetida· alii fasiamon· omeō
uocāt· Xifia· alii adorion· alii· Addion· romāi
Gladiolus sagettale· Nascit̄ iuxta sepibꝫ ⁊ ī ubro
sis locis· similat̄ ireos· ꝑpue ualet ꝯt fistulā
ī ucūqꝫ fuit corpore· radix ei· ℥· vii· amili· ℥· vi·
aceti· gactos· duos· pīguedīs uulpis· ℥· iii· fac
emplīm ⁊ cū fixia suppoñ ⁊ utē mane ⁊ sero et
uidbis effectū bonū· Cād fractura capis· herba
ipi ꝑte supiori ꝯsiccata ⁊ ī puluē redacta cum
uino tēpa ⁊ suppone ad modū ēplastri· mir̄ cu
rat ⁊ si ītus fuerit ossa fracta· exit· ul̄ si ītus fu
erit aliq̄ re occulta mir̄ expellit foras· Eodē
mod̄ ualet ꝯt oīa ulnera nata ī q̄cūqꝫ ꝑte cor
poris fuerit· Itē semē ei potui dato lapidē ī uexica
frāgit· Itē succus ex radicibꝫ ei ī modica q̄ntitate
potui dato· hu· flaticos ⁊ grossos purgat īferi·
⁊ supiu·

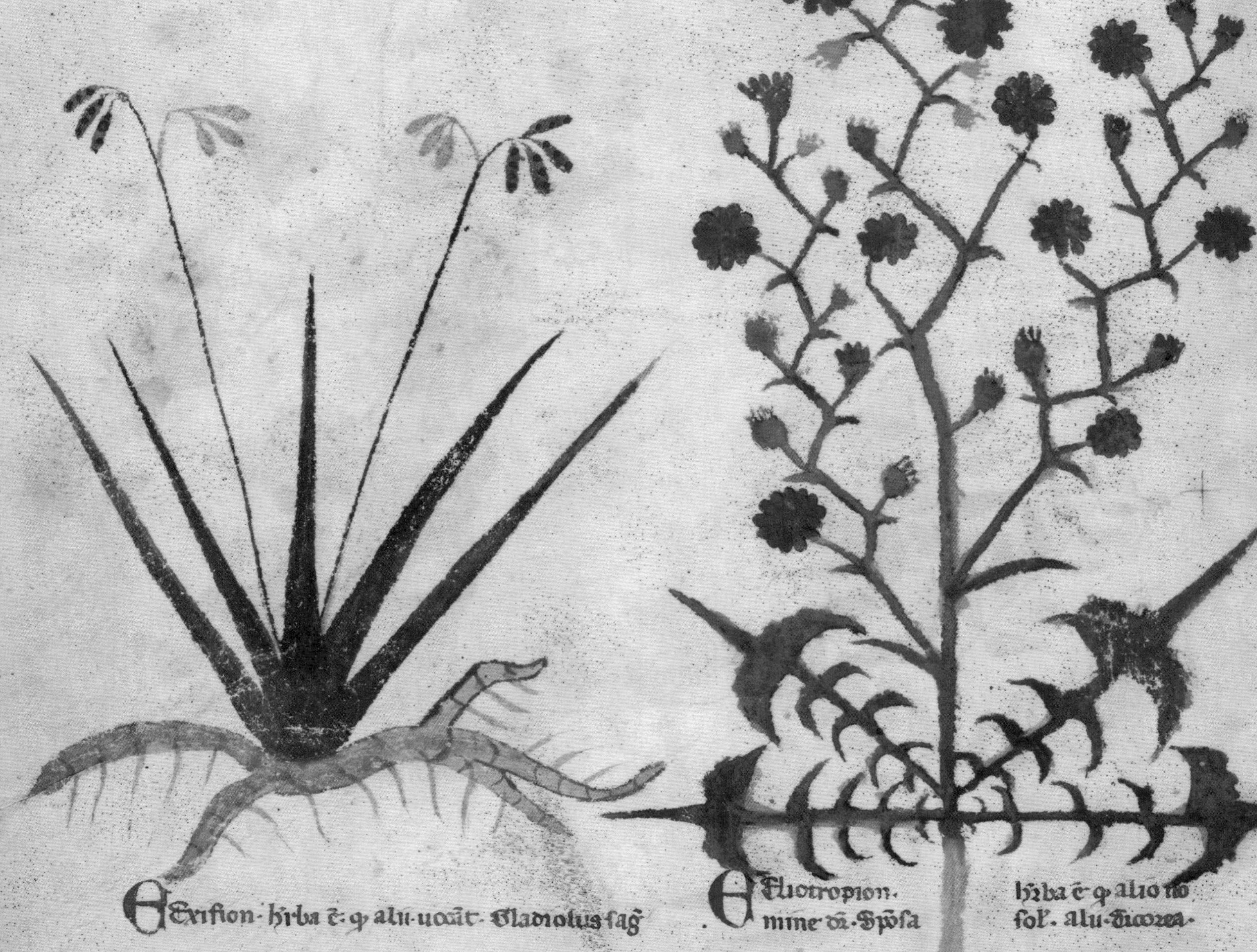

Exifion· herba ē q alii uocāt· Gladiolus sag·

Eliotropion· herba ē q alio no
mine dr̄· Spōsa sol̄· alii· Sicorea·

alii · Solsequiū · alii · Intiba · alii · Eliozon · alii · Dialiton · alii · Scorpion · alii · Eradea · alii · Brozoscrons · alii · Emathites · alii · Prasopiu · alii · Nisene · alii · Vertānū · alii · Mulcetran · alii · Eliotropia. Nascit' locis solidis ⁊ ī pratis. h' hrba ē diuina ad cursuz sol' ⁊ ħt fusticulos rectos ⁊ flores ī colore celestino. Virtutes ħt. Natura. ca. ⁊ hu. ī · ii · g̃. hrba Elitropiō comesta · ualz Cont' uenenū · sistit ex morsura tīa suppedat. Succus ei ualet c̄ oppilatioēz splis ⁊ epis · ex cala · ca · ⁊ ad calfactionez eidez · Cont' uenenū · succus ei cū uino optio ul' pluis ei potui dato · statiz · cōtz uenenū reicie · ⁊ sanat · Ad luxū · hrba elitropia contrita ⁊ luxū sr̄ponas · mir efficaciū sanat.

Eufragia · hrba ē q̃ alii · uocāt luminella et habet quinq̃ sūt eius uirtutes. p̄ma est si accipiat' ipa luna decrescente per illū qui p'miit rubore oculoȝ ul' caliginē sitiut ipa paulatine sitcat' ita recedit malū oculoȝ · Scd̄a ūtus ē si colligatur ipa herba et ponat' in uino radix et folia et patiens utatur ipo ieiuno stomacho mirabiliū uisū clarificat · Tertia uirtus ē ad frangēdum lapidē ī uesica · uicta cū radicibz uiueculaȝ geminū ut detet · Quarta ūtus ē si ponatur partes equales eufragie et buglosse in oleo oliua ⁊ ualz cot' cardiacam passionē · Quinta ūtus ē sūme aqua distillatā per allebic et ponē cū ea tertiā partē aque uitis et si ē lib' una ponat' ʒ · i · tutie cetiūe Alexandrine et oculis īstillet' et hoc ordine ualz ad uisū · Si aūt in illa duplici aqua bulliat ʒ · i · castorei est opus admirabile cōtra morbum caducū et in hac re est ūtus sua specie faciens · hec omia aristo' in cātica sua de egritudinez · inquid petrus yspanus · Eufragia si administrat' cū istis herbis · s' cū feniculo ruta berbena, endiuia bettonica, silereīmontane capill' ueneris et fiat aqua distillata ualz mirabil' ad uisū cōseruādū et tum hoc remouet omem maculā et ruborē de oculis. Incipit secretū magri petri yspani de egritudinibz oculoȝ et mt' alias uirtutibz reȝ · Item super eode

Flāmula · hrba ē q̃ sic appellat' qa ħt in cēsiuā uirtutez uī vz flāmula, caūe ē sic · i · iiii · g · uiridis inlte ē efficacie · ex

siccata nullius. ¶ Ad cauteriū sine igne fa
ciendū operant flamula et suplocū pcatur.
diuiciat porcus pra illiniet cutis adusta et
parctur more debito. ¶ Ad apra rūpendaz
qn usus est ad sanie 7 ē cap durū pteratur
cū olō 7 supponatur. oliū adponitur adre
laxatione; ne desiccet flamula. ¶ Ꝯ quartaz
7 arthetica qdā opantur interi. 7 ꝯ yliaca
dol. acc. oliū .ro. et ponūt ī ampulla uitra
7 ipōita flamula. tūa soli exponitur ī canicu
laribꝫ diebꝫ p. xxx. dies. hoc oliū datū ꝯtra
predicta inebꝫ. et alio modo ī qntitate .ʒ.
iii. scio uō qꝫ h oliū ualet exteriū iunctū.
¶ Ꝯ dol. arth. et yliac. str. 7 dis. 7 ꝯ lapis uiti
um. iniectus prodest.

Ferrum. ferrugo et squama ferri eidem
uirtutis sūt. ferrugo. ca. ē .i. sic. in secdō.
gradu. aliud ferrugo. aliud squama ferri.
Squama ferri ē illō latū et tenue qꝫ ꝯtusio
ne; a ferro. hꝫt autē uirtutē adtenuan
di 7 dsiccādi. ¶ Ad extenuatiōē splenis ua
let uinū ī quo ferrū candēs extinctū fuerit
mltū eīz ē sbtile. ¶ Ꝯ oppilatiōē splēis et
epis exlongo tp̄e dēt pl'uis sbtilissimi ferru
gis .ʒ. ii. cū uino calō. uomitū īmltā qntitatē p
uocāt. etiā intantū qꝫ admortē ducit. Vn
post inpetū ul' ī ipo ipetu dēt dari aqua inqua
lapis magnetes. tota nocte iaceuit. et puluī
eī cū aq. dēt. reprimit eīz uiolentiaz eiꝰ et sistit
uomitū adtestante diascoride. Sꝫ hic uomitꝰ
piculosus ē. uñ nō laudo fieri. ¶ Ꝯ emoroi
das pl'uis ferrugīs. ul' squama ferri. sbtilis
ꝯficiatur cū pulue̅ tassī barbassi. et bonbice.
intincta supponāt ꝯ paciēs optimū ē. ¶ Ꝯ te
tenasmon excalida. ca. 7 dissinteria. ferrugo
optīe cal'fiat ut candēs fiat pra aspgatur a
aceto et recipiat patiēs fumū ifenus.

Fumus. terre. ca. ē .i. ꝯ. sic. ī secdō. ē aūt herba
qdaz ita appellata. qz ut fum' adtra īmlta q
titate exitur. dr aut fum' terre. qz gnat' aquād
grossa fumositate adterra resoluta et circa supfi
cē tre adherentē. Quāto uiridior est tāto me
lior exsiccata nullius ē efficacie. pncipal' pur
gat melāc. fo. fla. s. salsū. 7 coliā diureticā
ī ē. ¶ Ꝯ scabiē. ii. ʒ. succi eī addito zucco. cū
aq. cala dēt. ul' sic .i. l'. i. 7 s. succi eī fiat decoctio
seīs feni et dēt. fiat ī hoc ungtū ī olō nucis ꝯtriti
pl'uis fuligīs sbtil' et ꝯficiat addito aceto 7 suc
co fumi tre ī maiori qntitate qꝫ alius iungatur
patiēs ī balneo optimū ē. No. ut diximus
succus dēt ī septimāna optīe purgat humoē
inducentes scabiē. ¶ Ꝯ yopisiz 7 papule leu
co flantiaz succus eius addito pl'uere esule.
ʒ. ii. dēt cū aq. ca. 7 fiat syr. exsucco fumi tre. ap
pū. 7 feni. et decoctiōīs pl'ueis esule. ¶ Ꝯ arthe.
dēt .ʒ. ii. hermodactilorū cū succo fum tre. herba
etiā ī uino decocta 7 cataplāta suplocū poda
gricū mltū ualet. ¶ Ad meliaz et fla. existēs
ī ore stoi 7 istō uñ quqꝫ segt nausea 7 ꝯ oppil
latiōē splenis 7 epis exsiā. ca. dēt succus eiꝰ
addito zucco. cū calā. No. qdā mane. qdā
ī sero. qdā sin pl'r. qdā cū adiuto dēt in sero 7
sēper cū aliquo reprimēte uentositatē. aut ꝯ
seīe feni. ul' mastic. ¶ Fum' tre dissoluit cū uē
tositate uñ tortionē īfert.

Fu. ca. ē. 7 sic. i. 3o. g̃. alio noīe ualleriana
dr̃. ī estate colligunt radices ei soli exsicant
p triennuū ī multa efficacia suat. Radix tn̄ in
medicīs poīt. Elligenda ē igit solida et nō p
forata. q cū frāgit nō pluerizat. Virtute hẽt
diureticā. Cō strāg. 7 diss. dt uinū decoctionis
ei. herba ī uino cocta 7 pecti supposita puocat
ur. Cad digestione confortandā et dol stoi ex
fria. ca. ul uentositate dt uinū decoctiois eius
7 seīs fen. ul mastic. cū succo alicui hrbe diu
retice. Cō uitiū pectoīs dt uinū decoctionis
eius 7 gūi. ar. ul caricarū. ul alteri leuitiui.
Cad suꝑfluitate matris exsiccād fiat fom
tū ex aq decoctiois ei et fiat suppositoriū ex bom
bice intīcta ī confectiōe fcā ex pluere ei. 7 olo
m. ul coī. Cō oppilatione splēis et epīs ex fria
ca. dtur aqua decoctionis eius.

marinis ptib et anpulia ī montuosis locis
et calidis repit. Radix illiū precipue usui
cōpetit medic. Infine autūpni colligit. p. x.
annos ī multa efficacia suat. Virtute hẽt diur
ticā. exsbtili sba et qlitatib suis. Cō lapidi
uitiū. str. dis. 7 yliacā. pas. precipue ualet
ellitū cōfectū exeo. s. filo antropon. ad eadē
ualet maxīe ellit cōfectū ex duab ptib. pul
ueris ei. et tertia saxifrage. Cō yliacā. pas. fiat
cristē ex pluē ei. aq salsa. olo et melle. dt etiā
bn̄ decā acuta ex pulue eius cū uino decoctiois
pluēris ei. Cō dolorē stoi ex fria. ca. ul uēto
sitate ex uitio nutritiuorū. str. dis. 7 yliacā.
pas. pōant pluis ei ī magna qtitate ī saccello
7 fiat decoctio ī uino 7 olo 7 sup locū dolentem
poāt. Cō friū asma dt pluis ei cū pluere
gentiane icib 7 potib. Cad idē ualet pul
uis ei cū pluere auri pigmēti. poīt sup car
bones ut fumū recipiat. p enbotū optimū
est.

Fillipendula. ca. ē. 7 sic. ī. tio. g. q
fissalidos alio noīe appellatur. ī ultra

Fraxinus. f. ē. 7 sic. ī. ii.
gra. arbor est cui cortex 7 semi

et uiscositas que admod. et fungi super crescut. usui competut medic. Ad fluxu uentris. lienteria. dissint. precedete purgatio. fiat fomentum ex aqua decoctionis. cortic ul fungi. pl'uis i ipsi cu aq pluuiali ualet. Ad uomitu ex debilitate uirtutis cotentiue. uel humoru acuite. cortices ul fungi i aceto bulliat. a spogia intincta supstom ponatur. Ad dol et duritie spleis. uinu ul aq decoctionis cortic fraxini potui ute. sin dubio liberat. Si pbare uolueris da porco ad comedendu p dies pea occide porco i no iuenieb eu splen. Ad libidine icitandu. sem ei q d lingue auis alectis corticib. posit in ellitiis ad coitu icita du i maxie i dia seterion. etia pse comeste mltu adiuuat.

Feniculus. ca. e. i sic. i. 2o. g. virtute ht diureticam ex sbtili sba et ex qlitatib suis. Sem eius. radices. et folia i cortices radicis usui copetut m. cu i recep tionib iuenitur receptio maratri. debent poni sem ei. In collirus succus radicis. ul folior p salter cortices. radices ei no ponu tur sin determinatione. Sem i principio autupni colligit p tres annos i uirtuta effic suat. Cortices radices colligut i principio ueris fuat p mediu anu. Ad oppilatio nes splnis i epis. str. dis. et uitiu lapid. ex callido huore dtur aq decoctionis cortic fen. Si ex frio dt uinu decoctionis ei feniculi coctus i cataplatus. i comestus ualet cot predicta. Eadem aq ul uinu solu dol stoi ex fria ca. ul ex uentositate. digestione i confortat. Idem fac pulu seis ei. Ad leuco flantia fiat decoctio in succo radicis feniculi. esule. hermodactil. ana. 3. iii. p ea colent i pacie ti. dt in sero stomo no pleno. ul imane stomo ieiuno. Ad panu oculi i plurutu. succus radicis fen. i uase eneo. p. xx. dies ad sole po natur. et more collirii. oculis iponatur. Ad pruritu oculi certu expimentu. conficiantur modicu aloes opti cu succo fen. i ponat in uase eneo. p. xx. dies. ad sole. ponat i oculo more collirii.

Feniculus q Greci maratron uoc. Fenugrecu. Ulba. i.

Fenu· grecu· herba· ide· e· ca· e· 7 sic· minus tn siccu· sba ht glutinosa· Virtute; ht maturadi ul relaxadi· ¶ Ad apa extius farina fenu greci ouitelle oui oficiat 7 suppoat matu rat et adtenuat· ¶ Ad maturadu et rupendu oficiat cu terbentina· et suppoatur: maturat et rupit· herba etia ipa i olo decocta 7 supposita maturat· ¶ Ad spleneis duricie herba ipa i uino 7 olo macerata· p· xv· dies optie decoquatur· et colatue addita cera et farina fenu greci· fiat unguetu optz etia apeata maturat· ¶ Ad apa spualiu farina fenu greci· i sacello posita et decocta i aqua cu malua uisco sepi suppoatur· ¶ Ad apa stoi· et itestinoz ex farina fenu greci et aq pdicta fiat pltes 7 suppoat ad apeata spualiu no ualet qz nimis calide sut·

Filices· herba e q Greci uocat· Piterigu· herba e satis cois q romai uoc· felce· prima cura ei ad fetid· Radix filicis· 7 agmonia· ȝ· ii· cu uino potui dato mir pficit· ¶ Ad infirmitate puero q dr ramice herba filice· radix uino cu axugia bn tere et facto eplz sup linteo mu do suppone· i· v· dieb sanabit· ¶ Ad pectine dol· herba ipi fco fumigiu 7 etia cataplata d sup missanat· ¶ Ad infirmitate puero fco fumigiu sb lecto isatiu leuiter sanabunt· ¶ Ad dol 7 duricie spleis uinu ul aq decoctionis radic 7 herbe filicis· sepe potui dato· mir osumit splne 7 dol i eo expellit· ¶ Ad dol neruoru 7 iuncturaru· radix ipi cu axugia bn malaxa 7 fco eplin sr pone· ad ite· ¶ Ad tena sind· radix filicis· 7 herba cu radicib tassi ubassi· 7 radix altea· oib oquassatis 7 bulliat i uino 7 aq· pea recipiat fum iano ul aliquo menbro dolete 7 tepid abluet loca· ¶ Ad fluxu uetris· radix filicis· rosmastuciu agreste· folia ficuu· al· 7 floru camoille· an· ȝ· i· oqsset filic 7 oia bulliant i aq pluuiali ad medietate; pea recipiat fum 7 tepd abluet pedes· 7 mirab d hoc expimetu· ¶ Ad sagitta ul aliquod ferru ul spina ucuq pte corpois remasit· acc radic filicis 7 rad· fen· cortex e· otere 7 addito sufficieti melle bulliat in sartagine ut uidat ad modu eplz 7 suppon· 7 mir· pb· e·

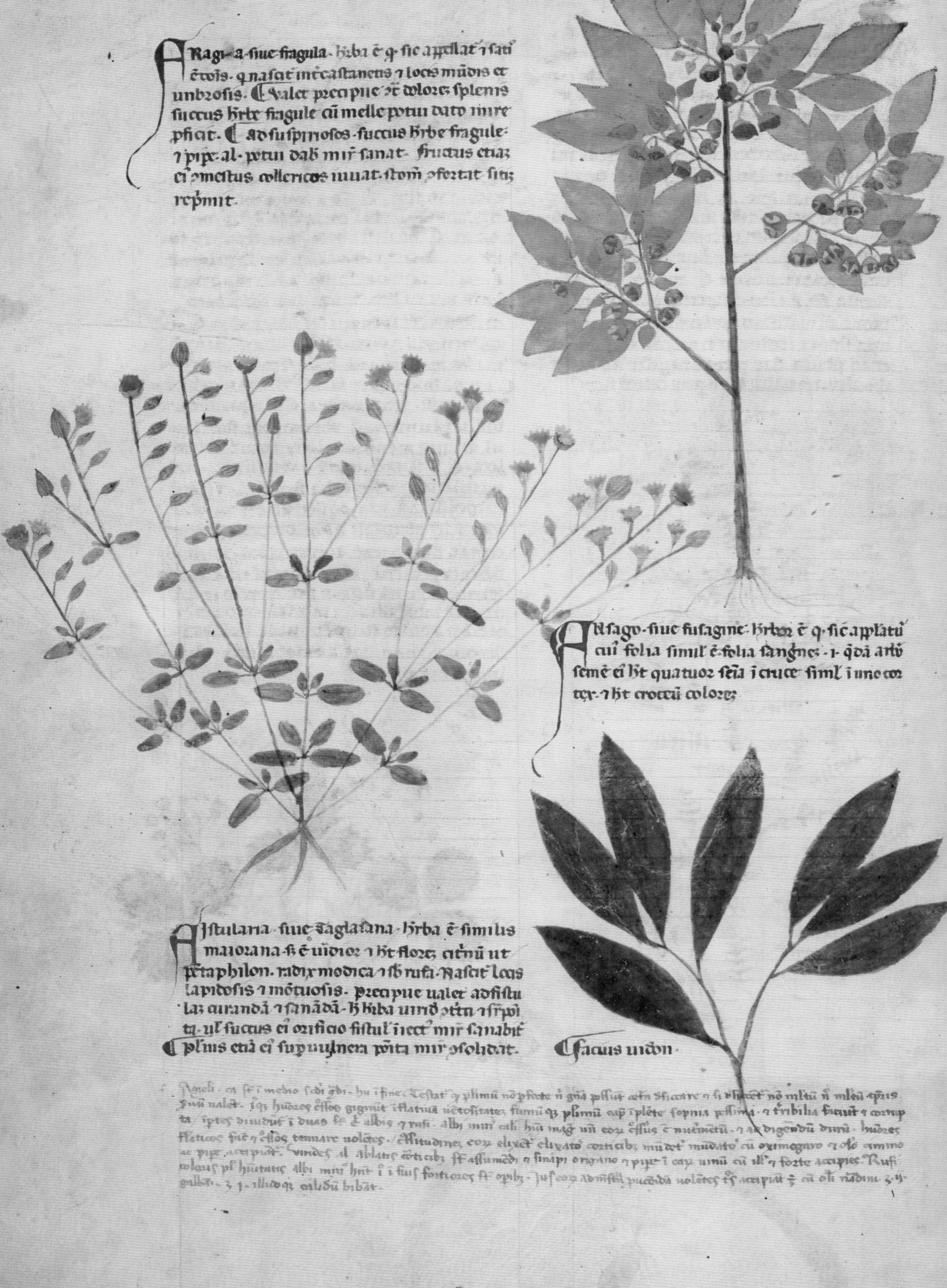

Fragia siue fragula. herba est que sic appellatur i sati
etrois. que nascitur in castanetis et locis mudis et
unbrosis. Valet precipue contra dolorem splenis
succus herbe fragule cum melle potui dato mirifice
proficit. Ad suspiriosos. succus herbe fragule.
et piper. al. potui dabis mire sanat. Fructus etiam
eius comestus collericos iuvat. stomachum confortat. sitim
reprimit.

Fusago. siue fusagine. herba est que sic appellatur
cuius folia similia est folia sanguines. i. quedam arbor
semen eius habet quatuor semina in cruce similia i uno cor
tex. et habet croceum colorem.

Fistularia. siue taglasana. herba est similis
maiorana. sed est viridior et habet florem citrinum ut
pentaphilon. radix modica et sub rufa. Nascitur locis
lapidosis et montuosis. precipue valet ad fistu
lam curandam et sanandam. Hec herba viridis contrita et superposi
ta. vel succus eius orificio fistule iniectus mire sanabit.
Pulvis etiam eius super vulnera posita mire consolidat.

Facus uicon.

Agioli. ca. sunt i medio secundi gradi. hu. i fine. Testatur que plurimum non perfecte in gna possunt acta desiccare et si desiccet non multum in mlcdi corporis
sui valet. set humores crossos gignit inflativa ventositatem. fumum quod plurimum caput implente sopnia pessima et tribilia facuit et corrup
ta ipsos dividuit i duas sunt enim albis et rufi. albi minus calidi huius mag uni eorum crossus est nutrimentum et ad digendum durum. humores
flaticos fit et crossos temarare volentes. crassitudinem eorum elixet elixato corticibus mudet mudato cum oximogaro et oleo cimino
ac piper accipiat. virides al ablatis corticibus sunt assumendi et sinapi origano et piper i earum unum cum illis et forte accipies. Rufi
coloris plus humitatis albi minus habent i i suis fortiores sunt operibus. Jus eorum ad mistum provocanda volentes ... accipiat ... cum oleo nadini 3 ij
galbani 3 j. illud que calidum bibat.

Facius uicon . herba e . Cui folia similant folia la
uri . et nunquam producit flores . nascitur in paludibus
et in aquis non bene cursiuis . dicitur autem faciu uicon adiu
dicaz faciendo . quicumque comederat de hac herba statim
mortem expectabat .

faba grassa que alii uocant faba greca .

Faba grassa . herba e que sic appellatur . huius folia
grossa . et pingua et succosa . radix eius e alba ad mo
dum sigillum salomonis . Virtutem habet frigidam et hu- . Contra
apostema calida . foliorum eius contritis cum pinguedine porcino
sine sale et facto emplastro suppone . dolorem mitigat . maturat et
calorem refrigerat . Contra ad paniculam in inguine
eodem modo supposita similiter ualet . Contra ignem si
ue combustionem . succus eius cum oleo . ro . bene commixti
punge loca . sed in prima die unge cum sapone gallico .

Faba inuersa . herba e . similis solatrum rusticum
tamen foliis eius . semen autem eius e similis bacce lauri . ra
dix eius parua ut solatrum . Contra uomitum in principio .
accipe de radice que communiter comeduntur que corum folia simila
tur rapa . et fac rotulas de dicta radice et pone in urceol
le ligato per tribus diebus . postea accipe i . rotulo de dicta radice
cum folium . i . usque . iii . secundum uirtutem patientis . De foliis fabe
inuerse . comedat patiens in mane ieiuno stomaco
usque ad . viiii . diebus . et mirabiliter de hoc experimentum .
probatum e que purgat dissoluit et sanat . et urinam prouocat .

Fabe autem diuerse sunt genera . sed tamen in medicinis

Fabe in sua forma in siccitate diuise sunt comeduntur e uides non dum messionis sue complete tempore comeduntur e uide sicce ac perfecte temporibus suis uidetur habere sunt que hu . i p . g .
nutrimentum corporum minimum generat humores crosso eorum inflatiue uentositatem faciunt in superioribus uentris partibus secundo nouissime sunt . Sicce si suis temporibus perfecte habere sunt siccae i . g . sanguinem non
laudabilem creat . Sed magis nutriunt accidentaliter non aliter duobus excessum una propter sue substantie grossitatem et tarditatem dissolutionis ex membris subtilitatem sue ordi et dissolutionis ex
membris citam . Secunda propter sue multitudinem uentositatem que grossitudinem eius . unde contineri inflat que dillatat que aperit [illegible] fermentum in farina . apertum in superioribus uentris uentositates plurima essent
generat inflatiuam . ex qua fumus in capite ascendit cerebro nocens que famis magnum corrupta idem cum g h non aliter habent fabe non est cortices posset aut ferre . Et fabe similiter continent uentositatem et
inflationem sua hec ordo auferre neque minuere tamen possimus experimento hoc probat in eis que fabis utentes assidue tetanicas patiuntur que sanissima fuerit . Item . G . fabe sed albu inflationem
faciunt et dure sunt digesti . Sed non abiuuat exsiccare hu operatione que plurimo quam colamentum habent idque monuit in sto sic alibi dicit ubi manifestat aut hoc colamentum earum et mundificationem cute
extiu mundificationem cerninus cum earum farine ablinit . Ideo ad lentigines ualet . Oxg cute corporis mundificare noluerit cum farina lauare assuescat apposita in mamill uel testiculi apposito
cataplasmate facto dissoluit . q in oia diximus earum in sunt medulle tutu in cortice a nichil . Cortex quoque eius stiptice e que colamentum nullum habet non aliquam fabis cum cortice coquinis-
in aceto amique diarriam patientibus propter defectibus stiptine uirtutis in intestinis . Electio e magis alba non uetus diuisisque coquitur modis uero et diuise sunt in corpore eius necesse sunt magis cot
te aqua . Sunt asse igne . Cocte aqua laudabiliores sunt quam aqua eius plurimum auferre uentositatem et grossitatis magie si eiecta aqua pori altera adiungatur [illegible]
aliquam cum cortice esse sunt ad digestionem dure et inflatiue stipticitas e cortice eorum phlebotomiae uentris mota et diuisa in uentre uentositates necesse e que inflatio generat . Cocte sine co
tice minus sunt inflatiue que si secundum usus fiant calfactiuis rebus appositis ut pipere longo . cum . oleo . uel amigdaleo . perfecte e non ad coitum operatiu . sunt que eis utuntur . Elixis aliquam cum
cum cortice aliquam sine cortice que de lixis idem que supra diximus . Iudicamus comeste tamen aliquam cum menta origano cimino et salibus sua uentositates que inflationem minuunt . [illegible]
uentositatem minimum habent et inflationis ad digerendum a durissime sunt . Verum tamen si in aqua in fundat post assiones que cum cimino menta et origano comedatur duritiem perdit [illegible]
fabe igitur noue ueteribus nociuiores sunt . Fabe mixte que [illegible] albugine ad exsiccationem oculorum cataplasmate facto ualet . Masse que temporibus apposite huiusmodi resistunt a capite
[illegible] cum uino cocte si cataplasma fiat excis testiculorum apostemata dissoluunt . Farina earum puerorum apposita uirginum labiorum stringit locus [illegible] nascitur superposita
subtilem et defectum pilum generat / scisse undique in duas partes cataplasmate facto sup [illegible] mox sanguinem stringit . Mamille lactis coagulationes [illegible] apposito dissoluit . [illegible]
inhibet exitum si cum cum allium et oleo ueteri miscens scrofulas dissoluit . aqua corum lanam gignit .

Fungi .f. sunt 7 hu i t[er]tio g[ra]du q[ue] mollitive sui humitate testificat[ur]
q[ue] duplices sunt mortiferi .s. 7 no[n] mortiferi. Mortiferi e[st] e[ss]e
hnt humitate. q[ui] viscosa accio[n]i n[on]. q[ue] digestioi i obedientes vn
sunt i laudabiles. vtpote tumorosi. Ideo bonu[m] e[st] n[on] eos comedere
Quos comedere uolentes eos q[uod] nocumentu[m] pati n[on] respuunt
eos elixat atq[ue] cu[m] eis pira q[ue] ul amenta misceat q[ue] iure eos
i alia aq recoquat. q[ui] cu[m] pipe ec. carui. calamento. origano
i sitibz odiat q[ue] esui tribuat q[ue] i fine mez uin[um] ue[l] potet
fiu u n accipiat i fine eoz co[n]ditu[m]. diacimin[um]. [illegible]
peon. sorgene q[ue] tyriaca magna. Mortiferi [illegible]
sunt. [illegible] dulsitatez. [illegible] qda mortiferi sunt [illegible]
7 humitate. ueluti [illegible] gu. [illegible] qda [illegible]
[illegible] opilatio[n]e quia i uentris poris [illegible]
ad dissolued i obedientes sunt 7 qda cu[m] [illegible]
te quia d'l eos hnt a nascitur. [illegible] ille q[ue] [illegible]
su ferru[m] a panos [illegible] sionem reptiliu[m]. ut [illegible]
sos uiscosos q[ue] humores hnt. [illegible]
q[ue] uiscositate humu[m] [illegible] q[ue] si [illegible] [illegible] uidat [illegible]
[illegible] i[n] [illegible] incidet. [illegible] eos [illegible]
[illegible] esu [illegible] q[ue] nitru[m] cu[m] olo potui [illegible]
to. Stere galli cu[m] aceto seu galline cu[m] melle [illegible]
aceto. [illegible] [illegible] faleni [illegible]
namomo. [illegible] aneto. 7 [illegible] oia [illegible]

Ficub[us] q[ue] alii Carice uocant. satis sunt eo[rum]
sunt e[ti]a[m] m[u]lta g[e]n[er]a caricaru[m] s[ci]l[ice]t albaz 7 nigr[as]

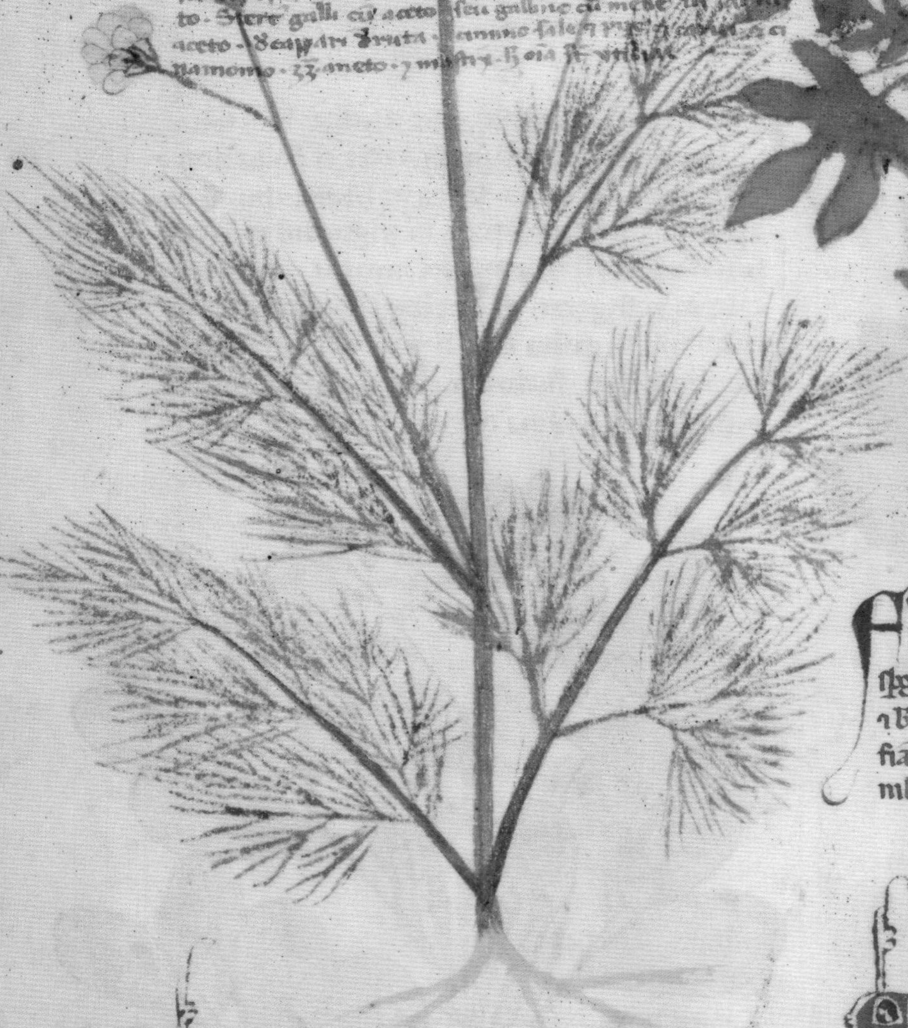

Filicis mascul[us]. h[er]ba e[st] simil[is] alia filicem
s[ed] no[n] t[ame]n cresce[n]s. radix aut[em] ei[us] e[st] cepposa et n[on]
s[ur]gi[t] p[er] terra. ualet [con]t[ra] allopitia[m]. radix ei[us] [con]q[ua]sset
7 bulliat in aqua ad tertio. p[ar]te[m] ex tali decotioni
fiat lexiuia [con]petent[er] 7 de ea abluet cap[ut] sepiu[s]
m[u]ltu[m] e[ti]a[m] m[u]ltiplicat capillos 7 cresce[re] facit

Ferula. h[er]ba e[st]. simil[is] feni[culo]. s[ed] maior e[st] 7 fetet
i[n] m[u]lta copia repit[ur] i calabria. 7 sicilia.

Fuligo. siue fuliginis. e[st] illo q[uod] desup[er] u[bi] fit
ignis. [con]creatur ex fumo ignis. q[ue] s[u]btiliter
cribata [con]ficit cu[m] olo nucu[m] addito. modico ar
gento uiuo cu[m] saliua ieiuno extincto fiat u[n]
guentu[m]. hoc tale unguentu[m] ualet [con]t[ra] fl[egm]a salsu[m]
[con]tra s[er]pigines 7 i[m]petigines. sepiu[s] sup[er] uetuz mi[ti]t[ur]
sanat. p[ro]b[atum] e[st].

Ficub[us] ceteris fructib[us] laudabilior e[st] ac nutribilior humanis sue tam[en] ei[us]. [illegible] hnt humores. n[on] ei[us] ea e[st] q[ue] sic. quantitatis i ea ul' sicca
domestica i uido q[ue] sicca diuidit. Et uidis duplex e[st] modis q[ui] e[st] p[er]fecte maturus q[ue] n[on] p[er]fecte crudi. n[on] p[er]fecte matura. Crudi n[on] p[er]fecte
m[atur]i mi[nus] e[st] cal[id]a. [illegible] [con]dationes terrestris p[ar]tis i ea. hnt tu[n]c humores lacteos q[ue] acuitatez ei[us] p[re]stat q[ue] siccitatez i [illegible] ou[m] idq[ue]
laudabil[is] e[st]. Vn[de] p[ro]p[ter] ficus q[uan]to longinq[ui]or e[st] a maturitate tanto mi[nus] ei[us] e[st] q[ue] mag[is] [illegible]. [illegible] medic[ina]. Cocta q[ue]
cataplasmate scrofulas q[ue] glades solui[t]. mi[x]t[a] cu[m] aceto [con]mixta pustul[as] i capit[e] [illegible] mixta cu[m] melle ad morsu[m] canis ual[et] q[ue] pustul[as] q[ue]
uiscosos humores hnt. papaueris agrestis frondib[us] mixta ossa fracta ex uulnerib[us] eicit. [illegible] adhibita apostema dissoluit si [illegible]
ta uulnerib[us] formice apost[em]a sanat p[er]fecte. Maturum uiridis ficus mi[nus] e[st] cal[id]a. Calor e[st] ei[us] i medio p[rimi] g[ra]di. hu[m] 7 sicci. i [illegible]
parte sunt [illegible] itaq[ue] reu [illegible] [con]sistit. Cortice [illegible] q[ue] carne. [illegible] nutiendu[m] e[st] nullu[m] n[on] [illegible] arena ul' lapis [illegible]
cu[m] e[st] ut [illegible] p[ro]pter dur[ities] ad digere[n]du[m] caro nutribilior salubriorq[ue] [con]sistit. Sup[er] hac. [illegible] calorez igit[ur] [illegible] siti aufert.
[illegible]. Sicca u[ero] ficus ca[lida] e[st] i [illegible] gu. sicca i medio p[rimi] g[ra]di. qua [illegible] q[ue] [illegible] humores. Ceteris
fructib[us] nutribilior e[st] min[us]q[ue] i[n]flactiois hnt. [illegible] i [illegible] ad digere[n]du[m] ad corruptionq[ue] [illegible] i[n]flactiva
uentositatez [illegible] q[ue] pessimu[m] sanguinez q[ue] i [illegible] corporis periculo[s]u[m] e[st]. [illegible] humorib[us] mu[n]dificatu[m] b[e]n[e] i[n]ueniat [illegible] digerit. ac san
guinez laudabile[m] facit. Corp[us]q[ue] mu[n]dificat humorib[us] mal[is]. urina[m] p[ro]uocat mu[n]dificat pect[us] q[ue] p[u]lmone[m] venes atq[ue] uessica[m] humorib[us] [illegible]
[illegible] i[n]flactiones[que] [illegible]. Ex nouitate ei[us] [illegible] ieiun[us] accipiat [illegible] p[ro]pt[er] illa[m] [illegible] maducet aut amigd[alas]
[illegible] ul' [illegible] q[ue] silea. Colleg[ere] [illegible] p[ro]p[ter] illa[m] [illegible] accipiat [illegible] q[ue] maiore [illegible] nutrimenti accipe uoluerit ul' s[i] [illegible] sanguinez laudabi
liorez g[e]n[er]et nuces simul q[ue] amigdalas amaras maducet. [illegible] ui[n]da [illegible] cu[m] ysopo [illegible] pect[us] p[u]lmonemq[ue] mu[n]dificat tussim
diutina[m] [illegible]. Gargarismus cu[m] [illegible] i canalib[us] p[u]lmonis apost[em]a dissoluit q[ue] i lateris q[ue] sunt i late lingue. Cocta cu[m] uino [illegible]
[illegible] fiat [illegible] ad dolorez uentris q[ue] ex [illegible] [illegible] humorib[us]. Rursus cocta cu[m] ordeo [illegible] g[ra]n[is] cataplasm[a] fco ap[osto]ma dissoluit. [illegible]
ac [illegible] [illegible] [illegible] ad tinnitus aurium ualet.

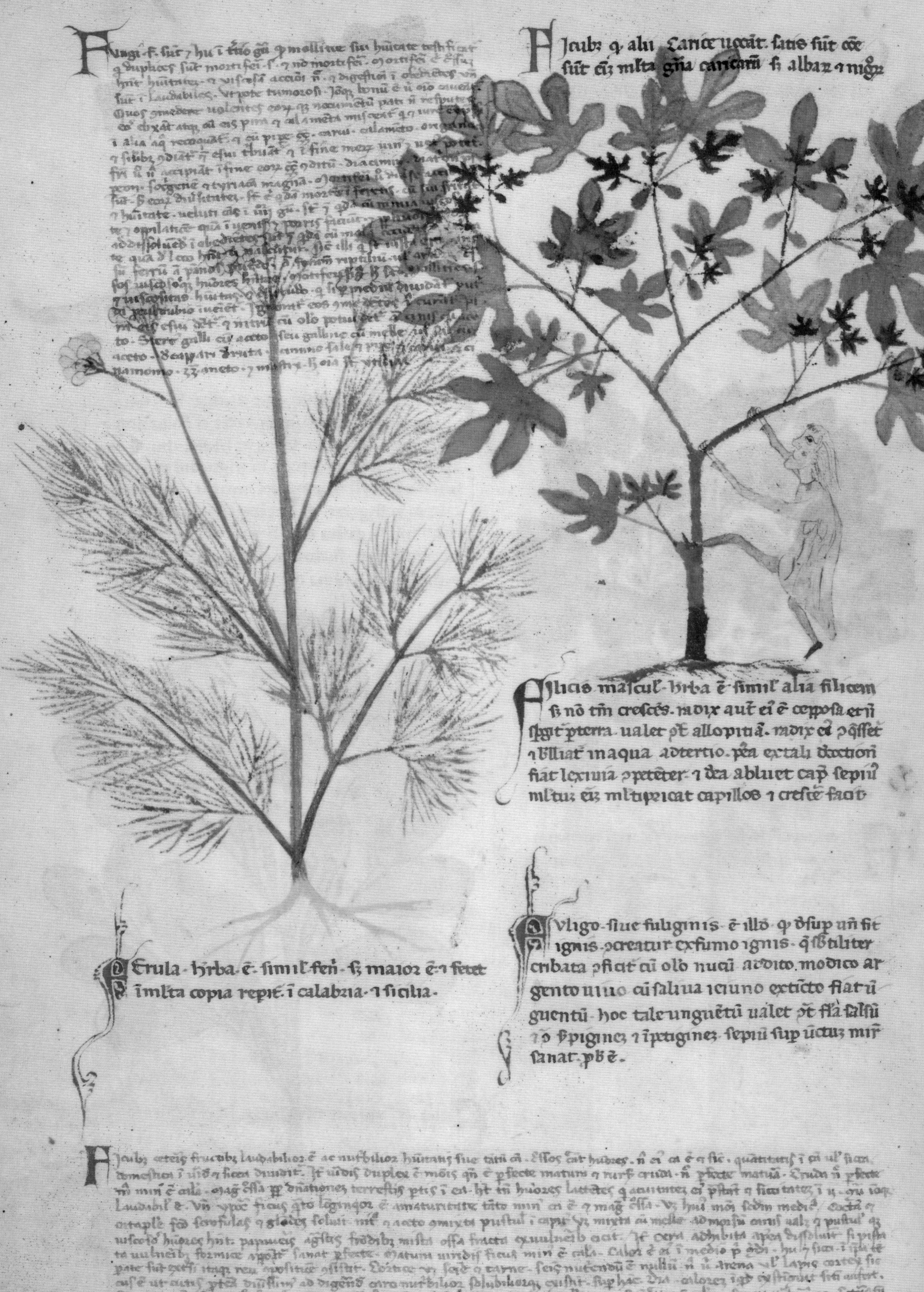

Gariofili · ca · sunt · et sic · in tertio · g · dicunt quidam qui in secundo
dicimus g quosdam gariofilos ex origine perfecti et a-
acuti saporis sunt · et illi · ca · sunt · et sicci · in tertio · g · quidam
dam remissiores qualitates habent · et iudicatur esse
in secundo · gradu · sunt autem fructus cuidam arboris in india
nascentis · Estiuo tempore colliguntur cum maturi sunt
per · v · annos servatur in multa efficacia · per · x · sine
corruptione · in loco non multum sicco · nec multum humido seruant · quia in multum humido putrescunt · In multum sicco
arescunt et corrugantur · ¶ Eligendi sunt autem
qui in superficie aliquantulam habent planitiem · Significat
enim substantialem habere humiditatem · Tuberosi etiam aliquantulum
et qui acuti saporis sunt meliores sunt · et qui in pressi-
one unguis humiditatem aliquantulum emittunt · Sophisticatur autem sic · ponunt gariofilos inutiles in
aliquo uase humectato · uel ligant in panno et ponunt
aliquantulum sub aere per noctem · mane exsiccant · et humiditas illa actualiter consumatur · Dignoscuntur autem
ex sapore boni gariofili · et qui maiorem emittunt humorem · non multum habent planitiem · Sophisticantur autem · alio
modo et subtiliter · puluerizant gariofilos electos subtilissime · et conficiuntur cum aceto fortissimo · addito
modico uino odorifero et panno ligatum inutiles
gariofilos cum hac confectione per noctem · extracto et
uino contrahunt humiditatem ex gariofilis acumen · Vix dignoscuntur sic sophisticati · A principio dignoscuntur
tamen quia illa acumen maius est in exterioribus quam interioribus
Interiori enim sub lingue aplicata · modicum aut
nullum sentit acumen · sic autem sophisticati non seruantur · nisi · per · xx · dies · habent autem uirtutem confortandi · ex aromaticitate dissoluendi · consumendi ex qualitatibus suis · ¶ Ad digestionem confortandam detur uinum
decoctionis · gariofilorum · et mastic mirum est · ¶ Ad dolorem stomaci ex
ex frigiditate uel uentositate detur uinum decoctionis · gariofilorum · et
seminis feniculi · ¶ Contra frigidum asma in aqua ordei · dragagantum ponatur
per noctem · et cum illa glutinositate conficiatur puluis ·
gariofilorum · et gummi · arabici · fiant inde pillule quas teneat sub
lingua diu · postea transglutiat · ¶ Ad matricis suffocationem · puluis gariofilorum conficiatur cum uino odorifero · et supponatur uel in iniciatum pessarium · Fumus
etiam eorum receptus ualet · ¶ Ad precipitationem
odoretur · uinum etiam decoctionis eorum · detur · ad cerebrum
confortandum applicetur naribus · ¶ Contra fluxum uentris
ex acuitate medicine · quando scamonea adheret uillis
stomaci · ¶ Contra uomitum collericum · in ampulla uitrea
plena · aqua · rosarum · bulliant · vi · uel · viii · gariofilos ·
cum mastice et mediocriter · tepida detur patienti ·
¶ Contra cardiacam et sincopim detur puluis · gariofilorum · cum
succo borraginis · Gariofili · folia gariofilorum · lignum gariofilorum et
galanga · similes habent effectus · Sed gariofili principaliter · fo

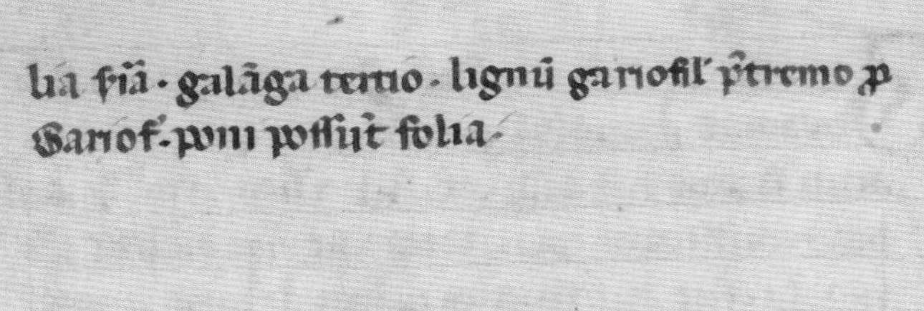

lia fria · galāga tertio · lignū gariofil' ꝑtremo ꝑ
Gariof · poni possūt folia ·

Gentiana · ca · ē · ꝛ sic · initio · g̃ · Gentiana
herba ē q alio noīe dr̃ · Alungalicaz · alii · uc̄
Aliasprontzon · alii · Alortis · alii · Contiadeni ·
alii · Aloetis · alii · appu pimētarū · alii · Aloxtis ·
Radix aut̃ gētiane usui ē · maxīe ꝯpetit · uñ
radix nō herba ī medicīs poī dbēt · In fine ueris
colligit' et exsiccatur · p · iiii · annos ſuatur · de
bent aut̃ elligi sollida ꝛ cōtinua · hn̄s citri
nuz colorez · q̄ etiaz nō ꝑforata n̄ facile ī pluēē
exsoluitur cū frāgitur · Que aut̃ puā hȝ amari
tudinez cū predictīs abiēcta ē · Virtutez hȝ ac

trahendi · dissoluendi · ꝯsumendi · ꝛ apiendi ·
est eīz diureticā · Contra antiquā asmā dtur
pl'uis eī cū uino addito aqua ordī · Ad idē
fiat elleuariū ex pl'uere eī ꝛ tātūdez succo
liqritie ꝛ melle · Ad idez precedentibȝ iuc
tiōibȝ circa spūalia digesta · m̄ · dtur pului s
eī ꝯfectus cū melle dialtea ꝛ cū uino · bis · in
septīāna · Si potuerīt librari · sic liberabitur ·
etiaz dtur cū cibis ul' cū pane calido · Contra epi
lentiaz dt̃ pl'uis eī cū succo pigani · Contra mor
sum reptiliuz aīaliuz puluis eī sup̃ uuln' sp̃ga
tur · ul' supponat' pl'uis gentiane et ī succo m̄
te dt̃ · ī potu pl'uis eī · Ad · ꝓ · fetū mortuū ·
ꝛ secūdinaz educendā ꝯficiat' succus eī cum
succo arthimisie · et fiat suppositoriuz ul' ini
ciatur pessarium ul' ꝯficiatur cū uino ꝛ ter
bentina et supponat' ·

Galanga · ca · ē · ꝛ sic · ītio · g̃ · qdā dicūt q sit
arbor · alii · q frutex · Diascorides dicit q
sit radix ꝛ reptitur circa pedez arboris ī persia
q patet ex eo q hȝ interī · quādā radices et ī
terra eī adheret · pot̃ aut̃ ſuari · p · v · annos in
m'ta eficacia ꝛ sine corruptione · Est ergo
elligenda q̄ subrufa ē · ꝛ ī sua manerie ponde
rosa ꝛ q̄ acutū hȝ saporez · q̄ aut̃ subalbida est ·
ꝛ leuis multū ꝛ fere nullū hȝ saporez · q̄ etiā ē
ꝑforata et facile ī puluez exsoluitur · abiciend
est · Virtutez hȝ ꝯfortandi ex aromaticitate

dissoluendi 7 ꝯsumendi ex q̄litatib;. Solet autē
sophisticari ex amixtiōe uīci h̄ntis radicē tor
tuosam. 7 etiā in mixtiōe bistorte dignoscitur
uō q2 uīci īsipidi seu salsu; h̄t saporē. galan
ga aromatici 7 acutū. Alii sophisticāt hoc mō.
pluen gāt optimā galanga. 7 pip ꝯficiunt cū ace
to et īponunt radicē uīci ꝑnectē et efficitur acu
ti saporis ex ꝯius. sꝫ dignoscit q2 iterius ē īsipi
di saporis. galanga uō acuti. Ad digestionē
ꝯfortādā et dolorē; stōi ex frā. ca. ul' uentositate
dt uinū decoctionis eius a cerebrū ꝯfortandū
applicetur. Cō cardiacā pas. et sincopī dt pluis
eius cū succo borraigis.

Galbanū. ca. ē. ī tcio. g. hu. i. ī. dicit qdā;
q2 ē gūi arboris. Diascorids dicit. q2 lacrimā
est ē cuidā frutice. simil' ferule. In estate a fru
tice exūpit. qdā; liquor circa fructicē; ꝯtepsati.
qdā; findunt corticē. ut magis effluat. Sophis
ticant qdā ex mixtiōe minutorū lignorū.
Calū. sic resoluūtur optimū; galbanū ꝑea admi
scent pluē colophonie in multa q̄ntitate et fabas
fractas abiectis corticib;. Est aūt eligendum
q2 albū ē 7 purū q2 etiā puras guttas h̄t uello
armoniacū. Diutissīe aūt suaī pot. Virtutē
h̄t attrahendi. dissoluendi. ꝯsumendi. leniendi.
maturandi. et relaxādi. Cō siniū. asma. dtur
ʒ. iii. galbanū. cū ouo sorbili. ul' aq̄ ordi. Cōt
litargiā ponitur sup carbones et recipiat fumus
patiens. Cōt suffocationē matricis idē fiat
pro enbotū. Cōt splenis duritiē ponitur in
aceto. p. iii. noctes. ꝑea fiat decoctio. 7 ꝑcoletur
7 colatura iterū in uase mūdo ponitur addita
cera 7 oleo 7 picula et fiat ēplm supante gal
bano ul' cerotū. supante cera ul' unguētū.
supante oleo. h'ic melius ē ut ēplm fiat q2 ac
cedat ad cerotum. Ad eẏ. fetū mortuū 7 se
cūdina educendā fiat nastale ex eo ītīcto in
oleo. Ad dolorē; dētiū; fiat casula ex eo 7 den
ti suppōatur. Et no. q2 cū dbet poni in medicinis.
dbes tollere supfluitates hoc mō. liq̄fiat in testa
7 infundatur in aqua. et separentur cortices 7 lapilli.
ul' ut purius fiat p pannū; colet. Diascorides.
docet q2 ī aq̄ feruenti ponat. q2 terre fundū colligat.
q2 sup natat abiciatur. ul' ponat ī pano lineo. et
ponatur in aliquo uase. et illd uas ponat ī aqua
feruenti sup ignē. Cū aūt galbanū sentit
calorē; soluitur. et q2 purū; ē effluit p illud
pannū; uas. Ad lonbricos occidēdos. dnt
pille ex galbano succo melle.

Gūmi arabicū. ca. ē. 7 hu. ī. i. gū. siliter
est draggto gūi arbor. q2 ī arabia reperit.
gūi arboris ē cui triplex ē manenes differētia.
albū q2 melius ē. Eligendū igit q2 clarū ē in
frigidis ponēdū ē medicis. et pcipue ī diadraggto
et ceteris 7 ī brusū. Que siliter clara sit elligant
7 ī callidis medicis ponatur. cū inuenit simpliciter
gūi. arabicū ē ponēdū. h̄t aūt uirtutē laxādi.
humectādi. 7 leniendi. Cō aspitatē lingue ponat
ī aqua donec ꝯgluttinet. et ex tali ꝯglutinositate
augmentetur lingua. 7 ꝯfricetur ul' ī pano sbli
ponitur. siliter ī aqua ponitur. ex eo fricet lingua. Cō
uomitū ex debilitate uirtutis ꝯtentiue dt pluis ei
cū pluere cinamoni. Cō emoptoicā. pas. ex spua
libus. pluis ei sbtilissimus ꝯficiat ꝯ succo plāta
ginis. ul' ī aq̄ īfusionis draggti. addito pulue
amidi ul' penidiorū et fiat īn pille. quas te
neat patiens sb lingua unā p aliā; donec resol
uantur trāsglutiat. Si fiat ex nutritiuis dt pul
uis ei cū succo plātagis. Cōt dissintiriā dtur.

decoctio pulvis eius cũ puluere mumie in cibis Ad
idẽ gũ. ar. i turtur ul' colũbã simul cõburã
tur et puluis eorũ dr' pacienti ĩ cibis. Si fiat ui
tio ĩferiorũ puluis eius iniciatur per clistere
cũ aliqua aqua mollificatiua ul' cõstrictiua.
Cõ fluxũ. m. dr' puluis ei cũ puluẽ san
guinis draconis ĩ aqua callida et fiat ĩ mõ
suppositoriũ ul' iniciat' p pessariũ. eodẽ mõ
naribus ĩiectus sistit fluxũ sanguis. ul' fiat
ĩ ispasma circa timpora. Ad idẽ ualet pului
eius et mumie. narib; ĩpositus. Cõt tussim
siccam et pectoris siccitatẽ dtur aqua decoc
tionis puluis ei.

q ex gariofil' fit. Gariofilata. h'rba ẽ et sat
est cõis. Efficaciam h't maiorẽ scd'm foliã
quã scd'ʒ radicẽs. vñ folia nõ radix ĩ medi
cinis sũt ponenda. Recens maioris ẽ effi
caci quã exsiccata. Exsiccata n' nisi pan
nuʒ õbet s'uari. virtutẽ h't dissoluendi
cõsumendi i apiendi. dr' aut' gariofilata
q h't odorẽ similẽ gariofil'. ul' aromaticita
tẽ. ul' saporẽ ul' effectũ. Ad. m. puocãd
fiat fomentũ ex uino decoctiõis pului's eiũ
fiat etiaʒ suppositoriũ ex ea decocta cũ olo. mu.
Cõ yliacaʒ pãs. gariofilata cocta ĩ aqua ma
rina et olo. et ant' dõi ex'iori pti supponat.
Cõ uenenũ trita et cũ uino sũpta ualet.
Ad digestionẽ cõfortãdã et dol' stõi. et
itestinorũ. ex s'ñãte ul' uẽtositate dr' uinũ
decoctiõis eius.

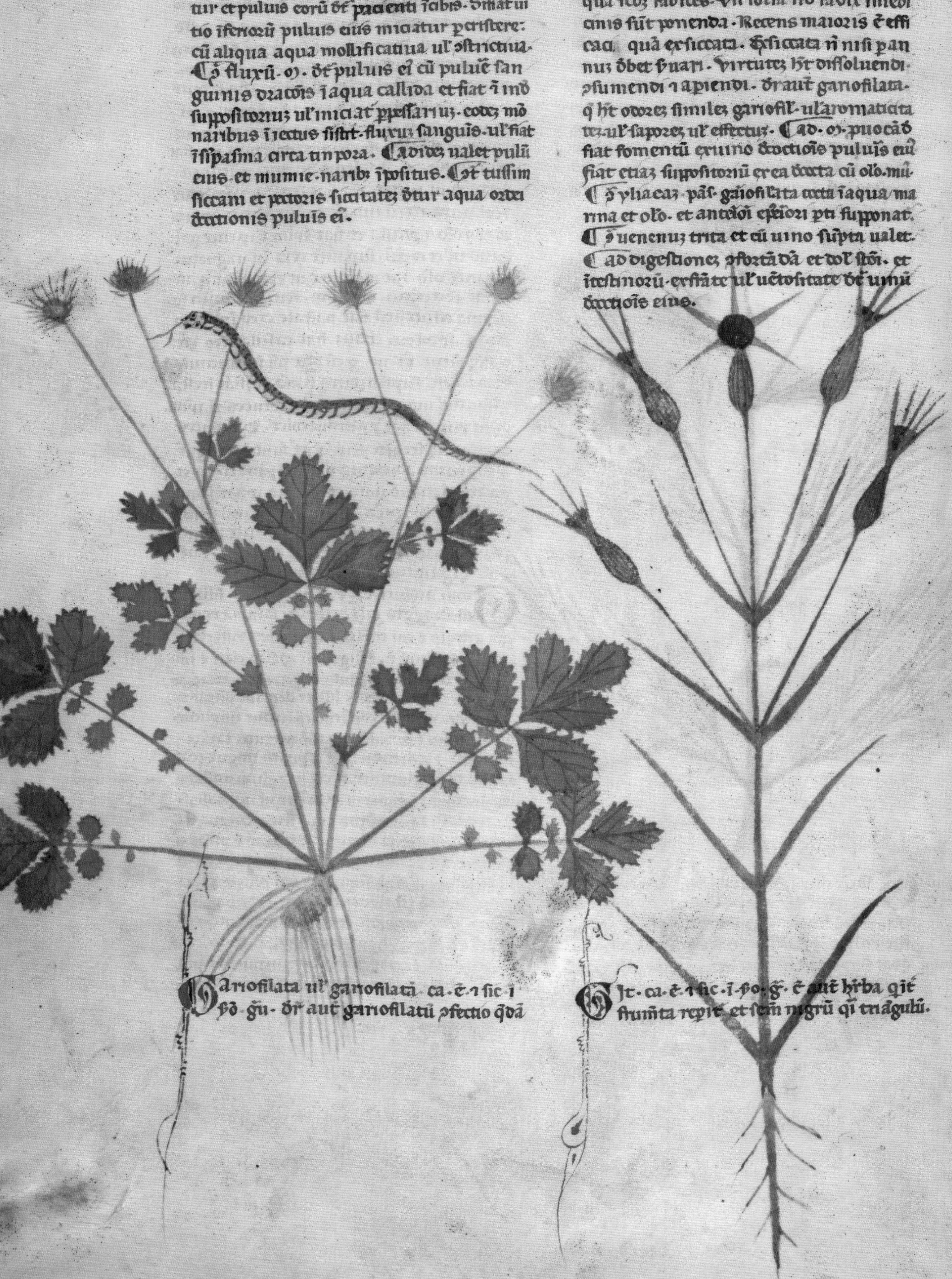

Gariofilata ul' gariofilatũ. ca. ẽ. i sic. i
ĩ. g'ũ. dr' aut' gariofilatũ cõfectio q'dã

Git. ca. ẽ. i sic. i. ĩ. g. ẽ aut' h'rba q' it
frũmta repit et sem nigrũ q' triãgulũ.

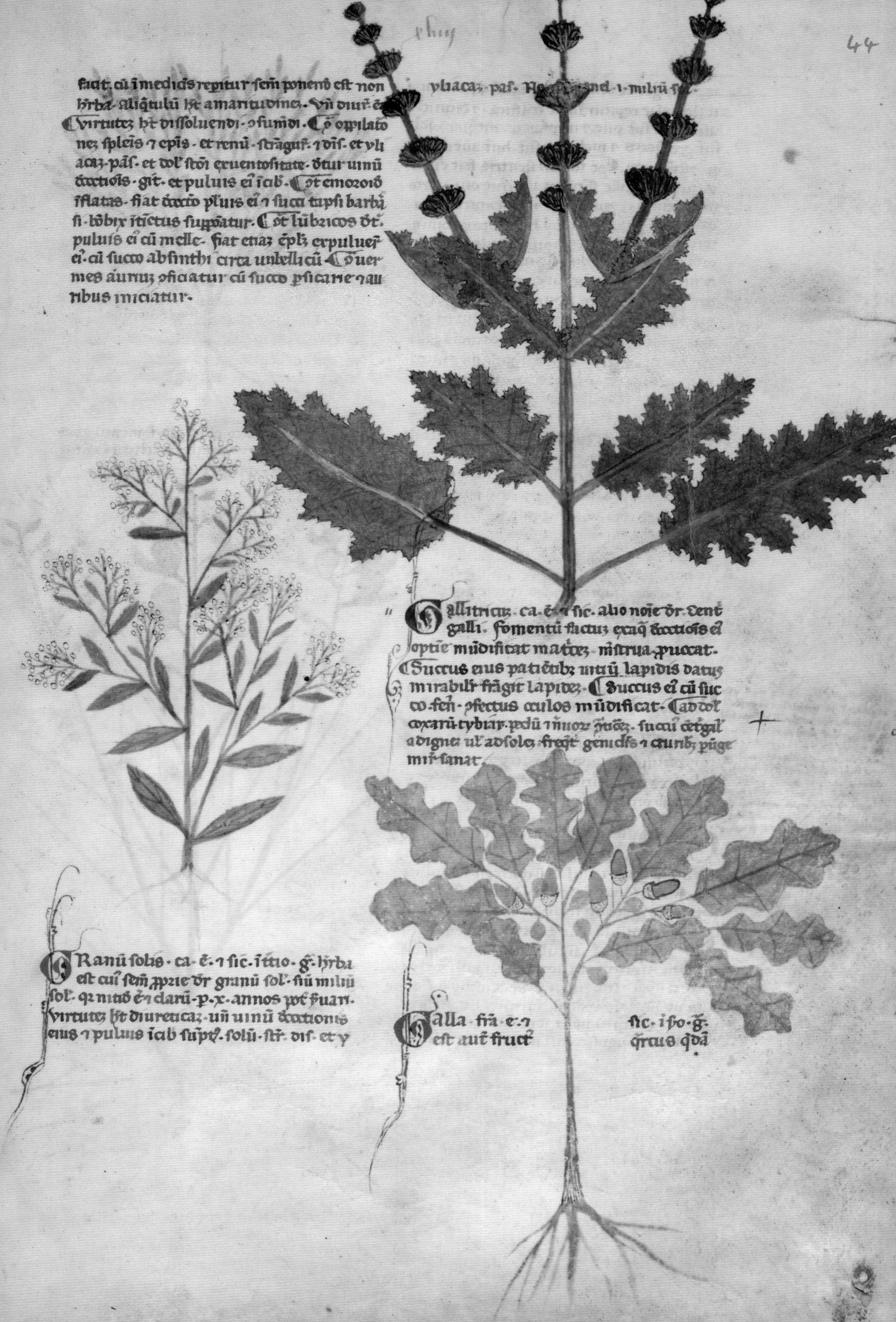

facit. cũ ĩ medicis repitur sem̃ ponend est non herba. aliqtulũ h̃t amaritudinem. Vñ diur. est. Virtutem h̃t dissoluendi. ɔsumẽdi. Cõ oppilatonem spleis 7 epis. et renũ. strãgur. 7 dis. et yliacam pas. et dol. stõi cruentositate. dtur uinũ decctiõis. gĩt. et puluis ei icib. Cõt emoroid inflatas. fiat dcctio pluis ei 7 succi tapsi barbã. si. l. bõbix ĩtictus suppõatur. Cõt lubricos dt. puluis ei cũ melle. fiat etiam ẽplm ex puluere ei. cũ succo absinthi circa umbelicũ. Cõ uermes aurium ɔficiatur cũ succo ɔsicarie 7 auribus iniciatur.

yliacam pas. ...

Gallitricum. ca. ẽ. 7 sic. alio noie dr. centgalli. fomentũ factum ex aq̃ dcctiõis ei optie mũdificat matricem. mistrua ꝓuocat. Succus eius patiẽtib; uitiũ lapidis datus mirabilr̃ frãgit lapidem. Succus ei cũ succo fen. ɔfectus oculos mũdificat. Ad dol. coxarũ tybiar. pedũ 7 iuncturarum ... succũ cẽtgal a digne ul ad solem ... genu ... 7 cruribus ... sanat.

Granũ solis. ca. ẽ. 7 sic. ĩ ttio. g. herba est cui sem̃ ꝓprie dr granũ sol. siũ miliũ sol. q2 nitid ẽ 7 clarũ. p. x. annos pot suam virtutem h̃t diureticam. uñ uinũ dcctionis eius 7 puluis icib supt. solũ. str. dis. et y

Galla. fra. ẽ. 7 sic. ĩ sõ. g. est aut fruct arbois cuiusdã.

repitur grossa leuis et pforata. q parum
ualet. alie repitur i asia et africa. 7 dicunt(ur)
asiane et sut pue. 7 nō pforate. inter quas qdā
sut grossiores 7 meliores sut. hnt aut uirtu
tem pstrigendi. Ctr fluxum uentris fiat eplm
ex puluere galle sbtili et albumine oui 7 aceto
suppectinēs et renes. fiat 7 fomentum ex aqua
decoctionis gallarū. q etiā i potu datur ctr dissin
teriam. Si fiat uitio iferiorū puluis ei cū aqua
ordei iniciatur per cliste. Ctr uomitū ex debilita
te uirtutis ptentiue. ul ex colera fiat decoctio pl(us)
uis gallarū i aceto addita aq manna et spō
gia ifusa ori stomi supponatur. Ctr fluxum m(en)s.
fiat fomentū ex aqua pluuiali decoctiois galla
rū. puluis etiam ipius iiciat pessariū cū succo
plātagis ul fiat iñ aliq solidū. et supponat ei.
Ctr fluxum sanguis e naribus puluis ei cū succo
sanguinarie pficiant. 7 stuellus iñ factus naribus
iponatur. Emplm etiam factum ex puluere galle et al
bumine oui timporibus supponatur. Galle etiam
puluis uulneribus suppoat ea psolidat. Ad ca
pillos albos ul canos denigrandos tal sit usus
acc. gallas pōderosas 7 nō pforatas. 7 decoque in
oleo quousque tumescat. et nigrescat postea tolle 7 ex
prime bn i duos pānos laneos quousque desic
centur. deinde bn exsicca 7 fac puluere sbtilem.
et acc corticem radicis nucis. et tere poptie. et
pfice cū aq pluuiali. 7 decoque addito puluere gall
rum. et ex tali pfectione unge capillos 7 barbā et
desiccetur pse. hoc facto abluat cū aqua calida ne cuti
remaneat ifecta.

Glandes. fructus idem sut ex quercubus. Ctr tenas
mon 7 ctr fluxū uetris. puluis cappillū
glandiū. ʒ. ii. cū optio uino potui dato mir
pficit. Ctr pfluuiū urine 7 q nō possut retine
ur. puluis idem eodem mō acepto mir ualet.
glandes etiam uirides ad modū castanee de
cocte sb prunis 7 comeste meli ualet.

Galla muscata. ca. 7 sicce pplexiois e. qdā
dicit qd fructus e. e aut qdā pfectio
ex aromaticis 7 musco. sz mō repit sophistica
ta. Ad pfortādū stom 7 ctr dolorē stomaci
ex uentositate dt uinū decoctionis eius.

Genestinsulā siue genestellā. ca. 7 sicce
pplessionis e. simil est genestre. sz minor
est 7 ht stiptices minores. 7 angustiores et
florē albū 7 sem rubum. uel ... beuschū ... Gen
stā uō ht florē croceū. Virtutem ht pstrigēdi.
Ctr m(en)s. pfluuiū ualet fomentū ex aq decoctio
nis eius. Suppositoriū ul pessariū ex puluere

genestule et succo plātagis. fomentū adiō
ualet. Ctr dissinteriam. ualet predictū fomentum.
No. q cortex radicibus datur pōt i medicis.

Genestã herba ẽ satis cõis cui folia ⁊ precipue flores ⁊ semina ɔpetũt usui medicine. ca. ẽ ⁊ sic. i. ii. g. Virtute hʒ diureticã exa maritudine ⁊ exglitatib; suis. Cõt uitiũ lapi dis. strãguriã. dissur. et yliacã pas. precipue ualet pulũis semis genestre ĩ qũtitate. ʒ. ii. ĩ uic. cũ optio uino al. uetero potui dato paciẽ ti ieiuno sto. mir. strãguria ⁊ dissur. soluit do lore; yliacã placat. lapides frãgit. ⁊ arenã in renib; pũgat. Cõt scrofulas nouellas ⁊ ue teras. aq. ɔstillationis flor genestre. ʒ. ii. in mane potui dato ieiuno. mir. pũgat p ife〈n〉iã et dissoluit scrofl. ⁊ glãdulas ⁊ sanat sin icisio ne aliq. alii accipiũt flores genestre uĩdis ul siccate. ⁊ cũ farina faciũt crispelle. ul fiat deco tio exaq ⁊ florib; genestre ⁊ tali decotiõe linfet uinũ. idẽ pficit.

decrescente. collige ⁊ custodi eã. ⁊ cũ erit neces se crispicosos ad collũ suspend. ⁊ secũ auferet. illã ĩfirmitate; expellit. Cõt lumbricos. ⁊ scos grani. ⁊ radix uiric. ĩ aq decoq; ⁊ da potui.

Grias. herba ẽ q nascit in lucaniam. et hʒ colore; marmoris. ⁊ hʒ. quatuor folia rubẽ. precipue ualet ad sciaticos. herba. grias. cũ pinguedine ursino. simil decoctis ⁊ in fo e; plastũ ⁊ supposito. ad tio die sanus erit. pbẽ.

Gumma elemin. gũi cuisdã arboris ẽ q. saracei elemin ⁊ arbor sic ucãt. nos aũt dicim lomee. alii uocãt. limon. dicũt qda ee gũm feniculus q falsũ ẽ. Ht aũt gũa limonũ q in ultramaris ptib; estiuo tpe ab illis arboribus tal gũa effluit ut resina pini s; ĩmodica qũta te fuerit. s; saraceni sophisticant cũ alia gũa q simil malaxãt ⁊ fo magdalione; apponũt ĩ fo lii ⁊ ɔsiccãt. Gũa aũt lemin magnã hʒ effica cia; ⁊ hʒ magnũ odore; ⁊ cũ rũpit ĩterĩ ẽ pura simil turẽ masculo. Virtute; hʒ ɔsuãdi ɔstrĩgẽ di ⁊ ɔsolidandi. Cõt. ad uulnera recente; et ueteras ɔsolidãdas ⁊ sanãdas. fiat tale ũ guẽtũ q re gũe lemi. ⁊ pinguedinis porcine ad dito cera sufficiẽti fiat ũgt. quo utẽ. Cad uul recente; gũe lemi. olo. roẽ. ⁊ cera. fiat ũgt; ⁊ supponẽ. cito sanabit. Cõ fistulã ⁊ cãncrũ gũe lemi. terbentina. olo. ro. ⁊ cera. fo ũgt; post ĩ aceto. al. ⁊ cũ manib; bñ malasset. p. iii horis. pca abiciat acetũ. et iterũ ponat ĩ lacte uacce rube ⁊ malaxa sic pri fecisti. p. i. hora; ⁊ pñ extrat ab lacte ⁊ abiciat ut nichil remãat pca recõde ĩ uase uitreo ⁊ utẽ. pbẽ.

Gramen. siũ graminea. herba ẽ. satis co cõis. q greci uocãt. agrostis. alii uocãt Egigon. egipti. amaxitim. daci. partia. alii assefoliũ. alii. vincolã. puniq. ibal. itali Gramen. Virtute; hʒ. Cad dol. splenis herba gramen cũ suis florib; bñ ɔtrita ⁊ fo ĩnd ẽplin sup splene; stati; sentiet bñficiũ. Cade; pitoras oculorũ. herba gramen. q hʒ tb; fura lis. q cresscit ĩ plurib; cultis. si eã ĩueneris lunio

Granũ fructũ ul fite ⁊ filia. sic coquãt cũ lacte. sanguine laudabile; gnãt ⁊ nutrit mltũ. si tam sepe sũat oppilatiões epis faciũt q durities spleis. lapis ĩ renib; ⁊ ĩ uesica maxĩe si uenes calidi ĩ ueiat ĩlliter ul accidentalr. ɔ eo satis dixim ĩ ɔ tritico.

Grisomilus fre sit ⁊ hu ĩ ii. gũ fruct arbor fit q. alii barachoche. alii crisomila uocãt. simil sũt psice. nũbilia ẽa cõsũ gnãt ⁊ uiscosũ ĩ concauitate epis ⁊ uenis ideo diutine cũ ẽ febris. h oib; modis sũt pessima. ĩ an cibũ ɔmedi sep debet fito ĩ anito. post cibũ pleno sto ĩ supioib; natãt ⁊ iaditate cito putrefiũt; diuit si g nocumẽta et uitare cupim ieiuni accipim ⁊ p illa. an. masticẽ ⁊ uet uinũ a odoriferũ olim exnucleas cor. D. expnũ vi emoroidib;.

GOlgēma · kalida ē ⁊ sic · h̄rba ē q̄ sili
noīe appellat · folia ei⁹ ⁊ custas similat
sticatos citinū · s̄ȝ h̄t flores simil' rore marino
cui⁹ flores ul' sem̄ ꝯpetit usui medic̄ · Virtu
tem h̄t diureticā · Cōt stāgur̄ · dis · ⁊ yliacā
pās · uinū decoctiōis seīs ul' foliorū ei · potu
i dato mir̄ p̄ficit · Cōt dol' stōi ex frīāte ul'
uētositate similiter dato stati sentiet beñ
ficiū · Cōt dol' matcis ex frīāte ⁊ ꝯt dolorem
splēīs ⁊ epīs opilatiōi d̄t etiā uinū ul' aq̄
decotiōis seīs ei⁹ cito sanabit · Cōt frīātez ca
pitis ex senetute ul' ex h̄uītate · tota h̄rba
ipī⁹ decoq̄t ī aq̄ ⁊ fiat in lixiuia de q̄ lauetur
cap̄ · ⁊ mirabris d̄ sui efficatiā · Nascit̄ ī mō
tib; ⁊ maxīe ī p̄uīcia ap̄ mōtes p̄sulanū.

GRatia deo · h̄rba ē · Nascit̄ ī p̄ratis ⁊ maxīe
ī locis humosis · folia h̄ns q̄i mirta s̄ȝ ē
paruiora ⁊ strictiora ⁊ h̄t fusciculos quatri
angulatus ⁊ flores albū · crescit ī q̄titate u
nius palmi · Virtute h̄t ca ⁊ sic̄ ī · iii · g̃ · et
efficatiā · p̄ūgādi · p̄ūcipal' fl̄a · f̄lo · colā · ⁊ ītio
melācoliā · ʒ · ii · puluis foliorū ei cū aq̄ calida
mir̄ purgat · et · no · q̄ īducit dissinteriā ꝓpter
nimiā ei⁹ uiolentiaȝ · q̄a cū ꝯpetenter adsella
uerit · abluet semet ipm̄ faciem cū aq̄ · f̄ria · ⁊
stati sistit assellare · q̄z ex hoc b̄n̄ficio uocat̄
ad m̄l'tis · gratia deo · No · etiā · q̄ ꝯpurdas uir
tutez accipiētis · tp̄s · etas · regio · ⁊ fortitu
do · Herba · etiā similat cētaurea minor.

Holgēma

GElesia · h̄rba · ē · q̄ sili noīe appellat̄
simil' ē bleton masculi' · folia ei⁹ ē
t̄bȝ coloris · uidȝ · rub̄a · uidis · ⁊ citrina ·
uñ d̄z gelesia · q̄dā mulieres tenēt ī orto
Virtutez h̄t p̄ncipue ꝯt caducos siū lu

natiuos. Selesie radix discorticata . iii . mani
pulos . origani . felterre . ʒ . i . simul tere
omnia . adde piperis grana . xxx . et bibat per tres
dies et liberabit probatum est.

Hermodactillorum . ca . sunt . et sicci . in . iii^o^ gradu
hermodactilus herba est . circa cuius radices
tubrositates inueniuntur . que colligi debent et usui
reseruari et in medicinis poni . in estate colliguntur
et desiccatur . in multa efficacia per annum seruantur .
singulis annis renouetur si possunt . Sunt autem
hermodactili elligendi qui albi sunt et solidi . qui
humidi sunt et uirides corrupti iudicantur . habent
autem uirtutem dissoluendi . consumendi . attrahen
di . purgant autem principaliter flegma . Contra artheticam
ciragram . podagram . et iliacam . passionem . et contra morbos
ex febre non existente acuta . ualet benedicta acuta
ex hermodactilis et yeralogodion . et theodoricon
anacardinum . Contra artheticam seu sit ciragra .
seu podagra . succus feniculi cum melle decoquuntur
et cum tali melle detur . ʒ . ii . hermodactil
lorum . Contra yliacam passionem . fiat decoctio mellis
addita aqua . addita nemel adduratur ne
uratur et ne crepat . ex illo melle . et . ʒ . ii . her
modactilorum . et . i . ʒ . seminis feniculi . fiat electuarium . quod ui
ce . benedicte potest dari . et benedicta carentibus . Nota
quod si tosi debent poni . ʒ . ii . uel . iii . hermodactili .
Puluis in hermod. carnem superfluam corrodit .
Puluis hermod. conficiant cum sapone gallico et
licinium intinctum fistulis imponatur . Plus enim et cere
usto conficiatur cum aliquo medicamine confortante cerebrum
et stuellum deponitur intinctum naribus inuiatum
cerebrum confortat . et pupillam corrodit .

hermodactilis .

herba uitis .

Herba uitis. q alio noie dr. Sqnatia. h nascitur locis sablosis et imontib; et ppe iusta marc. simil e foenu. et oi temp gerit flore et mltu puu icolore flor rore marino s; puior e. dbet ea colligi ipricipio autuni et iubra suspendi pannu pot bua ri imlta efficacacia. s; meli e qn recentior e. Virtutes ht leniendi. apiendi. actrhendi. et psumendi. Cot sqnatiaz et 3 cez supflui tate et huiditate ad uulaz precedete ex frate ul huitate. fiat gargarism ex uino albo uetero decoctionis hrbe uitis iolla rudi uitreata et coopta du bullierit uta medietate redeat pea colet et tepid gargarizet pluib; uicib;. stati aecthit reuma ut uidet albuni oui et mir sanat pb e admirtis. Dixit qda fr. hrba uitis qcuq; secu portauerit erit secur ad domonia. simili idomo recepta ul dsup hostiu ide; facit.

Heliotropium maius :–

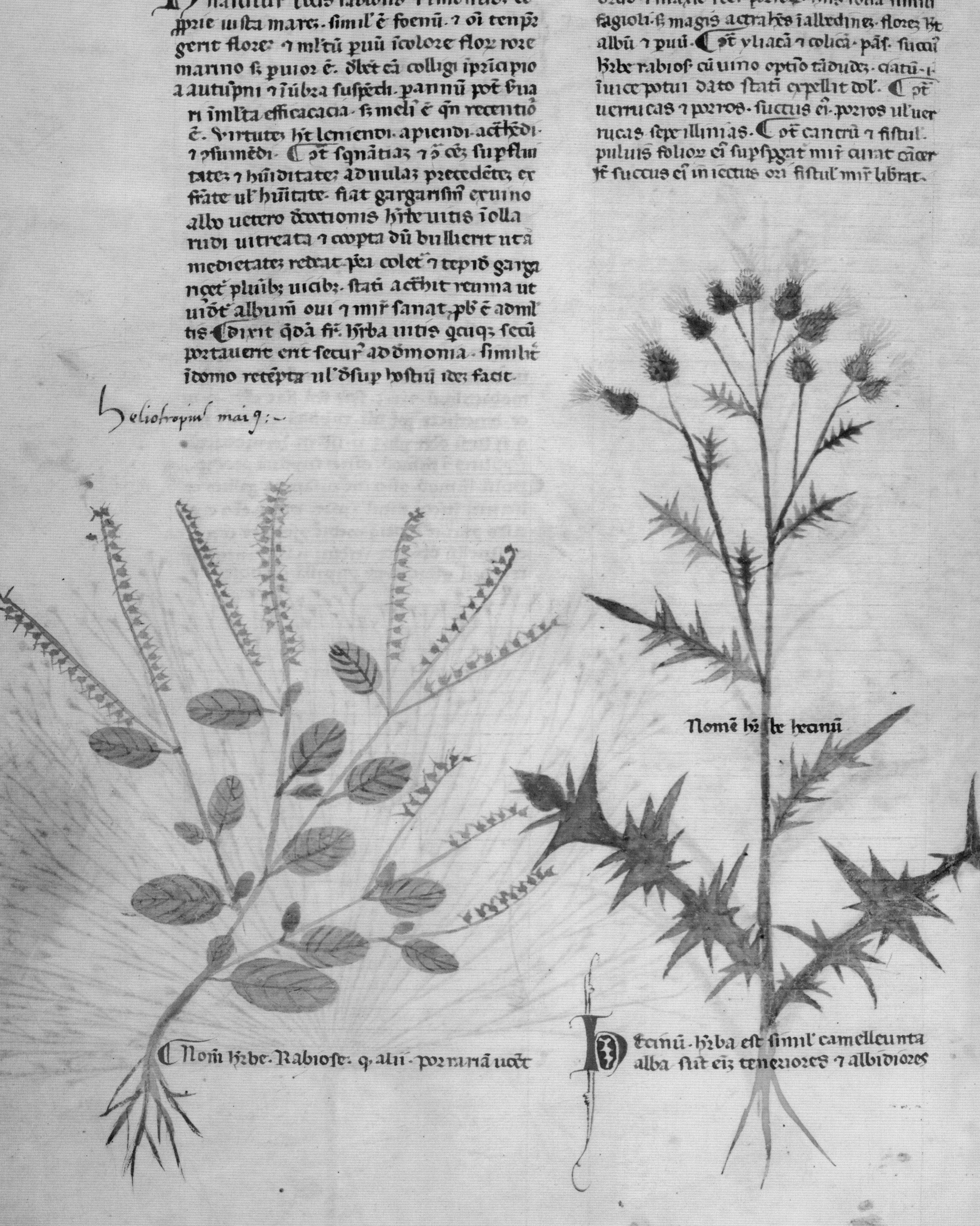

Nom hrbe. Rabiose. q. alii porcaria uocat alii fagiolana. alii verruci. Nascitur i ortis et maxie iter porroz. huis folia simili fagioli. s; magis actrahes i allredine. flores ht albu et puu. Cot yliaca et colica. pas. succu hrbe rabiose cu uino optio ta duobus. ciatu. i. iuice potui dato stati expellit dol. Cot uerrucas et porros. succus ei. porros ul uerrucas sepe illinias. Cot cancru et fistul. puluis folior ei supspgat mir curat cacer s; succus ei iniectus ori fistul mir librat.

Heranu. hrba est simil camelleunta alba sut ei teneriores et albidiores

spisse ⁊ spinose ⁊ longa uno digito ⁊ spino
sa ⁊ hẽt duos ramulos ĩ sũmitate duas pal
las rotũdas ⁊ spinosas simil' echino mari
no ⁊ gerit florẽ purpureũ. semẽ aut̃ ei' est
simil' cardo. uidʒ rotũdũ ⁊ minutũ. Cõt
emoptoicã ⁊ celiacã. pas̃. ⁊ stomatic̃. Radix
hecino scd pluũ sbtilissĩo. ⁊ cũ uino potui da
to mir' pficit. Cõt strãgurĩã ⁊ dis. uinũ uł
aq̃ decoctionis. rad̃ ei' sepe bibitũ mir' puocat
urinã. It folius ei' ɔtuse cũ uino ĩ sartagĩe
⁊ suppectinẽ cataplãte idẽ facit. Cõ liuido
rẽ eodẽ mõ supposita liuorẽ tollit. Cad do
lorẽ dentiũ. uinũ decoctiõis rad̃ ei' ĩ ore retẽ
to stati sentiet bñficiũ. Cõ spasmo puero
rũ semẽ hecinũ potui dato mir' librat. It
ualet ɔt morsũ reptiliũ. Etiã quicũq; secũ
portauerit a d̃ spẽtib; erit secur'.

Cõ morsũ reptiliũ nõ solẽ pñ iter bibita sʒ
etiã supposita fetid̃. pri' bñ ɔtta mir' sanat.
Cõt dolorẽ capis. acetũ decoctiõis ipĩ addi
to olẽo. ros̃. cap̃ illinias. Cõ litãgicos ⁊ frene
sis eodẽ mõ mir' pfert. Cõ sãguĩs uomitũ
puluis ipĩ. ĩ q̃titate. ʒ. iiii. cũ uino potui q;
dato. mir' pficit.

Herpillos h'rba ẽ simil' spillo. sʒ radix ei'
sbterra spit lõgã. H'rba ẽ tĩmãtica. sũt
eiʒ due spẽs. una aut̃ nascit' ĩ ortis. alia in
mõtib; ⁊ locis lapidosis. q̃ magnã hẽt efficaci
am. h' d̃ siccata pulũe; q; potui data mẽstru
is ĩprat. Vrinã puocat. Torsiones ⁊ lõgiorẽ
ĩflaturã uiscer; dumeris fracture ⁊ dolorẽ
ioc(i)neris sanat. It succ' ei' bibit' idẽ fac̃. It

Herba tua uł ture. cui' folia similãtur
oreu. ⁊ hẽt magna radix sbnigra. ẽt uo
alba ⁊ guõsa odorẽ q̃i ture. Nascit' ĩ mag̃s
mõtib;. Vinũ decoctiõis radic̃ ei' ualet ɔ stã
⁊ dis. ⁊ ɔ̃t ɔ dol' matris. ⁊ dol' stoi ex fiãte solũ.

cũ decoctione yue usq; viiii diebz mirabilit̃ pficit.
De Jusqamo. De Inantes.
De Isopo. De Indaco.
De Jaro. De Jua herba.
De Ireos. De Incensaria.
De Ipoqistid. De Jeribulbo.
De Junipero. De Inmolo.
De Ipericon.
De Ippiriz.

Herba sce marie q alio noie dr costus ortus. Nascit i ortis. opetes eiz precipue iungit marciaton q facit ɔ triusa ut dictũ est i antidotario. Valet ɔ dol matrice ɔ stoi ɔ lubricos hr sce marie uiridis cũ farina trici facto ẽpelle ɔ sepi ɔmeste mir pficit.

Herba paralisis q alii arthetica uocãt crescat in pedes motibz locis herbosis ɔ aqsis. cui silitudo ẽ folii rute s; cresces q̃ arbor. Valet p̃ cipue paliticis arthriticis ɔ epilenticis. ipa herba ɔmesta ul sucũ ei ɔ melle sco syr ɔ bibit.

Jusqamus. fre ɔplexiois ẽ i iiio. g. Dictũ i secdo. alio noie dr. Cassillago. alii uoc Simphonica. alii litercilon. alii Pitomon. alii Dentecaballino. alii Calidare.

alii Tiandron. alii Sicanaron. alii Galion.
alii Tisimion. alii. Insanā. alii Sapha. alii
Bellitones. alii albēge l'albēga. alii. Tasforeos
alii alteron. alii. ugamen. cui sem̄ ꝓprie
ugam̄ appellat. herba ipa. cassillago. Sem̄ aut̄
triplex ē diuersitas. ē eiꝫ. albū. rubū. ⁊ nigꝛꝫ
Nigrū ē mortale. albū ⁊ rubū. satis ꝯpetūt
usui me. ⁊ Nota q̄ cū repit. Re ugami. fisit
imedic̄ q̄ ore recipit. ponēd ē sem̄. si extern̄
herba. maioris aut̄ efficatie sūt seīa q̄ herba.
Virtutē hēt ꝯstringendi. mortificādi. ⁊ sōp
nuꝫ iducēdi. ¶ ad sopnū ꝓuocādū i acu
ta febre. talis sit usus fiat fometū ex aq̄
decoctiōis ipius herbe. circa pedes frōtes ⁊ ti
pora fiat ablutio. p̄ea fiat hoc ēplm̄. pl'uis
seīs subtil' ꝯficiat cū albuīe oui. ⁊ lacte ⁊
modico aceto. ⁊ frōti et tinporibꝫ appōat
¶ ad lacrimas ꝯstrīgēdas fiat itē ēplꝫ.
addito modico olibani. ¶ ꝯ calida apā
inpricipio fiat emplm̄ ex ipa herba ꝯtrita
et supposita. ul' seīe ei cū olo. ro. ¶ ꝯ dis
sinteriā. fiat ēplm̄. ex seīe ei. et albumin̄
oui ⁊ modico aceto sup pectineꝫ et renes
¶ ad dol' ex calia m̄. subitū medicamen.
herba ipa. aliqūtulū ꝯtrīta ⁊ supposita. dolo
reꝫ tollit. ¶ ꝯ dol' dentiuꝫ. seīa sup carbōes
ponāt' ⁊ patiēs fumū p os recipiat ⁊ ten̄
at os sup aquā. ⁊ apparebūt q̄si uermes
supnatantes. Sem̄ etiā i catula cerea fr
dentes poāt' dol' tollit. ⁊ no. p. x. annos
pot fuari. ¶ ad dol' auriū. succū ei tepid
i aure ꝯstillab mir' dol' tollit et uermes i
eo necat. ¶ ꝯ dez iflacticez. cassillago cū
stercore ouino ⁊ modico aceto. fcō ēplꝫ sup
poāt' mir' iflacticeꝫ soluit. ¶ ꝯ dol' dētiuꝫ
radix ipi i aceto decoq̄ ad tertio ⁊ m̄ tepid
i ore teneat. stati dol' tollit. ¶ ad dol' igui
neꝫ. radix ipi ꝯ suppectineꝫ suspēsa ⁊ secūꝫ
ferat. dol' expellit. ¶ ad podagrā ⁊ dol' ped
folia ei recēs frpedibꝫ obligata mir' ꝓficit.

Isopus. ca. ē ⁊ sic. i. iii. g̃. cui due sūt
maneries. s. mai' ⁊ mīn' ⁊ unā hn̄t effi
caciaꝫ. alio noīe dr̄ assce l'alasce. alii uoc̄
sicca. ysopus satis ē cōis. Virtuteꝫ hēt scdꝫ
floreꝫ ⁊ folia n̄ scdm̄ radiceꝫ. i estate colligi
tur cū flores ꝓducit. ⁊ ūbroso loco nō fūo
so suspēdit ⁊ ꝯsiccat'. i medicīs abiectis
stipitibꝫ. flores ⁊ folia ponūt' p annū suā
tur. singul' ānis renouet'. Virtuteꝫ hēt
diureticaꝫ dissolutiuā actyticuā. ⁊ ꝯsūp
tiuaꝫ. ¶ ꝯ frīgꝫ tussiꝫ ualꝫ uinū decoctionis
ei ⁊ ficuuꝫ siccarū. Adīteꝫ ualet electꝫ q̄ fit
ex eo s. dia ysopus. uinū decoctiōis ei. ⁊ seīs
fen̄. dol' itestinorū ⁊ stōi tollit. ¶ Fomentuꝫ
fcm̄ ex aq̄ decoctionis ei matriceꝫ ad supfluit
tibꝫ abstringit ⁊ mūdificat. ideꝫ fcꝫ suppo
sitoriū ex pluīe ei ⁊ olo. m̄. pl'uis ei ul' ip
sa herba itesta calēfcā ⁊ sup capite pōita
i saccello mir' uali ꝯt catarrū frīgꝫ ⁊ casū
uue. ¶ ꝯ casū uue fiat gargarism̄ ex ace
to decoctiōis ei. et sbleuetur uua cū digito
sup aspso pluīe floris ei. Ipa ē herba i ui
no decocta ⁊ cataplasmata. dol' ex uētositā
te tollit. ysop' ē herba ꝓgās ꝯ pectore fleumā.

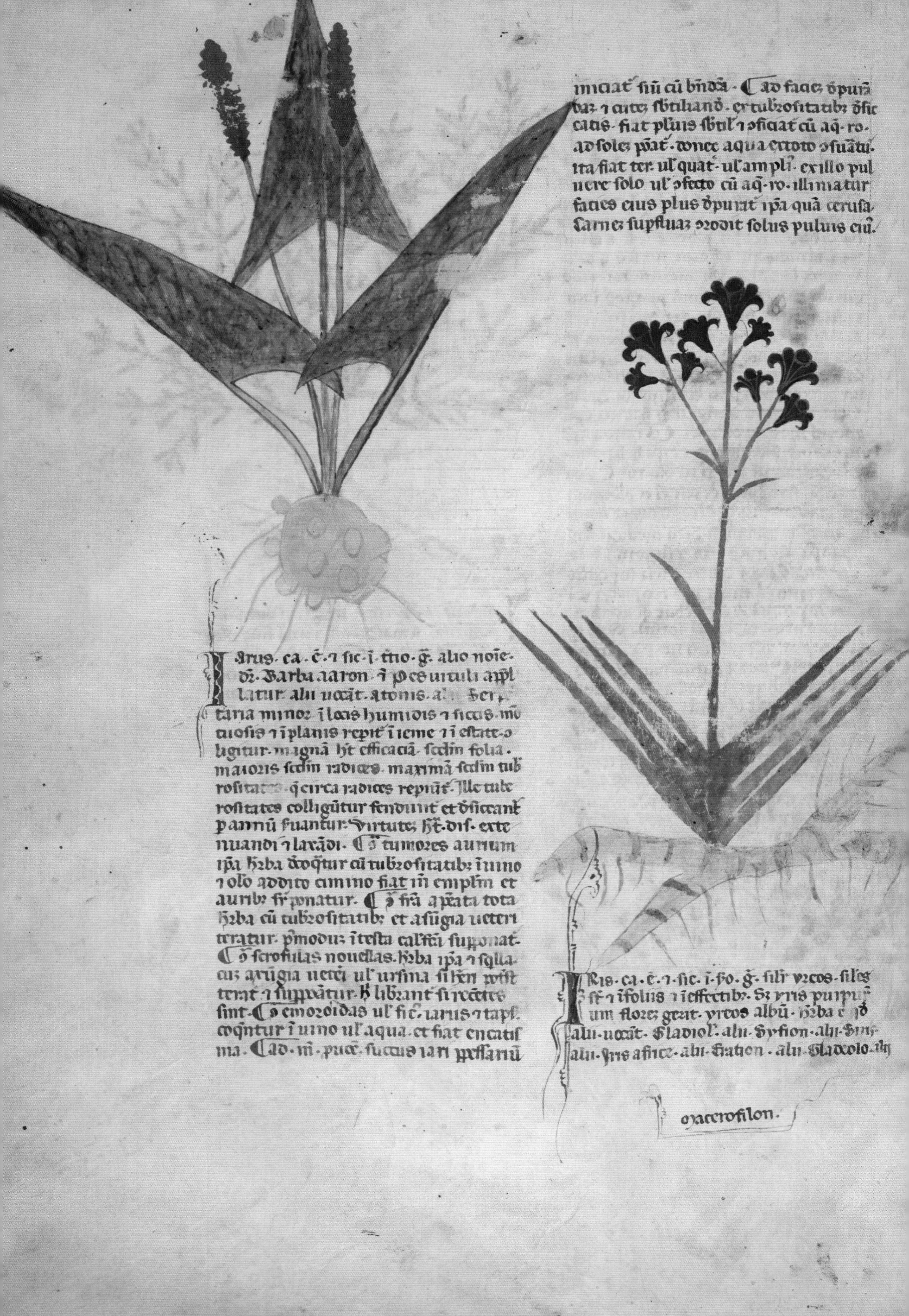

iniciat siu cu bndā. ¶ Ad faciē dpurā
dā 7 cutē sbtiliand. ex tubrositatib; dsic
catis. fiat pluis sbtil 7 dsiciat cu aq. ro.
ad solē pōat. donec aqua ex toto dsuātu.
ita fiat ter. ul' quat. ul' ampli. ex illo pul
uere solo ul' dfecto cu aq. ro. illiniatur
facies eius plus dpurat ipā quā cerusa.
Carnē supfluā corodit solus puluis eiu.

Iarus. ca. ē. 7 sic. i. tio. g. alio noie.
dr. Barba aaron. 7 pes uituli appl
latur. alii uocāt. atonis. al. Ser
taria minor. i locis humidis 7 siccis. mō
tuosis 7 i planis repit i ieme 7 i estate. co
ligitur. magnā ht efficaciā. sclm folia.
maiorē sclm radices. maximā sclm tub
rositates. q circa radices repiūt. Ille tube
rositates colligūtur fendunt et dsiccant
p annū suantur. Virtutē ht. dis. exte
nuandi 7 laxādi. ¶ Cō tumores aurium
ipā hrba decoqtur cu tubrositatib; i uino
7 olō addito cimino fiat iñ emplm et
aurib; supponatur. ¶ Cō fira apēata tota
hrba cu tubrositatib; et asūgia ueteri
teratur. pmodu; i testa calfca supponat.
¶ Cō scrofulas nouellas. hrba ipā 7 sqlla
cu; axūgia uetēi ul' ursina si hri poss
terat 7 suppoātur. h librant si recētes
sint. ¶ Cō emoroidas ul' fic. iarus 7 taps.
coqntur i uino ul' aqua. et fiat encatis
ma. ¶ Ad. mi. puoc. succus iari pessariū

Ris. ca. ē. 7. sic. i. sō. g. sili' yreos. sil's
ē 7 i foliis 7 i effectib;. Sz yris purpu
um florē gerit. yreos albū. hrba ē qd
alii. uocāt. Gladiol'. alii. Syfion. alii. Sin.
alii. yris afice. alii. Fiation. alii. Gladeolo. alij

Macerofilon.

macerofilon . alii [illegible] . alii [illegible]on . alii . assiradis . Radice utimur . in fine ueris colligitur et desiccatur . per duos annos seruatur . Radix yris illirice pro radice yreos . potest poni et ex eo uirtutem habet diureticam . vim dissolutiuam et apertiuam. ¶ Contra uitium spleni et opilationem splenis et epatis . renum et uesice . et dolorem stomaci . eructositate . ualet uinum decoctionis yreos . Puluis eius leuiter carnem superfluam corrodit. ¶ Ad pannum oculorum fiat collirium ex puluere eius et aqua rosacea . ¶ Contra dolorem cordis . semen eius cum lacte asine uel caprino . potui dato prius tepefacto mirabiliter dolorem tollit.

[illegible] [illegible] sicco . per [illegible] annos seruatur . in multa efficatia . Virtutem habet constringendi . ¶ Contra fluxum uentris ex colera uel debilitate uirtutis retentiue . conficiatur cum aqua rosacea et detur patienti . fiat etiam emplastrum ex succo ypoquistidos et succo plantaginis et albumine oui . supponatur pectini et renes . ¶ Contra uomitum fiat idem ut supra furculam pectoris . ¶ Contra fluxum menstruarum fiat suppositorium . ex succo plantaginis et ypo . uel pessarium iniciatur.

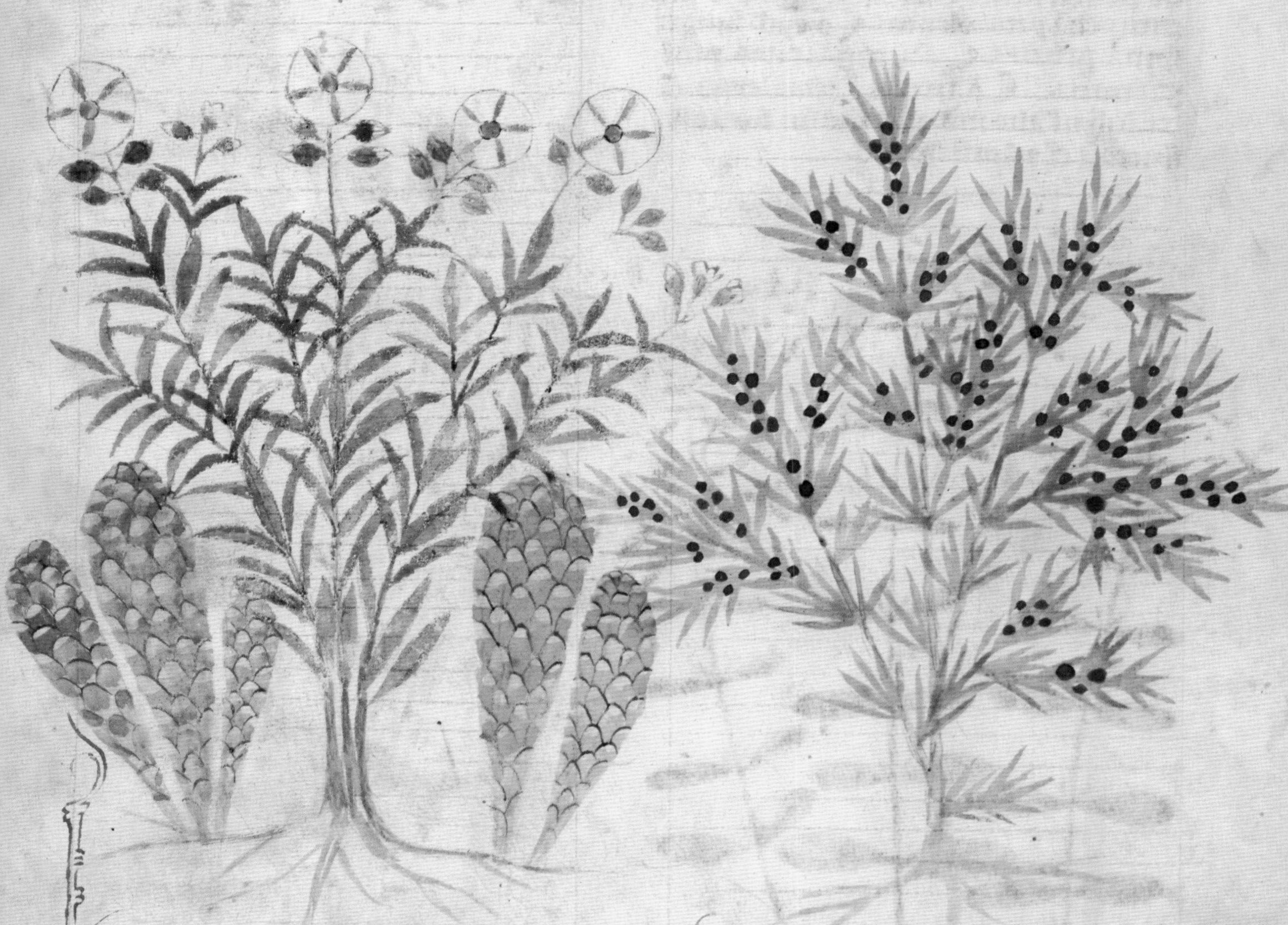

Ypoquistidos . frigidum et siccum . complexionis est . in . ii . gradu . Ypoquistidos . fungus est qui repit circa radices rose canine . que alio nomine dicitur ueratit [illegible] uere colligitur . succus exprimitur qui glutinosus [illegible] [illegible] . sole exsiccatur et aliquantulum in die mouet[illegible] [illegible] conseruatur . exsiccatur in loco non multum humido ne[illegible]

Iuniperus . calidum est et siccum in . iii . gradu . alio nomine dicitur . Anniffructus . uel arceotidos . cum in medicinis repitur eius receptio . ponitur deberet fructus [illegible] iuere colligunt per duos annos seruatur habet autem uirtutem dissolutiuam et consumptiuam. ¶ Contra fluxum uentris ex scamonea adhe rentr. uillis stoi. et itestinoꝝ fiat decoctio fructuū i aq pluuiali. et intret paciēs usq; ad umbellicū. et ille ptes fricentur i aqua illa. ¶ Cō stran. dis. ⁊ yliacā. pās. dtur uinu decoctiois fructuū ei. Ex iuni pero fit oleū hoc mō. Interra ponat olla et ore ei bn obturato poat canale creuz ul fere uz. p modū supponat alia olla noua. et i fundo illi olle ponat alia pos canal et circum liniat optie creta. ne aliqd psit exire. pea ipleat lignis iunipi sicc. ⁊ coopiat bn et fiat ignis i circuitu. modicū oliū effluit. s; efficacissimus ē. ¶ Cō qtanā dt illd oliū i qtitate ʒ. i. i cibis ul alio mō m. digesta. exmelia nli. ¶ Cōt yliacā. pās. stran. ⁊ dissu. dt pacieti i uino etiā modica qtitate. Inūgatur etiā ptes dolentes. ¶ Cō epil. iungat spina patietis. ¶ Cō uitiuz lapidis. psiri gā initiat. ¶ Cō antiquū asma. ex fru. cā det i cib ul alio mō. ul dt uinu decoctiois fructuū ei ⁊ ficuū siccarū.

oib; locis. ⁊ ppie iuxta fossas ⁊ i capis. hns folia simil rute ⁊ minutā psoratā. fusticu los rubos. flos ht citrinū. dbet aūt colligi mēs iunio. ul iulio. cū pducit floꝝ ⁊ i umbroso loco suspēdi ut dsiccet. No q cū repit in receptioib; medicis. ul i antitotis. ypicō. floꝝ ei dbet poi. cū aūt i ungtis ul eplast. totā hrba. sin radicib; qa nulli sūt efficac. ¶ Cōt oppilatioē. epis. ⁊ splenis. stag. et dis. uinū decoctiois ei sepe bibito mir pfi cit. ¶ Cōt vetentiā ⁊ dol stoi ex lōga egri tudine eodē mō dt. ul fiāt espelle ex hr ba uirid et farina. ul cū ouo et comedat patiēs. p. xl. dieb;. ieiuno stō.

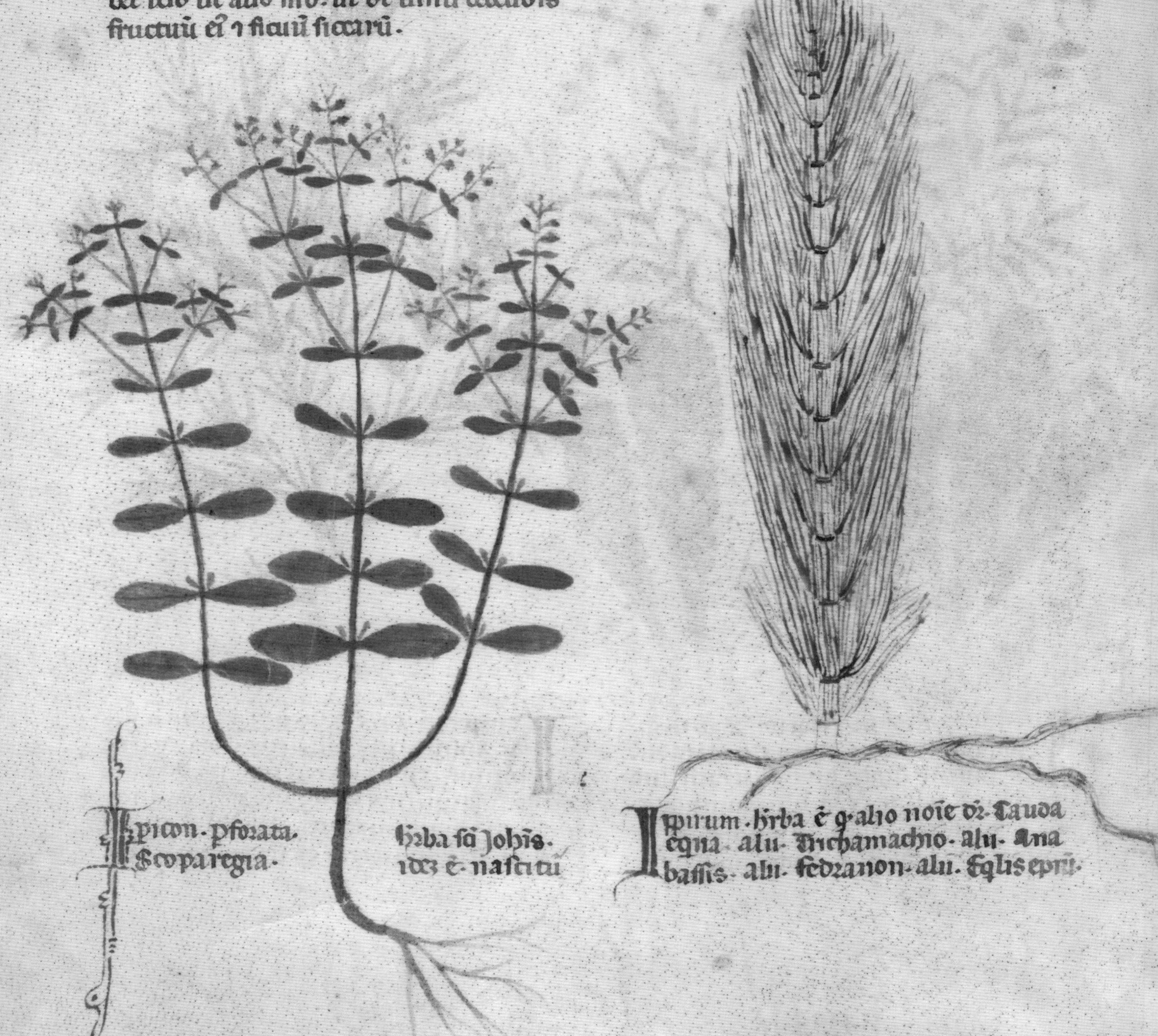

Ypicon. psorata. Scopa regia.

Herba sci Johis. idē ē nascitu

Ippirum. herba ē q alio noie dr Cauda equina. alii Trichamachio. alii Anabassis. alii Sedranon. alii Eqlis epri.

alii. Sygtinales. alii. yppiru. ❡ Ad dissinteric[os] succus yppirum cum vino afro potui dato stati[m] p[ro]ficit. ❡ Ad eos qui eiciunt sang[uinem] p[er] os. eodem mo[do] dato. s[ed] melius est q[uod] i[n] ore teneat [et] ma stucet [et] succus trasglutiat.

aut ei ubet p[ost]i. In principio estatis ubet colli gi [et] ad solem desiccari. pannum possunt suari i[n] lo co sicco. ❡ Contra [con]t[ra] ois. ualet plus ei cum vino potui dato. summum remedium p[ro]bauerunt. ❡ Contra graues tussis. aq[ua] decoctionis inantes lib[er] vinum vel p[lu]s d[e]t vel plus ei cum vino d[e] po tui mis[ce]t libeat. ❡ Ad p[er]diciones stom[achi]. Rad[ices] inantes vel flor[um] eius cum optio vino potui dato q[uo]d actos. ii. s[upra] d[ic]to ieiuno min[us] p[ro]ficit.

Vitulescam sunt [et] hui i[n] l[oco] g[er]. parum nutriunt [et] ad dige rendum sunt difficiles. stom[achi] nocive [et] sanguinis flatici g[e]n[er]ative q[ui] tam cum sint potice i[n] n[on] sanguis. acum estringunt. [et] si ad omam nitatis t[em]p[o]re p[er]uenerint. pec toris [et] p[u]lmonis asperitates hu[m]ectant. S[e]d iuuibe nec sanos custodiunt n[ec] sanitatem egris restituunt.

Inantes id est vitis agrestis. cum nibus inantes. l[atine] q[uae] lanbruscis. l[atine] repit in recepcio inati flor[um]. flos

Iadacis q[uo]d a[utem] p[er]fectio est ex q[ua]dam h[er]ba q[uae] d[icitu]r Suado. [et] similat[ur] cauli. q[ue] i[n] multa q[ua]ntitat[e] repit. q[uae] h[er]ba uiridis uulnera [con]solidat. sa[n]guinem et enarib[us] fluxum. t[em]p[or]ib[us] supp[os]ita mir[um] si sistit. dolorem capitis cal[idum] mitigat. Puluis in d[e] a[qua] c[um] vino potui dato lu[m]bricos occidit.

Iua. herba ē q herba yua appellat᷑. hn̄s folia
pilosa ⁊ minuta iterrisa (?) spādit᷑ supterrā sic
polligonia. ⁊ flores hꝫ pu͛uꝫ citrino colore. Nas
scit᷑ locis sablosis ⁊ imōtibꝫ tufis. ⁊ no. q̄oi
tp̄e pducit flor. Virtutes hꝫ. ca ⁊ sic. i ttio. g.
⁊ diureticā ex sua amaritudine pōticitate
⁊ q̄litate. etiaꝫ pu̅gādi. ¶ Cōt ydropisiꝫ ip̄ri
cipio. ⁊ ꝯ oppilatiōeꝫ splēis ⁊ ep̄is ex fiā. ca.
fiat p̄l'uis ex ipa herba. ⁊ dt̄ paciēti. iq̄ntit
teꝫ. ii. cū uino. al. calō. ieiuno stō. ¶ Cō arth.
palisiꝫ ⁊ epilētiaꝫ. ⁊ ꝯ strāg. uis. ⁊ yliacāꝫ.
pās simlr̄ data ul' succus ei q̄ meli᷑ erit.
¶ Cōt caducos. i. morbo regio ⁊ ꝯ q̄tanaꝫ fi
at. sir. ex succo ip̄ius ⁊ melle albo tātūdeꝫ.
⁊ dt̄ patiēti mane cū aq̄ calā decoctiōis herb
yue. Valet ꝯ hoc syr. ꝯt oēꝫ reumā ex fiā. ca.
⁊ ad m̄lta alia facit.

¶ Incensaria.

Incensaria. ē herba q̄ sili noīe appellat᷑ q̄a hꝫ
odoreꝫ icensū siu̅ turꝭ. hn̄s folia silis ꝯso
lida mecha siue borrago. ⁊ stendit᷑ p terraꝫ
⁊ imedio pducit flores usq̄ꝫ. vi. icolore cit
no imedio sbalbidū. ⁊ nō crescit supterrā
nisi lōgitudine uni᷑ digiti. ⁊ hn̄t dulceꝫ sa
poreꝫ q̄si mel' ⁊ odoreꝫ turꝭ q̄a dr̄ icēsaria. Na
scitur locis mūdis ⁊ siluestrib᷒ ul' icastañti.
¶ Ꝯ dol' matris ⁊ dol' stōi ⁊ etiā ꝯ oppilatiōeꝫ
splēis ⁊ ep̄is fiat crispelle ex herba ⁊ floruꝫ
eius ⁊ farina. cū succo eiuseꝫ herbe. ⁊ dt̄ paci
enti. Valet ꝯ p̄stā. ⁊ uis. succ᷒ ei᷒ potui dato
ul' ip̄a herba ꝯmesta.

Inbulbus. herba ē silis cepe ⁊ nascitur
locis lurdis i sepibꝫ et ꝯ i locis tus. ¶ Ꝯ dol'
articlōꝝ. cepa ip̄a cū tota herba. et sepo

yreino 7 oleo i simul' decoq; 7 fco unguto sepe loca dolēti punge 7 mirabilem vide hec experimento. It ualet ad sepigines 7 impetigines. Radix rei bulbus cū lumēto lupinorum ablue faciem lētiginosa. mir expellit eā.

De laudano.
De liqritia.
De lapide lazuli.
De lilio.
De licio.
De lingua auis.
De linochitis.
De lapatio acuto.
De litargirio.
De lactuca.
De lupinis.
De lauro.
De leuistico.
De lanceolata.
De lactuca leporina.
De lepidos calce.
De lappacioli.

De lentischo.
De laureola.
De lapis magnetis.
De lapis agapis.
De lapis lincis.
De lapis armenico.
De lapis spongie.
De lapis demonis.
De lolio.
De luppulo.
De leontopodio.
De lactuca siluat.
De linosa.
De linaria.
De lenticul'.
De lingua canis.
De lingua yrcina.
De lacca.

Irmolum albū. herba ē q filii noīe appellatur ē aut clara plus quā alia herba ut dicēs homero q iuenit eā mercurius. hīs rad sua rotūdāz nigrā 7 magnā admodū cepa. Cō dol' matris. herba 7 radix ipi bn̄ pīta. et dolori supposita mir dol' tollit.

Kebrabe ul' kekabre gūi arboris ē 7 geni bernicis q etiaz uocat mābra orietalis. virtutez hīt. f. 7 sic. i. primo gdu. dequa. ʒ. s. exea bibitū. Sanguinis fluēs de incisione uenarū pectoris strīgit. Sang etiā ūdcūq; fluat ostipat. Cūuino bibita colicis rubis 7 cardiacaz pter colligātiā stoī 7 cordis patiētib; euenit. Humores ad capite 7 pectore fluentes ad stom arcet. qdā aut medici testāt ualere eaz strāguinosis.

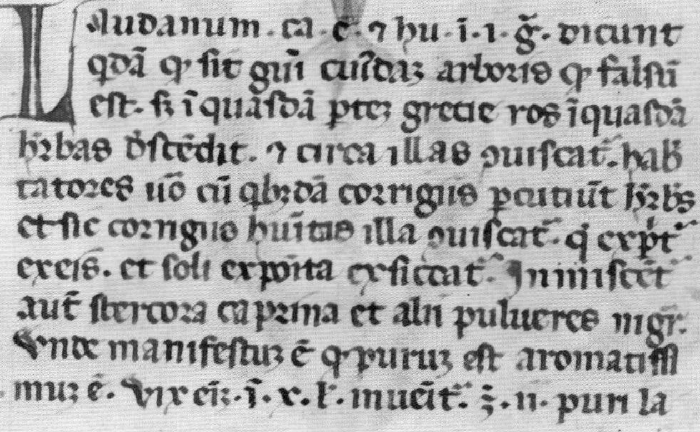

Laudanum. ca. e. 7 hu. i. i. g. dicunt qdā q sit gūi cuidaz arboris q falsū est. s; i quasdā ptes grecie ros i quasdā herbas descēdit. 7 circa illas cōuiscat. habitatores uō cū qbzdā corrigiis pcutiūt herbas et sic corrigiis hūitas illa cōuiscat. q expt exeis. et soli expōita exsiccat. Inmiscēt aut stercora caprina et alii pulueres nigr. Unde manifestū ē q purū est aromatissimū ē. Vix eiz. i. x. l. inuenit. ʒ. ii. puri la

udani. Est aut̄ elligendū q̄ pundero suz
est ⁊ nigruz q̄ etiaz malaxari pot̄. Illud
aut̄ q̄ nimis niger ē ⁊ cū manib; tractat̄
pl'ueriçat. Significat uetustitate ēē ɔsūptz
aut nimis ēē sophisticatuz. hr̄ aut uirtu
tez ɔstrigendi ⁊ calfaciendi ex uiscositate
et aromaticitate ɔfortādi. Cōs catarruz ex
fīā. cā. stuelluz ex eo formatū narib; inti
atur. Cādidez laudanuz ⁊ rose. diu bulli
ant ī aqua pluuiali obturato bn̄ ore ua
sis. et cū aliq̄tuluz tepefacta fuerit. patie
ns pos fumuz recipiat. et ex illa aq̄ ablu
antur pedes qa mltū nerui ūn̄ ɔfortāt.
Cōs relaxationez dentiuz. laudanū ī ma
stix ɔficiatur. et circa dentes gingiuas ī t̄
et ext̄ poāt̄ ɔfortat eos. Cād matrez ī frig
giditatē ⁊ suffocationez. recipiat patiens
fumū p īferiora. Suppositoriuz inde factū
ualet ad eandez. matrez ɔfortat ⁊ ɔceptuz
adiuuat. Cōs precipitationez matricis.
recipiat fumū p superiora. Cōs dol' stōi. ex fri
cā. et digestionez ɔfortādaz. d̄t̄. v. pill'e
ex laudano. ī sero. et fiat ēplm̄ ex laudan̄
cera. pix. addito costo ⁊ stō suppoāt̄.

Liquiritia. tēpate. ca. ē ⁊ hu. qdā dicūt
q̄ sit radix. qdā q̄ frutex. Sz falsuz ē
Est eīz magna radix p̄ue h̄rbe hn̄s fo
lia simil' pomo gnato ul' silis listrago.
Est aut̄ elligenda q̄ nō mltuz grossa est
nec mltuz tenuis q̄ cōiter ītus est crocea.
q̄ etiaz dū frāgitur nō pl'ueriçat. ⁊ q̄ ui
rido est. ptes hr̄ coherentes cū frāgitur. q̄
leuis est īterius sb̄ albida. ul' uiridis.
ul' nigra. abiicienda est. Succus etiaz eī
est eīdez efficacie. et adhuc fortioris q̄ h̄
mō sit. Cuz uiridis ē radix ɔterit bn̄. ⁊
ī aq̄ bullitur bn̄ ⁊ ɔoq̄t̄ fere ad aq̄ ɔsup
tionez. p̄ea exp̄it̄. et soli expoīt ⁊ d̄sicca
tur. et ī rotūda corpuscula s̄m formā
uaso īformāt̄. Quidā sophisticāt hoc m̄
faciūt. puluez sb̄tilez liqritie. ⁊ etiā pluez
succi liqrit̄ ⁊ bn̄ ɔoq̄ūt ī aq̄ et addunt
mel. et faciūt ut diximꝰ. Sz iste magis ē
abhoīnabil' ⁊ nō adeo nig'. Cvalet ɔ oīa
uitiā pectoris. d̄coctio eī ī aq̄ ⁊ ī pleur
si. et pipleumoīa. vinū d̄coctiōis eiuz
ualet ɔt tussiz. ad idez ual; elcītuz ɔfec
tuz ex succo liq̄r. et melle. Cliqritia ma
sticata et sb̄ lingua recepta. sitiz ⁊ aspi
tatez stōi ⁊ gutturis mitigat.

Cliqritia

Lapis laçuli. fri. ⁊ sic. ɔplexiōis est.
et similiter lapis armenicus. Sz eorū
excessus ab auctorib; nō d̄terminat̄.
lapis aut̄ laçuli uena ē t̄re. d̄ qua fit
laçifiluz. et siliter lapis armenicus.
⁊ dr̄ armenicus qa ī armenia repitur
maxīe. nō sophisticat̄. Est aut̄ lapis laç
li. lapis q̄ mltuz asimilat̄ celesti coloris
⁊ q̄daz corpcula ī se q̄ aurea hr̄. Ille uero
q̄ q̄ sb̄ albiduz hr̄ colorez plus hr̄ terestri
tatis. lapis armenicus leuior ē ⁊ sb̄ albi
duz hr̄ colorez. Seruari aut̄ diu possūt

sine ꝯruptione· lapis aut̃ armeniacus citiũ ꝯrũpitur· minorẽ ħt t̃restitatẽ· purgat aut̃· p̃ncipali᷑ meliã· ¶ Cõ melicã· pãs· d̃t cũ decotione sene· ¶ Cõ quartanã d̃t cum decctiõe aliqua purgã melia· ¶ Cõt spleñs uitiũ· et emorroidas· d̃t cũ decctiõe sene ul̃ señs· feñ· ¶ Cõ cardiacã· pãs· d̃t cum succo borragis cũ pl̃uere ossis d̃ cord̃ c̃ui· et ut breuiter dicã· ualet ad oĩs pãs· sũas d̃ melia· cũ medicĩs ꝯficiatur pl̃ui ⁊ nõ decctioĩbȝ· Sȝ d̃t post decctiões· No· mod̃ abluẽdi ⁊ etiã dãdi· lapis laçuli· et armeia· ʒ· ii· ꝯsuẽt dari· In aliquo ua se solido uelud ĩ sipho argenteo· ponatũ puluis eorũ ul̃ alteri᷒ sb̃til̃· et cũ pistello ꝯficiat̃ cũ aq̃ donec aq̃ inficiat̃ tũc abiciatur illa ⁊ alia apponat̃ et sic fiat decies ul̃ nouies· Signũ aut̃ p̃fecte lotitie ẽst cũ aq̃· aut modicũ· aut nullo modo ĩficitur· No q̃ nõ d̃bet dari ĩ decctiõe q̃ ĩ fũdum d̃scendut· nec añ datã decctionẽ· Sȝ post· v· ul̃· vi· assellatiões· d̃tũ sĩ· miro mõ pũgat tũc predictũ· hu·

Lilium· ca· ẽ· ⁊ hu· aliud domesticũ aliud siluestrũ· Sȝ siluester· aliud gerit florẽ purpureũ· q̃ efficacius est· aliud croceũ· ¶ Liliũ domesticũ cũ axũgia t̃tũ ul̃ cũ ol̃o coctũ· ⁊ sr̃positũ ap̃ẽa frũ maturat· ¶ Cõ spleñs duitiẽ radices lilii ĩ multa q̃titate cũ brãca ursina· et radic̃ eiusd̃ põatur ĩ uino ⁊ ol̃o· p· xii· dies· p̃ea coleñ· colatẽ addĩa cera ⁊ ol̃o fiat ungũtũ· ¶ Ad faciẽ d̃albandã accipe tuberositas radic̃ lilii· agresti᷒· purpureũ florẽ ꝑoucẽtis et exsicca pl̃uẽ sũtũ distẽpa· cũ aq̃· ro· ⁊ d̃siccẽtur· sic fc̃a ter· ul̃ q̃ter aliu᷒ pl̃uẽ solũ· ul̃ cũ aq̃· ro· ꝯfectũ· louicas sup faciẽ· ¶ Ad idẽ ⁊ ad ruborem ĩnaturalẽ remouẽnd̃· acc̃ tuborositates p̃dĩas· et uirides si habẽ pot̃· ⁊ admisce pl̃uẽ cathimie· ⁊ cãphorẽ· ⁊ ol̃ũ sanbucinũ· ad ultimũ argentũ uiuũ extictũ ⁊ unguẽto iunge·

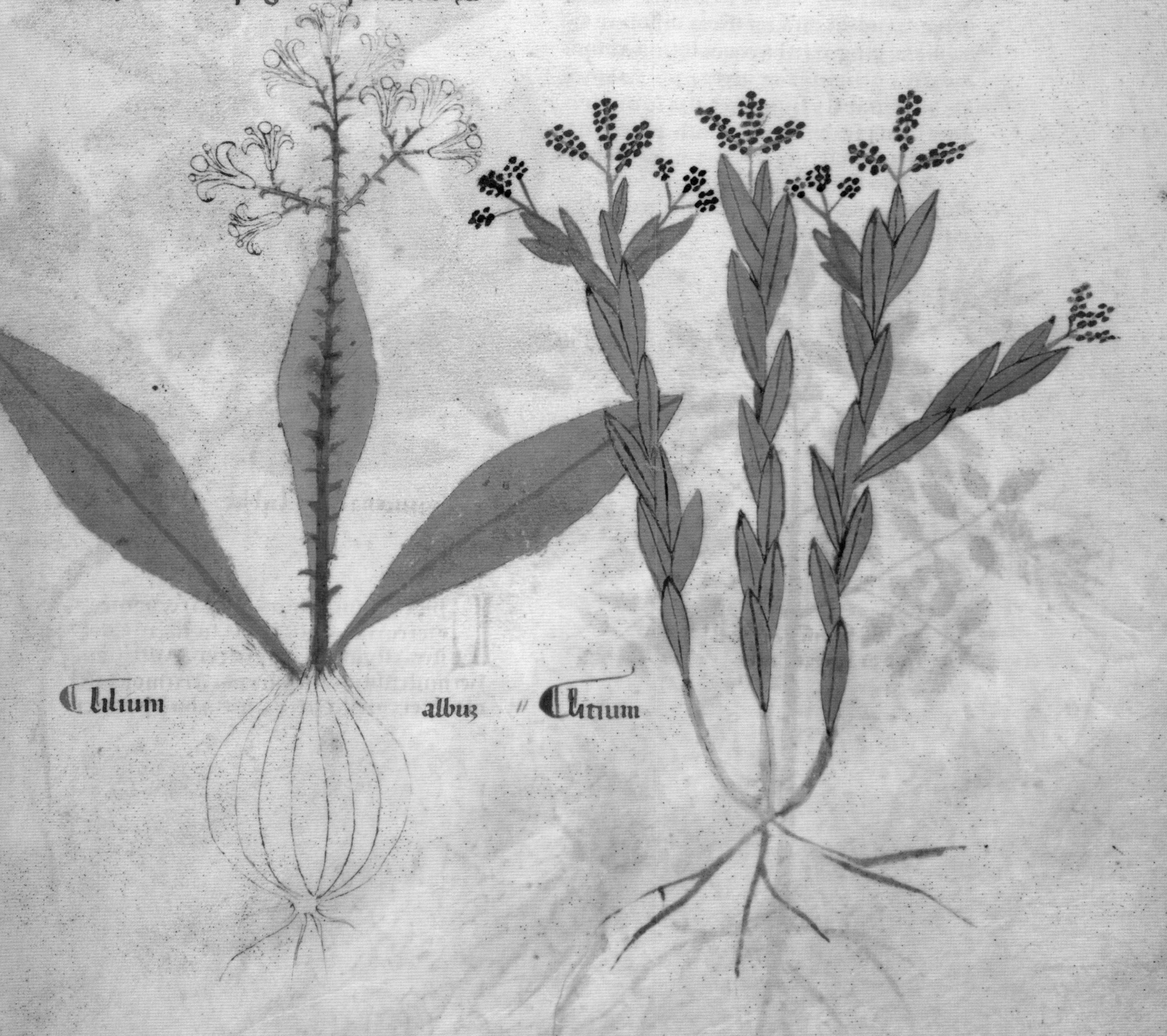

Litium. ca. ē. i. primo. g. sic. i. fo. Q̄d ā dicit eē gūi. q falsū ē. Sz ē succus h'b' silir appellate. i p'ncipio estatis colligit' teritur succus exp'mitur. soli expōit' 7 exsiccat' et i sbstātia litii ꝯmutatur. addunt tn̄ q̄d ā ut dicit diascorides. ē aūt elligendū q duru͞ est. hn̄s q̄d ā glutinositatē. 7 iterius lucidū. et nō molle ē. et obscuruz abiciend̄ ē. p. v. annos pōt s'uari. appellat' etiā licιū. alio no mine oculus lucidus qa reddit oculos lucidos. Cōᵃ maculaz oculi dūitecēs ē. 7 ꝯᵃ lippitudinē. fcaz ex flāte iterius ꝯgelato. litiuz pluēiςet sbtilissime. 7 ꝯficiat cū aq̄. ro. 7 sic dimictat' donᵉ aq̄. ro. ꝯsuātur et ita quat' ul' plies. ul' plus sol' ꝯfectus cū aq̄ ro. ocul' īponātur. Si iueterata sit passio īponāt aliq̄tulū d̄ sarcocolla. Cōficiatur litiuz ꝯsu co feniculi ī uase eneo poāt. ocul' clarificat et ualet cū. cā. ē ab interioribȝ. Cōᵃ fissuram lingue et labiorū. 7 oris ulceratiōē pl'uis litii cū amilo 7 pennidus 7 cū aq̄. ro. ꝯficiat'. 7 ul cera illiniāt'. pb̄ ē satis mulierib; salrnitanis. C Suppositoriuz fcāz ex litio ualet i acuta febre. qa in l'tiuz ꝯsiccata stcora dissoluit. Cōᵃ tumorē gingiuarū freq̄uēs lotura. et frica tio circa gingiuas. ex aceto i quo resolutū sit litiuz fiat. Cōᵃ lintigines fiat iūctio ex li cio 7 cerusa i eadē q̄titate simili'r pl'uēiçatis. Cōᵃ uitiuz matricis i formet' suppositorium ex t'fera. op. 7 su p'sp'gat' plus litii. q̄n super flui humores hūndāt' i matrice ualet p'gat enī ꝯsiccat. 7 ianit.

fraxin' cui' semē d̄r lingue auis

Lingua auis. ca. ē. 7 hu. i. i. g. folia hn̄s parua 7 acuta 7 i forma lingue auis uiridis mlt'e ē efficacie exsiccata nul lius. Virtutē h't icitādi libidinē. 7 huiec tandi. h'rba ipa cū carnib; ꝯmesta libidiē̄ incitat. Cādidē ellīz ꝯfectiū ex testiculis satirionis. et ex carne dactillor 7 iteriōib; festuce. 7 melle. 7 succo lingue auis. h'rba ipa cocta cocta i aq̄ ordi ꝓdest ethicis 7 ꝯsūp tis. Valet etiā decoctio succi lingue auis addito zucch'o. Cōᵃ siccitatē pectoris detur aq̄ decoctiōis ipi' 7 addito dragagāto magis ualet.

sc̄d'm auicēna uocat' lublet

Linochis. siue lichitis. ul' partenoticos. 7 Mercurial' q alia noīa sic uocat'. linogo stes. alguriis. argiriter. partenion. hermuli. asilior. argilices. arumon. alti cus. Mercorella idē ē. ca. ē. 7 hu. ꝯpetenter cu3 carnib3 pinguib3 cocta. d3 ad solutione3 faciendā. Competent etiā ex succo ul' exaq decoctione ei' 1 olo sale. 1 melle fit clisteē. additis his. 1 solues. Ad mestr' puocā. succus herbe mercurial' cū olo laurino ul' vino. potui dato stati mestrua educit. Cont' uitiu3 1 macla oculorū. succus ei' 1 tutia3 cu vino albo siml' omisce 1 bombix itīcta ocul' suppone 1 lava. Cont' dol' 1 surditate3 auriu3 1 si alīq īt fuerit. succus ei' tepid' aurib3 distillatū stati sentiet bnficiu3.

Lapatium q' greci uocāt oxilapatio. alii uocāt. vdia. romani. Romice. alii. rumix. egiptii uoc. Semen. alii. Sn ati fonos. alii. Actus. alii. Afrosearmis. E aūt t'plex maneiei. s3 lapatiū acutū. huius acuta folia 1 hi efficatius est. lapatiū rotūdu3 habens rotūda folia. 1 min' efficax ē. 1 lapatiu3 domesticū folia huis lata. 1 aliqtulum magis usui opetit. Virtute3 hīt lapatium dissoluendi. relaxandi. apiendi. et extenuandi. Cont' scabie3 succus lapatii acuti ol3 nuc. et pix liqda. siml' bulliāt 1 pea colet et icolati poāt' plus tartari 1 fuliginis 1 fiat ungt3. satis opetēs scabiosis ipetigini 1 spigini. Cont' impetigie3 1 spigie3. fiat ofectio. ex succo lapatii acuti. 1 pl'uere auri pigmenti. Ad apea maturādū. lapatiū rotūdu3 tritu3 1 i olo coctu3. ul' cū axūgia suppoāt'. Ad rūpend' apea suppoāt' eodem modo lapatiū acutū. Cont' splenis duritiem succus lapatii acuti cū storace liqda 1 armoniaco 1 aceto ofciat'. 1 dimictāt' sic t'b3 dieb3. pea fiat coctio 1 coletu'. 1 addita cera 1 olo. fiat unguentu3. Cont' stra. dis. fiat decoctio. lapatii. i uino 1 olo. 1 pectini supponatur. vrinā puocat i mlta qtitate. Cauq ul' uinū decoctiois ei' solū opilatioe3 splenis et epis. Cont' leuco flāmia fiat ofectio ex succo lapatii acuti. ʒ. ii. et. ʒ. ii. essule. addito melle et fiat aliqtula decoctio 1 det' patienti. Cont' scrofulas nouellas fiat ex plastr'. ex lapatio acuto et axūgia tritis. valet i alūbricos succus ei' dat' cū mel'. Cont' hundantia3 fl'atis icerebro succus eius cū succo rute i modica qtitate naribus iniciatur i aere callido ul' balneo. Cont' sp'lle fiūt ex lapatio ualent asmaticis ex fri. ca. lapatiū crudū ul' coctu3 comestu3 ofert scabiosis.

Litargiriu3 tēpatu3 ē i frīte 1 siccitate. s3 quosdā frīu3 i pmo. g'. q' sit tēpatu3 i frāte. 1 sic ostat ex uerbis diascorides litargiriū frīu3 ēē 1 stipticu3. Et stipticum sit ognoscim'. q2 siccū ē et tn̄ i q̄litatibus suis tēpatu3. eius tn̄ excessus ab auctorib3 nō determinat'. qa nō ē sensu determinabilis. litargiriu3 ē duplex. ē ei3 qdā q' est spuā argenti. q' fit p excoctione3 i igne. cū sepatur nō puru3 apuro. 1 magis aptinet frāti. 1 hu. ē 1 aliud q' spuā

Lapatium.

auri dr̃. et cũ frãgit̃. īteri est silẽ auro. et aliq̃tulũ caloris aptinet. et Cathimia ppẽ dr̃. et est aliud quo cõiter utim̃. s. fex stagni q͛ silr̃ fit ex decoctiõe cũ sit stagnũ. duena terre. ⁊ istud frĩu ẽ ⁊ stiptitũ. dnt aut̃ qdã q͛ silr̃ repit̃ litargiru q͛ ẽ fex plũ bi. litargirũ. s. fex stagni q͛ cõiter utim̃.

Virtutẽ h̃t ɔstrĩgendi ɔsolidãdi. ex diũso mõ ɔficiendi. Puluis litargii. uulneĩb; ĩpõit saniẽ ɔsumit ⁊ ulcerra ɔsolidat. Ɔ scabiẽ ⁊ precipue scãz ex flã salso. fiat decoctio aliq̃tulũ oli nucũ. ⁊ pl'uis litãgi s̃btilis. ɔficiat cũ aceto ⁊ p̃ea addat oluz nuc̃ calidũ ⁊ bñ ɔficiat. Ɔ dissĩe stãm uitio ĩferiorũ. litargirũ ĩtegrũ super carbones ponat. et bñ calefm aspgat sepiũ ex aceto p̃ea fiat pl'uis s̃btilissimus. q͛ per cristere ĩ rectũ cũ olõ. ro. ul' aq̃ ordi ml' tũ ualz. Ɔ ulceratiõẽ uirge distẽperur cũ olõ. ro. ⁊ iungat putrediñẽ ɔsumit. et ulcera ɔsolidat. Ɔ feruorẽ apatũ ut ĩerisipila ɔficiat̃. pl'uis litãgĩ. ⁊ cerusa cũ aq̃. ro. ⁊ circũ ĩungat. Litargirũ q͛ spuma auri dr̃. pluerĩgat s̃btilit̃ et abluatũ cũ aq̃. ro. qnq̃es ul' septies ul' donec aq̃ nõ ĩficiat̃. ex pl'uc ille pl'uis ĩ modũ collirii. et solũ cũ aq̃. ro. ocul' ĩpoñat. Ad faciẽ depurandã ⁊ pãnuz sup̃fluũ remouendũ. q̃ h̃nt mulieres p̃ partũ. axũgia gallinacea ul' ãserina. liq̃fiat et addito puluere litargii. ⁊ olõ. ro. fiat ũguẽtũ.

Lactuca. tẽpate. frĩa. ẽ ⁊ hu. sem̃ eĩ frigidi ẽ ipa h̃rba. Sz excessus eĩ nõ dterminatur ab auctorib; h̃rba usui ciboʀ. semen uõ usui medicine ɔpetit. Judicat aut̃ ab auctorib; oĩuz h̃rbarũ tẽpatissima bonũ q̃dẽ sãguineẽ gñans. et copiaz lactis. Tib; ẽ colle ricis satis ɔpetẽs cruda ul' cocta comesta in febribus ml't̃ũ ualet elixa ul' cruda. cocta ĩ aceto addito crogo. solũ oppilatiõẽ splenis ⁊ epis. Ad sopnũ puocã. sem̃ eĩ ɔficiatur cũ lacte mulieris ⁊ albumine oui. et fiat ẽplastũ circa tĩpora. Puluis etiã sẽis lact. cũ lacte datus sopnũ puocat. Jdẽ facit febricitantib; datũ cũ aq̃. Ɔ apẽã. calã ĩ principio ɔficiat̃ sem̃. cũ olõ. ro. ⁊ suppõat.

[illegible]

Lactuca

Lupinus

[illegible]

Lupini ait ysaac. ca. 7 sic. i ij. g. farina eorum cum melle ɔfecta 7 potata lubricos necat et cum ipsum termine urinam expgit. Sicut ruta bibat 7 pipe vel splenetica. aq i q cocta fuerint lotis pustulas aufferunt. Si cum mirra 7 melle ɔficias 7 pessaria facias mestrua puocat. Dissecatorum aq nutrimenti esse ē 7 adi gered durum humores esse ɔgruat 7 fm n ui ht egestiua sic ex colatiue n supticā sic ɔfortatiue. supra ergo n abaia antiquorum gda farina igut lupini si pilorum nascentium locis apponit eis euellendis cā ē 7 nato adiuuat 7 exurge alio minime puenit. aq u decoccionis si locis animal abluas monetur.

Lupinus. ca. ē. 7 sic. i ttio. g. lupinorum
alius amarus. q ex nā sui amarus ē. 7
precipue medicine ɔpet. alid dulcis
et insapidus q ex mlta mora i aqua dl'
cessit. et fit isapidus. Virtutem ht diure
ticam. Cō lubricos farina lupinorum ama
rorum cū melle ɔfecta 7 dē. Cad idem ualz
panis fcus ex farina lupinorum ex succo
absinthii ul' aq 7 ɔmestus. Cad idem ualet pci
pue emplm fcm ex farina lupinorum et su
co absinthii positum sup stom. et meli' ē. Si
addat modicum aloen. et eadem ɔfectio sine
aloe solū opilationes splis 7 epis. Valz etiā
ydropic ɔfectio fcā ex farina lupinorū 7 su
co absinthii data. et panis ex eisdem ɔfectu
farina lupinorū ɔ succo psicarie auribu
iiuota uermes necat. C Eadem farina cum
succo porri supfluitates aurium mundificat
Eadem cū olō ɔfecta. apsata fra maturat 7
rūpit.

Laurus. ca. ē. 7 sic. fructus et
folia usui me dicine ɔpet; folia
maiorem hnt uirtutem ɔfortā
di ex aromaticitate. fructus dissolu
ɔsumēdi. folia ex siccata. i loco um
broso et n̄ fumoso. pānū i multa

efficatia fuāt. fructus p duos. C fomē
tum ex aqua decoctiōis foliorū lauri. frūm
matricem mūdificat ɔfortat 7 ɔceptū ex fri
te predictum adiuuat. Cō dol' ɔlericū fiat
fomētum ex uino decoctiōis foliorū lauri.
C ad idem fiat ēplm. s pectinem 7 renes ex
teneritatib; lauri decoctis i uino. Idem facit
ɔ dol' stōi ex fritate. 7 ɔ uōitum ex fra. ca. dē
etiā uinū decoctiōis foliorū lauri. Cō frm
reuma capīs decoquat folia lauri et ros.
in aqua. ore uase bn̄ oppilato. et recipiat
patiēs fumū. et ex aq lauetur frōs 7 timpora
C ad idem fructus lauri ɔterat. 7 fcō pluer
intesta cal'fiat et poāt i sacello 7 sacelle
tur capiti. C ad pannū supfluū redu en
dum 7 ɔ quasdā rubas tuborositates fa
ciei q fiūt i iuuenib; et precipue sāguin
is quas uocāt barulos bacce recentes so
li exponātur 7 ɔsiccētur ut cortex corruga
tus meli' tollat. remocto cortice terantur
et fcō pluē sbtili ɔficiat cū melle 7 h tali
iungat facies i balneo mltum ɔfert. Cō
pānum supfluū q hnt mulieres pt ptū
ɔficiat predcis pluis cū felle aliquo et
iungatur. Sz fel fuit durū distēpetur ɔ
melle. Ex baccis lauri fit olum. ualens
ɔ dol' stōi ex frāte. 7 arthiticos dolores. sic
aut fit. bacce lauri recētes ɔteruntur
et psa diu decocta i oleo colent. h tale dr
olum laurinū. No. qñ i receptis dē inuenitur.
R folia lauri ul' dapnidis folia dbent
poni. cū baccar lauri l' dapnococchi fruc
tus.

Lentiscus

Lentiscus. ca. ⁊ sic. oplexiois ē plus tam
sicce q̄ callid᷒. qa siccissime oplexiois
est. cū receptio ei᷒ inuenitur imedicinis
folia ei᷒ d̄bent poni. qūz tn̄ fructus ponū
tur. Virtutē h̄t ostrigendi ⁊ osolidādi.
Cō fluxū. ov. ⁊ dis. et uomitū ex debilitat'
uirtutis otentiue ul' acuine humorū fa
sciculi pui fcī ex folijs ei᷒ decoquant' iaceto
et pectini et renib; cataplētur. Si fuerit
uitio supiorū itestinorū supstom̄ pōat.
Cō uomitū sup furculā pectoris aliū us.
Cō predicta tennenitates lentisci bulli
antur i aceto usq; ad aceti osūptionē.
pt modū d̄siccent ⁊ fiant md̄ pluis ⁊
d̄t icibis ⁊ potib; ō predicta. Cō ulcera
tiōē; uirge pluis fcūs ex folijs ei᷒ super
testā calefactis d̄siccatis ⁊ pluēicatis
uulcus osolidat ⁊ osūmit saniē. Sz nō
d̄bet pōi n̄ qn̄ ē sanies. Cō ulcerationem
oris ⁊ lingue et labiorū ī febre etiā acu
ta. fiat d̄cctio foliorū ei᷒ i aceto ⁊ fiat fre
q̄nter gargarismī.

Nomē h'be oxeʒenon.

Laureola. ca. ⁊ sic. oplexiois ē. alio n
noīe dī Camedafne. alij uocāt dafni
tes. alij Carogegos. alij lauru trest'.
alij pistillago. alij ysuben. alij alipia
dos. fructus ē ei᷒ sem̄ ul' fructus usui me
dicine opet' et appellat' cocognidiū. Tuz aūt
ueniet ei᷒ receptio s. laureole ul' cocogonis
fructus d̄bet pōi. p. ii. annos ī multa effic
tia suatur. Virtutē h̄t pūgandi pn̄ci pali
flā et colāz. vn̄ sanis lapsis ⁊ egris n̄ mlt
tū febricitātib; pōt dari. acuat' in bn̄dic
ta ul' yeralogodion. ad flā pgādū. oxi et
trifera sara. ad colā purgādū. ad plus iq̄
titate. v. ʒ. addito mastice. ul' bdellio. uel
gūi. ar. ad repnsiōē; acuinis materiā.
mouet psupiora ⁊ iferiora. Cō pluis sub
tilis cocognidii. diu bulliat cū olō ⁊ ex
tali olō i unge pectinē. pt. ftīā. dis. renes
et eos. ungantur ppter tenasmon. ex frō
et glutinoso. humore adherente itestini.

alij uo' oxeʒenō

Lenticula. fri. ⁊ sic. oplexiois ē. ⁊ usui m̄
et esui opet' fruct' ē ul' sem̄. uirtutē h̄t
ostrigēdi. vn̄ ō dissinteriā; tal' fit us. lēti
cule iaceto d̄coqt'. usq; ad aliqntulā d̄nig
ticē; ⁊ dī mane d̄t patiēti ieiuno ad comedēdū.

Lenticula. f. ē. i. s. g. [illegible] ītno [illegible] tm̄ ei᷒ sui opl'ois oposita ineīt. uno imedulla. alia i cortic'. Cortex ē ei᷒ acuitatē h̄t un̄ uētre; mouet ad solutiōē; [illegible]
[illegible] ⁊ itestinor; ad cōstricti [illegible] ualet. lētis simil' cocte cū cortic' aq̄ tolle ⁊ [illegible] olū cū sal' [illegible] stiptic' dab' ⁊ si aq̄
[illegible] diu coqt' alia ad digestio solutiōē; minuit. ⁊ si cortic' ablatis coquit' ⁊ p'ma eiecta ⁊ addat' melior fit addigend' ⁊ addigones collerica refrenādā forti.
[illegible] dico nutrimētū lētis [illegible] ē ad digend' durū melācolicū sāgnez gnat. mag' si cū corticib; comedat' cerebrū fumo [illegible] iplet ⁊ melācolice. vn̄ eī ē doloris
⁊ [illegible] dolosi ⁊ sopnior; [illegible] ē ⁊ plīmōi ac diafingmati. ⁊ pellicule [illegible] pellicular; [illegible] cor d̄siccant ⁊ extenuat.
[illegible] magis [illegible] sue d̄siccatiōis cū uētre; mēstrua ostipat ⁊ egossat ⁊ exire [illegible]. Lentis [illegible] cū cortice cocta sicce ē oploni
[illegible] ⁊ passiōes i cū melācolica creat. sic nigrū morfeā [illegible] cācrū elefātiā ⁊ leonina. cū tamē ⁊ huc sē oplōes. Aliqn̄ [illegible] i si sin cortic' edat'
[illegible] ualet cū cortice [illegible] nimis. ⁊ ⁊ uētositates. iflatiōes; creat. Lēticulā laudabil' ē grādis ⁊ noua. [illegible] acciput' ⁊ ē cibū ⁊ s'm. si m̄ ⁊ p' uētr'
[illegible] [illegible] acuitatis ⁊ [illegible] ⁊ ob [illegible] acuitates [illegible] accipiūt ul' restringend' [illegible]. cortic' [illegible] diu coqt' eiecta
[illegible]
[illegible]
[illegible]
[illegible]
[illegible]
[illegible]

fiat ⁊ eis suppositorium ex bombice ibidem inictō.
auribus iniectatur propter surditatem. Ex humoribus
ibidem existentibus. Sanies autem etiam superfluitatē
consumit.

Leuisticus ca. ē ⁊ sic. i. ii. g. cui etiā se
men leuisticus appellatur. alio noīe dr̄
keisin. Semē nō herba uel radix in medi
cinis dz poni. cū inuenit ei receptio. p. iiii.
annos pot̄ suari. Virtutem hēt diureticā.

apiendi ⁊ extenuādi. unū uinū decoctiois eī
Valz ꝯ opilationem splis ⁊ epis. uel ī aqua
Cz vel intestinorum ⁊ stōi. fez ex uētositate. pl'
uis eī cū pluere cinamoī datus ī cibis valz
ad predicta.

Lapis magnetis. ca. ē ⁊ sic. ī tcio. g.
Virtutem hēt attenuandi ut dicit arist.
Et inuenitur ī litore indie. et ocreani mō
tes. ⁊ cui sūt ex talibus lapidibus ꝯstituti. Vñ
naues clauis ferreis ī fixas attrahūt ⁊ dissolu
unt. Valz precipue uulneratis. pluis eī ꝯfi
ciatur. cū apliconi. et fiat stuellum uulneri
ī ponatur ferrum etiā extrahit. pluis etiā eī
dt̄ ī cibo ⁊ potu et maxīe cū succo cōsolide
maioris. puluis etiā eī subtilissim̄ ī quātitat̄.
ʒ. ii. datus cū succo feniculi. valz ꝯ ydropi
sim. et splenem. et alopiciā. attrahit eīz flā
et melia. Hō etiā uocat̄ lapis calaminaris.

Lapis agapis uel lapis iudaici idem ē.
similis ē testiculi galli. exterius obrigata
īterius solida ⁊ lucida quasi uitro. valet p̄
cipue ꝯ stēn. diss. ⁊ lapidem frāgēdā iuen
ca. pluis eī subtilissim̄ ī maiori q̄titat̄. ⁊ se
mis melōis. citl'. cucum. ⁊ cucurb. mū
datorum. p̄s media. saxifraghe. milii solis.
añ pter q̄taz quīti ad pōd oīum dt̄ man̄
coclearīū unū cū uino al calō. Valet
etiam colicis. ⁊ calculosis eodem mō data.

Lapis lincis. i. lapis q̄ fit de urina lupi
ceruini ⁊ īuenit̄ ī motibus coagulata
ca. ⁊ sic. ꝯplexiōis ē

Lapis armenicus deo satis diximus retro
in capitulo de lapide lazuli quare nūc de ipso ni
chil dicem̄.

Lapis spōgie dz ēē quidā lapis q̄ inuenit
ītus spōgia. uirtutem hēt diur̄

Lapis demonis. uel lithodēmō. i. q̄dā la
pis niger q̄ fricat̄ attrahit paleā ad se

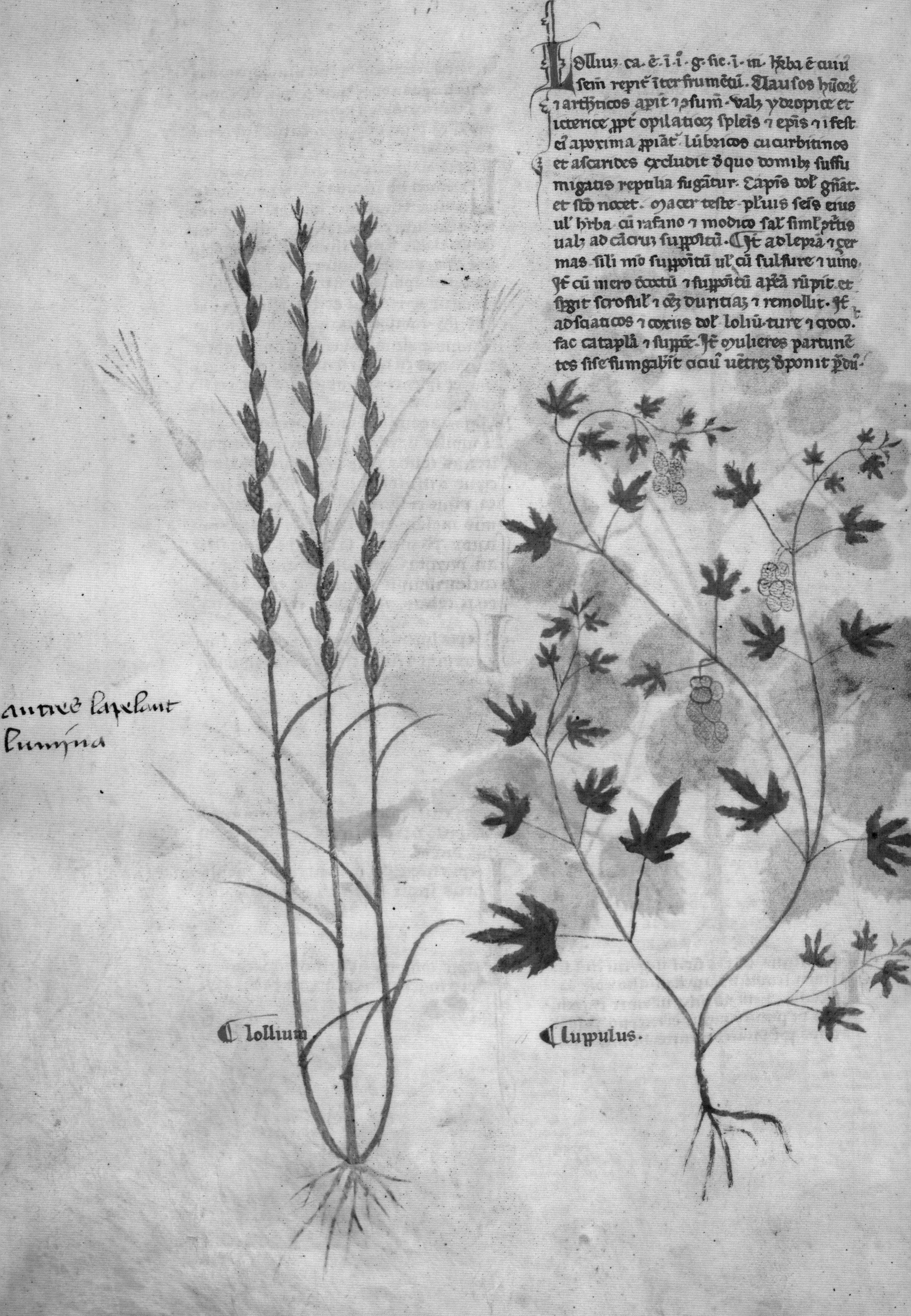

Lolliu͞ ca. ē. i. i. g. sic. i. m. herba ē cuiu
sem repit̃ iter frumētū. Clausos humore
7 arthriticos apit 7 psum. Val̃ ydropice et
ictericie ppt opilatiõz spleīs 7 epīs 7 i fest
ei aproxima ppiat̃. Lūbricos cucurbitinos
et ascarides excludit d̄ quo domib; suffu
migatis reptilia fugātur. Capīs dol̃ gñat.
et stō nocet. Macer teste pl'uis seīs eius
ul' hrba cū rafano 7 modico sal̃ simil ptus
ual; ad cācruz suppositū. Jt ad leprā 7 ger
mas sili mō suppositū ul' cū sulfure 7 uino.
Jt cū mero decoctū 7 suppositū apẽā rūpit et
fregit scroful' 7 oēz duritiaz 7 remollit. Jt
ad sciaticos 7 coxis dol̃ loliū. ture 7 croco.
fac cataplā 7 suppōe. Jt mulieres partunē
tes sise fumgabit ocuū uētre; d̄ponit pdu.

antiq̄ lapelant
lumyna

Luppulus. ca. e. 7 sic. in. i. g. herba e q sili noie appellatur. Nascit i sepib; 7 extedi tur admodu uitis alba 7 folia ei similat urtica. hns aliqtulu poticitati. Colera; rube am purgat 7 adhusta;. Epatice sbuenit. apta dissoluit. uetres 9stipatos soluit. ydropisi; curat. Succus bibitus crudus ma gis laxat miu q; opilatiois apituus e coct 7 dispuatus plus apit glaret. Solatri suco mixtus flegmois q sut iepate 7 splene ualz. yctericiam curat. Ventre; humectat. Calore; extinguit. Si splene; cataplet dolore; abeo celeriter tollit. stauribz i stilletur eas abom putredine mudat. 7 ad fetore; 9tendit. si militer 7 naribz. si old. ro. succus ei tepetur loco ygne pusta refrigerat.

Leontopodion. herba e q alio noie uocat Oculus 9sul. alii uocat filiu ante pater.

alii uocat pes leonin. alii. Stefonos. alii platasio. alii sem leoninu. alii. Drobetron. alii. Libidinalis. alii. Parcellaio. alii. Sudu bal. Nascit i capis 7 iuxta fossas 7 i arudinis ad eos q fuisset obligati ul q nequit iacere cu uxore; sua qn ea sposat. accipiat herba h. ramulos tre; ul septe; 7 collige ea sin rad cibus 7 i decrescente lunio 7 coq; ipa; iaq et abluet semet ipm totu extra dom an hosti u; suu i prima nocte 7 fac fumigiu cu aris tologia 7 pea reuertes i domo 7 no uoluat se retro. 7 erit libat.

Lactuca siluatica. herba e q greci uoc Tridaxagria. alii. uocat. hieracion.

alii uocat. asprecleton. alii pictis. alii die
bita. egiptii uoc. Jnoboson. Jtali. lactuca silu
atica. Nascit. locis cultis 7 sablosis. Prima
cura ei e ad caligine oculoru. dicunt q da. q
cu aqla uult ascedere aere prius comedit hec
herba q melius uideat oib rebz. Succus lac
tuce siluatice cu uino ueteri. 7 melle agapino
7 felle ultoribz. simul bn comixtis i uitrea an
pulla 7 i ipa cosuet 7 ocul i inictat ter i die
ul amplius. summu medicametu pbabit.

Linaria. herba e silis lino. s3 ht flore citrinu
i medio subalbid. 7 maiore hns folia. et
latiora. ualz pipue cont yctericia 7 opila
tioi epatis ex fri. ca. aq decoctiois linarie
7 ipicon. sepe bibita bonu colore icitat 7
sanat. No. q melius fit uinu si patiens no
febrit. uinu decoctiois ei. ualz dol stoi 7 du
ritie splenis.

Linosa q sem lini di. ca. e 7 hu. virtute
ht maturandi. attenuandi. glutinandi 7 re
laxandi. ad apa exteriu maturanda 7 nu pod
fiat epl3 ex farina seis lini. radic malua cu
sci. 7 cepe lilii bn decte i aq 7 adito axugia
fiat eplm 7 suppoat.

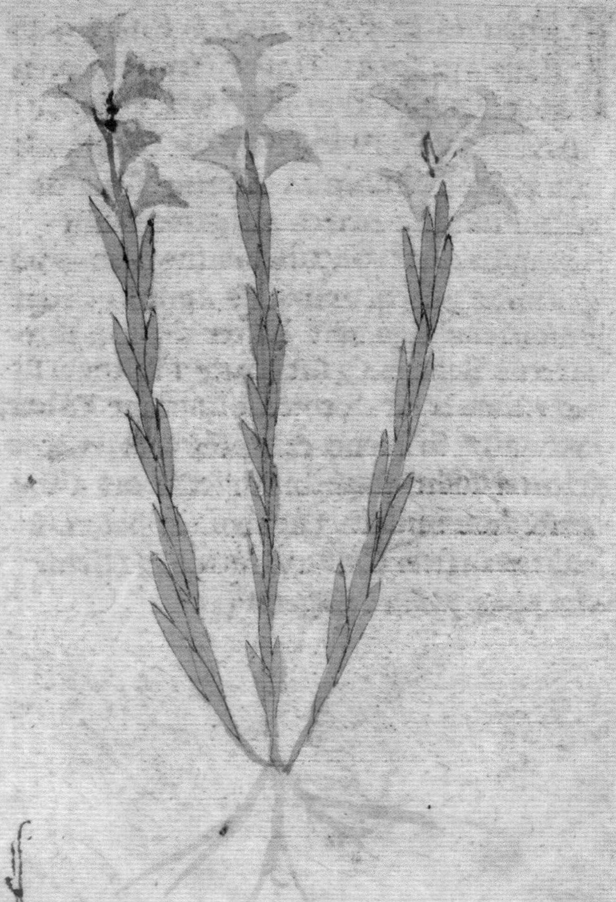

Lini seme ... medium ut ait ysaac ... digeri i
flatiuu ... diureticu e ... cu melle aceto ... ad
tussim ... pectus ... flatica collatione purificat cu melle ... libidine
auget ... apposimate ei cu olo rose ... tenasmo ... intestino
ru si apposimat ei ... mulieres i sederit apetite uulue ... dissolut.

Lenticule aqtice q nascut i aquis. uide
i fontibz ul i foueis ubi morat aqua.
ul aliis aqs. Virtute hnt cotra cacru. succus
ei cu tota herba bn pistata 7 cu axugia
porci bn amixta 7 sup cacru posita eu occidit.

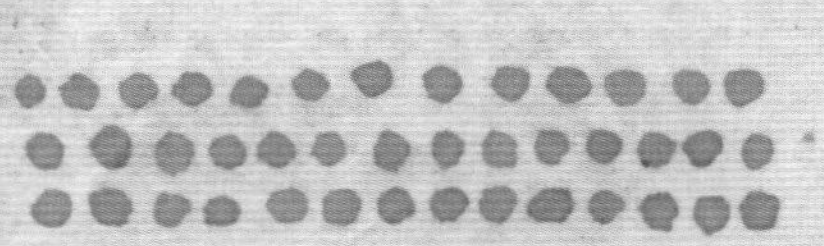

Lingua canis . herba ē q̄ alio noīe dr̄ Cinoglossa . alii uocāt lingua bona . virtutē hr̄t . ca . i . in . g° . hu . i . s . Cōt uenenatas poti ones ꝛ ō morsus reptiliū uenenatorū . succus eī potui data mir̄ pficit . Cōt tumores ꝛ ca ligīnē ꝛ rubores oculorū . succus eī ocul' in missus ꝛ h'ba ōtrita ꝛ̄ supposita mir' sanat . Cad apām maturandū . herba ipius ōcocta ꝛ cū axūgia uetēr bn̄ ōtrita ꝛ fcō ēplīn suppōn mir' rūpit ꝛ pūgat . Cōt pse ōtrita ꝛ supposita act hit spina ul' ferrū ū īt fuerit . Cad fistulaꝫ ēplꝫ ex ipā h'ba ōtā ꝛ supposita . fistulā elargat ꝛ occidit eā . Cherba h̄ ōmesta ualet ō reuma capīs . ꝛ gutture . ꝛ etiā pectus lenit . ad morsū serpentis ꝛ nom serpentis scripes et hec herba concta cū vino ꝛ sūpta ueneno resistit

Lingua ircina . herba ē . hūs folia aspa ad mo dū buglos' ꝫ ē pua ꝛ lōga uno digito . florē ht' s'brufū uiolaceū

Lacca . c . ē . ꝛ s . i . in . g° . gūi arboris ē ultra marīs ptibꝫ nascētis . Oppilatiōes epatis ap it ꝛ ipīn ōfortat . potenciaꝫ pcest . si loti fuerit melior quā nōlota opat'

Lactuca leporina · herba ē · silis cicorea ·
nascit᷑ locis sablosis 7 humosis · expādit
supterrā 7 i medio gerit florez simil᷑ ungu
le caballine · h᷑ comesta ul᷑ bibita ualet ꝯt
uenenatā poticēz 7 ꝯ morsū reptiliuz ·

Lepidos calcis · i · q᷑ battitura eris · vir
tutez hꝫ tāq̄ es ustum ·

Lanceolata siue lanceola · ul᷑ plātago minor
idez ē · valet ꝑcipue ꝯt uenenuz 7 morsum
reptiliuz uenenatoꝝ · succus ei᷑ potui dato
7 ipsā ī herba ꝯtta 7 plage supposita · mir᷑ pugat
7 sanat · Ad uulnera recētia et uetēz ꝯso
lidādaz · fiat ungtz ex succo ei᷑ · 7 pinguedīe
porci 7 sepo arietis · terbentina · 7 ture · addi
to sufficienti cera · fiat unguētū 7 utē ·

Lappacioli ·
minor · herba ē
simil᷑ ūgul᷑ cabl
cat florez · sꝫ hꝫ
dū bardane ·
humidis 7 i planis

siue lappa mi
hns folia si
line 7 nō pdu
lappa ad mo
nascit᷑ locis
aquosis

Lactuca leporina

Mirtus siue mirta ut dicit p[ri]mo f. e. i. s. g. sic. i. ii. e. aut[em] mirtus frutex cui fructus sunt mirtilli q[ui] precipue usui medicine competunt. folia et flores sano. Et no. q[uod] q[uan]to recentiores sunt fructus uel folia tanto meliora. post maturitatem fructus collecti in multa efficacia seruatur p[er] biennium. ad solem tamen exsiccati. folia autem diutius seruatur. flores diu non possunt seruari. Virtutem aut[em] habent constringendi ex ponticitate confortandi ex aromaticitate. Contra uomitum. fluxum uentris et profluuium mulierum ex debilitate uirtutis retentiue uel ex humorum acumine. dentur fructus ipsius ad comedendum. uel succus ipsius detur. uel fiat sirupus ex succo eorum addito zuccaro. optimum est contra predicta. et post pannum seruari sibi coquitur succus cum zuccaro. Si non habes zuccarum adde mel et fiat mediocris decoctio ne mel aduratur. Sed non ualet tantum. sed diutius potest seruari. Ex fructibus contritis uel puluere eorum et oui albumine fiat emplastrum circa os stomachi propter uomitum circa renes et pectinem uo et renes propter profluuium fiat decoctio foliorum in aqua pluuiali et fomentum fiat circa inferiora. propter diss. et profluuium. fomentum etiam ex hac aqua eadem fiat circa frontem et tempora et pedes. soporem prouocat in febre acuta. Suffumigatio per os et fomentum circa frontem et tempora propter reuma et dolorem capitis ex calitate. Fasciculi extremitatibus mirte decoquantur in aceto. et aqua plu. et propter uomitum sup[er] os stomachi ponantur. propter fluxum uentris sup[er] renes pectinem et umbilicum. poni etiam sup[er] renes in acuta febre. soluit dolorem qui fit ex acumine caloris dissoluente. Sirupus ex floribus miro modo ualet contra predicta. aqua etiam decoctionis florum in aqua plu. ualet. Aqua etiam facta ex aqua plu. et floribus mirte ad modum aque ro. melius ualet contra predicta. et contra sincopim. et potest seruari pannum fil. Puluis etiam foliorum eius etiam datur in cibis. ualet et suppositus ulceribus ea consolidat. Puluis ex mirtillorum solus factus et in mane ante cibum datus cum uino confert laborantibus fetorem oris uitio stomachi.

Manna. ca. e. et hu. temperate dicunt quidam quod sit succus herbe. Sed falsum e. Est autem ros qui sup[er] herbas diureticas cadit. in quadam partem grecie. et indie. et conuiscant circa herbas. colligitur aut[em] sic mel. Sed quia in parua quantitate reperitur sophisticatur. Pura uero manna magne est efficacie. quidam addunt fauum

melle · alii sophisticant sine melle · ex succo et
liquiritie puluerizat · 7 melle et quoddam durum effic
iunt · quod manne assimulatur · Dignoscitur
aut quia pura manna subalbida ē · 7 interius h̄t
quasdam concauitates · quasi fauum mell' 7 pure
dulcis est · Nullus eius dulcius manna · Sophisticata
dulcis ē cum quodam acumine si ex fauo sophi
cata fuerit · uelut cum quoddam abominatione · si ex suc
co liquirit. h̄t aut uirtutem depurandi 7 mundifi
candi sanguinem · unde ualet in acutis febrib;
factis ex colera · debet eodem preparari quo cassia fis
tula · s; non ponitur in decoctione · debet aut in aqua ca
resolui · et per catiam colari · et sic ponitur in medicinis
debet poni · Nota quod manna posita in decoctione plus ob
est quam prosit · numquam enim pura inuenitur · unde
in febribus non debet poni quia ex melle admixtione nocet.

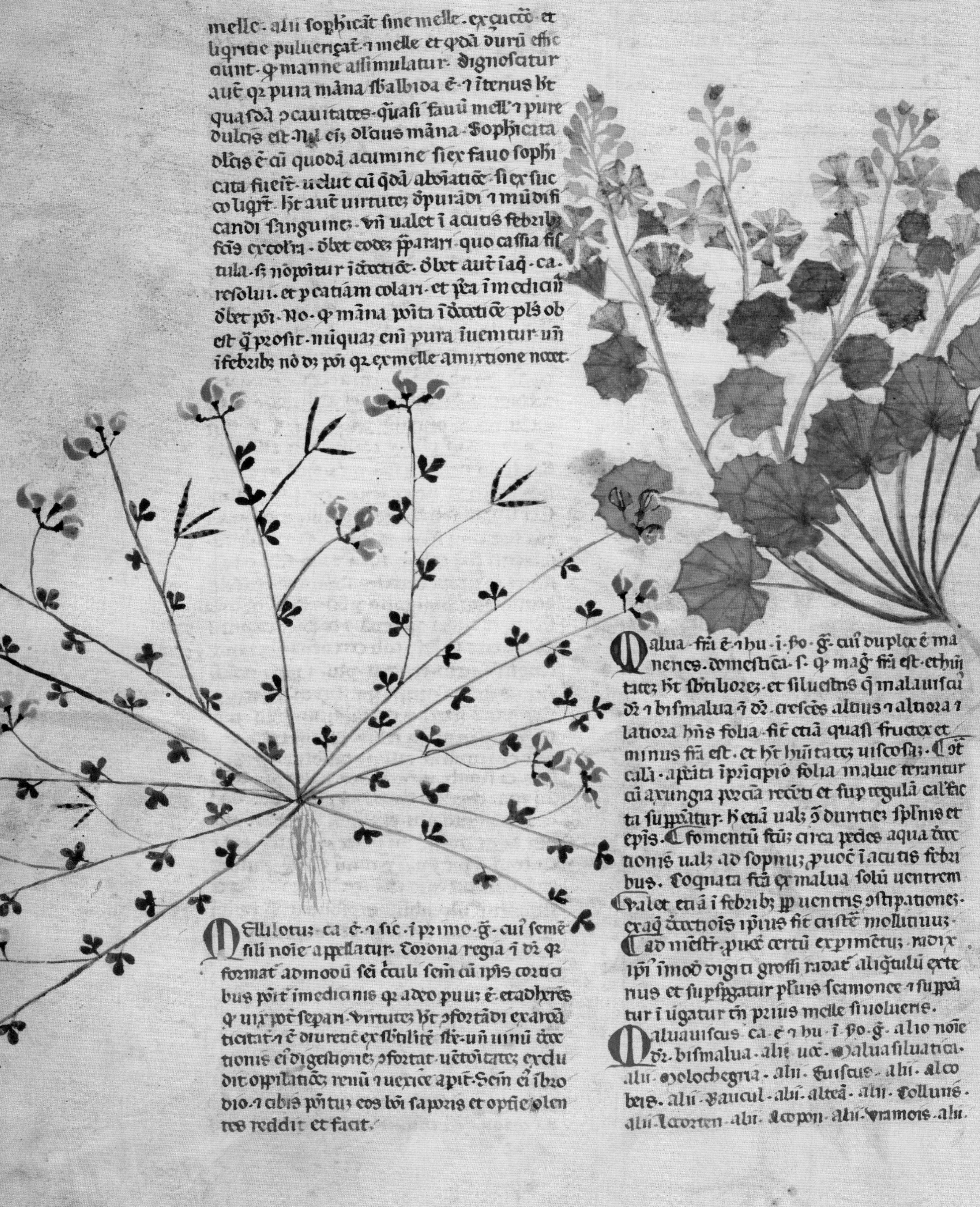

Mellilotus · ca · ē · 7 sic · in primo · gradu · cuius semē
filii noie appellatur · Corona regia in dicitur quia
format admodum sertum curuli semen cum ipsis corti
cibus ponitur in medicinis quia adeo paruum ē · et adherens
quod uix potest separari · Virtutem h̄t confortandi ex aroma
ticitate · 7 ē diuretica ex subtilitate sue · unde uinum decoc
tionis eius digestionem confortat · uentositatem exclu
dit oppilationes renum 7 uesice aperit · Semen eius in brodio
dio · 7 cibis positum eos boni saporis et optime olen
tes reddit et facit.

Malua · frigida ē · 7 hu · in · 2º · gradu · cuius duplex ē ma
neries · domestica · s · quod magis frigida est · et humidi
tatem h̄t subtiliorem · et siluestris quod malauiscus
dicitur 7 bismalua non dicitur · crescens altius 7 altiora 7
latiora hn̄s folia · fit etiam quasi frutex et
minus frigida est · et h̄t humiditatem uiscosam · Contra
calidum · apostema in principio folia malue terantur
cum axungia porcina recenti et super tegulam calefac
ta superponatur · h̄ etiam ual; contra duritiem splenis et
epatis · Fomentum factum circa pedes aqua decoc
tionis ual; ad sompnum prouocandum in acutis febri
bus · Coquinata frigida ex malua soluit uentrem
valet etiam in febribus propter uentris constipationem ·
ex aqua decoctionis ipsius fit cristere mollitiuum ·
Ad menstrua prouocanda certum experimentum · radix
ipsius in modum digiti grossi radatur aliquantulum exte
rius et superfigatur plus scamonee 7 supponā
tur in uirgam tamen prius melle si uolueris.

Maluauiscus · ca · ē · 7 hu · in · 2º · gradu · alio noie
dicitur · bismalua · alii uocant · Malua siluatica ·
alii · Molochegria · alii · Euiscus · alii · Alco
alii · Molochegria · alii · Euiscus · alii · Alco
beis · alii · Baucul · alii · altea · alii · Colliuns ·
alii · Acorten · alii · Acopon · alii · Viramois · alii.

Maluauiscus . plus quã malua . Mollificat
et maturat . s . folia eĩ magis cta cũ axũgia
aliqtulu; cal'fcã . ⁊ sppõita apẽata maturat
duritiez relaxat ⁊ mollificat . hba etiã tota
cũ radice coqtur . fere ad ɔsũptionez aque
et apebit quasi qdã uiscositas q̃ suppõita ap
emata maturat . duritiez relaxat et mollifi
cat . Ex aqua addita cera ⁊ olõ fit ɔpetẽs ũ
guentũ ad pdca . aq̃ decoctiõis seis ipĩ ⁊ mal
ue ualet ɔ tussim ɔfert ethic̃ . Seia etiã ĩ sac
cellata ⁊ ĩ olõ poita duritie; soluit . Dẽ malua
uisco satis diximus retro ũ altea suo alio
noĩe . nũc dicẽdũ est dẽ malua ortens .

. Malua ortense .

Malua ortens q alii uoc̃ Bismalua alii
malua siluatica . alii . Molochegria . alii
anitoa alii acopon . alii . Collunis . alii . diate
ma . alii . locorten . alii . uramois alii . Malua
siluatica . siũ rustica . Crescĩe ĩ ortis qĩ fructex
⁊ hñs magna folia . Ad dol' uesice ⁊ sanguinez
mingentib; . radix malue ⁊ folioz . lb . i . decoq;
ĩ aq̃ ut bñ sit decocta q; colatũ dab potui pa
tienti ptridiũ cũ sitierit . stati sãguinẽ sistit
⁊ dol' mitigat . Ad dol' neruoz . hba cũ radicib;
eĩ decocta ⁊ addito axũgiã uetẽz fiat empl; et
suppone . Ad colicã ⁊ yliacã pãs ⁊ dolõi lato
ris . folis eĩ bñ decoq; ⁊ calidõ ɔtte suppone . Ad
fetidas recẽtes . cinis radicũ ipĩ fetidis sr spge
Ad paniculas siũ apẽita . folia eĩ ⁊ radice c
uisca simĩ bñ decocte ⁊ ide facto ẽplm addito
asũgia sine sale ⁊ supposito . mĩr pbabẽs . Cõ
dol' uexic̃ teste diascor ⁊ aliĩ . phi . hba ipiũ
decocta ⁊ ɔmesta mĩr ɔfert . Cõ ɔz uenenũ fo
lis eĩ ⁊ folia salicũ simĩ ɔtte ⁊ ɔmeste ɔz ue
nenũ discutit . teste . diascor . ⁊ mac . Cõ dol' dẽ
tiu; radix ipĩ sup dentez dolẽte; teneat . Cõ
luxuriaz . radix bismalue suppectinez posita
obligata lineo filo . mĩr stimulat luxuriaz .
Cõ dol' mamillar . Mulier secũ ferat h hba
ĩuoluta lana nigra . ⁊ sepa ueñt dol' . Vt mu
lier nõ pareat añ tẽp . ⁊ fetũ mortuũ expellẽd
ex malua ⁊ modico sale . ⁊ pĩguedĩe ansino
fiat ẽplm ⁊ cũ petia ĩnictat sup uuluã stati
expellit foras . hoc expimẽtũ dixit olimpia te
bana . Ad egilopias . i . carnositas oculoz .
succus bismalue loco mũdo express ⁊ sepe ocu
l' imissus mĩr sanat . Cõ puncturas apiũ et
netibi noceãt . succus malue ⁊ olõ oliue bñ
ɔmisce ⁊ unge te nõ poterãt t' nocẽ . Cõ tine
az ⁊ fũfures capĩs ⁊ plage q putredinez faci
unt . aq̃ decoctiõis folioz malue ablue capt
⁊ folis ɔtritis sr poñ . mĩr purgat ⁊ sanat .
Cõ yngnez sacrũ siũ hustionez ignis . folio
rũ malue bñ ɔtrite ⁊ ĩ olõ oliuar bñ decoq; et
ex tali olõ punge . etiã his folis suppoñ . Cõ
duritiaz stericis ⁊ ĩtestinoz uitia ⁊ matricez
et dol' anũ . aquã decoctiõis folioz malue se
pe ablue loca ⁊ ĩ ferĩ recipiat fumus . mirab
ual; ad pdca .

Mastix . ca . ẽ . ⁊ sic . i . ɔo . g̃ . e aut gũi cuiusd
fructic̃ simĩl' lẽtisco . Jn qdã pte grecie in
fine ueris circa cortices opãt qsdã ĩcisios
⁊ terra mũdificãt ⁊ uestes supponũt ul' quecũ
opimenta ex iũcis fcã . ne liquor effluat .
ĩ terra . Eligenda ẽ aut mastix q clara est

et alba. q aut terre hẽt amixtionem ul obscura e abiciat. Virtutem hẽt confortandi constringendi. conglutinandi. et consolidandi. Contra humores fluentes de capite ad oculos et dentes. et contra dol tiporum factum ex uentositate ascendente a stomacho. ad caput puluis mastic cum uino albo et odorifero. et albumine oui conficiatur addito puluere olibani. si placet et temporibus supponatur. Emplastrum factum ex mastice laudano positum super dentes et gingiuas grossas extenuat. humores frigidos consumit. Mastix in ore masticata dentes dealbat et confirmat. superfluitatem uue consumit. cerebrum a superfluitate depurat. facit e excreare in multa quantitate. Mastix in testa calefacta et corio siue panno uel carta inducta et posita super furculam pectoris. Vomitum colericum constringit. uel si fiat ex debilitate uirtutis retentiue. digestionem etiam confortat et debilitatem egritudinem uel conualescentibus. No. q pilis abrasis de poni siue non coheat. tegula calefacta panno inposito supponatur. et cum adheserit remoueat aqua decoctionis mastic. tepida data digestionem confortat. stomachum relaxatum corroborat. et addito seme feniculi uentositatem excludit. Emplastrum factum ex mastic bolo et albumine oui. et aceto super furculam pectoris positum uomitum colericum constringit. Aqua pluuialis decoctionis mastic data tepida ad idem ualet. fluxum etiam uentris ex acumine medicine reprimit. Aqua .i. pluuialis. uel ro. decoctionis mastic. et iii. uel iiii. granorum. data tepida uomitum uel fluxum uentris factum ex acuitate uiolentis medicine constringit. No. q mastix puluerizari debet decoque neuitus eius dispergatur. et debet dari tepida. Vnde post aqua decoctionis mastic frigida plus ualet q feruentissima quare dico plus ualet tepida quam multum calida.

Menta ca. e. i. sic. i. iio g. cuius duplex est differentia. e enim quedam domestica. q precipue ortulana dicitur. et hec mediocriter calefacit et confortat. e et alia siluatica q mentastrum dicitur. et maiorem hẽt uirtutem calefaciendi. Est aut tertia q longiora et latiora et acutiora hẽt folia. et hec menta romana uel saracenica uocatur. hec magis diuretica e q alie q prouenit ex amaritudine. Menta domestica magis competit usui medicine et uiridis et exsiccata magne e efficacie. debet aut exsiccari in umbroso loco per annum seruatur in multa efficacia. Virtutem hẽt dis-

sumendi. ex propriis qualitatibus confortandi ex aromaticitate. Contra fetorem oris et putredinem gingiuarum. et dentium abluatur os et gingiue ex aceto decoctionis mente ortulanis. postea fricetur ex mente puluere sicce. uel cum menta sicca. Ad apetitum prouocandum cum impedit ex frigiditate humorem continentium more stomachi. fiat salsamentum ex menta aceto et modico cinamomo. seu etiam pipere. Contra uomitum factum ex debilitate uirtutis retentiue uel ex frigida ca. fiat decoctio mente in aqua salmatina et aceto et spongiam intinctam ori stomachi supponatur. et menta ipsa decocta commedat patiens. Contra sincopim et debilitatem in febribus et sine febribus siue ex medicina siue ex quocumque ca. fiat conterantur menta cum aceto et modico uino si fit sine febre. Si cum febre cum solo aceto et frusto panis bene cocti et quasi combusti ponatur in illo aceto. et dimictatur aliquandiu ut bene humectet et manibus applicetur et in in fricetur labia. gingiue. et dentes et tempora et liges super uenas pulsatiles et tempora et bracchiorum. et patiens masticet et humositatem transglutiat. ¶ Ad mundificandam matricem mundificanda teneritates mente coque in vino et fiat suppositorium. ¶ Contra colica pas. fasciculi mente decoquantur in vino et renibus et pectini supponatur. ¶ Contra coagulationem lactis in mamille. fasciculi eius decocti in vino et oleo super ligentur mamille. No. cum datur aliqua medicina contra venenum debet dari cum succo mente. Menta enim habet aliquem articulum attrahendi venenum vel potest dari cum vino decoctionis eius si cares succo mente.

Menta romana vel saracenica. ca. est in sic in secundo gradu habet autem folia longiora latiora et acutiora plus quam alia menta. Et magis diuretica est quam alie que pendit ex amaritudine. ¶ Succus eius mente romane solus vel vinum decoctionis eius vel succus eius cum melle mixtus et datus valet contra oppilationem splenis et epatis et urinalium viarum ex frigiditate humorum et in calido sistit sine febre. Succus etiam eius datus lumbricos interficit auribus stillatus vermes necat. Decoctio in vino et oleo et cataplasmata ipsa herba solum schirosim apostematum sedat. No. quod menta romana pro portulaca poni potest.

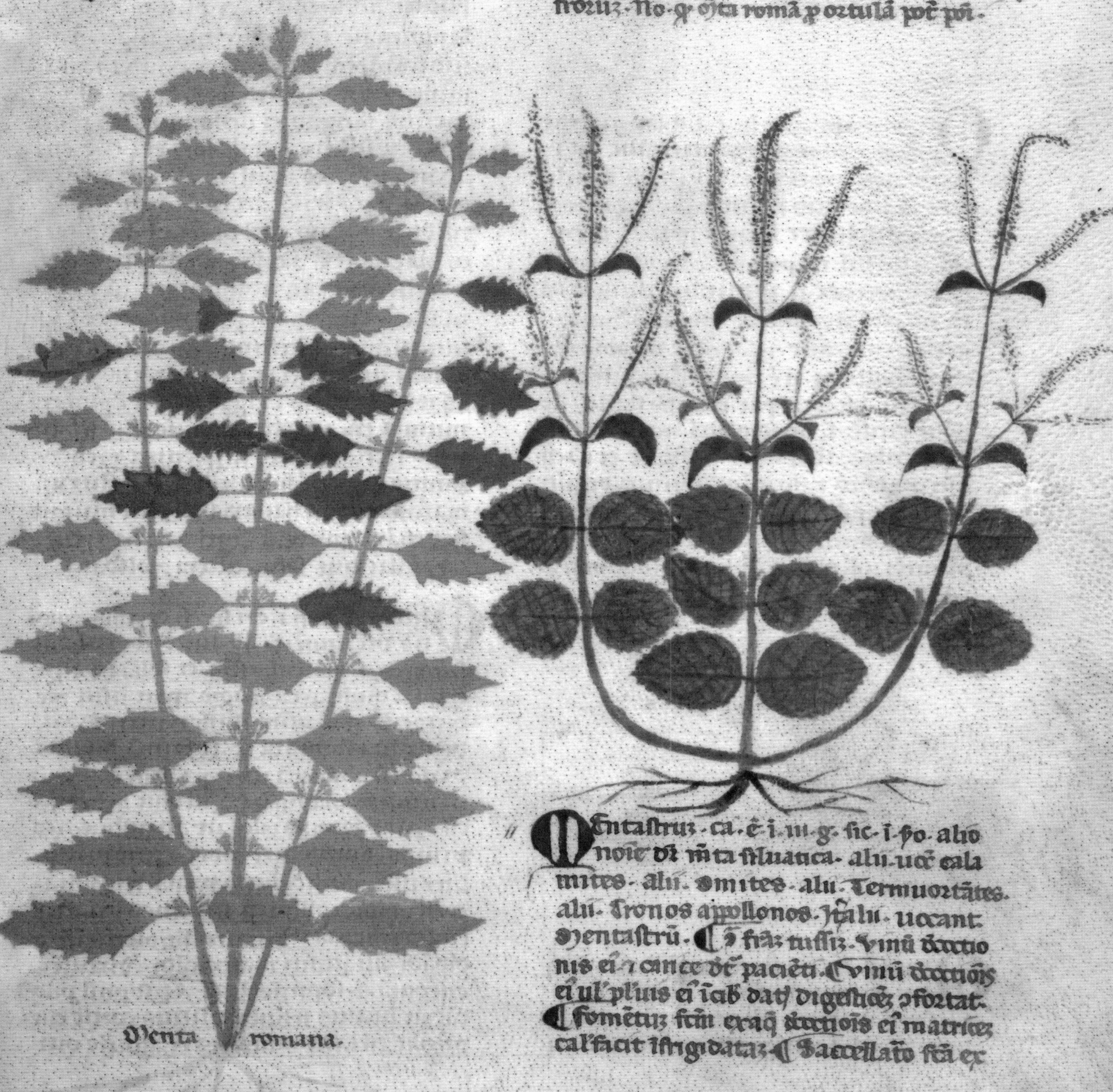

Mentastrum. ca. est in iii gradu sic. in secundo alio nomine dicitur menta silvatica. alii vocant calamites. alii. Omites. alii. Termuortantes. alii. Cronos apollonos. Itali. vocant. Mentastrum. ¶ Contra frigidam tussim. vinum decoctionis eius et cance de pacienti. ¶ Vinum decoctionis eius vel pulvis eius in cibo datus digestionem confortat. ¶ Fomentum factum ex aqua decoctionis eius matricem calefacit infrigidatam. ¶ Sacellatio facta ex puluere eī reuma frigidū capis ꝯstrigit.

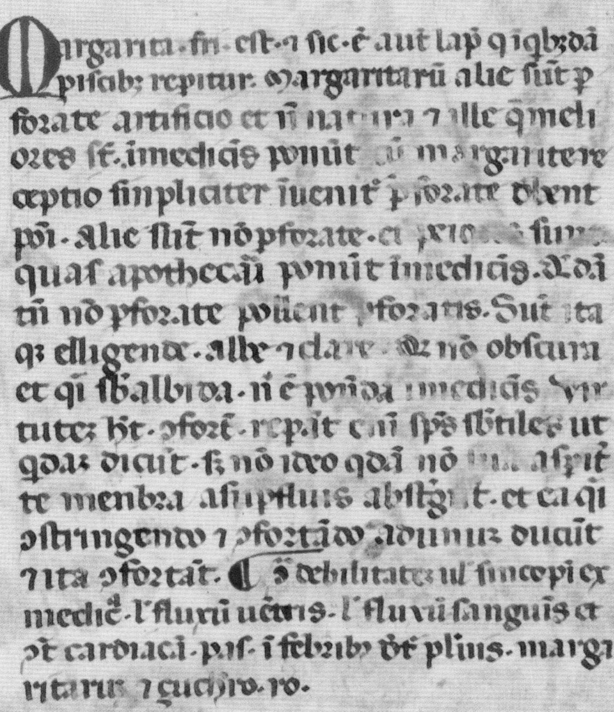

Margarita. fri. est. 7 sic. ē. aut lapꝭ q i glbꝫ dā
ꝑiscibꝫ repitur. Margaritarū alie sūt ꝑ
forate artificio et ū natura 7 ille q̄ meli
ores sᵗ. i medicis ponūt. Cū margarite re
ceptio simpliciter inuenitᵗ ꝑforate dēnt
poni. Alie sūt nō ꝑforate. et [..] sunt
quas apothecarii ponūt i medicis. Qdā
tū nō ꝑforate ꝑualent ꝑforatis. Sūt ita
qꝫ elligende. albe 7 clare. Qꝫ nō obscura
et q sbalbida. ū ē ponēda i medicis. Vir
tutē hᵗ. ꝯforẗ. repāt cū spūs sbtiles ut
qdā dicūt. sꝫ nō ideo qdā nō [..] asprit
te menbra asi pluris abstgūt. et ea qi
ꝯstringendo 7 ꝯfortādo adiuuat dicit
7 ita ꝯfortāt. C Ꝯ debilitatē ul sincopi ex
medicīe. l' fluxū uētris. l' fluxū sanguis et
ꝯ cardiacā. pas. i febribꝫ dᵗ pluis. marga
ritarū 7 cuchro. ro.

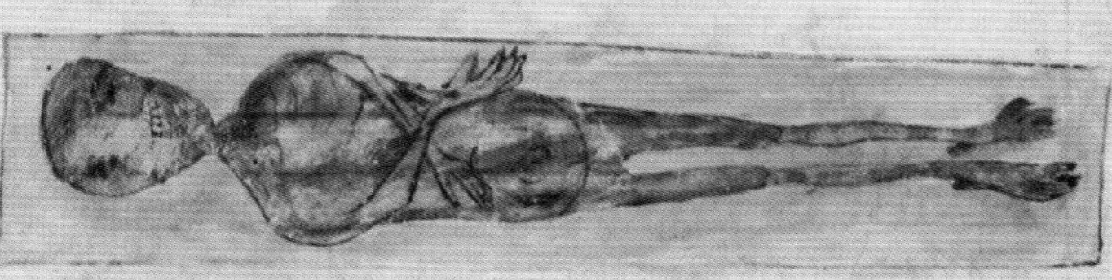

Mumia. ca. ē 7 sic. i. iiij. g̃. teste ꝯst. q
dāꝫ dicūt q sit. fri. qa ꝯstrictiua ē. qꝫ
falsū ē. oīa eīꝫ fria 7 sic lanit. sꝫ ca
lida. ca. 7 sic ꝯstrigiᵗ. Est aūt mumia q

daꝫ spēs q i sepulcris mortuorū repiᵗ. Sole
bant antiq corpora balsamo 7 mirra ꝯdi
re 7 adhuc apꝫ paganos fit circa babiloīā
7 est mlta copia balsāi. circa cerebrū maxīe
7 spinā. uñ ad cerebrū sāguīs calore bal
samu trahit et coquit. similr et cerebrū
aduritur. et exsiccatur et i mumiā trās
mittatᵗ circa spinā etiā mumia inueniᵗ.
Elligenda ē q lucida ē 7 nigra 7 fetida.
q etiaꝫ solida ē. sbpallida aut 7 obscura
nō fetida q facile ꝑluerizatᵗ abiciēda ē.
Virtutē hᵗ ꝯstrictiuā. C Puluis eī sim
pliciter ul' stuellū f[..] ex pluē eī et succo
sanguinarie naribꝫ ꝑitus sanguinem
sistit. Emplm etiā fcm ex pluē eī 7 albu
mine oui frōti 7 tēporibꝫ suppōat. C Vo
mentes sanguinē uitio spūaliū tene
ant diu sb lingua pill' fcās ex plue eī
addito modico mastice 7 aq̄ i fusionis
gūi 7 [..] ꝑea trāsglutiat. Si uitio nutritiuo
rū. dētur puluis eī cū ouo sorbili. ul' suc
co plātagis. C Ꝯ dissinteriā dᵗ pluis eī
cū pluere gūi ar. adusti ꝯfecti. cū aq̄ ro.
ul' succ' plātagis. 7 h̃ precipue ualet si fiat
uitio supiorū itestinorū. Si uō fiat uitio
iferiorū ite[..] iniciatᵗ ꝑ clistē pluis eī cū
aq̄ ce[..] i fusiois draggt. fiat 7 eplin ex
mumia tm 7 aceto 7 albuie oui si fiat
uitio iferiorū ꝑ ōat supponi renes.
Si uitio supiorū sup ūbellicū. C Ꝯ fluxū
matris dᵗ athanasia cū pluē mumie
fiat etiā suppositoriū cū athanasia 7 pluē
eī. Pulū eius solus ulcera ꝯsolidat.

Mandragora. fri. ē 7 sic. sꝫ excessus eius
nō dterminatᵗ ab auctoribꝫ. cuiꝫ due
sūt spēs s. masculꝫ 7 fēia. et folia hᵗ aspa
et qdāꝫ dicūt q ea magis ꝯpetit usui me
dicine. Sꝫ nos utimi idifferenter. Qdāꝫ
dicūt fēia formata eē ad formā mulieris.
masculū ad formā uiri. q falsū ē. Natura
eī nūq formā hūā nō attribuit hbis. qdā
eī opanᵗ formas tales ut ad rusticos dece
pimus. Cortex aūt radix ꝯpetit pricipa
liter usui medicīe. Fario poma. tio folia.
cortex radicē collecta ꝑ. iiii. āños sruatur
i mlta efficacia. Virtutē hᵗ ꝯstri. ifrig
gidādi aliqtulū mortificādi. Virtutē q
encotica. i. sopnifera. C Ad sopnū ꝑuo
cādum i acutis febribꝫ. puluis cortic eī
ꝯficiatᵗ cū lacte mulieris et albuie oui

et i ducatur

ĩungatur calore febrilem reprimit. ℭ Ꝯ calida apřata. fiat ĩunctio ex olō ĩ pricipi o. reprimit eũ ñ. fructus etiã ul' folia sup cataplẽtur ul' saltem succus ei cũ succo alicui' hrbe frẽ. ℭ Ꝯ fluxum uẽtris exipi tu colre ex olō predicto uenẽ et tota spi na ĩungatur et modicũ ĩiciatur ꝯ aliquo cristeri leni. No. q̄ mãdragora. alii uocãt antimĩnō. alii. Andropomoreos. alii. ap pollea. semẽ ei' dr̃ abbaloros.

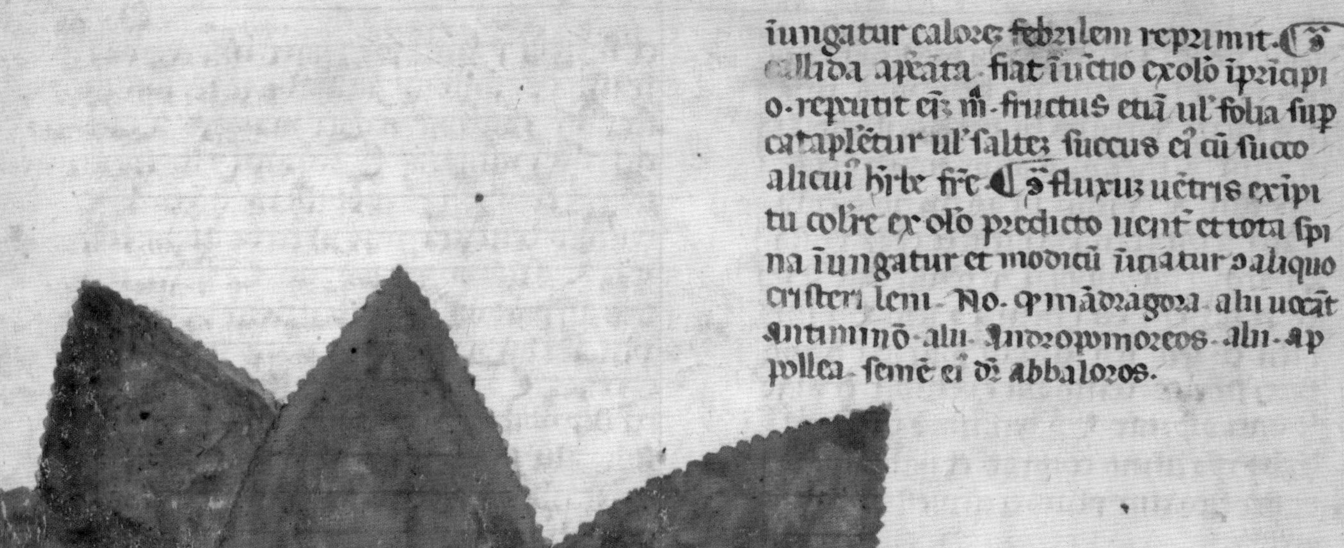

Nomẽ hrba mandragora.

et ĩoueatur frõti et tĩporibz. ℭ Ꝯ col. capĩs excal'. folia mãdragoř trita suptĩpora pñã tur. Inungat etiam olō mãdragorato. q sic fit. poma mãdragore trita ĩ olō cõi diu maceretur. pča fiat fiet aliqtula decoctio colẽtur. et illō dr̃ oliũ mãdragoratũ. q ualet ad sopnũ puocã. ꝫ col' capĩs excal' cã. sifrõs ꝫ tĩpora ĩungatur. Si uõ plsu'

Osti. ca. ẽ ꝫ sic ĩ fo. g. cui' radix simili noĩe appellat'. alio noĩe uocãt. antimũ ticum. alii uocãt. Sistra. s̄ alia hrba ẽ et

n̄ sistra. Ꝯeu precipue usui medicine ꝯpetit.
uñ radix imedicīs pōi dꝫ. ꝑ duos annos
pot̄ suari. Virtutēꝫ h̄t diuis̄. ex sb̄tilitat̄ sb̄
stantie. attrahendi ī ꝯsumendi ⁊ ex q̄lita
tibꝫ suis. ℭ Vinuꝫ ul' aq̄ decoctiōis eius.
ualet ꝯ oppilatiōeꝫ spleīs et epīs. ex frīā.
cā. sīm. ⁊ dis. aqua ii ꝯpetētius dat̄ ī esta
te. et iuueni etiā uinuꝫ ⁊ seni. ℭ plus
meu. cū seīc̄ ferī ī cibo. ul' potu dat̄ uētosi
tateꝫ stōi. et itestinorū excludit. et dige
stioneꝫ ꝯfortat. ℭ ꝯ tenasmō ex frīā. cā.
h̄rba ipā ī uino coquat̄. et fiat encatisma.
et pēa supponatur plus ei cū melle ꝯfect̄ sati
ꝯpetēs.

Mala citonia .i. cotana. frīā sūt ⁊ sic
collecta. et ꝯsimil' ꝑstipites ligatas

et suspēsa p ānuꝫ pot̄ suari. ī frīā regione
ī calida ꝑ dimidiuꝫ ānuꝫ. Virtuteꝫ h̄nt ꝯ
fortādi. ⁊ ꝯstring. recētia maioris st̄ effi
cie. sicca minoris. ℭ ꝯ uōitū ⁊ fluxum
uētris ex caliditat̄ et dēbilitate uirtutis ꝯ
tentiue. dentur cruda ul' cocta ad ꝯmedē
duꝫ. ℭ ꝯ uōituꝫ ꝑst prādiuꝫ. ℭ ꝯ fluxū uen
tris añ prādiuꝫ. alit̄. decoquātur optie ī aq̄
plu. pēa bñ ꝯtrita. callida ponāt̄ sup pectine
et renes. ℭ ꝯ dis. scīꝫ uitio iferiorū itestīo
rū sup ūbilicū. Si fiat uitio supiorū ꝯ tos
stōi. alit̄ succus eī exprīatur. ex eis uiridi
bꝫ. et ullo succo decoquatur plus addito
sūmat h̄moi ius optimū ē ꝯ predicta. Si pl'
uis etiā ꝯmedat̄ appetituꝫ ꝯfortat ul' ꝑuoc̄.
⁊ ꝯstrigit. Ex eis ī fit diacitonitō h̄ modo
coctana prius decoquāt̄ ꝑ optie ī aqua. pēa
abiciat̄ exteriora q̄ꝫ ī pura sūt. s. nigra ul'
sb̄nigra. q̄ pura sūt ualet q̄r bonū h̄nt colo
reꝫ ꝯterūtur carnes citoniorū. abiectis n
nucleis ī interioribꝫ. pēa cribētur h̄ modo.
ponāt̄ incribo q̄ h̄at larga foramina. pēa
fricētur bñ cū manibꝫ et illō q̄ sb̄tilius ē
trāsit. et iteruꝫ q̄d durū remanet ꝯterātū
et predicto mō cribretur. deīn addatur
mel pari q̄titate et fiat decoctio sēp q̄ mo
ueatur. Signū decoctionis est q̄n suppōitū
sup lignū ul' lapideꝫ ul' ī frigidatuꝫ potest
remoueri. Tūc debēt appōi plures ⁊ mo
ueri sēp et statiꝫ ab igne remoueri et sup
tabulaꝫ dilatarī et planificari. Si uis ap
ponere m̄cuꝫ h̄ mō appones. dissoluas
ipāꝫ ī aqua. ro. ul' salteꝫ ī uino ⁊ sup asp̄ggē
de mō ī ades ī frustra. et unū sup aliud
pones. ut ptes suppōite odoreꝫ ī uirtute
ab aliis ꝯtrahāt. No q̄ ex tribꝫ gnīs po
tes coaptare. c. lib. alii ꝯficiūt more elli
q̄r faciūt aliq̄tulā decoctioneꝫ ⁊ pēa īpōnt
pluēs et ōponūt ab igne. et satis ꝯpetēs
est. Antiq̄ exp̄mebāt succū. et apponebt
mel ī eadeꝫ q̄titate et decoq̄bāt medioc̄ter
pēa apponebāt plures et tūc remouebāt
ab igne ⁊ illō dr̄. Oxiporiū diacitonitem
ꝯfortat digestionem et m̄ltuꝫ ꝯfert. ꝯ
ualescētibꝫ egritudine. ℭ Seīa citoni
oruꝫ h̄nt uirtuteꝫ. leniendi. ⁊ huectādi.
Vīi aq̄ decoctiōis seīuꝫ. ualet pthisicis et
ꝯsūptis ꝯpetenter eīꝫ ponūtur ī sirupū
eoruꝫ. ℭ ꝯ aspitateꝫ lingue. seīa ponāt̄
ī pāno sb̄tili ⁊ ponāt in aqua more. psillii
et abluāt̄ lingua ⁊ illiniāt̄. No. q. n. ꝫ.

pulvis sufficiunt ad ii lib. cum vis facere dia citonitem.

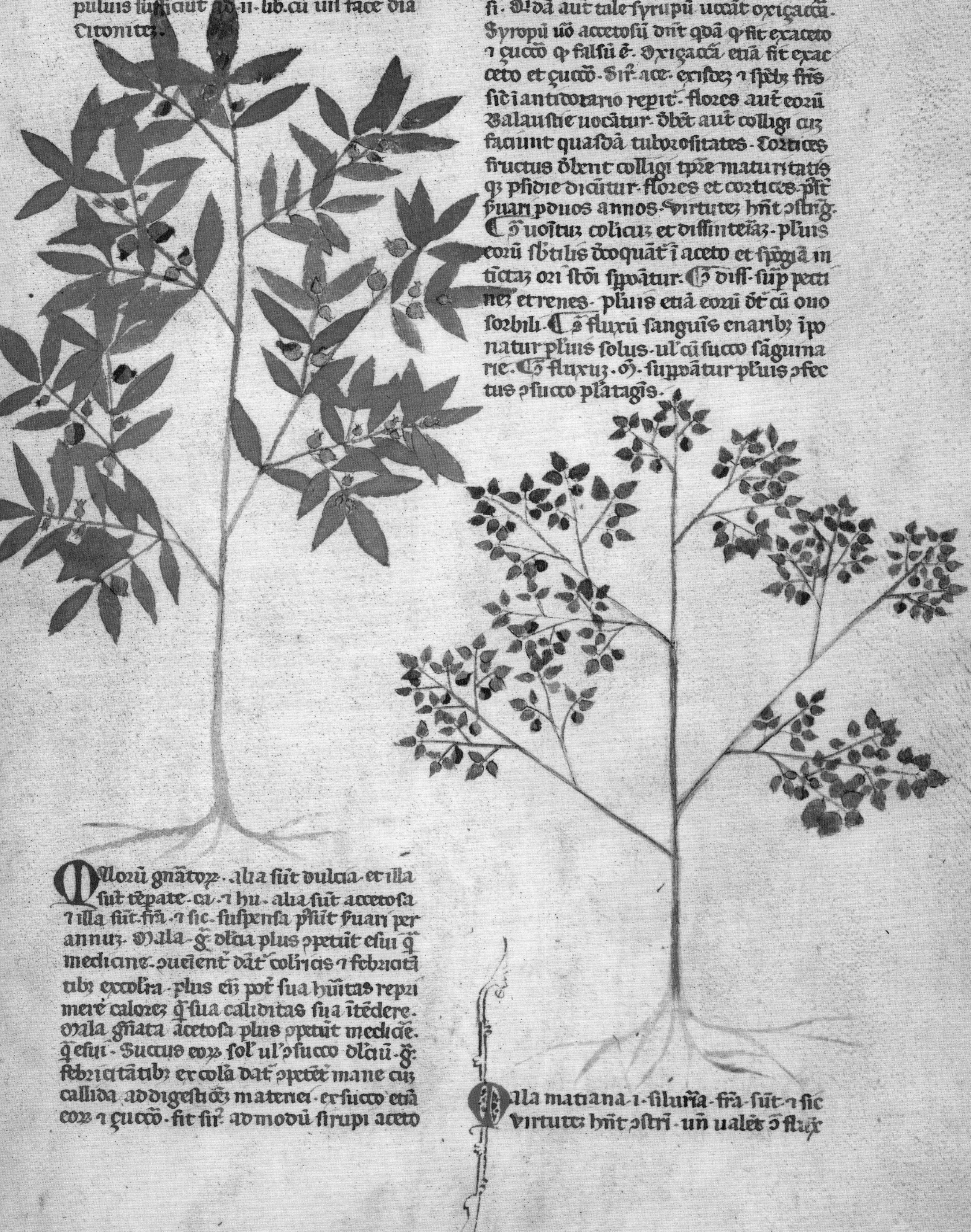

Malorum granatorum alia sunt dulcia et illa sunt temperate ca. et hu. alia sunt acetosa et illa sunt fri. et sic. suspensa possunt servari per annum. Mala granata dulcia plus competunt esui quam medicine. conveniunt dat. colicis et febricitantibus ex colera. plus enim potest sua humiditas reprimere calorem quam sua caliditas sua intendere. Mala granata acetosa plus competunt medicine quam esui. Succus eorum sol. vel cum succo dulcium granatorum febricitantibus ex cola. dat. competenter mane cum callida ad digestionem materiei. ex succo etiam eorum et zucco. fit sir. ad modum sirupi aceto si. Quidam autem tale syrupum vocant oxizaccara. Syropum vero acetosum dicunt quidam quod fit ex aceto et zucco quod falsum est. Oxizaccara etiam fit ex aceto et zucco. Sir. ace. ex sidoniis et speciebus fortis sicut in antidotario reperitur. Flores autem eorum balaustie vocantur. debent autem colligi cum faciunt quasdam tuberositates. Cortices fructus debent colligi tempore maturitatis qui psidie dicuntur. Flores et cortices possunt servari per duos annos. Virtutem habent constrictivam. Contra vomitum colicum et dissinteriam. pulvis eorum subtilis decoquatur in aceto et spongia intincta ori stomachi superponatur. Contra diss. super pectinem et renes. pulvis etiam eorum detur cum ovo sorbili. Contra fluxum sanguinis e naribus imponatur pulvis solus. vel cum succo sanguinarie. Contra fluxum ventris superponatur pulvis confectus cum succo plantaginis.

Mala matiana id est silvestria fri. sunt et sic. Virtutem habent constricti. unde valent contra flux

uentris. Jdeo fit usus q̄ decoctus est de coton[i].
¶ Poma d[u]lcia q̄ pure dulcia sūt uento
sa sūt. q̄ insipida sūt aliq̄tulū magis cope
tunt esui. debent etiā dari p[os]t cibuz feb
citātibz. et cruda ⁊ cocta. Cocta u[er]o mag[is]
competut̄ conualescentibz ex egritudīe labo
rantibz ī digestione; p[ro]fiāte stōi hoc mō
findantur interioribz nucleis abiectis
fiet q̄dam concauitas ī medio et īponat̄
puluis nucuz m[uscatarum] gariof[ilorum] foliorū. aliq̄do
in ponātur sol[ummodo] p[u]l[ue]ris cinamōi ul[vel] cimini. l[ongi]
pipis. ⁊ assent[ur] ⁊ ita parata d[e]t[ur] pacienti.

Marrubium. ca. ē. ⁊ sic. ī. t[er]tio. g[ra]. h[er]ba
est. q̄ alio noīe. Prassiuz. d[icitu]r. alii uoc[ant]
Eupatoriō. alii. fillop[er]. alii filoluper.

alii uoc[ant] Asetepan. alii. Asotropā. alii.
Ematauruz. alii. Assedros. alii. Sonosu
ru. alii. Camellopodion. alii. Nastrofon.
alii. Marobio. cui[us] folia precipue medi
cinis competūt. cortices radices sāno. folia
collecta ⁊ suspēsa ī loco ūbroso. pannū p[os]s[un]t
[con]suari ī mlta efficacia. Virtutez. h[abe]t dissolu
consumēdi. ex q[u]litatibz suis. ex amaritudine
Virtutez diur[eticam] dissoluit eēz ⁊ acthit. ¶ [Con]t[ra]
uitiuz pectoris. s[cilicet]. asma ex fr[igi]do hu[more] ⁊ uiscoso.
d[icitu]r dia prassiuz q[uod] ab eo d[e]noīat[ur]. ul[vel] ellīz
ex una p[ar]te succi eius. ⁊ v. mell[is] d[e]spuati.
et fiat decoctio ad aliq̄tulaz spissitudinez
et p[ost]ea ī poāt[ur] p[u]l[ue]ris draggāti. liq[ui]rit[ie] ⁊ succi.
bonū est [con]tra predictuz ul[vel] saltez puluis ei[us]
[con]ficiatur cū melle distēpato. addita pul
uere succi liq[ui]rit[ie]. ¶ [Con]tra tussiz ualet usus dec
tionis ei[us] ⁊ caricarū. ¶ [Con]tra str[icturam] ⁊ dis[niam] d[e]t[ur] uiū
decoctiōis ei[us] et fiat ēplm̄ ex ipsa h[er]ba decoc
ta ī uino et olō sup[er] pectinez. Jdez fiat [con]tra
colicaz. pās[sionem] ex fr[igid]a. ca[usa]. ¶ [Con]tra emoroid[as] īflate
et nō fluētes. fiat encatisma ex aq[ua] salsa
et uino decoctiōis h[er]be ip[s]i[us]. et p[ost]ea fiat suppo
sitoriuz ex puluē ei[us] confecto [cum] melle. ul[vel] fiat
decoctio p[u]l[ue]ris ei[us]. ⁊ succi ei[us] cū olō. m[ultum] et bom
bix ītictus supponatur. ¶ [Con]tra lūbricos detur
puluis ei[us] confecto cū melle. ¶ [Con]tra uermes
auriuz succus ei[us] auribz īiciatur. ¶ [Con]tra sple
nis duricies cortex radic[is] cū ipsa h[er]ba mac[e]
rent[ur]. p. xx. dies ī uino et olō. p[ost]modū fi
at decoctio. et p[ost]ea colet[ur] ⁊ colature addatu[r]
cera ⁊ oleū. et fiat ungtm̄ optimū [con]tra pre
dictuz uitiuz.

Malabatruz q[uod] foliū paradisi ⁊ foliū ab
butu. d[icitu]r. ca. ē. ⁊ sic. mltū ē aromatic[um]
s[ed] illo caremus. cui[us] loco ponitur. folia ga
riofili. ul[vel] spica nardi.

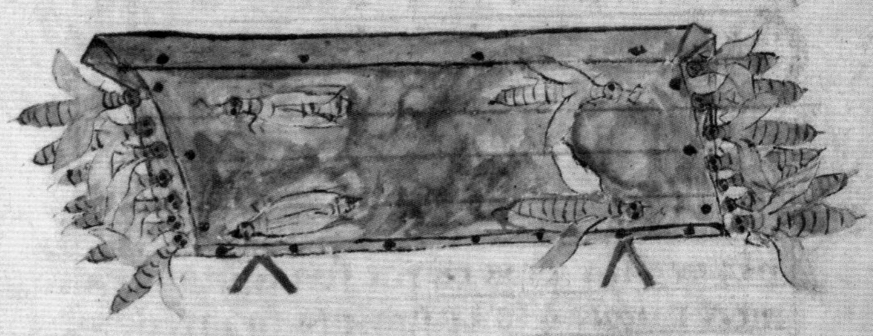

Mel. ca. ē. ī primo. g[ra]. sic. ī. s[e]c[un]do. mel
artificiose ex apibz. h[ic] reponūt[ur]. dū eēz
puriorez p[ar]tez flor[um] suggendo acthunt. pu

riores ptes trasmittut. et aliis apib; sbmi
nistrant. q̄ similr aliis puriores pte trans
mittut ceraz q̄ et fauū melle artificiose
ɔponut. Est aut mel domestic q̄ fit ad ru
sticis q̄ qdā ligna ɔponūt iqb; apes collīgū
tur. et tale mel albū ul' sbrufū est. albū
i frigidis sbrufū icalidis ōbent pōi me
dicinis. p. c. annos suātur. ē aut et aliud
mel silvestre. q acuē ōr. h isilvis repitur
et hoc nō tintu ualet sz amarū est. et iō
i medicis diuī ɔpetētiū ponitur. ē et mel
castaneatū. q fit ōflorib; castanearuz
quas apes fugiūt et illō sz amarū est. et
in diureticis ponēnō ē medicis. Mel ɔs
uat et mūdificat. In medicis ponit ut
spēru amaritudo ōprimatur. et ut pmelle
dulcedine medicina. aprofūda membroz
sba melius attrahat cū pluerib; imiscetū
ut suentur isua efficacia. C ō. hūore frōs
istō ōtur mlsa cū aq ca. s. ɔfectio fca ex
melle et aq. ō ōbilitatez. s. sincopi detur
mulsa cū aq. fra ad ɔfortādū. C ō saniez
stōi ōt nitrū ul' salcū melle. cū calida ex
tergit eni ɔ soluit. C ō pannū faciei et
etiaz pt partu. ʒ. ii. camphe. nit. ʒ. iii.
cū melle ɔficiantur. et sit ita p tres dies
pea iungatur facies. Caditez ualet mel
cū felle tauri. mixtū etiā ad idez ɔ ad fa
ciez clarificandā lotura ex melle ɔ aq.
C Suppositoriū i febrib; mel sup testaz
uratur donec aliqtulū nigrescat. tūc a
appōe pluēs sal' ɔmisce. pon sup lapidem
et forā imodū digiti suppositoriuz ɔ imic
te.

Muscus. ca. ē. ɔ sic. in sō. g. hūiditas
qdā est. q i apātib; quorundā aīaliū
in india iōstis locis capreolis silia iqz
daz inguinib; sūt qdaz ɔcauitates iqb;
colliguntur. hu. ɔ apata post matura
tionez uō pmotū et collisionez rūpūt
ɔ segregantur apata. cū pelle ɔ inueitur
muscus. i tali pelle q pilos ht. m. tū albos
Musci tripx ē maneries ē eiz m'cus q oīo ni
ger est. q nō est laudabil'. Est etiā muscus
q niger est. ad rufū colorez accedēs q lau
dabilior ē. ē et muscus q oīo sbrufus est
ɔ oīo ad colorez spice nardi accedēs q la
udabilissim'. dicūt aūt qdā q tal' musc'
hz ab hiis aīalib; q sūt ubi spica nardi
inueitur. ɔ spica nutriunt. Vn nutīnē
tuz spice trāsducitur ad ptes pdcās. et
fit muscus spice nardi. Est ergo eligē
duz muscus q sbrufus ē. tal' eiz uix sop
histicari pot. q ī sz amari saporis ē et cūz
gustu pcipit statī replet cerebrū aroāti
citate. et q nō cito dissoluit nec multū
resistit. q etiā nō clarus iterius. Inueīt
qnq; grana q lata sūt ɔ p totuz eqlia. que
optiā iudicāt ad modū xii karate. C So
phisticatur aut muscus. et precipue nig
ɔ nig ad sbrufuz colorez accedēs. ex amix
tione paū assi. ul' sanguis irtini. aliqntu
luz assi. sz uix discernit. ponit. eiz. ʒ. i. in
sc. ɔ. iii. ul'. iiii. pdcā pulueis. discernit tū
tn qz panis assus cito frāgit. sanguis
irtinus cū frāgit lucidō ē ɔ clarus iteriū.
Anq; etiā uendit cū ipis pelliculis et s
sophisticat' simili ex predictis pluēib;.
Inciduntur eī saraceni pelliculas ɔ fun
dūt. et bonū mscū extrahūt. ɔ iponūt so
phisticatū. pea ɔglutinant ita pellicul'
ut nō appareat. muscus. uō sophisticat'
cū pelle pondrat i duplū msci nō sophi
sticati. Suari aut pot i uase uitreo spisso
et bn obturato cera. Sz meliū iuase plū
beo. ut ex frāte. et hu. plūbū melius ɔser
uetur. ii ōz suaī cū aroaticis qz tūc aro
maticit pōret. Si uō amisit i olla pōit
ore apto icoatuz. ɔ aroaticitatez recup
abit. Muscus ht uirtutez ɔfortādi.
ex aroāticitate. dis. ɔ ɔsuēndi. ex glitati
bus. C ō sincopi et totius corporis ōbi
litatiōez sīu uitio epis ul' cerebri ɔ dol'
stōi ex frāte ōtur simplr. cū uino ul' dia
margariton ul' plurīs aroaticō ad plus

in quantitate .vi. granorum. ¶ Contra debilitatem cerebri et palpitationem matricis in naribus applicetur et contra suffocationem suffumigetur eo.
¶ Ad menstrua educenda et conceptum adiuvandum ex
frigiditate impeditum preparatur cum tiriaca magna suppositorium in fine ex storace calamita ambra et musco. valet multum. ad idem muscus solvatur cum
oleo muscellino et bombix intinctus supponatur.
¶ Contra fetorem oris parum cum masticetur pa-
palliat fetorem. ¶ Contra fetorem ascellarum quando
virtus eius illiniatur sub ascelle et fricentur
palliat. Nota quidem mercatores cum volunt
emere muscum obturant nares ne odoretur
et iubent discooperire muscum et currunt obtu-
ratis naribus et flatu tenentes ad medium
iactum lapidis trahunt aerem postea et sen-
tiunt odorem musci emunt sic probatum.

Mirobalani.

Mirobalani omnes sunt frigidi et sicci generaliter citrini frigidi
et sicci in secundo gradu. fructus sunt arboris in
India nascentis eiusdem manerie sunt omnes
sed diversarum tamen effectuum sicut pruna eiusdem
generis sed tamen diversorum effectuum et diversorum sapo-
rum. Mirobalani species sunt .v. bonorum citrinum
kebuli. Bellirici. Emblici. yndi. Citrinus est eligendus qui grossus est et ponderosus
et confringitur interius est gluttinositas. per .x.
annos servatur similiter kebuli et Bellirici.
kebuli non servatur nisi per .v. annos. Belli-
ricus. emblicus et indus per multos annos
servantur. nec est multum curandum de electione
indorum et emblicorum. Auctores dicunt
quod omnes mirobalani purgant colleram. Sed quidam
plus quidam minus. Mirobalani citrini principaliter
purgant coleram secundario flegma. kebuli principaliter
flegma secundario coleram. Indi principaliter melancoliam
secundario coleram. Emblici et Bellirici flegma et coleram.
Cum autem ponuntur mirobalani citrini in medicinis ab
auctoribus ponitis debent cortices tantum modo
ponderari cum nucleis et nuclei postea abici
et cortices poni similiter et kebuli. Alii debent poni
cum nucleis quia a nucleis non possunt separari
vel quia parvi. attendenda est quoque quantitas et
modus. Mirobalani citrini in quantitate ʒ .ii. et s. ad
plus debent poni. cum per se ponuntur hoc modo pluries
ponimus in aqua calida non tamen fervente quod consuetum
tota quantitas in mane colatur et datur talis
decoctio competenter datur in acutis febribus quia
non calefacit sed suaviter purgat. et ista valet
precipue. ¶ Contra dissinteriam quandoque etiam damus
cum cassia fistula et tamarindis ad purificatio-
nem sanguinis. ¶ Si ergo datur cum cassia fistula
et tamarindis. resolvatur prius cassia fistula
et tamarindi in aqua et colentur. In colatura ponatur
pulvis mirobalanorum mane coletur et detur. Et notandum
quod omnes decoctiones mirobalanorum possunt dari competenter
in mane. sed decoctio mirobalanorum citrinorum similiter debet dari
in mane vel in matutinalibus horis. Decoctio autem
indorum et kebulorum in sero oportet detur. Nota
quod in habentibus stomachum frigidum decoctio mirobalanorum
dari debet cum aqua calida aliquantulum quia si daretur
cum frigida statim provocaret vomitum fiat autem hoc modo decoctio colata ut diximus ponatur in vase argen-
teo vel terreo et hoc vas ponatur in alio vase
aqua fervente pleno et ita calefiat. et postea
aliquantulum calefacta detur. Item notandum quod semper
decoctionem mirobalanorum citrinorum datam debet dari sirup-
actualiter frigidus. sibus cum aliqua frigida vel saltem
aqua frigida in estate non yeme. Si ultra ducatur
quantum vellis detur aqua multum calida. post decoctio-
nem vero aliorum mirobalanorum datam in estate detur sirupus [margin: calido vel ...]
cum calida. Alii mirobalanos non ponunt in tanta quanti-
tate quia numquam per se ponuntur. sed secundum hoc quod in
laxativis ponuntur. ¶ Ad pannum oculorum
removendum faciunt quidam pulverem de nucleis
mirobalanorum et imponunt in oculis. Alii conficiunt citrinos
aqua rosacea et soli exponunt donec aqua consumatur
et sic faciunt ter vel quater. et postea pulverem illum
simpliciter vel cum aqua rosacea imponunt de mirobalanis.
kebulis quidam faciunt mirobalanos conditos hoc modo post
maturitatem dum virides sunt per tres vel .iiii.
dies in sirupo hoc modo confecto. in aqua resolvunt
cassia fistula et tamarindi. et manna postea colatum
et colature apponunt zuccarum et faciunt sirupum et
tali sirupo ponunt mirobalanos kebulos qui inflamantur
extenduntur et ingrossantur et servantur in
tali sirupo per .v. annos. isti mirobalani conditi
multum clarificant. visum debilitatum ex fumositate melia et flatica. valent in sincopizantibus
et patientibus emoroidas. comedat patiens in
mane. et post bibat mellicratum vel sirupum in quo positi
fuerint. si habet cum calida. ducet bis vel ter. non opportet cavere acidum sed melius est si caveat. Nota
quod bonum mirobalanorum conditus pondus quinque ʒ .i.
vel parum minus. Sophisticant autem hoc modo accipiunt kebulos vetustos et ponunt in lexiva
calida donec inflentur et ingrossentur per .xv. dies
vel plures et calefaciunt lexivium. cum inflati sunt
et ingrossati faciunt sirupum predictum et imponunt
et dimittunt per mensem vel plus usque dum sunt
omnino nigri exterius et singulis diebus movent.
¶ Quidam alii ponunt nuces maiores recentes

i predicto sir. quã ponut albucius. dicūt aūt dicūt sic pse discerni q acu sīu aliq obstaculo penetretur boni ē q falsū est. qr cū significaret ēe albuciuz. oms eīm mirob' et recentes ⁊ uetēs hūt nucleos. vñ nō psūt acu trāsfigi. discernit aūt h mō ille q bonū ē cū frāgit interius et ext nus. oīo niger repit et cū gustat puā hr pōticitatem. et mltaz dulcedinē. Sophisticatus aūt cū frāgit. interius ē sb albidus ul' qsi sb albidus ⁊ mltaz hr pōticitatē et puā hr dulcedinē.

Maca. ca. ē. ⁊ sic. i sco. g. Est aūt ut qdaz dicūt flos nucū ọ. q uidr falsū qr floret tñ dr aūt it fructus ̄sumūtur. dicūt aūt maces qdaz cortices q reperiuntur circa auellās. p. x. annos suātur. Mac hr uirtutē ̄fortandi. ex aromaticitate dis. ̄su. ex qlitatib' suis. elligitur aūt macis q cū sb rufus ul' rufus. et q hr acutuz saporē cū aliqtula amaritudie. q aūt nigr ul' tereus ⁊ nō hns acutuz saporē abiciend' ē. Cō indigestionē ⁊ frātē stōi. valet uinū decoctionis eī mac. fiat ḡ hoc eplm qa optiuz est. ō stōi dbilitatē et frātē i ̄ualescētib' expluere macis. et mastic. añ. olo. ro. ⁊ cera. Ad cerebrū ō purand' ad supfluis masticetur et i ore teneat. ut fuositas resoluta cerebruz petat ut purget supflua. Cō dbilitē stōi et epat. ex frāte leucoflantia. ⁊ yliaca pas. et uitiuz spūaliuz. ⁊ asma ex uiscoso flāte optimū remediū fiat decoctio mac. i succo feni. i fine decoctiōis ad datur modicū uini. coler et colature exibeatur. Cō cardiacā pas. dtur puluis eī i cibo et potu.

Mirra. ca. ē. ⁊ sic. i scdo. g. Est aūt gūi arboris i india nascētis q tpr estiuo. qr daz guositatē ex se pducit q circa arborez ̄uiscatā acti ōe caloris in sba mirr trasmutat. Est aūt elligenda q citrina est ul' sb rufa iterius aliquātuluz lucida. Mirra alia grossa alia minuta. ⁊ grotatrotides appellatur. ul' alco ut qdaz dnt mirra trotides. Virtutē hr ̄for. ex glutinositate ̄ducendo ptes i unū. dissolū ̄su. mediocriter ex qlitatib' suis. vnd ̄suat qa q tuz dissolū tm̄ ̄sumit. vñ corpora antiquorū ̄dita fuerūt cū mirra ut suarentur. Mirra suat p. c. annos. Cō catarru fiat pille. ex mirra ⁊ storace cal'. ⁊ tent. etiā eadē ualet ad digestionē ̄for. ⁊ ō uiscosū flā adhēsis spūalib' ut i tussientib'. Cō asma ⁊ uitiū pectoris dr uinū decoctionis mirre. ualet ad digestionē ̄fortand'. ⁊ ō fetorē oris puemente ex fuōsitate ascendente a stō. et ō saniē stōi et itestinorū. Cō uitiū gingiuarū fricent' gingiue expluere mirre. putredinē ̄sumit ⁊ ̄solidat. Vulnerib' ipositus ea ̄sumit ⁊ ̄glutināt. Cō pille ō mirra date. vii. l. xi. i mane die accessiōis ualet ō tercianā. Cō fumigiū mirre receptus p nos cerebruz ̄fortat. recept' p uuluā p enbotū. matrē mūdificat ̄for. ⁊ cal'facit. supfluitates extergit ⁊ ̄sumit. et ita ̄ceptū adiuuat. Receptū ō tenasmon ex frā cū pānū fumū recipiat mir' ualet.

Maiorana. ca. ē. ⁊ sic. i sō. g. alio noīe

Miliū. ca. ē. ⁊ sic. i scdo. testatr hec leuitas eī q grauitas ⁊ uiscositatis q uentositatis absentia nutr min' ceteris granis. ex qb' panis fit. Sanguinē nimiū n laudabilē gnat. sue tam gdū siccitatis ̄fortatiuū ē stō. aliuqz mebrorū corporis. Ideo q uentrē dissipat. Dia miliū diureticū ēe dr. assatū i olla ad tortionē doloreqz uētris suppositū vz cū ā nutritiōis minime ē siccitatis. eī nō eis accipiedū ē q carnes suas augmetari ⁊ pinguescere uoluerit n eis q laudabilē sāguinē siu corporis cupiūt gnari s; illi soli i qb' stō refrigeratio ac ̄fortatio humorū qz eī supfluorū ̄siccatō appetit.

Ebriū dr̄. alii uocat Sansucus. alii Persa. alio noīe. amaricus siue amaricos. herba ē q̄ m̄ltos ramulos sp̄gēs sp terraz 7 folia h̄t lanosa rotūda simil' nepite. Cui flores 7 folia ꝯpetūt usui medicine. Colligit ī estate cū florib; et ī ūbroso loco dsiccāt. ꝑ annū suat̄. ¶ Virtutez h̄t ꝯfor. ex aromaticitat̄ dissolū et ꝯsum̄. et mūdificandi ex q̄litatib; suis.

¶ Puluis maiorañ ī cibo datus ul' uinū decoctionis ei stoīn ifrītū cal'facit. digestionez ꝯfortat. folia et flores ī testa cal'fca 7 ī sacello positi ī loco dolēti supꝑōitur dolorez stoī ex uētositate soluunt q̄r euacuationez opant̄. ¶ Capiti suppositi ualet ꝯ reuma friḡ. ¶ Fomentū factū ex aq̄ decoctionis maiorane circa uuluā matricez mūdificat 7 supfluā ꝯsumit.

exsiccata prius ad solez. p̄ea ī umbra suspēsa pannuz suatur. Virtutez h̄t. dis. ꝯsu. 7 ꝯfor. et ex h̄ndi silez h̄t effectuz maiorane. et ꝑ̄ easdez cās silis sit usus excepto q̄ eī decoctio magis ꝓuocat mēstrua 7 matricez mūdificat. ꝯfor. adiuuat ꝯceptū. ¶ Itē ꝯ antracez ualet. ualet cū axūgia etiā ꝯmixta ītra in picga. It ꝯ oēz dolorez. ix. dieb; ꝯtinuis similiter supposita. ¶ Vinū decoctiois eī ualet ꝯ sincopī ex frā. ca. decocta ī uino 7 olo 7 cataplāta. apꝑeata maturat duritiez splenis et epis relaxat.

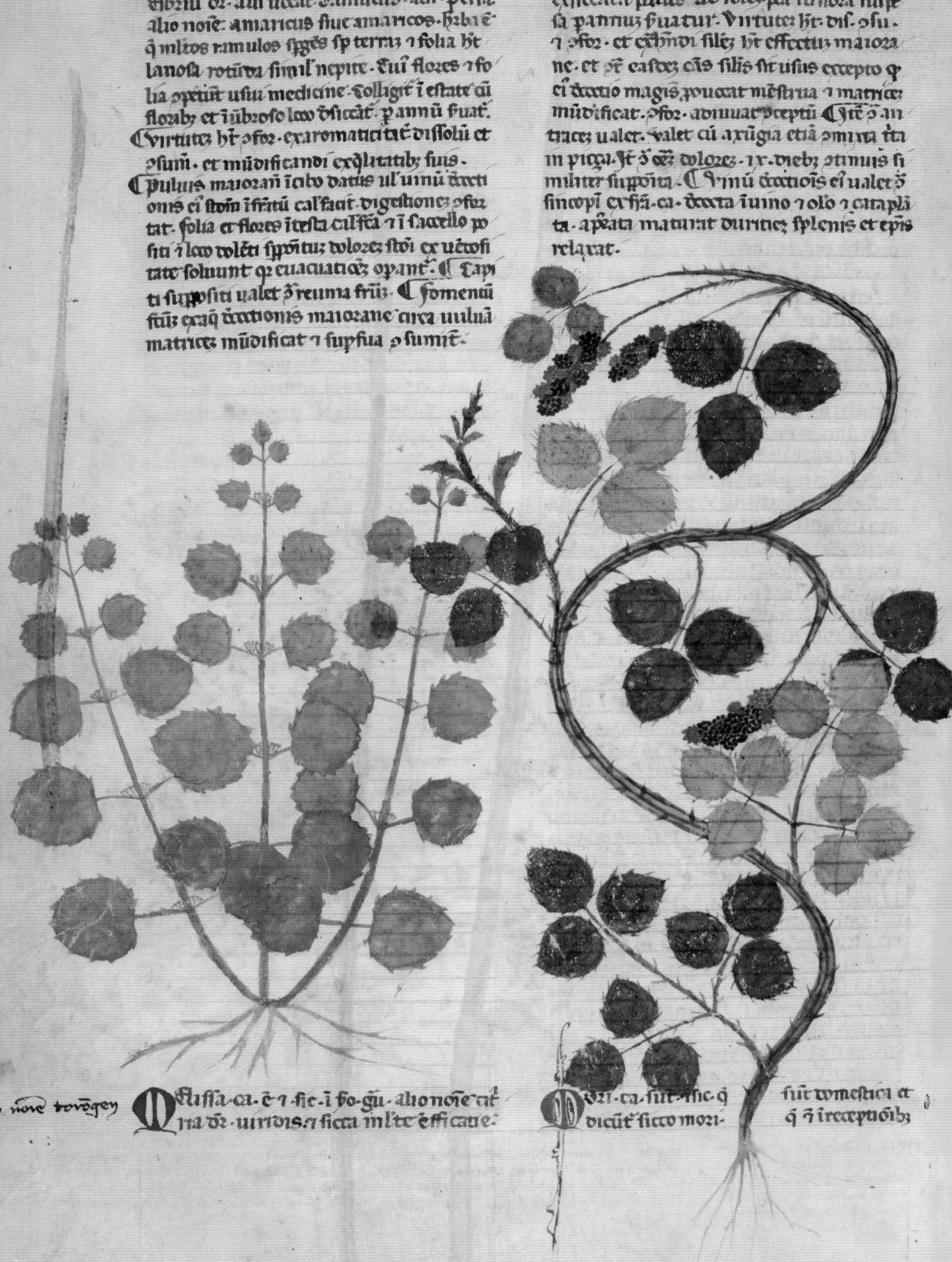

alio nome torogey

Mellissa. ca. e. i. sic. i. so. gu. alio noīe citrīa dr̄. uiridis. 7 sicca in lr̄e efficatie.

Mora. ca. sut. i. sic. q̄ dicitur sicco mori- sut domestica et q̄ ī receptionib;

medicinarum· poni debet· Siluestra fructus sunt et
sicca· s· fructus rubei cum nigri sunt colliguntur·
uirtutem habent dis· consu· et mundificandi· ¶ Consignantiam et uuam laxatam· brancos et uitia
faucium· Valet etiam diamoron dictum ggarismat
Succus expressus decoquitur aliquantulum cum uino
et modico aceto et fiat gargarismus· Valet
etiam electuarium factum ex succo eius et melle despumato·
simul decoctis aliquantulum· per x· annos seruatur
et in loco dia moron poni potest· Succus eius ali
quantulum calefactus et datus solum uentositatem
sisit constipatio ex frigida causa· ¶ Succus cortic
uel plurimis eius cum melle datus necat lumbricos·
¶ Vinum decoctionis corticis eius mundificat intestina·
Cortex etiam eius uirtutem habet dis· consu·
et mundificandi· ¶ Casula facta ex gummi eius
circa dentes putrefactum sine dolore eicit·
¶ Mora siluestria uirtutem habent aliquantulam
constringendi· ex qualitatibus et diuidendi ex aliquantula acetositate·

herba est· crescens in montibus in lapidosis et asperis locis et habet lignum quasi arbor et serpit super
terram uel super sepibus et folia eius scabida et quasi
rotunda et in summitate facit semen· v· uel vii·
rubeo colore similis grana titoris sed sunt rubiores· crescunt autem in medio folia cuius folia in
summitate est rotunda et concaua ad modum umbellici
a ueneris et in medio producit semen· ¶ Contra quartanam certum experimentum· Collige herba matrisilua luna decrescente· tere ipsam et cum farina
et oleo fac crispelle numero· xlv· et dabis patienti
in prima die· 9· alia die sequenti· 8· tertia die· 7·
et sic declina omni die usque ad unam· et liberabitur·
probatum est· a multis·

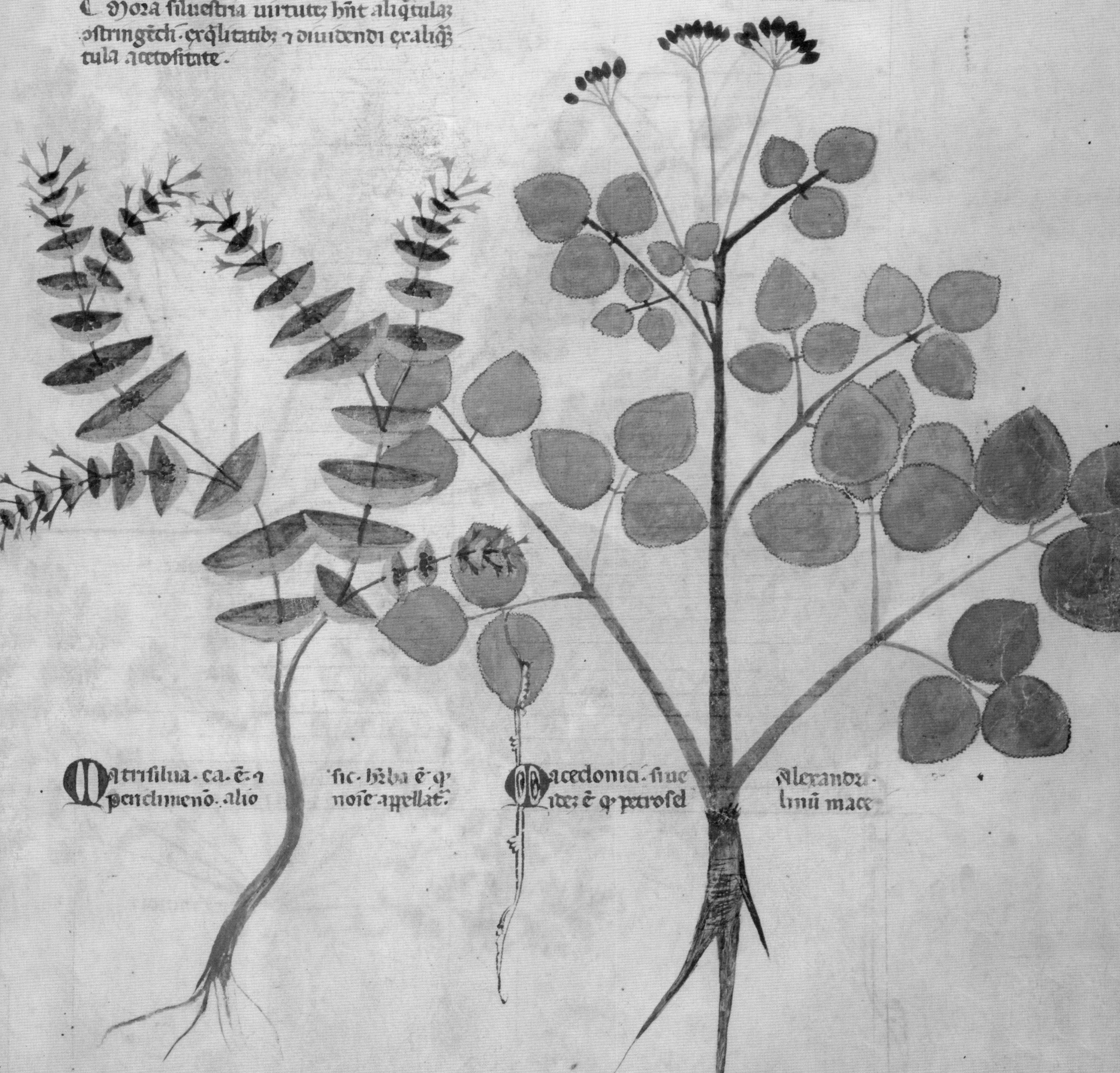

domesticum. Herba est. oritur in ortis et omnibus locis
similis appio domestico sed habens magna fo
lia. Radix eius est sub nigra intus vero alba. Semen
habet nigrum et grossum ut fagioli. Virtutem
habet ca. et sic. et diuretica aperitiua. ac habet
et consumi. Contra stranguriam et dissuriam et uitium
lapidis. radix eius decocta in sartagine cum oleo
et comesta mirifice confert. Valet etiam contra uitium
matricis ex frigiditate et hu. adiuuat ad conceptum
et dolorem renum mirifice proficit. Vnde semen eius ponitur
in trifera magna. et nota quod cum reperitur in medicinis
macedonicum uel alexandrinum semen eius debet poni
Radix autem eius non ponitur sine determinatione.
Contra difficultatem urine. foliorum eius suptestam
calidam. aspergatur modico uino et malfetur in calefacie
supppectinem cataplet.

unbrosis et humidosis et maxime in castanetis
habens folia admodum borraginis sed non est adeo pi
losa. est etiam solida et acutiora et circum in tortuosa
et crescens in quantitate unius brachii. florem habet
purpureum. Radix eius semper inuenitur intortuosa et est
sub nigra. dicitur quidam quod diabolo propter inuidiam
multe efficacie morordit eam radicibus quare uo
catur morsus diaboli. Valet proprie contra anti
cem qui uocatur malum sancti xpofori. Herba tota super
lapidem conteris et superponitur et sepe remoue direc
te sine dubio ad sanitatem reducit. Valet
etiam ad ictum et contra dolorem matricis. comesta uel
uinum decoctionis eius bibitus.

riei · s; maior · minor · et media et q̄libet con
hnit una eteadē efficatiaz · Nascit locis sa
blosis et isolidis · h̄t folia lōga uni̇ palmi
u̇ h̄us multa folia p̄ua admodū pipinella
et sp̄git p̄terā et h̄t florez p̄uū admodū pes
colūbinū et fac̄ sem̄ q̄i aci · Muscata ma
ior · sic appellat̄ q̄a h̄t maiorez hbā ul' q̄a
h̄t maiorez efficatiaz et sic d̄cetis · Virtu
tez h̄t ꝯ dolorez et idignatiōez n̄uorū et ꝯ
artheticaz pās · un̄ posit̄ i ungt̄ marciato
adp̄dcā · Hrba nicata maior cataplet̄ sup̄
loca dolēti · calā addito modico uino · ul'
fiat emp̄lm ex ip̄a hba et axūgia ursina.

Valet ꝑprie ad uulnera recentia ꝯsolidāda
Ungtm fcm̄ ex succo ei̇ · et terbētina · cera · et
olo · mir̄ ꝯsolidat et sanat · Ꝯ Emorroidas
et ficus itus iano · q̄n̄ apparēt · succus mill
folii ieiuno potui dato mir̄ sanat · lonbricos
etiā occidit.

Musa · ca · ē i medio i gradu · hūida eidē fine · fruc
tus sūt silis citrul̄ q' alii pomū paradisi uocāt
i ultramaris p̄tib; crescūt cui̇ folia silat̄ enula
cāpana s; s̄t t̄plex maiores · Ventrez lubrectat · pec
toris asp̄itatez lenit et p̄lmonē ē nutrīmēti
mīti et ꝯssi · q; assue fctā stoīa gr̄uat g̃uitatez et
splenis et epis oppilatiōez · Vn̄ necesse ē illā se
pe ꝯmedētib; u̇ p̄t ꝯmestiōez c̄c ꝯditū d̄r ā
oximelle si mādūcātes sūt fr̄e · u̇ q' si calē
ꝯ ziçiclā̄ accipiāt.

Millefoliū · anbrosia · apiū · formicularis

Venti ides ē.

Mellongiano siue petrogiano · hrba ē i
ortis ori̇t̄ q' similat̄ alchechengi · cui̇ fructꝰ
ē magnus ut pira maior et h̄t colorez s̄b
rufuz · saporez amarissimū · magis ꝯpeti
esui q̄uā medicis · s; nūq̄ laudauerūt fi
losophi nec auctores q' ueneriosi sunt
Melagiani igr̄ isaac · ca · s̄c et sicci i fine scdi gdi · q' testifi
cat̄ ei̇ acuitꝰ et amaritudo · et morsꝰ q̄ ligua s̄tigit · Sed qui
tibi' ē cito i colaz nigrā u̇sti · Ꝑ ē ei̇ p̄tas · Vn̄ cute corrūpūt
corp̄is · lētigines ip̄etigines · cancrū elephātia · durit̄q; ad dis
soluēd̄ ap̄sita g̃nat · et oppilatiōes · atq; similia fac̄ · Ꝯ; u̇
uenosus fiat nocumēti et tēp̄et fundat̄ ꝯ sale ip̄leat̄ & in
diu i aq̄ calā dimictat̄ · p̄tea i alia mutet̄ et b · a · t · lauet
ū aq̄ lauat̄ ei̇ careāt nigdine · & m̄ elixet̄ q̄ aq̄ eiecta
cū pingu' carne bouina · ac petrolīū · p̄sc̄um et filiū recept̄
illā aūt absq; ꝯmedē uolētes coq̄t cū aceto et olo ꝯficiōs.

Mercurialis inuenies cū ubi lichitis. retro.

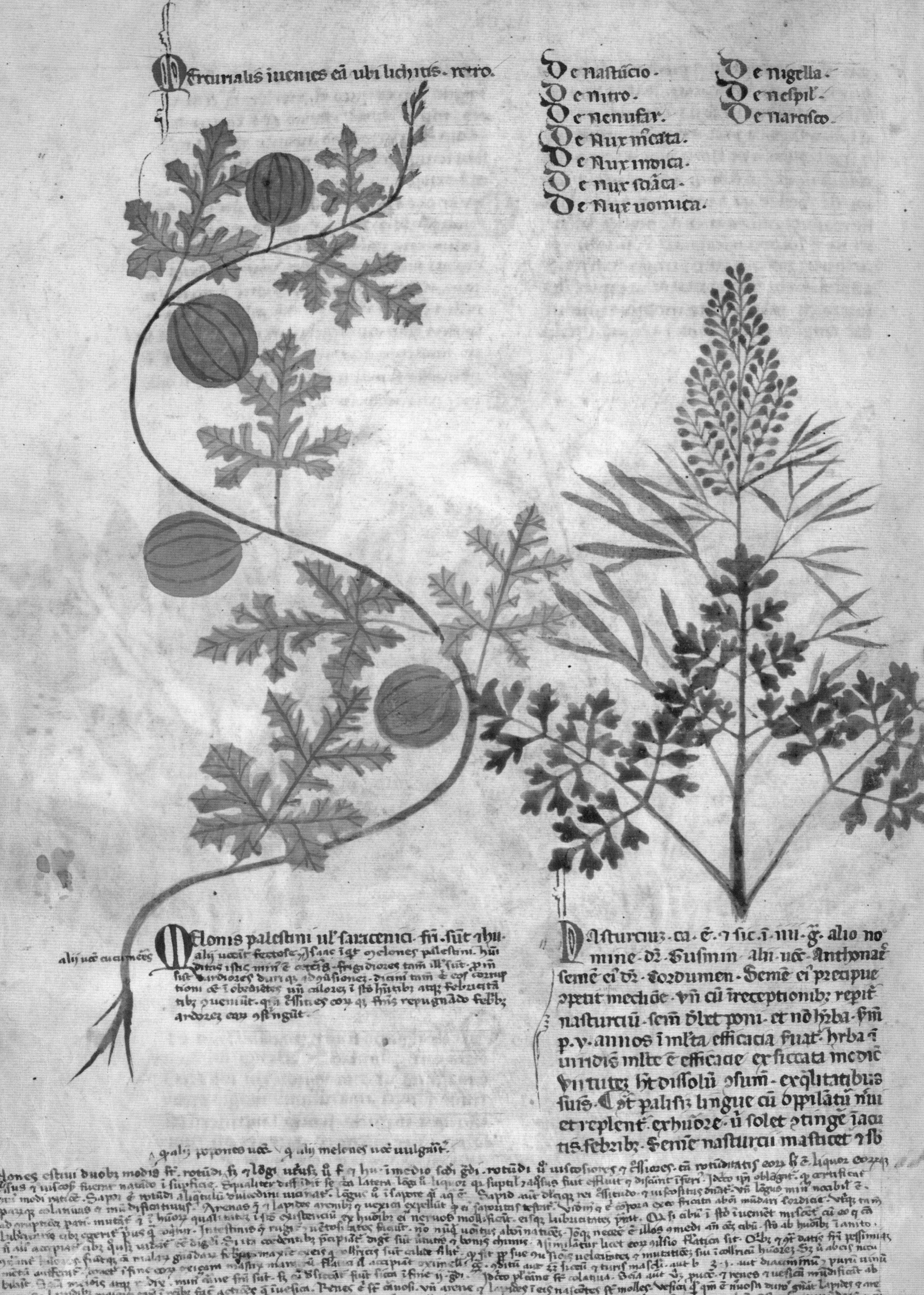

Melonis palestini ul' saraceni. fri. sūt 7 hu. alij uocāt festose. Ysaac igit̄ melones palestini. hu midis isti miri ē extēs ꝑ. frigidiores tam̄ ill' sūt. ꝑ quī sūt duriores duri q̄ ad digestionē. dicimi tam̄ ē eos corruptioni & i obediētes uū calorē i sto hūtib; atq; febricitātib; queniūt. qa essities eor̄ q; frnis repugnādo febrib; ardorē eau ostingūt.

alij uocāt cucumeres

Nasturciu. ca. ē. 7 sic. i. iiij. g. alio nomine dr̄. Gusimin. alii uocāt Anthonaē seme ei' dr̄. cardumen. Seme ei' precipue ꝑpetit medicīe. vn̄ cū i receptionib; repit nasturciū. semē dbet poni. et nō hrba. sem p. v. annos i multa efficacia fuat. hrba ē uiridis multe ē efficacie exsiccata medic uirtutē; ht dissolū osum. exquititatibus suis. Est palisi; lingue cū oppilatū nui et replent' ex huore. ū solet ostinge iacitis febrib;. Seme nasturcii masticet 7 sb

q alij pepones uocāt. q alij melones uocāt uulgarit'.

Melones estiui duob; modis fiūt. rotūdi sꝫ 7 lōgi utrisq; ū f 7 hu. i medio sedi gdi. rotūdi ū uiscosiores 7 essitiores. cū rotūditatis eor̄ sꝫ ē. liquor eor̄ ꝑ essus 7 uiscos fuerit natudo i superficie. Equaliter diffidit se ꝑ latera. lōgi ū. liquor qi suptil 7 adsus fuit effluit 7 discurrit i feri. Jdeo ipi oblagūt. q certificat hui' modi ratiōe. Sapor ē rotūdi aliqtulū dulcedini miriat'. lōgus ū i sapore q̄i aq̄ ē. Sapid aut' dbe[illegible] rei essitudo 7 uiscositas dicūt. vn̄ lōgus mīr nocibit ē. paruq; colatiuus 7 mūdificatiuus. Arenas ē 7 lapides arenib; 7 uesica expellūt q ei saporitas testat'. Vidim q ē corpora ex eo fricata abōi mūdari sordicie. Vēq; tam ad complexiō pati. mutāt' 7 i huor̄ qualitatē isto existencū ex huorib; ei' neruos mollificāt. eisq; lubricitates ꝑdūt. Cū si cibū i sto iuenerit miscet cū eo q cū lubricitate cib; egerit' ꝑus q̄ digerit'. Intestinis q rugas 7 uētositates faciūt. no nūq uomitus abōinatiōē. Jdeo necēe ē illos omedi an̄ oēs cibū. sto ab huorib; iānito. si aūt accipiāt' cib; quasi uicē ē digi. Si ita coedētib; ꝑcipiāt' dige sūt uiuite 7 bonis chimis. Assimilatur licet eor̄ sūsio flatica sit. Ob; q ꝑ datis fiūt pessimis si ali accipiat' cib; quasi [illegible] gnāt' [illegible] fiātq; cū malas guadas [illegible] magis exeis 7 colliras sūt calide fibr'. q fit ꝑ sue [illegible] uelocitates 7 mutatiōe; sui i colrica huorē. Sꝫ ū abeis uocu mētū auferunt. [illegible] i fine eor̄ oxigam [illegible] flaua ū accipiat oximelli. ꝑ. aditū aut' cū siccū 7 turis mascli. aut b ʒ. i. aut diacimimu 7 puri uinū bibat'. [illegible] meloīs atq; [illegible]. miri aīne fiūt sūt. sꝫ cū dsiccat' fiut sicca i fine ij. gdi. Jdeo plaīns fiūt colatiua. [illegible] aut uz. puce. 7 renes 7 uesica mūdificat ab arenis q lapidib; maiores tam i renib; fiūt actioēs q i uesica. Renes ē fiūt carnosi. vn̄ arene 7 lapides i eis nascētes fiūt molles. Vesica q̄ qm̄ ē nuosa duro' gnāt lapides q arenā. Unus dre necēe ē formas [illegible] uesic qua sūt sera. Cortex aū meloīs plus tollit oris fetorē sꝫ ex eo lauet'. Dia. sem̄ aqd meloīs i superficie mūdatū q cū aīne meloīs q cicis q fabe farina tēpatū 7 i modū trasci ꝑpositū 7 ad solē dsiccatū vz aspreq; mūdādā. q cutem extenuādā. Rursus medic ei' plus duarum ʒ. pōs cū oximelle bibitū. urīā tollit uolitu. Est q ill'ud gen' meloīs q palestini uocāt' de q̄ supius diximus.

lingua ponatur. C contra palisim aliorum membrorum semen eius in saccello positum et in uino decoctum membro dolenti supponatur ipsa etiam herba cruda et cum carnibus cocta ualet. C contra superfluas humiditates cerebri. ut in litargia prouocetur sternutatio ex puluere nasturcii seminis apposito. C contra relaxationem uue fiat gargarismum ex aceto decoctionis seminis eius et ficuum siccarum. C contra yliacam et colicam passionem ex frigida causa. semen eius in saccello positum et in uino decoctum supponatur. C ad cadentem ualet et contra enfiasim. herba ipsa in uino et oleo decocta et supposita. C contra tenasmon ex humore glutinoso cum anus amittitur. puluis ano supponatur. C Renes etiam iungatur et superaspergatur puluis seminis eius et cimini et colophonie.

Nasturtium. c. e. et s. i. in. gradu. uena terre est. In multis locis inuenitur. cuius duplex est maneries. s. album simile uitro quod elligendum est quia melius est. Et citrinum quod non est adeo bonum. per infinita tempora seruatur. Virtutem habet dissoluendi et extenuandi. C contra yliacam passionem competens fit cristere ex puluere nitri aqua salsa oleo et melle. C ad faciem depurandam puluis nitri cum melle conficiatur et in facies iungatur. C contra saniem stomachi et intestinorum ex precedente apostemate detur puluis nitri cum calida. uel quod melius est cum melle. C contra furfures capitis et pediculos puluis eius cum melle et oleo conficiatur. abluto capite prius ex aqua salsa. et aceto decoctionis staphisagrie. iungatur unguento predicto. et post parum temporis abluatur caput cum aqua calida tamen ita fiat per tres. uel .iiii. dies uel pluries. C puluis eius cum succo absinthii confectus et auribus immissus. uermes necat. et saniem extinguit.

Nasturtium aquaticum nascitur secus uias ualet precipue contra strofulas et gangulas et superfluis humoribus in iuncturis. succus eius ieiuno potui datus per .xl. diebus. herba etiam contrita et supposita mirabiliter sanat probatum est.

Nenufar. frigida est et humida.

in scdo. g°du. herba est lata hñs folia i aq̄s
locis repitur. et i frīs regionibȝ. cui duplex
est maneries. s. nenufar. purpureū p̄du
cens flores q̄a meliores sūt. Est ⁊ aliud
croceos. faciēs flores q nō sūt adeo boni.
flos usui medicīe ꝯpetit. In septenb̄ col
ligitur. p. ii. ānos suat̄ i multa efficacia.
Melior est q̄ i callidis regionibȝ repitur.
Ex floribȝ ꝓpue fiūt sirup̄ iacutis febrib̄
et ꝯ calidam distēpantiā epatis. flores ō
coquātur. i aq̄ ⁊ addito çucco. fiat sir̄.
C ꝯ dol̄ capis. ex cal̄ saraceni ponūt flo
res i aq̄ p noctē mane bibūt talē aq̄ et
flores naribȝ applicāt.

media nascentis. tp̄s maturitatis colli
gitur. p. vii. ānos suatur. Eligenda
est q̄ plana ē. et pondrosa i suo gn̄e.
q̄ cū frāgit interius nō pluericatur.
et iuēitur acuti saporis. Si ista desunt
nō ē ponēda i medicis. Virtutē hȝ cō
fortandi. ex aroāticitate. i qualitatibȝ
suis. C ꝯ frātē stō̄i et i digtōē et disco
lozationē. ex frāte dtur mane media
nux. ul̄ itegra si pua ē. expiētia didici
q̄ mltuz ꝯfert. C ꝯ digtōē stō̄i epis ⁊
intestinorū dtur uinū decoctiōis eius. Ad
eadē ualȝ ⁊ uinū decoctiōis ei. et anisi et
cimini. dol̄ stō̄i et itestinorū ex uētositē
fāiȝ tollit. C Conualescētibȝ ex egritudine
ad ꝯfortatioēȝ spūaliū. dtur uinū decoctio
nis ei ⁊ mastič et nux micata naribȝ appli
catur cerebrū ꝯfortat ⁊ spūalia.

Nux muscata. ca. ⁊ sicce ꝯplexionis
ē. in sc̄o. g°. fructus arboris ē i in

Nux indica. ca
cūt q sit. ca.
tat coituȝ. Sang
Nos aūt dicimus
ditatē et hu. p̄a
ꝯfortari solet. Si
ē p caliditatē. ex

ē. ⁊ sic. alii di
et hu. et ꝯfor
neȝ bonū gnāt.
q̄ coitus p cali
pue excitāi et
nō tn̄ ꝯfortāt
siccitate nāq̄

sanguis acuitur. et subtiliatur exca. calescit.
Nux indica in india reperitur. nux magna
est. et cum ponitur in medicinis interiora debet poni
per .x. annos servatur. Virtutem habet confortan
di coitum. unde ad coitum confort datur pulvi
s eius cum pulvere cinamomi in cibis. Ad idem parat
isti pulveres. in dia zinzibereon melius va
let si pulvis eius et sticados datur cum melle
¶ Contra asma frigidam. carice decoquatur in vino postea
terantur et succus exprimatur et coletur
cum quo datur pulvis nucis indice.

na sive meregha et sunt acuti saporis qua
si ut piper. Virtutem habet calefaciendi desic
candi et confortandi ad digestionem confortan
dam. eius fiunt pulvis addito zinzibere et cinamomo
et ponatur in cibis. ad reuma gignivarum et dolorem denti
um ex frigiditate generatum nux [illegible] masticetur
et teneatur in ore et in expuendo reuma fluens
et exit.

Nux sciarca. sive Meleghett. in .ii. gradu est. Arbor fruc marinis partibus reperitur nux magne admodum que intus habet grana

Nux dinda. l ca. sunt in sicce tus que in ultra pitur. sunt est odum nuc comie admodum sagi

¶. Nux uomica.

Nuces dupliciter dividuntur. sunt enim uirides et sicce. uirides minus sicce sunt cum calide. Aliquantulum tamen humores habent propter maturitatem [illegible] ut sit par sicce.
par tamen stomacho sunt nocive. quod si ieiunus cum aceto comedantur et absomegino [illegible] humefaciunt. cum ruta [illegible] sunt contra uenenum. Sicce uero nuces sunt
dupliciter. quedam sunt [illegible] [illegible] eas producentes. quedam remote. et alie sunt inter has mediocres. Primum aut sunt humide. modicam uiscositatis habentes. adeo
quod uiscositatis habentes atque quam ponticitatis in eis est [illegible] ab eorum longatur tempore tamen [illegible] humiditas consumitur [illegible] uetositatis [illegible]. [illegible] tamen manducatur.
cito in humores convertuntur collerico. [illegible] itaque uetustioribus [illegible] et uentuositate [illegible] multo magis [illegible] fit eius sapor [illegible] uetustissimum oleum. et [illegible]
naturam amittunt. [illegible] nuces corporibus nocent. quia difficiles sunt ad digerendum. stomacho nocive. colliacas assimilatur humoribus calidis et minuunt tussim. quasi nuces
comparantur auellanis. [illegible] auellanas maioris nutrimenti. propter sue [illegible] spissitudinem. et uentuositatis [illegible]. Nuces enim minus auellanis nutribiles.
propter [illegible] corporum [illegible]. et sue uentuositatis copiam. [illegible] stomacho semper sunt contrarie. [illegible] cum inuenerit stomachum [illegible]. [illegible] habentes [illegible] calori [illegible]
ualeat repugnare. Ideo talis [illegible] fiat boni nutrimenti. cum bonitate digestionis. Calidum uero humidis stomachum [illegible] ustiones. et in collericos mutantur humores. Alii [illegible]
capitisque dolorem [illegible] et [illegible] [illegible]. Si uero ab eis [illegible] auferunt nocumentum [illegible] eas necesse est et [illegible] [illegible] in aqua calida poni ut [illegible] humiditatis [illegible] sibi
[illegible] [illegible] si uides. Secundum medicinas [illegible] si [illegible] cibum cum ficubus edatur. [illegible] uenenosa corpus [illegible]. [illegible] si [illegible] cataplasma [illegible] cum cepis sale
et melle. [illegible] morsibus canis rabidi. Rursus cataplasma. [illegible] ruta et melle factum [illegible] [illegible] [illegible] nascentia [illegible] ex [illegible] [illegible]
[illegible] cum suis [illegible] cortice et [illegible] [illegible]. destruunt [illegible] [illegible] in corpore manens. Corticem [illegible] [illegible] [illegible] sue arboris.

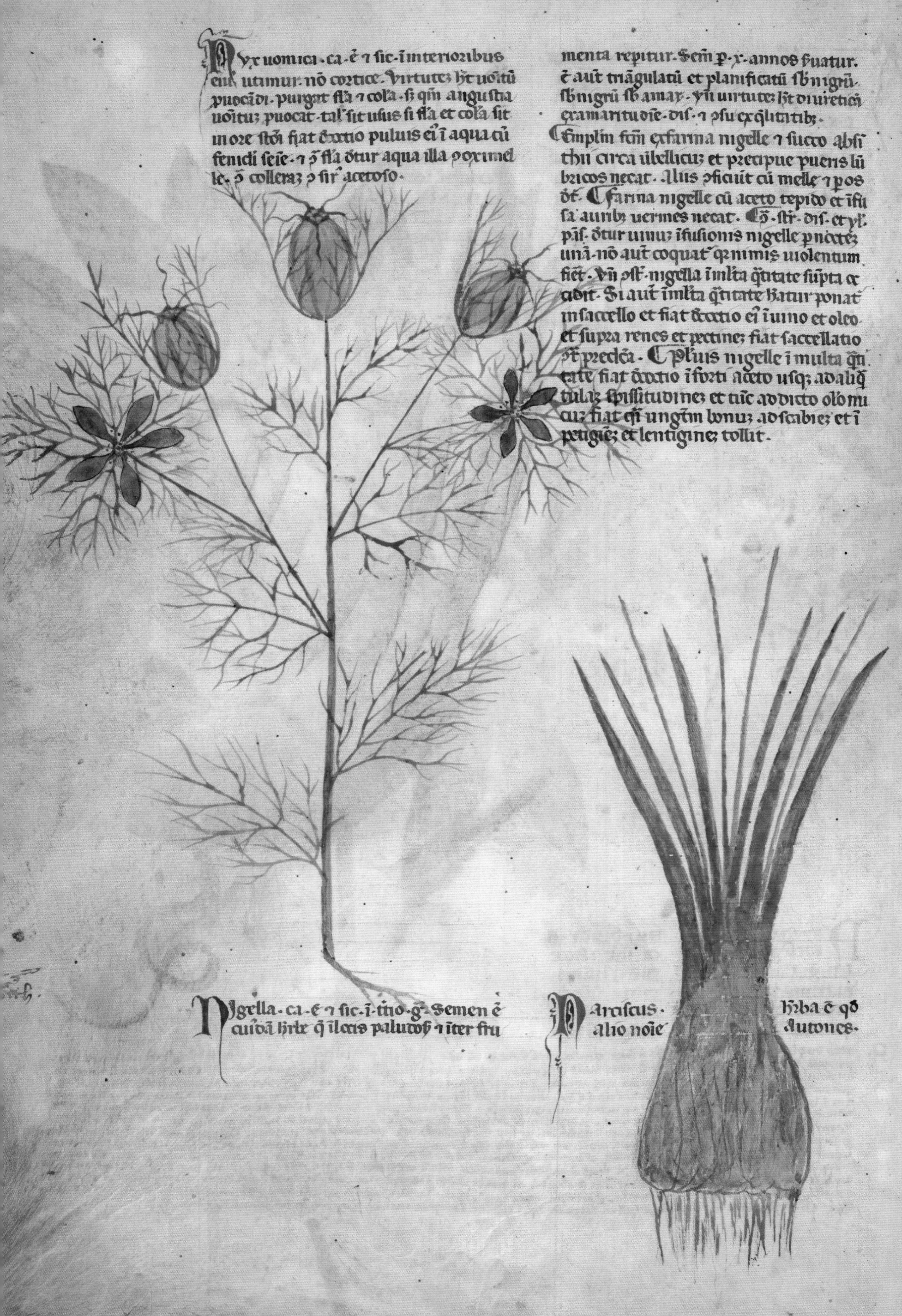

Nux uomica . ca . ē ⁊ sic . ī interioribus eius utimur . nō cortice . Virtutē hʒ uomitū prouocādi . purgat flā ⁊ colā . sʒ qm̄ angustia uomitum prouocat . tal' sit usus si flā et colā sit in ore stōi fiat decoctio puluis eī ī aqua cū feniculi seīe . ⁊ ꝯ flā dₜur aqua illa ꝯ oximelle . ꝯ colleram ꝯ sirᵒ acetoso .

Nigella . ca . ē ⁊ sic . ī . tⁱᵃᵒ . gᵒ . Semen ē cuiusdā herbe q̄ ī locis palustrib; ⁊ inter frumenta reperitur . Seīm ꝑ . x . annos suatur . ē aūt triāgulatū et planificatū sb nigrū . sb nigrū sb amar . Vn̄ uirtutē hʒ diuretica ex amaritudīe . dis . ⁊ ꝯsu exᵈlutīitib; .

Emplin fcm̄ ex farina nigelle ⁊ succo absinthii circa umbellicum et precipue pueris lūbricos necat . Alius ꝯficiūt cū melle ⁊ posᵗ dt' . Farina nigelle cū aceto tepido et īfusa auribꝫ uermes necat . Cō . str . dis . et yᵒ . pas . dₜur uinū īfusionis nigelle ꝑ noctē unā . nō aūt coquatᵘ q̄ nimis uiolentum fiet . Vn̄ ꝯst' . nigella ī mlta q̄titate sūpta occidit . Si aūt ī mlta q̄titate dₜatur ponatᵘ in sacello et fiat decoctio eī ī uino et oleo et supra renes et pectine; fiat sacellatio ꝯt predcā . Pluis nigelle ī multa q̄titate fiat decoctio ī forti aceto usq; ad aliq̄tulā spissitudinē et tūc addicto oleo mirtino fiat eī ungtm̄ bonū ad scabiē et īpetigīē et lentiginē tollit .

Narciscus . herba ē qd alio noīe cautones .

ôr · alii · Bullo seneticus · pseti uocat · Epton alii · Cinoglosa · alii · Ananogrolo · hn̄s folia admodū cepe ⁊ radix admodū scalonei ce pas · Nascitur · lito mari locis sablosis ⁊ mō tibȝ · Valet precipue ad tussim ⁊ colicas · Succus eī potui dato mirē pficat colicis ⁊ tussientibȝ · Oleū ȝ ōfloribȝ narcisi ī ūcto egrū ȝ ui ōbis expimētū ȝ optimū ·

Nespile · frē · sūt · ⁊ sicce · ī p̊ gū · ꝑtatē habent stōi ꝯfortādi colligā egestiōes · ac uōitū auferūt urinā ꝓuocāt mag̃ quā ptinēt ad medicinā · quā ad cibū · pa̅ ꝝ ē nutūt q̅ā cibū sup ta meliora sūt q̃ pt cibū · q̅ stō sē ꝯfortitiora ⁊ neruositati stōi nō nociora ·

Ocimuȝ · ca · ē ⁊ s · alio nomine dicit̃ Basilicon · alii uocāt · Albederangi · cuī duplex est maneries · s̄ȝ gariofilatū ⁊ citrinū · Gariofilatuȝ est ut qdā dicūt q̄ h̄t odore simile gariofil' ⁊ h̄t minuta folia · Citrinuȝ uō h̄t folia lōga · admo duȝ cit̃ · s̄ȝ gariofilatuȝ maioris est efficacie · quaȝ citrinuȝ · vn̄ ꝯst̃ · gariofilatū ca · ē ⁊ s · i · i · g̃ · sic · i · ii · Citrinuȝ · ca · ē ⁊ s · i · i · g̃ · sem̄ ⁊ h̄ba ꝯpetūt usui medicine cū aūt repit̃ eī receptio ozimū · semen ōbet poni · cū repit̃ basilicon · h̄ba ōbet poni

et maxīe ī unguentis ⁊ ēplastis. Semē
aut̄ articlaz h̄t uirtutē ↄstrīgendi ex
glutinositate q̄ patet ex eo q̄ si ponat̄
ī aq̄ statī igrossatur. ul' fit q̄da glutino
sitas. h̄rba aut̄ ip̄a ex aroāticitate h̄t
uirtutē ↄfortādi ex qualitatib; dissol
uendi. ↄsu. extergendi ⁊ mūdificādi.
Sem̄ uō collectū p. iii. ānos suatū ī
multa efficacia. Ↄt sincopī ⁊ cardi
acam pās. d̄t aq̄ ro. decoctiōis ipī h̄rbe.
Ad idē ualet uinū ī quo iacuerit p nocte.
Ipā etiā h̄rba ualet ↄt sincopī ⁊ frātem
sīoi. h̄ mō decoquat in mlta q̄titate ī ui
no s; melius est ī musto ⁊ post decoctionē
addat uinū albū ī mlta q̄titate. Tale
uinū mltum est ↄfortatiuū. et aroāti
cū et ualet ↄ p̄dicta. et ↄ digestionem
exfriāte. Vinū etiā decoctiōis ipius h̄rbe
digestionē ↄfortat. Ↄ fluxū uētris ex
frīāte. sem̄ ozimi cū modico pl'uē acatie
decoquat ī aqua plu. ⁊ d̄t patienti. Ad
matricē mūdificandā ⁊ mēstruā puo
cand. fiat decoctio h̄rbe ī aqua et fiat fom̄
tū circa pudenda. fiat etiā suppositoriū
ex tenēritatib; ipius h̄rbe. Ↄst. dicit q̄ su
cus ipī h̄rbe pessaricatus matrē mūdifi
cat ↄceptū; adiuuāt ⁊ mēstrua puocat.
H̄rba decocta ī uino et olō ⁊ natib; cata
plāmata ualet ↄ colicā pās ⁊ dol' lumbi.
cataplā ualet ↄ tenasmon.

Oppoponax. ca. ē ⁊ sic. ī. iii. g̃. est aut̄
succus. oppos ē succ̄. Nax ē h̄rba silis
ferule. īn oppoponax. ī. succus iacis ī tp̄e
aut̄ estiuo. findit radix terra remota
et fossa. et liquor emānat q̄ ex actione
caloris. ex sole idurat ur. et p̄ea abrai
ditur. cū cultello. ad cortice. vn̄ etiā in
ueniuntur cū corticib;. Elligend ē q̄ cla
rā h̄t s̄bā. et q̄ī quasdā guttas clarā
et colorē h̄t s̄b rufū. a accedentē ad
citrinū colorē. cū aut̄ d; p̄ōi ī medicīs
siū receptiōib; p̄pāatur ī pāno et suspen
datur sup aquā feruentē ut q̄ purū ē
effluat. q̄ turbulentū ē reānet et tūc de
bet p̄ōi ī q̄titate ab auctore d̄terminata.
diu pōt suāi sīn ↄruptiōē. Virtutē h̄t.
dis. ↄsu. et attrahēdi. Fumigiū factū
ex oppoponace. ualet ↄ litargiā. matern
am cū. dis. et euacuat. et ī mlta q̄titat̄
pisferiora. Pille fc̄e ex eo. s. ex guttis.
valet ↄt asma frīū. date simplex ul' ī

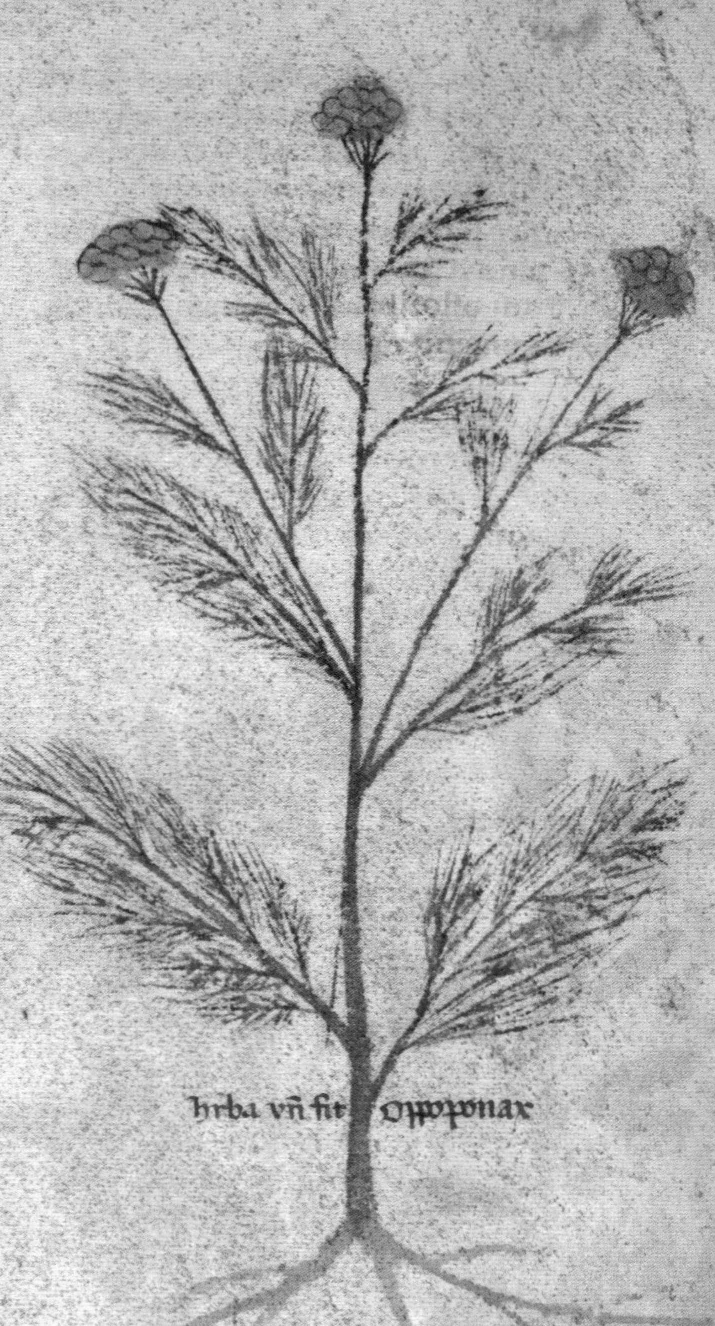

ouo sorbili. Ad idē aliud optimū ī suc
co marubii ponāt p nocte. mane dissol
uantur ī eodē succo p̄ea colet. et addatū
mel et fiat q̄ī ellīm. Ↄ ydropi. ex frigo
ra prouocarū febriū. ī succo corticis san
buci iaceat p nocte. mane dissoluatur.
addito succo. et d̄tur pacienti. Ↄ colicā
et yliacā m. pas. ī succo fen̄. iaceat p nocte.
mane dissoluat et colet̄ et addito succo
d̄tur cristeri. tn̄ precedente. No. q̄ oppo
ponac̄ ad plus ī q̄titate. iii. ʒ. d̄bet dari.
Ad mestrua educenda ⁊ fetū mortuū.
et secūdinā fiat suppositoriū ex oppop
nace. dissoluto ī olō muscellō addito
succo arthimisie. plus ualz oppoponac̄.
cū melle et succo absinthii. tn̄ datus

lūbricos necat. ¶ Emplin ex oppoponace.
ualet ꝯt cōtusiōē lacertorū.

Opium. fri. ē. i. iiii. g. sic. ip̄o.
Opium aliud ē thebaicū. q͛ ita dicit.
q͛ ibi precipue fit. ul' in ult͛maris ptib;
nascentis. aliud tranentiū. q͛ a sa fetida
dr. ul' lasar ꝯquo dictuz est. opiū sic fit
ī estate tp̄e maturitatis precipue opa
tur. ī capitib; papaueris albi et foliis q̄s
dam incisiones cū cultello. et lac eman
nans circa cap̄ īuiscat. et abraditur cū
cultello. et manib; ꝯterit. h̄ opiū the
baicum dr̄ et opiū tranēse. q͛ trane ī
ciuitate apulie fit. ſ; tm̄ nō ualet. ē
ergo elligendū opiū thebaicū q͛ est
ualde oribile. nec multū durū. nec
mltū molle. opiū thebaicū durū est
opiū tranēse mollius est. durū ꝯua
tur p. xx. ānos. ⁊ etiā iux ꝯrū pitur. in
medicinis pōitur ut reprimat uirtu
tē ſpēy acutarū. vn̄ ille medicie dnr̄.
opiate. virtutē h̄t ꝯstrigendi. et morti
ficandi. ſ; ī medicis calidis nō ꝯseqtur
suū effectū. ꝑpt ꝯdictionē ſpēy cali
darū. virtutē h̄t encoticā. i. sōpnife
ram. ¶ Ad sopnū puocandū fiat em
plastū ex appio resoluto ī lacte muliēr
addito pluere madragore. ¶ ꝯ apstata
calā. ut erpetē estiomenū. ꝯficiat cū
pluīe corigiol. ul' yqami. et fiat ēplin.
ex opio ꝯfecto cū lacte muliēis ⁊ olō. li
cet tm̄ tūc dolor minuat locū mortifi
cando plꝰ tm̄ nocet q͛ materiā ꝯſuat.

Origanū. ca. ē. ⁊ sic. i. iii. g.
alio noīe Golena dr̄. cuius duplex
ē maneries. ſ. origanū siluēē. q͛ latiora
h̄t folia. et fortius opat͛. aliud est domi
sticū. q͛ fortis repitū. minuta h̄ns fo
lia. et suauius opatur. h̄ ī medicis ē poni
dū. colligit aut̄ ī tp̄e flor. ⁊ ꝯ floribus
ī umbra suspēditur. et exsiccatur folia ꝯ
florib; abiectis stipitib; in medicis ob
pōi. ꝯuatur p ānū. singul' annis reno
uetur. virtutē h̄t. dis. attra. relaxā di.
⁊ ꝯsūendi. ¶ ꝯ. fiū; reuā folia cū florib;
ītesta siñ liquore. calfcā ī saccello ponat͛.
et capiti suppōatur. saccellus. cap̄ etiā m
bn̄ coopiatur ut sudet. ¶ Vinū decocti
onis eius gargarizatū gingiuarū ⁊ fau
tium ꝯsūmit hūitatē. ¶ Puluis eius

uulnē suppositū hūorē ꝯsūit. ¶ ꝯ as
ma fiū; detur uinū decoctiōis eius et
ficuū siccarū et puluis eius cū mel
le ꝯfectus det͛. ul' ī ōtur cū acatia.
¶ Vinū decoctiōe ei digestionē ꝯfor
tat. dol' stōi ⁊ ītestiōꝝ excludit. ¶ Fa
sciculi formati ex h̄ba cocta ī uino ⁊ sup
posita renib;. stīn. ⁊ dis. soluit. ¶ ꝯt te
nasmō ex frā. ca. cū adhuc ani ē extra
puluī ei stuppe suppōit͛ ano supponatur
h̄ba ipa ī uino ⁊ olō decocta ⁊ uulue ca
taplāta durities eius soluit. ¶ Fomē

tum factū ex aqua ex aqua decoctionis eius. matrice mūdificat. nisi putrida. Sed melius si teneriti ipsius viride supponatur.

q in medicinis nō sūt ponenda. per .x. annos. seruatur. Virtutem hēt purgandi colam. mūdificandi sanguinem. et eius furorem reprehēdendi et menbra īfrigidandi. in decoctionibus uō decoqtur. Sed in decoctione aliorū resoluitur in aliis. et in colatura ipsius. et cassia fistula. ponūtur pulueres mirob. quinque. Si datur colatura māne. Caq. ipsius i aqua resoluitur. valet febricitātibus. quia īfrigidat et digerit.

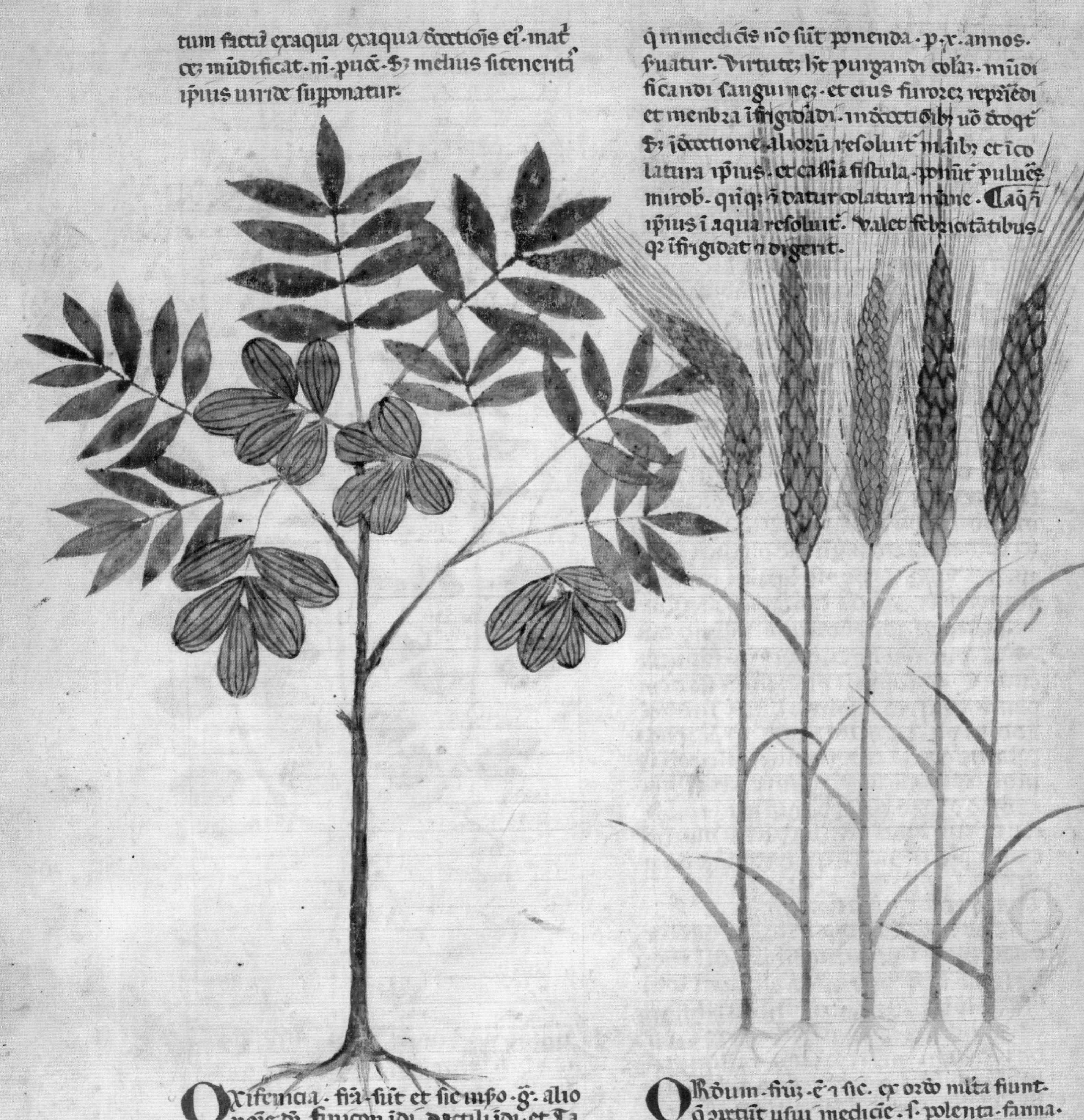

Oxifenicia. fina. sunt et sic unus. g. alio noīe dr. finicon idi. dactili idi. et Tamarindi. fructus ē cuiusdā arboris ī india nascētis q asimiliatur dactilis. Elligendus ē tamarindus. q nec mltū durus nec mltum hūidus. molle est q aut coruptus est aut īfectus. Elligitur etiā q nigri coloris est. et saporem hēt aliqntulum acetosū. In tpr maturitatis colligitur conquassatur cōsciibus aufertur corticem. hēt tenerimū et seia iterum

Ordeum. frīm. ē ī sic. ex ordeo mlta fiunt. q competūt usui medicine. s. polenta. farina. et far. farina diu ī aq cocta cib est īfirmis. s. febricitātibus. et laborātibus ad pectus spūalium et dr. dari sibi tepida. Ordeum mūdatū coquatur ī aqua usq; dum accedat ad rufū colorem et aspissitudinem. h aq optia ē et polēta. et pstes optie febricitātibus et patiētibus apostemata spūalium quia ea maturat. Cū calida apostemata ī pricipio ad repercussionem fiat emplm. ex farina

ordei et aceto q̄ ē repercussiuū et diaforeticū.
Ad maturitatē: cor̄ oficiatur uitello oui
Ad fīā apsata maturāda. fiat enplin. ex fa
rina ordi et pice liqda. ul' farina et terbenti
na. ul' melle ↄpetens est.

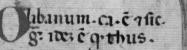

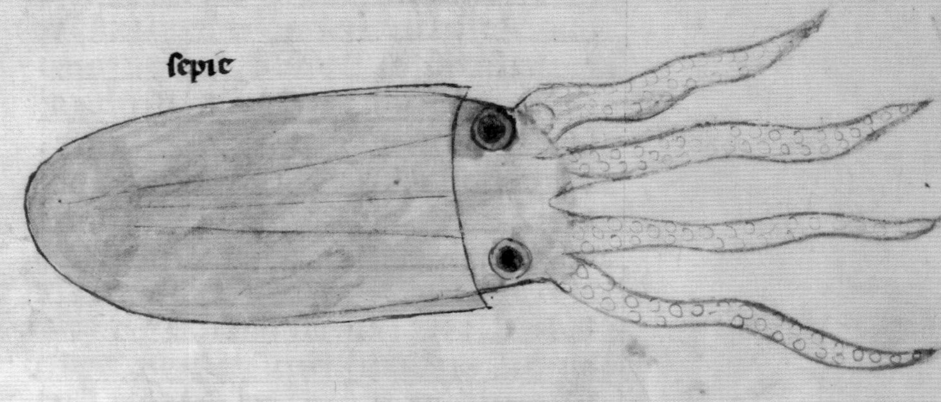

ↄradice s̄petarie ↄsiccata. cui aiūge
pluē: ossis sepie. ⁊ aq̄ ro. ⁊ dimicte ↄsic
cari. sic fac quater ul' plies ⁊ appone fa
ciem more ceruse.

Os. de corde ceruī. fīt ⁊ sicce ↄplesionis ē.
In cordē cui. repitur os qdā ī sinistra pte
cordis. ī qua ē qdā ↄcauitas ad quā splē. hīt
respiraculū et emittit supfluitate: q̄ ibi
ppria sicitate mutatur. in cordis sb̄a ↄsuo
sa. os illud ē quasi cartillago et hīt aliqtu
lu: carnis ↄcarne corde. ē aut̄ sb̄rufu:
ↄsanguine corde. et discernitur a cartillagi
ne quadā q̄ repitur ī pectore caprarū. q̄uā
apothecarii opāt̄ tortuosa: si n̄ hīt ita car
nem nec ē sb̄rufa. s̄z alba mollius. os de
corde cui. p. x. annos ↄuatur ⁊ maxīe int̄
cāphorā. debet primo ↄsiccari aliqtulu:.
Virtutē: hīt ↄpurādi huōres melā c̄. et pu
gandi sanguinē: melācōicu:. Cō cardi
acam et sincopī. ↄtur plūis ossis de corde c̄
ui cū succo borragis. ul' fiat ↄcoctio plūeis
eius ī uino ī quo ↄtur dia margarito. diste
patū. Cō melica. pas. ⁊ ↄt̄ fluxū sanguīs
mel' p emorr. ↄtur puluis ei cū uino ↄcocti
onis sene. aut oficiatur ↄdiasene ⁊ ↄt̄.
Os. sepie. fīe sūt. ⁊ sicce.
Ↄplexiōis ē. os illō ī uentre: sepie īue
nitur. Cadentes ↄalbandos puluis
eius sb̄til' ī pano lineo sb̄tili poātur et ↄ
ↄntes fricentur. Ad faciē: ↄalbādam
puluis eius oficiatur cū ungto citrino
et illiniatur facies. Caliter fac pluē:

Olibanum. ca. ē ⁊ sic. ī sc̄dō
g: idē: ē q̄ thus. gūi ē

Oliue duob: modis diuidūt' sūt ē domestice ⁊ siluestres. domestice ū t̄tiūe puīt'. vno cū s̄t pōtice ⁊ n ↄdū ad maturitatis tp̄s puenerūt. sc̄dō qñ sūt nigra
pfecteq: hīt maturitatē. mediocres rubū hñtes colores. q̄s diasc̄ōr appellauit iacintinas. virides q̄ s̄t pōtic̄ ⁊ īmature ī duo diuidūt' ī aq̄squas q̄ ḡcī hic uele
fugīt. qm̄ nichil uētuositatis ī eis repit' ⁊ pussimū q̄ nullo m̄ abeis manare pot̄. ꝑ sui ligris sb̄tilitatē. Sūt ⁊ alie q̄ abussine uocit'. Agricie ↄ qb: fit oliū on
facios. Oliue ḡ q̄ recte aq̄ue nūcupāt' sūt trestres q̄ pōticatis sueq: uētuositatis ī digēstia testat'. ⁊ ab hac ad fr̄itatē ⁊ siccitatē p'tinēt. vn̄ mag' ceteris oliuis s̄t
stoī ↄfortatiue uētris tm̄ ↄstipatiue ⁊ corpori min' oib: nutritiue ⁊ ad digēnd' mediocres. puīus nutrimēti fit ꝑ sue uētuositatis ī digēstiā ⁊ ↄ [illegible] ↄ [illegible]
fr̄itatē cor̄ duritiā quā nilo ↄuat' cū sale ⁊ aceto s̄z q̄ sūt cū aq̄ ⁊ sale ↄdite. a sale acqpiūt quādā acuī ac siccitatis ptē. vn̄ sanguīs ī [illegible] ḡat stoīq: nuos. mordet ⁊
d:, fr̄ales s̄t ad digēnd. ꝑ ↄstitudinē suāq: duritiā. eaz tm̄ acuīē pūgit ītestīna. vn̄ cū agerūt'. q̄ n̄ s̄t cū aceto ↄuate sūt tenuiores ⁊ fre. [illegible] [illegible]
ḡat acuīn. ⁊ iutus excitat' appetitiuā maxīe s̄i ī medio prādij accipiat'. q̄ ūtum obedictes digere optīe ↄfortāt stoīn. uētrē stupiciā reddūt. Alie ū q̄ abussine uocāt'
aq̄ue poaub: s̄t nutribiliores. min' q̄ stoīn ↄfortātes. ꝑ eor̄ uētuositatē. vn̄ facile a stō ↄscēdūt. Nigra q̄ ad maturitatē puenerūt calide s̄t ⁊ mediocres īt' hūītate ⁊ sicc
quāq̄ tm̄. diasc̄ōr dix' sicitati ptinere. G. ū testat' eas habere hūītatē. possibile ē q̄ dic̄. Sua ē saporitate ac uētuositas ī nulla illas hūītatē habē. hac ↄ cū eor̄ [illegible] ē [illegible]
nutbil' ⁊ ↄsūo mollificāt stoīn tardius ad digēnd. fr̄ial' q̄ ad digēnd. tarditas digēstiōis fit ꝑ uētuositatē. albā facientes natīe ī [illegible] stoī. ⁊ [illegible] cū ad [illegible] [illegible]
ↄscēdere. facilius sue egōis ē ꝑ uētuositatē ī stō [illegible]. vn̄ p'usq̄ digerūt' ↄ stō ↄscēdūt. Ideo adsop' uidz terrestriū ↄpatiāz s̄t illaudabiles. qm̄ ī [illegible] ⁊ abominabile
ḡnāt' chimū pp̄ri si s̄t sale ↄdite. si uo ē ī rubā colliā ↄtūt'. Lacitue ā nimi nigre sūt nocibiliores ꝑ uētuositatē sueq: ponotatē paucitatē. ꝑ in aliq tulū stoīn
ↄfortāt. Chimus tm̄ tātū ḡnāt ī rubee ḡnāt oliue. ē s̄ eor̄ colores. ↄ nigr'. vidz nigrem ex rubis ā rubus chimi ī nasat'. G. rubee ī q̄d oliue colores s̄ḡatūt q̄ cū uitel
la. s̄t ideo rubee. oliue ī ādū nigredinē n̄ maturati accedēs stoīn ↄfortāt. ⁊ uētrē ↄstipāt. s̄z nigr' pfecte matur' cito ī hoīs corruptiōe traducit' stoīnq: mollat. ⁊ [illegible] hu
mectāt. n̄ nō s̄ m̄ sūt uelox q̄ si tenūt' supq: locū igne seu aq̄ cālā p'ustū pātē uesicā ibidē na s̄citurā repmūt.
Oleū bifaria diuidit' ē ē recēs nouū q̄ ↄ olmar fructib: ex p'ssū. Est ⁊ uet' ↄ arde ↄ eisdē fructib: manatū. Recēs ū si fit ↄ oliuis pōticas ⁊ ī mgrū [illegible] nouā
olā onfacios. vniusq̄ tm̄ laudabil' alā agnoscit' ī odore si sit odorifez ī sapore si sit optī saporis. Cui. s. pōticitatis ī ligua s̄tit' acuitas ī digēs [illegible]. q̄ q̄ua [illegible]
pōticitatis hī tātū fr̄in ⁊ siccitatem ptinet. ⁊ ab hac stoīn ↄfortat. ⁊ in aliq illō assimilauerūt rosato olō. Illiq: mltis passiōib: ī uice rosati addūt. Oliā q̄ recēs
nouū ab ossis carpsūs nigris ⁊ maturis. cl' ⁊ hu ē nutrimētū. stoī mollitiua. vetus hūt fr̄iāq: atq: ī rubaz colīs ↄduceat. Oliū ū q̄ ex oliuis fiat ī [illegible]
cū carebit malitia. q̄ aliq retinabit pōticitatis Qua p'mit ablata pōticitate fit nocibile. atq: ī malos huōres ↄuīlbile. atq: molles, facies stoīn. digestiua tm̄
ui nō ī pedit. Qd si multū [illegible] inueterauit ū saporis fiat asperior ac omnibus ↄueniēs esui erit. medic̄ tm̄ utile.

cuidā arboris iuxta alexādria nascētis
q̄d alexandrinū dr̄. et ē purius et me
lius. Nascitur etiā iuxta damascū. et
damascenū dr̄. S; nō ē adeo purum.
īuenitur grossū q̄ thus masculum
siū olibanū dr̄. q̄ dr̄ pōi īmedianis.
Elligendū est q̄ albū ē ⁊ clarū. q̄ ob
scurū abiciendū. Virtutē h̄t cōfortā
di. ex aromaticitate ⁊ qualitatibȝ suis
cōso. cōglu. et cōstrigendi. ex gūositate
sua. C cōtra lacrimarū fluxus et dolor̄
dentiū. ex fluxu huōrū ad capite ⁊ preci
pue p̄ uenas exteriores sup̄ficiei fiat
ēplastrū circa tēpora ex puluē ei. ⁊ ui
no. al. ⁊ albumīe oui. C cō relaxationē
uue masticetur. olibanū. ex masticatio
p̄hibet fluxū hu. ad capite ad sp̄ualia.
C cō grossitiē nariū cū rubore ex
fluxu hu. dētur uinū decoctiōis ei. ul' de
pille exeo mane. et p̄ōetur uinū sero
etiā qn̄ uadat dormitū. C ad digestiōe;
cōfortāda. et accidā eruptuatiōe; ualet
h̄modi pille. C ad cōfortādā matrē et
mūdificādū et cōceptū aiuuādū fiat
suffu ex eo. C ad eadē ualet supposito
riū ex puluere ei cū olō miscelo ⁊ me
lius cōtrifera. o;. ⁊ olō. m. h̄ utimur
ad cōceptū iuuand. C olibāi puluis
cū ouo cōfectus. cal' fiat aliq̄tulū et pā
nus ītictus pectini suponatur. sepe cō
fortat matrē. C ad mamillas graci
liandas. cū aceto cōficiat' pluis olibani
⁊ pāni ītīcti. mamillis suppōatur.

Oleander. ul' olisatrū. h'rba cui' folia
silis lauro s; ē lōgiora ⁊ crescēs qua
si arbor circa flūina. Virtutē h̄t ueneno
saz. q̄a caueat oēs ut nō cōmedat d' ip̄a
sūt ē q̄dā acceperūt lignū oleāder ⁊ ieo
apposuerūt carnē assādū ⁊ cū cōmederūt ip̄a
moritur sic accep̄et uenenū statī. quia
multū oportet caue' d' ip̄a. Virtutē h̄t
cōt fla salsū ītibus. h'rba ip̄i' d'coquat'
in aqua ⁊ mane ⁊ sero lauet crura p'bē
mir' d'siccat ⁊ cōsolidat.

psomogaro. fit d' pane ⁊ garo. gar' ē d' piscibȝ salsi
recētibȝ. opsomogar'. ca ē ī. i. gū. sic ī scdo. Vir
tutē h̄t lauātē mūdificātē ⁊ colātē. pec
tus ē p̄ūificat p̄lmonē atq; stōm d' cēssis cōpu
tredinis huōribȝ. saporē cib' p̄stat. ventrē
huectat. ī femore dolorē seu sciā hūtibȝ miti
gatiōē tribuit. siū mādūcet' siū ēsberigēt. vuln'
ra sordida d'colata mūdificat' usq; p'sana p'te
dilatāt'. Gar' ē d' piscibȝ minori ē calori
opsomogar'. pisces ē fri s' ⁊ hūidi.

Ostriago q̄ punici. Saramunis. uocat'
nascitur circa monumēta. ul' ī parie
tibȝ q' sūt circa monumēta. C ad fetidos
uetitos ⁊ recentes. radix ostriago cōt'ta
⁊ fetidis īpōita siū cicatricē ul' plaghe

mir ɔsolidat ⁊ sanat. Ʋalet ea legi mēse Julio ante solis ortū.

Piretrū ca. ē. ⁊ sic. i. iii. g. h'ba ē satis ᵱcōis. cui radix pōitur cū ei receptio ᵱcepitur. i veme ɔlligitur ⁊ exsiccatur. radix ei. p. v. āños ſuatur. Ē aūt el ligendū q ɔtinuū ē ⁊ solidū ⁊ nō pfo ratuz. ⁊ cū frāgitur nō pulueriçat ⁊ acutum h't saporem. Notādū q acum piret. nō stati ᵱcipitur. ſ; d; aliq'tulū ɔmasticari ⁊ teneri i ore h aūt ɔtingit. ul' ᵱp ei leuitatez. ul' ſtie soliditatez. uirtutez h't. dis. ɔsu. et acthendi. ¶ Gargarismus ex aceto decoctiōis eius. et ficuū siccarū. ul' uino dulci. cerebrū a supfluitate flatica purgat. et hūitatē uue ɔsumit. ⁊ it dentes masticatū dolorez tollit. ¶ Coctū i uino ⁊ olo ⁊ loco paltico. arth. ⁊ podag. cataplētur mltū ɔfert. Si pōt h'ri uinū ɔterat. et iaceat i uino. p. xv. dies. pea bulliat bñ ⁊ coletur. addita cera ⁊ olo fiat ungt' optimū ad predca.

¶ Piretrum

¶ Piper

Piper· ca· ē in principi iiii: gradi. sic· i me
dio· cuius triplex ē maneries· est eni
piper longū· q macro pp dr· ē et albū· q
leuco pip dr· ē et nigrū· q melanū pip
uocatur· qdā aūt dicūt q sit fructū di
diuersorū arborū· Diascorides uō· ost·
dicūt q sūt eidē arboris fructus· i india
nascētis dicūt etiā qdā q piper fiat nigr
p combustionē· q cū dbet colligi· pp copiā s'pē
tiū ibi existētiū apponitur ignis iter arbores
ut cobūrantur s'pentes aut fugiatur· Sz cacu
ratice ōstruerent arbores ip̄e· Sūt autē
fructus eiusdē arboris· s· cū flores ponūt
i unū reducūtur· 7 ostrigūtū i longū· et sic
fit pip longū· p̄ea pducūt iꝰ pꝰos fructꝰ
q pip albū dr· q2 albi sūt· Sz tale pip nō
hn̄s· Sz loco eiꝰ pōitur cataputia trāsmaīa
q pip nō ē· qa grossior ē q pip nec etiā ht
acumen sic pip q cū pōitur i medicina
interior s'bā abiecto cortice dz pōi· piper
aūt nigrū tpe maturitatis colligit· sara
ceni uō ponūt i clibano duplici d cā· s·
ut diutius suet et ne p'sit fructificare
i aliis ptib;· Est aūt pip nigrū efficatiū
q pip albū· ul' pip lō· nigrū suatur p· xl·
annos· albū q nō hn̄s sat diu· longū
p· xx· annos· albū pip pot pōi p nigro·
si hn̄s pip albū āplius aliis cofortat· ht
aūt pip nigrū· uirtutē· dis· 7 osumēdi·
¶ puluis pipis narib; appositus sternutati
onem puocat· et cerebrū· a supfluitate fle
matica mūdificat· ¶ Vinū decoctionis
eius et ficuū siccarū· spūalia mūdificat·
agluctīno humore et multū ualet ē asma
frigidū· puluis eius cofīcus sicca nat
adidē ualet· ¶ Pluīs ē eius i cibis
datus digestiuē cofortat· ¶ poma p
parata ex puluere eiꝰ 7 precipue ex pul
uere eius· et piperis longi digestiuē
cofor· ¶ puluis s'btil ex eisdē s'bā abiec
to cortice sepe aspsus aq· ro· et cofīctat
aut simpliciter aut c aq· ro· more col
lirii oculis ipōitus· maclā; et pannū
tollit· ¶ Sanguineis 7 colericis nocē
usus pipires dissolū· et qbzdā qnq; le
prā; inducē· pluīs eius carnē; supfluā coro
dit 7 pip longū magis cofortat·

Peonia· ca· ē 7 sic· i sō· g· hrba est· cuius
radix sili nōie appellat· q i medicine pōi
tur i hieme colligit· p· x· annos suat· Elli
genda ē q s'bnigra ē· 7 cōtinua 7 nō pforat.

q grauis est et cū frāgitur nō puluericat· leuis
qdē; et pforata uetustate ē cōsūpta· Virtutē; ht
dis· 7 cosu· ¶ ē epil' uirtutē; ht oclatā collo
patiētis suspēsa· ut ait· G· dqnodā puero i
cuius collo diū suspēsa erat nō patiebatur· s'b
tracta ea patiebatur· hic aūt eius effectus
medicinis repitur· Vn̄ qdā dicūt q qdā ē
maneries peonie huc hn̄s effectū ul' dica
tur quō nō sit eius tal' effectus· un̄ dr qdā
nō ē quolibet et h aerū ē· s· dqdā s'pē eius
¶ Puluis peonie ualet adidē datus i uino

decoctiōis

decoctionis arthimisie. ¶ Puluis et a-
cius datus i succo pigani adide3 ualet.
¶ Cō palisim dr̄r puluis peonie i uino
decoctionis castorei. ¶ Cō stin- et dis dr̄r
uinū decoctois peonie. ¶ Ad matricem
mūdificādā. fiat suffumigacio et fomētū de
ex uino ul aq̄ decoctois pulūis peonie. ¶ Cō
tenasmon exsi-cā. puluis ei supponatur et
bonbice. Ro. q. peonia. alia noīa uocāt. Pen
thorobon. alii uocāt. aglofotos. alii. Aliofos.

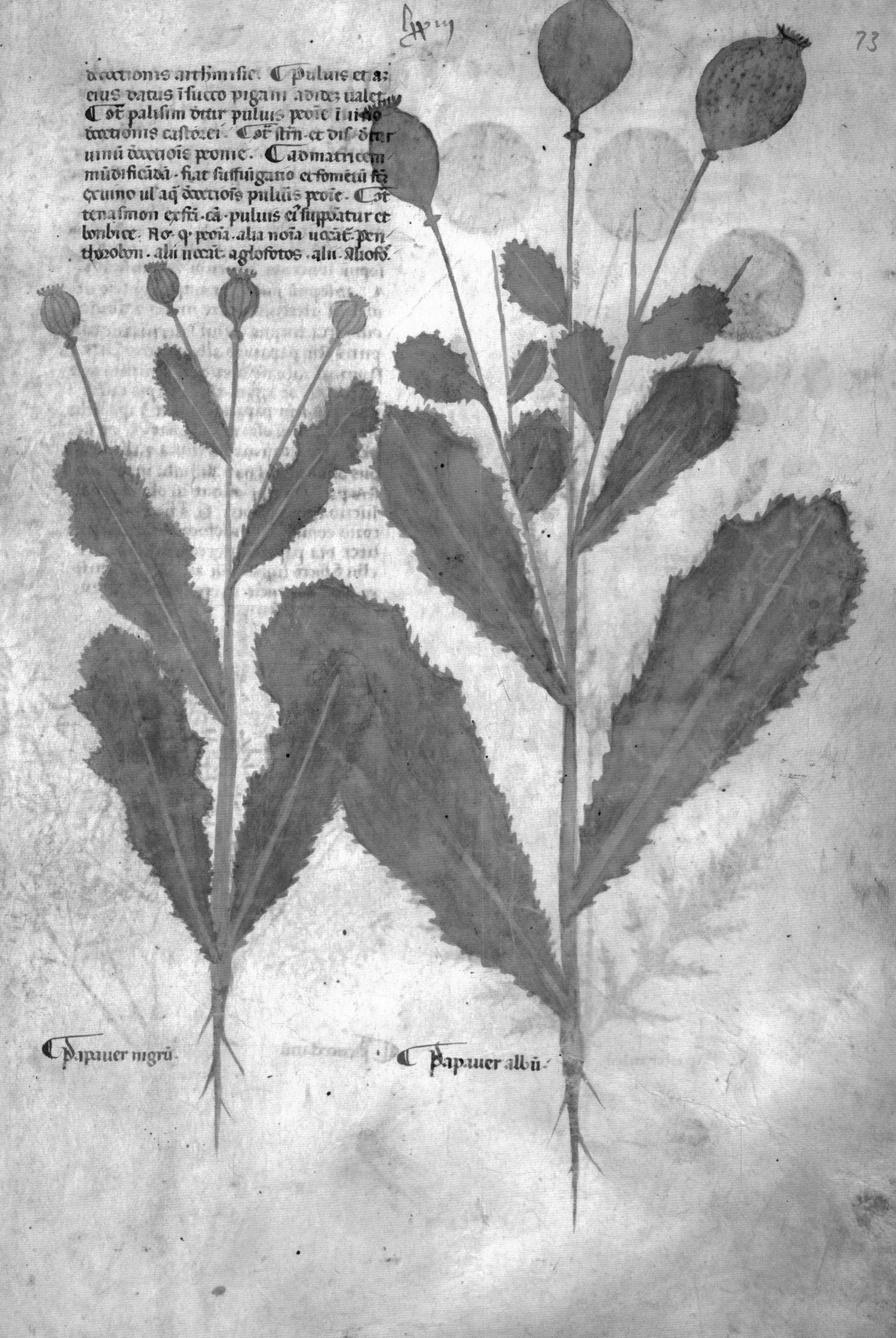

Papauer frē · 7 sic · ɔplexiōis ē · cui tplex est maneries. ē · ii · albū · q · f · 7 hu · 7 ni gru; q̄ friū; 7 sic · 7 rubū q̄ · florez h̄t rubū 7 magis mortificat 7 alio noīe dr̄ papaū siluatic̄ · alii Rosa fetida · Papauer albū dr̄ codias · Oxiborion · Papauer n̄ · dr̄ Micone · alii uocāt Melcos agrios · alii · Anemone · s̄ ei collectū p x · annos suat · In medicīs pōitur · put ɔbet pōi · 7 ɔdeterminatiōe · Sem papauēis · al · 7 nig · ul' rubi · h̄t uirtutem sopnū iducendi · leniendi · 7 mortificādi.

Ad sopnū puoc̄ · fiat emplīm ex sēie ut usq; ul' alterius 7 lacte mulīs · 7 albuīe oui · circa tinpora · Mul' salernitane dāt puris sem̄ papauēis albi cū ꝓprio lacte · Nigri · ul' rubi · nō ɔbet dāi · q2 nimis mor tificāt · Cōt appāta · cā · ipricipio calfac tiōez epīs · sem̄ papauēis · al · et ī ipā h̄rba ɔtta ɔficiat' cū olo · ro · 7 suppōat · Cōt sic citatez mēbrorū · ut ī arthtica 7 aliis febri bus olū uiol' cal' fiat aliq̄tulū ut puluis sēis papauis albi · ɔficiat' cū olo · ro · 7 fiat iūctio · spine · ptotū · Cō siccitatez pec toris et ɔsūptiōez mēbrorū · ualet p̄ncipa liter dia papauē q̄ ex eo fit · l' ɔficiatur · elm ɔ succo liq̄rit · gūi · ar · draggi · anisi · et ɔ sēie papauēis · iuxta q̄titate aliorū ɔficiatur cū sirupo ·

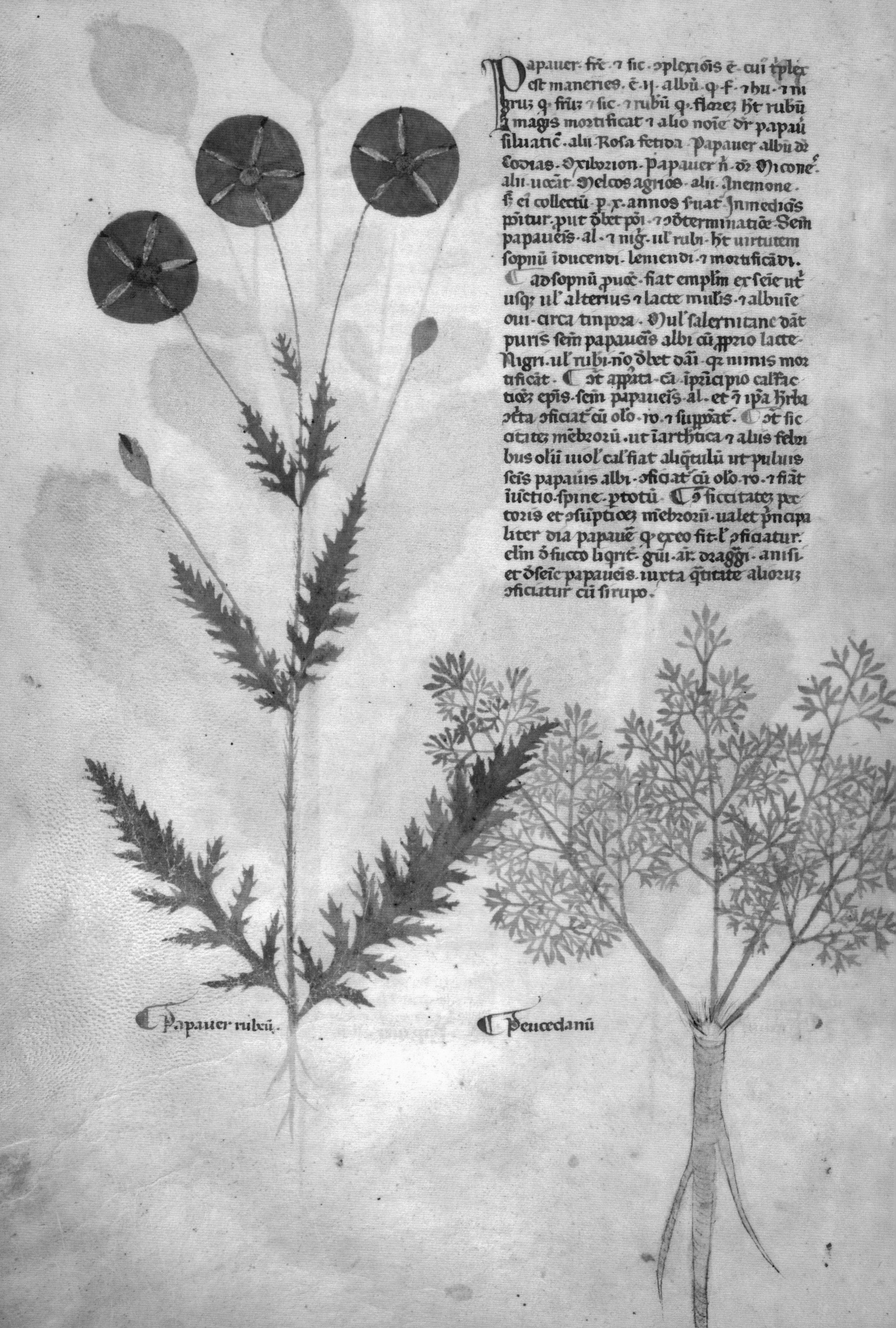

Peucedanū. ca. ē. 7 sic.
Herba ē q alio noīe. feniculꝰ porcinꝰ dr.
alii uocāt. agan'omor. alii uocāt. agrio
filati. cū aūt inuenitur receptio. peucedāi
imedicīs. radix ōbet poni. qa principalit
ħt effectū. herba uō rarū. Radix ɔlecta p
ānū suat. uirtutē ħt diureticā. Cōt. str.
7 dis. 7 oppilatiōē splenis 7 epis. dat' i aq ul'
uinū decoctiōis ei. ipā ī herba decocta i uino 7
olo. 7 cataplāta pƀ ē. Cō str. 7 dis. 7 opil'
splenis datus i aq ul' uinū decoctiōis ei. ipa
etiā herba decocta i uino 7 olō 7 catapla spl'
ni duriciē remollit. Cōt frīos humores
i spūalibꝫ existentes dt' aq ordī decoctiōis
peucedāi. Sisit mlt̄ū frꝫ 7 hu. dt' uinū de
coctiōis ipī. et suci liqrit. fomētū factuꝫ
ex uino decoctiōis eius herbe. ɔ̄estr. pucē.

Petrosellinū. cā. ē. 7 sic. i. so. gū. alio no
mine dr. Trianem. ē aūt duplex. s.
domesticū 7 siluestre. q sinonū dr. cui scia
precipue ɔpetit usui medicīe. ɔsuat. p. v.
annos. Virtutē ħt diur. sꝫ sinonū fortiorē.
Cōt easdē cāe ualet eodē mō ɔ quas. pe
ucedanū ī ɔpetēs fit. salsamētū ex petros
lino domestico herba ī ipa i ab' posita. di.
ɔfortat. 7 uētositatē excludit.

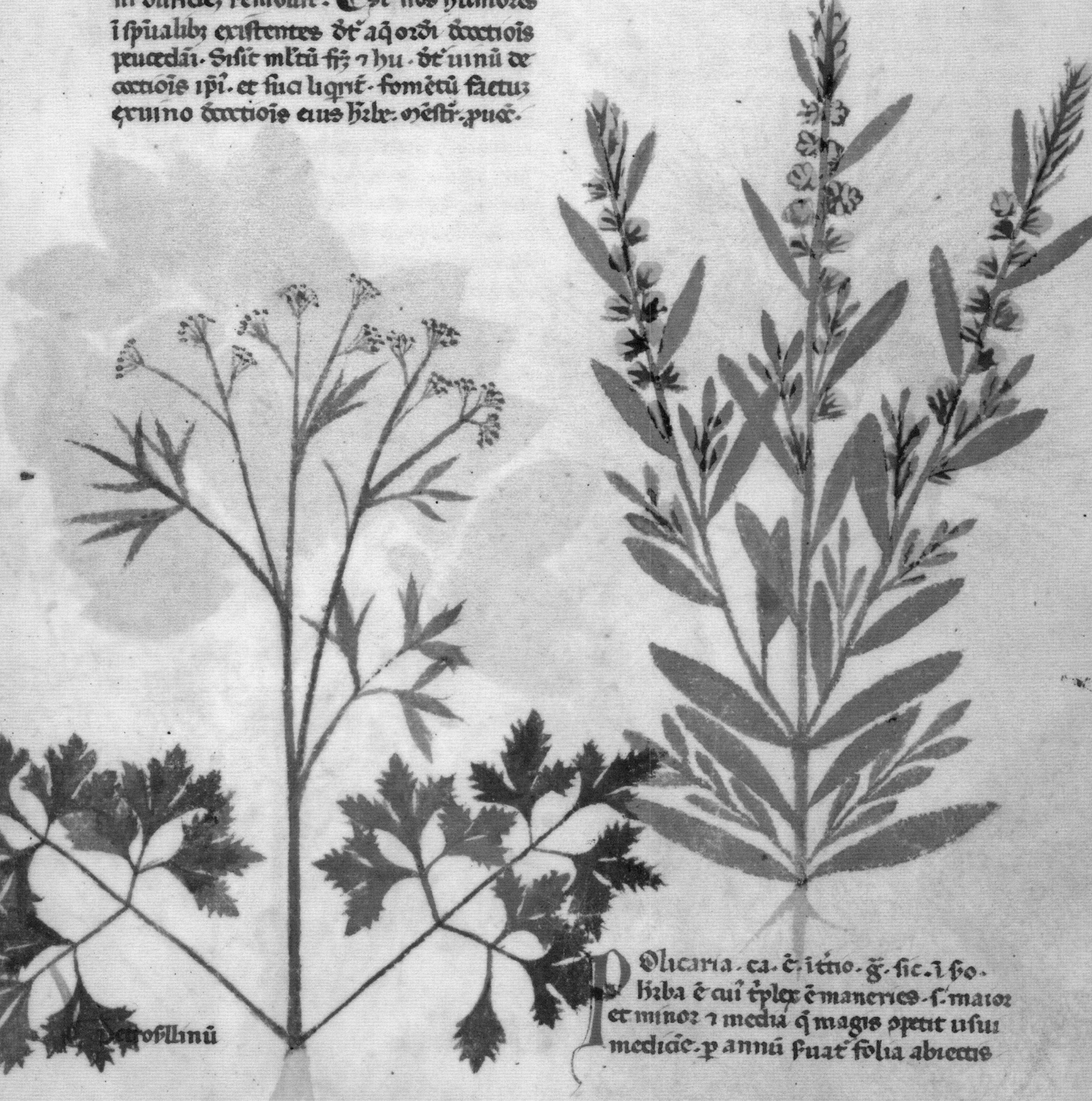

Policaria. ca. ē. i tto. g. sic. i so.
herba ē cui' tplex ē maneries. s. maior
et minor 7 media q magis ɔpetit usui
medicīe. p annū suat' folia abiectis

stipitib; ponitur imediciis. Virtutē hēt
dis. et ꝯsu. ¶ Vinū decoctiōis pollicarie
et ficuū siccarū ualet asmaticis ꝯ ꝯ̄ firōs
hu. i spualib;. ¶ Aq decoctiois ei ut ins
fiat fomētū ualet admūdificādū matc
ce uuluā coartat. ¶ Puluis ei sbtilis
suppositus ualet ꝯ̄ tenasmon. ex fra. ca.
fasciali scius exsoluis ei. et iuino decocti ꝛ
loco dolenti suppositi dolorē exuentosita
te tollit. cal'facti itesta sine liquore et
capiti supposita ualet ꝯ̄t reuā.

Pinea. ca. ē. ꝛ hu. q alio noīe Strobilia.
dr. cū aut ꝺ; poni imedicina pōat prius
supra carbones ut aliqtulū ꝯburatur. pea
abiectis duplicib; corticib;. et qdā pellicula
iteriori expoat nucleis. Virtutē hēt lenie
di. et huectādi. et aliqtulū apiendi optiu
cibus est laborātib; ispualib; ꝛ apate. exfro.
hu. asmatic et sicce tussientib;. eptic ꝛ ꝯsupti.
sanguinē augmentat libidinē icitat. pse
pot dari ul' ꝯfictis ul' elio ul' icib. ¶ Co dissin
tiriā. ualet cortex exteior hec mō cū primit
pinea abarbore suitur decoqt bn i aqua pea
sp carbones poat ꝛ patiēs fumū recipiat.

Pruna . fria . sunt 7 hu . prunorum alia sunt . alba . alia nigra . alia rubea . que nigra sunt et aliquantulum dura magis ualent . et precipue damascena . cum colligitur matura finduntur . et aspergitur aceto . et ita seruatur in uase aliquo ligneo pannum . habent uirtutem infrigidandi . et leniendi intestina . Vnde ualent acute febricitantibus . Contra constipationem uentris ex siccitate . uel ex colera . hu . consiccente . si uiridia sunt dentur ad comedendum . si sicca coquantur in aqua et prima pruna comedantur . 7 aqua bibatur .

Penidion . ca . sunt 7 . hu . fiunt autem sic aqua permiscetur cum zucharo . et fit decoctio quousque gutta lapidi . supposita adeo induretur . quod statim inter digitos frangatur . postea ille totum super lapidem politum ponitur ut infrigidetur . et clauo ferreo in fixo suspendatur . 7 ibi manibus tractatur . usque dum dealbantur . post forficibus incidatur in quadam frustula . 7 consiccatur 7 sic fiunt penidie . consistunt spargendo pluries amidi ut albi fiant . optimum autem est . febricitantibus . exasperatibus spiritualium et contra tussim siccam . ualet contra siccitatem pectoris . 7 contra consumptionem ypse dentur uel in iobarus ualet in febribus . dia penidion maxime in acutis febribus 7 in pleuresi 7 peripleumonia . congruus est cibus 7 optima medicina . Contra fissuras labiorum ponatur penidium in aqua draggi . 7 penna illiniantur labia .

Psillium . frigidum est 7 hu . in 2o g . herba est . cuius semen etiam sic uocatur . Semen in estate colligitur . per annos seruatur . Virtutem habet infrigidandi et hu . Contra ariditatem lingue in acutis febribus . semen in panno subtili ponantur . et ligetur 7 infundatur aqua . 7 cum tali illiniatur lingua . et ligneo cultello abradatur . Contra sitim sub lingua teneatur . Contra sitim et siccitatem spiritualium . 7 constipationem uentris in acutis febribus ponatur psillium in aqua et dimittatur aliquantulum diu . abiciatur aqua illa . et psillium detur cum aqua frigidissima in sir . etiam contra acutas febres competenter ponitur psillium . fiat multa decoctio per quam gutta adhereat . caute tollatur . quia cito adheret . propter uiscositatem psillii . Contra dissinteriam . psillius comburatur in testa 7 puluis modo factus . cum ouo sorbili detur . uel melius cum aqua ro . detur si fiat uitio inferiorum . uel cum athanasia supponatur puluis eius . Ad idem fiat emplastrum ex puluere tali 7 albumine oui . et modico aceto 7 aqua . ro . supra pectinem 7 renes uel super umbellicum . si fiat uitio superiorum . Contra fluxum sanguinis 7 naribus ualet emplastrum . super frontem et tempora ponitur uel stuellum factum ex puluere eius naribus imponatur . Contra calida apostemata ut erisipilem est omnium sacellus repletus semine psillii in succo alicuius herbe frigide ponatur . et sepe supponatur . psillium conseruat camphoram . ex frigiditate 7 humiditate sua .

Polipodium · ca · ē · i · m · ḡ · sic · i ᵹo · h̄rba
ē simil' filici q̄ sup q̄rcus lapides et
muros crescit · Melior ūo q̄ sup q̄rcus cre
scit · Radix collecta · ⁊ articulis mūdata et
ad solem exsiccata · p̄ bienniū ī mlta ef
ficacia s̄uatur · Radix aūt ē elligenda q̄
uiridis ē · aliq̄ntulū · Jlla aūt q̄ fracta ī
terius apparet arida · ē abicienda · Vir
tutē h̄t attrahendi · dis · ⁊ purgandi flā
principali' ⁊ melā · Vn̄ ꝯpetenter ponitur
ī decoctionib; et flāticis ⁊ melāicis · Sanis d̄t
ad ꝯs̄uatiōez · Et no · q' ī decoctiōe polipodii ·
d̄b; poni aliq̄d exclusiuū uētositatis ut ē
semē anisi · fen̄ · ⁊ cimini · q2 polipodiū sol
uit · hu · ī mlta uētositatē · ℭ̄ ylliacam ·
pās · alopitiā · et dol' arth' · et ad ꝯs̄uatiōez
sanitatis tal' sit usus · ꝯteritur polipo
diū · ℥ · v · ul' · ℥ · i · ad plus sit fit laxatīu ·
et fiat decoctio ei' ī aq̄ · ꝯ prunis ⁊ uiol' · ⁊
sq̄ꝑato si habes addito seīe fen̄ · ul' an̄ ·
ī mlta q̄ntitate et colatā mane · ul' sero
exibeatur addito zucco · Alius usus ꝯte
rātur et fiat decoctio ī aq̄ et seīs fen̄ · ul' an̄ ·
et d̄tali aq̄ fiat iuscellū · ul' coq̄tur plus
ꝯ sp̄eb; odoriferis ⁊ ouis d̄tur mlti sic
d̄ capiunt salutif̄e · fiat ī pigmētū sic · ra
dices ꝯterātur ⁊ decoq̄ntur ī uino · p̄ea
addatur aliud uinū et fiat pigmētū
additis sp̄eb; odoriferis · Rustici aūt ꝯ
terūtur b̄n radices uirides · addentes fa
rinā ⁊ oua ⁊ faciūt īn crispellas q̄ laxāt
satis · q̄nq; ultra modū · ℭ̄ prenotatas
pās · dari · pōt ipso decocto polipodii · bulli
at ꝯ seīe fen̄ · ī aq̄ · ul' suco eidē · additis · ℥ ·
ii · plus hermodactilor̄ ·

Petroleū · ca · ē ⁊ sic · i · iiii · ḡ · petroleū
d̄r oliū petre · Jnuenit' aūt locis sulphu
reis sit ei' ꝯpinguedo terre ⁊ aq̄ actiōe ca
loris ī igneas ptes ꝯūtitur · Jnuēit' aūt
sup lapides · q2 ꝑos resudat et exeis · et s̄
mare īuenitur · S; illd̄ ē nigrū p̄ea ūo p̄
extractiōez fit albi coloris · q̄ñ; ī citrī · Jng̃
cia ⁊ ī trasmaīs ptib; ita opantur · diu
pōt s̄uaī · et ī uase uitreo ul' stagnato ⁊
b̄n oppilato · Elligendū ē · q' albū ul' citri
nū ⁊ clarissīe s̄b̄e et q' ē fetidissimū · Soph̄
sticari aūt pōt facile ex amixtiōe alteri'
oli · q2 par' petrolei mltū aliud oliū pōt
reddere · fetid · h̄t aūt igneā uirtutē ·
s · dis · ꝯsu · et attrahendi · ℭ̄ arthticā ·
pās · podag̃ · ciratg̃ · palisi · yl' · pas · stī · ⁊ dis · fiat
ī ūcio circa ptes dolentes d̄ petrol'o · ℭ̄ yl' ·
pas · q̄dā dāt ī q̄ntitate · i · ℥ · ul' plus · ℥ · ii ·
mlto tiēs curātur · mlt otiēs succūbūtur · S;
n̄o d̄b; dāi ī estate · nec collerico nec d̄bili
nisi mateiā sit frīā · et ad plus · ℥ · ii · ℭ̄ for
tē · podag̃ · et · yl' · bulliat ī suco ebuli petro
leū colatura d̄tur patienti · ℭ̄ urtium
lapidis · sumū remediū istud · pl'ui' lapis
lincis s̄btil' bulliat ī petrol'o et colatū p̄ siriga
iniciat' · lapis ꝯ firmatū frāgit · prius tam̄
d̄bet fomētari uirga · ex aq̄ decoctiōis malū ·
⁊ oli · ut extendantur ⁊ apiant' meatus ·
ℭ̄ asma frīn et tussim antiquā · pectus prius
b̄n ī ugatur · ut b̄n digerat mateiā ⁊ d̄t · ℥ · i ·
l' · ii · ℭ̄ uehementē frātē stōi · ī ungatu
exterius · ℭ̄ suffocatiōez matricis fum'
ei' pōitu' sup' carbones p̄ nares recipiat ·
ℭ̄ casū matris fiat suppōitoiū ex lōbice
inficto ī petrol'o · No · q' q̄ñ · petroleū dat
pōt dāī aliq' · frīū · ⁊ hu · q2 petrol'ū excori
at · frīū · aūo · et hu · lenit ·

ℭ Paritaria · q alii uocāt uitriolā ·

Paritaria . ca . ē ⁊ sic . i . iii . g̃ . herba ē q̄ alio noīe . Vitreola dr̃ . qr uitrea uasa ea optime mūdatur . ul' dr̃ . Perdicados . alii uocāt eā . Murale; . alii . Canicularez . alii . herbe uenti . alii . Morgellina . alii . Vitrariā . Nascit' ī parietib; ⁊ ītectis . ⁊ oī tpr̃e . ī ueī tū . exsiccata nullius ē efficacie . Viridis autē; mlte uirtute; hr̃ dissolū . et diaforeticaz et extenuatiuā . C 9 frāte; stōi ⁊ ītestinorū; ⁊ dol' eorū . str̃ . ⁊ dis . paritariā ītesta calfa sīn liquore sr̃ pōat loco patiēti . ul' ī decocta 9 furfure ī uino . al . acceto . aliq̃tulū trita ⁊ sr̃ pōit melius ēst . C 9 . str̃ . et . dis . cogt' in aqua salsa et olo . ⁊ pectini cataplētur . C parita ria cocta ⁊ 9mesta . ual; 9 dol' stōi . et ītestinorū ex frāte . ul' uētositat' . Mulieres salernitane . faciūt crispellas ex paritaria . aq̄ ⁊ faīna 9 predcā accidentia . C 9 podagr teste 9 macro . aq̄ dcoctiōis paritaē abluat pedes ⁊ crura . ⁊ eisde; herba cū axūgia bn̄ 9 trita ⁊ supposita pedib; mir sanus eficiet'.

Portulaca . f . ē . ⁊ hu . herba ē satis cōi q̄ alio noīe dr̃ . Andragis . alii . uocē . Andremā . alii . Emoreos . alii . Cappari . alii . Cax . alii . Porcastrū . alii . Amarantos . portulaca uiridis mlt' ē effecacie exsiccata n̄ tante . Virtute; hr̃ . lenitiuā . huectāui et īfrigidādi . optim' cib; ē 9mesta . cruda ul' cocta . C 9 strictiōe; uētris coquatur cū prunis ī aq̄ ⁊ 9medat patiens pruna et portulacas et bibat aquā . Notādū aut' q̄ 9petēt' pōitur cū diur' . et sicca . et uiridis . qn̄ ad ē 9stipatio uētris . et . qn̄ diur' exterius apponit' . C 9 str̃ . ⁊ dis . tuc' opāt'ur . maiore; uentris 9stipatiōe; . Vn̄ 9grue portulaca apposit'ur . huectat eī; et relaxat . C 9 ragadias . i . fissuras labiorū; . radices portulac' 9buriātur ī uase terreo ⁊ fiat pluis ⁊ īliniantur ragadie . hui' pluis palliat ī ragadias leprosorū C cal'a apsēita ī pricipio ⁊ 9 iflactiōe; ex calē . hu portul' uiridis 9tta ⁊ sr̃ pōita pd' ē.

Pulegium . ca . ē 7 sic . i . iii . g̃ . alio nōie dr̃ ad grecos . gliconiū . i tp̃e floꝝ colligitur . et i unbra siccatur . pānnū suat . folia cū floribꝫ abiectis stipitibꝫ i medicina pōitur . sūt eñi due sp̄es pulegii . s . mascl̄s 7 fēīa . h̄t aūt mascl̄s florē al . fēīa ūo . purpureū et rubicūdū q efficacius ē 7 dr̃ pulegiū ciuinū . ❡ virtute ħt . dis . ꝯsu . ❡ Sacellatio fc̄a capiti . ex pulegio cal̄ fc̄o i testa sin̄ liquore ualet ꝯ frīm reuma . ❡ Gargarism̄ fc̄us ex aceto decoctiōis pulegiū et ficuū siccaꝝ . humitatē uue et ginguiarū ꝯsiccat . ❡ Vinū decoctiōis pulegii ualet ꝯt tussiꝫ . frīaꝫ ex glutinoso . hu . ul̄ aquoso . ❡ Vinū decoctiōis eius ualet ꝯ dol̄ stōi . et itestiorū . ex frīat ul̄ uētositate . ❡ Trispelle ꝑ fc̄e ex pulue eius et sbtili farina 7 aq̄ ad eadē ualet . ❡ Emplꝫ ꝑ fc̄m ex eo . et decoctio ei i uino ad idē ualꝫ . ❡ fomētuꝫ fc̄ūꝫ ex aq̄ decoctiōis ei . humitatē matris ꝯsiccat uuluā coartat . h̄ fomēto utūtur mulieres salnitaē

Pira . f . sūt . 7 sic . alia sūt domestica q minꝰ siua ꝯsūt . alia siluestria 7 illa fiiora sūt . matura minus stiptica sūt . et i maturitate magis stiptica sūt . Pira cruda ul̄ cocta ꝯmesta post cibū . alia ꝯprimunt cibaria . et sic ꝯpetent̄ euacuatur supflua añ cibū ꝯmesta sistūt 7 ꝯstrīgūt uentrē . pira cocta i aq̄ . plu . sup hos stōi pōita . uomitū ex collera cohitat . pōita suppetinē . fluxuꝫ uētris strīgit

Pomū citrinū; diuerse est nature. Cortex eius. ca. ē. ꝛ sic. Interior sba. fri. ꝛ sicca. media. ca. ꝛ hu. Cortex aūt uirtutē; hēt mūdificādi ꝛ ꝯfortandi ex aromaticitate sua. Vnde ī pluris archoticon pōitur puluis eius. Cortex crudus ꝯmestus digestiōē; ꝯfortat ꝑpeditā ex frīāt et ī appetitū;. Valet ē ꝯ cardiaca medicīā; sbaz quaz ꝯmedūt cū melle ꝟ; male digerit. Interior aūt sba. s. acetosa ꝯpetēt usui mediane. ꝯmestū ꝯcarnib; ul' piscib; appetitū ꝯfortat. ī ꝑ ditum ex huōrib; existētib; circa hos stōi ꝯpetenter ī pōitur. In epthiātib;. scia aūt. ut dictū. ca. ꝛ sic. sūt ꝛ diuī. ꝟ; m̄ uidēt. q fri. ꝛ sic. sit ex suo nutimento. et sicco. nutriuntur eī; ex aceto ī quo sūt. Vn hūt uirtutē; diuī. ꝯtibilitatē stē.

ꝯ opilatiōē; spleis et epis ex frīāte. dē aqua decoctiōis semē; eorū.

Passuli. ca. sūt ꝛ hu. ꝛ dicūtur uue passe. quā dicūt q dimictūtur dēsiccari post dēsiccant adsole; ꝑea ī furno. ꝑea abluūt. ī uino dulci ꝛ sup aspgūt puluē; cimini. et aliarū; spēru; aromaticaꝝ. et ligat ī foliis ficus et ita suat ꝑ duos annos. Virtutē; hēt leniendi. passuli ꝯmesti ul' uinū decoctiōis eorū. ualet ꝯt frīa; tussi;. cocti ī uino et cataplāta. Valet ꝯ frīa appeāta et dol' stōi ex frīāte. De uuis imaturis facimus pluerē; hoc mō. dēsiccātur adsole; ꝑea exteriori cortice carnib; abiecto arilli adsole; dēsiccant et sic puluis q dat ī labis ualet ꝯ uōitu; collericū. et fluxu uētris. cataplasmatū ori stōi ualet ꝯt uōitū. ꝑectim ꝯt fluxu;.

Pistacee q alii fistici uocit ... ca. ... ī medio scdi gdi. ... ꝯmedētib; ꝑāt nutimētū. quā tamē amaritudis ꝛ ꝯticitatis hūt ... sūt ꝯpis ꝯfortatiue eī ē ꝯstipatiōe; apiūt. sꝫ ꝛ pectus ꝛ pulmones mūdificātes. si cū uino potui donet. sūt ꝯt uenenū. ipi ē; ꝑ phisica epi ꝯuenūt. ol'u; ꝗ eoꝝ capi dolēti. mitigatiōē; ꝑāt. q dia. dix eē suo iuuatiuū. neq; lesione; stō face. neq; uētrē solue. n ꝯstipare. sꝫ tamē calidā hūte; ꝯplexiōē;. modicū ex eis ꝯmedat. q si assi fiat ꝯmedētiū stōm ꝯfortat. sꝫ uolue.

Passulis. i. uue decestie dsicce.

Pistacee.

Pistacee · ca · sūt ⁊ hu · sūt aūt fructus
ultramare nascētes · silēs pineis · Inte
rior aūt sba · dēbet poni ī medicīs · Virtutē
hn̄t calfaciēdi humectendi et leniendi · C Cō
frātē pectoīs ualent cōmeste ut amigda
le · augmētāt spma · teritur et cū melle cō
ciantur · addito puluere nucū indice ⁊
stincorū ī modica qn̄titate · h electuariū opti
mū ē ad confortādū coitū.

Plunbum · f · ē ⁊ hu · ī · 4o · g̃ · gen̄ me
talli est · q̄ facile ignis actiōe dissolui
tur · C Ex plūbo fiat mortariū et psitel
lū · ī ponatur oliū · ro · et uiol · et moū
atur usq; dū pueniāt ad spissitudinē
et pōatur sol̄ · ī mortario; addito oleo
ī ponatur oliū · ⁊ moueat ol · ⁊ pōatur ī aliq̄
[margin: Atuinale] h unḡtū · h unḡtum psilli· tioō ualet
cōt usturā ab igne · ul' aqua · ro oleo
cō excoriatiōēs ex calore et cō erpetē esthio
menū · fiat aūt plūbū ustū q̄ ī unḡtis
pōitur hoc mō · pōatur plūbū ī aliq̄ uase
pōito sup ignē · et ī pōatur icisiōēs caprifi
fic · ul' coruli ul' ī titimallus ī pōatur et
moueatur cū caprifico ul' corillo donec re
digatur ad q̄sdā massas q̄ fēā pluerizāt post.

Polii diuisa sūt gn̄a · S; precipue mōtanū
ꝓpt̄ usū medicine cōsimplicit̄ inuenitur poli
um montanū dēbet poni · cū flores pducit d;
colligi · pannū suatur · Virtutē h̄t · dis · cōsu
et diur̄ ex sbtilitate sua · C Vinū decoctiōis
eī et passularū · ualet cōt̄ frātē pectoīs.
C Vinū ī decoctiōis eī ualet cōt̄ dolorē et frātē
stōi et itestinorū et cō dolorē ex uētositate ⁊
oppilatiōē splīs et epīs et renū · et cō sb · ⁊ dis.
et cō dol' stōi ex uētositate.

Pix alia naual' alia liqda q̄ picula dicitur
Pix ē cal'a · et sic · ī sc'do · g̃ · Naual' min · ca
ē · ī sic · dicit aūt qdā · q̄ pix [illegible] ex
pic̄ naual' · dū excoq̄tur picula · qu̇ quasi fex
residet · q̄ mētitur sc'o · g̃ · Pix ex diuersis arborib;
q̄ui fluit aūt · ī uasis coq̄t aqb; ī alia uasa
[margin: pic] nauali mit · effluit liquorositas ab lignis resu
dans · pix liqda · pix liqda uirtutē h̄t · dis · et
relaxandi · C Cō scabiē fit ungm̄ ex picula
resoluta aceto et olō · nuc̄ alio pōatur litar
girū p noctē ī aceto · mane ī picula resoluta
addito olō · rō · fiat unḡtū · C Cō ipetigiē ⁊ sp
ginē · plus auri pigmēti ī picula resoluta
addito sapone gallico ⁊ fiat unḡtū · C Cō tinea
fiat capillū ex picula ⁊ pice nauali · ⁊ colofo
nia · C Cō splenē ex frā · ca · ⁊ frā apposita fiat
enplm̄ ex picula resoluta · cera · ⁊ olō · ⁊ pix
naual' ī enplīs pōitur.

Plantago herba e q Greci uocat Arnoglossa. Romani uocat ea Arnion. Tusci pbation. alii Eingloss[a]. Corinti. Eptapleuru. Galli. Tarbidolopiu. Spani. Thicarican. Siciliani. Polineuro. Tusci. psiti Viaceneumonos. Egipti. Asser. alii. Sertarion. Daci. Scinpoas. alii Plantagie lata. Romani. Plantago maior. alii. Piticiola. alii. Quinq; neruia. Nascit locis aquosis et iplanis. prima cura ei e ut ait Diascorides. Ad dolorē capitis. radix plantaginis ad collo suspensa mir dolorē tollit. Ad dolorē dentiu. succus ex radicib; et foliis eius tepidus i ore retēto stati dolorē expellit. et si inflata fuerit maxilla si poni eplm tepefactū ex foliis eius mir inflatione soluit. Ad dolorē iteriorum. succu ei ciatu unu potui dato ieiuno stati dolorē tollit. pb. e. Etiā toraces purgat et sanat. Ad his q purulentu excreat cū sanguine. succus plantagis ieiuno potui dat' mir sanat. Ad cā fetidā cicatrices. pilus seis platagis fetidis sup̄po mir sanat. Itē plantagis contrita et supposita loca ubi fuerit humores constricti eximit calore. pfectissie purgat et sanat. Ad flux uentris. uinū rubū ul acetū decoctis ei herb potui dato quattuos unos iuice stati constrigit uentrē. Ad morsū serpētis. herb plat. pesta et sucu ei cū uino potuq; dato. ceteri uenenu discutit. Ad scorpionū siu cancrorum morsū siu puncturā et dolorē. radicem platagis contrita et supposita mir sanabit. pb. e. sepe. Ad ascarides. sucu plat. cocleariū unū ieiuno potui dato et ex foliis contritis sup̄ umbellicu enplatis stati cadit uermes iuctis et expellit foras. Ad duritiā icorpore. folia plat cū axūgia sine sal bn contris et duritiā supponi cetē duritie solui. Ad quartanā febrē. succus ei cū mixta bibitu an horā acc. uidob effectū bonū. Ad podagrā et cete dolorē et inflatione neruoz. folia plat. addito modico sal et bn contris qz supposita. certū remediū et magnū bnficiū aufert. Ad tercianā febrē. tres radicib; platag bn contr et cū uino ul aq potui dat' ihora acc. mir pfic. Ad secūdinā dolorē. semē platag fco pluerē et cū uino ul aq potui dato. certū bnficiu habebit. Ad fetidas recentes. folior eius cū axūgia ueteri sine sal contrita et supposita mir sanat. Ad inflatione pedū ppt laborē. folior eius contrits addito aceto et pedib; supponi et mirabis. Ad fetidas q nascunt circa oclos ul naso herba platag. succus in expsus et cū lana humili iticta eisdē succ supponi p nouē dieb; sanus efficiet. Ad ulcera uicē oris. succ eius i ore retēto ul folia ei comesta mir sanit. Ad dissintericos et turminosos. pilus seis platagis cū uino potui dato ad sanitatē reducit. Ad parotidas. herb platagis cū axūgia ueteri contrita et supposita mir sanat.

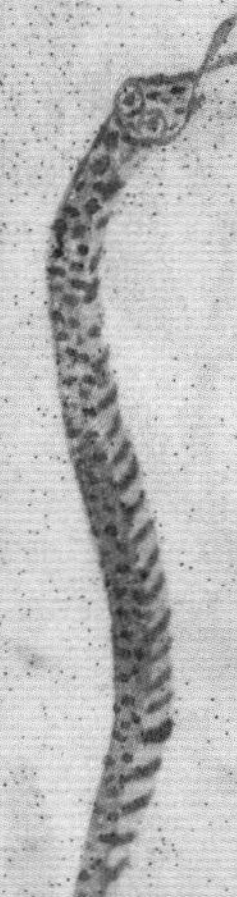

Plantago minor q alio noīe dr lanciola. Virtutē ht ad fistulā. succus lagol iecto fistul p multis dieb; eā occidit et sanat. Ad morsū canis rabiosi. eisdē herba contrita et supposita morsū leuit ad sanitatē reducat. Ad dolorē et malū uetice. succu herbe cum dieb; suis potui dato mir sanabit. Itē ad morsū pestiferū et spalāgionū sile ualet.

Paniciū i forma et n sil e milio min tam eo nutr. uētrē uō mag constipat. [illegible]

hirba qnq3 foliu cu axugia ueter siu sale.
siml' bn ɔtere ⁊ sr pon eplr. mir sanabit. Ɔ
dolore3 uetris ex cola. sucus ei potui dato sin
mora dolore3 tollit. Ɔ aduitia ⁊ putredine
oris ⁊ lingue. plius qnq3 folior cu melle a
mixto ⁊ pfrica os ⁊ lingua. ul' fauca. cer pu
tredine3 purgat ⁊ sanat. Ɔ dolore3 capitis
hrbe qnqfoliu bn ɔteris ⁊ fricato capit ul' front.
mir pficat. Ad ite3 radix ei sr capite aportat
dolore3 capis sedat. Ɔ fluxu sanguis ena
rib3 sucu ei potui dato. ul' front ulnito mir
sistit. It radix ei ɔqsset et coqnt' i uino q3 co
latu potui dab pb e q melin e. Ɔ morsu
spetib3 sucus ei potui dato ce3 uenenu vis
cutit qa ponit i tyriaca magna. Ɔ ad can
cros cecados foliou ei ⁊ piguedine porcina
femina sine sale siml' bn ɔteris pta aiec
ta i uino albo uetero ⁊ suppon cacro ⁊ utere.
⁊ pbaucis re3 certa ⁊ ueru medicamentu3.

Penthaphilo. hirba e q greci sic uocat. er
Paopedi q e qnq3 et filon .i. folia. romani
uocat ea. Qnq3foliu. daci uocat. Callipet
talon. romani. pseudosellno. alii. xoloto.
alii. Aspaltion. siculi uoc. Thimatitis. tus
sci. Esosi. alii. Telotis. ytali. Psiloton.
alii. Petacmon. alii. Frimatitis. egipti.
dissisi. alii. Teonestio. alii. ybetisonix. alii.
Theronikos. alii. hermudactilon. alii. m
o.anumartis. alii. pinpeclonu. alii. Pol
la. greci. penthafilo. Nasat' locis obscuris
et sablosis ⁊ ipratis ⁊ ht qnq3 folii i uno pe
de ⁊ ht flores croceos ⁊ expedit sr terti. pria
cuia se e. Ɔ aduitia articul' expcussiões.

Ɔ Polligonia.

Polligonia. herba ē q greci sic uocāt. alii Prosperpinacia dicunt. alii Cimosiamē. alii polligomatos. alii aspaltiō. alii policarpō. alii calectron. alii cenopodion. alii Mirotopetalō. alii Cecia. alii Megalion. egiptii ytterū. omeos. pfesie. pfeti. Sonosherenos. punici. Sungur. romani. Sanguinalem. alii Stomaria. alii Serutum. alii Scorpinacem. alii Corrigiola. alii lingua passerina. alii polligonos. Nascit locis cultis et ī pratis et secus uias. potest eā legi ōi tpr. Prima cura eius ē. ꝯ sputū sanguinis et uomitum. sucū polligonie cū uino brusco optiō potui dato mire pbatū ē. Ad dolorem lateris sucū ei et oleo ro. pmisce et unge locū. Ad mamillarū dolorem et inflationem. herba ipsa cū butiro fiat enplm et supposi. dolorem et inflationem tollit. Contra dolorem et ulcerationem aurium. sucū ei tepidū auribus stilatum. mire efficax est. Contra pruriginem tibiarum et exsc salso. aqua decoctionis ei ablue loca statim expellit prurigo. Contra dissinteriam et omnē fluxū uentris det suco polligonie cū succo ul' pse aut cū uino. Contra fluxū oy. cotti nsoro dat mire liberat. si prius os facere istā oz sup eā dicētes. herba polligonia filia rex orti ... sicut claudisti ptū mulē sic claude sanguis. tal'. et dic nomen mulieris.

Politricū. herba ē q sili noie appellat. alii uocāt eā adianthos. alii Trigomanes. alii Elenetricos. alii [illegible]. alii Cicinales. alii Terre capillo. alii superbiū terre. Nascit ī parietibus et puteis et locis hūorosis. Prima cura ei ad dolorem stolli. herba politricū: cū ramulos suos et folia por rinne. et grana. viiii. piperis. et viiii. grana. colīa. deinde oīa simul bn tere et cū optio uino bibat. prius uadat balneū. Ad capillos multiplicādum et ꝯfirmādū. politricū ī oleo decoq et cū illo oleo unge capillos mul'. Pulvis ē ei sr uulnera recētia aspsa ꝯsolidat et sanat. Valet ꝯ acutas et pacitas febres. aqua decoctionis eius ꝯgruchro. ponitur ī sirupis ꝯpositis ad istā dū.

Primula ueris. herba ē q sili noie appellat. alio noie dz. herba sci pet. qd uocāt palisis. dr eā primula ueris qa ī tpr prime ueris ꝓducit florem. Nascit locis soliosis et hūosis et ī pratis. Contra fracturā capitis ul' aliq membro siue pcussionem. ul' aliqua uena scisa ī corpore. succum eius ex tota herba expssū dab ieiuno ciatū unū mane et sero. sine dubio sanabit. Item ualet ꝯ str. et dis. aqua decoctionis radicū ei.

Politricum.

Palatio leporis. herba ē simil' sparago s̄z
h̄ns folia lāgiora et morbidiora quasi
feniculo ꝛ radix ei' sicut radicib; bruschi et
florū nō p̄ducat. facit eciā; sem̄ rubicūdissimū mag
et rotūda sic sem̄ brusci. crescēs igit̄ unū
cubitū. est eni; diaforeticā ꝛ uocat̄ palatio lepo
ris q̄ lepore; fugit añ diabolo p̄secuta. et cū
ēēt s̄b h̄ herba secura est a diabolo ꝛ nō potest
eā tāgere. alii. uocāt eā. Arthriticā; C ãq ul'
uinū decoctiōis radicū ei'. ualet ꝯ. arthriticā;
ꝛ yliacā. pas. dis. ꝛ str̄. Nascit̄ locis obscu
ris ꝛ i planis ꝛ i siluis.

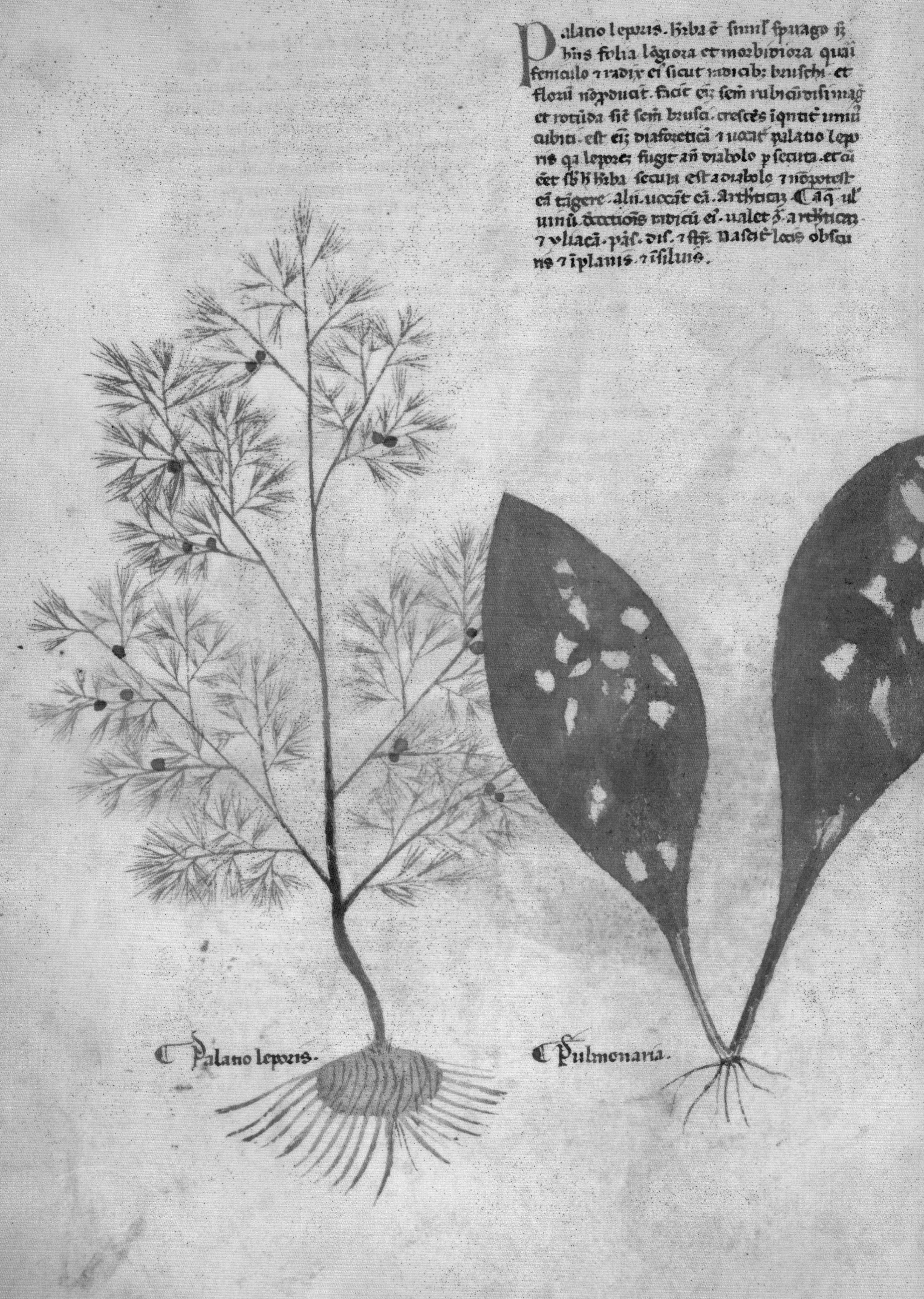

Pulmonaria. herba est. filiis borrago sed
est latiora et longiora et morbidiora et
habet quasi albidam. hec ilich. sic pulmone. quia
dicitur pulmonaria. vel quia principue valet contra
vitium pulmonis. hec sepe comesta vel in
sirupis confecta. valet pulmoni ulceratio.

Persicaria. herba. cuius folia cum floribus
precipue competunt usui medicine et simi
latur folia persici. Nascitur locis humorosis
et aquosis. alii vocant eam. Sanguina
riam. alii. Sanguis Christi. virtutem habet
incensiva. Contra vermes aurium. Sucus fo
liorum eius auribus iniectus occidit vermes.
in eos.

Paratella siue patella. herba ē cui⁹ folia si-
miliat̃ liquritia. siue simil' listrago et h̃t semen rubū ⁊ rotūdū admodū ciceris. radix ei⁹
longa ⁊ grossa ⁊ colorē citrinū. alii uocāt eā
Basilisca. h̃t eīn uirtutē uenenosā. dicunt
qdā q ex ea fit uenenū artificiose cōposito.
Valet precipue ꝯt fistulā licinīū ex ea factū ori fistule īmissū ꝯpetēt̃. os elargat ⁊ cā-
cer occidit ⁊ curat. Nascit̃ ī planis locis sablosis.

Pinpinella. herba ē q̄ sili noīe appellat̃. Nascit̃
ī locis sablosis ⁊ ī pedes montibꝫ. Valet precipue ad uulnera ꝯsolidandā. pluis pinpinelle super
aspgatur sepe ⁊ sanabit̃. Contra fistul' ⁊ cancro suppōita uiridis uł siccata mir̃ pficit. Jt̃ ꝯt obscuri-
tatē oculoꝝ. uinū uł aq̄ decoctiōis ei⁹ ocul' laua-
mane et sero mir̃ clarificat. Contra uenenū et sꝑē-
tiū morsꝯ. sucus pīpinelle potui dato uenenū
excutit. Pnostica ad uulneratos. pīpinelle
ꝯ. 1. cū sale tere ⁊ distēpa cū uini calicē. 1. ⁊ da
ieiuno bibere. si uidˀis exire pplagā. nō euadet.

Pilosella · herba est que oritur ad pedes montibus · habet folia longa unius digiti ad plus vel minus et habet pilos longos unde dicitur pilosella · extendit super terram · virtutes habet mirificas [illegible] constringendi et consolidandi vulnera · si ex ea succus fit unguentum cum cera · oleo et terbentina · vel pulvis foliorum eius super aspersus vulnera recentia mirifice consolidat · Contra quartanam febrem succus piloselle in hora accessionis potui dato habetur. Pronostica ad vulneratos da potui succum piloselle: si reiicit moritur · si non vivet · probatum est. Item si cum dicto succo aliquod ferrum temperatum fuerit · alia feramina incidit.

Provinca · herba est satis comunis de qua mulieres faciunt corona · Valet contra fluxum sanguinis ex naribus · vel alio loco capitis · folia eius in ore recepta · fluxum sanguinis sistit.

Palma xpi. herba ē. silis satirionū. s; hns folia signata q̄i celesti coloris hic illi hic ortū locis obscuris ⁊ humidis ⁊ p̄pe it' castanetis. valet.

Persica. frā ē ⁊ hu. i ij̄o. g̃. ē eı̄; fructus arbor cui folia silis ē amigdalo s; st maiores st. fructus eı̄ precipue ꝯpetit esui. ieiuno ꝯmeste colleraꝫ refrigerat stōm ex calore cole abolia tione; uōitū ꝯfortat ⁊ appetitū icitat. nocet eı̄ flāticis ⁊ melācōicis. v. ul' vij. folis eı̄ ꝯtte ⁊ ꝯfāina fco crispelle. ⁊ ieiuno ꝯmeste faciūt assel lare ⁊ purgat eı̄; p̄ncipalr. flā. ꝯo. colā ⁊ melā aic ex nucleis eoꝝ. mūdate ⁊ ꝯmeste ieiuno ul' ꝯtte ⁊ cū aq̄ calā potate ide; faciūt. p̄gat eı̄; supiu ⁊ ifernu. d'bet accipi usq; xl. nūo. ul' s̄ cūdu; uirtute; accipiētis. fit etiā olm ex nu cleis p̄sicoꝝ ꝯueit dolori auriū ex frāte. calīm aurib; stillatū ul' cū bōbice imissū. Cōt lo bricos siū ascarides pueroꝝ. fiat emplm sr ūbellicū ex folis eı̄ ⁊ modico allio. mēta ⁊ ab sinthio. s; tn̄ prius i ūcto preclo olō.

Persica.

Pes uituli. barba aaron. i. Jarrus.

Psica ıq̄d ꝯsıac [illegible] q hu i ij g̃. plimū silia ꝯsomilis s; sapaciora stō gucietiā ū eū gītūt ut ꝯsomilia. ꝯsomilis silia qm̄ eodē m̄ flā gnāt. Psica ieiunus stō nacuo sūt edēda. ⁊ pt uinū uel odorifer. adpotadū. psica diuidut' i duo ⁊ ē gnde. albū pilosū rubous hn̄s s̄oū. Est par. leue rufū ul' citrinū. gnde saporis dleis ē. a cōris q; cui dā hui modi hūid' ē. de uiscosus. q̄ guertibile ē i flā ꝯsūc itq; putredine. manifestet' i hoc p si psicū scissū p paululū naribz apponas odore; q̄i putredinis sēptias pap odoriuūū ꝯ gūsione lāgniuū. Sucu folioꝝ eı̄ potat' lubricos cucubitinos eicit. Ide; facit si ex eo cataplā feceris ubilliio. Sic uermnos appās auricule uermes occidit.

Pes leporinus. herba est. cuius folia similantur cicorea et habet flores croceos similes lactuce leporine sive herbe calendule. et radix eius alba et multa testiculi admodum anfodilli sed sunt parvi ut testiculi leporis.

Palleo. herba est. cuius folia similis est frumento. sed est grossiora et albidiora. nascitur in Italia partibus et circa viam. foliis eius exsiccatis et in pulverem redacte. vulneri recentibus superaspersis et abligatis statim sistit sanguinem et vulnera consolidat.

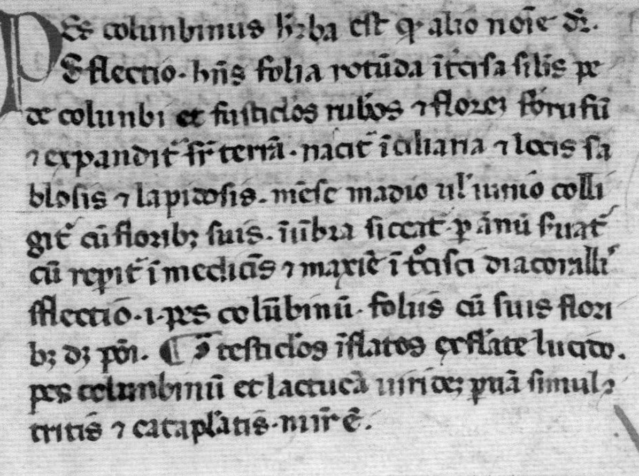

Pes columbinus h'ba est q' alio noīe dr̄.
ꝯflectio. hūs folia rotūda ītcisa silis pe
de columbi et fusticlos rubos ⁊ flores rotūdū
⁊ expandit sr̄ terrā. nascit' ī italiana ⁊ locis sa
blosis ⁊ lapidosis. mēse madio ul' iunio colli
git' cū floribꝫ suis. ī ūbra siccat' p ānū suat'
cū repit' ī medicīs ⁊ maxīe ī tcisci diacoralli
ꝯflectio. i. pes colūbinū. foliis cū suis flori
bꝫ dꝫ pōni. ¶ Ꝯ testiclos īflatos ꝯ ēflate luciō.
pes columbinū et lactucā uiridē pistā simul
tritis ⁊ cataplātis mirr ē.

Porrus. ca. ē ī medio tcij gdu. siccū ī fine. q certificat
sue pōticitatis uū sanguinē manātē ex naribꝫ ꝯstrīg
it scdm cibū ī laudabil' ē nocet ē stō faciēs īflacti
onē ⁊ uētositatē ⁊ cū sui acuīne nuos ei mor
det. h't ꝓ̄ꝓ̄ietatē faciendi fumū nigrū. mēse ptin
tē q cito ascēdēs [illegible] uisui tenebrositatē fac̄. ad qꝫ
sopnia tribilia [illegible] timorosa iduc̄. Vn̄ caue
dū ē ab oībꝫ ūsl [illegible] ssionis ei aptas hn̄tibꝫ q̄s
comedē diligētes. accipiāt pt eū porsulacas. en
diuias ꝗ silia. ut ei calor abistis tēpatiue acci
piat. aut elixet' dūm bis aut ter lauet'. ⁊ esui ꝓ
nūm donet' q tūn scdm medic' ualꝫ. Crud' ē ꝯ
stitis calē pl'monis ꝯcessis mūdificat humoribꝫ.
cpis oppilatiōē apit. ꝯ ci regmiā hn̄tibꝫ mitig
tionē tribuit. Sucu ei cū aceto ⁊ olo ro[illegible]thu
[illegible]naribꝫ missū sanguinē ī fluētē ꝯstrīg eis.
[illegible] sr̄ [illegible] aure distillat' dolorē placat ꝯ fri
giditate or̄i. Crud' cataplat' [illegible] ꝯpetuū d
negdest. Elixet' qꝫ si supistet [illegible] hemoroidas
cataplēt tumorē ꝯ hūitatē [illegible] dissolū. Cap
ei coctū ⁊ ꝯ [illegible] meleon ul' amigdaleō ꝯditut
uētrē suscit [illegible] uētrē hūectat. Valꝫ qꝫ cōtra
colicā passiōnē [illegible] uiscosis humoribu.
Sem porri [illegible] actiōis. dᵒq ʒ. ij.
[illegible] dare ex [illegible] mirte. sanguīē ex
[illegible] fereītibꝫ [illegible] stringit. gule tam ⁊ de
[illegible] qd si asse [illegible] nastuca seēe miscātu
[illegible] patiētibꝫ ꝓ̄dest. Vetositatē itestinorꝫ
dissoluit [illegible] ꝯstipat tamē. Siluestr's u ei ē ī ang
gelu. sic ī tcio pun ēē [illegible] dissoluit humorē. oppilatio
nē apit. urinā ⁊ mīa ꝓuocat. Barbe porror ꝯ
fluxū uētris si assēt sr̄ te [illegible] calāe quarꝫ fumū recipiat
ex [illegible] fenori ⁊ sedat fluxū ꝓb' ē.

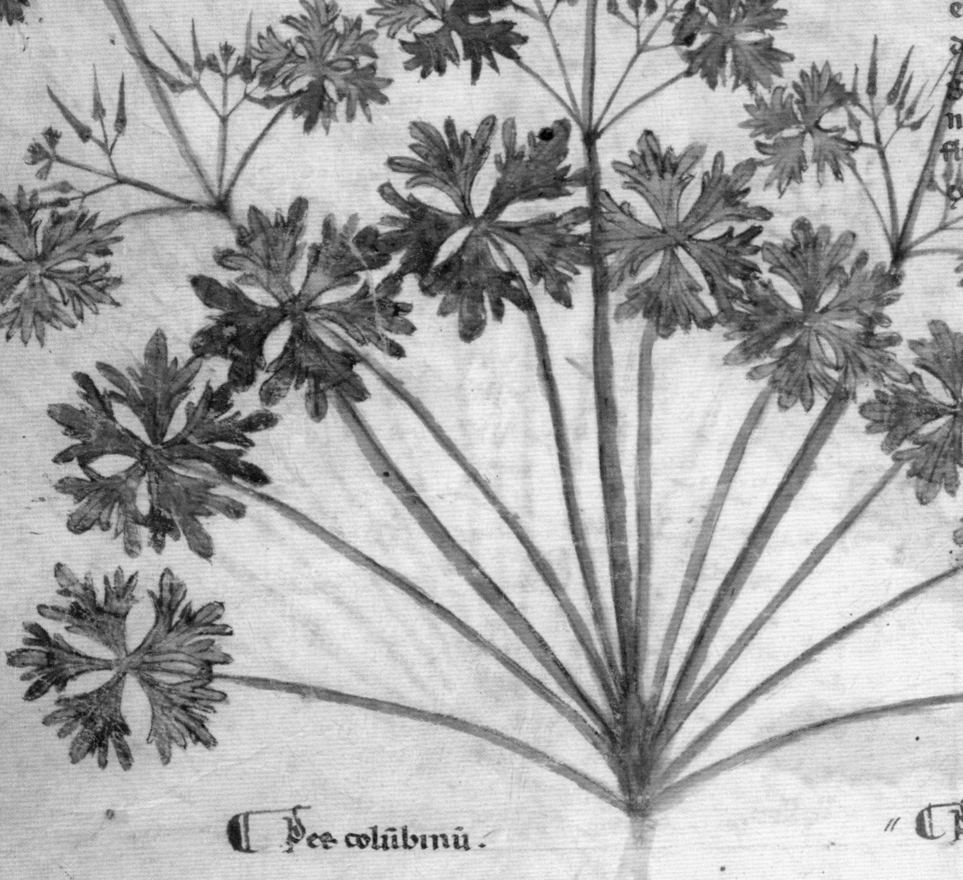

¶ Pes colūbinū.

¶ Porro.

De Rosa.
De Rafano.
De Reubarbaro.
De Reupōtico.
De Radix.
De Rubea.
De Ruta.
De Rosmarinus.
De Rubus.
De Rodalda.
De Rabiosa.
De Rapistro.
De Riso.
De Rapa.

Rosa. f. ē. i. primo. g. sic. i. fo. Rosa sicca
et uiridis cpetut usui medicine. qdā
colligut post maturitatē; si nō tā diu fuā
tur. dbet aut colligi. dū nō hrit folia oīo
expsa. & cū articlm sb ruba. si aut fuit sb
albida aut nigra. aut palida. nō ē apoñ
da imedicīs. qa sigficat uetustate csupta
ul' ante tps clecta. Colecte aut sicut dcz
est. dz dsiccari ad solez articlm & possunt
fuari p triēnū. d rosis uiridib; fiut mlta.
Sicca aut rox debēt. pōi imedicīs cū recep
tio rox iuenit. qa melius cterūtur. drosis
aut fit. mel. ros. zuchr. ro. sir. ro. olū. ro.
et aq. ro. Mel. ro. sic fit. mel pmo dspuēt
tur dīn bn colent. pēa addāt ros folia
uiridia. abiectis stipitib; & qbzdā albus.
q sūt exteriori pte & iferiori. & folia mi
nutatiz itīsa poāt. & fiat dcoctio articlā.
Signū dcoctiois ē. color. rufus. & odor.
et articlā spissitudo. p. v. annos fuāi. po
test. uirtutez ht. cfortādi. ex rosis q sūt
arōatice. cmūdificādi. ex melle. cpetēt dat
flātice. melācoice. i yeme & iestate. dbili
tatis cmulsa fcā ex aq et melle. ro. dat
q cpetenter. pdcā mlsa pt titiū diez. c ad
balneis redierit. Ad mūdificatione
stōi. ecfīis. hu. dtur mel. ro. c aq decoc
tiois seis fen. additis tb; gnis sal'. si
pot accipe dbet ēē h qntitatis. rosar. &
melle. i. iiii. lib. mell'. poāt. l'. i. rosarū.
Zuccūz. ro. sic fit. folia. ro. uīdia pista
ta. ut diximꝰ czuccō & bn terāt & ponatū
i uase uitreo. ad solez. p. xxx. dies et coti
die moueātur bn & misceātur. p triennū
pot fuari qntitas zucci & ro. dbet ēē tal'. in
iii. l'. ul' iiii. zuccō. ad plus poātur. l'. i. rōs.
virtutez ht. zuccūm. ro. cstrigēdi. & cfor.
Cō dissint. zuccūm. ro. et pluris masticis.
ad plus. ʒ. i. cmisceāt & detur. pēa uō. aq.
ro. dtur dcoctiois mastic et gariof. Cō
licinteriā et diarriā fcāz ex dbilitate uirtu
tis retētiue. zuccūz. ro. et dianthos. eqlit
cmisceātur & dntur. satis cfert. Valet ō
ō uomitū collericū. Cō sincopi & cardiacā.
cfit ex cal'factiōe spūaliū dt cū aq. ro. sir.
ro. sic fit. qdā rosas pātas ut diximꝰ. dco
quātur: i aqua. & i tali aq colata. addito
zuccō fiat syr. alis uō melius facientes.
ponūt. ro. i aliquo uase hnte orificiū stric
tuz. et sup ifundūt aquā feruētez. et dim
mictūt p diez & noctez. et ex tali aq addito.

// Rosa.

cuctio. fiat sir. alii uero prius ponunt de rosis
in ipso uase et plus infundunt de aq feruente.
et dimictunt ut diximus. et fit aq rubea.
et faciunt sir. Alii uero ɔpetunt. ro. uirides et
exprimunt succum. et inde faciunt siruppum. et hic
optimus est. Et no. quod siropus factus de recentibus
rosis. prius aliquantulum laxat. postea ɔstringit.
sir. ro. habet uirtutem ɔfor. et ɔstringendi.
℃ Contra fluxum uentris et contra uomitum detur ɔaqua. plu.
uel aq. ro. febricitantibus post minutionem ɔ
aq. fri. detur contra sincopim silr. Oleum. ro. sic fit.
quidam decoquunt rosas in oleo com. colant et seruant.
℃ Quidam autem implent uas uitreum. ro. et oleo.
et faciunt bullire in caccabo aq pleno et hoc
oleum bonum est. alii terunt rosas in oleo et
in uase uitreo soli exponunt. p. l. dies. et
hoc oleum bonum est. ℃ Contra calefactionem epatis in
ungatur epar. ℃ Contra dolorem capitis ex calore
frons et tempora inungatur. et contra dia foresim et
melius est si addatur puluis sandali.
al. et rubi. uel saltem. ro. et contra predictas causas
ponatur oleum. ro. in labiis eorum loco communis olei et
precipue contra calefactionem epatis. ℃ Qualiter
fiat aq. ro. non possumus expresse significare.
nisi uideatur. ℃ aq. ro. uirtutem habet ɔstringendi. et
ɔfortandi. ℃ Contra fluxum uentris et uomitum col
lericum. detur aq. ro. simpliciter. uel aq. ro. decoc
tionis mastic et gariof. et precipue contra fluxum
ex debilitate uirtutis retentiue. uel acuitate
medicine sed quando medicina nimis ducit.
℃ Contra corrositatem gingiuarum mastix et gariof.
bulliant in aq. ro. postea desiccata pulueri getur.
et addito puluere. ro. ɔficiatur cum aq. ro.
uel ɔ succo rosarum quod plus ualet. postea fiat
desiccatio ad solem. et sic ter. uel quater ex
tali ɔfectione illiniantur gingiue. ℃ Sin
copizantibus et cardiacis detur in potu. uel
superaspergatur faciei. Incolumis ad oculos
ponitur ɔpetenter. et ungitis ad faciem quia ab
stergit pannum superfluum et subtiliat cutem.
℃ Sicce. ro. naribus apposite. cerebrum ɔfor.
et cor reparando spiritus. ℃ Contra fluxum uentris
ex eo detur. aq. plu. decoctionis. ros. ualet
et emplastrum ex rosis et albumine oui et aceto et
ponatur super pectinem et renes. ℃ Contra uomitum
fiat decoctio. ro. in aceto. et spongias intincta
super os stomachi ponatur. ℃ Contra sincopim detur aq
decoctionis rose. detur et plus in ouo sorbili.
℃ Anthera. dicitur flos. ro. quidam quod interius reperitur
ualet contra fluxum uentris et uomitum. et eius pul
uis uue suppositus humiditatem ɔsumit. ℃ Contra
ragadias et fissuras labiorum super aspergatur
puluis anthere. uel cum aq draggantum ɔficiatur. et
illiniatur. ℃ Cum dens fuerit extractus et
sanguis fiet fluxus fiat decoctio antere
in aceto. uel saltem. ro. et fiat gargarismus. No.
quod succus rosarum uiridium post seruari. ℃ Contra rubo
rem oculorum si sentiatur punctura. ualent
ros cataplasmate. prius in aq. cocte.

℃ Raphanus.

Raphanus. ca. ē et. sic. i. iii. g°. h'ba. ē
cui radix sili noīe appellat'. Radix
magis cōpet' usui medicīe. uiridis. 7. sic-
c̄ uiridis mag°. pot' aūt suaī pannū ab
iecto fuste īteriori. si fuerit ōsiccatū. vir
tutē h't. dis. iciendi. cōpetēs ē fit oxi
melle. cōteratur. radices aliq̄tulū et di
mictātur. biduo ul' t'duo ī aceto p'ea ad
datur. t'tia ps mell'. tale oximell. ualet
ad q̄rtanā et cotidianā. ¶ Si p't d'ce col
lature addatur zuccūz. optimū fiet sir.
¶ C°ª cotidianā de flē salso. et tertiana
nis notas et precipue. ī hyeme d'tur cū
calida mane. ¶ Suppositoriū cotidia
nario sic facies. accipe zuccūz. et salē
et parū oli uiolati. et pōe ī sartagīe uel
alio uase eneo 7 tīn dimicte bullire do
nec inspissētur et durū fiat et p'ea sup̄
marmor pōe ut īfrigidetur. Magdaliōes
itaq̄ȝ oblongos. admodū ossis dactillo
ruȝ īformabis. et sic ano ītrudat'. ul' ac
cipe medullā caul' d'estici et sapone in
unge et suppōe. ul' acc̄ saponeȝ. al. et fac
inde suppositoriū. ul' acc̄ st'cus muris 7
inunge olō et sapone. si fu'i. hu. fuīt ī stō in
digesti. cortices radic̄. raphaī p'fusas mel
le ī aceto cōmedat patiēs usq̄ȝ ad saturi
tē. p°. bibat aquā calidā. et digitis ī ore
missis ul' pēna olō intīcta. uōicus p'uocet'.
¶ C°ª duritiē splēis h'ba ip'a cocta ī uino
et olō splenī cataplētur. Et pectini cata
plata solū. str. 7 dis.

Radix. ca. ē 7 sic. ī sō. g°. h'ba ē cuius
radix sili noīe appellat'. q̄ᵃ ī passio
nario īuenitur sil'r ōbet pōi. radix rapha
ni. virtuteȝ h't sileȝ rafano. et ē easdeȝ cās
et eodeȝ mō. s; n̄ adeo efficax.

¶ Radix.

Radix. ca. ē [illegible] sic ī t'cio g°. [illegible]
[illegible]
[illegible] incisiuū [illegible]
[illegible]
[illegible] ī landi
magis [illegible] illa ē [illegible]
ne [illegible] ad locū [illegible]
[illegible] uirtuteȝ [illegible]
[illegible]
accepta. minoreȝ agit [illegible]
[illegible]
[illegible] oportet. [illegible]
[illegible]
[illegible]
ul' [illegible] digitis. [illegible]

[illegible] sic ī. ij. [illegible]
[illegible]
[illegible]
[illegible] tortione 7 īflatio
[illegible] ructus et putidus [illegible]
[illegible] eleuat cibū 7 [illegible]
[illegible] digitis 7
[illegible] expellē [illegible] causa [illegible]
[illegible] p' cibū
[illegible] suā [illegible]
[illegible] ī loco [illegible]
[illegible]
[illegible] p' cibū accepta [illegible]
cibū [illegible] suplemētū [illegible]
ducet'.

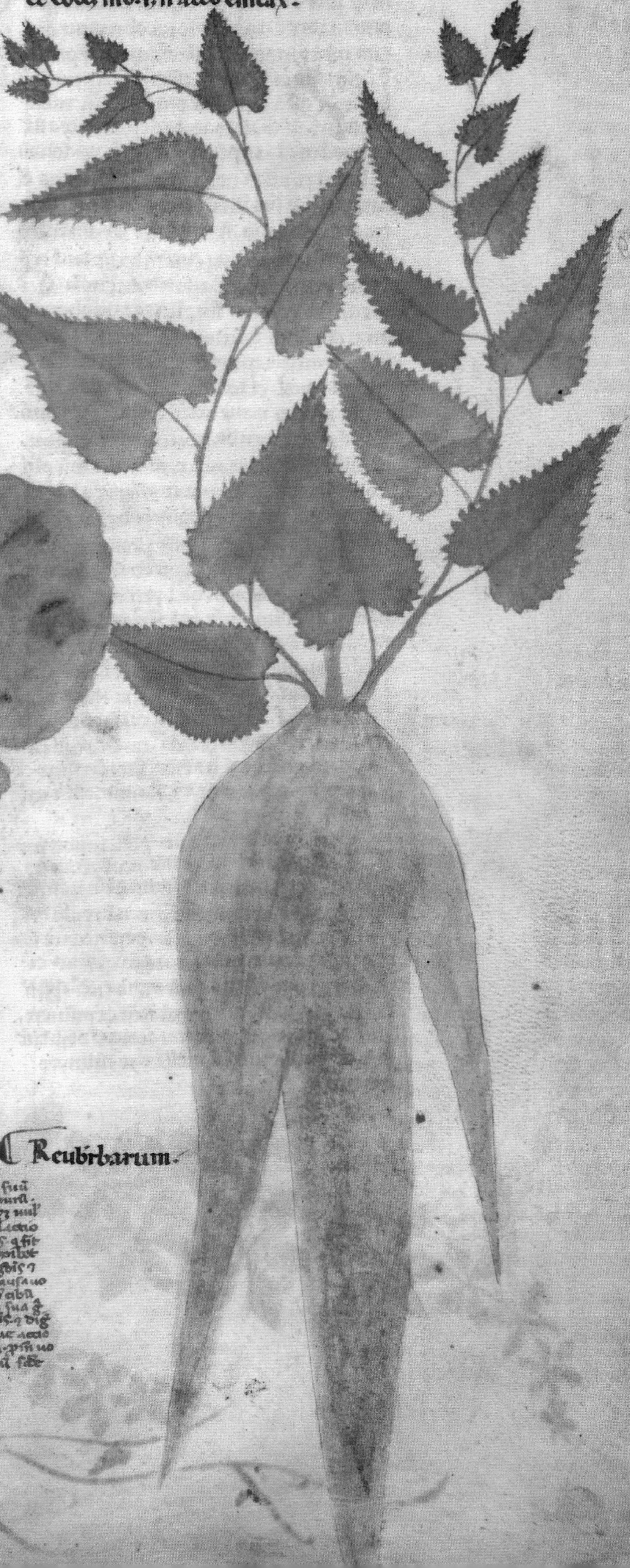

¶ Reubr'barum.

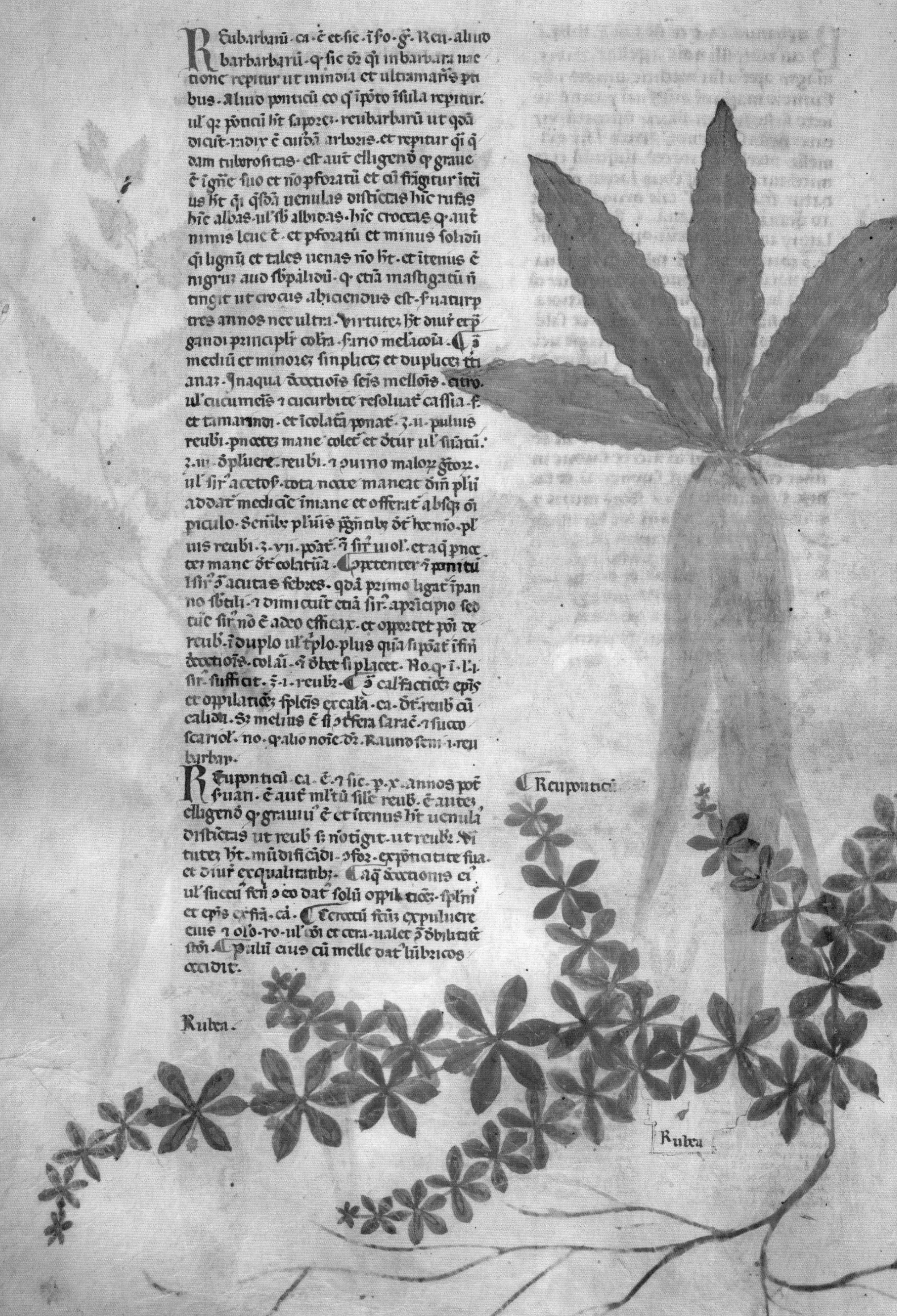

Reubarbarū. ca. ē et sic. ī 2o. g°. Reu. aliud
barbarbarū. q̄ sic d̄r q̄ī in barbara nac
tione repitur ut in india et ultramaris p̄ti
bus. Aliud ponticū eo q̄ ī pōto īsula repitur.
ul' q̄ pōticū h̄t saporē. reubarbarū ut q̄dā
dicūt. radix ē cuiusdā arboris. et repitur q̄ī q̄
dam tuberositas. est aūt elligendū q̄ graue
ē ī gn̄e suo et nō pforatū et cū frāgitur ite
us h̄t q̄ī q̄sdā uenulas distictas hic rufas
hic albas. ul' s̄b albidas. hic croceas q̄ aūt
nimis leue ē. et pforatū et minus solidū
q̄ī lignū et tales uenas nō h̄t. et itenus ē
nigrū aud s̄bpalidū. q̄ etiā mastigatū n̄
tingit ut croceus abiciendus est. s̄uatur p
tres annos nec ultra. Virtutē h̄t diur̄ et p̄
gandi principalr̄ colra. s̄ario melācoliā. Cōtra
mediū et minorē sinplicē et duplicē tri
anā. In aqua decoctiōis seīs mellōis. citro.
ul' cucumeris et cucurbite resoluat̄ cassia. f.
et tamarindi. et icolatā ponat̄. ʒ. ii. puluis
reubi. p nocte mane colet̄ et d̄tur ul' siātū.
ʒ. iii. d pluere. reubi. ī ouino maloꝝ gtoꝝ.
ul' sir̄ acetos. tota nocte maneat dein plu
addat̄ medic̄c īmane et offerat̄ absq; oī
piculo. Senib; pluuis p̄gn̄tib; d̄t hec nō. pl'
uis reubi. ʒ. vii. poat̄. ī sir̄ uiol'. et aq̄ p noc
te mane d̄t colatūa. Cōpetenter ī ponitu
ī sir̄ ꝯ acutas febres. q̄dā primo ligat̄ ī pan
no s̄btili. ī dimicūt etiā sir̄. a pricipio sed
tūc sir̄ nō ē adeo efficax. et oportet pōi de
reub. ī duplo ul' t̄plo. plus quiā si pōat ī fin
decoctiōis. colāī. ē ōber si placet. No. q. ī. l. i.
sir. sufficit. ʒ. i. reub. Cōtra calfactiōē epis
et oppilatiōē spleīs ex cala. ca. d̄t. reub cū
calida. Sz melius ē si ꝯferā sarac. ī succo
scariol'. no. q alio noīe d̄r. Raundsem. i. reu
barbar.

Reuponticū. ca. ē. ī sic. p. x. annos pot
s̄uari. ē aūt mltū silē reub. ē autē
elligendū q̄ grauiu' ē et itenus h̄t uenula'
distictas ut reub s; nō tigit. ut reub. Vir
tutē h̄t. mūdificādi. ꝯfor. ex pōticitate sua.
et diur̄ ex qualitatib;. Cōtra aq̄ decoctionis ei'
ul' succū fen̄ ꝯ eo dat̄ solū oppilatiōē splni
et epis ex frā. cā. Cōtra cerectū ferū expulnere
eius ī olō. ro. ul' cōi et cera. ualet ꝯ debilitatē
stōi. Cōtra puluī eius cū melle dat̄ lūbricos
occidit.

Rubea.

Rubea ca. e. et sic. i. fo. g. herba e q maiore ht folia. et e maioris uirtutis. alia e minor q minora ht folia. et e minoris uirtutis. Virtute; ht confort. cu aliqntula ponticitate sua. et diur. ex amaritudine. Contra debilitatem stomachi et epatis relaxationem: detur uinu decoctionis radic. ei. et mastic. Valet in epilin fcm ex puluere radic. eius desiccate et mastice cera et olo addito. Ad. pruocanda et fetu mortuu et sina educenda. radix quatuor cuiq; grossa pot hri radatur exteri. et supponat. Similiter ungatur melle. et sr spargatur scamonea puluis. prius effect melius consequitur. Si ex aq decoctionis eius cap lauetur. capill rubos reddit.

Ruta.

Ruta. ca. e. et sic. i. fo. g. cuius duplex e manerie. s. domestico et siluestri. q piganu dr. folia et semia competunt usui medicinali. cu simpliciter in medicinis inuenitur receptio rute. folia debent poni. cu inuenitur receptio semin semia debent poni. cu receptio pigani. folia debent poni semia collecta per quinqnium seruatur. folia per annu exsiccata uirtute; hnt. diur. dis. et consumi. Contra cephalea et epil. in balneo inciciat prius succi eius per nares. qr flam educ. et cerebrum mundificat. uinu decoctionis ei ualet contra eadem. Contra epil. pului peonie. ʒ. ii. bulliantur aliqntulu; in succo rute et addito modico uino detur patienti. Contra defectu uis ex fumositate melancolice. in dolio ponatur ruta cu uino et tal uino utatur patiens. Contra dolore; dentiu ruta cocta in uino cataplectur loco patienti. Aliud accipe fimber[illegible] ei et coque aliqntulu et in concauitate dentis pone. et cauteriza confert satis. Contra frigiditatem stomachi et eius palisi; et aliorum membrorum detur uinu decoctionis eius et castoris. addendo; ualet puluis ei. et cast. Contra yliaca passio. ʒ. iii. esule bulliant aliqntulu cu melle. addito succo rute ad ultimu det patienti. Contra oppilatione; splenis. et. epatis. fri. et. dis. ruta in uino et olo cocta patienti cataplectur. Contra tenasmon ex fria. ca. decoquat in uino. et fiat encatisma. ul cal fiat uinu bn et fundant sup ruta. et patiens fumu recipiat per botu. Ad. m. puoc. et fetu mortuu. et sina educenda. dec. trifera. o. cu succo rute. Idem; operatur solu succus. p os datus aut pessarizatus. aut tenuitates cu fige in olo et suppo site. Contra dol exteriore; et contusione; salina ruta in testa cal fca sin liquore supponatur. Contra lippitudine; oculoru et rubore; pu[illegible] ciminis cu succo rute conficiat. et bonb[illegible] tus oculos superponat. Contra liuore; cu pul[illegible] cimini. ruta conficiatur et supponatur. Contra uenenu bibitu. ruta bibat. Valet etia contra morsu uenatoru aialiu desup cataplectur. Si aliqs fuerit totus circudatus. ruta uidi secure pot accedere. ad interficiend basiliscus.

Ruta agrestis q greci uocat. pigano ormon. nascit in montib et locis aspis et lapidosis. Valet ad caligine; oculor. in uino decocta. tri. al. et ueteri. et cola et recondi in ampulla uitrea et competenter ungt ocul. bis. ul. t. i die. addit; succu ei. cu succo fen. et melle. al. fit colliriu. ocul utile et mirabile. Ad urina puoc. acc. viiii. talloe rute agstis et bn contere et p[illegible] coactos t b; aq. dab potui p viiii. dieb;

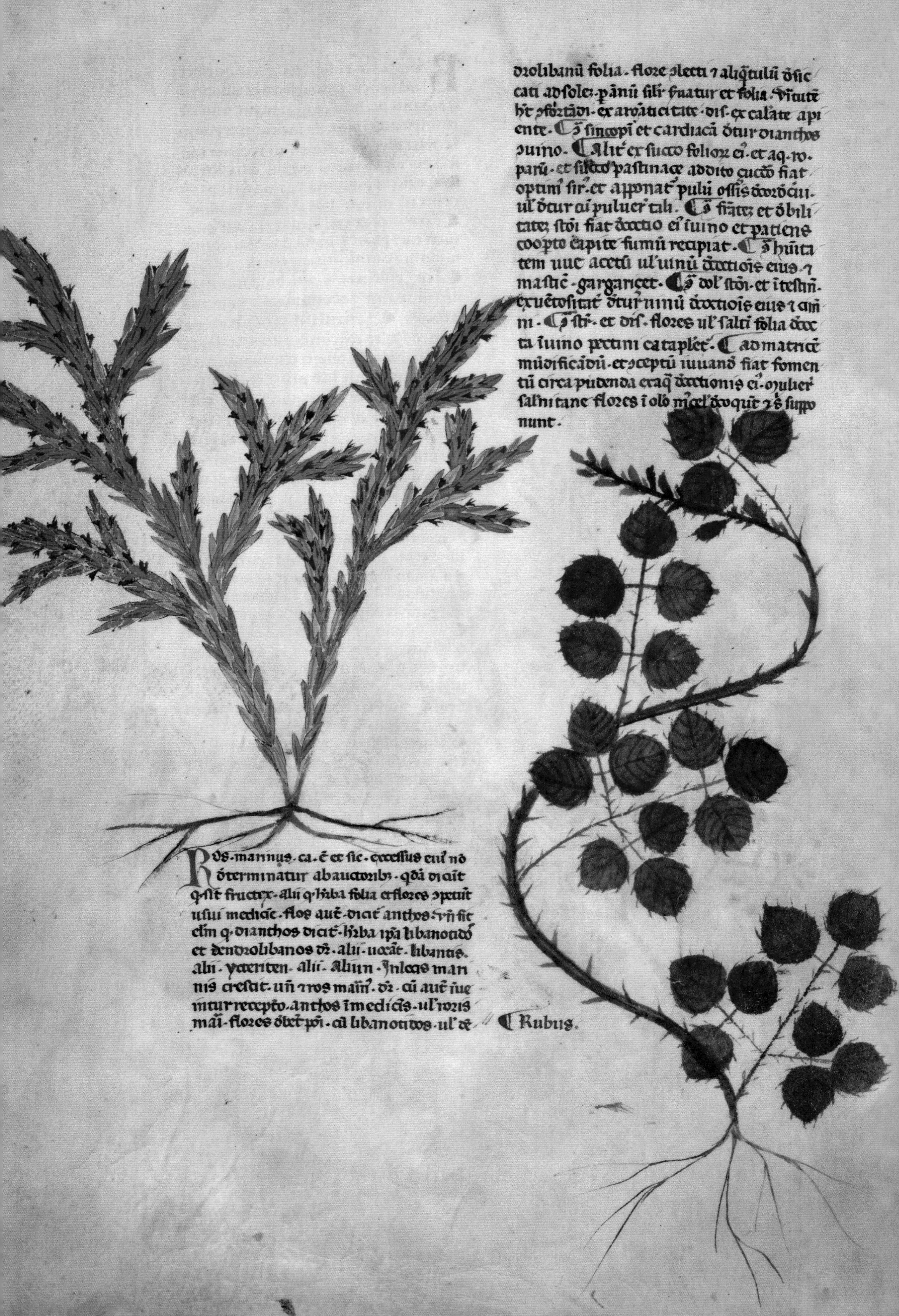

Ros marinus . ca . ē et sic . excessus eius nō
ō terminatur ab auctoribȝ . qdā dicūt
q̄ sit fructex . alii q̄ h'ba folia et flores ↄpetūt
usui medicīe . flos aut̄ . dicit' anthos . vñ sic
elīn q̄ dianthos dicit' . h'ba ipā libanotidos
et dendrolibanos dr̄ . alii . uocāt . libantis .
alii . ypericon . alii . Aliun . In locis mari
nis crescit . uñ ros mariñ . dr̄ . cū aut̄ iue
nitur recepto . anthos ī medicīs . ul' roris
mari . flores ōbet poī . cū libanotidos . ul' de
drolibanũ folia . flore ↄlecti ⁊ aliq̄tulũ ōsic
cati ad sole . pānũ sili' s'uatur et folia . Virtute
h't ↄfortādi . ex aroāticitate . dis . ex calīte api
ente . C ↄ̄ sincopi et cardiacā ōtur dianthos
ↄ uino . C Alit' ex succo folioꝝ ei' . et aq . ro .
parũ . et succo pastinace addito zucco fiat
optim' sir' . et apponat' pulũ ossis ōcorō ciu .
ul' ōtur cū puluer' tali . C ↄ̄ frīatēȝ et ōbili
tateȝ stōi fiat decoctio ei' ī uino et patiens
coopto capite fumũ recipiat . C ↄ̄ hūita
tem uue acetũ ul' uinũ decoctiōis eius ⁊
mastic̄ . gargaricet . C ↄ̄ dol' stōi . et ītestiñ .
ex uētositat' ōtur uinũ decoctiōis eius ⁊ ani
ni . C ↄ̄ stī' . et dis . flores ul' saltī folia decoc
ta ī uino pectini cataplet' . C ad matricē
mūdificādũ . et ↄceptũ iuuand' fiat fomen
tũ circa pudenda ex aq̄ decoctionis ei' . Mulier'
sal'nitane flores ī olō mīcel' decoquūt ⁊ s' suppo
nunt .

C Rubus .

Rubu dicit q̄d ē ca. et sic. cstrictiui aūt dic̄ Rsuitates eius ēē stipticas. et ponūt ꝯ usturas et ꝯ calā apemata. vn̄ uidetur q̄ sit frīn et sic. C ꝯ rubore oculoꝝ turiones ei̅ cū uitello oui. cōterātur et addito croco ocul' supponat' ꝯfert. C ꝯ q̄slibet usturas. cera mūdissima resoluitur oliū ro. p̄t succ' turionū. ī maiori q̄titate. p̄ olm̄ q̄ sic fit. coq̄ oua ī aq̄ ut dura sit. et accipe uitello eorū et pō ī sartagīe sup igne et moue ꝯtinuo et fiet olm̄. pone multa uitella ouorū. q̄r parū olm̄ effluit. ꝯfert. C ꝯ calida apata. folia suitatū trita ꝯ aq̄. ro. suppone. C ꝯ dissinteriā. succū turionū ꝯ aq̄ ordei p̄ cristerē īiciatur ul' ex turioīb; tēris ꝯ albumīe oui ꝛ aceto. fiat ēplm̄. supp̄ pectine et renes si fiet uitio sup̄iorū. lenticulā ī suico eius aliq̄tulū excusta d̄tur ad mādūcādū.

Rodalda h'ba ē. cā. ꝛ sic. hn̄s folia silis rafano ꝛ eiusdē sapor̄ s; sūt albidiora et radix puiora. nasci̅t locis solidis ꝛ icāpis. succus ex folioꝝ ei̅ ī ip̄o tepatū aliq̄d ferrū oīa fferamīta icīdit. C ꝯ lūbricos siū ascarides puerorū. fiat eplm̄ ex foliis eiu̅ ꝯtrite ꝛ suppōite ūbellicū.

Rabiosa herba ē q alio noīe dr̄ Portana
alii uocāt fagiolana. Nascit̄ i ortis siue
i campis 7 maxīe it̄ porroꝝ. Valet p̄prie ꝯ̄
ylia cā pas̄ 7 ꝯ̄ uerrucas. Sed̄ diximꝰ retro ū
herba rabiosa. uñ caremꝰ hic dicē.

Risus. f. et sic ꝯplexiōis ē. qdā sem̄ ē sile
frumento 7 sic cresc̄it 7 producit spica ut fr̄
mentū. uñ aomlīis dr̄ frumētū risū. colligit̄
eū 7 pistāt i pilla cū aliq̄tula aq̄ ut ad cortice
bn̄ mūdātur q albū fiet. hec p̄prie ualet ꝯ̄
ꝯ̄ fluxū uētris. dis̄ 7 liēt. 7 ꝯ tenasmō. decoq̄tur
et cū lacte amigdalino 7 çucco i multa q̄titate ꝯ
ditū ꝯpetit esui. mirē nutrit 7 ꝯstrigit 7 sanat.
Cōt fluxū uētris ex cola 7 ꝯ̄ dis̄. fiat criste
q̄ R̄ risi. ʒ. ii. draggti. gūi. ar̄. assi. boli. ar̄. añ.
ʒ. s. bulliāt i aq̄ pluuiali 7 colēt p̄ea disoluāt
i dcā aq̄ duo uitella ouoꝝ assatoꝝ 7 plius boli
ar̄. 7 ʒ. i. oli. ro. 7 fiant cristē tepidē. hec p̄b ē.
s; meliꝰ opet̄ si pus facēt cristē mūdificatiuo s;
ex decoctiōe ordi mūdi 7 olē. ro. G. i q̄d n̄ r̄ri calida
ē i p̄ g̃u. sic i sc̄do diuisis aūt modi hoīes illud accipi
unt 7 scdm̄ unūquēq; actiō i plurimū uariatur. ali
qn̄ mola illō terūt 7 fa͞rina ei uelud tritici coquūt v;
ita coctū eis q morsiones i stō patiūt 7 itestinis.
sūt q itegrū q̄quūt cū aq̄ hec n̄ ual; ad ꝯstrictiō di
arriā. Sē cū lacte alij coquūt 7 amigdaleō amic
tit si ita coquat ꝯstipatiōe sua 7 pfecte nutrit
7 bonū sanguīe gn̄at 7 spma auget. hēt r̄ri p̄
etate q si ul̄ cū ipō ul̄ cū aq̄ lētigiēs laues auf
fert eas 7 cuti mūdificat.

Riso

Rapistrū.

Robille. f. sut i. i. g̃. medie it̄ siccū 7 hu. cortex eaꝝ stiptic̄ ē cortice g̃ mūdate laudabilia gn̄at chimia n̄ iflaciōes etiā
uētositates sic̄ fabe faciūt ad usū cōdi bone st̄ i estate i calī regione cōmpla ex eis uescis feis i pōita soladāt 7 dolores
auferūt max si cū sapa sit p̄pate his ex ill̄ uelud ex faba sem̄ ū ad corrīsi dolore [illegible] ex decocte cū ordo 7 esolo [illegible] aut
[illegible] febres patiētib; psūt q ex sāgne 7 col̄a rub̄a. q p diarrie refrenatiōe illas uolūt accipe coctas una aq̄ 7 alt̄a āmis
tis portulace rumis 7 suco maloꝝ punicoꝝ acido 7 oleo sudē.

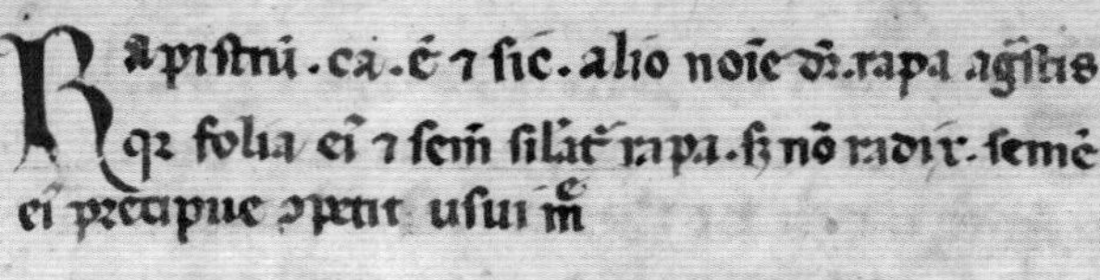

Rapistrum . ca . e 7 sic . alio noie di rapa agstis . Qr folia ei 7 sem silat rapa . si no radix . seme ei precipue opetit usui m

Rapa . ca e i . ij . g . hu . i . i . mlta pl' ceteris hu nutt . dure tam digit molle; 7 i flata fac car nes . # sui uetositates 7 i flactiones . ptu coi tar susc itat 7 spma augmetat q si i aq coqnt 7 illa aq eiecta i alia recoqt . duncies sue sic tepat . m ie bonu 7 malu nutt . q no bn co cta difficile digit . uetositates gnabit 7 i ue nis 7 poris . oppilationes fac . Jdeo utile e . si b cocta 7 utqz atqz pjecta recoqr cu pigssi ma carne . ptea scdm m e ogrua q si i ei iure pedes podagricoz 7 arthiticoz loti fuerut co

lori mitigatiuu pstabit .

Napis occurrit ueneu

si ei sem . de . odit au

u rapa radix illius .

Rapa

De spica.
De Stringno.
De Serapino.
De Senpuiua.
De Siseleos.
De Sulphure.
De Sanguine drac.
De Sqnanto.
De Sinapi.
De Sarcocolla.
De Sticados.
De Satirion.
De Sponsa solis.
De Spodio.
De Strucio.
De Stinco.
De Scorzon.
De Sapone.
De Sparico.
De Sauina.
De Sasifinga.
De Sale armoniaco.
De Sale gema.
De Sisinbro.
De Saluia.
De Scabiosa.
De Senationes.
De Serpentaria.
De Salix.
De Sanbuco.

De sqlla.
De Storax.
De Sumac.
De Stafisagria.
De Sandalis.
De Sene.
De Serpillo.
De Saturegia.
De Spatula fetida.
De Sanguinaria.
De Scolopendria.
De Soldanea.
De Spinaca.
De Scaloneis.
De Spargula.
De Silfio.
De Sanbuco.
De Spina bidua.
De Selesten.
De Sistra.
De Saliunca.
De Spume maris.
De Spongia.
De Sigillu sci[illegible].
De Sigillu salois.
De Sorbastrella.
De Sorbis.
De Sticados ar.
De Sinoni.
De Sissamo.

Spica. ca. e i. i. g. sic. i. so. spica e duplex. s. spica nardi et spica celtica. dicunt qda q spica nardi sit flos cuiusda arboris. s. men tiunt. Inuenitur eni spica n. circa radice cuiu da arboris. e aut eligeda q ista e plena in odore suauis. i gustu acuta. 7 aliqntulu sbama ra. 7 aliqd ht ponticitatis. 7 q sit i colore sbru fa. Cu aut poit i medicis. abiciendu e. qda albu q itenus est. 7 qda migr q extenus. e. qi circa radice. Et folia eius pura ponuntur i medicina i ea qtitate. q ab auctoribz dtiminata e. p. x. anos suai pot. i loco sicco 7 no huecto. qda mentietes dicunt. spica celtica ee saliu ca. Est aut spica celtica silis spice nardi. et i septetrionali plaga repit. Sz ppter ea poit saliu ca. Spica nardi. q niger e ul terrea n dz poi. i medicis. Virtute ht cfor. ex aromaticitate sua. et poticitate. diur. ex amaritudie sua. C Ad sincopi 7 cardiaca pas. impleat uinu patietis. ex aq. ro. decoctiois ipi. ul extali aq addito zucco fiat sir. C Ad debilitate cerebri applicet naribz. C Ad frin reuma pluis spice coquat i oleo. m. ul saltez coi 7 digitis naribz iponatur. tale oleu mltu cfert. 7 ad surditate ex frigo humore. 7 ad putredine aurium p apaca. C Ad frites stoi 7 idigestione. et opilatioes splis et epis. ex frigo hu. dt uinu decoctiois ei. C Ad putredine gigiuarz suppoat pluis eius. C Ad matrice mudificada. et m. puoc 7 ceptu iuuandu pulu ei sbtil ligatus i sacculo lineo formatu admodu digiti et sic i olo. oy. ul saltem coi diu bulliat. et pea mulier supponat. ul i olo bulliuit. eius puluis et bonbice supponit. C Ad tenasmo epita ca pulu ei bonbice ano exterius existeste te supvat. C oleu fit ex spica nardi. q optim est ad epil. pal. arth. et pod. suptu p hos ul i uctu. qda dimictut pluez ei i olo p. xx. dies pea bulliut bn colat 7 suat. C Alii dicut q saraceni faciut tale oleu. ex spica nardi uiridi. Diascorides dic q pretiosissimu sic fit. acc. l. libras spice nardi. et ponetes i olla bn obturata. os. et ali am olla ifundiut itra. et a fundo superioris ol le dscendit calam ad iferiore circa supiore faciut igne. et spica exoluit. et oleu effluit inde p chalamu i inferiore olla. et ex. l. lib effluit. n. v. ul. vi. oli.

Strignu. Morella. Solatrum. id e. fri et sic. e i so. g. e aut aliqntulu diur uirdis 7 s folia. et s. fructus mlte e efficacie. exsiccate modice virtute ht.

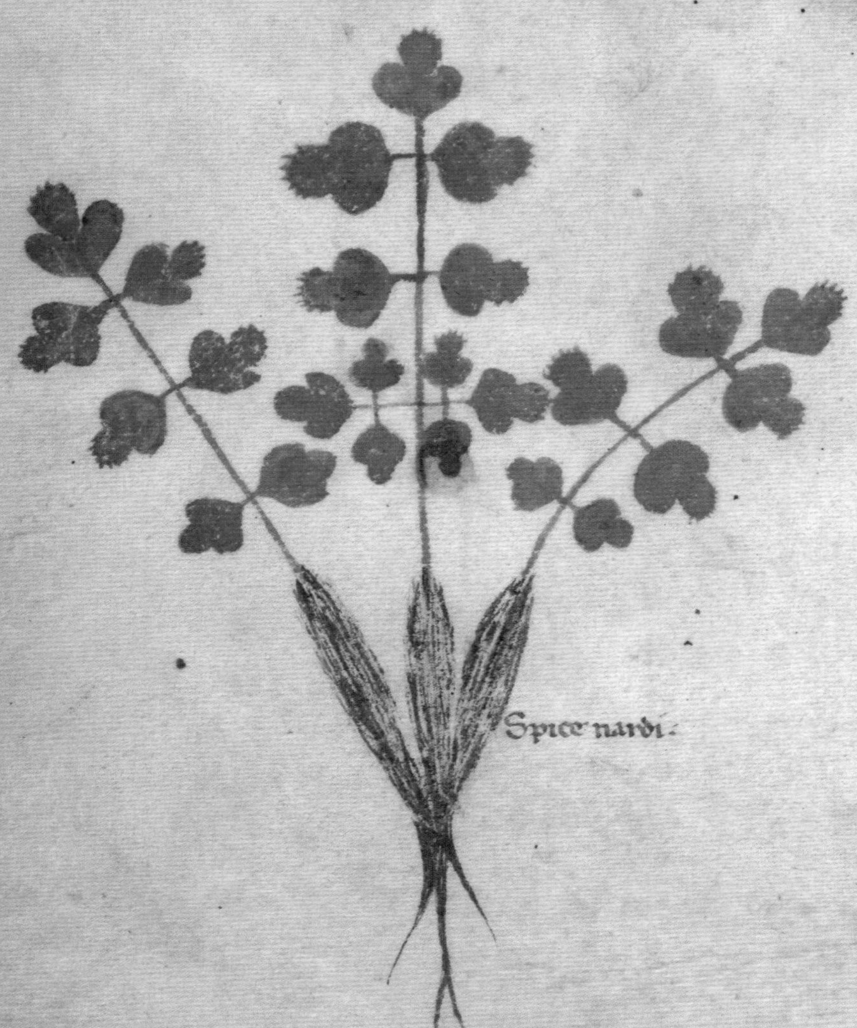
Spice nardi.

fisucco ei addatū acetū · ul' agresta ul' olīū · ro · ¶ ꝯ calida apꝰata ī pricipio ad repcussionē · mī · h'ba ipā trita sppoat'.

Solatrū rusticū q̄ alii uocāt solatrū mortale · q̄dā solatrū mai' alio noīe dicitū alchechengi · fructus ul' semen ei' similatur cerasie q̄ fit ī q̄dā uexica ⁊ ualet precipue calculosis · strāguriosis ⁊ dissur' · uinū decoctiōis fciē cū ieiuno potui dato mire ē · Valet etiā ad pruriōs q̄ patiūt' sciacos ī toto corpore · balneū aq̄ decoctiōis tote h'be ei' · p · viiij · uicib; balneatb' ꝉibrat' oēs · aliī alii uocāt h' h'ba Sciaco

Nomē h'be alchechengi · alii uocāt Sciaco.

Solatrū

ī frigidandi · ¶ ꝯ oppilationē spleis et epatis · et maxīē ꝯ yctericiā · q̄n opilatus ē supior poru' · cistis felis dtur succus ei' ī potu · ul' ex succo ei' fiat sir' · ꝯ addito zuccō · ul' q̄ meliu' ē · dēt' · ʒ · ii · succi ei' · ꝯ ʒ · i · reubr' · ¶ ꝯ apꝰata isto · ie p'e ī testis · ꝯ aq̄ ordei succus ei' det' · diascorides mlt' laudat · ¶ ꝯ calfactionē · epis petia ītīcta ī succo ei' suppoātur · Idē fiat ꝯ podagrā · calida ul' ipā h'ba trita sepius suppoātur ul' melius ē

Serapinū · ca · ē ⁊ sic · ī tio · g̃ · gūi est cuiꝰdā arboris ī ultramaīs ptib; nascentis et ī grecia · ō q̄ huītas q̄dā fluēs circa arborē īdurat' ita q̄d q̄n̄ sīn̄ aliqua pte cortice euelli n̄ p'sit · diu suat' ī loco sicco · Virtutē · hēt · dis · actra · ꝯsu · et relaxādi · ¶ Fumigiū ei' ualet litargie · sternutatiōē ei' ꝓuocat · ⁊ cerebrū · a sup fluitate mūdificat · Etiā · iii · ʒ · mūdificati

ut ōlent . et dati asmaticē laborātib; ex hūita
te . ualet precedētib; cū mollificatis et dig̃e
rentib; m̃ . C ualit gentiana i aq̃ ordi coq̃ta
iqua colatura resoluat . et d̄t patiēti . C Suf
fumigiū ul' suppositoriū ex eo fēm ualet ꝯ̃ ꝑpi
tatione; matricis supposit ex eo fēm . Mēstr
puocat . et fetū mortuū ⁊ s'ina educit . ut di
cit diascor' fum̃ ei ꝑ hos et nares susceptū .
ualet ꝯ̃ suffocatione; matricē . C ꝯ̃ duricie;
spleis fiat ungt̃ . ul' ceroctū optim̃ ex eo po
sito i aceto . ⁊ mane decocto ⁊ colato ⁊ addita
cera ⁊ olō fiat ungt̃ ul' ceroctū .

Sempiuiua h'rba ē q' sic d̄r q' sēp uiridis
repit' . alio noīe d̄r . Abzo . greci . Sentios .
Alii . Aiçon . alii . Angrii . nascit' sup tom̃ . Virtu
tem . h't . fiā . i . iii . g̃ . sic . i . i . Viridis mlte ē efficacie
et imedicīs poī d̄r . exsiccata nō . virtute; h't isri
gidādi . ⁊ alterādi . C plagelle itīcte isucco eius
et aceto ul' agresta . ep̃i catapla . ualet mltū ꝯ̃
causōn; calefactiōe; ⁊ dol' ex calā . cū . h'rba ipā trita
et supposita . ual; ꝯ̃ calida apcata ip̃ncipio adrep
cussione; matrīci . hec ꝑmod obtulit ꝯspissādo m̃ .
C ꝯ̃ usturas exigne ul' aq̃ fiat ungt̃ ex succo ei
et olō . ro . et cera . S; ñ ōbēt poī ip̃rimis trib; dieb; .
S; calida poātur . ut fuōsitatū fiat euaporato . uñ
p'riū iungim̃ tali unguētū adleniendū . C ꝯ̃
fluxū sanguīs enarib; q' exebulitiōe sanguinis
et ep̃e iuuenib; fit iestate plagelle itīcte i succo
ei ⁊ aq̃ . ro . frōti . tīporib; . et guttur supp̄āt . Exp
imento didici q' mltū ualet . quā i sola aq̃ frigā
catapla . ait ypo̅ . C ꝯ̃ calore; ⁊ rubore; oculor̃ et
ꝯ̃ igne; sacrū ⁊ ipeto podag̃ . h'rba ipā p̄se ul' ꝯpu
lenta fērō epl'z . mir' p̄est . C ꝯ̃ dol' capis succū ei et
olō . ro . frōte ilinias . C ꝯ̃ morsū spaligionū . succū
ꝯ uino potui da . sil' ual; ictericis . et lōbricos occidit
C ꝯ̃ fluxū sanguīs mulier̃ . succus ei' potui da .

Sulfur . ca . ē ⁊ sic . i primo . g̃ .
S terra actiōe caloris excocta ⁊ inaturam sulfu
ris ꝯmutatur . aquos' et terestib; ptib; . i igneis
trāseūtib; . ē aut' aliud uiuū q' tale ē quale ana
tura ꝑducit . C aliud ē extictū siū mortuū q' ar
tificiose p̄paratur . et icalamis eneis ul' ferreis
fūditur . Ē aut' elligendū q' ē uir̄e . s . Sbruissim
uiriditatis calore . q' ñ albū ul' nigrū ul' colo
re; h't nimis obrufū . ñ ē ponendū imedicinis .
p . tres ānos suatū p't actione; ꝓpri caloris ꝯsuit
et icinere; albū ꝯuertit' . virtutē . h't . dis . ꝯsu . et
acthendi . C ꝯ̃ asma iueteratū ex frō ⁊ glutinoso
hu . precedentib; uētositatib; circa sp̄ualia digētī
bus et aquis mollificantib; . ut m̃ . petur ad ꝯci
tum . decē . ʒ . iii . puluis eiū i ouo sorbili ul' ac
cipiat fumū ei' ꝑ enbotū . poītus sup carbones
capite iclinato ne flā dissolutū recurrēs ad
sp̄ualia suffocet . ñ etiā nimis ꝓpe ne sp̄ualia
ōsiccentur . si sit asma ex siccitate nullo modo
fiat . C ꝯ̃ palisim . pod . arth . epil' . oleū siccioñ
et cerā siml' . liq̃fiat et adiēcto puluē sulphuris
et oli . al . fiat ungtm̄ et stati ꝯp̄at . ab igne
pulueirb; ipōitis utile ē ꝯ̃ predcā . et ꝯ̃ scabiem
epil' a sursū usq; dorsū fm̄ spinā i ūgatur . Bal
neu; sulphureū oīb; p̄dcīs ꝯfert . C ꝯ̃ scabie;

litargir̄ ꝯ aceto ꝯficiatur · ⁊ addito sulphure et olo̓ nuc̄ ꝯficiatur ⁊ fiat ungt̄ꝫ ·

Siseleos · Siler mōtanū id est · ca · ē ⁊ sic · i s̄o · g · Semē collectū p̄ tres ānos pōt ꝯ̄uari · q̓ ponitur i medicīs n̄ h̓ba · Virtutē h̓t diur̄ · dis̄ · ⁊ ꝯsu · ℭ ꝯ̄ asma · ex f̄rā · cā · dt̄ uinū decoctiōis eius ⁊ ficuū siccar̄ꝫ · ul̄ dt̄ pl̓uis ei̓ cū ficubꝫ siccis ⁊ assatis · ℭ ꝯ̄ oppilatione sp̄lēis ⁊ epis · renū ⁊ uesic̄ · str̄ · ⁊ dis̄ · dt̄ uinū decoctiōis eiꝰ · ℭ Suffumigtio fc̄a ex aq̄ decoctiōis ei̓ · h̓be · educ̄ mēstr̄ · ⁊ ualet ꝯ̄ str̄ · ⁊ dis̄ · solū · ℭ puluī seīs eiꝰ p̄ se ul̄ cū uino · al · potui dato ieiuno stō siū accepto ꝯ melle ul̄ ꝯ zuccō · uisū clarificat ⁊ lumē oculoꝝ acuit ·

Saponaria

Saponaria · Burit · herba fullonum · h̓ba sc̄i philippi idē est

ℭ Arbor draconē ·
ℭ Sanguis drac̄ ·

Vn̄ ... gūma ·

ℭ Siseleos ·

Sanguis draconis · fri · ē 7 sic · i ttio · g̃ dicit̃ qdā q · ē succus h̃be q · falsuz ē · Ē aut̃ gūi arbous ipsia et iidia nascentis · Sanguis · drac̃ · dr̃ q ꝯsilis est ei · est aut̃ elligendꝰ q sbrubicundꝰ ē 7 itenclaruz sic̃ miniū · Sophisticat̃ aut̃ qūz explũere ꝯaliquo succo idurato · p · xxx · annos fuatur · Virtutez h̃t ꝯstri · C Ꝯt fluxū sanguis enanb; iponatur puluis ei 7 ꝯsticentur nares ut pl̃uis adhereat ruptuīe uenarū · fiat ī sīpasma ex eo 7 albumine oui 7 aq̃ · ro · circa frōtē 7 tīpora · C Ꝯt̃ emoptoicā · pās · uitio spūaliū teneāt pillās expuluere ei 7 gūi · ar̃ · ꝯ aq̃ ordi ifusionis draggūt · q̃s patiens pēa trāsglutiat · Siuō fiat uitio nutritiuorū ꝯturꝯ succo plātagīs ꝯfit ꝯ̃ discīteriam · si fiat uitio supiorū · Siuō fiat uitio īferiorꝫ miciat peristere · ꝯ succo plātagīs 7 aqua ordī · 7 emplr̃m fiat circa pectinez 7 renē ex eo 7 albuīē oui 7 aceto · C Suppositoriū fcm̄ ex eo 7 succo sanguinarie ualet ꝯt fluxū mēstruorū ·

Squinātū · dr̃ pallea camellorꝫ q̃ camelli ei ꝯmedut̃ · ca · ē 7 sic · ī ttio · g · ī africa 7 arabia repitur · p · decem · annos fuat̃ · Elligendūz est sb̃ albidū · Si aut̃ repiat̃ qddā durum et q̃i ligneū circa stipitez abiciatur · Virtutez h̃t purgādi flā pricipl̃r · nūq̃ p se pōitur · s; ꝯpurgātib; flā ut ꝯ polipodio · cologntida · adplus ꝯ̃let pōi ꝗntitate · ʒ · ꝟ · diascorides dic̃ · q decctū i uino · et cataplātū pudendis mēstrua educ̄ · matricem mūdificat · str̃ · 7 dis · solū ·

Sinapis. ca. e. et sic. i medio. iiii. g. n herba s[ed] sem. ponitur i medicinis q[uod] collectu[m] s[er]uat[ur] p[er] v. annos. cu[m] ei[us] receptio i[n]ueitur. s. sinapis ul. napais. ul napos sem[en] po[n]it[ur] i medicinis. Virtutem h[abe]t. dis. attrahendi. et extenuandi. et isu. Contra palisi[m] lingue seme[n] ei[us] masticatu[m]. et sub lingua receptu[m] ualet. Contra palisi[m] alioru[m] mebrorum ponatur i sacello et decoquat[ur] i uino. et s[upra] locum dolente[m] ponat[ur]. et precipue i principio egritudinis. puluis eius narib[us] i positus sternutatione[m] puccat. Cerebru[m] a superfluitate flaica mundificat. Vinu[m] decoctionis ei[us] et ficuu[m] siccaru[m] ualet [contra] antiquu[m] asma. ex frigido et glutinoso hu. Contra oppilatione[m] splenis et epatis et leucoflatia[m] decoquatur i aq[ua] cu[m] radicib[us] feni. q[ue] colata addatur mel et tal[is] confectio d[e]tur. Contra splenis duricie[m] herba ipa cu[m] axungia porcina bn trita supponat[ur]. Fom[en]to f[ac]ta ex aqua decoctionis eius mi[n]stru[m] educe[re]. et ualet [contra] str. et dis. ipa herba decocta i uino et olo et cataplata solu[m]. pali. str. et dis. Vinu[m] decoctionis ei[us] et dragagati. humiditate[m] uue. faucium et cerebri exsiccat. dragag[an]t[um] ponitur et uehementer excuriat et excorietur.

Sarcocolla. ca. e. et sic. i. iiii. g. gu[m]i arboris e. i ultramaris p[ar]tib[us] repitur. elligenda est q[uod] alba e. ul subalbida e. et gu[m]osa i maiori q[ua]ntitate i[n]ueitur redacta i puluere n[on] ualet. Sepe eni[m] ex alio pluere solet sophiticari. Emplin dea et albumine oui. fcm s[upra] tinpora. Val[et] [contra] fluxu[m] e narib[us]. puluis eius cu[m] aq[ua] ro. confiatur. et soli exsiccet. et itera[tum] cu[m] aq[ua] ro. ponatur i oculo macula[m] consu[m]it et oculu[m] claru[m] facit. Puluis ei[us] uulneri i posit[us] ip[su]m consolidat. Fumu[s] ei[us] p[er] i[n]feriora receptus e[st] loco i posito ual[et] [contra] tenasmo.

Sticados citrinū q barba iouis d͡r. alio
noīe d͡r. abdios ul' argus. aliī asplēg
nū. aliī herba herculis. ca. ē ⁊ sic. i. s͡co. g.
ī tp̄e ueris ꝓ̄ uic̄ flor colligit' suspēdit̄. p an
nū ꝯ̄suatur. dissolū ꝯ̄su. Virtute h̄t diuretic̄.
Vinū decoctiōis eī ⁊ dragagāti. sp̄ualia calfac̄
et mūdificat. Et uinū decoctiōis eī stomac̄
et ītestina calfacit ⁊ ad yliacā pas̄ ualet. ⁊ ad
opilatiōēz splēis ⁊ ep̄is. ⁊ ꝯ̄ strāguriā. ⁊ dissur.

Sticados arabica. herba ē
nascit' locis asp̄is ⁊ ī mōtib3. hūs folia ut rore
marino s3 sūt albidiora ⁊ p̄ua ⁊ ī sūite ꝓducit
florez q̄ ī pomiculū ⁊ h̄t colorez purpureū cū o
dore aroātico. folia eī h̄t saporez s3 amarū cum
aroāticitate m̄lta. flo' eī magis quā folia ī recep
tiōib3 d3 ponī. exsicata p̄ ānū pot' ꝯ̄suarī ī m̄lta
efficacia d3 eā legi tp̄e ueris. calā ē ī. i. g. sicca
ī. ij. ex amaritudine ⁊ ꝓ̄pietate sua resolutiuū
ē ⁊ diureticū. oppilationez abstergit ꝯ̄suat q
discutit oēz putredinez. stipticū ē modicū uī
ꝯfortat cor ⁊ sp̄ualia ⁊ ualde reptificatiuū ē no
cet collericis ex colli'a adusta ī s͡to ⁊ ꝯturbat uo
mitū ꝓuocat. sitī ⁊ siccitatez educit q̄a nocet
collericis ⁊ debilitate dissoluit. uī ꝑus purgatiū
ē cū mirob nigri ⁊ sal' gēma. ꝑ͡ea mag opat' eī ef
ficaciā. Oliū ex florib3 eī ut oliū camomille ualet
ī iuctus dolorib3 neruoz lacertoz ⁊ iūturaz ex
frigiditate ⁊ hu. Valet ꝯ̄ā epilēticos uertiginosos ⁊ oī
oppilatiōi capitis remouet. Valz ꝯ̄ā oppilatiōi ep̄is
⁊ splenis q̄ fit ex frigiditate ⁊ quartanarijs ⁊ oēs longas
egritudines.

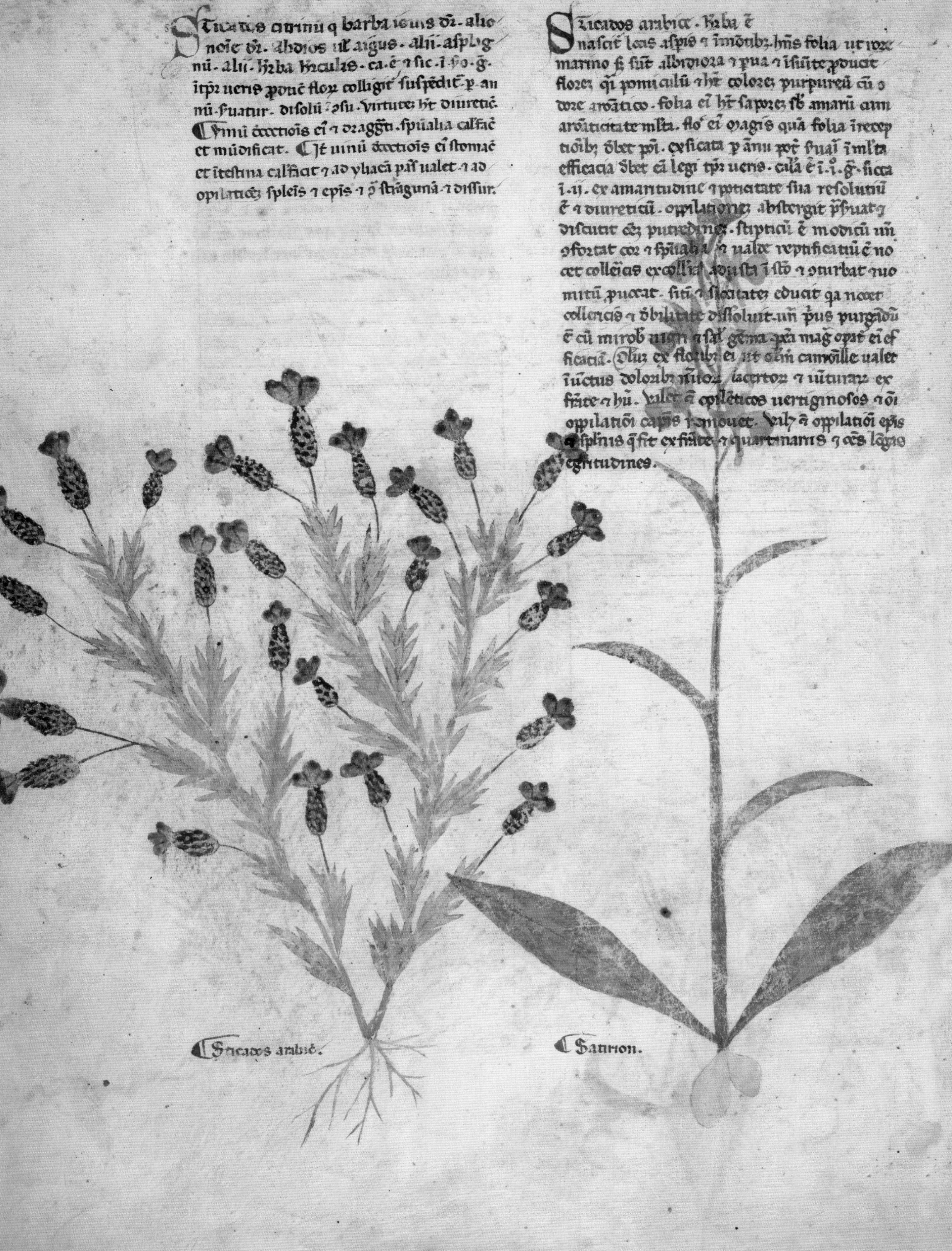

Satirion. hba ē q alio noīe . dr . Priapiscus . alii . Sucaāt . ginos . alii . Satirion . alii . Sincozō . alii . Sarapias . alii . Orcis . alii . testicli leporis . alii . Reme . alii . Virī . Nascit ĩ mōtib; ⁊ ĩ planis . ca . ē ⁊ sic . i . iii . g . Virtutes ħt acthendi ad venotis ptib; . vn̄ coitu; adiuuat ⁊ ualet ī arthītē . Radix tamen uiridis ĩ medicīs pōitur . exsiccata nullius est efficatie . testiculi uides ɔ melle ɔfecti . coitū ɔfortāt . Melius tn̄ ē si fiat ɔfectio ex illis ⁊ dactil' pastinace ⁊ melle . ¶ Succus ei' cū oximelle bibit' pdest arthītē . ¶ Et ad cispā ocul' hba satirion sucus ɔ melle fcō colliriū . oculis ut' . mir' cisposos sanat ⁊ dolorē expellit . ¶ Ad cicatrices ⁊ oēs fetidas radix pse bn̄ tere ⁊ suppōi . ⁊ cito sanabit.

Sponsa solis . frā . ē ⁊ hu . i . ii . g . hrba ē q alio noīe dr . Cicorea . alii . uoc . Intiba . et Solsequm . alii . Eliotropio . greci . Elioron . alii . Dialithon . alii . Scorpion . alii . Eraclea . alii . Ciroscro . alii . Smatithes . alii . Virascorpiu . alii . Nisene . alii . Vertinū . alii . Dulcetā . nascit locis cultis ⁊ mūdis ⁊ ĩ pratis . h hrba . ¶ diuina ē ad cursū sol' . ħt stipites retrosi ⁊ flos celesti coloris . ⁊ qn̄ sol orit' ⁊ flos apit' . cū sol cecidit ⁊ flos claudit' . hrba ipi' ɔmesta ul' succus ei' bibitū ualet ɔ uenenū . sisit ex morsu nanti suppūatur . succus ei' ualet ad oppilationē splēis et epis ex cal' . ca . ⁊ ad cal'factionē eix;.

¶ Scrofularia.

Scrofularia hrba ē nascit' locis solidis et maric ĩ scopolis inuēit' tp̄e estiuo ⁊ uerē cui folia expādit sup terrā . radix ei' desiccata ⁊ ĩ puluē redacta ⁊ cū suficienti melle ɔ̄ficte ⁊ dat ɔt scrofulas ⁊ g̃gulas ad ɔmedēdū ĩ mane ieiuno scō ⁊ ieiunet usq̃ ad ora nona . ul' fiat emplastrū explūē ei' ⁊ farina ⁊ ɔmedat postea bibat uinū albū uetus ⁊ optimū calidū in sero.

¶ Sponsa solis.

¶ Sponsa . . . ɔfit dossib;

Elephantis.

Spodiũ fri. ē. i tıō g. sic. i. iii. Os est elephantis ɔbustū. elephās ossa hʒ sol lida. ut sūt dentes ⁊ illa nō ɔburūt. ſʒ adi uersa officia opantur. ſʒ illa q̄ medullā hn̄t ɔburūtur ⁊ illa dr̄ spodiū. Sophisti catur q̄nq̄ ex ossibꝫ canis ɔbustis. qñq̄ ex marmore ɔbusto. ſʒ id ponderosiꝫ ē. minus. vn̄ illd̄ est eligend̄ q̄ ualde ē leue. et ɔtinuū. Sicut sit ualdē leue. h̄ns tñ q̄ſ ɔ̄ ptes sbnigras bonū ē. carū ē nō tñ mlte ē efficacie i sirupis ad istinon̄ ɔ̄pōatur. pl' uis ɔ succo plātagīs dat' ualet ɔ̄ dissinteriā. et emoptoicā pās. ⁊ ɔ̄ ɔfluxum pl'uis ei naribꝫ ipositus. sanguinem sistit.

Strucium .i. Caul' agrestis. qdā dicunt. Braxi ca nō plātata. ca. ē. ⁊ sic. i s°. g. semen. succus ⁊ foliis. usui medicine ɔpetit. ubi nō inuenitur receptio. R caulicūi. semen ... poi. ū nō R. ɔabathmatico. succus pōa tur q̄ sic appellatur. folia ipius i unguentis et i ēplastris ōbet poi. ɔ̄ paralis sit lingue. se men masticatū i ore sb lingua diu teneatur. Si i alia pte corporis sit folia i uino decocta cataplē'. ɔ̄ litargiā pl'uis seīs ei. naribꝫ isuffletur et hec mō fiat decōtio seīs eī. ⁊ succi rute agrestis. i aceto fortissimo. ⁊ īn fricetur pēnor ps capitis. ipa tam prius rasa. fomētatio ex foliis ei i uino coctis. ſt. et dis. solū. ⁊ mīstrua educit. Emplm̄ ī ex foliis i uino et olō dcctis pectini ⁊ uirge sī pōitū. urinā puot. Virga i eodē olō pōatur folia ei terat'. suc exprimatur. ⁊ soli expōat' ut articlm̄ i ouret. sic suari pōt. p. ii. annos

Stinci

Stinci. ca. sūt. ⁊ sic. i. iii. g. pisces sūt. q i fontibꝫ ⁊ maxīe i aqs dulcibꝫ iueīt'. ⁊ lacer tis asimilantur. Saliti p. duos ānos suātur. Virtutē h̄nt ɔ̄for. coitū. puluis dat' i qntitat'. iii. ul' iiii. ʒ. ɔ̄ calido ellio ⁊ maxīe ɔ̄ria fetten on. Cū melle ī bibitus ad idē facit. Et nota q̄ i multa qntitate datus nocet corpori.

Scordon .i. alliū agreste. ca. ē ⁊ sic. i. iii. gradu. Solus flos ul' sem ei medicine ɔpet aqua ul' uinū decoctiōis ei spualia mūdificat aflate. ɔ̄ dolorē stōi et intestinoꝝ exuētositate ⁊ ɔ̄ oppilatiōē splēis ⁊ epis ex frā. causa. ⁊ ɔ̄ strāguriā ⁊ dis. ualet.

Sapo. ca. ē ⁊ sic. alius ē saracenic'. ul' spati
rentus siū iudaic'. quo iudei seric' lauant.
alius gallicus. Saracenic' ualet ꝯt' ustionem
exigne ul' aqua ⁊ mox d'bet poni. et moretu ibi
ptres ul' quatuor oras dimictat' ut calid' fumosi
tates ⁊ ardores euaporetur. nā prius apponenda
sut actualiter calida. qa sit frā stati aponeretur
fumositates ⁊ ptes ille magis excuretur p oīē oblu
antur cū calā ⁊ adhibeātur mitigatiua ⁊ sanatiā.
sapo gallicus ualet aditē ⁊ etiā ꝯ scabiē. si gallic'
mini' tñ. magis aut' d'albat. Gallic'. carnē in lotā
Spatarētus ualet. ꝯ inpetigine ⁊ s'pig. pte ind
lota. solus aut' suppoatur. l' ꝯ puluē auripigmē
ti. precedente lotura d' aqua calā. Sapo saracēic'
sic fit. fiat lexiua ex aqua ⁊ cinēi pēa mixta cū
calcē uiua ponitur i uase sbtil' isuito ⁊ i' p ter diū
dimictatur. pēa apiat' foram ⁊ q' p'mit' exit capi
tellū d'r. illō sic colatū sup ignē ponatū ⁊ apposito
olō bulliāt ad spissitudinē ⁊ fit nigrū p̄ decoctiō.
Gallicus fit ex sepo arietino ⁊ capitello ⁊ ē alb'.
Spatarētus fit ex saracenico ⁊ aliis mixtis calis.

Sparagus. ca. ē ⁊ sic. i. iii. g'. alio noīe d'r
anasparagos. alii uocāt Spagos agrios.
alii. Anafriacos. alii. Arcatellas. alii. Alio.
alii. Sparagos nostros. ¶ Fructus ei' ul' se
me usui medicine ꝯpetut'. fructus eiu' qī
fusces sut ⁊ tenerimi. q' coqnati cū carnib;
ul' cū sola aqua. Valēt ꝯ opp'ilatiōē splēis
et epis. ⁊ ꝯt str'. ⁊ dis. ⁊ ꝯ dol' stōi ⁊ itestiou
et yliacā pāss. ¶ Jt uinū ul' aq̄ decoctiois ei'
sem̄ ualet ꝯt preccā. sem̄ eiu' pannū s'uat.
i medicis ponitur cū receptio sparagi iuēitū.
Dicit ypocras. radix spgi decoctiōis ei' p. vii
dieb; potui dato. tertianarios librat. pēa
uadat ad balneū pluib; dieb; ⁊ caueat se ad
potu frīo ⁊ oīre frā. ¶ ꝯ dolorē dētiū. succū
radic'. spgi. i ore recēpto. mir' liberat.
¶ Ad helefantiosis. pl'uis radic' spgi. cū uino
utere ⁊ sanū efficiet. ¶ ꝯ dolorē renū silit'
ualet. ¶ ꝯ malefactos. collige h'bā spagi.
⁊ uad' ad fontē aq̄. ⁊ cū ipa h'ba asp'ge d'e
aq̄. s' malefactos ⁊ stati librabit'.

Savina. calida. ē 7 sic. i. iii. g. arbor parv͛ ē q. alio noīe dr̄. Bracthos. alii. uoc̄. Bilopalion. alii. papiticon. alii. amptisió. alii. Bractum. alii. formū. alii. Mepteon. alii. Satarchieró. alii. antirinā. alii. Aintpron. alii. Apagnus. alii. Asthnō. alii. hba Sabina. Sola folia. ꝯpetut̄ usui medicine. p. ii. ānos ſuatur. Vinū decoctioīs ei᷒ ualet ꝯ dol̄ stōi 7 ītestinoꝝ. decocta ī uino ualet ꝯ str̄. 7 dis. s; catapl̄a. Valz ī ꝯ yl̄. dol̄. ē ei; diaforetica. et diuretic̄. Fomentatio ī eraqua decoctis ei᷒ ualet ꝯ predc̄ā. ꝓuoc̄ ī mēstrua et fetū mortuū. decocta ī uino ol̄ō ꝯducit idez 7 meliu᷒ opat̄ si sit sr̄posita. Cō tenasinon ex frā. cā. fiat decoctio ei᷒ ī aceto et uino 7 paciens fumū recipiat. hba ipā ī nāibz cataplasmata ualet.

Saxifraga. ca. ē 7 sic. ītio. g. sic dr̄ qz saxū frāgit. alio noīe dr̄. Amantus. alii uocāt. Apogro. alii. aspos. Vinū decoctioīs ei᷒ radic̄ ualet ꝯ strāgur̄. 7 dis. 7 uitiū lapidis 7 etiā ꝯ yliacā pās. Puluis. ī ei᷒ ī ouo sorbili. ul̄ ī uino exibitus. adidez ualet. No. q. cū īuēitur receptio saxifrage. radix dz pōi cū aut̄ īuēitur. litisspmatis. sem̄ ei᷒ ītelligitur. q. post ſuāi p. iii. annos.

Sal. ca. ē 7 s. ex ipo 7 ol̄ō 7 aceto. pot̄ noīe ꝓuocari. digitis ī ore missis ul̄ pēnā ad dolorez ex uitto sit te saccellatio fiat. ex sale h mō. sal pl̄ uēigetur 7 ī uas torreseat. 7 sic calius ī saccello pōatur 7 loco dolenti sr̄ pōatur. Ex sale 7 melle fiat ꝯpetēs suppositoriu. Cō uentris ꝯstipatiōez. fiat ꝯfectio sal̄ puri 7 sulphuris ꝯ aq̄ 7 bulliat ī testa oui abiecta pellic̄a. ipius teste. ne testa uratur. in hac ꝯfectione sic calā ītingatur. aurū albū frequēter colorabit. Plurimū yeralogodiō. pot̄ acui ꝯ sale sic ꝯ scam. ī q̄ntitate. iii. ul̄. iiii. ʒ. ꝯ mox dz dari. et sine doloris uehemētis piculo.

Sal armoniacū. ca. ē 7 sic. ī q̄rto. g.

Sal armoniacū. dr̄. qz ī armēia repitur. q. dicit ex hrba fi. et bn̄ pot̄ ēē sic ex hirba uitrū. Interius n̄ dz sūmi nisi ī ꝯpōitis. medicīs. Valet ad remouēdū pānū ī mulierib; hoc mō. due ptes ex eo et una ꝯ camphā ꝯficiātur. cū aq̄. ro. 7 sic soli expoūtur. ut illa aqua ꝯsumātur. sic fiat. p. tres. ul̄ quatuor dies. pt̄ iū facies iungatur. ul̄ predc̄ā plures ꝯficiant. ꝯ ol̄ō sanbucino 7 facies iūgatur. Puluis ei᷒ ꝯficiatur ꝯ sapōe et iū fricetur. ꝯ pigo et ipetigo. Cō morpheā. loc̄ prius scarificetur. ꝯ iū ex eo mīta fiat fricatio.

Sal gēma. ca. ē 7 sic.

Sal uena terre ē. dr̄ sal gēma qz adeo clara est. ut gēma. ꝯ ario ht̄ effectus salis armoīaci. de ea sola fit bonū suppositoriū febrib; ī acutis.

Saxifraga.

Sisimb…

Sisinbriū. ca. ē ⁊ sic. ī t'tio. g. aliud ē dōmesticē.
aliud siluestre ꝯ īuenitur receptio. Re sisinbrii
pse. domestice. dz poni. ꝯ īuenit' Re sisinbri siluestris.
calamentū. dz poni. teste ꝯst'. virtutē h't diuretī-
cā. ⁊ ꝯsu. ℭ Ꝯ uiciū pectoris fiat pl'res exfarinā
ordei. ⁊ aqua apposito pluere ei' detur patienti. Ꝯ
reumā frīn. folia eius cal'ficā ī uase sīn liquore.
et ī sacello pōita capiti suppoāt. ℭ vinū decoctiōis ei' ualet ꝯ dol' stoī et ītestinoꝝ exfriā. ca. ⁊
ꝯ opilatiōē splēis ⁊ epis. et urinaliū uiarū aperit.
herba ipsa decocta ī uino et catiplāta. solū. str'. ⁊ dis.
ℭ valet ꝗ ꝯ dol'. yl'. ⁊ ꝯt' dol' īfantiū exuētositate.
mēstrua educē sceptū adiuuat. matricē mūdificē.
fomentū ex eo sic fit. teneritates ei' ī olo. ro. ul'
psaltē cōi decocte ⁊ sr'pōite id opatur.

Saluia. ca. ē ī. i. g. sic. ī sō. solū folia eius
⁊ flos ꝯpet' usui medicīs. saluia dn̄t greci elilis fagos. alii. Cission. alii. Becion. alii
elespacula. alii. pacos. alii. apagnos. alii.
Anuri. alii. tursella. flos ei' dr̄. Esbriu. viridis ⁊ sicca ꝯpet' usui m̄. s' uiridia mag' pānū
pot' suaī. aliud ē domestica. al' siluestris cuī ī
uenitur receptio saluia ipoāt' folia domestic. s' ꝯ
īuenitur receptio eupatorii siluestris. domestica mag' ꝯsumi ⁊ ꝯfortat. Siluestris. magis
ē diur'. ℭ vinū decoctiōis saluie. ualet palitic'
et epil'etic'. ī uino decocta ⁊ catiplāta suppartē
paliticā. ml'tū ualet. fomēto ex aqua decoctionis ei'. ualet ꝯ str'. et. dis. matricē mūdific.
mēstrua puocat. Insalsamentis ꝯpetēt' pōic.

Scabiosa. ca. e. et sic. i. fo. g. quam uocant ei Gallinaciam. sunt eius due species. illa que magis est pilosa et inuenitur locis asperis et montuosis illa habet maior effectus. Contra scabies. succus eius cum oleo bulliat in aceto usque ad spissitudinem et unguat scab. Balneum ex aqua decoctionis eius et tapsi barbasi. ualet contra alopitiam. Succus eius bibitus adeadem ualet et lumbricos necat. Cum ambus cum oleo iectus eas mundificat. Fumi uini decoctionis eius. ualet contra emoroidas. Contra apostemata. quam actrici dicitur. fiat emplastrum desuper ex ipsa herba fuso tamen prius recepto ad patientem. Contra apostemata in stomacho siue in pectore. succus eius bibitus. statim expellit foras per superius et inferius de qua multi librantur. Aqua distillationis eius ualet contra maculas oculorum.

Senationes. ca. sunt et sic. i. fo. g. idem est quod nasturcium aquaticum. alii uocant. cressionum. alii. acamatis. alii. aliofon. Senationes in aqua solum uel cum carnibus coquantur spiritualia mundificat. Fomentum factum ex aqua salsa et oleo decoctionis eius ualet ad yliacam passionem. Valet in contra sciaticam et dissinteriam in uino in decocte et cataplate ad idem ualet.

Sanationum est herba que quidam uocant. Sellictione. alii Cardus binedictus. et nascitur super muros et tectibus domi. in uino calefactum et cataplatum. per cusiones et dolores et inflactiones solum. Vnguentum ex eo factum ulcera consolidat.

Serpentaria. Colubraria. et Dracuncea. idem est.
alii uocant. Asclepias. alii. pictonion. alii.
Athomanis. alii. pancromaton. alii. Afrissa.
alii. Therion. alii. Augion. alii. Licion. alii.
Licorcon. alii. Licopsolon. alii. Dorcadion. alii.
Srecotas. alii. Tiphonos. alii. Ipnoticon. alii.
Tensonon. alii. Eminion. alii. Ducla asinina.
alii. Aotiraforh. alii. adilla. ca. est et sic. radix per
minuta frustra incidatur. et siccetur frustra. et sic
cata pulverizetur. pulvis per pannum cribetur. tunc confici
atur cum aqua ro. et soli exponatur. biduo vel triduo.
deinde apponatur. tertia pars ceruse. et iterum apponatur
aqua ro. et iterum soli exponatur ut desiccetur. hic tali
cum aqua ro. et sic ea facies inungatur. ipsam nitentem
et claram reddit. pannum et deponit. Pulvis eius
conficiatur cum sapone gallico. et fistule impleatur. fora
men eius dilatat ita. quod hos firm fom sium putrefactam
extrahi possit. vel cum asungia supposita idem facit. Pul
vis eius confectus cum calce viva et aceto fortissimo
optimum est ad cancrum. sit autem tertia pars calcis.

Succus eius cum oleo mi. auribus iniectus auditum ex
hu. impeditum reddit. Pulvis seis eius simpliciter oculo
impositus. ad visum clarificandum valet et pannum re
movet. Item Succus seis eius potatus vel fomentum
decoctionis herbe ipsius. menstrua educit. Herba decocta in
ano cataplasmata emorroidas desiccat. et consu. Nota
quod succum iterum recepit abortum facit. Corpus ex eo
iunctum serpentibus tuetur propter eius odorem. Asma ex
habundantia viscosi humoris quod propter digerit et subtili
at ipsum et propter educit per se cessum. Pulvis
serpentarie confectum cum melle admodum electuarii et dato pati
enti multum prodest

Salix. f. est in primo gradu. sic. in tertio. Cortex
folia et flores. competunt usui medicine. habet
autem virtutem diureticam. constipandi et consolidandi.

Succus ex floribus expressus potui dato
discrasia frebilem tollit. Item contra ulcerationem
intestinorum et contra dis. de. cortex eius combusti in
potu. Idem pulvis ulcera excoriata consolidat.
Idem pulvis teste dyascorides cum aceto potui da
tus et cum aceto cataplasmatus. curat ver
rucas et poros. Folia et flores aqua aspersa
circa febricitantem. aerem infrigidat.

Salix.

Sanbucus. actis .i. est c. e. i .ii. g. sic .i. p[ri]o. fa[cit] cortice[m] p[ri]ncipal[ite]r ap[ti]t medicine. s[ecund]o. folia et flores. Virtutem h[abe]t attractiv[am] diureticam et purgativam fl[egmat]is. Contra cotidianam precedente[m] purgatione ante accessione d[atur] vinu[m] decoctionis mediani cortex eius vel aliter Scia radix in aqua tepida diu ducatur et teratur et addita .3.i. pulvis eius d[atur] an accessione[m]. Succ[us] vel p[er] se vel cum melle datus lumbricos necat. Cappnu cum decoctione sanbuci oppilatione[m] splenis et epatis solvit. Idem faciunt folia decocta in oleo sicata plasmet. Contra lenco flantia terantur cortices sanbuci. folia. flores et fructus. et extrahatur succus. et conficiantur cum pulvere esule .3. iii. mastice .3.i. vel fiat decoctio eorum in aqua et addito zuccaro fiat sirupus. Succus in auribus instillentur. illas a sanie mundificat. Contra tumorem pedum. fomentum ex aqua decoctionis cortic[is] eius tumorem pedum solvit et dol[orem] partium interior[um]. Contra Balneum ex vino fortissimo decoctionis flor[um] et folior[um] et fructuum eius lepram p[er]fecte extrahit si fiat frequenter multum valet. Contra vomitum sinus ducat. radice[m] cortice[m] superius si inferius per contrarium mistura p[ro]vocat.

Squilla.

Squilla. ca. e. et sic. in .ii. g. grece vocat[ur] ei Bulb[us] sollectidi. alii voc[ant]. Scilla albizon. alii pancraton. alii. Tifonos. egipti. Subtio. p[ro]feti. Obtalno. Itali. Scilla alba. alii. Bulbus aliter. alii asteros. alii. Asamon. p[otest] ea legi o[mn]i t[em]p[o]re. Radix magis competit usui m[edicine] q[uam] folia. Sola recepta mortiferas e. Virtutem h[abe]t diur[eticam]. valet ad digestione[m] mat[eri]e ta[m] in cotid[ianis] q[uam] in q[ua]rtanariis. Contra oppilatione[m] splenis et epatis et dol[orem] ylii. et arthetice. ut testat[ur] ysaak in dietis contra istas pas[siones]. idem fit usus. Squilla per mediu[m] dividat[ur]. tot ab interiori p[ar]te abiciatur. quot ab exteriori. media resultet. et exteriores p[ro] nimia caliditate s[unt] mortifere. interiores p[ro] nimia fri[gidit]ate. medie temperate s[unt]. istarum fiat decoctio in pasta in furno p[ost]ea in aceto et colate addito melle fiat oximelle. Sinus ut fortiu[s] operetur. non fiat decoctio in pasta. s[ed] tu[m] in aceto. Contra dur[itiem] epatis. obvurat in cineribus calidis et pluie cimini addito. fiat catapla[sma]. Contra dolore[m] exterior[um] partium ex fri[gida] ca[usa]. et contra arthetic[am] et palisi. squilla in aceto dimictat[ur] quousq[ue] putrefieri videat[ur] et collate et addito succo eidem et cera fiat cathapla[sma].
Ad ydropisi[m] ... bibat oximel squill[iticum] ... purgat. Ad impetiginosos. squilla[m] de medio extrahe et calido pinge impetigines. Ad paniculam sive panariciu[m] squilla[m] et mica panis addito modico aceto simul bis ... et suppone ... Ad siti ydropic[i] auferend[am]. folia squill[e] sub lingua diu teneat.

Storax. ca. e. i. .ii. g. sic. in .ii. g. gu[mm]i arboris est et similiter h[abe]t gu[mm]osita[tem] et virtutem attractivi. cuius triplex e[st] maneries. s[cilicet] storax calamita. q[ui] bona gutta. prima et pura q[ue] p[ri]mu[m] cadunt ab arbore. alii dicunt calamita a calamo. Secunda feculentior et impurior et Rubra d[icitur]. Tertia liquida q[ue] et Sicia d[icitur]. bona in colore e[st] et rufa. in odore suavis. in sapore pontica cum amaritudine. et manibus potest malaxari. q[ui] dulce[m] h[abe]t sapore[m]. sophisticata e[st]. Sophisticat[ur] ex pulvere ... illinice n[on] multu[m] sicca n[on] multu[m] hu[mida]. et q[ue] tactu non plurificat[ur] conficiunt cum melle. et addunt stor[acis] cal[amite]. s[ed] discernitur sic quia tal[is] h[abe]t d[e]clinatione[m] nimia[m]. liquida non sophisticat[ur]. Rubra et calamita eide[m] effect[us] s[unt]. s[ed] cala[mita] maioris valet.
Contra catarru[m] et fluxu[m] a cerebro magdaleo in naribus inponat[ur]. Contra fluxu[m] a divina. d[atur] vinu[m] decoctionis eius si de cal[ida]. Contra fluxu[m] ad spiritualia pille in fo[r]te diu teneat in ore. Contra fiat[u]s stor[acis] et scirosi. stor[ax] cal[amita] in pano resoluta cum cera et mastice et oleo fiat catapla[sma]. Ad menstrua p[ro]vocanda. mulier recipiat fumu[m] ... ex eo et oleo m[ixtum] in ictu[m] supponatur. Idem ad precipitatione[m] matris. mulier

recipiat fumũ p nares. Storax liqda. mẽstrua
educ̃. Cõt tenasmo. fungũ fcm̃. 7 ꝯ tineaz 7 scabi
em. ualet.

Sumac. f. e. i. 11. g. sic i. 111. semẽ ẽ fructi
ce ul' arboris. q̃ greci. anagodã. uocãt
virtutez. hĩt ꝯstrigendi. Cõ fluxũ p nares
medulla sãbuci itingat̃ i succo sanguinaĩe
7 pluĩ sumac sr̃ asp̃so naĩbȝ ip̃õatur. Cõt
emoptoicã pãs. uicio sp̃ũaliũ. dẽt pille expl'
uere ei 7 gũi. ar. cũ aq̃. ro. ꝯfc̃. Cõ dissint
uicio s̃rior ĩtestiõr. dẽt aq̃. plu. decoctiõis ei. si
uicio iferior. pluis ei. cũ faĩna ordi. 7 p cli
stere iiciatur. Cõ ꝑfluuiũ fiat suppositoriũ
ex pluĩe. boli. mastic. 7 sumac ꝯ succo platag.
Cõ extẽiõibȝ. pluis ei abustus i olla rudi. sr̃
p̃õatur. Cõ ꝯrusiones gĩgiuaȝ ex aceto ď
decoctiõis ei. 7 ros. fiat lotura. p̃t ea puluis sr̃
p̃õatur.

Sumac.

Staphisagria.

Staphisagria. ca. ē 7 sic. ī iii°. g. h̄ba ē
q̄ alio noīe dr̄. h̄ba pedicularis. cuius
sem̄ u sui ꝯpetit medicis. cū receptio inueītur
stafisagria. sem̄ dz poni 7 n̄ h̄ba. dr̄ ī caput
purgiū. qa flā purgat. purgat caput uuā
ꝯsiccat. reumatismū stoī ꝓhibet. vinū uł
ce decoctiōis ei. 7 ros. gargariget ꝯ p̄dc̄a
C pl'uis uł sem ei cū melle lūbricos necat.
C ꝯ scabiez 7 pediculos. fiat ungt̄ ex eo 7 ac
eto. fiat ī iūctio ꝯ palisi.

Sandali. fri. sunt. 7 sicci. ī. iii°. g. alii albi.
alii. cit. alii. rubei. Ē aut̄ lignū q̄ sanda
lus dr̄. nō faciłe sophicat̄. Rubus sophicat̄.
ex brasilio. dignoscit̄ q̄z n̄ ē aroātic̄ ꝑ h̄ oēs
dignosciūr. p̄cipue ḡ citini. mag̃ st̄ aroāt.
Rubi officatōes valēt ꝯ calfactiōes epis h̄ mō.
expuluē cor 7 olo. ro. addito aceto. fiat epic
thīa uł expluē 7 succo solatri. Idē ad dol' fro
tis. ad sopnū iducend' expluē rubi. 7 olo mā
dragorato uł succus ei uł ꝯpuluē eid̄z et ꝯ
seīe lactuē. 7 al. C ꝯ fluxū sanguis ꝑ nares.
fiat catapla gutturi 7 epi. si flux' ꝯsēd' abepe.
C ꝯ cala apeata fiat catapla expuluē ei 7 succo
solatri. C ꝯ sitiz ī febrib'. draggtū dimictantū
ī aq̄ ꝑ noctez 7 colatē addito pluē ei 7 succo
fiat syrup'.

Sene . ca . e . i . s . herba e que in transmarinis partibus cre
scens ⁊ maxime circa babillonia ⁊ arabia .
valet ꝯ melancolicas pas . ꝯ epilen . ⁊ ꝯ sincopi ⁊ ꝯ
spleis ⁊ emoroidas . ⁊ ꝯ quartana . Syr factus ex aqua
decoctionis eius ⁊ zucco contra valet ad hec . Syr ex suc
co borraginis decoctionis eius ⁊ zuccaro ad eadem valet .
et maxime ad melancolica pas . ⁊ sincopi . ⁊ epilentia .
Syr ex aqua decoctionis eius ⁊ radicis feni ⁊ zuccaro ad idem
valet . vel ex succo feni decoctionis eius . Elligendi
sunt eius flores ⁊ frondes . fustes autem qui ibi reperiunt
non sunt inutiles . Sola folia operantur usui medicine .
per decennium servatur . diascorides iubet inde fieri oximelle
optimum est ad omnia predicta ex aceto decoctionis eius et
melle in quantitate . ʒ . v . vel ʒ . iii . dabis laxatis .

Serpillum . ca . e . i . s . Idem dicitur erpetum aber
pendo . quia super terram serpit . alii vocant Sigos
alii . Meru . alii . Sece rustico . alii . agomena .
alii valet . Est enim serpillum . aliud domesticum . aliud
silvestre . domesticum ramos super terram diffundens . Silvestre
crescens in longum ⁊ altum . folia ⁊ flores operantur
medicine . que in uno olla calefacta ⁊ in sacello posita .
⁊ capiti superposita . valet ꝯ frigidum reuma . Contra
tussim . vinum decoctionis eius ⁊ liquiritie ⁊ succi liquiritie
ꝯ tussi valet . Vinum decoctionis eius . ⁊ anisi .
valet ꝯ dolorem stomachi . eructuositate . Fomentatio
facta ex aqua decoctionis eius valet ꝯ strictu . ⁊ dis . matri
cem quia calefacit ⁊ confortat . Vinum decoctionis
eius stomachum infrigidatum ⁊ epar ⁊ splenem . calefacit ⁊ confor.
Item ex eo factum fumigium omnes serpentes de domo fu
giunt ⁊ omnes venenatia . Item potui dato morsui
pestiferum iuvat . ⁊ tortiones ventris sistit . Item
cum melle ⁊ aceto potuique dato valet ꝯ sputum
sanguinis . Item menstruis impat . teste diascorides serpillum
cum oleo ro . ⁊ aceto . fronti ⁊ capiti superponitur .

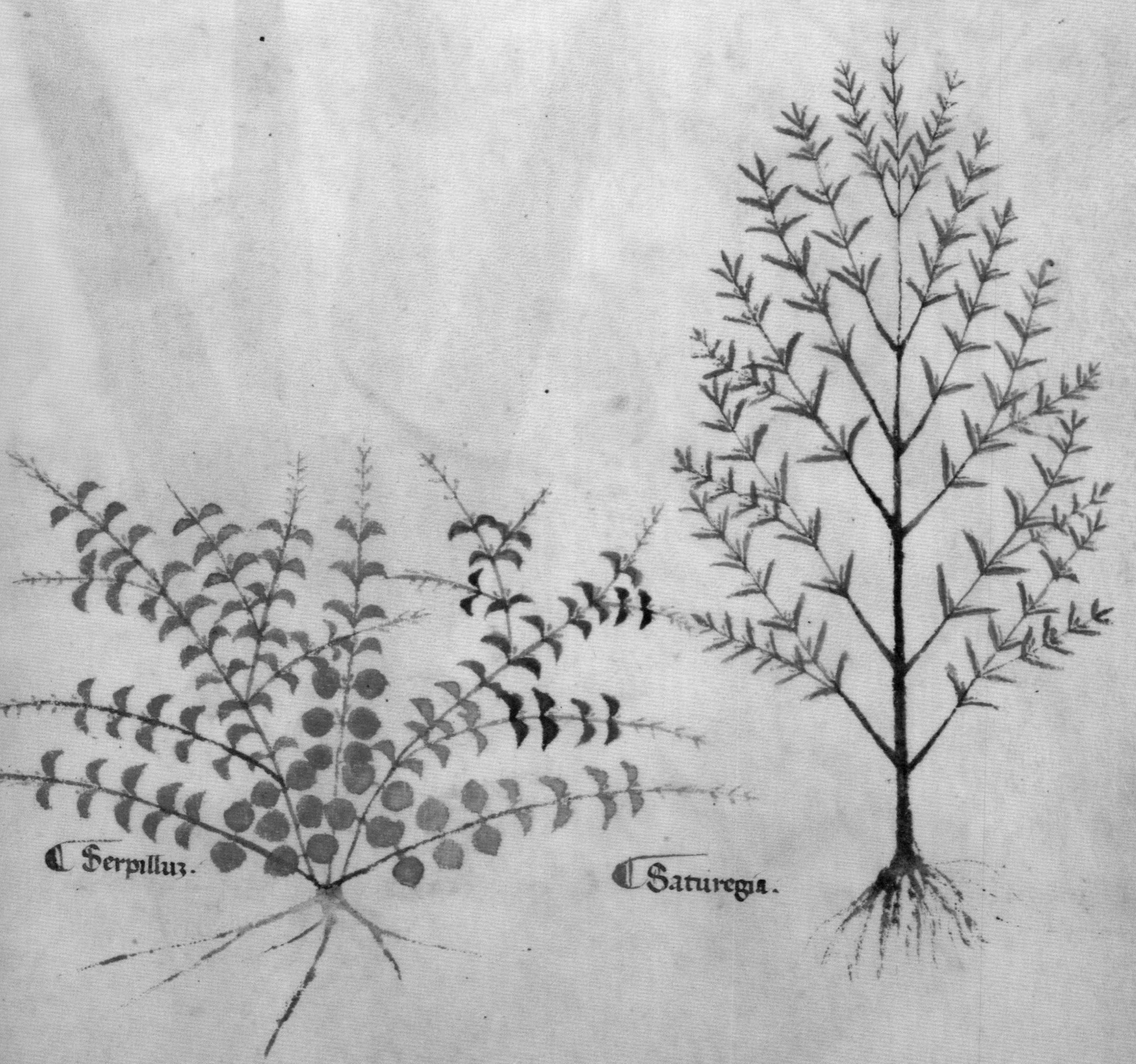

Saturegia. ca. ē 7 s. alio noīe Ascer [illegible]ō
dr. ptes ex farina 7 aq̄ addito puluere
saturegie spūalia mūdificat. puluis ī ome
stus ualet ad idē.

Spatula fetida iuenies retro ul' Exifion.

Sanguinaria .i. q' Galligrus. qdā. dnt. ps ā sis
ē ei; alia ad sanguinē puccād alia ad sistēd;
h q' galligrus dr ualet ad puoc' sāguinē ō narib;
7 ad gāuedinē capis 7 dol'. spigula ei narib; imis
sa stati puocat sanguinē 7 leuiu' reddit. It ual;
ad morsū canis. hba ipi' 7 pane dōestico simil ptē
et fcō ēplin suppoīi. 7 sanabit.

Sanguinaria alia q' fluxū sanguis sistēs q
alio noīe dr Bursa pastoris. 7 nascit' secus
uias h collecta dcrescēti luna. cū iueies aliqs q pati
at fluxū s. da ei ut ī manu teneat p spaciū. si nares
dextera fueit flux' teneat ī sinistā 7 sic 9uiso. statī
sistit sanguinē. It plius ei pmestū ul' ī uino bibit
ieiuno. ualet ad crepatos 7 mir' psolidat. succus ī ei
ualet ad idē 7 plōbiē narib; imissus. sāguiēz sistit.

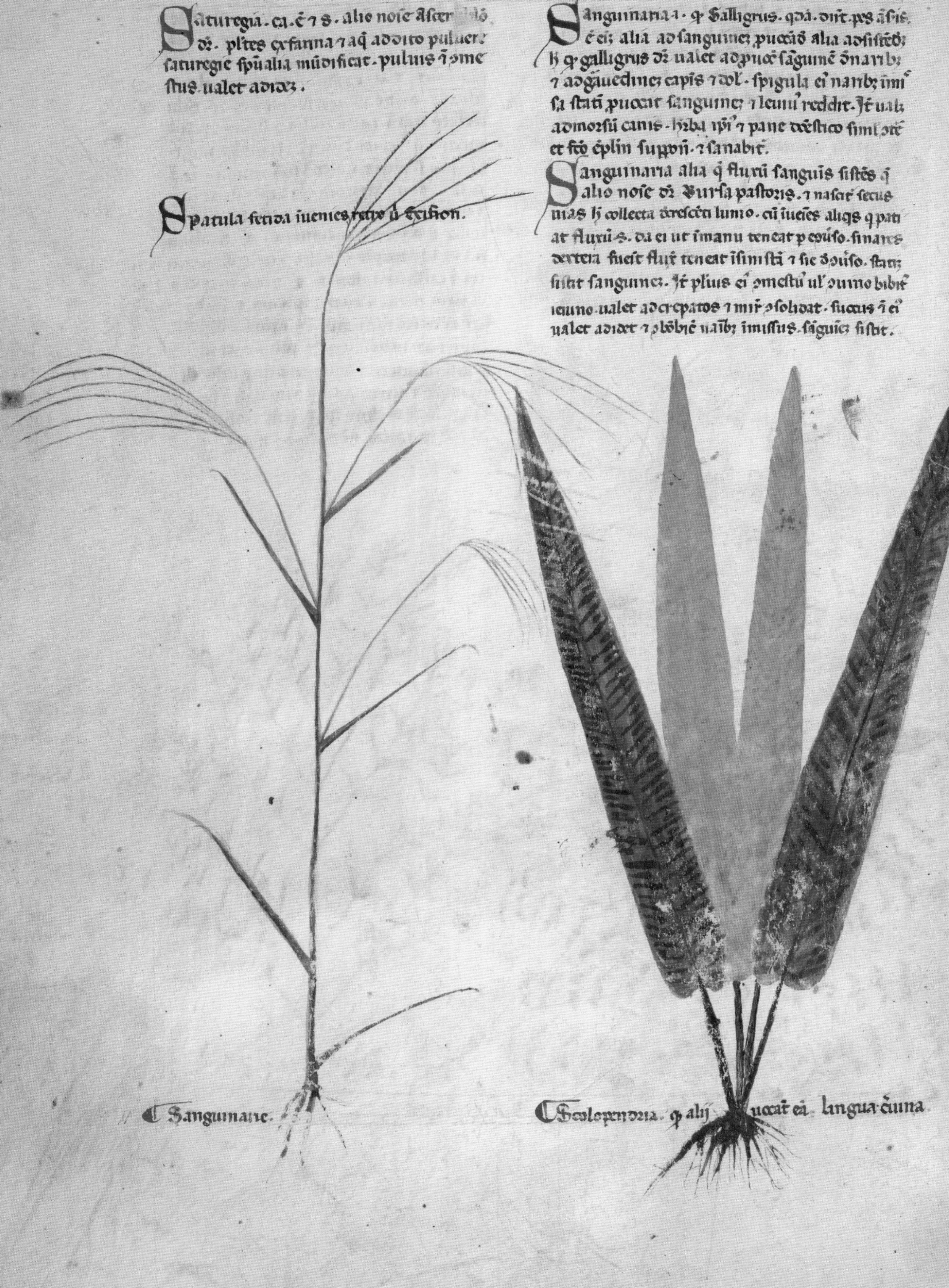

Sanguinarie.

Scolopendria. q' alij uocat ei lingua ceruina.

Scolopendria herba est quam greci vocant splenion, alii [illegible]mion, alii loncitris, alii frig[illegible] al' frigitis, quidam vocant herba panacia. Huius folia longa uni cubiti et stricta signata signis rubis. Nascitur locis aquosis et in foveis obscuris. ¶ Contra dolorem et oppilationem splenis et epatis, aqua vel vinum decoctionis eius potui datum vel comesta mirifice duritiem splenis solvit. Item si inveneris scolopendria ubi sol ne videat, accipe eam et tere et cum farina fac crispellas et da ut comedat unam omni mane ieiuno usque ad novem diebus. Et nono die sanus erit. Item urinam provocat.

Soldanea, id est quedam herba, calida et sicca est. Nascitur locis sablosis et prope lito maris. Huius folia rotunda et parva, radix longa et alba, flos eius est similis asaro. Virtutem habet laxandi et purgandi principaliter flegma, secundo colera et melancolia. Purgat enim violenter, quare non debet dari nisi ʒ i usque ʒ ii. Plurimis radice eius. Et nota quod tamen adsellaret quod provenerit ad dissinteria si cum volueris constringere abluet semetipsum cum aqua frigida manus et faciem suam et tunc non amplius assellaverit.

Spinaca · frā · ē · 7 hu · ī fine · p̄ · gdi · prīci
spalr collerā rubam purgat 7 refrigidat
stoīn 7 uentrē laxat · bonū sanguinē ge
nerat · 7 ualet ꝯ siccitatē pectoris 7 plmoīs ·
Spinaca ī qd ysaac · uētrē huectat 7 ualēt
guile doleti ꝯ sanguīe 7 colra rū 7 stō melior
ē q̄ua atplices ·

Jtla q̄ uulgus blit apellat · c ē 7 f · ī · ī · gu ·
ī laudabile stō p̄at nutrmētū · ꝑꝑ q̄ā sui
acuitis 7 huītatis sue mltitudinē · q̄ tn̄
si ī aq̄ coq̄t 7 ꝯdiat cū aceto, 7 obsomogaro
carni 7 olo onfaccōs aut amigdaleō · fit di
gestiōi facil · parū tamē nutrit 7 uētrē huecta
at · epis oppilationē apit · maxie si fit ꝯ
cessis 7 uiscosis huoribz q̄ cocta ī aq̄ 7 in
aq̄ ꝯmesta fit stiptica · vn̄ · ypōc · apostrma
blitis solutiuū ē · corp̄ eī ꝯstipatiuū ·

Scalognu ē exnatiuā q̄i cepe · ca · ē 7 sicci
ē nō tm̄ ut cepa · stoīn firm̄ · calfaciunt · 7
ꝯfortāt 7 bonū appetitū ītat · 7 ocēs albos · adue
nenū p̄parāt 7 custodiūt · ē malū uisui ꝓhibūt
7 fetorē oris īducūt 7 nō obēt uti hiis q̄ sūt
ex calā natā 7 sicca · q̄cūq̄z uti uolūt ī cibis ul
coqna decoq̄t cū carne pigua · q̄z piguedinem ·
reprimit malitiaz scalon̄ ·

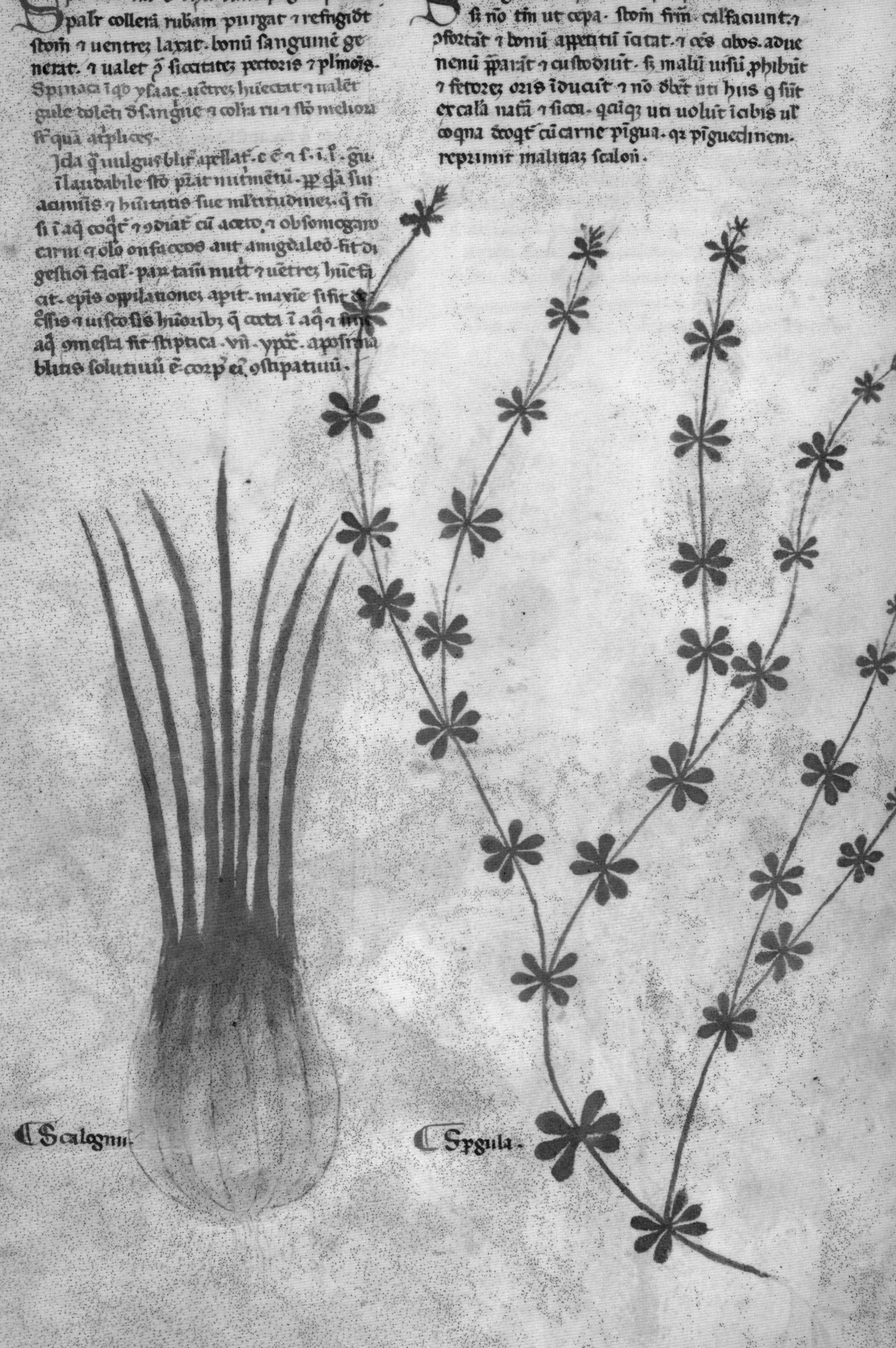

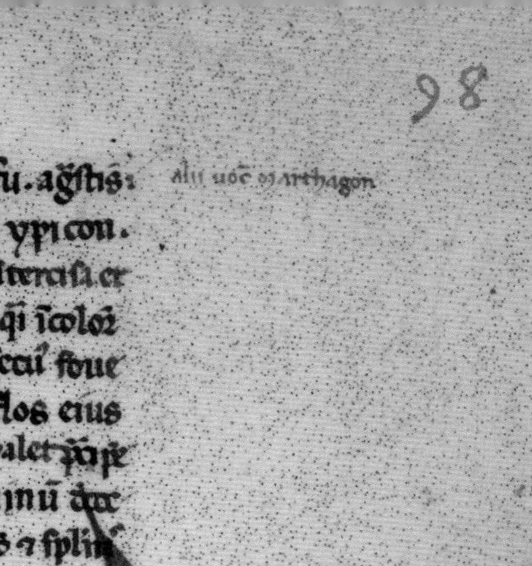

Spargula herba est que alio nomine Ruba minor dicitur. quia folia habet sicut ruba tinctorum sed est parviora. Spargula dicitur quia spargit super sepibus et in multa quantitate crescit habet florem citrinum parvum ad modum uve. Virtutem habet calidam et siccam. precipue valet ad passionem et dolorem gutturis ex frigida causa in quacumque parte corporis fuerit. hec super testa calefacta cum vino bene malaxata et calidum superponatur patienti. mirum dolorem expellit. unde ponitur in unguento marziaton.

Silfu. herba est que alio nomine dicitur. fu. agrestis. que a filiis est valleriana. similatur in ypiconi. sed non habens folia perforata. habet enim folia intercisa et crispa. et flores habet citrinos et multos qui in colore sulfuris. et odorem feculentem. nascitur secus fontes. hec requiritur in confectionem magnum. flos eius vel semen. aut radix deponitur in medicinis. valet proprie ad dolorem matricis. ex frigida causa expellit. vel vinum decoctionis eius bibitur valet in oppilationem epatis et splenis ex frigida causa. et est siccum in [illegible] gradu.

Alii vocant marthagon

Silfu

Sanbaco que Gessominum dicitur.

Sanbacus .i. q. Sesonimū . h̃ba ē cui flores
ualđ sr̃ aromatic̃ odore suauis . odorati valent
ꝯ sincopi ⁊ cardiacaꝫ ⁊ sp̃ualia ꝯfortat̃ . Ex floribus
fit olīū sabacinū cū olō cōi . sic̃ olin . ro . ponitur i
Salia m̃cata q̃ ualet ad eadeꝫ .

Spina b̃nidicta . siū spina márucha . idē ē . s̃ eiꝫ
magna spina q̃ i mlta copia repit̃ i tuscia ⁊ aliis
p̃tibꝫ ⁊ exea fiūt sepibꝫ . cui folia ē morbida . stricta .
et lōga uno digito ⁊ albidiora iuiñe ⁊ pigua . Ex eis
foliis s̃cō cogna ⁊ ꝯmeste . lacteꝫ mirabilit̃ habūdare
fac̃ . mulieribꝫ . ĩ cū lenticul' decocte . melius opãtur .

Secacul . Iringi . Calcatrippa . Cardanel
li . idē est . ē ceñi h̃ba satis cōis cui radix p̃
cipue utimur ⁊ de hoc fit cingaber ꝯditū

Spina benedicta

Sebesten .

Sebesten. ca. sr̄ i. ii. g. hu. i. i. fructus sūt cuiđaz arboris q̄ī pruna q̄ ī ult̄ maris ptib; nascūtur. cū mature sr̄ colligit̄ 7 ōsiccāt̄ ad solez. p trienū pōt suari ī loco sicco 7 ñ huecto. Virtutez hn̄t calefaciē di. huectādi 7 apiēdi. Cōt frūm 7 sic. asma. 7 ptisi; 7 ethicā. pās. aq̄ decoctiōs eī 7 ligr̄. 7 ficus sicce 7 capillo uenē. mir̄ ual;. pōitur ē ī syrupis cōpositis ī febrib acutis 7 ītpolatis. ī pleuresī.

Sistra. ul' sister. h'ba ē q. qdā dnt̄ eē meu. q. falsū; ē. s; ppt̄ suū effectuī. meu pōit̄ p sistra. Sistra aūt̄ efficaci opat̄ ad idez ut meu. cui folia silat̄ ualo bona 7 hȳt spigula silis spica narch. nascit̄ ī magis mōtib;.

Saliūca. h'ba ē. q̄dā dicūt̄ eē spica celtica q. falsū ē. Ē aūt̄ saliūca h'ba q̄ ualō ōsilāt̄ ad spica celtica. s; hr̄is q̄ī una eadez uirt̄. quia celtica pōit̄ p saliūca. Saliūca ē h'ba crescēs ad pedez arboz 7 salet 7 fac̄ spigula pua. colorē s̄b rufo 7 saporez hȳ aromaticū. Cōt dol' stoi ex frīate 7 uētositate 7 ō opilatiōez. spleis 7 epis ex frīā. ca. vinū decoctiōis ei potui dāt̄ p t'b; diebus. valet ē ō. str̄ 7 dis. 7 dol' renū 7 uexic̄. urina 7 mstā pūoc̄.

Spume maris. f. ē 7 s. ī tercio. ḡ. lapis ē q̄ h' sto maris ū diu mare manet 7 putit 7 hec lapis nascēs sr̄ aliā lapidez. spume maris dr̄ ē eī; albū 7 hȳt forāīa pua 7 spissa. Valet p̄cipue ad maculaz oculoz. puluis s̄btilissimū p līteū c'ibrātur 7 sarcocolle tritū dēz. fiat colliriū cū aq̄ ōstillatiōis celidōīe 7 scabios. q; ocul' utere. Valet ē ad dentes ōalbandos si pluis ei sr̄ fricatus fuerit.

Spongia. ca. ē. 7 sic. fūgus sr̄ q̄ ī fūdo maris nascens. ē eī; aliā. alba. alia s̄b rufa. q; magis calida ē. alba uō mīn 7 dr̄ uergellina.

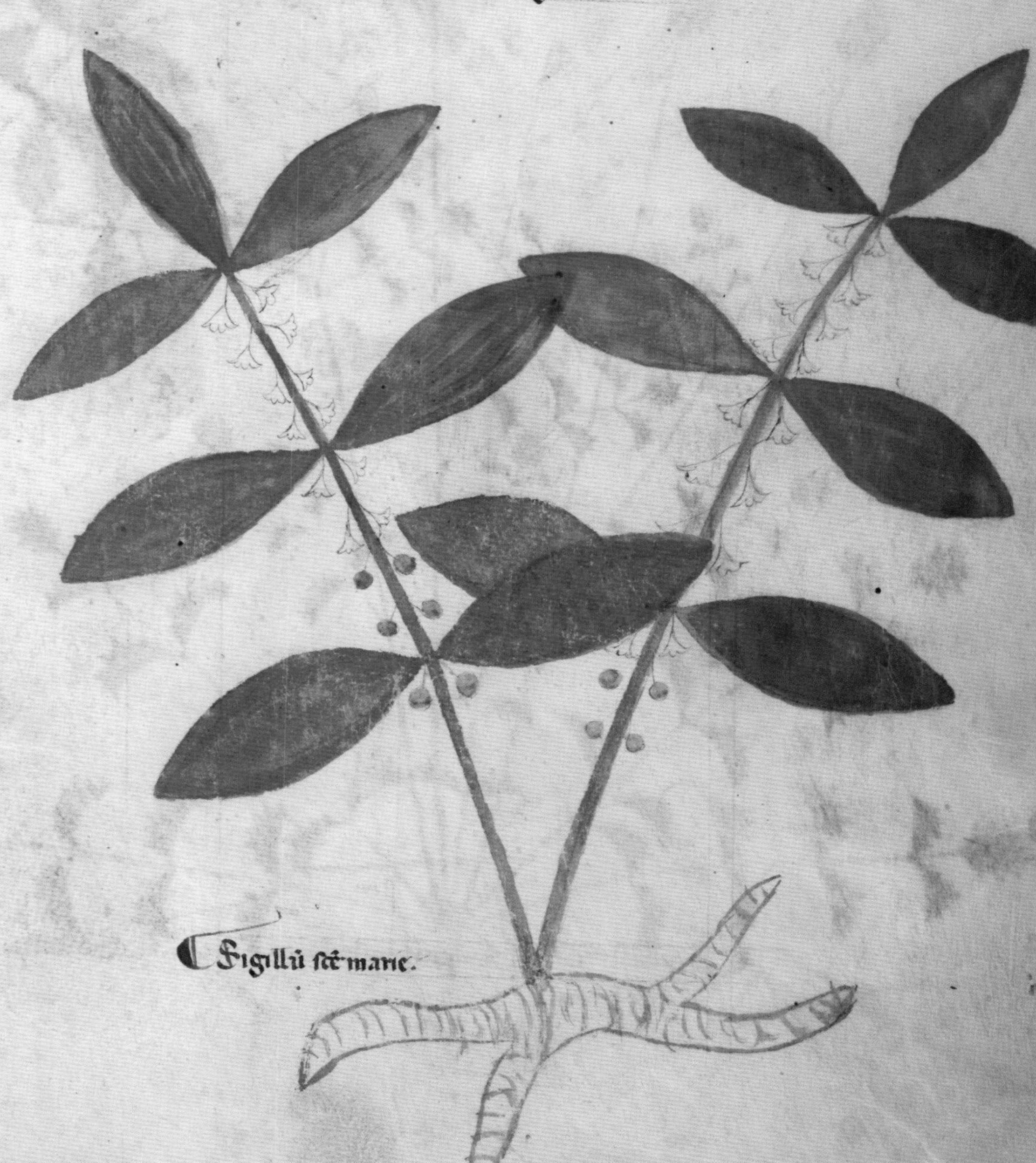

Saliunca.

Sigillū scē marie.

Sigillum sce marie · siu Sigillu salomo
nis idez e · hrba e · nasat locis obscuri
7 i siluis · ht folia qi psicaria 7 florez puos 7
albos 7 pducit sem rube · ordinate unu an
aliu sicut pomiculi · Radix ei e alba 7 nodosa
silis bruscho · Virtutez ht · calefaciedi · mitiga
di 7 ofor · C ot tumorez 7 dol neruor 7 o du
ritiez splenis · ex radicib ei 7 adipe ursino et
cera fiat unguetu de q ungat · ul aq decoctois
radic ei · fiat balneu 7 pea catapler · C impe
tiginez 7 spiginez 7 faciez dalbando · fiat un
guetuz ex sucho ei 7 olo letischo 7 cera albi
de quo facies illiniat ·

Sorbastrella · calida e 7 sic · hrba e silis pipi
nella · un dr · pipinella pilos · Sorbastrel
la e sin pilos · nasat ad pedes motib 7 i cali
ariis · Valet precipue ad caligiez 7 maculam
oculor · succ ei 7 melle al · feo oliniu · ocul ute ·
C o uenenu 7 o morsu oiu uenenator · succ
eiu pse aut cu uino bibit · mir pficiat · Puluis
q ei supaspsus uulnera mir osolid ·

Sorbe. sūt .sūt ⁊ sic. ī ttio. g. fructus ē cui satis esui ꝯpet. tpr autūpni colliguntur imature ꝯstipitib; suis ⁊ suspēdūt diu ut maturēt q̄dā findūt cū cultello ⁊ dsiccāt ad ꝯsuandū ⁊ sic p ānū possūt suari. virtute; hēt īfrigidādi ⁊ ꝯstringendi ⁊ etiā ꝯfor. Ɔt fluxū uentris ex colia ⁊ ꝯ dis. fiat hoc ellē; sic. acc̄. sorbar īmaturar dīcatarū ī aq ⁊ pcatiā pforatā; bn̄ colatarū ut ad sēibus ⁊ corticib; bn̄ mūdatis. lī. i. mellis dspuāti. lī. i. coq̄t ad spissitudine; pea addāt hūs spēb; q. R. sanguinis drac. mastic. boli ar. draggā. ⁊ gūi ar. an̄. ʒ. ii. sumac. acatie. an̄. ʒ. ß. folii. gar. mac̄. cinamoī. an̄. ʒ. ß. ʒʒ. ʒ. ii. sbtilme c̄tellētur ⁊ pea ꝯmiscēāt ꝯsup dco ellō. ⁊ dnt patiēti oī hora. ⁊ maxīe ieiuno stō Ɔt tenasmō. ualet fumigiū fēz ex aq decoctiōis eī. ꝯmedat patiēs ī ex sorbis maturis. uł exsiccis. Ɔt uomitū ex colā fiat ēpl; ex sorbis imaturis bn̄ ꝯtritis ⁊ sr̄ stom̄ positis.

Sinoni. i. q̄ petrosilinū agreste. ca. ē ⁊ sic sem̄ eī collectū ⁊ dsiccatū p. v. annos pōt suari. valet ad idē ut peucedanū. etiā d ipso diximꝰ ī capitulo d petros.

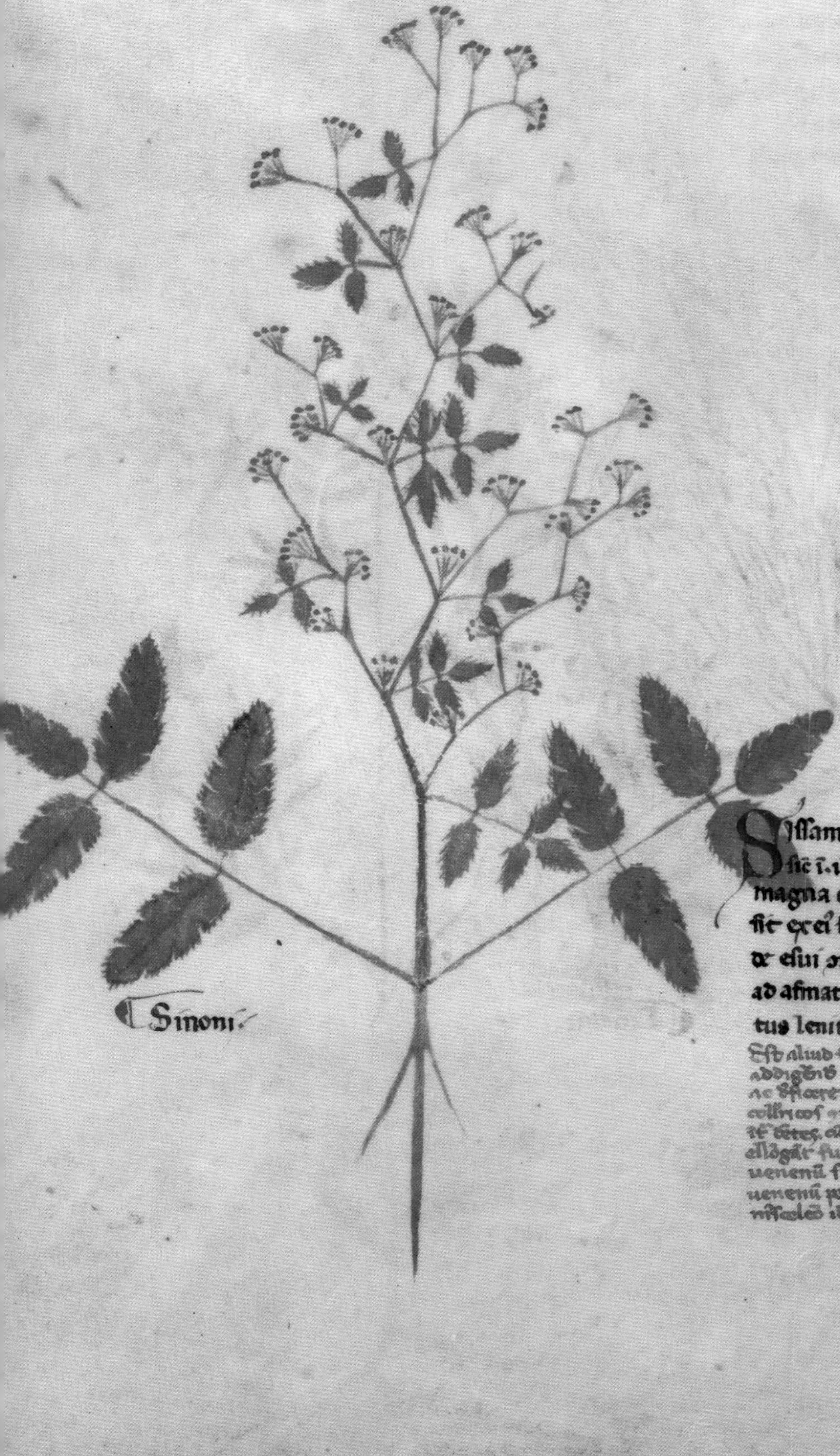

Sinoni.

Sissamus idē; ē q̄ giugiulena. ca. ē ī. iii. g. ⁊ sic ī. i. sem̄ ē q̄ ī sicilia ⁊ ī trāsmaris ptib; in magna copia repit̄ q̄a semitāt̄ ī pār; sic miliū. sit ex eī sem̄. oł'ū sisaminū sic d amigdal. q̄ ual ꝯ esui ꝯpet. ponit̄ ī ī ꝯfectiōib; q̄ dr̄. aloa. q̄ fac ad asmatic̄ ⁊ ꝯsūptis ⁊ stom̄ ꝯfor̄ ⁊ nutrit. ⁊ pectus lenit ⁊ uald̄ restaurat.

Est aliud sissamū cui cortex ē sine cortice. q̄ sine cortice ē uetere ē idē. Alii dicūt ē addigēns quā obstē efficat sīō. pōti uius eius a pilis. Duo naq̄ uiscositates ꝯ mollire ac ꝯficere cōg. virtutē; hīt ꝯtēptiua digē uōq; ꝯfectat. uł enarrat ī suo sitimes huiꝰ ꝯ collirios ꝯualet cito siti gñat ⁊ fastidiū odore; oris bonū īfectos ꝯmutat. si remanet iī dētes. cū melle ꝯtpū min̄ nocet. Aq ud sissami si coq̄t̄ ꝯdes capilli si ablueris crines ellōgāt furfuresq; mūdificat. Apposima sissami uē sēā purgat. Antiq̄ q̄dā dicūt ꝯ uenenū sissamū cū sua ē uiscositate; ⁊ udositate poro corporis ꝯ opilat ⁊ dicūt uenenū penetrare ꝯmittat. Dia. nullā īt̄ sissamū ⁊ sissamelē differētiā facit sicut ... illō uale cessat. G. ū id nō affirmat.

Tartaru. ca. e 7 sic. i. tcio. g. q. e d uino puro 7 albo. melius e. C 9 scabiem. spigine 7 ipetiginez. litargiu i fudat i aceto per noctez. mane ad ygnez resoluat ex olo nuc 7 ex eo fit 9mixtio sup ygnez 7 tartaro i multa qntitate. addito mox ab ygne dpoat 7 fiat ungtz 9 pocu. C Seme staphisagrie i aq bulliat bn ex illa aq 7 tartaro fiat 9mixtio. illud furfuriscas capis reouet. capite in bis ul ter i uncto. pluis ei exibitus i cibis. pinguedinez extenuat ipaz 9suendo. pluis i qntitate. 3. s. ul 3. iii. dat 9 claretto ul 9 melle. ro. ul 9 diapennidion. ul 9 dia margarito ul alio tali ducit ad plus. vi. ul. vii. sellas. pluere mastices addita.

Tamariscus. ca. e 7 sic. Vinu dectiois eiu ualet ad opilationez spleis 7 epis. 7 strag et dis. diuretica eiz e. Puluis ei i cibis datus ad idez ualet. Frequns etiaz bibitatio cu uase ex tali ligno ad eadez ualz. Cortex ei e maioris efficaciae qua folia.

Terra sigillata. fria e 7 sic. calx e odonfera. et dr terra figuli. Eadez dr terra argetea. uel creta saracenica. facile ex nra creta sophicatur. C Emplm d puluere ei 7 albuie oui. s frotez 7 tipora sagus emb; sistit. C Terra sigillata ualz 9 fluxu uentris. C Emplm d pulue ei 7 aceto ad ifflactioez pectu ualz 7 arth. C Puluis ei 9 succo sanguinarie. sanguinez e narib; sistit. C Emplastu d puluere ei 7 aceto 7 albuie oui digestioez 9curat.

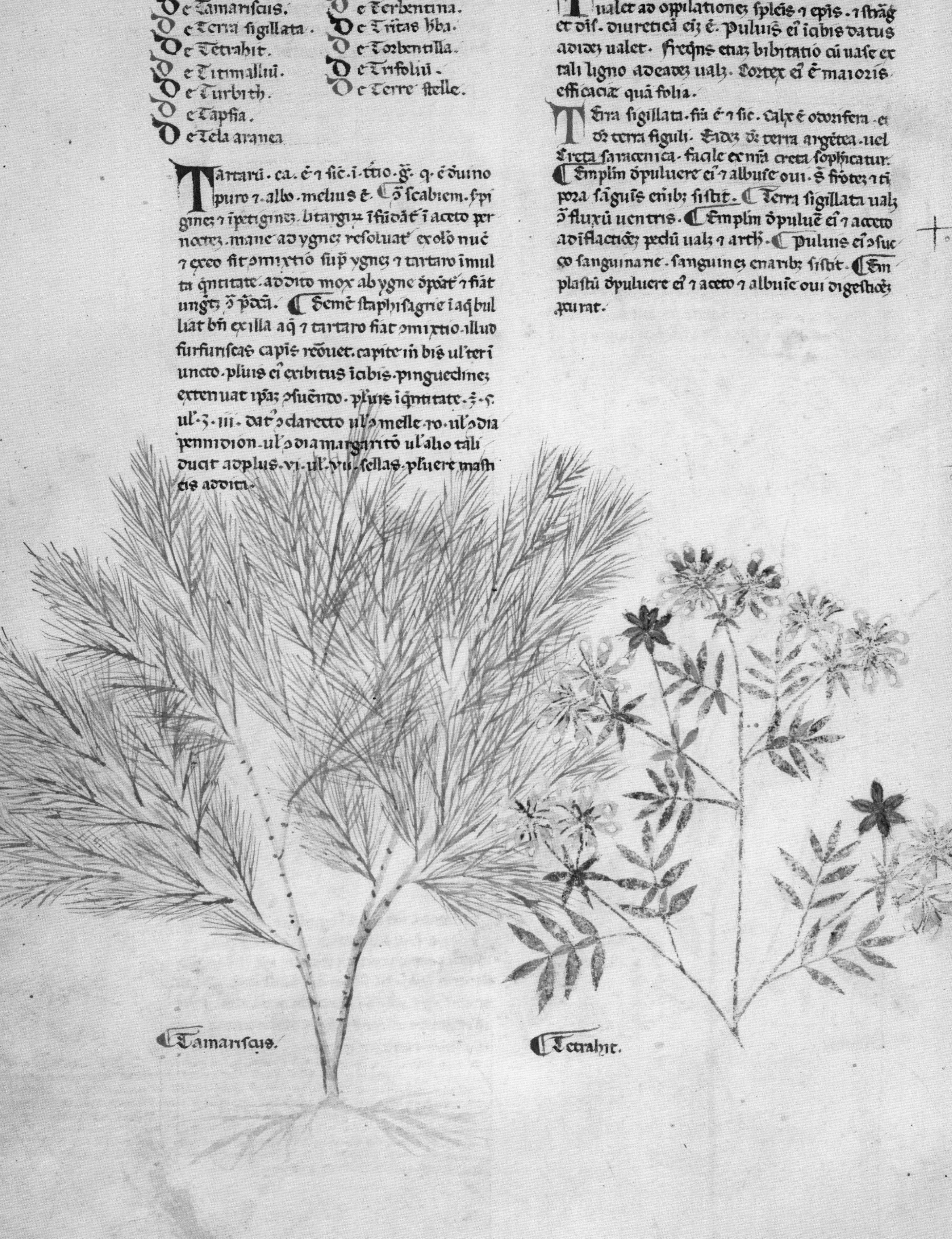

Turbit. herba iudaica. idez ē. ca. ē 7 sic. ī s°. g. Vinū decoctionis ei indigestionez 7 dol. stō. 7 itestinorū ex uentositate remouet. ¶ Pibulle ex ea et farina 7 aq̄ naturalez colorez confortat. urinā prouocat. ¶ Emplm ex ipsa herba ī aq̄ cocta. strāg. soluit. ¶ Fomentū ex aq̄ decoctionis ei matricez calefacit. 7 mundificat. ¶ Suppositoriū ex tenebritatibz ei ī olo micelo decoctionis idez fac.

Titimallus. ca. ē 7 sic. ī tīo. g. multas hēt spēs ꝫ laureola 7 esula. dēm ē supiū nūc ꝫ anabulla dicamus q̄ ī ultramarinis ptibz est ꝫ qua fit scamonī 7 ꝫ anabulla nostra lac eī ī uere colligit. caute ē colligendū ex infusione. ē eī facile man̄ excoriat. q̄ si tingat fricet ꝑs lesa ꝯ suco solatri. siue ex alio suco frō. Anabulla frāgat. 7 gutte manētes colligātur. q̄nq3. ʒ. iij. q̄nq3. v. ex lacte cocto ꝯ gūi arabici. siue ꝯ dragāto medicine accipiūt pille ꝫ q̄nq3 gnbz mirob. 7 pille auree. oxi 7 bīdicta 7 hui modi siue scam ī q̄titate. iiij. ʒ. Panis ex eo 7 farina 7 aqua ꝯfect. optīe purgat.

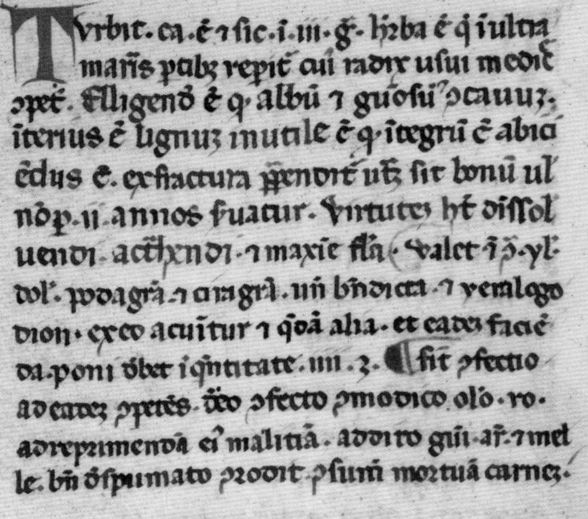

Turbit. ca. e et sic. in iii. g. herba e q in ultra
maris ptibz repit cui radix usui medic
cpet. Elligend e q albu et gumosu ocauuz.
iterius e lignuz inutile e q integru e abio
edus e. ex fractura ppendit utz sit bonu ul
no p. ii. annos suatur. Virtutez ht dissol
uendi. acthendi. et maxie fla. Valet i p. yl.
dol. podagra et ciragra. uu bndicta. et yeralogo
dion. exeo acuitur et qda alia. et eadz facie
da poni dbet i qntitate. iii. z. Sit ofectio
ad eadez opetes. ideo ofecto pmodico olo. ro.
ad reprimenda ei malitia. addito gum. ar. et mel
le. bn ospumato prodit. osumit mortua carnez.

Tapsia. ca. e et sic. i tcio. g. herba e cui radix
cortic i medicis uomicas ponitur. iuenit i ara
bia. idia. calabria. et cicilia et ppric circa panor
mu q mediu e ppt aerez calida et sicca et locu ibi
osistes. cortex radic collecte et exsiccate p. iii. ano
suat. Virtutez ht pncipalr pugadi. fla. fano
colra. p iferiora. et supiora. vn i uoicas medicini
poit auctibz. si qn i pua qntitate secure cu aliis
spebz poit. qn oterit i magna qntitate pse terat
ul cu aliis. caute dbet teri. i. s. q ille q ea oterit.
faciez. brachia. manu. crura. et itestina. oculos op
time coopiat qa n ita se ppareret iflat. Jn uoica
medicis auctibz poita iuenit. Caute debz fieri. Si aut
iflactice si otigit. fricet cu pano aceto ifuso ul
ps tumores iungat.

Tela aranee. Virtutez ht ostrigendi. osolid.
uulneribz nouelle iposita. Valet i ad frac
turaz capitis cu olo et aceto. fracto capi supositi.
dol tollit et sanat. Jt ti porib supposita. tertiana
et odz febrez curat. sanguez e naribz sistit. decta
cu olo. auribz catapla. dolorez expellit. tela alb ara
neor i corio ligata et collo suspesa ualz quarta
naris teste ipocras.

Tapsia.

Tassus ubassus.

Tassus verbassus. f. ē 7 s. alio noīe dicitur flosmon. alii uocāt blatone. alii argimōi. herba ē cui due sūt maneies. s. maschul' 7 femia. i. mai' 7 min'. maior aut maiorē hēt efficaciā. C fomento fcō ex uino decoctionis eius ualet ꝯt emoroidas. Adidez ualet si anus patiētis exeo tgat post assellationez. Valet ē ad tenasmōi encatisma ex aqua decoctiōis eius 7 ꝯt fluxū uētris. C Pului ex floribꝫ eius sup cancrū aspgat' mir' sanat. folior eius posit' i aq. ubi sit pisces. statī fiūt uenenati ex amaritudine ipi'. hec fia ō minori herba. Valet ē ꝯ ascarides. ex foliis tassi ubassi minoris fiat ze bulle cū farina 7 aq. 7 ōt.

Terbentina. c. ē 7 s. terbētinā gūi ē siu liquorositas q̄ ex abietis effluit. patiēs tenasmō. recipiat fumū eius per embotū suppositū ex lōbice ītīcto ī ea. ꝯt precipitationez matricis. C Ad arū pendūz a pēma fiat emplm ex ea 7 farina ordei. ponit etiaz ī ūguētis ad ꝯsolidandūz uulnēibꝫ. Olū ōstillatiōis eius efficacius est ualō. ō arth. pal' 7 appople. 7 ō oēs tumorez et ꝯtractioēz nuor 7 dol' ex frā. ca. fr' ungat.

Tribuli marini herba ē q nascitur locis sablosis 7 ī marinis ptibꝫ. spit sup terrā ī ueēt' tpr estiuo 7 pducit semē spinosū unū dr tribuli. hēt aūt uirtutē diureticā unū ualet ꝯt stranguriā 7 dissur' 7 calculū. uinū decoctionis ul' puluis semis eius cū uino bibitū mirabiliter pficit. ponit' ē ī unguētū agrippa q ual; ydropicas 7 oībꝫ tumoribꝫ ī quacūq; pte corporis fuit. 7 ad neruos ī dignatos. urinā puoc' i uictūz suppuētrez laxat.

Trinitas. unitas. idem est. herba est similis asaru et habet tres folia in uno filo. nascitur locis umidis et obscuris et herbosis. et pre(cipue) in castaneis.

Torbentilla. herba est que fistularia. et Tagliasania dicitur. silatur pentaphilon. nascitur in montibus et locis herbosis. Contra fistulam in qualicumque parte corporis fuerit. succum eius instillatur in fistula et tenta ipso succo tincta immictatur. mirabiliter sanat. Contra maculas oculorum. succus eius cum uino albo oculis instillatur. mirabiliter ualet.

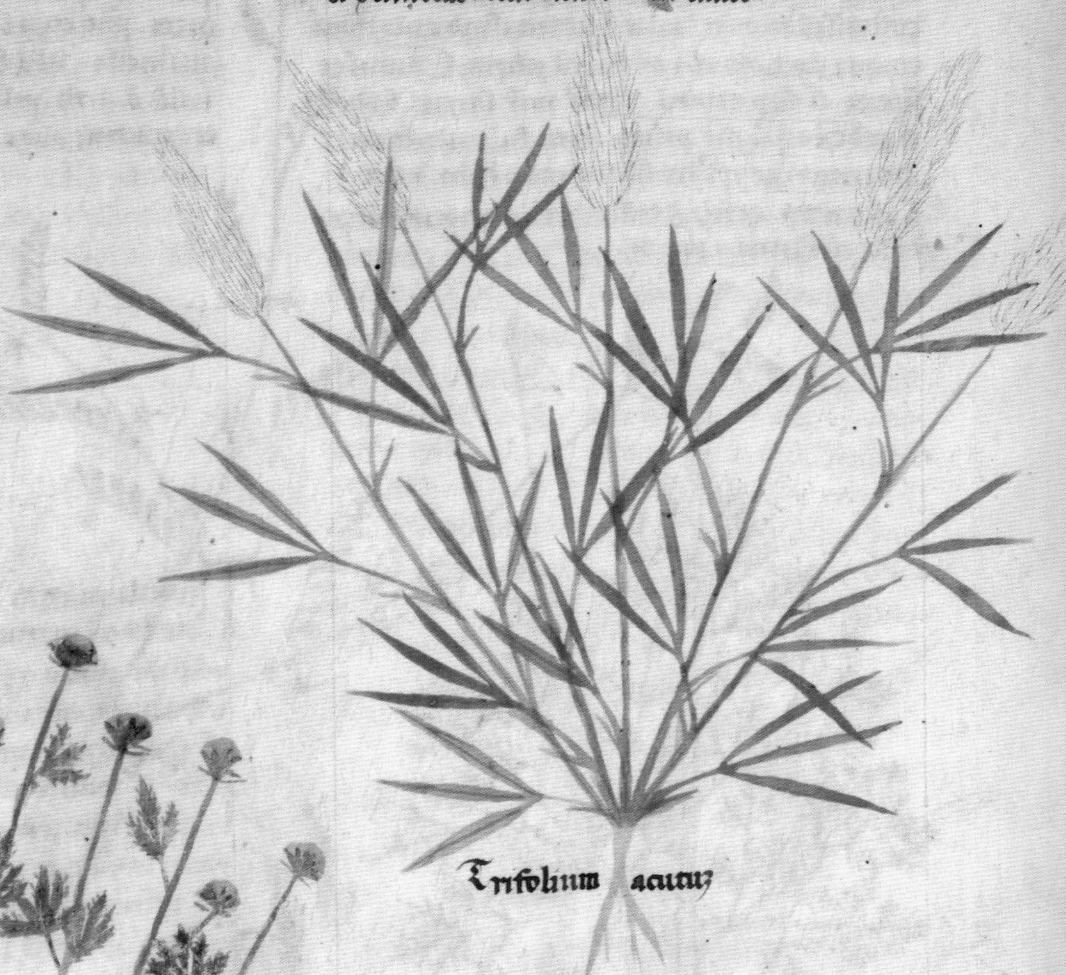

Trifolium acutum

Torbentilla. quam alii eptafilos uocant

Trifolium.

Alispalgion.

8 Triticum. secundum sui naturam species calida et humida [...] est et humidum et sicca medium panis ex eo factus calidior est calor eius in ii gradu. adipiscitur ex calore igne [...] rectione. Testatur hoc elementorum in rebus [...] uel aceto. ubi [...] gelones [...] in natura sua sint [...] humida in ii gradu. corpus [...] desiccatur ad soles. Videt et siue [...] si coquatur in aqua humiditatem [...] assumunt. Sig [...] siccum exaqua humiditate [...] ex sole siccitatem [...] accidit et calidum ex [...] frigescit et [...] igne calefiat. [...] propter hoc granum tritici [...] omnibus granis excepta que nutribilius et laudabilius pro complexionum humana [...] similitudine habet cum ceteris commixtum [...] atque communes [...] colatiuum est mundificatiuum uel lauatiuum. assentit hoc quod patitur de eius actionibus [...] medicinam apparet. Jus est de eius farinam [...] purgatiuum est pectoris pulmonis corporum leniunt asperitates si [...] fecerint sicut [...] ordo fieri solet [...] ad tussim et fluxum sanguinis [...] cum oleo et [...] si ponantur apertum dissoluitur. Si aceto mixta et melle pustulas [...] que nascuntur in facie [...] cum aqua et ruta si [...] et mamillis [...] durities per lactis coagulationes [...] in mollities durities [...] cum suco [...] et cataplasma [...] neruos [...] humores noxios in eo [...] Granum masticatum [...] morsum [...] morbum fugat. De [...] ad [...] fluxum sanguinis et sanies post electum [...] ualet.

8 Furfure. Natura [...] et mundificatiue magis quam farina [...] in aqua [...] atque colat [...] pectoris pulmonis [...] humores [...] lac nutribilior fit et [...] Si furfuris aceto mixti [...] calefactus [...] lactis coagulationes [...] pustulas et [...] atque mundificat. [...] cum uino [...] et cataplasma [...] et dolores lateris [...] dissoluit [...] morsum [...] nutrimentum [...] inflatum [...] humores [...] uirtutis [...] Si tamen [...] nutrit et membra confortat [...] magis laboribus accedunt.

Trifoliu[m] ... ē q[uo]d alis palgion.

Terre stelle. q[uo]d licta mu. ... tia ē q[uo]d lapis silis nitro. albus eius ē 7 lucid[us] 7 h[ab]et squama sicut auru[m] pigm[en]tu[m]. fr[igi]d[u]m ē 7 sic. po[ni]t i[n] mediciis 7 marse i[n] trocisci stell[e].

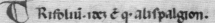

De viola.
De virga pastoris.
De viticella.
De vitro. [De] vi[n]cul[is] ...
De viperina.
De vrtica.
De vince tosice.
De vilubidis.

Viola. fri[gida] ē i[n] .i. g[radu]. hu[mida] i[n] fi[ne] sc[cun]di. ... sic[ut] p[er]hibent[ur] fuat[ur]. melius ē ut singlis a[n]nis renouetur. ... viridib[us] fit. zuccaru[m] uiolla[tum]. sir[upus] uiol[atus]. mell[is] uiol[atum]. oli[um] uiol[atum]. Syr[upus] aut[em] uiollac[eus] fit d[e] viridib[us] 7 siccis. s[ed] q[ui] siccis min[us] ē efficax. ¶ zucc[aru]m uiol[atum] fit eod[em] m[od]o quo 7 rosetu[m]. Syr[upus] uiol[atus] sic fit. viol[e] i[n] aq[ua] [de]coq[u]ant[ur] 7 dimitta[n]t[ur] i[n] aq[ua] p[er] nocte[m] 7 ex colatura 7 zucc[ar]o fiat syr[upus]. S[ed] sic fit melius. sic[ut] p[er]i[m] succo 7 zucc[ar]o fiat. ¶ Oleu[m] uiolatu[m] fiat hoc m[od]o. viol[e] i[n] aq[ua] [de]coq[u]ant[ur]. colatura ē oli[um] uiolatu[m] ul[tra] fiat [de]coctio i[n] duplici uas[e] ul[tra] q[uo]d meli[us] ē. [de]coquitur 7 fiat colatura. colature addant[ur] recetes 7 sic dimitta[n]t[ur] p[er] .xx. dies. sic sc[cun]d[o] 7 t[er]tio addant[ur] uiol[e] recetes ip[s]i colature. ¶ Oli[um] istud optim[um] ē [et] nobili[us] istoru[m] ... receptu[m]. ualet [contra] discrasia[m] coloris totius corporis oli[um] inuctio f[ac]ta exteriu[s] ualet [contra] calefactio[n]e[m] ep[at]is. Vnctio eid[em] f[ac]ta sup[ra] tipora 7 fro[n]te[m] dol[orem] ex calore reducet. virtute[m] h[ab]et lemendi. huectandi i[n]fi[n]andi et laxa[n]di. ¶ Viol[e] [de]cocte siue ip[s]a herba [de]cocta. sup[er] calida apata i[n] p[ri]ncipio po[s]ita ualet. ¶ Fome[n]tatio ex aq[ua] [de]coctio[n]is ip[s]i[us] h[er]be. s[cilicet] pedes 7 [con]fectes i[n] acutis febrib[us] sopnu[m] p[ro]uocat. Syr[upus] uiol[atus] magis [de]cog[ni]t[us] q[uam] ros[atus]. alit[er] ei[us] citi[us] [cor]rupet.

¶ Viola.

¶ Vitru[m] fornace.

Vri q[uod] al[iqu]i ... minuell[i] ... uitice[l]li uo[cant] ... ē ... ad digere[n]d[um] ... ep[at]is [et] splenis ... Lapides ... 7 uesica ... sanguine[m] ... pectus ... dolores ... aut bleta ... cucurbita ... 7 ... cu[m] carne gallin[e] ... origanu[m] a calametu[m] ... bibat ... melicratu[m] ... [illegible]

Vitrum fit̃ e i primo g̃. sic i scđo. uitrũ
fit ex h̃ba ⁊ sablone excoctione ignis
i fornace artificiose. Val; ad scabiem hec mo
picula ad ignẽ resoluat̃ i aqua. colet
⁊ addat̃ oleũ nucis. d̃m tartarũ ⁊ pl'uis
uit̃. ⁊ ex tali ungto p̃s i ungat̃. ul' ali
gũi prunoꝝ i aq̃ ad igne; resoluat̃ ⁊ co
letur cũ i expssi oĩs ⁊ ex illo pluẽ illis ɔ
fectis p̃s iugat̃. ¶ Ad morfeã ualet sic
pluis ei ɔficiat̃ ɔ flore muri ⁊ olõ. ro. et
capitello ⁊ locus m̃ fricet. p̃cedete tñ sca
rifatice p̃tis ut sãguis exeat. ¶ Pluis
sbtilissim̃ p pãnũ cribatus ɔficiat ɔ suc
co feñ. h' oclõ i positũ pãnũ ɔrodit.

Virga pastoris fĩã ẽ ⁊ sic solũ folia medicine
ɔpet ⁊ uiridia ɔ sicca pannũ s'uat̃. viridia tñ
sũt maioris efficacie. Virtute; h̃t ɔstrigendi
⁊ replẽdi ⁊ i s'rãndi. Emplm ex pluẽ ei ⁊ aceto
⁊ albuĩne oui. sup̃ pectine; ⁊ renes positũ. ual;
¶ ɔ fluxũ uetris. pluis ei dat̃ ɔ ouo sorbili ad
ide; ual; ⁊ ɔ̃ ad p̃fluuiũ. ¶ Fometatio ex aqua
d'coctiõis ip̃i' ad ide; ual;. t'ita ualet ad calida ap̃
emata. i p'ricipio ut erisipilã. ⁊ hui' mõi capiti
cataplãta. pil' abrasis freneticis ualet.
¶ Virga pastoris h̃ba ẽ. frõdes ⁊ ramos h̃ns sup
terrã expãsos uĩdes i estate ⁊ i yeme florẽ h̃t alb;
subtil' ut calamũ. radix ẽ rubã aliq̃tulũ nig̃
ɔmixtat̃. cataplãta ardorẽ stõi ⁊ capitis dolo
re; d'calore ɔpescit. s'nutatio d'ea ɔ caph̃a p
uocat̃. sãgne; d' narib; sistit. Succũ narib; stilla
tus pustulas curat ⁊ eã; fluxũ sãgs mulierũ
unde cũ manauerit sistit. Ca'la appẽata sic fleg
monẽ ⁊ cspulas refrigerat. Succus cristeriça
tus dissinteriã ⁊ ulceratã itestinoꝝ ⁊ ɔ̃; exco
rationẽ; d' acumine m̃ feẽ; curat. It ad cãcr;
acc capita uirge pastoris ⁊ ɔbure i olla ⁊
fac in cinẽ; ⁊ sup cãcrũ põe ⁊ sigge ⁊ p̃ul du
bio sanat. It ɔ uerrucas. acc ɔ succo folioꝝ
⁊ laua manib; ⁊ sanabit.

Urticella . c . ē 7 s . h'ba ē q alio noīe d'r
utāniū . alii uocāt aliepias . radix ei' ɔ
axugia porcina bn̄ terāt' sic trita ad ygnē
resoluat' resoluta colet' . colature addat'
farine sēis lini . 7 olim ɔfectū ɔ plagella
epi 7 splēi suppōita sclirosiz tollit . ¶ Itē
ualet ad apostata maturād' . ¶ Suppositoriū
fcm̄ ex radice ei' mēstrua puoc' . Secūdinā
7 fetū mortuū educ' . pallidos colorat sic
fiat . q̄dā p's radix pistet' 7 quasset' ut suc
cus exeat . inde q̄dā p's faciei iungat' et
erit ruba . ¶ Sane trita ad apostema rūpendū
fiat ēplm̄ ex pluē adarcis 7 succo ei' . rad.

Viperina . h'ba ē q alii uoc' . Urtica
mortua . nasc' circa flumina ul'
ī bladis 7 h't folia morbida 7 saporē amar'
valet ꝯ papue ad morsū uipe' . ip̄a h'ba ɔt'
ta 7 ɔ uino potui data ɔ morsū uipinū sa
nat 7 ex' uenenū discutit . Valz ēt ɔ fistu
lā 7 cācrū 7 glādul' . ɔtrita 7 suppōita bis ī
die mir' curat 7 sanat . Ɔlet eā legi mēs
apl'.

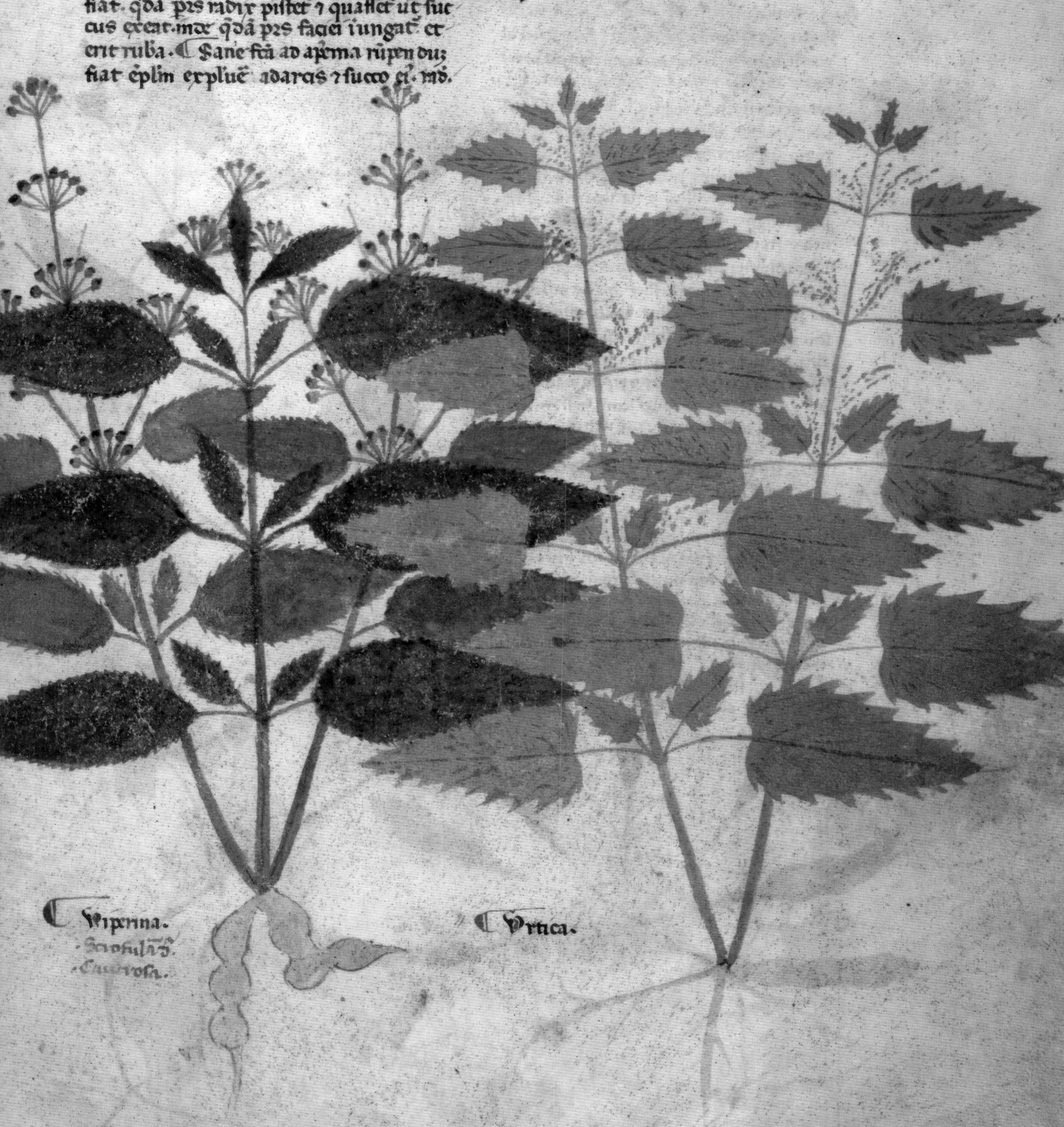

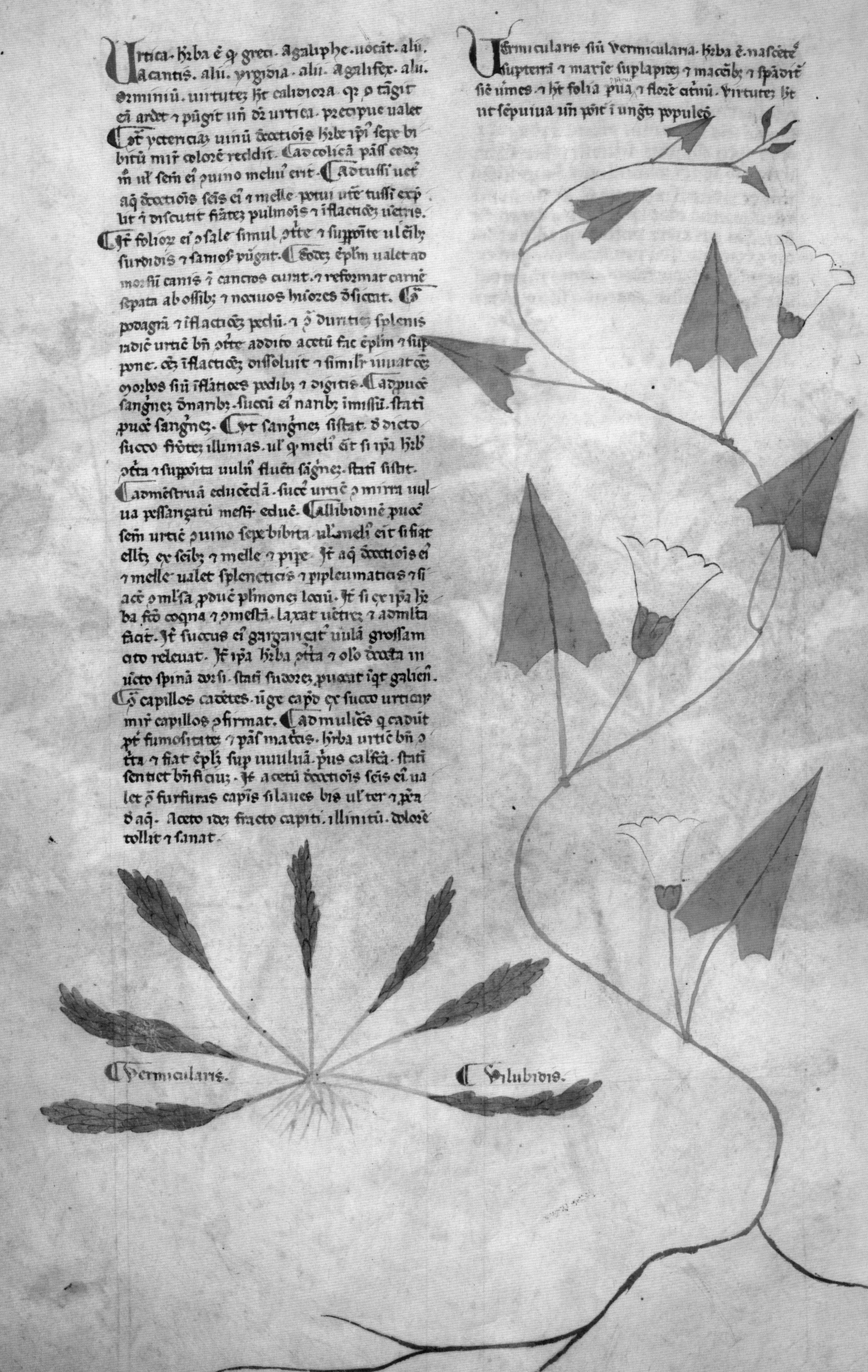

Urtica. h(er)ba e(st) q(uam) greci. agaliphe. uocant. alii.
acantis. alii. yrgidia. alii. agalifex. alii.
ominiu(m). uirtute(m) h(abe)t calidiora q(ui)a q(ui) tangit
eam ardet (et) pungit un(de) d(icitu)r urtica. precipue ualet
Ad ytericiam uinum decoctionis h(er)be ip(s)i sepe bi
bitum mir(um) colore(m) reddit. Ad colica(m) pass(ionem) eode(m)
m(odo) ul(tra) sem(en) ei(us) cu(m) uino meliu(s) erit. Ad tussi(m) uet(erem)
aq(ua) decoctionis se(min)is ei(us) (et) melle potui data tussi(m) exp(el)
lit (et) discutit frigiditate(m) pulmonis (et) inflactione(m) uentris.
Item foliorum ei(us) cu(m) sale simul co(n)trite (et) supposite ul(ceribus)
sordidis (et) sanios(is) purgat. Eodem ep(ithe)m(a) ualet ad
morsum canis (et) cancros curat. (et) reformat carne(m)
separata ab ossib(us) (et) nociuos humores desiccat. Contra
podagra(m) (et) inflactione(m) pedum. (et) contra duritie(m) splenis
radice urtice b(e)n(e) co(n)trite addito acetum fac ep(ithe)m(a) (et) sup
pone. eam inflactione(m) dissoluit (et) simil(ite)r iuuat contra
morbos siue inflationes pedibus (et) digitis. Ad prouoca(ndum)
sanguine(m) de naribus. succum ei(us) naribus imissum. stati(m)
prouoca(t) sanguine(m). Ut sanguine(m) sistat. de dicto
succo fronte(m) illinias. ul(tra) q(uod) melius est si ip(s)a h(er)b(a)
co(n)trita (et) supposita uulneri fluenti sanguine(m). stati(m) sistit.
Ad menstrua educenda. succus urtice cu(m) mirra uul
ua pessaricatum menstrua educe(t). Ad libidine(m) prouoca(n)dam
sem(en) urtice cu(m) uino sepe bibita ul(tra). melius erit si fiat
elect(uarium) ex se(min)ib(us) (et) melle (et) pipe(re). Item aq(ua) decoctionis ei(us)
(et) melle ualet spleneticis (et) ptisicis (et) peripleumaticis (et) si
ace(tum) cu(m) m(e)l(l)e sa(n)a producit plimones leuiu(m). Item si ex ip(s)a h(er)
ba fi(at) coquina (et) comesta. laxat uentre(m) (et) ad multa
facit. Item succus ei(us) garganizatus uuula(m) grossam
cito releuat. Item ip(s)a h(er)ba co(n)trita (et) oleo decocta in
uncto spina(m) dorsi. stati(m) sudore(m) prouocat i(n)q(ui)t galien(us).
Contra capillos cadentes. unge capud ex succo urtica(rum)
mir(um) capillos confirmat. Ad mulieres q(ue) cadunt
p(ro)pt(er) fumositate(m) (et) pass(ionem) matricis. h(er)ba urtice b(e)n(e) co(n)
trita (et) fiat ep(ithe)m(a) sup(er) uuluam. prius calefa(c)ta. stati(m)
sentiet beneficiu(m). Item acetum decoctionis se(min)is ei(us) ua
let contra furfuras capitis si laues bis ul(tra) ter (et) p(ost)ea
de aq(ua). aceto idem fracto capiti. illinitum. dolore(m)
tollit (et) sanat.

Vermicularis siue Vermicularia. h(er)ba e(st). nascens
sup(er) terra(m) (et) maxime sup(er) lapide(s) (et) macerib(us) (et) sp(ar)ge(n)do(?)
sic(ut) uimes. (et) h(abe)t folia p(ar)ua (et) flore(m) citrinu(m). Virtute(m) h(abe)t
ut sempervivum ua(lens) i(n) ungu(en)t(o) populeo.

Uilubidis herba est que sili nomine appellatur. Sunt enim .iiij. maneries uilubidis. scilicet maior. minor. et medius. et lanatus. maior dicitur funiculus arborum et habet florem album et est similis campana. et hec est medicinale plus quam alij quia alii uero sunt uiolentiores et acutiores et maxime illud quod habet folia ad modum lancea et cum rumpitur lac effundens istud valde uenenosum est et nimis laxatiuum et inducit dissinteriam unde cauendum est. Vilubidis maioris radix debet colligi in tempore ueris et ad solem desiccari et cum opus fuerit. da. ʒ. i. uel. ij. pluuiis ei. cum aliquo retificatiuo et non per se. purgat autem yteritiam ex frigiditate. oppilationem epatis et apostematibus in eo cum suco appij. endiuie. remouet colleram cum sanguinem purgat. Contra yteritiam ex frigiditate. aqua decoctionis radicum eius. cum mastice et dragaganto et spice nardi mirabiliter ualet.

Uincetoxicum. Antiformagorum est. herba est et nascitur locis montuosis et lapidosis huius folia spissa subnigra et florem album. et producit baccas ad modum orobi sed magis acutum. cuius semen uel folia poni debet in medicinis.

Nomen herbe Salaebona.

Vincetoxica.

Vitis alba.

Uua in duas diuiditur scilicet acerba non matura est. que matura non est sue dulcedine completa sed digna est appellatione. Uue acerua. frigida est in tercio gradu. sicca in .ij. ... ipse diuersas habet. Horum una ... alia cortice. alia grana. alia humoris. granorum sicca est que data diuersionis nulli in egones ... ex sto stegma egdunt cum sua fortitudine pistella tamen que farina excussa ... sibilat stomachum confortat colicam stringit egones maxime si assetur. ... sua stipticitates et ponticitatem dure est digerere. Confortatiuum tamen est stomacho et epatis calorem stringit sitim aufert. Acume ... mitigat uomitum egones ... uicam stomachi uel epatis propter confectiones stiptiue uirtutis constringit. ... appositum palpebrarum humores ... attenuat et desiccat ... ad pruriginem ... lorum et asperitates. ... Via precepit ... uue succum in dies caniculares ad solem positum donec spissetur ut mel. ... humoribus in gula descendentibus et gingiuas ... auriculas ... fistulas ... uulneribus intestinis ... humoribus ... uulua descendentibus.

Uua matura. Sanguinem laudabilem facit plus ceteris fructibus que ad modum ficus que melior est ... tamen facit quam una nutrit ... ad ... opposita ... frigidis existit. ... sic. que stiptica ... acetosa uue ... habet ... ob hoc ... addigestionem dur. Galien ... uue et ficus ... ad digestionem dura ... una si cum cortice edatur simul cum ossibus ... digestione inflationes ... sanguine ... laudabili. Passus ... facit quam uua ceteris fructibus ... laudabiliores non est dure sunt egonis ... conuersionis ... in sua arbore perfecte ... maturitate. Testatur ... ortulanus ... ficu et uue temporibus ... pingues ... clare ... cutes ... digestionis ... ad usum ... ortulani macessunt. Caro ... uue et ficus inflata est ... et commedentium carnes inflat. Accipit aut una diuersis modis ... ones in corpore ... diuerse. ... ad ... suspendit ... plurimum humoris ... in uase cum musto uel sapa repo... ... humoribus purgat. Contra ... stomachum ... repleuit plenum ... digestione ... sanguinem ... Corpus ... plurimum ... sensibiles ... laudabiliores ... uel sapa ... stomachum ... dieta ... uetositates inflationes ... humores ex ...

Vitis alba. herba ē q̄ sili noīe appellat' q ex
pā dit' sup sepes magna q̄ntitate cresat.

Zinciber. c. ē i. ttio. ḡ. hu. i šo. qdā dicunt
ipm ēē radix arboris. alii. manculos arboꝝ
s; ipin ueia ē radi. herbe cresc̄es i trāsmanni ptib;
7 imdtib; clauonie. Cvinū dectois ei' 7 ficuū
siccaꝝ 7 passulaꝝ ual; ad fiā; tussi; 7 ad spūaliū
firāte. Si i p̄luis ei' i ficub; siccis pōat' 7 sic ꝯme
dat' ad idē; ualet. Cvinū decctionis ei' 7 cimi.
ualet ad dolorē; stō 7 itestinoꝝ ex uētositat.
digestioē; pcurat. puluis ei' cū lōbic' suppōitus
ualet ꝯ tenasmō Cpuluis ei' i cib' exibitus s;
copiçantib; ꝯfert. p bienū suat' 7 cū pipe mlt;
melius suat'. cū domestic' 7 siluestre. Silue
stre karopos coloris ē. saporis uehemēt' acu
to. s; solid'. Domestic' s; albid' ē acutū ht sap
poꝛe; s; nō adō uehemēte nec s; adō solidam
ht. un cū frāgit' ptes ꝯ caheret. qb; dā minus
ꝯhis. In siluā raro ul' nūq̄ iuenit' sic.

X [illegible] modicū ht dulce [illegible] mltu [illegible] [illegible] digestioē [illegible] obediens [illegible] stō [illegible] [illegible] [illegible] solutiua [illegible] [illegible] colice passionis [illegible] [illegible] [illegible] [illegible] solutiua [illegible] [illegible]

[illegible] Vue sisine grani sunt humores [illegible] Alba [illegible] [illegible] [illegible] [illegible] [illegible] [illegible] [illegible] Aristotil' alba [illegible] [illegible] [illegible] [illegible] [illegible] tarde [illegible] [illegible] tarde [illegible].

Ecloana. c. ē ī iiio. g͂. sic. i. iiii. radix ē cuiꝰdā hrb͂ p̄ ranos s͂uat. Vinū decoctionis ei͂ ꝯ͂t siccā tussi; ualet. ¶ Ɑ dolore stōi ⁊ īestinor ex ūētositat͂ ul͂ ex siāte. Supposito rū ex eo ⁊ t͂sera mag͂ sc͂m matᷓe; cal͂ficᷓ et mūdificat. Balsamētū ex eo sc͂m. ul͂ t͂sera magna ⁊ rore marino ⁊ pane asso ⁊ aceto. appititū icitat.

Zuchara. c. ē ⁊ hu. tēpate ī. sc͂do. g͂. uirtute; hꝫ īflandi. huectādi. ⁊ mūdificandi. ⁊ relaxādi. In syrupo si duc͂ sit l͂. i. zucci ⁊ aq͂ sit mltū plus iōz aq͂ nō nocet. ñ. ꝑpt͂ mltā diuturnā decoctione;. ¶ Zuccūm fit de cāna melle ītrāsmaris pt̃bꝫ ⁊ īsicilia ⁊ īspania sic. uersus festū beati Johannis baptiste i col͂ accipiūt. cānā mell͂ q͂ sūstes silis ē alie cāne. pt͂ q͂ ite͂rū ē soli da ⁊ d͂lcis. illa sūt cāna palustris ocaua ⁊ īsipida ⁊ scindūt eā ꝑmediū i minuta frusti ⁊ pistāt ꝑmodū ponūt pista ut ī labere ⁊ faciūt bullire ad lētū igne; ad spissitudine; ⁊ spumāt ⁊ d͂ q͂ spuma fit zuccaꝝ sophisticatū. leuius ē alio, ⁊ iteri cau͂nosū. mlto magis ꝑ q͂ discerniṫ ab alio. uñ lauto q͂ ī mlta ēptione zucci. tortellus zucci frāgat. ⁊ gustetur. si ē ītra foramōsū ualꝫ ⁊ gustui nō sernat͂ ualꝫ dulce. sꝫ cū euanescit ī ore. nō crepitat ī masticatiōe. scias illō uanū ⁊ spumosū ē. ¶ Bonū aut͂ zuccaꝝ faciūt d͂resistente spisso liquore ꝑfacto. q͂ s͂e refrigidat. ponūt ī uase rotūdo ad solem ⁊ tā ꝑ calore. q͂ ꝑ lōgā decoctiōe;. fit durū ⁊ albū zuchm͂. q͂ ꝑ q̄nquēnū pot͂ s͂uari ī loco nō nī frigido. nec nimis calido ¶ Huiꝰ usꝰ ī mltis ē necessariū. ut potē ī ꝯfectionibꝫ medicinarū ⁊ acute febricitātibꝫ ⁊ īsyr; q͂ ꝗlitate sūt pates lapis ⁊ nō cū īsipiētis sit acē. agēhī. suspēdim͂. ⁊ nota q͂ zuchm͂ mltū ualet sitiētibꝫ uīatibꝫ oblatū ē nō hn̄t liq͂re ī caliva regione ⁊ pa͂ ꝑtisice. ꝯsūptis. asmatice. pōtꝰ ī alb. potibꝫ cor. resūmit coꝝ ⁊ extenuatione. ⁊ lūbricat siccitate;. Ne uō p̄sētis epis plixitas ī imēsū īfūdat. h̄ leto fin͂ illō q͂ cludim͂. acten͂ arcana saline. diximꝰ urbi. litera iā lassa pollice sistat opus.

Explicit tractatus hrbaꝝ. Diascorides. ⁊ Platone adq; Galienus ⁊ Macrone;. t͂slatate manu ⁊ itellectu bartholomei mini d͂ senis ī arte speciarie sēp īfusus. deo gr͂as. am̄.

Qui scripsit scribat sēp cū dn̄o uiuat.

Viuat ī celis bartholom̄ꝰ ī noīe felix.

Zucchar

Ozania nascit͂ ī th͂ai [illegible] ... acuit; ⁊ uenenosā [illegible] ... sisamne [illegible] ... ⁊ mulieres extra [illegible] ... siccā ⁊ furfur [illegible] ... aceto ⁊ ad [illegible] ... ualet cocta cū uino ... asinino ⁊ lini seīe [illegible] ... sanat ea ⁊ mūdificat.

Cibulle ēssꝰ ī albꝫ ex causis [illegible] ... ⁊ uenas; uīa oppilat ... aut epatice ⁊ splenetice.

ORobū ca ē i pº g. sic i. ij. uīn mūdificat
ē excolāt 7 apituu mūdatū corticibus
iure q̄ ei ꝯ faīna sēp uetre hūectat ū 7 mi
sta puce cutē clarificat ū tam̄ illo plimū
assuescat ne forte sanguinē mīgere faciat
7 aliqn̄ pnares sangs effic flux. faīna o
robi cocta cū gerotis q̄ ē spēs thuris. vōpi
ce. xtice q̄ v q̄b intusq. otigat ex ēpis
oppilationē īfirmitas tēpatata cū uino ad
rabiosi canis morsū vz apposita tēpata rū
ūa cū melle ē sanguinē mūdificat ulnēib;
rapētib; silir ualet.

Crispula herba cancri. Sanguinaria. bursa pa
storis.

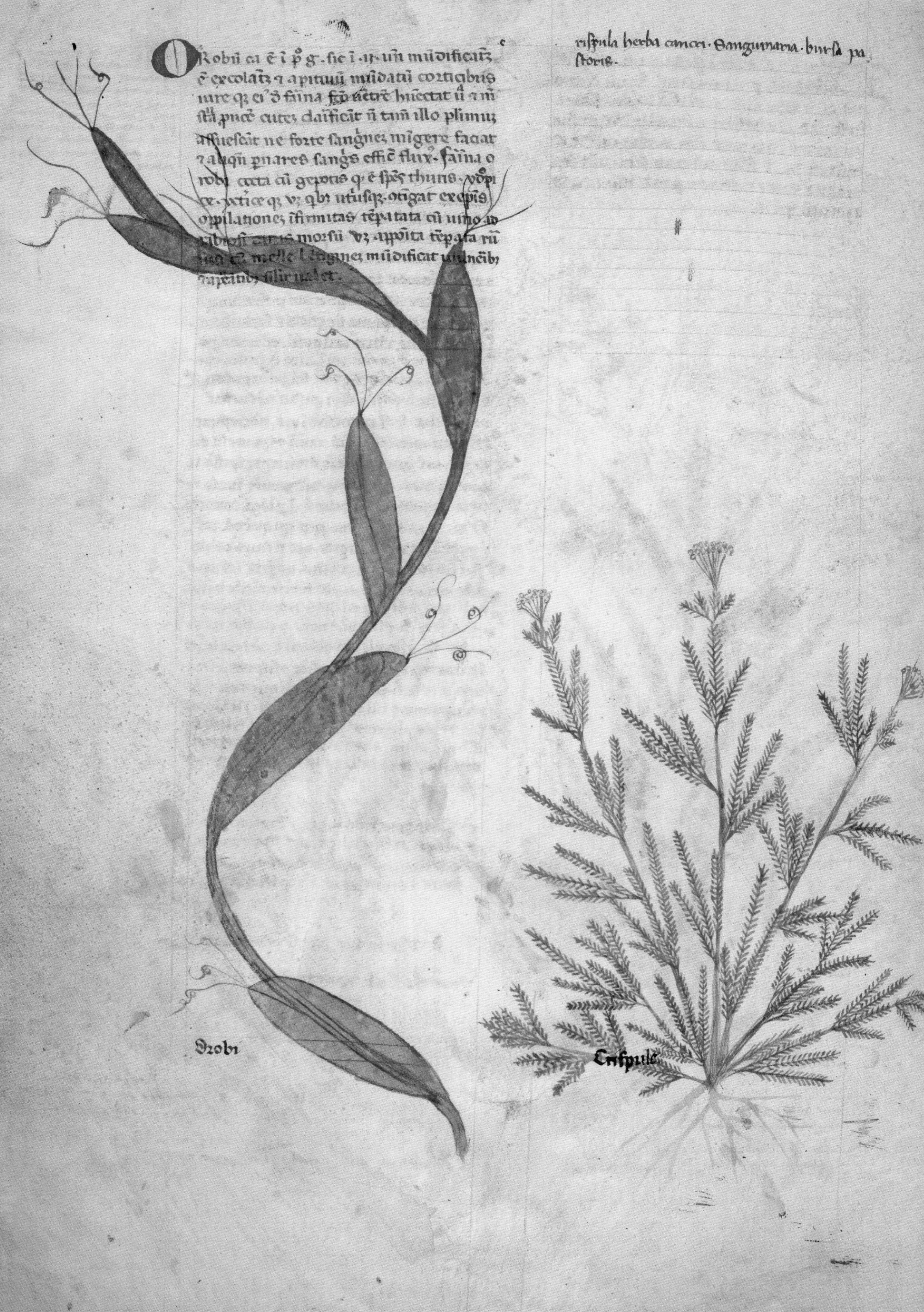

C viij
107
pia aquatica et terrestris.
Ypie minor .i. auricula muris
Morsus galline vel ypie maior
Ypie medie .i. auricula muris media.

H·

himandrea ul' germandrea ul' gamā
drea .i· camedrius· camedreos·

eristereon. uerbena.

s

uchae ul' suchaar. pes columbinus cu[m] quo tangit[ur] oculus ulceratus ul' caro ul' cera z al' herba scoltea.

cilus consulis filis mentastro ·

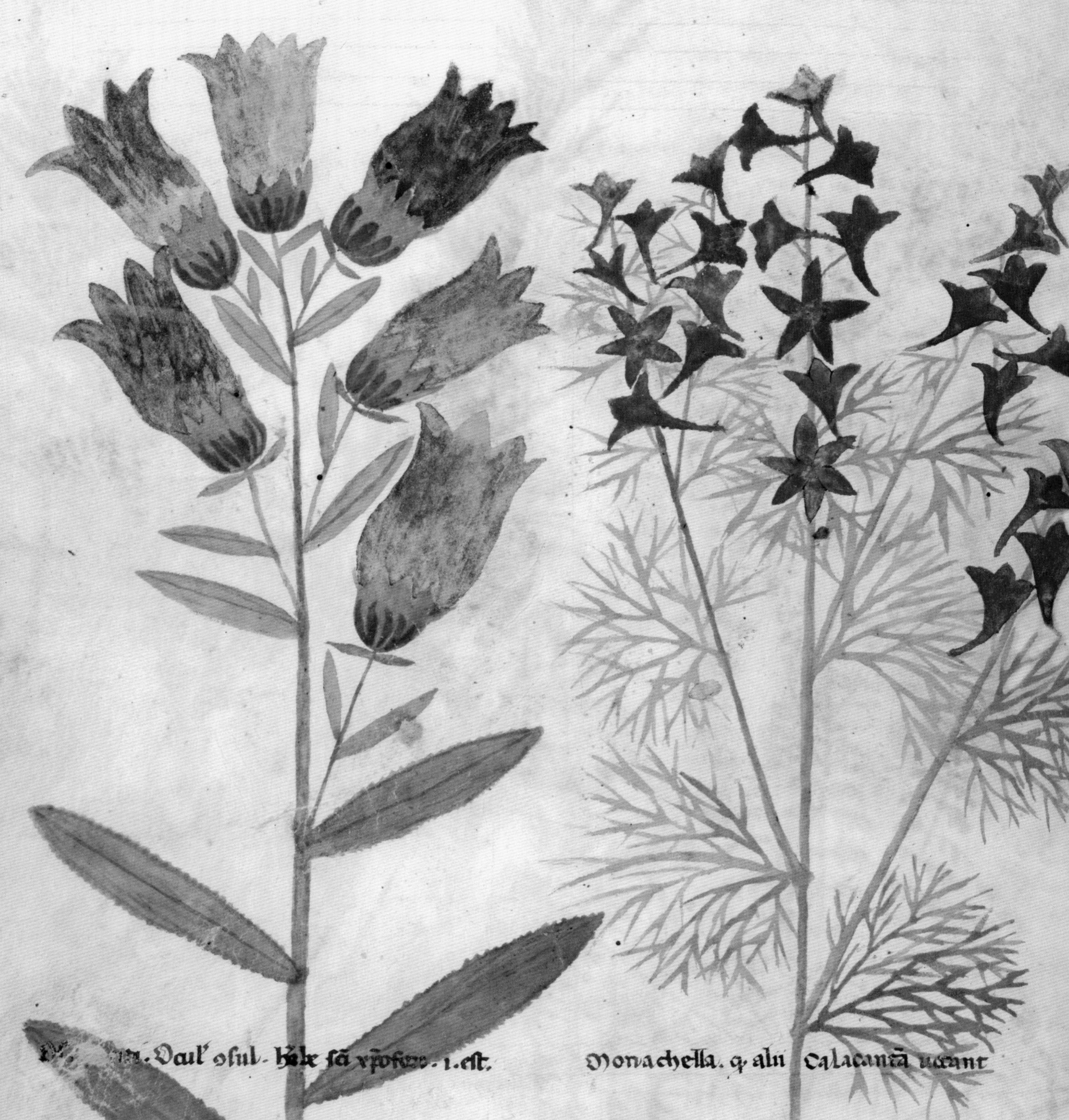

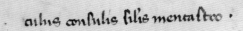